Machine Translation Summit XVII

Volume 1: Research Track

Dublin, Ireland
19-23 August 2019

ISBN: 978-1-5108-9292-7

Machine Translation Summit XVII

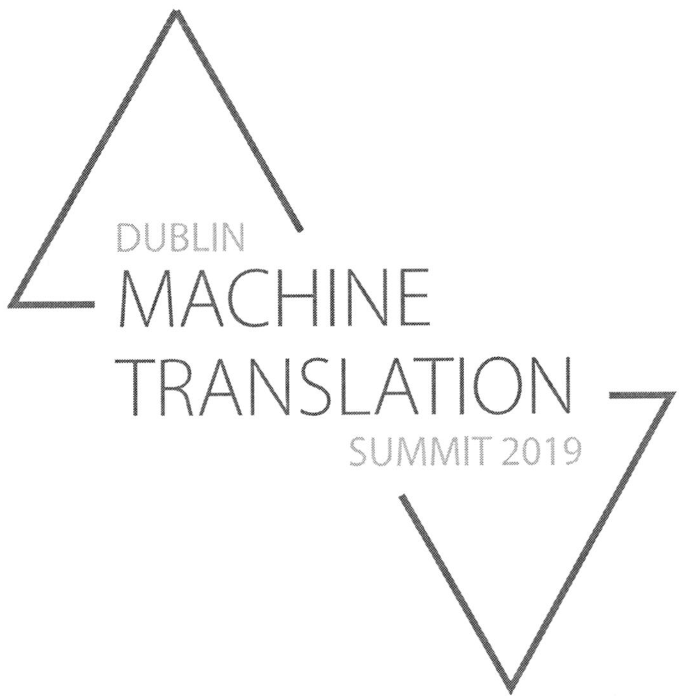

Proceedings of Machine Translation Summit XVII
Volume 1: Research Track
https://www.mtsummit2019.com

19–23 August, 2019
Dublin, Ireland

Proceedings of Machine Translation Summit XVII
Volume 1: Research Track

https://www.mtsummit2019.com

19–23 August, 2019
Dublin, Ireland

DCU

Foreword by the President of the IAMT and the EAMT

Céad míle fáilte romhaibh!

It's a pleasure for me to warmly welcome you all to the 17th Machine Translation Summit.

Every two years, the International Association for Machine Translation (IAMT), an umbrella organization comprising the Asian Association for Machine Translation (AAMT), the Association for Machine Translation in the Americas (AMTA), and the European Association for Machine Translation (EAMT), jointly call everyone related in some way or another to machine translation and translation technologies to the most inclusive MT conference in the world, a real Summit. It brings together senior and junior researchers, developers, vendors and all kinds of users, coming from academia, industry, or even as freelancers, to share and become aware of any new developments in the field.

This is the sixth such summit held in Europe, after having visited Munich (1989), Luxembourg (1995), Santiago de Compostela (2001), Copenhagen (2007), and Nice (2013).

The organizers have assembled an excellent programme; after two days with a wide offer of tutorials and workshops, the main conference features four tracks: the research track, the users' track, a new translators' track, and the usual projects track, and includes three invited talks, poster sessions and oral sessions. Everyone will find something going on that interests them throughout the event.

Every six years, the EAMT organizes the MT Summit in Europe. The EAMT is a growing association, which organizes a yearly conference, sponsors research, development and community outreach initiatives, and annually grants a Best Thesis Award. Individuals, institutions and companies from Europe, Africa and the Middle East can join the EAMT for a modest fee and benefit from all these activities. In addition to that, EAMT members (as AMTA and AAMT members) enjoy attractive discounted fees when attending EAMT, AMTA and AAMT conferences. This is possible thanks to our members but especially to my colleagues in the EAMT Executive Committee —coming from both academia and industry— who work hard to make it all happen.

The XVII MT Summit would not be possible without the hard work of our local organizers, headed by my predecessor as EAMT president and current Executive Board member, Andy Way, who have, with the help of other MT actors from the Adapt Centre and the professional collaboration of Abbey Conference & Events, put together an excellent conference. I am very thankful for their hard work and for having put their local MT expertise at the disposal of the EAMT (and the IAMT).

Bainigí taitneamh as, that is, enjoy. Enjoy the programme, the company, and the city. Ten years ago, I lived here and worked here for a year and I'll miss it every day of my life. And I'll tell you something: it is especially the local people that makes Dublin —and all of Ireland— one of the best places in the world to hold a conference like our Summit. I'm sure you'll bring home sweet memories of it!

Baile Átha Cliath/Dublin, Lúnasa/August 2019

Mikel L. Forcada
President of the IAMT and the EAMT
Professor of Computer Languages and Systems Universitat d'Alacant
Alacant, Valencian Country, Spain.
Email: `mlf@ua.es`

Foreword by MT Summit 2019 Conference Chair

Back in 2017, on behalf of the International Association for Machine Translation (IAMT), the European Association for Machine Translation (EAMT) entrusted me with hosting this conference that you are currently attending.

While I was grateful for the trust shown in me, as a previous IAMT/EAMT president, I was acutely aware of the need to deliver; compared to our annual EAMT conferences, MT Summits provide us with the opportunity to show our Asian and American friends and colleagues that we can put on an event that all three regional associations and the IAMT can be duly proud of; if you mess up, Europe has to wait 6 years to try to put it right!

After two years of hard work, I can say with some confidence that we have achieved this. One of the first things I did was put together a very strong support team. I would really like to thank our seven co-chairs of the four tracks, namely:

- Research track co-chairs: Barry Haddow & Rico Sennrich (University of Edinburgh, UK)

- User track co-chairs: John Tinsley (Iconic Translation Machines, Ireland) & Dimitar Shterionov (ADAPT Centre, Dublin City University, Ireland)

- Translator track co-chairs: Celia Rico (Universidad Europea de Madrid, Spain) & Federico Gaspari (ADAPT Centre, Dublin City University, Ireland)

- Projects chair: Mikel L. Forcada (Universitat d'Alacant, Spain)

I am also very grateful to Laura Rossi (Lexis Nexis, The Netherlands) and Antonio Toral (University of Groningen, The Netherlands) for acting as excellent Tutorials and Workshops Chairs, respectively. I hope you all benefited from attending these pre-conference events!

For the most part, it is these 9 individuals who have put together the programme assembled before you. Each of them will comment on their Tracks later in these proceedings, but they all deserve our heartfelt thanks, as do the panels of reviewers they assembled which helped improve all our papers. From a personal point of view, I am delighted that we have – for the first but surely not the last time – included a Translator track; I have advocated for some time now that it is only through dialogue that MT developers and the translator community can advance our field. I have been very keen to take up a number of recent opportunities to speak at translator conferences, so I am especially pleased to welcome translators to this event; thank you for coming!

I am of course grateful to everyone who submitted a paper; whether your work was selected for presentation or not, if no-one had submitted, we wouldn't have had a conference. For those of you whose work was selected for presentation, many thanks for coming to Dublin, and to DCU, which have been my home and workplace now for 28 years, half my life. All of you would have interacted via EasyChair, and I am grateful to Carol Scarton, EAMT secretary, for her effort in setting up the various accounts which enabled the submission and notification processes to run so smoothly.

When you act as IAMT/EAMT president, or edit the Machine Translation journal, or act as track chair at major conferences, sometimes you have to be a bit of a pain, because you are often asking busy people to do things, mostly for free! Having been around the block a few times, I have lots of contacts in the industry, so I made myself responsible for bringing in sponsorship. I know they will say I was close to pestering them on many occasions, but I am truly grateful for the hugely generous support we obtained from our sponsors from the translation and CAT industry:

- Silver sponsors: Microsoft, and STAR

- Bronze sponsors: Pangeanic, text & form, CrossLang, Flitto, VistaTec

- Other sponsors: Welocalize, Iconic, XTM, Unbabel, DCU, ELRA, Tilde, Springer, Apertium

I am also extremely grateful to Fáilte Ireland for their generous support of this conference, which helped my ADAPT@DCU colleagues Joss Moorkens and Sharon O'Brien present our bid in Nagoya in 2017, as well as supporting our excellent invited speakers: Laura Casanellas, Helena Moniz, and Arianna Bisazza. With many women in our team, it's extremely important to have strong female role models, and we could not have asked for better from Laura, Arianna and Helena; many thanks to all of you for agreeing to share your expertise with us!

We took the decision a while back to try to be as green a conference as possible. You will already have noticed that, in order to reduce waste, there is no delegate bag. To reduce paper, we are not producing paper proceedings, and the normal programme booklet has been replaced by a smaller 'bradge' which doubles as a name badge. We are hoping to have a tree-planting ceremony during the conference in order to reduce the carbon footprint of the Summit. To reduce transport costs, we are using onsite accommodation at DCU, and will promote the use of public transport to the off-site events. Thanks to DCU Sustainability Manager Sam Fahy for her support in these efforts.

While we decided not to produce printed proceedings, they still needed to be put together in electronic form. I am grateful to Jenny Walsh for producing such an excellent conference logo, but huge thanks are due to Alberto Poncelas for putting together the proceedings, and for helping workshop chairs to produce theirs. Alberto has also liaised with Matt Post to ensure that your papers are indexed in perpetuity on the ACL Anthology!

I have two final people to thank. Firstly, I am very grateful to Grainne McQuaid and her team in Abbey Conference and Events for their professional support of the conference. You will have met them at registration, and they are available throughout the event to ensure your needs are met. We have been engaging with them for 2 years now, and this has been a true partnership that has made this journey an enjoyable one. Secondly, I am especially grateful to my colleague Jane Dunne, for managing the planning of the conference, and for managing me too. Jane has done this over and above her work on a European project, and I could not have chosen a better, nicer person to engage with over these past two years – thank you Jane on behalf of everyone; we are all deeply grateful for your huge effort in getting us to where we all are today!

Finally, I really hope that you all enjoy the conference, that you benefit from the excellent programme that has been assembled, and that you go away from here having made new friends. I am fortunate indeed that many of my very best friends are in the MT community, and I hope to meet as many of you as possible during the event.

Andy Way
Chair, MT Summit 2019
Deputy Director ADAPT Centre School of Computing Dublin City University
Dublin, Ireland.
Email: `Andy.Way@adaptcentre.ie`

Foreword by the Research Track Program Chairs

It is with great pleasure that we present the proceedings of the research track at MT Summit XVII. We solicited full papers that present novel research contributions across all areas of MT, particularly encouraging submissions that are oriented towards building robust and practical systems.

We received 57 submissions for the research track. Out of these, 1 was withdrawn before the notification of acceptance, and 31 were accepted (54%). 4 were withdrawn after the notification of acceptance, resulting in 27 papers being presented at the MT Summit.

The selected papers span a wide range of topics in machine translation. Major themes include translation from other modalities than text, especially speech, the analysis of MT models and automatic translations, and the integration of MT into translation workflows, with studies on post-editing and constrained/controllable MT.

We would like to thank the members of the Program Committee for their timely reviews.

Barry Haddow and Rico Sennrich

Organizers

President of the IAMT and the EAMT
Mikel Forcada   University of Alicante
MT Summit 2019 Conference Chair
Andy Way   ADAPT Centre

Programme Chairs

Research track co-chairs
Barry Haddow   The University of Edinburgh
Rico Sennrich   The University of Edinburgh
User track co-chairs
John Tinsley   Iconic Translation Machines
Dimitar Shterionov   Dublin City University
Translator track co-chairs
Celia Rico   Universidad Europea de Madrid
Federico Gaspari   Dublin City University
Projects track co-chair
Mikel L. Forcada   University of Alicante

Program Committee

Research Track

Alberto Poncelas	DCU
Aizhan Imankulova	Tokyo Metropolitan University
Aleš Tamchyna	Memsource a. s.
Alon Lavie	Carnegie Mellon University
Anabela Barreiro	INESC-ID
Andreas Maletti	Universität Leipzig
Andrei Popescu-Belis	HEIG-VD / HES-SO
Ankur Bapna	Google
Ann Clifton	Simon Fraser University
Annette Rios Gonzales	University of Zurich
Anoop Kunchukuttan	IIT Bombay
Antonio Toral	University of Groningen
Antonio Valerio Miceli Barone	University of Pisa
Arturo Oncevay	The University of Edinburgh
Arul Menezes	Microsoft
Arya McCarthy	Johns Hopkins University
Atsushi Fujita	National Institute of Information and Communications Technology

Barry Haddow	The University of Edinburgh
Boxing Chen	Alibaba Group
Carla Parra Escartín	Unbabel
Carolina Scarton	European Association for Machine Translation
Celia Rico	Universidad Europea de Madrid
Chenhui Chu	Osaka University
Chris Brockett	Microsoft
Christian Dugast	tech2biz
Christian Federmann	Microsoft
Christian Hardmeier	Uppsala University
Christoph Tillmann	IBM
Christos Baziotis	The University of Edinburgh
Colin Cherry	National Research Council Canada
Constantin Orasan	University of Wolverhampton
Cristina España-Bonet	UdS and DFKI
Dakun Zhang	Systran
Daniel Marcu	ISI/USC
Daniel Ortiz-Martínez	Unversitat Politecnica de Valencia
Dario Stojanovski	Ludwig Maximilian University of Munich
David Vilar	Amazon
Devendra Singh Sachan	CMU
Deyi Xiong	Tianjin University
Dimitar Shterionov	Dublin City University
Dušan Variš	Institute of Formal and Applied Linguistics; Charles University in Prague
Duygu Ataman	University of Trento; Fondazione Bruno Kessler; University of Edinburgh
Ekaterina Lapshinova-Koltunski	Saarland University
Ekaterina Vylomova	The University of Melbourne
Eleftherios Avramidis	German Research Center for Artificial Intelligence (DFKI)
Eva Hasler	The University of Edinburgh
Eva Vanmassenhove	DCU
Fatiha Sadat	UQAM
Federico Gaspari	Dublin City University
Felipe Sánchez-Martínez	Dep. de Llenguatges i Sistemes Informàtics. Universitat d'Alacant
Felix Hieber	Amazon
Felix Stahlberg	University of Cambridge
Ferhan Ture	Comcast Labs
Francis Tyers	Indiana University Bloomington
Francisco Casacuberta	Universitat Politècnica de València
Francisco Javier Guzman	Facebook
François Yvon	LIMSI/CNRS et Université Paris-Sud
Frederic Blain	The University of Sheffield
George Foster	NRC
Gholamreza Haffari	Simon Fraser University
Gonzalo Iglesias Iglesias	SDL
Graham Neubig	Carnegie Mellon University
Gregor Leusch	eBay inc
Hainan Xu	Johns Hopkins University

Helena Caseli	Federal University of São Carlos (UFSCar)
Helmut Schmid	Ludwig Maximilian University of Munich
Hiroshi Echizenya	Hokkai-Gakuen University
Houda Bouamor	Carnegie Mellon University
Huda Khayrallah	Johns Hopkins University
Iacer Calixto	University of Amsterdam
Isao Goto	NHK
Jan Niehues	Maastricht University
Jesús González-Rubio	WebInterpret
Jiajun Zhang	Institute of Automation Chinese Academy of Sciences
Joachim Daiber	Apple Inc.
John Henderson	The MITRE Corporation
John Tinsley	Iconic Translation
Joke Daems	Ghent University
Jonathan Mallinson	The University of Edinburgh
Joost Bastings	University of Amsterdam
Jörg Tiedemann	University of Helsinki
José G. C. de Souza	ebay
Josep Crego	SYSTRAN
Joss Moorkens	ADAPT Centre
Juan Antonio Pérez-Ortiz	Universitat d'Alacant; Departament de Llenguatges i Sistemes Informàtics
Julia Ive	King's College London
Julia Kreutzer	Heidelberg University
Julian Schamper	DeepL GmbH
Katsuhito Sudoh	Nara Institute of Science and Technology
Ke Hu	ADAPT Centre; Dublin City University
Kenji Imamura	National Institute of Information and Communications Technology
Kenton Murray	Carnegie Mellon University School of Computer Science
Laura Jehl	Institut für Computerlinguistik; Universität Heidelberg
Laurent Besacier	Laboratoire d'Informatique de Grenoble
Lemao Liu	NICT
Lexi Birch	The University of Edinburgh
Lieve Macken	Ghent University
Linfeng Song	University of Rochester
Luisa Bentivogli	FBK
Maja Popovic	ADAPT Centre; DCU
Manny Rayner	University of Geneva
Mara Chinea Rios	Universitat Politècnica de València
Marc Dymetman	Xerox Research Centre Europe
Marcello Federico	Amazon AI
Marcin Junczys-Dowmunt	Microsoft
Marco Turchi	Fondazione Bruno Kessler
Marianna Apidianaki	CNRS
Marija Brkic	Department of Informatics; University of Rijeka
Marion Weller-Di Marco	University of Amsterdam
Mark Fishel	University of Tartu

Markus Freitag	Google AI
Marta R. Costa-Jussà	Institute For Infocomm Research
Martin Popel	UFAL; Faculty of Mathematics and Physics; Charles University
Martin Volk	University of Zurich
Masaaki Nagata	NTT
Masao Utiyama	NICT
Mathias Müller	University of Zurich
Matīss Rikters	Tilde
Matt Post	Johns Hopkins University
Matteo Negri	Fondazione Bruno Kessler (FBK-irst)
Matthias Huck	Ludwig Maximilian University of Munich
Mattia Antonino Di Gangi	Fondazione Bruno Kessler; University of Trento
Maximiliana Behnke	The University of Edinburgh
Mercedes García-Martínez	Pangeanic SL
Meriem Beloucif	The Hong Kong University of Science and Technology
Michael Carl	Kent State University
Michel Simard	National Research Council Canada (NRC)
Miguel Domingo	Universitat Politècnica de València
Mihael Arcan	Insight Centre for Data Analytics; National University of Ireland Galway
Mihaela Vela	Universität des Saarlandes
Miloš Stanojević	The University of Edinburgh
Miquel Esplà	Universitat d'Alacant
Mireia Farrús	Universitat Pompeu Fabra
Mirjam S. Maučec	FERI; University of Maribor
Myle Ott	Facebook
Nicola Ueffing	eBay
Nikolay Bogoychev	The University of Edinburgh
Niyu Ge	
Nizar Habash	Columbia University
Núria Bel	Universitat Pompeu Fabra
Orhan Firat	Google
Ozan Çağlayan	Le Mans University
Parnia Bahar	RWTH Aachen University
Patrick Simianer	Lilt.
Paul Michel	Carnegie Mellon University - LTI
Pavel Pecina	Charles University In Prague
Petra Barančíková	Charles University in Prague
Philip Williams	The University of Edinburgh
Philipp Koehn	Johns Hopkins University
Praveen Dakwale	Informatics Institute; University of Amsterdam
Preethi Raghavan	IBM TJ Watson Research
Qun Liu	Huawei Noah's Ark Lab
Rabih Zbib	Raytheon
Rachel Bawden	The University of Edinburgh
Raj Dabre	IIT Bombay
Rajen Chatterjee	Apple Inc.
Rebecca Knowles	Johns Hopkins University
Rebecca Marvin	Johns Hopkins University

Rico Sennrich   The University of Edinburgh
Roland Kuhn   National Research Council of Canada
Roman Grundkiewicz   The University of Edinburgh; School of
                                     Informatics

Rudolf Rosa   Charles University
Saab Mansour   RWTH Aachen University
Sadao Kurohashi   Kyoto University
Sameen Maruf   Monash University
Sameer Bansal   The University of Edinburgh
Samuel Läubli   University of Zurich
Sarah Ebling   University of Zurich
Sergio Penkale   Lingo24
Shahram Khadivi   eBay
Shankar Kumar   Google
Sharon O'Brien   Dublin City University
Sheila Castilho   Dublin City University/ADAPT Centre
Stephan Peitz   Apple
Surafel Melaku Lakew   University of Trento
Tamer Alkhouli   RWTH Aachen University
Taro Watanabe   NICT
Teresa Herrmann   Fujitsu
Tim Anderson   Wright-Patterson Air Force Research
                                     Laboratory

Tomáš Musil   Charles University in Prague
Toshiaki Nakazawa   The University of Tokyo
Tsuyoshi Okita   Kyushu Institute of Technology
Ulrich Germann   The University of Edinburgh
Víctor M. Sánchez-Cartagena   Transducens Research Group; Departament de
                                     Llenguatges i Sistemes Informàtics; Universitat
                                     d'Alacant

Viktor Hangya   Ludwig Maximilian University of Munich
Vincent Vandeghinste   Instituut voor de Nederlandse Taal, Centre for
                                     Computational Linguistics, KU Leuven

Vishal Chowdhary   Microsoft
Vu Hoang   The University of Melbourne
Wei Wang   Google
Xing Niu   University of Maryland
Yinfei Yang   Redfin Inc.
Yuki Arase   Osaka University
Yunsu Kim   RWTH Aachen University
Yvette Graham   Dublin City University

Translator Track

Adrià Martín-Mor   UAB
Alberto Poncelas   DCU
Ana Guerberof Arenas   DCU/ADAPT Centre
Bogdan Babych   University of Leeds
Carolina Scarton   European Association for Machine Translation
Celia Rico Perez   Universidad Europea de Madrid
Federico Gaspari   Dublin City University
Ignacio Garcia   University of Western Sydney
Joss Moorkens   Dublin City University

Katie Botkin	MultiLingual magazine
Mary Phelan	Dublin City University
Minako O'Hagan	The University of Auckland
Mirko Silvestrini	UNILINGUE
Olga Torres-Hostench	Universitat Autònoma de Barcelona
Oliver Czulo	Universität Leipzig
Pilar Sanchez-Gijón	Autonomous University of Barcelona
Sarah Bawa-Mason	University of Portsmouth/Institute of Translation and Interpreting
Sharon O'Brien	Dublin City University
Stephen Doherty	The University of New South Wales
Valeria Barbero	MT Summit

User Track

Alberto Poncelas	DCU
Aljoscha Burchardt	DFKI
Alon Lavie	Carnegie Mellon University
Bram Bulté	Katholieke Universiteit Leuven
Bruno Pouliquen	World Intellectual Property Organization
Carlos Collantes Fraile	TransPerfect / Universidad Complutense de Madrid
Carmen Heger	SZ
Carolina Scarton	European Association for Machine Translation
Chao-Hong Liu	ADAPT Centre, Dublin City University
Charlotte Tesselaar	LexisNexis Univentio
Chris Wendt	Microsoft
Christian Federmann	Microsoft
Christian Eisold	berns language consulting GmbH
Dag Schmidtke	Microsoft
Daniel Stein	eBay Inc.
David Vilar	Amazon
Declan Groves	Microsoft
Dimitar Shterionov	Dublin City University
Eva Martínez Garcia	Vicomtech / Universitat Politècnica de Catalunya
Eva Vanmassenhove	DCU
Evgeny Matusov	eBay
Félix Do Carmo	ADAPT Centre
Fred Blain	The University of Sheffield
Gema Ramírez-Sánchez	Prompsit Language Engineering, S.L.
Guodong Xie	ADAPT Centre, Dublin City University
Heidi Depraetere	Cross Language NV
Jean Senellart	SYSTRAN
John Tinsley	Iconic Translation Machines
José G. C. de Souza	eBay Inc.
Keith J. Miller	The MITRE Corporation
Kim Harris	text&form GmbH
Laurent Chevrette	Mondzo
Maxim Khalilov	Unbabel
Mercedes García-Martínez	Pangeanic SL
Nathalie DeSutter	Untranslate
Nicola Ueffing	eBay

Olga Beregovaya — Welocalize
Patrik Lambert — Pompeu Fabra University
Phil Ritchie — Vistattec
Raj Pate — CDAC
Rohit Gupta — Iconic Translations Machines Ltd.
Saša Hasan — Apple
Silvio Picinini — eBay
Steve Richardson — The Church of Jesus Christ of Latter-day Saints
Thierry Etchegoyhen — Vicomtech-IK4
Tony O'Dowd — Xcelerator Machine Translations Ltd.
Yury Sharshov — LexisNexis Univentio

Project Track

Alberto Poncelas — DCU
Carolina Scarton — The University of Sheffield
Mikel Forcada — University of Alicante

Contents

Online Sentence Segmentation for Simultaneous Interpretation using Multi-Shifted Recurrent Neural Network

Xiaolin Wang   Masao Utiyama   Eiichiro Sumita

Advanced Translation Research and Development Promotion Center
National Institute of Information and Communications Technology, Japan
{xiaolin.wang,mutiyama,eiichiro.sumita}@nict.go.jp

Abstract

This paper is devoted to developing a recurrent neural network (RNN) solution for segmenting the unpunctuated transcripts generated by automatic speech recognition for simultaneous interpretation. RNNs are effective in capturing long-distance dependencies and straightforward for online decoding. Thus, they are ideal for the task compared to the conventional n-gram language model (LM) based approaches and recent neural machine translation based approaches. This paper proposes a multi-shifted RNN to address the trade-off between accuracy and latency, which is one of the key characteristics of the task. Experiments show that our proposed method improves the segmentation accuracy measured in F_1 by 21.1% while maintains approximately the same latency, and reduces the BLEU loss to the oracle segmentation by 28.6%, when compared to a strong baseline of the RNN LM-based method. Our online sentence segmentation toolkit is open-sourced [1] to promote the field.

1   Introduction

Simultaneous interpretation (SI) is to translate one spoken language into another spoken language in real time. Automated SI typically requires integrating two fundamental natural language processing technologies – automatic speech recognition (ASR) and machine translation (MT). Both technologies have become quite capable after half a

even cats were watching this video cats were watching other cats watch this video but what 's important here is the creativity that it inspired amongst this techie geeky internet culture there were remixes someone made an old timey version and then it went international there were remixes someone made an old timey version

Table 1: Illustration of Input for Sentence Segmentation

century's intensive study, but one problem makes it difficult for them to work together – the raw transcripts generated by ASR contains no segmentation (see Table 1 for an example), while MT expects segmented sentences as input.

Online sentence segmentation smoothly bridges the gap between ASR and MT through segmenting the transcripts generated by ASR engines into sentences in real time. As a matter of fact, the task is non-trivial. The example presented in Table 1 is extracted from a TED talk [2], which is used in the experiments of this paper. Readers may find the raw sequence of words difficult to read. However, the readability is greatly improved once it is segmented as follows,

- even cats were watching this video

- cats were watching other cats watch this video

- but what 's important here is the creativity that it inspired amongst this techie geeky internet culture

- there were remixes

- someone made an old timey version

[1] https://github.com/arthurxlw/cytonNss

[2] https://www.ted.com/

- and then it went international

- there were remixes someone made an old timey version

Therefore, sentence segmentation is a meaningful natural language processing task. Correctly segmenting an ASR transcript requires a certain level of understanding the content.

This paper proposes a multi-shifted RNN to approach the problem of online sentence segmentation, which shifts target signals by multiple durations of time as illustrated by Table 2. This design emphasizes two central elements of the task – accuracy and latency. Usually, predicting a sentence boundary immediately after a last input word is not wise. Instead, waiting and checking a few words to make sure that a new sentence has started can raise the accuracy at the cost of latency. Shifting the target signals n time stamps right implements the idea of waiting and checking more words, but the optimal n varies on different textual contexts. Therefore, the proposed network learns multiple shifted target signals during training, and maintains multiple pathway of trading latency with accuracy during test. Experimental results demonstrate the effectiveness of our proposed method.

The contributions of this paper include,

- proposing a multi-shifted RNN for online sentence segmentation;

- achieving competitive performance on a real-world corpus;

- releasing the source code for reproducibility.

The rest of the paper is organized as follows. Section 2 reviews a baseline n-gram LM-based method which serves as a foundation of our method. Section 3 describes our method from the aspects of training, decoding and tuning. Section 4 presents the experiments. Section 5 compares our method with some related works. Section 6 concludes this paper with a description on future works.

2 Baseline: N-gram LM-based Method

N-gram LMs are used to segment unpunctuated transcripts by Stolcke et al. (1996; 1998) and Wang et al. (2016). They view sentence boundaries as hidden events occurring between the input words, and use n-gram LMs to compute the likelihood of the input words with or without sentence boundaries. Among them, the work of Wang et al.(2016) is the most related to this paper, because it addresses segmenting in an online manner for SI. Suppose an input sequence of words is $\cdots, w_{t-1}, w_t, w_{t+1}, \cdots$. The following two hypotheses are considered,

- *Hypothesis I*: there is no sentence boundary after the word w_t, which assumes that the underlying input remains the same as $\cdots, w_{t-1}, w_t, w_{t+1}, \cdots$.

- *Hypothesis II*: there is a sentence boundary after the word w_t, which assumes that the underlying input is $\cdots, w_{t-1}, w_t, \langle/s\rangle, \langle s\rangle, w_{t+1}, \cdots$.

The segmentation is predicted by comparing the probabilities of the two sequences as,

$$
\begin{aligned}
s_t &= \frac{P_t^{\langle\text{II}\rangle}}{P_t^{\langle\text{I}\rangle}} \\
&= p(\langle/s\rangle|w_{t-o+2}^t) \cdot \frac{p(w_{t+1}|\langle s\rangle)}{p(w_{t+1}|w_{t-o-2}^t)} \\
&\quad \cdot \prod_{k=t+2}^{t-o+1} \frac{p(w_k|w_{t+1}^{k-1}, \langle s\rangle)}{p(w_k|w_{k-o+1}^{k-1})}
\end{aligned}
\tag{1}
$$

where o is the order of a n-gram LM, and s_t is the confidence score of placing a sentence boundary after w_t. The left hand of the formula has one item for $\langle s\rangle$, w_{t+1}, ..., w_{t+o-1}, respectively. Theoretically, the o-1 future words w_{t+1}, ..., w_{t+o-1} are required when predicting the segmentation for the time stamp t. Empirically, it is found that 1 or 2 future words is enough for accuracy while having the merit of low latency.

N-gram LM-based methods are effective. However, they have two shortages. First, n-gram LMs cannot capture the long-distance dependencies required by the task, as the length of a sentence is typically larger than the order of n-gram LMs. Second, they are generative methods as the prediction is made by comparing the generative probability of two sequences. The accuracy of generative methods is known to be lower than that of discriminative methods. In the paper, we explore using RNN LM (Mikolov et al., 2010) to extend the n-gram LM-based method to address the first issue. This method turns out to be quite effective and serves as a strong baseline in this paper, though it does not address the second issue. Our

Time Stamp	1	2	3	4	5	6	7	8	9	10	11	12	13	...
Input	i	'd	like	some	tea	and	cake†	that	will	be	a	very	nice	...
Target	0	0	0	0	0	0	1	0	0	0	0	0	0	...
Shift by 1	0	0	0	0	0	0	0	1	0	0	0	0	0	...
Shift by 2	0	0	0	0	0	0	0	0	1	0	0	0	0	...
Shift by 3	0	0	0	0	0	0	0	0	0	1	0	0	0	...
Shift by 4	0	0	0	0	0	0	0	0	0	0	1	0	0	...

Table 2: Illustration of Multi-Shifted Target Signals for Sentence Segmentation. The input is a sequence of words. The target signals are 0's and 1's where 1 means a sentence boundary after the current time stamp. The last four rows shift the target signals by 1 to 4 time units. † Suppose the sentence ends here.

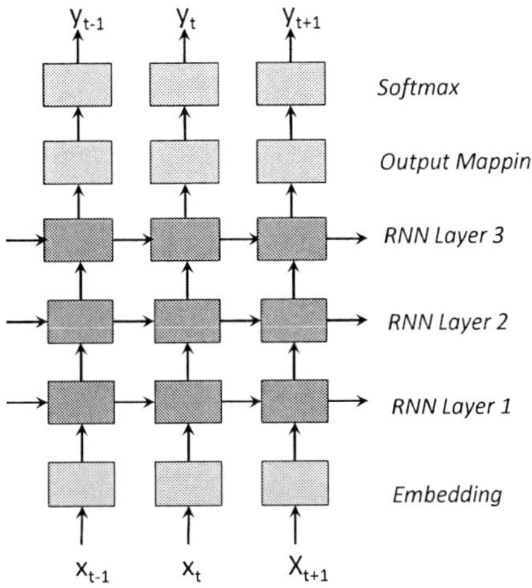

Figure 1: Network Architecture of Multi-shifted RNN Sentence Segmentor

proposed method addresses both issues; thus, it achieves even higher accuracy.

3 Our Method

3.1 Network Architecture

A network architecture inspired by RNN LM is adopted (illustrated by Figure 1). The network works in an online manner by taking one word x_t at each time stamp t as input, and outputting y_t for sentence segmentation.

The output y_t is an $(m + 1)$-dimensional vector $(y_t^{\langle 1 \rangle}, y_t^{\langle 2 \rangle}, \ldots, y_t^{\langle m \rangle}, y_t^{\langle m+1 \rangle})$, where $y_t^{\langle k \rangle}$ ($1 \leqslant k \leqslant m$) presented the confidence of putting a sentence boundary after the k-th word before the time stamp t, while $y_t^{\langle m+1 \rangle}$ is imposed by the softmax layer to sum up the probabilities to one. To be precise,

- $y_t^{\langle 1 \rangle}$ indicated segmenting after w_{t-1} ;

- $y_t^{\langle 2 \rangle}$ indicated segmenting after w_{t-2} ;

- $\ldots$

- $y_t^{\langle m \rangle}$ indicated segmenting after w_{t-m} ;

- $y_t^{\langle m+1 \rangle}$ equals to $1 - y_t^{\langle 1 \rangle} - y_t^{\langle 2 \rangle} \ldots - y_t^{\langle m \rangle}$.

In contrast to LM-based methods, this design removes the use of a fixed number of future words. It enables the network to predict a sentence boundary flexibly to time stamps.

3.2 Training

The proposed network is trained on the samples extracted from neighboring sentences, and the training target is to match the output y_t with the oracle segmentation signals. The following two paragraphs explain these two aspects in details.

3.2.1 Extracting Training Samples

Suppose $\mathbb{S} = (S_1, S_2, \ldots)$ is a sequence of sentences which are taken from continuous text. In other words, S_{i+1} is the succeeding sentence of S_i.

Suppose $S_i = (w_1^i, w_2^i, \ldots, w_{n_i}^i)$ where w_t^i ($1 \leqslant t \leqslant n_i$) are the n_i words in the sentence.

One training sample (X_i , n_i) is extracted from (S_i, S_{i+1}) as (illustrated by Figure 2),

$$x_t = \begin{cases} w_t^i & 1 \leqslant t \leqslant n_i \\ w_{t-n_i}^{i+1} & n_i + 1 \leqslant t \leqslant n_i + m \end{cases} \quad (2)$$

where $X_i = (x_1, x_2, \ldots, x_{n_i+m})$ is a sequence of input words.

3.2.2 Training Criterion

The desired value of y_t is formulated as,

$$y_t^{\langle k \rangle} \doteq \begin{cases} 1 & 1 \leqslant t \leqslant n_i, k = m+1 \\ 1 & n_i + 1 \leqslant t \leqslant n_i + m, k = t - n_i \\ 0 & \text{otherwise} \end{cases} \quad (3)$$

Therefore, minimizing the cross entropy between y_t and the desired value is taken as the train-

3

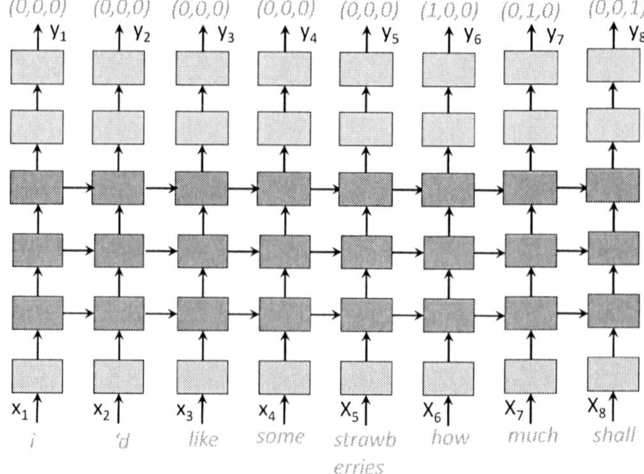

Figure 2: Unrolling a Sample on Multi-shifted RNN Sentence Segmentor. The ASR transcript is "i 'd like some strawberries how much does it cost" where the first sentence ends after "strawberries". Note that y_t's last dimension $y_t^{\langle 4 \rangle} = 1 - y_t^{\langle 1 \rangle} - y_t^{\langle 2 \rangle} - y_t^{\langle 3 \rangle}$ is omitted for simplicity.

ing criterion,

$$\mathbb{E}(\mathbb{S}) = -\underset{(X_i, n_i)}{E} \left(\sum_{t=1}^{n_i} log\, y_t^{\langle m+1 \rangle} + \sum_{t=n_i+1}^{n_i+m} log\, y_t^{\langle t-n_i \rangle} \right) \quad (4)$$

Note that the equation 4 treats each dimension of the output y_t separately. Other sophisticated training criteria that encourage the cooperation among different dimensions have been tried, such as

$$\mathbb{E}(\mathbb{S}) = -\underset{(X_i, n_i)}{E} \left(\sum_{t=1}^{n_i} log\, y_t^{\langle m+1 \rangle} + \underset{t=n_i+1}{\overset{n_i+m}{max}} log\, y_t^{\langle t-n_i \rangle} \right) \quad (5)$$

which requires only one of the output to be 1 if the corresponding position is a sentence boundary. However, decrease of segmentation accuracy is observed from this kind of training criteria. We suspect that these criteria introduce dependency among the different dimensions, which reduces the robustness of the method and eventually harms the performance. Therefore, the idea has been avoided.

3.3 Decoding

Decoding on the proposed network is to infer the position of sentence boundaries from a sequence of real-number vectors y_t. The decoding method should be both simple enough to

cause no additional latency, and effective enough to achieve competitive accuracy. Therefore, the threshold-latency hybrid decoding strategy proposed by Wang et al. (2016) is extended for the proposed network (illustrated by Figure 3).

The extended decoding strategy uses an m-dimensional threshold vector $\theta = (\theta^{\langle 1 \rangle}, \theta^{\langle 2 \rangle}, \ldots, \theta^{\langle m \rangle})$ to deal with the m-dimensional output y_t. The strategy works as, for each time stamp t,

1. if $y_t^{\langle k \rangle}$ exceeds $\theta^{\langle k \rangle}$ ($k = m, m-1, \ldots, 1$), set $\hat{t} = t - k$ and go to 3;

2. if the buffered input exceed the maximum length, find $argmax_{t',k}(y_{t'}^{\langle k \rangle} - \theta^{\langle k \rangle})$, set $\hat{t} = t' - k$ and go to 3;

3. predict a sentence boundary after $\hat{t}$, and restart the decoding from $\hat{t} + 1$.

The method of tuning θ is described in Section 3.4.

3.4 Tuning

This subsection first defines an empirical score to measure the overall performance of online sentence segmentation, which serves as a target for tuning; then presents an algorithm to search for the optimal threshold vector to maximize the score.

3.4.1 Performance Measurement

An F_1 score calculated on the base of sentences is adopted to measure the accuracy of sentence segmentation. According to our observation, SI

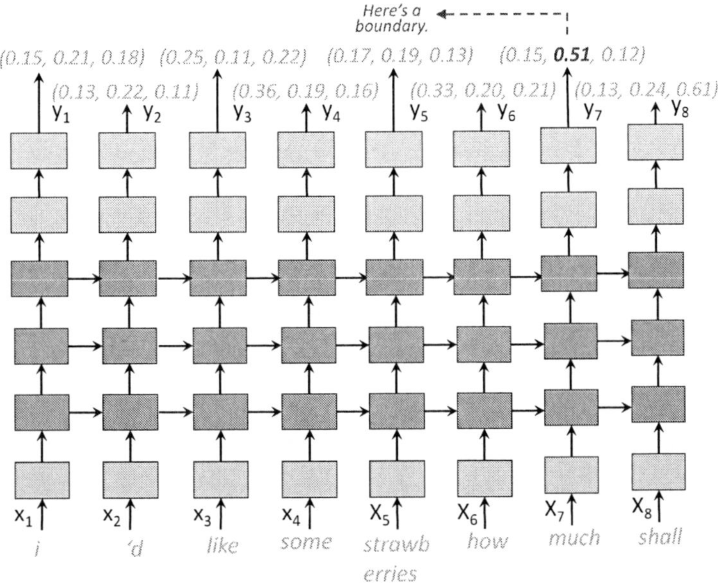

Figure 3: Decoding a Sample on Multi-shifted RNN Sentence Segmentor. Suppose the threshold vector is $(0.40, 0.50, 0.60)$. $y_7^{\langle 2 \rangle}$ is the first value that exceeds the corresponding threshold $\theta^{\langle 2 \rangle}$. This correctly predicts a sentence boundary after the time stamp 5. Note that y_t's last dimension $y_t^{\langle 4 \rangle} = 1 - y_t^{\langle 1 \rangle} - y_t^{\langle 2 \rangle} - y_t^{\langle 3 \rangle}$ is omitted for simplicity.

users often judge the performance based on sentences – how many predicted sentences are correct and how many oracle sentences are recalled. The F_1 score summarizes the precision and recall through calculating the harmonic mean as,

$$F_1 = 2 \, \frac{precision \cdot recall}{precision + recall}. \tag{6}$$

The latency of sentence segmentation is measured as the average distance per word between the time stamp when a word is input to the segmentor, and the time stamp when this word is output as part of a sentence. Please see Section 4.2 on calculating the latency of the oracle segmentation for an example.

An empirical score is proposed to summarize accuracy and latency, calculated as

$$score = F_1 - \alpha \cdot latency, \tag{7}$$

The trade-off existed because a segmentor could either trade latency for accuracy by waiting for more input words to re-evaluate a prediction, or trade accuracy for latency by predicting boldly without waiting for more evidence brought by input words. The trade-off ratio α is set to 0.01 in this paper according to our observation on SI users and our test on practical sentence segmentors. Note that this ratio can be changed to fit

practical applications without the need to revise the proposed method.

3.4.2 Tuning Algorithm

Manually tuning the threshold vector θ for the proposed network is unfeasible as it has m dimensions. Therefore, we propose to use a heuristic greedy search to maximize the score on a develop set, presented in Algorithm 1. The algorithm increases the efficiency by,

- prioritizing the threshold vectors whose parent have achieved high scores;

- pruning the search space by the heuristic that the $\theta^{\langle k \rangle}$ ($k = 1 \ldots m$) should be in descending order.

The intuition for the second point is that a higher threshold should be given to the value derived from fewer future words, because the evidence under that circumstance is weaker.

4 Experiments

4.1 Experimental Setting

The corpora from the shared task in the international workshop on spoken language translation (IWSLT 2015) are used as the experimental corpora (Cettolo et al., 2015)[3]. The task is to translate

---

[3]https://wit3.fbk.eu/mt.php?release=2015-01

Algorithm 1 Tuning Threshold Vector

Require: θ_0 $\triangleright$ a seed threshold vector
Require: $\mathbb{D}$ $\triangleright$ a development set
Require: μ $\triangleright$ a search step on threshold
Require: ν $\triangleright$ a margin on score

1:   $\Theta \leftarrow [\theta_0 : 0]$ $\triangleright$ a sorted list of threshold vectors descending on the scores of their parents
2:   $s^* \leftarrow -\infty$ $\triangleright$ the best score
3:   $\theta^* \leftarrow \theta_0$ $\triangleright$ the best threshold vector
4:   $dict \leftarrow \{\}$ $\triangleright$ a dictionary of visited threshold vectors
5:   **for** θ in the beginning of Θ **do**
6:   remove θ from Θ
7:   **if** θ' not in $dict$ **then**
8:     $dict \leftarrow dict \cup \{\theta\}$
9:     $s \leftarrow$ decode $\mathbb{D}$ using θ and evaluate
10:     **if** $s \geqslant s^* - \nu$ **then**
11:       **if** $s > s^*$ **then**
12:         $s^* \leftarrow s$
13:         $\theta^* \leftarrow \theta$
14:       **end if**
15:       **for** k in 1 to m **do**
16:         $\theta' \leftarrow$ increase/decrease $\theta^{\langle k \rangle}$ by μ
17:         **if** $\theta'^{\langle k-1 \rangle} \geqslant \theta'^{\langle k \rangle} \geqslant \theta'^{\langle k+1 \rangle}$ **and** $0.0 \leqslant \theta'^{\langle k \rangle} \leqslant 1.0$ **then**
18:           $\Theta \leftarrow \Theta \cup [\theta' : s]$
19:         **end if**
20:       **end for**
21:     **end if**
22:   **end if**
23: **end for**
    return θ^*

English TED talks into Chinese. Table 3 presents the statistics of the corpora. The news commentary corpora (Tiedemann, 2012)[4] and a subset of the OpenSubtitles corpora (Lison and Tiedemann, 2016)[5] are used to scale up the in-domain training set in order to achieve higher performance.

The corpora are pre-processed using standard procedures for MT. The English text is tokenized using the toolkit released with the Europarl corpus (Koehn, 2005) and converted to lower case. The Chinese text is tokenized into Chinese characters and English words using the tool of *splitUTF8Characters.pl* from the NIST Open Machine Translation 2008 Evaluation [6]

[4] http://opus.nlpl.eu/News-Commentary.php
[5] http://opus.nlpl.eu/OpenSubtitles2016.php
[6] ftp://jaguar.ncsl.nist.gov/mt/resources/

Two operations are applied in order to simulate the transcripts generated by ASR following the setting in (Wang et al., 2016) and (Cho et al., 2017). First, because ASR engines normally do not produce punctuation, punctuation is removed from the text. Second, because ASR engines split output based on long pauses, and each of the output contains multiple sentences; every 10 neighboring sentences in the development and test set are concatenated to form an input for sentence segmentation.

Two baselines are used in the experiments. The first baseline is the n-gram LM-based method proposed by Wang et al. (2016). The toolkit of SRILM (Stolcke, 2002)[7] is used to build n-gram LMs with Kneser-Ney Smoothing and an order of 6.

The second baseline is an extension of the first one by replacing the n-gram LM with an RNN LM. The settings of RNN LM follow the large LSTM setting used by Zaremba et al. (2014) which consists of two layers of 1500 LSTM units (Hochreiter and Schmidhuber, 1997), and a vocabulary size of 10K. A dropout of 0.65 is applied to the non-recurrent connections.

The proposed neural network adopts three layers of 512 LSTM units, and an input vocabulary size of 20K according to our pilot experiments. The output dimension m is 6. A dropout of 0.50 is applied to the non-recurrent connections. Larger networks have been tried in our experiments, but no significant improvement has been observed.

Both the proposed network and RNN LM are trained using SGD with a start learning rate of 1.0. The cross-entropy on the development set is measured after each epoch. When the development cross-entropy stops decreasing, the learning rate starts to decay by 0.5 per epoch. The training terminates when no improvement is made during 3 continuous attempts of decaying learning rates.

The numbers of future words for the two baseline methods are enumerated from 1 to 6, and the decoding thresholds are tuned by a grid search from -1.6 to 1.6 with a step of 0.2. The decoding threshold vector for the proposed method is tuned by Algorithm 1 with $\theta_0 = (0.9, 0.8, 0.7, 0.6, 0.5, 0.4)$, $\mu = 0.1$, and $\nu = 0.04$. The maximum sentence length is set to 40 for all the methods, which covers approximately 95% development and test sentences.

[7] http://www.speech.sri.com/projects/srilm/

Corpus	Sentences	Src. Tokens	Trg. Tokens
IWSLT-Train	209,491	4,270,869	6,050,169
News Commentary	223,153	5,689,117	5,660,789
OpenSubtitle(subset)[†]	1,000,000	8,682,476	1,047,208
Dev (test2010 test2011)	2,815	55,426	83,317
Test (test2012 test2013)	2,658	52,766	74,822

Table 3: Experimental Corpora. [†] The subset consists of the first one million sentence pairs.

The software is implemented using C++ and NVIDIA's GPU-accelerated libraries. The experiments are run on a workstation equipped with an Intel Xeon CPU E5-2630 and a GPU Quadro M4000.

4.2 Evaluation after Training on Standard Set

The three methods – two baselines and the proposed method – first learn their models on the source side of the standard training set (Table 3). The n-gram LM-based method learns a 6-ordered n-gram LM whose perplexity on the development set is 148.17. The RNN LM-based method learns an RNN LM with a development perplexity of 62.93. The proposed method learns a network model with a development cross entropy of 0.441. After that, each method tunes its decoding parameters on the development set to maximize the score (the equation 6). In the end, each method decodes the test set using its learned method and tuned parameters. The evaluation of the results is presented in Table 4.

The proposed method outperforms the stronger baseline of the RNN LM-based method by 18.8% on the measurement of score, which is quite large. The improvement is caused by the rise of the measurement of accuracy – F_1 – which is improved by 13.5%, and the stableness of the latency which is only enlarged by 3.4%. This result indicates that the architecture of the proposed network suits the task better than that of RNN LM. In addition, the RNN LM-based method outperforms the n-gram LM-based method by 67.7%. This confirms our expectation that RNN can model a sentence better than n-gram as it can capture long-distance dependencies.

The table also presents the latency of the oracle segmentation which assumes that every sentence is submitted to MT engines as soon as it ends. Suppose the i-th sentence has l_i words, the average latency per word would be $\frac{\sum_i l_i \cdot (l_i-1)/2}{\sum_i l_i}$. On the ex-

perimental test set in, the latency of the oracle segmentation is 8.126, and the latency of the proposed method is 12.386. This approximately means a delay of 4.2 words per sentence, which is acceptable in a real-world environment.

4.3 Evaluation after Adapting Models Trained on Scaled-up Set

Luong et al. (2015) and Cho et al. (2016) show that large-scale out-domain training data and model adaption can effective improve the quality of NMT models. They first train models on the union set of in-domain and out-domain data, and then adapt the models by resuming training on in-domain data only. Inspired by their work, we scale up the standard training set to pursuit better performance for sentence segmentation (see Table 3 for details) .

Through scaling up training set and model adaptation, the development perplexity of the RNN LM is reduced by 8.06% (from 62.93 to 57.86), and the development cross entropy of the model learned by the proposed method decreases by 0.082 (from 0.441 to 0.359).

The n-gram LM is adapted by linear interpolation. The mixture weight is tuned to minimize the development perplexity, whose value turns out to be 0.7. The development perplexity of the n-gram LM is reduced by 8.25% (from 148.16 to 135.93)

Each method again tunes its decoding parameters, and then decodes the test set as described in Section 4.2. Table 5 summarizes the results, and compares them with the previous ones on the standard training set. The performance of all three methods is found to be improved, while the proposed method achieves the largest improvement.

The detailed comparison between the two results (the last row in Table 5) shows that all the individual performance measurements have been improved. Moreover, the optimal thresholds generally get lower. This clearly indicates that the quality of the trained model has been improved, which is quite impressive. The same effects also

Methods	Parameters		Performance				
	n_f	thresh.	Precision	Recall	F_1	Latency	Score
Oracle			1.000	1.000	1.000	8.126	0.9187
n-gram LM	1	-0.6	0.1402	0.2432	0.1779	8.3410	0.0945
	2	-0.6	**0.1862**	**0.3087**	**0.2323**	**9.6480**	**0.1358**
	3	-0.6	0.1928	0.3005	0.2349	11.2520	0.1224
	4	-0.6	0.1944	0.2993	0.2357	12.2930	0.1128
	5	-0.6	0.1935	0.2959	0.2340	13.2410	0.1016
	6	-0.6	0.1927	0.2937	0.2327	14.1570	0.0912
RNN LM	1	-0.8	0.2686	0.3213	0.2926	10.3503	0.1891
	2	-0.6	**0.3289**	**0.3683**	**0.3475**	**11.9733**	**0.2277**
	3	-0.8	0.3255	0.3743	0.3482	12.7531	0.2207
	4	-0.8	0.3372	0.3845	0.3593	13.8317	0.2210
	5	-0.8	0.3342	0.3822	0.3566	14.8643	0.2080
	6	-0.8	0.3256	0.3740	0.3481	15.7449	0.1907
Proposed	$1-6$	$(...)^\ddagger$	**0.3583**	**0.4387**	**0.3945**	**12.3863**	**0.2706**
Improve[†]			8.9%	19.1%	13.5%	-3.4%	18.8%

Table 4: Performance after Training on Standard Set. [†] Improvement versus the stronger baseline of RNN LM. [‡] The optimal threshold vector is (1.0, 0.8, 0.8, 0.5, 0.5, 0.3).

Methods	Parameters		Performance				
	n_f	thresh.	Precision	Recall	F_1	Latency	Score
n-gram LM	1	-0.6	0.1349	0.2541	0.1762	7.6290	0.1000
	2	-0.4	**0.2054**	**0.3163**	**0.2490**	**10.3310**	**0.1457** (+0.0099)[†]
	3	-0.4	0.2125	0.3148	0.2537	11.6760	0.1369
	4	-0.4	0.2129	0.3129	0.2534	12.7040	0.1264
	5	-0.4	0.2125	0.3099	0.2521	13.6660	0.1154
	6	-0.4	0.2120	0.3080	0.2512	14.5780	0.1054
RNN LM	1	-1.0	0.2574	0.3269	0.2880	9.7292	0.1907
	2	-1.0	**0.3205**	**0.3894**	**0.3516**	**11.2249**	**0.2394** (+0.0117)[†]
	3	-0.8	0.3383	0.3856	0.3604	12.8106	0.2323
	4	-1.0	0.3315	0.3894	0.3581	13.6455	0.2217
	5	-1.0	0.3302	0.3871	0.3564	14.7268	0.2092
	6	-1.0	0.3295	0.3845	0.3549	15.7642	0.1972
Proposed	1–6	$(...)^\ddagger$	**0.3959**	**0.4605**	**0.4257**	**12.1118**	**0.3046** (+0.0340) [†]
Imp. vs. RNN LM			23.5%	18.3%	21.1%	-7.9%	27.2%
Imp. vs. standard[†]			10.5%	5.0 %	7.9%	2.2%	12.6%

Table 5: Segmentation Performance after Adapting the Models Trained on Scaled-up Set. [†] Compared to the best score of each method on the standard training set. [‡] The optimal threshold vector is (0.9, 0.8, 0.5, 0.5, 0.5, 0.4)

happen on the RNN LM-based method. Therefore, adapting neural network models through resuming training is a very effective technique.

4.4 Evaluation of End-to-end Translation Quality

The best segmentations of each method, which are listed in Table 5 in bold font, are post-processed to recover case and punctuation, and then piped into an English-to-Chinese NMT engine. The post-processing is conducted by a monotone phrase-based statistical MT system, which is trained to translate lower-cased unpunctuated sentences to cased punctuated sentences. Moses toolkit (Koehn et al., 2007) is used. The NMT engine is an implementation of attention-based encoder-decoder proposed by Bahdanau et al. (2014) and Luong et al. (2015), and the model is trained and tuned on an

Methods	BLEU	Loss[†]
Oracle	19.73	
n-gram LM	18.98	0.75
RNN LM	19.38	0.35
Proposed	**19.48**	**0.25** (-28.6%)[‡]

Table 6: Evaluation of End-to-end Translation Quality. [†] Compared to the BLEU of the oracle sentence segmentation. [‡] Compared to the stronger baseline of RNN LM.

in-house parallel corpus of approximately 21 million sentence pairs from various domains.

The translations are evaluated following the official guidelines of IWSLT 2015. The translations are aligned to reference sentences through edit distance (Matusov et al., 2005). BLEU is calculated on cased tokens including Chinese characters and English words. Table 6 presents the results.

The results show that the proposed method achieves the highest BLEU, which is lower than that of the oracle segmentation only by 0.25. The improvement compared to the stronger baseline of the RNN LM-based method is 0.10 BLEU point, or 28.6% calculated by 0.10 / 0.35.

5 Related Works

Segmenting the unpunctuated transcripts generated by ASR have attracted attentions from many researchers. A large variety of methods have been proposed.

Conditional random fields (CRFs) are used to approach the problem. Hassan et al. (2014) did a thorough treatment of this problem in 2014. However, CRFs have been outperformed by neural networks recently.

MT systems are used to approach the problem by Cho et al.(2015), Ha et al. (2015), Kzai et al. (2015), Cho et al. (2017), Pham et al. (2016), Klejch et al. (2016; 2017) and Przybysz et al. (2016). This approach builds MT systems to translate unpunctuated text into punctuated text which contains full stop marks as sentence boundaries. The drawback of this approach is that MT systems normally expect complete sequences as input, which prevents them from working in an online manner. Cho et al. (2015; 2017) address the issue using sliding windows. A fixed-length subsequence of words are extracted from the stream of words, and then feed into MT systems. The shortage of this method is that the dependencies outside the sliding windows are ignored, which will de-

crease the accuracy. In contrast, our RNN-based method performs incremental decoding from the beginning of sentences, so it can capture all the dependencies within a whole sentence.

Pauses, or precisely the duration of silence between two spoken words, which can be captured by ASR engines, are used to predict sentence boundaries by Fügen et al. (2007) and Bangalore et al. (2012). However, studies on human interpreters reveal that segmenting merely by pauses is insufficient, as human speakers might not pause between sentences. The mean proportion of silence-based chunking by interpreters is 6.6% when the source is English, 10% when it is French, and 17.1% when it is German (Venuti, 2012). Therefore, this paper focuses on using linguistic information. Nevertheless, pauses can be directly integrated into our proposed method to boost performance.

There are several segmentation methods that target at splitting an input sentence into smaller pieces for simultaneous interpretation, such as Yarmohammadi et al. (2013), Oda et al. (2014), and Fujita et al. (2013). However, these methods often assume that ASR transcripts have already been segmented into sentences, which is the task addressed by this paper. Therefore, our method is orthogonal to these methods, and it is possible to pipeline our proposed method with them.

6 Conclusion

In this paper, a multi-shifted RNN is proposed to solve the problem of segmenting the unpunctuated ASR transcripts for SI. The multi-shifted RNN addresses the trade-off between accuracy and latency which are the two central elements of the problem. The experiments show that the proposed method greatly outperforms an n-gram LM-based method and an RNN LM-based method on accuracy, latency and end-to-end BLEU, under both a standard training set and a scaled-up training set.

Acknowledgement

This work was partially conducted under the program "Promotion of Global Communications Plan: Research, Development, and Social Demonstration of Multilingual Speech Translation Technology" of the Ministry of Internal Affairs and Communications (MIC), Japan.

References

Bahdanau, Dzmitry, Kyunghyun Cho, and Yoshua Bengio. 2014. Neural machine translation by jointly learning to align and translate. *Proceedings of the 3rd International Conference on Learning Representations.*, pages 1–15.

Bangalore, Srinivas, Vivek Kumar Rangarajan Sridhar, Prakash Kolan, Ladan Golipour, and Aura Jimenez. 2012. Real-time incremental speech-to-speech translation of dialogs. In *Proceedings of the 2012 Conference of the North American Chapter of the Association for Computational Linguistics: Human Language Technologies*, pages 437–445. Association for Computational Linguistics.

Cettolo, Mauro, Jan Niehues, Sebastian Stüker, Luisa Bentivogli, Roldano Cattoni, and Marcello Federico. 2015. The IWSLT 2015 evaluation campaign. In *IWSLT 2015, International Workshop on Spoken Language Translation.*

Cho, Eunah, Jan Niehues, Kevin Kilgour, and Alex Waibel. 2015. Punctuation insertion for real-time spoken language translation. In *Proceedings of the Eleventh International Workshop on Spoken Language Translation.*

Cho, Eunah, Jan Niehues, Thanh-Le Ha, Matthias Sperber, Mohammed Mediani, and Alex Waibel. 2016. Adaptation and combination of NMT systems: The KIT translation systems for IWSLT 2016. In *Proceedings of the 13th International Workshop on Spoken Language Translation (IWSLT 2016).*

Cho, Eunah, Jan Niehues, and Alex Waibel. 2017. Nmt-based segmentation and punctuation insertion for real-time spoken language translation. *Proc. Interspeech 2017*, pages 2645–2649.

Fügen, Christian, Alex Waibel, and Muntsin Kolss. 2007. Simultaneous translation of lectures and speeches. *Machine Translation*, 21(4):209–252.

Fujita, Tomoki, Graham Neubig, Sakriani Sakti, Tomoki Toda, and Satoshi Nakamura. 2013. Simple, lexicalized choice of translation timing for simultaneous speech translation. In *INTERSPEECH*, pages 3487–3491.

Ha, Thanh-Le, Jan Niehues, Eunah Cho, Mohammed Mediani, and Alex Waibel. 2015. The KIT translation systems for IWSLT 2015. In *Proceedings of the twelveth International Workshop on Spoken Language Translation (IWSLT), Da Nang, Veitnam*, pages 62–69.

Hassan, Hany, Lee Schwartz, Dilek Hakkani-Tür, and Gokhan Tur. 2014. Segmentation and disfluency removal for conversational speech translation. In *Fifteenth Annual Conference of the International Speech Communication Association.*

Hochreiter, Sepp and Jürgen Schmidhuber. 1997. Long short-term memory. *Neural computation*, 9(8):1735–1780.

Klejch, Ondřej, Peter Bell, and Steve Renals. 2016. Punctuated transcription of multi-genre broadcasts using acoustic and lexical approaches. In *Spoken Language Technology Workshop (SLT), 2016 IEEE*, pages 433–440. IEEE.

Klejch, Ondřej, Peter Bell, and Steve Renals. 2017. Sequence-to-sequence models for punctuated transcription combining lexical and acoustic features. In *Acoustics, Speech and Signal Processing (ICASSP), 2017 IEEE International Conference on*, pages 5700–5704. IEEE.

Koehn, Philipp, Hieu Hoang, Alexandra Birch, Chris Callison-Burch, Marcello Federico, Nicola Bertoldi, Brooke Cowan, Wade Shen, Christine Moran, Richard Zens, et al. 2007. Moses: Open source toolkit for statistical machine translation. In *Proceedings of the 45th Annual Meeting of the Association for Computational Linguistics on Interactive Poster and Demonstration Sessions*, pages 177–180. Association for Computational Linguistics.

Koehn, Philipp. 2005. Europarl: A parallel corpus for statistical machine translation. In *Proceedings of MT Summit*, volume 5, pages 79–86.

Kzai, Michaeel, Brian Thompson, Elizabeth Salesky, Timothy Anderson, Grant Erdmann, Eric Hansen, Brian Ore, Katherine Young, Jeremy Gwinnup, Michael Hutt, and Christina May. 2015. The MITLL-AFRL IWSLT 2015 systems. In *Proceedings of the twelveth International Workshop on Spoken Language Translation (IWSLT), Da Nang, Veitnam*, pages 23–30.

Lison, Pierre and Jörg Tiedemann. 2016. OpenSubtitles2016: Extracting large parallel corpora from movie and TV subtitles.

Luong, Minh-Thang and Christopher D Manning. 2015. Stanford neural machine translation systems for spoken language domains. In *Proceedings of the International Workshop on Spoken Language Translation*, pages 76–79.

Luong, Thang, Hieu Pham, and Christopher D. Manning. 2015. Effective approaches to attention-based neural machine translation. In *Proceedings of the 2015 Conference on Empirical Methods in Natural Language Processing*, pages 1412–1421, Lisbon, Portugal, September. Association for Computational Linguistics.

Matusov, Evgeny, Gregor Leusch, Oliver Bender, Hermann Ney, et al. 2005. Evaluating machine translation output with automatic sentence segmentation. In *IWSLT*, pages 138–144. Citeseer.

Mikolov, Tomáš, Martin Karafiát, Lukáš Burget, Jan Černocký, and Sanjeev Khudanpur. 2010. Recurrent neural network based language model. In *Eleventh Annual Conference of the International Speech Communication Association.*

Oda, Yusuke, Graham Neubig, Sakriani Sakti, Tomoki Toda, and Satoshi Nakamura. 2014. Optimizing segmentation strategies for simultaneous speech translation. In *ACL (2)*, pages 551–556.

Pham, Ngoc-Quan, Matthias Sperber, Elizabeth Salesky, Thanh-Le Ha, Jan Niehues, and Alex Waibel. 2016. KIT's Multilingual Neural Machine Translation systems for IWSLT 2017. In *Proceedings of the 14th International Workshop on Spoken Language Translation (IWSLT 2017)*, pages 42–47.

Przybysz, Pawel, Marcin Chochowski, Rico Sennrich, Barry Haddow, and Alexandra Birch. 2016. The Samsung and University of Edinburghs submission to IWSLT17. In *Proceedings of the 14th International Workshop on Spoken Language Translation (IWSLT 2017)*, pages 23–28.

Stolcke, Andreas and Elizabeth Shriberg. 1996. Automatic linguistic segmentation of conversational speech. In *Spoken Language, 1996. ICSLP 96. Proceedings., Fourth International Conference on*, volume 2, pages 1005–1008. IEEE.

Stolcke, Andreas, Elizabeth Shriberg, Rebecca A Bates, Mari Ostendorf, Dilek Hakkani, Madelaine Plauche, Gökhan Tür, and Yu Lu. 1998. Automatic detection of sentence boundaries and disfluencies based on recognized words. In *Proceedings of 5th International Conference on Spoken Language Processing*, pages 2247–2250.

Stolcke, Andreas. 2002. SRILM - an extensible language modeling toolkit. In *Proceedings of the 7th International Conference on Spoken Language Processing*.

Tiedemann, Jörg. 2012. Parallel Data, Tools and Interfaces in OPUS. In *LREC*, volume 2012, pages 2214–2218.

Venuti, Lawrence. 2012. *The translation studies reader*. Routledge.

Wang, Xiaolin, Andrew Finch, Masao Utiyama, and Eiichiro Sumita. 2016. An efficient and effective online sentence segmenter for simultaneous interpretation. In *Proceedings of the 3rd Workshop on Asian Translation (WAT2016)*, pages 139–148, Osaka, Japan, December. The COLING 2016 Organizing Committee.

Yarmohammadi, Mahsa, Vivek Kumar Rangarajan Sridhar, Srinivas Bangalore, and Baskaran Sankaran. 2013. Incremental segmentation and decoding strategies for simultaneous translation. In *IJCNLP*, pages 1032–1036.

Zaremba, Wojciech, Ilya Sutskever, and Oriol Vinyals. 2014. Recurrent neural network regularization. *arXiv preprint arXiv:1409.2329*.

Robust Document Representations for Cross-Lingual Information Retrieval in Low-Resource Settings

Mahsa Yarmohammadi[1], Xutai Ma[2], Sorami Hisamoto[3], Muhammad Rahman[4], Yiming Wang[5], Hainan Xu[6], Daniel Povey[7], Philipp Koehn[8] and Kevin Duh[9]

Center for Language and Speech Processing,
Johns Hopkins University, Baltimore, MD, USA
{mahsa[1],xutai_ma[2],sorami[3],mahbubur[4],yiming.wang[5],phi[8]}@jhu.edu
{hainan.xv[6],dpovey[7]}@gmail.com kevinduh@cs.jhu.edu[9]

Abstract

The goal of cross-lingual information retrieval (CLIR) is to find relevant documents written in languages different from that of the query. Robustness to translation errors is one of the main challenges for CLIR, especially in low-resource settings where there is limited training data for building machine translation (MT) systems or bilingual dictionaries. If the test collection contains speech documents, additional errors from automatic speech recognition (ASR) makes translation even more difficult. We propose a robust document representation that combines N-best translations and a novel bag-of-phrases output from various ASR/MT systems. We perform a comprehensive empirical analysis on three challenging collections; they consist of Somali, Swahili, and Tagalog speech/text documents to be retrieved by English queries. By comparing various ASR/MT systems with different error profiles, our results demonstrate that a richer document representation can consistently overcome issues in low translation accuracy for CLIR in low-resource settings.

1 Introduction

Cross-lingual Information Retrieval (CLIR) is a search task where the user's query is written in a language different from that of the documents in the collection. There are some important niche applications, for example, a local news reporter searching foreign-language news-feeds to obtain different perspectives for her story, or a patent writer exploring the patents in another country to understand prior art before submitting her application, or an aid worker monitoring the social media of a disaster-affected area, looking for unmet needs and new emergencies. In all these scenarios, CLIR increases the user base by enabling users who are not proficient in the foreign language to productively participate as knowledge workers. Even if the user requires manual translations of the retrieved documents to complete her task, CLIR can at least provide a triage/filtering step.

CLIR performance depends critically on the accuracy of its underlying machine translation or bilingual dictionary component. Recent advances in MT suggest that it is now ever more possible to build CLIR for practical use. In particular, the availability of large amounts of parallel text in some language-pairs (e.g. English sentences and their aligned German translations from European Parliamentary proceedings) had led to dramatic improvements in MT quality. However, there are many language-pairs–what we term "low-resource" settings–where parallel text is limited and the challenge is to make CLIR robust to translation errors. Missing words in translation may lead to degradation in recall, while extraneous words may lead to degradation in precision.

In this work, we focus on the document translation approach to CLIR, where all foreign documents in the collection are translated into the language of the user query prior to indexing and search. While the use of N-best translations in CLIR is not a new idea, the contribution of the paper is a comprehensive analysis of how different kinds of document representations perform under low-resource settings. We compare whether indexing the N-best translations from MT leads to better CLIR than indexing only the 1-best (most-likely) translation. We also propose a novel bag-of-phrases document representation and show that it can be effectively combined with the N-best document representations. The idea behind the bag-of-phrases translation is the fact that less strict syntax is required in a CLIR system, which is often based on keyword search. The bag-of-phrases method relaxes the strict language grammar in the target language when producing translations, and instead, emphasizes the selection of translation words.

We perform comprehensive experiments on three low-resource test collections from the IARPA MATERIAL project (OpenCLIR Evaluation, 2018), where the documents are in Somali, Swahili, and Tagalog and the queries are in English. The inclusion of speech documents (audio files) in this collection means that automatic speech recognition (ASR) has to be run before MT, leading to further challenges in translation accuracy. Our results demonstrate that a rich document representation containing many translation hypotheses consistently improves CLIR performance in these low-resource settings.

2 Related Work

The key component in CLIR is translation, to resolve language gap between documents and queries. An appropriate approach is query translation (Oard et al., 2008), where the query is translated into the desired language based on a dictionary (Pirkola et al., 2001), or parallel corpora (Dumais et al., 1996). Query translation often suffers from translation ambiguity due to the limited amount of context in short queries. Another approach is document translation (Croft et al., 1991), which can produce more precise translation due to having more context. Several studies have compared the query translation and document translation approaches (Nie, 2010; Dwivedi and Chandra, 2016).

In recent years, deep neural networks have shown significant results on NLP tasks such as machine translation (Bahdanau et al., 2014), however, applying such models to information retrieval tasks has had relatively less positive results (Craswell et al., 2016). The reason is that, first, IR tasks are fundamentally different from NLP tasks, and second, the application of neural networks to

IR problems has been under-explored. Recently some work on CLIR adopt word embedding approaches to use unlabeled text to learn the representations in unsupervised manner, and use them for document search (Vulić and Moens, 2015; Litschko et al., 2018; Josifoski et al., 2019). Such methods allow to learn representations from comparable data or independent monolingual data and alleviate the need for full-fledged machine translation. However, these methods are mostly useful when operating at Web scale, such as searching in Wikipedia articles, is considered. In this study, we focus on searching on a limited set of given documents in foreign low-resource language.

3 Task

The goal of the task we focus on this paper is to develop ASR, MT, and IR methods to most efficiently respond to queries against multilingual speech and text data in low-resource languages. The system will take English queries as input, and returns retrieved documents relevant to the queries as output. To resolve language differences in documents and queries, we focus on the document translation approach: all source documents in the foreign low-resource language are translated into English before search. Since some of the source documents are speech documents (audio files), we first run our ASR system on those to convert them to text before translation.

For each input query, the translated speech and text documents are searched via standard monolingual information retrieval approaches (e.g., BM25), which match words between query and document. Translation errors will naturally make this retrieval step more difficult. The retrieved documents are sorted according to their match scores, and we evaluate performance by comparing with the true (human-labeled) relevance ranking using standard metrics like Mean Averaged Precision (MAP).

4 Methods

4.1 Index and Search

Our CLIR engine is based on the document translation approach, where all foreign documents are translated beforehand and the English is what is indexed. We use a pre-existing search engine implementation Elasticsearch [1] to index, search, and

---

[1]https://www.elastic.co/products/elasticsearch

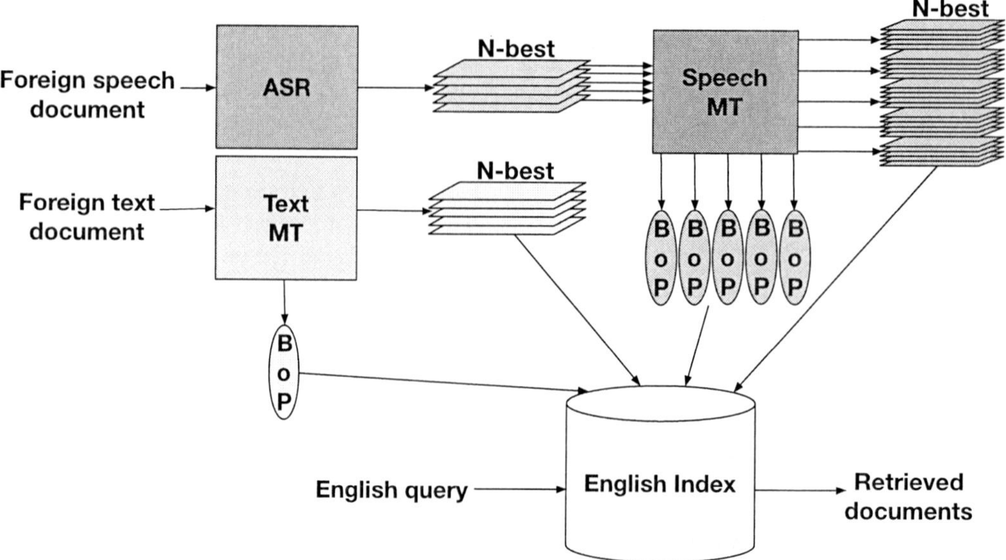

Figure 1: N-best+Bag-of-Phrases document representations for CLIR.

rank our translated documents. We use a standard built-in English analyzer to pre-process the document and query text. The analyzer conducts tokenization, word stemming, and stop word removal. We parse input query strings and convert them into Elasticsearch executable JSON format, then use those to retrieve search results from the Elasticsearch engine. We use Okapi BM25 (Robertson et al., 2009) algorithm to score the documents. BM25 is a popular algorithm to rank documents based on the relevance to a given query. We tuned the BM25 hyper parameters (for term frequency normalization and document length normalization), for each language to get the best CLIR performance. Finally the document ranking scores for each query are passed to the evaluation. CLIR performance is evaluated using the standard Mean Average Precision (MAP) measure.

4.2 Document Representations

To increase recall of documents and prevent error propagation from potential ASR or MT errors, we added multiple hypotheses capability to our CLIR pipeline. We implemented three types of pipelines, N-best decoding, bag-of-phrases, and combination of the two representations.

N-best decoding For speech documents, first, ASR generates N-best list for each input segment. Then MT decodes each of the ASR segment transcripts, generating M-best translations. The result

is an $N \times M$ list, which is indexed into the IR system with equal weighting. We explored two variations of N-best decoding, first where the full $N \times M$ matrix is included in the document to be indexed. The second variation is where we sub-sample the full $N \times M$ matrix to its diagonal elements, that is the best translation of the best ASR output, the second best translation of the second best ASR output, and so on and so forth. We did not notice gains in the CLIR performance from including the full matrix in the document as opposed to including only its diagonals. This shows that the redundancy of hypotheses in the full matrix is not necessary for CLIR. For simplicity, we only present results where N=M. For text documents, MT generates N-best translations of each sentence.

Bag-of-Phrases For speech documents, first, ASR generates N-best list for each input segment. Then we use the phrase-based MT system to generate all possible phrases whose source side matches the ASR transcripts. In other words, we output all the translation options but do not perform a full decoding search with language models. For each input segment, all of the output phrases are concatenated together to form the bag-of-phrases for that segment. For $N > 1$, bag-of-phrases of all of N-best lists are considered. These bag-of-phrases are then indexed into the IR system. The same procedure is applied to each sentence in text documents.

Combination of N-best decoding and Bag-of-

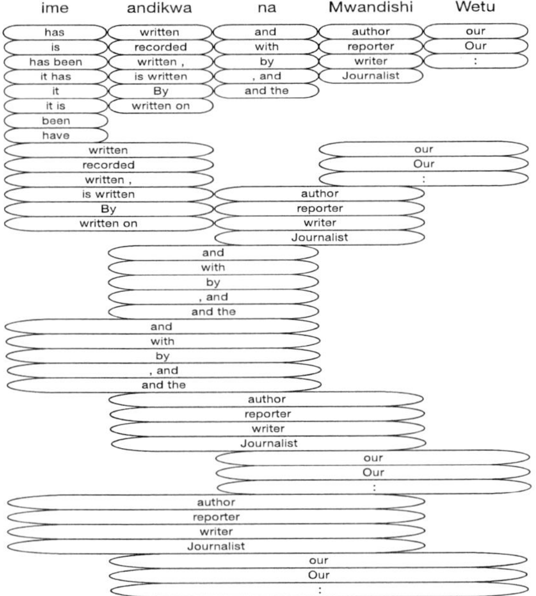

Figure 2: Bag-of-phrases (BoP) representation of the Swahili sentence "Imeandikwa na Mwandishi Wetu". The phrases in the boxes are all possible phrases that can be extracted from the phrase-based decoder.

Phrases Our IR system allows multiple "views" of the same document. We can index on both N-best decoding and bag-of-phrases (BoP). The search function will score documents based on how well the query matches either of the views. As shown in Figure 1, foreign text documents are run through a text MT system to produce N-best and BoP outputs. Foreign speech documents are first run through the ASR system to be transcribed to N-best hypotheses. The hypotheses are then run through the speech MT system, which is the same as the text MT system but adapted to interface better with ASR, to produce N-best and BoP outputs. Finally, N-best and BoP outputs from foreign speech and text documents are indexed and searched in response to English queries and relevant documents are retrieved.

By indexing and searching both N-best and BoP representations we not only consider the most accurate translations achieved via N-best but also take advantage of additional lexical variety provided by BoP. Figure 2 shows all possible phrases from the phrase-based MT decoder for the example input sentence "Imeandikwa na Mwandishi Wetu" in Swahili. These phrases, form the BoP representation of that sentence, and as can be seen, a variety of translations for different input spans

are produced (e.g., the translations "author", "reporter", "writer", and "Journalist" for the Swahili word "Mwandishi"). The N-best (N=5) translations of the sentence are all the same sentence "it has been written by our writer" with different probabilities. Although the N-best output is a descent translation of the input in this example, it does not have as much word diversity as we could get from the BoP translation, thus hurting the retrieval of documents relevant to the query. For example, the word "Journalist" that is present in the BoP representation does not appear in the top 100 translations of the N-best representation. Thus, if a query includes that specific word, the chance of retrieving the document decreases if only the N-best representation is searched.

5 Data

5.1 CLIR Data

Given a query the system should detect which documents out of a set of documents are responsive to the query. Queries are English word strings that may contain words from any part of speech. There are different types of queries such as a lexical query consisting of a single word (e.g., "ocean"), a lexical query consisting of a multiple words (e.g., "bicycle race"), or conceptual queries that are subject to semantic expansion (e.g., "expiration+"). The set of documents includes speech and text documents from different genres. Table 1 shows the number of queries and documents we used for testing our CLIR system. Number of text documents is almost as twice as number of speech documents in each language.

5.2 ASR and MT Data

To train our ASR systems, we used "train" and "tune" data, which are transcribed conversational audio, as training and development sets. In addition, we used a large amount of untranscribed audio, the "unlabaled" set, for semi-supervised training of the acoustic model, as described in Section 6.1.

	# queries (English)	# documents (Foreign)		
		speech	text	total
Somali	442	279	559	838
Swahili	547	266	547	813
Tagalog	537	315	529	844

Table 1: CLIR test collection statistics.

ASR	Length (hours)
train	~40
tune	~10
unlabeled	~250
test	~20

MT	train (# Eng tokens)		test
	baseline	crawled	(#sent)
Somali	800k	1.7M	9.5k
Swahili	808k	5.2M	11.7k
Tagalog	759k	12.3M	11.4k

Table 2: ASR and MT data statistics.

We used parallel corpora (bitext) of around 800k English words to train our MT systems for translating from Somali, Swahili, or Tagalog to English. This data is provided in the BUILD package of the MATERIAL project and contains news, topical, and blog texts with provided source URLs. In addition, we harvested and filtered bitext from Web to augment this baseline bitext. We made this data publicly available[2]. It is important to filter web bitext to reduce noise. We filtered the web bitext using Zipporah (Xu and Koehn, 2017) and chose filter thresholds optimized on tune sets. The crawled data improved the MT system by 1 point BLEU or more for these languages. We also added monolingual WMT news and LDC Gigaword data, which include 8.2 billion English tokens in total to train the language models of our MT systems.

The IR system indexes and searches "test" documents that are either speech or text. There are around 20 hours of test speech data and 10k foreign sentences of test text data for each language. We have the reference transcripts and translations of "test", hence, we can measure the performance of our ASR and MT systems on the test set in terms of WER and BLEU scores, and also investigate how ASR/MT systems with different WER/BLEU scores impact CLIR. Table 2 shows the statistics of the ASR and MT data. For information about the number of test speech and text documents in each language see Table 1.

6 Experimental Setup

6.1 ASR system

Our ASR system follows normal pattern for Kaldi-based (Povey et al., 2011) system build. Our recipe is publicly available at GitHub[3].

Acoustic and language model. We use GMM training to create alignments and lattice-free MMI-trained neural network (Povey et al., 2016) with factorized TDNN (Povey et al., 2018). We gen-erate lattices with n-gram ARPA-style language model and re-score them with an n-best RNN language model (Xu et al., 2018a; Xu et al., 2018b). Source-side bitext and crawled monolingual data are used in building the n-gram LM, RNNLM re-scoring, as well as extending the baseline lexicon.

In addition to supervised training, we ran semi-supervised training of acoustic models using the extension of lattice-free MMI to semi-supervised scenarios (Manohar et al., 2018). We added unlabeled audio to the labeled audio in the training set to train the acoustic model. Table 3 shows the WER improvements from supervised to semi-supervised setup for Somali, Swahili, and Tagalog. To study the effect of ASR errors on CLIR, we tried both supervised and semi-supervised ASR systems in our experiments.

ASR input and output. Test data come in long unsegmented files of over a minute. To deal with this, we split the input into equal-size (15 second) slightly overlapping segments and stitch together the ASR outputs. For consistency, we lower-case all text resources that are used in training the ASR system, which include transcripts and external resources for language modeling (source-side bitext, web crawled monolingual text). As a result, the ASR output would be all lower-case. However, the machine translation system expects inputs that have been tokenized and true-cased. Thus, we post-process ASR output to normalize punctuation, tokenize, and true-case using the models and scripts that are used in MT training and decoding. This post-processing helps passing names through the MT system, and improves the IR performance.

6.2 MT System

We tried phrase-based machine translation (PBMT) as well as neural machine translation (NMT) for Somali-English, Swahili-English, and Tagalog-English language pairs. The PBMT systems were developed using the Moses SMT toolkit (Koehn et al., 2007). We trained our systems with the following settings: a maximum sentence

---

[2] http://www.paracrawl.eu/
[3] https://github.com/kaldi-asr/kaldi/tree/master/egs/material

ASR		ASR1	ASR2
Somali	tune	57.8	57.7
	test	56.7	48.4
Swahili	tune	38.9	36.7
	test	39.7	32.9
Tagalog	tune	47.5	46.6
	test	51.4	40.3

MT	BLEU PBMT	BLEU NMT
Somali	18.31	18.83
Swahili	28.66	30.18
Tagalog	33.05	29.95

Table 3: %WER for supervised (ASR1) and semi-supervised (ASR2) systems, BLEU scores for PBMT and NMT systems.

length of 80, grow-diag-final-and symmetrization of GIZA++ alignments, an interpolated Kneser-Ney smoothed 5-gram language model with KenLM (Heafield, 2011) used at runtime, hierarchical lexicalized reordering (Galley and Manning, 2008), a lexically-driven 5-gram operation sequence model (OSM) (Durrani et al., 2013) with count bin features (Chiang et al., 2009), a distortion limit of 6, maximum phrase-length of 5, 200-best translation options, compact phrase table (Junczys-Dowmunt, 2012) minimum Bayes risk decoding (Kumar and Byrne, 2004), cube pruning (Huang and Chiang, 2007), with a stack-size of 1000 during tuning and 5000 during test. We optimize feature function weights with k-best MIRA (Cherry and Foster, 2012).

The NMT systems are LSTM sequence-to-sequence models (Luong et al., 2015). The layer size is 512, and the number of layers is 4 for Swahili and Tagalog, 2 for Somali. The models were developed using the Fairseq[4] toolkit. For NMT, we applied Byte Pair Encoding (BPE) (Sennrich et al., 2016) to split word into subword segments for both source and target languages. The number of BPE operations is 3000 for all three languages. We observed improvements in BLEU scores under small BPE settings for all three language pairs.

We filtered noisy crawled bitext using Zipporah (Xu and Koehn, 2017) and applied the unsupervised morphology induction tool Morfessor (Virpioja et al., 2013) to split words up into putative morphemes, with keeping numbers and names unchanged. We noticed that splitting the words to morphemes improves BLEU scores for Somali and Swahili, but does not help for Tagalog.

To better translate speech documents, we built systems that are adapted to interface better with ASR, which we refer to as speech MT systems. For

building speech MT systems, we removed punctuation and spelled out the numbers in the bitext before training the MT systems, which both improved BLEU scores.

7 Results

We run our CLIR system using document representations based on a combination of N-best transcriptions/translations and the novel bag-of-phrases output from ASR/MT. A simple baseline for comparison is the query translation approach, where each word in English query is translated into its most likely foreign word using dictionary extracted from bitext. This baseline achieves the MAP scores of 0.0967, 0.1204, 0.2293 for Somali, Swahili, and Tagalog respectively, which all are inferior to the results we present in this section.

Table 4 shows MAP scores for different MT/ASR and document representation combinations for the three languages. For N-best and BoP representations, the results for $N = 5$ are shown in the table. For text, top 5 translations for each sentence are combined and indexed as the N-best document. For speech, 5 translations of the diagonal of the ASR $\times$ MT matrix for each speech segment are combined and indexed as the N-best document. For speech, BoP is the aggregation of bag-of-phrases translations of top 5 ASR outputs.

We observe that N-best+BoP achieves the best MAP scores across all settings. For example in the Somali ASR1+PBMT / PBMT pipeline, N-best+BoP achieves 0.2444, outperforming the 1-best baseline (0.1894), and isolated N-best (0.1902) and BoP (0.1999). This result even outperforms the 1-best reference translation (0.1956), indicating that a richer document representation based on multiple ASR/MT hypotheses, even if potentially error-prone, is better than a single professional translator's result in the context of CLIR. This is likely due to the challenge of finding exact

---

[4]We used a PyTorch implementation : `https://github.com/pytorch/fairseq`

Somali	Speech/Text	1-best	N-best	BoP	N-best+BoP
	ASR1+PBMT/PBMT	0.1894	0.1902	0.1999	**0.2444**
	ASR2+PBMT/PBMT	0.1970	0.2182	0.2080	**0.2526**
	ASR1+NMT/NMT	0.1322	**0.1623**	n/a	n/a
	ASR2+NMT/NMT	0.1321	**0.1630**	n/a	n/a
	ASR2+PBMT+NMT/PBMT+NMT	0.1999	0.2231	0.2080	**0.2521**
	Ref transcript+PBMT/PBMT	0.1965	0.2169	0.2268	**0.2633**
	Ref transcript+NMT/NMT	0.1509	**0.1788**	n/a	n/a
	Ref translation/Ref translation	0.1956	n/a	n/a	n/a

Swahili	Speech/Text	1-best	N-best	BoP	N-best+BoP
	ASR1+PBMT/PBMT	0.2234	0.2398	0.2072	**0.2582**
	ASR2+PBMT/PBMT	0.2306	0.2474	0.2135	**0.2634**
	ASR1+NMT/NMT	0.1897	**0.2061**	n/a	n/a
	ASR2+NMT/NMT	0.1896	**0.2104**	n/a	n/a
	ASR2+PBMT+NMT/PBMT+NMT	0.2299	0.2516	0.2135	**0.2632**
	Ref transcript+PBMT/PBMT	0.2437	0.2600	0.2170	**0.2768**
	Ref transcript+NMT/NMT	0.1902	**0.2099**	n/a	n/a
	Ref translation/Ref translation	0.2408	n/a	n/a	n/a

Tagalog	Speech/Text	1-best	N-best	BoP	N-best+BoP
	ASR1+PBMT/PBMT	0.2947	0.3162	0.3114	**0.3355**
	ASR2+PBMT/PBMT	0.2945	0.3159	0.3392	**0.3617**
	ASR1+NMT/NMT	0.2226	**0.2437**	n/a	n/a
	ASR2+NMT/NMT	0.2470	**0.2683**	n/a	n/a
	ASR2+PBMT+NMT/PBMT+NMT	0.3150	0.3380	0.3392	**0.3623**
	Ref transcript+PBMT/PBMT	0.3660	0.3906	0.3884	**0.4187**
	Ref transcript+NMT/NMT	0.2803	**0.3039**	n/a	n/a
	Ref translation/Ref translation	0.3847	n/a	n/a	n/a

Table 4: MAP scores for various ASR/MT systems and document representations (N=5) on Somali, Swahili, and Tagalog test sets.

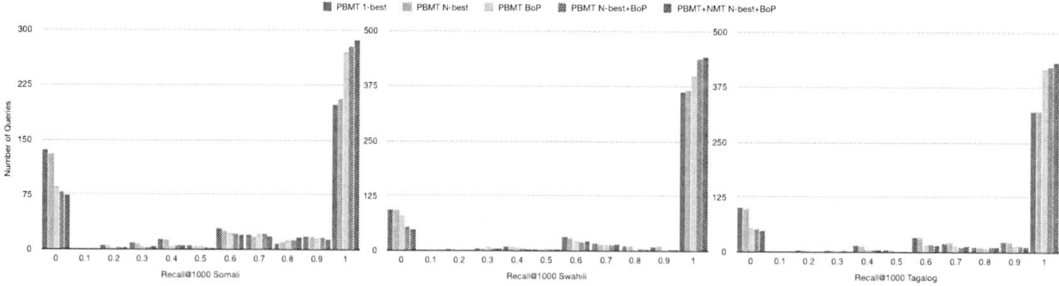

Figure 3: Per query recall@1000 for different systems.

match between the query and the document.[5] We also observe that the MAP scores from the ASR systems with lower word error rate (ASR2) are in general better than those from the ASR systems with higher word error rate (ASR1). This observation underscores the impact of a high quality ASR system on improving the performance of CLIR.

We noticed that NMT has much higher missed detection rate compared to PBMT, which turns into a low MAP score. Although the NMT model has comparable BLEU score, high missed detection indicate that NMT somehow fails to produce the tokens that IR system is interested in. More investigation of the reason is future work. We also use NMT translations as an additional field to PBMT translations (ASR2+PBMT+NMT / PBMT+NMT). We can observe that there is a small improvement over PBMT N-best+BoP method for Tagalog. We plotted number of queries versus the recall after 1000 documents are retrieved for different systems. As Figure 3 shows, when using N-best, BoP, N-best+BoP, and NMT as an additional feature, the number of queries with 0 recall decreases consistently in all three languages. This indicates that a richer document representation is indeed helping in retrieving relevant documents.

8 Conclusion and Future Work

The key component in CLIR is translation. The objective of translation in CLIR is different from Machine Translation tasks, as in information retrieval settings the goal is to retrieve relevant documents rather than having a high quality translation per se. In this study, we augmented high quality translation through N-best lists with the lexical variety of translation required for IR through BoP translations. We explored combinations of ASR and MT systems with different error profiles, and showed that our proposed N-best+BoP representation consistently performs well for CLIR on all three low-resource languages we studied. We plan to conduct various error analyses in future work to categorize the error types in our end-to-end CLIR system, as well as comparing PBMT and NMT systems. Another interesting future direction is to reinvestigate these representations in the context of

<hr>

[5]Note that these results are not necessary our best results, since we have not tuned for scoring function and various other hyper-parameters. This exercise is meant to compare multiple systems in a simple setting that varies only the document representation.

high-resource languages and stronger component systems, to contrast with the low-resource setting.

Acknowledgments

This work is supported in part by the Office of the Director of National Intelligence, Intelligence Advanced Research Projects Activity (IARPA), via contract #FA8650-17-C-9115. The views and conclusions contained herein are those of the authors and should not be interpreted as necessarily representing the official policies, either expressed or implied, of the sponsors.

References

Bahdanau, Dzmitry, Kyunghyun Cho, and Yoshua Bengio. 2014. Neural machine translation by jointly learning to align and translate. *arXiv preprint arXiv:1409.0473*.

Cherry, Colin and George Foster. 2012. Batch tuning strategies for statistical machine translation. In *Proceedings of the 2012 Conference of the NAACL-HLT*, pages 427–436. Association for Computational Linguistics.

Chiang, David, Kevin Knight, and Wei Wang. 2009. 11,001 new features for statistical machine translation. In *Proceedings of the 2009 Conference of the NAACL-HLT*, pages 218–226. Association for Computational Linguistics.

Craswell, Nick, W. Bruce Croft, Jiafeng Guo, Maarten de Rke, and Bhaskar Mitra. 2016. Report on the SIGIR 2016 workshop on Neural Information Retrieval (Neu-IR). *SIGIR Forum*, 50(2):96–103, December.

Croft, W Bruce, Howard R Turtle, and David D Lewis. 1991. The use of phrases and structured queries in information retrieval. In *Proceedings of the 14th ACM SIGIR conference*, pages 32–45.

Dumais, Susan T., Thomas K. Landauer, and Michael L. Littman. 1996. Automatic cross-linguistic information retrieval using latent semantic indexing. In *Proceedings of SIGIR Workshop on cross-Linguistic information retrieval*, pages 16–23.

Durrani, Nadir, Alexander Fraser, Helmut Schmid, Hieu Hoang, and Philipp Koehn. 2013. Can markov models over minimal translation units help phrase-based smt? In *Proceedings of the 51st Annual Meeting of the ACL*, volume 2, pages 399–405.

Dwivedi, Sanjay and Ganesh Chandra. 2016. A survey on cross language information retrieval. *Int'l Journal on Cybernetics & Informatics*, 5:127–142, 02.

Galley, Michel and Christopher D Manning. 2008. A simple and effective hierarchical phrase reordering model. In *Proceedings of the Conference on*

EMNLP, pages 848–856. Association for Computational Linguistics.

Heafield, Kenneth. 2011. KenLM: Faster and smaller language model queries. In *Proceedings of the sixth workshop on statistical machine translation*, pages 187–197. Association for Computational Linguistics.

Huang, Liang and David Chiang. 2007. Forest rescoring: Faster decoding with integrated language models. In *Proceedings of the 45th annual meeting of the ACL*, pages 144–151.

Josifoski, Martin, Ivan S. Paskov, Hristo S. Paskov, Martin Jaggi, and Robert West. 2019. Crosslingual document embedding as reduced-rank ridge regression. In *Proceedings of the 12 ACM International Conference on WSDM*, pages 744–752.

Junczys-Dowmunt, Marcin. 2012. A phrase table without phrases: Rank encoding for better phrase table compression. In *Proceedings of the 16th Annual Conference of the European Association for Machine Translation*.

Koehn, Philipp, Hieu Hoang, Alexandra Birch, Chris Callison-Burch, Marcello Federico, Nicola Bertoldi, Brooke Cowan, Wade Shen, Christine Moran, Richard Zens, Chris Dyer, Ondrej Bojar, Alexandra Constantin, and Evan Herbst. 2007. Moses: Open source toolkit for statistical machine translation. In *Proceedings of the 45th Annual Meeting of the ACL*, pages 177–180.

Kumar, Shankar and William Byrne. 2004. Minimum bayes-risk decoding for statistical machine translation. In *Proceedings of the Human Language Technology Conference of the HLT-NAACL 2004*.

Litschko, Robert, Goran Glavaš, Simone Paolo Ponzetto, and Ivan Vulić. 2018. Unsupervised cross-lingual information retrieval using monolingual data only. In *The 41st International ACM SIGIR Conference*, pages 1253–1256.

Luong, Thang, Hieu Pham, and Christopher D. Manning. 2015. Effective approaches to attention-based neural machine translation. In *Proceedings of the 2015 Conference on EMNLP*, pages 1412–1421.

Manohar, Vimal, Hossein Hadian, Daniel Povey, and Sanjeev Khudanpur. 2018. Semi-supervised training of acoustic models using lattice-free mmi. In *2018 IEEE ICASSP Conference*, pages 4844–4848.

Nie, Jian-Yun. 2010. *Cross-Language Information Retrieval*. Morgan and Claypool.

Oard, Douglas W, Daqing He, and Jianqiang Wang. 2008. User-assisted query translation for interactive cross-language information retrieval. *Information Processing & Management*, 44(1):181–211.

OpenCLIR Evaluation. 2018. `https://www.nist.gov/itl/iad/mig/openclir-evaluation`.

Pirkola, Ari, Turid Hedlund, Heikki Keskustalo, and Kalervo Järvelin. 2001. Dictionary-based cross-language information retrieval: Problems, methods, and research findings. *Information retrieval*, 4(3-4):209–230.

Povey, Daniel, Arnab Ghoshal, Gilles Boulianne, Lukas Burget, Ondrej Glembek, Nagendra Goel, Mirko Hannemann, Petr Motlicek, Yanmin Qian, Petr Schwarz, Jan Silovsky, Georg Stemmer, and Karel Vesely. 2011. The kaldi speech recognition toolkit. In *IEEE 2011 Workshop on ASRU*.

Povey, Daniel, Vijayaditya Peddinti, Daniel Galvez, Pegah Ghahremani, Vimal Manohar, Xingyu Na, Yiming Wang, and Sanjeev Khudanpur. 2016. Purely sequence-trained neural networks for asr based on lattice-free mmi. In *Interspeech 2016*, pages 2751–2755.

Povey, Daniel, Gaofeng Cheng, Yiming Wang, Ke Li, Hainan Xu, Mahsa Yarmohammadi, and Sanjeev Khudanpur. 2018. Semi-orthogonal low-rank matrix factorization for deep neural networks. In *Proc. Interspeech 2018*, pages 3743–3747.

Robertson, Stephen, Hugo Zaragoza, et al. 2009. The probabilistic relevance framework: BM25 and beyond. *Foundations and Trends® in Information Retrieval*, 3(4):333–389.

Sennrich, Rico, Barry Haddow, and Alexandra Birch. 2016. Neural machine translation of rare words with subword units. In *Proceedings of the 54th Annual Meeting of the ACL*, pages 1715–1725.

Virpioja, Sami, Peter Smit, Stig-Arne Gronroos, and Mikko Kurimo. 2013. Morfessor 2.0: Python implementation and extensions for morfessor baseline. Technical report.

Vulić, Ivan and Marie-Francine Moens. 2015. Monolingual and cross-lingual information retrieval models based on (bilingual) word embeddings. In *Proceedings of the 38th International ACM SIGIR Conference*, pages 363–372.

Xu, Hainan and Philipp Koehn. 2017. Zipporah: a fast and scalable data cleaning system for noisy web-crawled parallel corpora. In *Proceedings of the 2017 Conference on EMNLP*, pages 2945–2950.

Xu, Hainan, Tongfei Chen, Dongji Gao, Yiming Wang, Ke Li, Nagendra Goel, Yishay Carmiel, Daniel Povey, and Sanjeev Khudanpur. 2018a. A pruned rnnlm lattice-rescoring algorithm for automatic speech recognition. In *2018 IEEE ICASSP Conference*, pages 5929–5933.

Xu, Hainan, Ke Li, Yiming Wang, Jian Wang, Shiyin Kang, Xie Chen, Daniel Povey, and Sanjeev Khudanpur. 2018b. Neural network language modeling with letter-based features and importance sampling. In *2018 IEEE ICASSP Conference*, pages 6109–6113.

Enhancing Transformer for End-to-end Speech-to-Text Translation

Mattia A. Di Gangi[1,2]   **Matteo Negri**[1]   **Roldano Cattoni**[1]   **Roberto Dessì**[2*]   **Marco Turchi**[1]

[1]Fondazione Bruno Kessler
via Sommarive, 18, Povo, TN, Italy
surname@fbk.eu

[2]Università degli Studi di Trento
CIMeC, DISI
name.surname@unitn.it

Abstract

Neural end-to-end architectures have been recently proposed for spoken language translation (SLT), following the state-of-the-art results obtained in machine translation (MT) and speech recognition (ASR). Motivated by this contiguity, we propose an SLT adaptation of Transformer (the state-of-the-art architecture in MT), which exploits the integration of ASR solutions to cope with long input sequences featuring low information density. Long audio representations hinder the training of large models due to Transformer's quadratic memory complexity. Moreover, for the sake of translation quality, handling such sequences requires capturing both short- and long-range dependencies between bi-dimensional features. Focusing on Transformer's encoder, our adaptation is based on: *i)* downsampling the input with convolutional neural networks, which enables model training on non cutting-edge GPUs, *ii)* modeling the bidimensional nature of the audio spectrogram with 2D components, and *iii)* adding a distance penalty to the attention, which is able to bias it towards short-range dependencies. Our experiments show that our SLT-adapted Transformer outperforms the RNN-based baseline both in translation quality and training time, setting the state-of-the-art performance on six language directions.

1 Introduction

Neural encoder-decoder models (Sutskever et al., 2014) with attention (Bahdanau et al., 2015) is a general architecture that, by enabling to tackle sequence-to-sequence problems with a single end-to-end model, achieved state-of-the-art results on machine translation (MT) (Bentivogli et al., 2016; Gehring et al., 2017; Vaswani et al., 2017; Chen et al., 2018) and obtained increasingly good performance in automatic speech recognition (Chan et al., 2016; Chiu et al., 2018; Zhang et al., 2017; Zeyer et al., 2018; Dong et al., 2018). The advantages of end-to-end techniques, besides their conceptual simplicity, reside on the prevention of error propagation, and a reduced inference latency. Error propagation is particularly problematic for the SLT task (Ruiz et al., 2017), in which MT would be significantly penalized by errors resulting from the previous ASR processing step. For this reason, end-to-end solutions have been recently proposed (Bérard et al., 2016; Weiss et al., 2017; Anastasopoulos and Chiang, 2018; Liu et al., 2018; Di Gangi et al., 2018) but, in terms of performance, they are still far behind the pipeline approach. The reason of the worse performance for this task can be found in its intrinsic difficulty, as it inherits and combines the challenges of the two pipelined tasks. Indeed, SLT models map audio features into words, like in ASR, but the input is mapped into text in a different target language, like in MT. Thus, the problems of word reordering and ambiguous meaning typical of translation are combined with the ambiguity of speech signal and speaker variety. One possible approach to deal with this task is to start from an MT solution and adapt it to speech input. Transformer (Vaswani et al., 2017) is an encoder-decoder architecture based on self-attention networks (SAN, (Cheng et al., 2016)) that, because of its strong results, is the most popular architecture in MT, and is now used as a base for many NLP tasks (Devlin et al., 2018). While LSTMs are known to require long trainig time (Lei et al., 2017; Di Gangi and Federico, 2018; Kalchbrenner et al., 2016), Transformer reduces the training time by performing parallel computation along all the time steps, similarly to convolutional neural networks (CNNs). Despite the appealing advantages, the research on end-to-end SLT has focused so far on recurrent architectures, and only big industrial players have been able to train networks with many layers, many parameters, and additional synthetic data (Jia et al., 2018). In fact, for computational and modeling reasons, the application of SANs to speech input has to face additional challenges compared to handling textual data. In particular, these include:

1. SANs have a memory complexity that is quadratic in the sequence length. From a computational perspective, this becomes a problem when the input is an audio signal, which is typically represented as a very long sequence of log-filter-banks. For the same utterance, this type of input is considerably longer than the corresponding textual representation fed to MT encoders.

2. The bidimensional dependencies along the time and frequency dimensions in the spectrogram (Li et al., 2016). This 2-dimensional representation is more difficult to handle compared to the 1-dimensional input representation (i.e. along the time dimension only) processed by MT encoders.

3. The absence of an explicit bias towards the local context. Differently from MT, modeling long-range dependencies between words is logically preceded, as the input is unsegmented, by modeling short-range dependencies between time-frames belonging to the same linguistic constituents (Sperber et al., 2018).

Focusing on these problems, in this paper we explore different adaptations of Transformer to the end-to-end SLT task. Initially, we show that *as-is* and with a comparable number of parameters, Transformer is not competitive with LSTM models. In order to investigate the reasons of its lower

performance, we posit that the problem lies in the inability of the Transformer encoder to properly model long audio input. This hypothesis is checked by switching the encoders and decoders of the Transformer and LSTM architecture, which results in better performance when the Transformer decoder is preceded by the LSTM encoder. These results inform and motivate our enhancements to the Transformer architecture. To this aim, we proceed incrementally showing, through comparative experiments, that:

1. Sequence compression with CNNs and downsampling enables effective audio encoding while allowing to train the system even on single GPUs;

2. Modeling 2D dependencies produces more stable and better results;

3. Biasing the encoder self-attention with a distance penalty improves translation quality.

Our experiments are run on different datasets covering different languages. First, we evaluate our architecture on two relatively small corpora: Augmented Librispeech (Kocabiyikoglu et al., 2018) for English→French and IWSLT 2018 for English→German. Then, we broaden the language coverage through experiments with MuST-C (Di Gangi et al., 2019),[1] a large multilingual SLT dataset recently released. This allows to validate our findings on six language directions (En-De/Es/Fr/Pt/Ro/Ru).

Overall, our evaluation indicates that the proposed SLT-oriented adaptation of Transformer results in a model that significantly outperforms a strong end-to-end system both in translation quality and training speed. For the sake of results' replicability the code developed for the experiments described in this paper can be downloaded at `http://github.com/mattiadg/FBK-Fairseq-ST`.

2 Related works

Our work has been influenced by the recent works on end-to-end SLT, as well as the applications of SANs to the task of ASR.

End-to-end SLT. The first encoder-decoder architecture based on LSTM was introduced for SLT by Bérard et al. (2016) showing the feasibility of

---

[1] `http://mustc.fbk.eu`

directly translating from the audio signal. Weiss et al. (2017) enhanced this approach by exploring settings with different numbers of layers in encoder and decoder and testing various multitask learning strategies. Bérard et al. (2018) trained a single model to translate English audiobooks into French and shown that pre-training the encoder on ASR data improves the final result. All these works showed that the input sequence length has to be reduced to work with recurrent models. To cope with the lack of end-to-end data, different directions have been evaluated. For instance, (Anastasopoulos and Chiang, 2018) and (Weiss et al., 2017) performed analyses of different multitask settings to leverage more data. Bansal et al. (2018) shown that the pre-training of the encoder is also helpful when performed on a different language, in particular when the source language is low–resourced. (Jia et al., 2018) increased the training data by using a large quantity of synthetic data that results in an end-to-end system able to outperform the cascade model. Their architecture still relies on LSTMs. Transformer has been applied to this task (Vila et al., 2018) using only a small training set and taking advantage of the computational power of TPUs. Differently from these works, we enhance the Transformer architecture to be trained on GPUs, in shorter time compared to LSTM models, and without using multi-task learning.

Self-attention for ASR. Given the results of Transformer in MT, recent works on ASR proposed SANs for both acoustic modeling (Sperber et al., 2018; Povey et al., 2018) and end-to-end ASR (Dong et al., 2018; Zhou et al., 2018a; Zhou et al., 2018b). Some works trained Transformer for (multilingual) ASR with little modification to its architecture (Zhou et al., 2018a; Zhou et al., 2018b), showing the feasibility of this approach in terms of results. Dong et al. (2018) proposed the Speech-Transformer for end-to-end ASR with the goal of encoding efficiently an effectively audio input. They rely on CNNs to reduce the sequence length, and propose 2D self-attention to capture the dependencies in the two dimensions of a spectrogram (Li et al., 2016) that are out of the range of CNNs. In this paper we show that only Speech-Transformer is not enough to outperform an LSTM-based model on end-to-end SLT, because the lack of an explicit bias towards local context seems to be harmful for SANs when applied to audio input. In ASR to address a simi-

lar problem, Povey et al. (2018) use hard masking to force the self-attention into a local context, while Sperber et al. (2018) use a Gaussian distance penalty to reduce the attention weights according to the distance between input elements. Though effective, the results of this distance penalty are highly dependent on the initial value of the Gaussian variance. Our work tests, for the first time, the distance penalty in the task of SLT and proposes a penalty function that, without additional hyperparameters, allows the Transformer model to outperform the LSTM architecture.

3 Background

Sequence-to-sequence models map a variable-length source sequence into a variable-length target sequence. They are usually composed of three conceptual blocks. An *encoder* maps an input sequence $\mathbf{X} = (\mathbf{x}_1, \mathbf{x}_2, \ldots, \mathbf{x}_n)$ of n time steps into a hidden representation $\mathbf{H} = (\mathbf{h}_1, \mathbf{h}_2, \ldots, \mathbf{h}_{n'})$ of contextualized vectors, where n' can be different from n. A *decoder* generates a target sequence of tokens $\mathbf{Y} = (\mathbf{y}_1, \mathbf{y}_2, \ldots, \mathbf{y}_m)$ in an autoregressive manner. The connection between encoder and *decoder* is given by one or multiple *attentions* that weight the elements of $\mathbf{H}$ according to their relevance for the current decoder time step. Such a network is trained by minimizing the cross-entropy between the probability distribution of the target tokens estimated by the network, and the gold labels:

$$L(\theta) = \sum_{i=0}^{m} P(\tilde{\mathbf{y}}_i = \mathbf{y}_i | \mathbf{X}, \mathbf{y}_{<i}; \theta) \tag{1}$$

In this paper, $\mathbf{X}$ is a sequence of audio spectrogram frames, while $\mathbf{Y}$ is a sequence of characters in the target language.

Two encoder-decoder architecture that are relevant for this work are: the recurrent model for end-to-end SLT proposed in (Bérard et al., 2018), which is based on LSTM and CNNs, and the Transformer, as proposed for MT.

3.1 End-to-end SLT

Bérard et al. (2018) proposed a recurrent sequence-to-sequence architecture for SLT based on LSTMs. The encoder receives an input in the form of sequences of Mel-filterbanks. The input is first projected to a larger space with two affine transformations, each followed by ReLU activation. The expanded input is then reduced by a factor of 4 with two following strided 2D convolutions. Finally, the resulting tensor is linearized and processed as a sequence by three stacked bi-directional LSTMs.

The average of the encoder outputs along the time dimension is used to initialize the first of two LSTMs in the decoder. The output of the first LSTM is used by an attention network to compute a context vector of the source, which is fed as input to the second LSTM. The output of the second LSTM is used to compute the target probabilities and also as a hidden state for the first LSTM (deep transition LSTMS (Pascanu et al., 2014)). Hencefort, we will refer to this approach as **CNN+LSTM**.

3.2 Transformer

Transformer (Vaswani et al., 2017) is an encoder-decoder architecture entirely based on attention networks. Given three sequences $\mathbf{Q}, \mathbf{K}, \mathbf{V}$ the attention computes a context vector d_i for each query time step i ($\mathbf{Q}_i$) that is a weighted average of the values $\mathbf{V}$, where the weights are computed as a normalized score of the similarity between $\mathbf{Q}_i$ and all the key values $\mathbf{K}$:

$$d_i = \mathrm{softmax}(\mathbf{Q}\mathbf{K}^T / \sqrt{d_{\mathrm{model}}}) \cdot \mathbf{V} \qquad (2)$$

where $\sqrt{d_{\mathrm{model}}}$ is a constant scaling factor based on the layer size d_{model}. The core component of Transformer is the multi-head attention (MHA), a network that, given two input sequences $\mathbf{a}, \mathbf{b}$ computes attention between $\mathbf{a}$ and $\mathbf{b}$ in multiple, parallel branches. MHA is used to model dependencies both between encoder and decoder ($\mathbf{K}, \mathbf{V} = \mathbf{a}$ and $\mathbf{Q} = \mathbf{b}$), and within the two networks (self-attention, $\mathbf{K}, \mathbf{V}, \mathbf{Q} = \mathbf{a}$). As it is shown in Equation 2, MHA is fully content-based and, as such, it is position invariant. The positional information within the sequence is conveyed by summing the vector content with a fixed positional encoding based on trigonometric functions. Another relevant property of the MHA is the possibility to compute it in parallel for all the time steps in both $\mathbf{Q}$ and $\mathbf{K}$, as well as for all the multiple heads, but this comes at the cost of a quadratic memory complexity.

4 SLT Transformer

The application of Transformer to speech input is not trivial because of *i)* computational issues that hinder its use; and *ii)* modeling limitations that

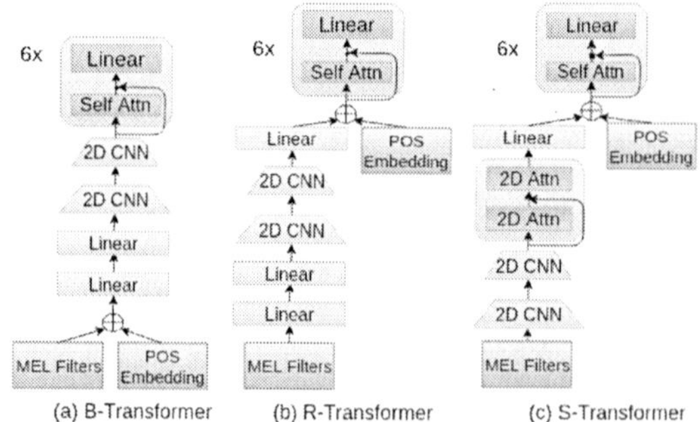

Figure 1: Three Transformer encoders for SLT. Components in grey are non-learnable.

harms its performance. The first issue to overcome is the quadratic GPU memory occupation of Transformer, which is particularly relevant on speech because the sequences are order of magnitudes larger than in text. On the modeling side, Transformer's performance is limited by the absence of a bias to capture short-range dependencies along time (Sperber et al., 2018; Povey et al., 2018), as well as the 2D joint dependencies over the time and frequency dimensions that characterize a spectrogram (Li et al., 2016). Strided 2D CNNs can compress the input sequence while also modeling 2D dependencies. However, the resulting sequences are still much longer than an equivalent text sequence, and thus we propose a distance penalty to enforce the modeling of short-range dependencies.

4.1 Encoding with 2D CNNs

In this section, we propose three variants of Transformer. B- and R-Transformer replace the LSTM layers in CNN+LSTM with Transformer encoder layers and differ in their use of the positional encoding. S-Transformer is a further improvement of R-Transformer that adds to the encoder the capability of modeling 2D dependencies in the input data. In all the three variants, the adaptations regard only the layers preceding the Transformer encoder. The following Transformer encoder and decoder stacks are left unchanged.

B-Transformer (Figure 1a). Our baseline model uses the same encoder as CNN+LSTM (Bérard et al., 2018) but replaces the LSTM layers with Transformer encoder layers. The replacement of LSTMs makes the encoder position invariant, and thus the sequential order is conveyed by summing the positional encoding directly to the input fea-

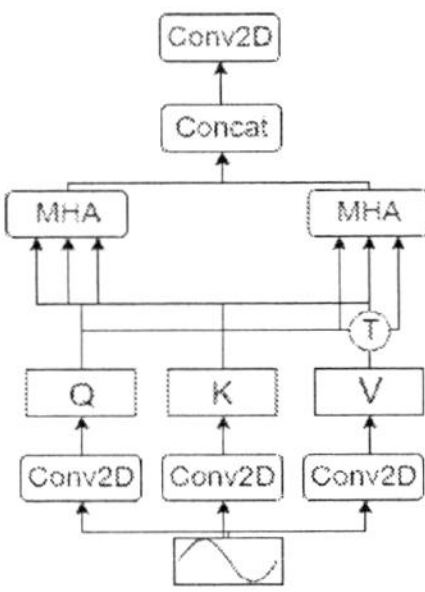

Figure 2: Schematic representation of 2D self-attention.

tures.[2]

R-Transformer (Figure 1b). As the positional encoding and the input are both fixed vectors, we propose to sum the positional encoding right before the Transformer encoder (the part of the network that requires a positional information). The sum is preceded by a linear transformation of the CNN output followed by ReLU non-linearity, whose goal is to transform its input into a space where the fixed positional encoding can be more effective.

S-Transformer (Figure 1c). Our second improvement follows the idea of modeling 2D joint dependencies in the input signal by applying a stack of 2D components to the input (Dong et al., 2018). The first two CNNs capture local 2D-invariant features (Amodei et al., 2016) in the input, while the following two 2D self-attention layers (Figure 2) model long-range context (Dong et al., 2018). The 2D self-attention computes the three tensors $\mathbf{K}, \mathbf{Q}, \mathbf{V}$ with three parallel 2D CNNs of its input with c output channels. Each of the c channels is used as an attention head in an MHA network. $\mathbf{K}, \mathbf{Q}$ and $\mathbf{V}$ are used to compute the attention over the temporal dimension as in Equation 2. Then, the three matrices are transposed and another MHA is computed over the frequency dimension. Finally, the $2c$ channels from the two MHAs are concatenated and processed by an additional $2D$ CNN with n output channels. The 2D attentions enrich the encoder representation by modeling 2D dependencies that cannot be captured by CNNs.

4.2 Distance Penalty

To further improve the encoder capability of modeling short-range dependencies, we introduce, besides CNNs, a distance penalty mechanism in the encoder self-attention. This mechanism biases the network towards the local context without imposing hard constraints that would prevent it from finding long-range dependencies. The attention computation (Equation 2) is modified as follows:

$$\mathbf{c} = \mathrm{softmax}(\mathbf{Q}\mathbf{K}^{\mathbf{T}}/\sqrt{d_{\mathrm{model}}} - \pi(\mathbf{D}))\mathbf{V} \quad (3)$$

where $\mathbf{D}$ is a matrix containing, in each cell $d_{i,j}$, the position distance $|i - j|$, and π is a distance penalty function.

In this paper, we experiment with distance penalty computed with two different functions. The Gaussian penalty introduced in (Sperber et al., 2018) computes a Gaussian-shaped penalty distribution with a distinct learnable variance σ for each head in the MHA as follows:

$$\pi_G(d) = \frac{(d)^2}{2\sigma^2} \quad (4)$$

This function gives to a network the flexibility to shrink or extend the attention span in each attention head. In this way, the network can extract different features from different heads in a layer, but also in different layers. Indeed, in (Sperber et al., 2018) only the first layer restricts its attention span in the best setting. The downside of this approach is that the initial value of the variance is an additional hyperparameter that highly affects the performance. In order to eliminate this additional hyperparameter, we propose to use a logarithmic function as a distance penalty:

$$\pi_{\mathrm{log}}(d) = \begin{cases} 0, & \text{if d} = 0 \\ \log_e(d), & \text{else} \end{cases} \quad (5)$$

The logarithm biases the network towards the local context but the penalty grows slowly with distance, and thus it does not impede the modeling of global dependencies.

5 Experiments

We run our experiments on three SLT datasets, of which two comprise a single language direction and one comprises 6 language directions. In all cases, English is the source language.

Monolingual datasets. The first one monolingual corpus is built from material released for the IWSLT evaluation campaigns, namely the En→De training data from IWSLT 2018 (Niehues et al.,

---

[2]Due to its high GPU memory occupation, we could not train a baseline Transformer (comparable in size to the other models used for experiments) without input compression.

Corpus	Hours	Train	Valid	Test
IWSLT (En-De)	273	171K	1000	1000
Librispeech (En-Fr)	236	95K	1071	2048
Multilingual				
En-De	408	234K	1423	2641
En-Es	504	270K	1316	2502
En-Fr	492	280K	1412	2632
En-Pt	385	210K	1367	2502
En-Ro	432	240K	1370	2556
En-Ru	489	270K	1317	2513

Table 1: Data statistics for IWSLT, Librispeech and our multilingual corpus. Train, Valid and Test are numbers of sentence pairs.

2018) and the test data from IWSLT 2014 (Cettolo et al., 2014).[3] The second dataset is the Augmented Librispeech corpus (Kocabiyikoglu et al., 2018) that is produced using English audiobooks of novels, and their translations into French.

Multilingual dataset. We have recently developed a large corpus from English TED talks, called MuST-C (Di Gangi et al., 2019). Unlike IWSLT and Librispeech, MuST-C covers multiple language directions (En→De/Es/Fr/Pt/Ro/Ru). We built it following the alignment-based approach proposed in (Kocabiyikoglu et al., 2018) and using English speech recordings and their translations available on the TED talks website.[4] For each target language, we aligned text in English and in the target language using the Gargantua toolkit (Braune and Fraser, 2010), then we aligned the resulting English sentences with the corresponding audio using Gentle,[5] a forced-aligner based on the Kaldi toolkit (Povey et al., 2011). In order to improve the alignment quality we performed two successive steps of filtering. In the first step, we removed all the talks where at least 15% of the words have not been recognized by Gentle. In the second step, we removed from the remaining talks all the sentences with no recognized words. For replicability of results, the corpus is released with a predefined train, validation and test split. The corpora statistics are listed in Table 1 and show that each language direction of MuST-C is considerably larger than the other 2 corpora.

Experimental setup. For a fair comparison of the different architectures, we first set the parameters of the recurrent baseline (CNN+LSTM, §3.1) similar to what reported in (Bérard et al., 2018). Then,

we adjust the Transformer to have a number of parameters similar to the recurrent one (∼9.5M). The CNNs have a 3×3 kernel and 16 output filters. The LSTMs in the baseline have a hidden size of 512, with 3 layers in the encoder and 2 in the decoder. The initial encoder states are learnable parameters, while the initial decoder state is computed as the mean of the encoder states. We found the learnable encoder states to be critical to reach convergence. The Transformer models have 6 layers in both encoder and decoder, with layer size of 256, hidden size of 768 and 4 heads in multi-head attention. To further asses the performance of our models, we also experiment with a BIG version with more parameters, featuring layer size 512, hidden size 1024, and 8 heads. set dropout to 0.2 for CNN+LSTM and 0.1 for Transformer. No dropout is applied in the recurrent connections. Training is performed using the Adam optimizer (Kingma and Ba, 2015) with learning rate 0.001 for LSTM and 0.0002 for Transformer. The learning rate is kept fixed for Transformer for the sake of a fair comparison with the baseline. B-Transformer serves as a baseline to evaluate the impact of the proposed adaptations. We train our R- and S-Transformer models with and without distance penalty, either Gaussian or logarithmic. We test all these configurations on the IWSLT and Librispeech corpora. Then, due to the higher number of directions in the multilingual corpus, we only run experiments on it with the best-performing system. Following (Bansal et al., 2018; Bérard et al., 2018), we first train a model with the ASR part of each corpus and then we use it to initialize the weights of the SLT encoder. All the experiments are run on a single GPU Nvidia 1080 Ti with 12G of RAM, and the code used for all the experiments is based on Pytorch (Paszke et al.,).

Data processing and evaluation. 40-dimensional MFCC filter-banks were extracted from the audio signals of each dataset using window size of 25 ms and step size 10 ms. The frame energy feature was additionally extracted from the LibriSpeech audio, similarly to (Bérard et al., 2018). All texts were tokenized and split into characters. Performance is evaluated with BLEU (Papineni et al., 2002) at token level after aggregating the output characters into words.

---

[3]We could not use the IWSLT 2018 test data, because the gold standard has not been released.

[4]http://www.ted.com – dump of April 2018

[5]`github.com/lowerquality/gentle`

Librispeech	Enc	Dec	BLEU ↑
CNN+LSTM	-	-	10.7
	✓	-	**13.2**
	✓	✓	13.0
B-Transformer	-	-	6.3
	✓	-	9.0
	✓	✓	**9.5**
IWSLT			
LSTM	-	-	8.5
	✓	-	**9.2**
	✓	✓	7.5
B-Transformer	-	-	**7.9**
	✓	-	7.3
	✓	✓	5.9

Table 2: Speech translation results for the Librispeech and IWSLT corpora wuth our two baseline models. A checkmark on Enc (Dec) means that the encoder (decoder) has been pre-trainined.

Enc / Dec	LSTM	Transformer
LSTM	13.2	11.9
Transformer	8.2	9.0

Table 3: Mixed-architecture experiments on Librispeech.

6 Results and Discussion

6.1 Baseline.

As a first step, we want to evaluate our baseline B-Transformer against CNN+LSTM to understand the effectiveness 2D convolutional compression with Transformer. We ran the experiments with no pre-training, by pre-training only the encoder or both encoder and decoder. As can be seen in Table 2, the best results with CNN+LSTM are obtained by pre-training only the encoder, while for B-Transformer the training is more unstable and this is reflected also in the results. Considering the results of CNN+LSTM and the relatively good results of B-Transformer when pre-training only the encoders, we decided to follow this practice in all the following experiments. When considering only the results with the pre-trained encoder, CNN+LSTM outperforms B-Transformer by 4 BLEU points on Librispeech and 2.1 BLEU points on IWSLT. To better understand the source of degradation for the B-Transformer, we performed an experiment switching encoder and decoder between the two architectures with pre-trained encoder (table 3) and evaluated them on Librispeech. When using CNN+LSTM encoder, the Transformer decoder causes a degradation of 1.3 BLEU points, while having Transformer encoder and LSTM decoder causes a degradation of 5 points over CNN+LSTM. Given these

Librispeech	BLEU ↑	Time (s)	Time/Ep.
CNN+LSTM	13.2	248K	~ 2.8K
B-Transformer	9.0	101K	~ 0.69K
R-Transformer	11.5	72K	~ 0.73K
- Gauss penalty	12.5	82K	~ 0.75K
- log penalty	12.3	64K	~ 0.75K
S-Transformer	12.5	76K	~ 0.79K
- Gauss penalty	13.8	88K	~ 0.86K
- log penalty	13.5	76K	~ 0.86K
IWSLT	**BLEU ↑**	**Time (s)**	**Time/Ep.**
CNN+LSTM	9.2	112K	~ 2.9K
B-Transformer	7.1	67K	~ 1.0K
R-Transformer	9.8	92K	~ 1.0K
- Gauss penalty	10.8	101 K	~ 1.1K
- log penalty	10.5	93K	~ 1.1K
S-Transformer	9.8	89K	~ 1.1K
- Gauss penalty	10.8	90K	~ 1.2K
- log penalty	10.6	81K	~ 1.2K

Table 4: Results on the Librispeech and IWSLT 2014 test set. Differences wrt the baseline (CNN+LSTM) are statistically significant (randomization test, p=0.05).

results, the following experiments all focus on enhancing the B-Transformer encoder. Despite the poor translation quality, exploring the Transformer is still interesting because of its reduced training time (listed on Table 4), which is reduced by a factor of 2 on IWSLT (67K vs 112K seconds) and even more on Librispeech (101K vs 248K seconds). These results show that input compression makes the training of Transformer feasible for SLT, but it does not result in immediate improvements over LSTMs.

6.2 Encoder Enhancements

In the following, we discuss the results obtained with our enhancements to the Transformer encoder, i.e. modify the use of position encoding, model 2D dependencies with CNNs and 2D self-attention, and insert a distance penalty to the encoder self-attention.

R-Transformer differs from B-Transformer in the layer where the position encoding is summed to the input. As can be seen in Table 4, this detail is very relevant as R-Transformer improves over B-Transformer by more than 2.5 BLEU points in both datasets with less training time. However, it is significantly worse than CNN+LSTM on Librispeech (−1.7 BLEU points) and slightly better on IWSLT (+0.6).

The next step is to evaluate the enhancements in modeling 2D input proposed in S-Transformer. Its results are 1.0 BLEU point better than R-Transformer in Librispeech, and equal on IWSLT, while having a similar parameter count and con-

Initial variance	Librispeech	IWSLT
5.0	13.8	10.8
100.0	13.1	10.9

Table 5: Results with different values of initial variance for Gaussian penalty and S-Transformer.

	LSTM	log	Gauss	BIG+log	BIG+Gauss
De	12.9	**14.5**	14.4	**17.3**	16.2
Es	17.9	18.4	**18.6**	**20.8**	20.1
Fr	22.3	23.1	**24.0**	**26.9**	24.7
Pt	17.1	18.6	**19.7**	**20.1**	19.3
Ro	13.4	14.7	**15.0**	**16.5**	16.1
Ru	7.2	8.8	**9.1**	**10.5**	8.5

Table 6: Results on six language pairs covered by the multilingual corpus. LSTM is the CNN+LSTM model. Results in columns 3-6 are computed with S-Transformer with logarithmic (log) or Gaussian (Gauss) distance penalty. Improvements over CNN+LSTM are statistically significant.

vergence time. Despite the improvement, S-Transformer is 0.7 points less than CNN+LSTM on Librispeech.

In Table 4 we show the results obtained using the distance penalties introduced in §4.2 to model short-range dependencies in the Transformer encoder. Distance penalties produce performance improvements for R- and S-Transformer that range from 0.7 to 1.3 BLEU points, with the Gaussian penalty (initial variance = 5.0) being $0.2 \sim 0.3$ BLEU points better than the logarithmic one. S-Transformer with Gaussian penalty obtains the best results in both corpora, with improvements of $+0.6$ and $+1.6$ BLEU points over CNN+LSTM on, respectively, Librispeech and IWSLT. The results with Gaussian penalty are computed using initial variance (for the ASR training) of 5.0. Using an initial variance of 100.0 (the value recommended in the work by Sperber et al. (2018)) we obtained a significant degradation on Librispeech with a BLEU of 13.1 and a comparable result on IWSLT with 10.9 (Table 5). These results show that biasing the self-attention with a distance penalty is critical to obtain competitive translation quality with Transformer and also outperform the strong CNN+LSTM baseline.

6.3 Gaussian variances

Sperber et al. (2018) have shown that the variances of the Gaussian penalty are smaller in the first layer and larger in the second layer of their 2-layered self-attentional acoustic model. Based on this observation, they suggest that it is better for the first layer to have a restricted range, while a global range is desirable for the upper layer. We performed a similar analysis for our models, but obtained quite different results. First of all, Table 5 shows that, in our experiments, the initial value of variance plays a role but it appears to be less critical. An inspection of the final variance values is shown in Figure 3, in which we do not observe any relation between the layers and the variance. On the contrary, we observe that different heads in the same layer can differ significantly. Additionally, the initial weight makes a big difference for

the final values but, as shown in table 5, this does not affect the performance significantly. To understand whether results' differences from the work of Sperber et al. (2018) are related to the task (SLT instead of ASR), we checked the weights of our ASR models and find that they do not differ significantly from the ones showed in Figure 3. The absence of a pattern in the distribution of the variance is a further justification to use a logarithmic distance penalty in all the layers.

6.4 Additional experiments

The previous experiments have shown that S-Transformer performs better than the other variants, and as such we report experiments on the larger MuST-C corpus only with S-Transformer and the two distance penalties. S-Transformer outperforms CNN+LSTM on all the 6 language directions with gains from $+0.5$ to $+1.6$ BLEU points with log penalty and from $+0.7$ to $+2.6$ with Gaussian penalty. Gaussian penalty generally achieves results only slightly better than the logarithmic one, except for the top improvements of $+0.9$ and $+1.1$ respectively on En→Fr and En→Pt. To explain this difference, it is useful to recall that the parameters of the encoders of SLT models (including their Gaussian variances) are initialized from a model pre-trained on English ASR. In particular, for the multilingual corpus we use the same model trained on the larger dataset. The inherited variance from this model may affect differently the different target languages.

Experiments with a larger model (S-Transformer BIG) show further improvements from a minimum of 1.5 points for En→Pt to a maximum of 3.8 points for En→Fr with log penalty, while the poor results with Gaussian penalty confirm that it is less stable than the logarithmic one. The number of training iterations is also reduced to less than half of the previous

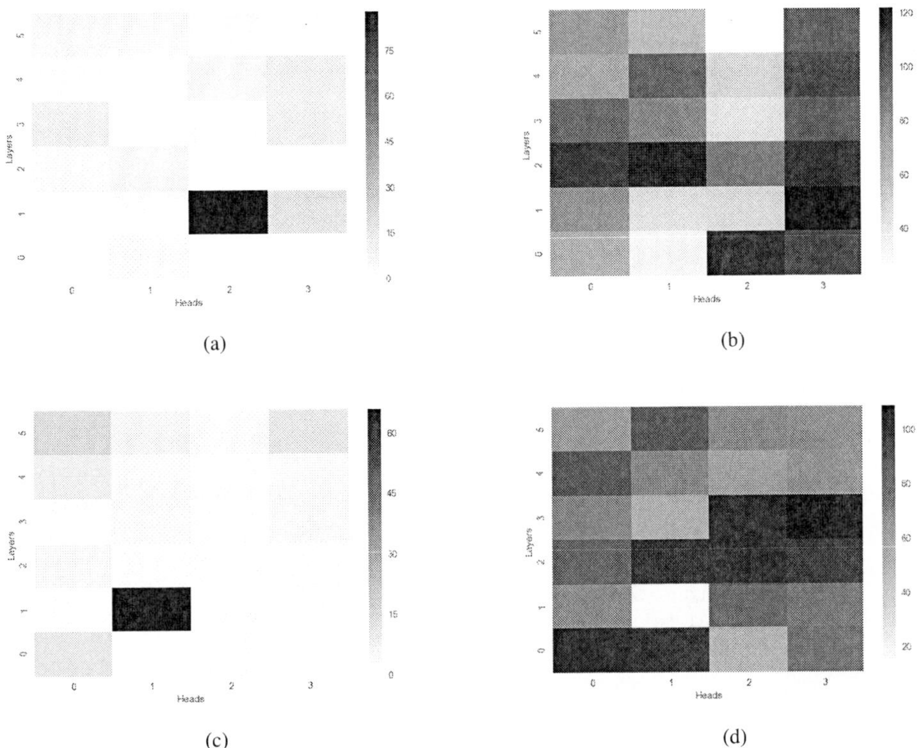

Figure 3: Final values of the variances for the SLT task in Librispeech (top) and IWSLT (bottom) with initial variance of 5.0 (left) and 100.0 (right).

experiments. The improvements obtained in this experiment, up to 4.6 BLEU point in En→Fr over the baseline, represent a step forward towards a translation quality that allows real-world applications for end-to-end SLT.

To conclude, our experiments show that: *i)* our task-specific adaptations make the Transformer trainable for the SLT task, also on a single GPU; *ii)* when both short-range and 2D dependencies are explicitly addressed in the model, they allow it to outperform a strong baseline based on LSTMs; *iii)* the logarithmic distance penalty can be preferable over the Gaussian one because it does not require additional hyperparameter tuning and results in competitive performance.

7 Conclusion

We have shown that the application of Transformer to end-to-end SLT is problematic in the encoder side. Consequently, we have proposed to enhance the Transformer encoder by taking into account the characteristics of a speech spectrogram. Our solution consists of: *i)* 2D processing of the input to compress it effectively before the self-attentional stack; and *ii)* a distance penalty in the encoder self-attention layers that forces the network to give more attention to neighboring time steps.We have shown that, although using a distance penalty is always beneficial, a simple logarithmic function can result in equal or better improvements than a learnable Gaussian penalty. Experimental results performed on three different corpora, for a total of 6 language directions, show that our approach outperforms a strong recurrent baseline in both translation quality and training time.

References

Amodei, Dario, Sundaram Ananthanarayanan, Rishita Anubhai, Jingliang Bai, Eric Battenberg, Carl Case, Jared Casper, Bryan Catanzaro, Qiang Cheng, Guoliang Chen, et al. 2016. Deep Speech 2: End-to-end Speech Recognition in English and Mandarin. In *International conference on machine learning*, pages 173–182.

Anastasopoulos, Antonios and David Chiang. 2018. Tied Multitask Learning for Neural Speech Translation. In *Proceedings of NAACL 2018*.

Bahdanau, Dzmitry, Kyunghyun Cho, and Yoshua Bengio. 2015. Neural Machine Translation by Jointly Learning to Align and Translate. In *Proceedings of ICLR 2015*.

Bansal, Sameer, Herman Kamper, Karen Livescu, Adam Lopez, and Sharon Goldwater. 2018. Pre-training on High-resource Speech Recognition Improves Low-resource Speech-to-text Translation. *Proceedings of NAACL 2019*.

Bentivogli, Luisa, Arianna Bisazza, Mauro Cettolo, and Marcello Federico. 2016. Neural versus Phrase-Based Machine Translation Quality: a Case Study. In *Proceedings of EMNLP 2016)*.

Bérard, Alexandre, Olivier Pietquin, Laurent Besacier, and Christophe Servan. 2016. Listen and Translate: A Proof of Concept for End-to-End Speech-to-Text Translation. In *NIPS Workshop on end-to-end learning for speech and audio processing*, Barcelona, Spain, December.

Bérard, Alexandre, Laurent Besacier, Ali Can Kocabiyikoglu, and Olivier Pietquin. 2018. End-to-End Automatic Speech Translation of Audiobooks. In *Proceedings of ICASSP 2018*, Calgary, Alberta, Canada, April.

Braune, Fabienne and Alexander Fraser. 2010. Improved unsupervised sentence alignment for symmetrical and asymmetrical parallel corpora. In *Proceedings of ACL 2010*, pages 81–89.

Cettolo, Mauro, Jan Niehues, Sebastian Stüker, Luisa Bentivogli, and Marcello Federico. 2014. Report on the 11th IWSLT Evaluation Campaign, IWSLT 2014. In *Proceedings of IWSLT 2014*.

Chan, William, Navdeep Jaitly, Quoc Le, and Oriol Vinyals. 2016. Listen, attend and spell: A neural network for large vocabulary conversational speech recognition. In *2016 IEEE International Conference on Acoustics, Speech and Signal Processing (ICASSP)*.

Chen, Mia Xu, Orhan Firat, Ankur Bapna, Melvin Johnson, Wolfgang Macherey, George Foster, Llion Jones, Niki Parmar, Mike Schuster, Zhifeng Chen, et al. 2018. The best of both worlds: Combining recent advances in neural machine translation. *arXiv preprint arXiv:1804.09849*.

Cheng, Jianpeng, Li Dong, and Mirella Lapata. 2016. Long short-term memory-networks for machine reading. In *Proceedings of the 2016 Conference on Empirical Methods in Natural Language Processing*, pages 551–561.

Chiu, Chung-Cheng, Tara Sainath, Yonghui Wu, Rohit Prabhavalkar, Patrick Nguyen, Zhifeng Chen, Anjuli Kannan, Ron J. Weiss, Kanishka Rao, Katya Gonina, Navdeep Jaitly, Bo Li, Jan Chorowski, and Michiel Bacchiani. 2018. State-of-the-art Speech Recognition with Sequence-to-sequence Models. In *2018 IEEE International Conference on Acoustics, Speech and Signal Processing (ICASSP)*, pages 4774–4778. IEEE.

Devlin, Jacob, Ming-Wei Chang, Kenton Lee, and Kristina Toutanova. 2018. Bert: Pre-training of deep bidirectional transformers for language understanding. *arXiv preprint arXiv:1810.04805*.

Di Gangi, Mattia A and Marcello Federico. 2018. Deep Neural Machine Translation with Weakly-Recurrent Units. In *Proc. of EAMT*.

Di Gangi, Mattia Antonino, Dessì Roberto, Roldano Cattoni, Matteo Negri, and Marco Turchi. 2018. Fine-tuning on clean data for end-to-end speech translation: Fbk@ iwslt 2018. In *International Workshop on Spoken Language Translation (IWSLT 2018)*, pages 147–152.

Di Gangi, Mattia A., Roldano Cattoni, Luisa Bentivogli, Matteo Negri, and Marco Turchi. 2019. MuST-C: a Multilingual Speech Translation Corpus. In *Proceedings of the 2019 Conference of the North American Chapter of the Association for Computational Linguistics: Human Language Technologies, Volume 1 (Long and Short Papers)*, pages 2012–2017, Minneapolis, Minnesota, June. Association for Computational Linguistics.

Dong, Linhao, Shuang Xu, and Bo Xu. 2018. Speech-Transformer: A No-Recurrence Sequence-to-Sequence Model for Speech Recognition. In *2018 IEEE International Conference on Acoustics, Speech and Signal Processing (ICASSP)*. IEEE.

Gehring, Jonas, Michael Auli, David Grangier, Denis Yarats, and Yann N Dauphin. 2017. Convolutional Sequence to Sequence Learning. In *Proceedings of ICML 2017*, Sydney, Australia, August.

Jia, Ye, Melvin Johnson, Wolfgang Macherey, Ron-J. Weiss, Yuan Cao, Chung-Cheng Chiu, Stella-Laurenzo Ari, and Yonghui Wu. 2018. Leveraging Weakly Supervised Data to Improve End-to-End Speech-to-Text Translation. *ArXiv e-prints arXiv:1811.02050*.

Kalchbrenner, Nal, Lasse Espeholt, Karen Simonyan, Aaron van den Oord, Alex Graves, and Koray Kavukcuoglu. 2016. Neural machine translation in linear time. *arXiv preprint arXiv:1610.10099*.

Kingma, Diederik and Jimmy Ba. 2015. Adam: A method for stochastic optimization. In *Proc. of ICLR*.

Kocabiyikoglu, Ali Can, Laurent Besacier, and Olivier Kraif. 2018. Augmenting Librispeech with French Translations: A Multimodal Corpus for Direct Speech Translation Evaluation. In *Proceedings of LREC 2018*, Miyazaki, Japan, May.

Lei, Tao, Yu Zhang, and Yoav Artzi. 2017. Training RNNs as Fast as CNNs. *arXiv preprint arXiv:1709.02755*.

Li, Jinyu, Abdelrahman Mohamed, Geoffrey Zweig, and Yifan Gong. 2016. Exploring Multidimensional LSTMs for Large Vocabulary ASR. In *Proceedings of ICASSP 2016*, pages 4940–4944. IEEE.

Liu, Dan, Junhua Liu, Wu Guo, Shifu Xiong, Zhiqiang Ma, Rui Song, Chongliang Wu, and Quan Liu. 2018. The ustc-nel speech translation system at iwslt 2018. In *Proocedings of IWSLT*.

Niehues, Jan, Roldano Cattoni, Sebastian Stüker, Mauro Cettolo, Marco Turchi, and Marcello Federico. 2018. The IWSLT 2018 Evaluation Campaign. In *Proceedings of IWSLT 2018*, Bruges, Belgium, October.

Papineni, Kishore, Salim Roukos, Todd Ward, and Wei-Jing Zhu. 2002. BLEU: a Method for Automatic Evaluation of Machine Translation. In *Proceedings of ACL 2002*.

Pascanu, Razvan, Caglar Gulcehre, Kyunghyun Cho, and Yoshua Bengio. 2014. How to construct deep recurrent neural networks. In *Proceedings of ICLR 2014*.

Paszke, Adam, Sam Gross, Soumith Chintala, Gregory Chanan, Edward Yang, Zachary DeVito, Zeming Lin, Alban Desmaison, Luca Antiga, and Adam Lerer. Automatic differentiation in pytorch. In *NIPS 2017 Workshop Autodiff*.

Povey, Daniel, Arnab Ghoshal, Gilles Boulianne, Lukas Burget, Ondrej Glembek, Nagendra Goel, Mirko Hannemann, Petr Motlicek, Yanmin Qian, Petr Schwarz, et al. 2011. The kaldi speech recognition toolkit. Technical report, IEEE Signal Processing Society.

Povey, Daniel, Hossein Hadian, Pegah Ghahremani, Ke Li, and Sanjeev Khudanpur. 2018. A time-restricted self-attention layer for asr. In *Proceedings of ICASSP 2018*, pages 5874–5878. IEEE.

Ruiz, Nicholas, Mattia Antonino Di Gangi, Nicola Bertoldi, and Marcello Federico. 2017. Assessing the tolerance of neural machine translation systems against speech recognition errors. *Proc. Interspeech 2017*, pages 2635–2639.

Sperber, Matthias, Jan Niehues, Graham Neubig, Sebastian Stüker, and Alex Waibel. 2018. Self-Attentional Acoustic Models. *Proceedings of Interspeech 2018*, pages 3723–3727.

Sutskever, Ilya, Oriol Vinyals, and Quoc V Le. 2014. Sequence to Sequence Learning with Neural Networks. In *Proceedings of NIPS 2014*.

Vaswani, Ashish, Noam Shazeer, Niki Parmar, Jakob Uszkoreit, Llion Jones, Aidan N Gomez, Łukasz Kaiser, and Illia Polosukhin. 2017. Attention is All You Need. In *Proceedings of NIPS 2017*.

Vila, Laura-Cross, Carlos Escolano, José AR Fonollosa, and Marta-R Costa-Jussà. 2018. End-to-End Speech Translation with the Transformer. *Proceedings of IberSPEECH 2018*, pages 60–63.

Weiss, Ron J., Jan Chorowski, Navdeep Jaitly, Yonghui Wu, and Zhifeng Chen. 2017. Sequence-to-Sequence Models Can Directly Translate Foreign Speech. In *Proceedings of Interspeech 2017*, Stockholm, Sweden, August.

Zeyer, Albert, Kazuki Irie, Ralf Schlüter, and Hermann Ney. 2018. Improved Training of End-to-end Attention Models for Speech Recognition. In *Proceedings of Interspeech 2018*, pages 7–11.

Zhang, Yu, William Chan, and Navdeep Jaitly. 2017. Very deep convolutional networks for end-to-end speech recognition. In *2017 IEEE International Conference on Acoustics, Speech and Signal Processing (ICASSP)*, pages 4845–4849. IEEE.

Zhou, Shiyu, Linhao Dong, Shuang Xu, and Bo Xu. 2018a. Syllable-based sequence-to-sequence speech recognition with the transformer in mandarin chinese. *Proc. Interspeech 2018*, pages 791–795.

Zhou, Shiyu, Shuang Xu, and Bo Xu. 2018b. Multilingual end-to-end speech recognition with a single transformer on low-resource languages. *arXiv preprint arXiv:1806.05059*.

Debiasing Word Embeddings Improves Multimodal Machine Translation

Tosho Hirasawa
Tokyo Metropolitan University
hirasawa-tosho@ed.tmu.ac.jp

Mamoru Komachi
Tokyo Metropolitan University
komachi@tmu.ac.jp

Abstract

In recent years, pretrained word embeddings have proved useful for multimodal neural machine translation (NMT) models to address the shortage of available datasets. However, the integration of pretrained word embeddings has not yet been explored extensively. Further, pretrained word embeddings in high dimensional spaces have been reported to suffer from the hubness problem. Although some debiasing techniques have been proposed to address this problem for other natural language processing tasks, they have seldom been studied for multimodal NMT models. In this study, we examine various kinds of word embeddings and introduce two debiasing techniques for three multimodal NMT models and two language pairs — English–German translation and English–French translation. With our optimal settings, the overall performance of multimodal models was improved by up to +1.62 BLEU and +1.14 METEOR for English–German translation and +1.40 BLEU and +1.13 METEOR for English–French translation.

1 Introduction

In **multimodal machine translation**, a target sentence is translated from a source sentence together with related nonlinguistic information such as visual information. Recently, neural machine translation (NMT) has superseded traditional statistical machine translation owing to the introduction

of the attentive encoder-decoder model, in which machine translation is treated as a sequence-to-sequence learning problem and is trained to pay attention to the source sentence while decoding (Bahdanau et al., 2015).

Pretrained word embeddings are considered an important part of neural network models in many natural language processing (NLP) tasks. In the context of NMT, pretrained word embeddings have proved useful in low-resource domains (Qi et al., 2018), in which FastText (Bojanowski et al., 2017) embeddings are used to initialize the encoder and decoder of the NMT model. They provided substantial overall performance improvement for low-resource language pairs. Similarly, Hirasawa et al. (2019) introduced a multimodal NMT model with embedding prediction that provided substantial performance improvement.

However, when word embeddings are used in the k-nearest neighbor (kNN) problem, certain words appear frequently in the k-nearest neighbors for other words (Dinu et al., 2015; Faruqui et al., 2016); this is called the hubness problem in the general machine learning domain (Radovanović et al., 2010). This phenomenon harms the utility of pretrained word embeddings. In the context of NMT, Rios Gonzales et al. (2017) reported that NMT models produce less-accurate translations for less-frequent words, but they are not aware of the hubness problem in word embeddings. Instead, they proposed annotating sense labels or lexical labels to address this problem. However, it is known to be effective to debias word embeddings based on their local bias (Hara et al., 2015) or global bias (Mu and Viswanath, 2018) for word analogy tasks, which does not require extra expensive annotations and references.

In this study, we explore the utility of well-established word embeddings and introduce debiasing techniques for multimodal NMT models. The main contributions of this study are as follows:

1. We show that GloVe word embeddings are useful for various multimodal NMT models irrespective of the extent to which visual features are used in them.

2. We introduce All-but-the-Top debiasing technique for pretrained word embeddings to further improve multimodal NMT models.

2 Related Works

With the recent development of multimodal parallel corpora such as Multi30K (Elliott et al., 2016), many multimodal NMT models have been proposed. Most of these models are divided into two categories: visual feature integration and multitask learning. In both categories, visual features are extracted using image processing techniques.

Visual feature adaptation Visual features are extracted using image processing techniques and then integrated into a machine translation model in many ways. These studies include incorporation with visual features in NMT models (Calixto et al., 2017; Zhou et al., 2018) and multitask learning models (Elliott and Kádár, 2017; Zhou et al., 2018), as discussed later in Section 3.

Data augmentation Owing to the lack of the available datasets, data augmentation is widely studied in multimodal NMT. Compared to a parallel corpus without images (Grönroos et al., 2018) and a pseudo-parallel corpus (Helcl et al., 2018), few studies have used monolingual data. Hirasawa et al. (2019) proposed a multimodal NMT model with embedding prediction to fully use pretrained word embeddings. However, the use of word embeddings has not been studied among various multimodal NMT models. We examine three different word embeddings for three multimodal NMT models.

3 Multimodal Neural Machine Translation

In this study, we measure the effectiveness of pretrained word embeddings for doubly-attentive NMT (Calixto et al., 2017), IMAGINATION (Elliott and Kádár, 2017), and visual attention grounding NMT (Zhou et al., 2018); these use visual feature integration, multitask learning, and mixed model, respectively.

First, in visual feature integration, visual features are incorporated into NMT models in different ways. Calixto et al. (2017) separately calculate textual and visual context vectors using an attention mechanism and then forward the concatenated context vector to output the probabilities of target words. Caglayan et al. (2018) use hidden states in the encoder to mask the local visual features and concatenate the textual context vector and the masked visual context vector to obtain the final context vector.

Second, in multitask learning, most multitask learning models use latent space learning as an auxiliary task. Models share the encoder between the main translation task and the auxiliary task, thereby improving the encoder. Elliott and Kádár (2017) proposed the IMAGINATION model that learns to construct the corresponding visual feature from the hidden states of the textual encoder of a source sentence.

Third, visual feature integration and multitask learning are not mutually exclusive and can be used together. Zhou et al. (2018) compute the text representation from a source sentence while paying attention to each word based on the paired image. This text representation is used in both the machine translation task and the shared space learning task.

All of these models tackle machine translation as a sequence-to-sequence learning problem in which a neural model is trained to translate a source sentence of N–tokens $x = \{x_1, x_2, \cdots, x_N\}$ into the target sentence of M–tokens $y = \{y_1, y_2, \cdots, y_M\}$.

3.1 Doubly-attentive NMT

Doubly-attentive NMT (Calixto et al., 2017) has a simple encoder and a modified decoder from Bahdanau et al. (2015) that uses two individual attention mechanisms to compute the textual context vector and the visual context vector.

Architecture The encoder is a bidirectional gated recurrent unit (GRU) (Cho et al., 2014), in which a forward GRU encodes source sentence x in the normal order to generate a sequence of forward hidden states $\overrightarrow{h} = \{\overrightarrow{h_1}, \overrightarrow{h_2}, \cdots, \overrightarrow{h_N}\}$ and a backward GRU encodes this source sentence in the reversed order to generate a sequence of backward hidden states $\overleftarrow{h} = \{\overleftarrow{h_1}, \overleftarrow{h_2}, \cdots, \overleftarrow{h_N}\}$. The final hidden states h for each position i are given as a concatenation of each forward hidden state and each backward hidden state.

$$\overrightarrow{h_i} = \overrightarrow{\text{GRU}}(\overrightarrow{h_{i-1}}, e_{enc}(x_i)) \quad (1)$$

$$\overleftarrow{h_i} = \overleftarrow{\text{GRU}}(\overleftarrow{h_{i+1}}, e_{enc}(x_i)) \quad (2)$$

$$h_i = [\overrightarrow{h_i}; \overleftarrow{h_i}] \quad (3)$$

where $i \in [1, N]$ denotes each position in a source sentence; $\overrightarrow{\text{GRU}}$ and $\overleftarrow{\text{GRU}}$ are the forward and backward GRU, respectively; and $e_{enc}(x_i)$ is the embedding representation for a word x_i.

While decoding, the model first computes a hidden state proposal s_j for each time step $j \in [1, M]$.

$$s_j = \text{GRU}(\hat{s}_{j-1}, e_{dec}(\hat{y}_{j-1})) \quad (4)$$

where $\hat{s}_{j-1}$ is the previous hidden state and $e_{dec}(\hat{y}_{j-1})$ is the embedding for the previous output word $\hat{y}_{j-1}$.

The textual context vector and the visual context vector are computed using two independent attention mechanisms. In each time step j while decoding, a feed-forward layer is used to calculate a normalized soft alignment $\alpha_{j,i}$ with each source hidden state h_i, and the textual context vector c_j^t is computed as a weighted sum of source hidden states.

$$z_{j,i}^t = v_t \tanh(U_\alpha^t s_j + W_\alpha^t h_i) \quad (5)$$

$$\alpha_{j,i}^t = \frac{\exp(z_{j,i}^t)}{\sum_{k=1}^N \exp(z_{j,k}^t)} \quad (6)$$

$$c_j^t = \sum_{i=1}^N \alpha_{j,i}^t h_i \quad (7)$$

where v_t, U_α^t and W_α^t are model parameters.

The visual context vector c_j^v is also computed from the spatial visual features v_i of the paired image in the same manner as the textual context vector along with the gating scalar mechanism, in which a scalar variable is computed based on the previous hidden state to decide how much attention should be paid to the entire visual features.

$$z_{j,i}^v = v_v \tanh(U_\alpha^v s_j + W_\alpha^v v_i) \quad (8)$$

$$\alpha_{j,i}^v = \frac{\exp(z_{j,i}^v)}{\sum_{k=1}^N \exp(z_{j,k}^v)} \quad (9)$$

$$\beta_j = \sigma(W_s \hat{s}_{j-1} + b_s) \quad (10)$$

$$c_j^v = \beta_j \sum_{i=1}^N \alpha_{j,i}^v v_i \quad (11)$$

where v_v, U_α^v, W_α^v, W_s, and b_s are model parameters. σ is the gating scalar function learnt while training; it projects a vector to a scalar value and activates with a sigmoid function.

The final hidden state $\hat{s}_j$ is computed using the hidden state proposal s_j, textual context c_j^t, and visual context c_j^v.

$$z_j = \sigma_z(W_z^t c_j^t + W_z^v c_j^v + W_z \hat{s}_j) \quad (12)$$

$$r_j = \sigma_r(W_r^t c_j^t + W_r^v c_j^v + W_r \hat{s}_j) \quad (13)$$

$$s_j' = \tanh(W_z^t c_j^t + W_z^v c_j^v + r_j \odot (U \hat{s}_j)) \quad (14)$$

$$\hat{s}_j = (1 - z_j) \odot s_j' + z_j \odot s_j \quad (15)$$

where σ_z and σ_r are feed-forward layers with sigmoid activation, and W_z^t, W_z^v, W_z, W_r^t, W_r^v, W_r, W_z^t, W_z^v, and U are model parameters.

The system output at timestep j is obtained using the current hidden state, previous word embedding, textual context, and visual context.

$$p(w|\hat{y}_{<j}) = \text{softmax}(\tanh(L^s \hat{s}_j + L^w e_{dec}(\hat{y}_{j-1}) + L^t c_j^t + L^i c_j^v)) \quad (16)$$

$$\hat{y}_j = \underset{w \in \mathcal{V}}{\text{argmax}}\{p(w|\hat{y}_{<j})\} \quad (17)$$

where L^s, L^w, L^t and L^i are model parameters.

Loss function We use the negative log likelihood of the probabilities to generate reference tokens as the loss function J for this model.

$$J = -\sum_{j=1}^M \log(p(y_j|\hat{y}_{<j})) \quad (18)$$

3.2 IMAGINATION

IMAGINATION (Elliott and Kádár, 2017) is a multitask learning model that jointly learns machine translation and visual latent space models. It trains an NMT model for a machine translation task and a latent space learning model for an auxiliary task, in which a source sentence and the paired image are mapped closely in the latent space. The models for each task share the same encoder in a multitask scenario.

Architecture The encoder is the same as that in the doubly-attentive NMT model described in Section 3.1. The decoder in the NMT model is the same as that proposed by Bahdanau et al. (2015); it first computes the hidden state proposal s_j, then estimates context vector c_j over source hidden states, and finally outputs the predicted word y_j for each time step $j \in [1, M]$.

$$s_j = \text{GRU}(\hat{s}_{j-1}, e_{dec}(\hat{y}_{j-1})) \quad (19)$$

$$z_{j,i} = v_a \tanh(W_a s_j + U_a h_i) \quad (20)$$

$$\alpha_{j,i} = \frac{\exp(z_{j,i})}{\sum_{k=1}^{N} \exp(z_{j,k})} \quad (21)$$

$$c_j = \sum_{i=1}^{N} \alpha_{j,i} h_i \quad (22)$$

$$p(w|\hat{y}_{<j}) = \text{softmax}(\tanh(s_j + e_{dec}(\hat{y}_{j-1}) + c_j)) \quad (23)$$

$$\hat{y}_j = \underset{w \in \mathcal{V}}{\arg\max}\{p(w|\hat{y}_{<j})\} \quad (24)$$

where W_a, U_a and v_a are model parameters.

The latent space learning model calculates the average vector over the hidden states h_i in the encoder and maps it to the final vector $\hat{v}$ in the latent space.

$$\hat{v} = \tanh(W_v \cdot \frac{1}{N} \sum_{i}^{N} h_i) \quad (25)$$

where W_v is a model parameter.

Loss function The loss function for IMAGINATION is the linear interpolation of loss functions of each task.

$$J = \lambda J_T(\theta, \phi_T) + (1 - \lambda) J_V(\theta, \phi_V) \quad (26)$$

where θ is the parameter of the shared encoder; ϕ_T and ϕ_V are parameters of the machine translation model and latent space model, respectively; and λ is the interpolation coefficient[1].

We use the loss function defined in Eq. 18 for the NMT model $J_T(\theta, \phi_T)$.

$$J_T(\theta, \phi_T) = -\sum_{j=1}^{M} \log(p(y_j|\hat{y}_{<j})) \quad (27)$$

The max margin loss is used as the loss function for latent space learning; it makes corresponding latent vectors of a source sentence and the paired image closer.

$$J_V(\theta, \phi_V) = \sum_{v' \neq v} \max\{0, \alpha - d(\hat{v}, v) + d(\hat{v}, v')\} \quad (28)$$

where v is the latent vector of the paired image; v', the image vector for other examples; d, the cosine similarity function that is used to calculate the word similarity; and α, the margin that adjusts the sparseness of each vector in the latent space[2].

[1] We use $\lambda = 0.5$ in our experiment.
[2] We use $\alpha = 0.1$ in our experiment.

3.3 Visual Attention Grounding NMT

Visual Attention Grounding NMT (VAG-NMT) (Zhou et al., 2018) uses a combination of the visual feature integration model and the multitask learning model, which also uses latent space learning as the auxiliary task.

Architecture The shared encoder of this model is an extension of Bahdanau et al. (2015), in which the model computes the sentence representation t by paying attention to the hidden states h_i based on the visual feature v.

$$z_i = \tanh(W_v v) \cdot \tanh(W_h h_i) \quad (29)$$

$$\beta_i = \frac{\exp(z_i)}{\sum_{k=1}^{N} \exp(z_k)} \quad (30)$$

$$t = \sum_{i=1}^{N} \beta_i h_i \quad (31)$$

where W_v and W_h are model parameters.

The decoder of the NMT model is the same as that used in IMAGINATION (Section 3.2) with a slight modification for initializing the hidden state with the sentence representation t.

$$s_0 = \tanh(W_{init}(\rho t + (1 - \rho)\frac{1}{N} \sum_{i}^{N} h_i)) \quad (32)$$

where W_{init} is a model parameter; and ρ, a hyperparameter to determine the ratio of text representation in the decoder initial state [3].

In latent space learning, both the sentence representation t and the visual representation v are projected to the latent space and made closer in the space during training.

$$t_{emb} = \tanh(W_t t + b_t) \quad (33)$$

$$v_{emb} = \tanh(W_v v + b_v) \quad (34)$$

where W_t, b_t, W_v, and b_v are model parameters.

Loss function The loss function for VAG-NET is given as described in Eq.26, and we use the loss function defined in Eq.27 for $J_T(\theta, \phi_T)$.

The max margin loss with negative sampling is used as the loss function for latent space learning.

$$J_V(\theta, \phi_V)$$
$$= \sum_p \sum_k \max\{0, \gamma - d(v_p, t_p) + d(v_p, t_{k \neq p})\}$$
$$+ \sum_k \sum_p \max\{0, \gamma - d(t_k, v_k) + d(t_p, v_{k \neq p})\} \quad (35)$$

[3] We use $\rho = 0.5$ in our experiment.

where d is a cosine similarity function; k and p is the index for sentences and images, respectively; $t_{k \neq p}$, the negative samples for which all examples in the same batch with the target example are selected; and γ, the margin that adjusts the sparseness of each item in the latent space[4].

4 Word Embedding

In this study, we compare three different word embeddings: word2vec (Mikolov et al., 2013), GloVe (Pennington et al., 2014), and FastText (Bojanowski et al., 2017). Section 5.1 describes the configurations to build each embedding.

When we use word embeddings of high dimension in the kNN problem in which the similarity of two words is computed using a distance function, certain words frequently appear in the k-nearest neighbors of other words (Dinu et al., 2015; Faruqui et al., 2016); this is called the hubness problem in the general machine learning domain (Radovanović et al., 2010). This phenomenon harms the utility of pretrained word embeddings. In the context of NMT, Rios Gonzales et al. (2017) report that less-frequent words are translated with low-accuracy; that may be influenced by the hubness problem.

To address this problem, localized centering (Hara et al., 2015) and All-but-the-Top (Mu and Viswanath, 2018) have been proposed in NLP literature, in which pretrained word embeddings are debiased using the local bias of each word or the global bias of the entire vocabulary. In this study, both debiasing techniques are tested for all embedding types.

Localized centering Localized centering shifts each word based on its local bias. The local centroid for each word x is computed and subtracted from the original word x to obtain the new embedding $\hat{x}$.

$$c_k(x) = \frac{1}{k} \sum_{x' \in k\mathrm{NN}(x)} x' \quad (36)$$

$$\hat{x} = x - c_k(x) \quad (37)$$

where k is a hyperparameter called local segment size [5]; $k\mathrm{NN}(x)$ returns the k–nearest neighbors of the word x.

---

[4] We use $\gamma = 0.1$ in our experiment.

[5] We use $k = 10$ in our experiment.

Language	Lines	Types	Tokens
English	96M	10M	2,347M
German	35M	11M	829M
French	39M	4M	703M

Table 1: Statistics of Wikipedia corpus for each language.

All-but-the-Top All-but-the-Top uses the global bias of the entire vocabulary to shift the embedding of each word. The algorithm of All-but-the-Top has three steps: subtract the centroid of all words from each word x, compute the PCA components for the centered space, and subtract the top n PCA components from each centered word to obtain the final word $\hat{x}$.

$$x' = x - \frac{1}{|\mathcal{V}|} \sum_{w \in \mathcal{V}} w \quad (38)$$

$$u_1, u_2, \cdots, u_D = \mathrm{PCA}(x' \in \mathcal{V}) \quad (39)$$

$$\hat{x} = x' - \sum_{i=1}^{D} (u_i^\mathsf{T} x') u_i \quad (40)$$

where D is a hyperparameter that is used to determine how many principal components of pretrained word embeddings are ignored[6].

5 Experiment

5.1 Word Embeddings

Training corpus As publicly available pretrained word embeddings use different training corpora, we created a monolingual corpus from Wikipedia for a fair comparison. We downloaded the January 20, 2019, version of Wikidump for English, German, and French[7] and extracted article pages. All extracted sentences are preprocessed by lower-casing, tokenizing, and normalizing the punctuation using the Moses script [8]. Table 1 shows the statistics of the preprocessed Wikipedia corpus for each language.

Training settings All embeddings trained on Wikipedia have a dimension of 300. The specific options set for training are as follows; default values were used for other options.

We trained the word2vec model[9] using the CBOW algorithm with window size of 10, nega-

---

[6] We use $D = 3$ in our experiment.

[7] https://dumps.wikimedia.org/

[8] We applied preprocessing using `task1-tokenize.sh` from https://github.com/multi30k/dataset.

[9] We train using https://github.com/tmikolov/word2vec.

tive sampling of 10, and minimum count of 10; the GloVe model[10] with windows size of 10 and minimum count of 10; and the FastText model[11] using the CBOW algorithm with word n-gram of 5, window size of 5, and negative sampling of 10.

Unknown words There are two types of unknown words: words that are a part of pretrained word embeddings but are not included in a vocabulary (Out-Of-Vocabulary (OOV) words) and words that are a part of a vocabulary but are not included in pretrained word embeddings (OOV words for embeddings). OOV words for embeddings only exist when using word-level embeddings (word2vec and glove); the embeddings of such words in FastText are calculated as the mean embedding of character n-grams consisting of the word.

The embeddings for both types of OOV words are calculated as the average embedding over words that are a part of pretrained word embeddings but are not included in the vocabularies, and they are updated individually during training.

5.2 Dataset

We train, validate, and test all multimodal NMT models using the Multi30K (Elliott et al., 2016) dataset. English is selected as the source language, and German/French are selected as target languages. All sentences in all languages are preprocessed by lower-casing, tokenizing, and normalizing the punctuation.

We run experiments without byte pair encoding (BPE) (Sennrich et al., 2016) for all models as BPE breaks a word into subwords, resulting in an increase in OOV words for word2vec and GloVe embeddings. In addition, we also run experiments using BPE with 10k merge operations to show the utility of pretrained word embeddings. The BPE subwords are shared for source and target languages and learnt from training dataset[12]. Table 2 shows the statistics of vocabularies in the Multi30K training data.

Visual features are extracted using pretrained ResNet-50 (He et al., 2016). We encode all images in the Multi30K dataset using ResNet-50 and pick out the hidden state in the res4f layer of 1024D for the doubly-attentive model, and that in the pool5

Language	Types	Tokens	OOV Vocab	OOV Embed
English	10,210	377,534	10M	129
German	18,722	360,706	11M	1,841
French	11,219	409,845	4M	89
with BPE				
English	5,199	397,793	N/A	N/A
→ German	7,062	400,507	N/A	N/A
English	5,830	394,353	N/A	N/A
→ French	6,572	428,762	N/A	N/A

Table 2: Statistics of vocabularies without BPE (upper) and with BPE (lower) in Multi30K training data. "Vocab" denotes the number of OOV words for the vocabulary. "Embed" denotes the number of OOV words for embeddings. "English → German" shows statistics of the shared subwords for English–German translation, and "English → French" for English–French translation.

layer of 2048D for IMAGINATION and VAG-NET, respectively.

5.3 Model

All models are implemented using nmtpytorch toolkit v3.0.0[13] (Caglayan et al., 2017).

The encoder for each model has one layer with 256 hidden dimensions, and therefore the bidirectional GRU has 512 dimensions. We set the latent space vector size for IMAGINATION to 2048 and the dimension of the shared visual-text space for VAG-NET to 512. The input word embedding size and output vector size are 300 each.

We use the Adam optimizer with learning rate of 0.0004. The gradient norm is clipped to 1.0. The dropout rate is 0.3.

BLEU (Papineni et al., 2002) and METEOR (Denkowski and Lavie, 2014) are used as performance metrics. As in (Qi et al., 2018), we also evaluated the models using the F-score of each word. The F-score is calculated as the harmonic mean of the precision (the fraction of produced sentences containing a word that is in the references sentences) and the recall (the fraction of reference sentences containing a word that is in the model outputs). We ran the experiment three times with different random seeds and obtained the mean for each model.

---

[10]We train using https://github.com/stanfordnlp/GloVe.
[11]We train using https://github.com/facebookresearch/fastText.
[12]We use https://github.com/rsennrich/subword-nmt to train and apply BPE.

English → German

Model	debiasing embedding	None BLEU	None METEOR	Localized Centering BLEU	Localized Centering METEOR	All-but-the-Top BLEU	All-but-the-Top METEOR
NMT	random	34.57	54.50				
Doubly-attentive	random	33.50	52.75				
IMAGINATION	random	34.97	54.21				
VAG-NET	random	35.55	54.87				
NMT	word2vec	34.23	52.83	34.14	53.09	33.88	52.66
	GloVe	35.49	55.14	35.33	54.89	**35.98**	**55.15**
	FastText	33.63	52.48	33.42	52.34	33.91	52.65
Doubly-attentive	word2vec	32.05	50.85	32.07	51.23	32.73	51.04
	GloVe	34.06	53.74	33.37	52.98	**34.77**	**53.86**
	FastText	31.14	49.29	31.04	50.33	30.86	50.13
IMAGINATION	word2vec	33.97	52.59	33.43	52.32	34.35	52.79
	GloVe	35.74	55.00	35.92	55.15	**36.59**	**55.35**
	FastText	34.21	52.53	33.69	52.22	33.83	52.31
VAG-NET	word2vec	34.32	53.01	34.10	53.40	33.91	52.70
	GloVe	36.01	**55.31**	35.56	54.61	**36.36**	55.17
	FastText	34.12	52.56	33.92	52.75	33.82	52.38

Table 3: Results obtained using Multi30K test2016 dataset for English–German translation. "NMT" shows the results of Bahdanau et al. (2015). When the debiasing is "None," we show the results obtained with raw pretrained word embeddings or random values.

English → French

Model	debiasing embedding	None BLEU	None METEOR	Localized Centering BLEU	Localized Centering METEOR	All-but-the-Top BLEU	All-but-the-Top METEOR
NMT	random	57.15	72.47				
Doubly-attentive	random	54.85	71.06				
IMAGINATION	random	57.38	72.57				
VAG-NET	random	57.78	73.21				
NMT	word2vec	55.65	70.79	55.82	70.90	56.20	71.20
	GloVe	58.14	**73.67**	57.76	73.00	**58.24**	73.40
	FastText	55.13	70.18	55.24	70.56	55.42	70.60
Doubly-attentive	word2vec	52.32	68.06	53.30	68.98	52.95	68.68
	GloVe	**56.25**	**72.19**	54.58	71.23	56.12	71.91
	FastText	50.46	66.35	51.02	67.20	51.22	67.09
IMAGINATION	word2vec	55.94	70.91	55.63	70.73	55.96	70.93
	GloVe	57.89	73.09	57.65	73.16	**58.10**	**73.26**
	FastText	55.12	70.17	55.52	70.77	55.52	70.42
VAG-NET	word2vec	56.23	71.14	55.79	70.82	56.33	71.34
	GloVe	**58.45**	**73.59**	57.31	73.16	57.94	73.40
	FastText	55.25	70.45	55.33	70.51	55.49	70.63

Table 4: Results obtained using Multi30K test2016 dataset for English–French translation. "NMT" shows the results of Bahdanau et al. (2015). When the debiasing is "None," we show the results obtained with raw pretrained word embeddings or random values.

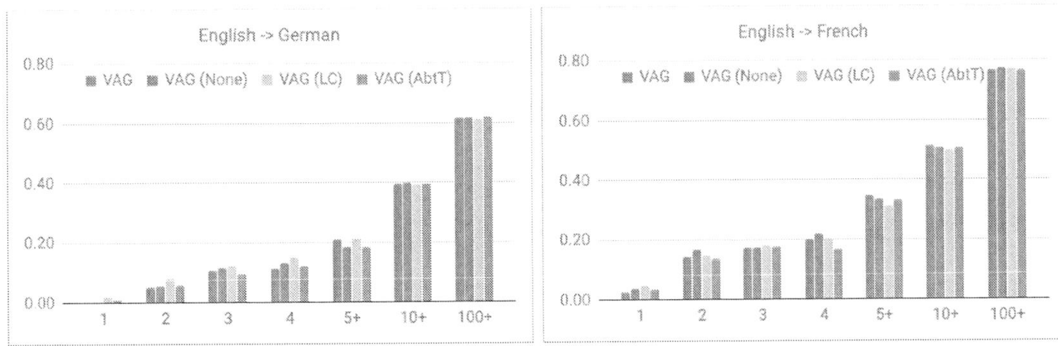

Figure 1: F-score of word prediction per frequency breakdown in training corpus. The model without brackets is initialized with random values: "(None)," GloVe without debiasing; "(LC)," GloVe with localized centering; and "(AbtT)," GloVe with All-but-the-Top.

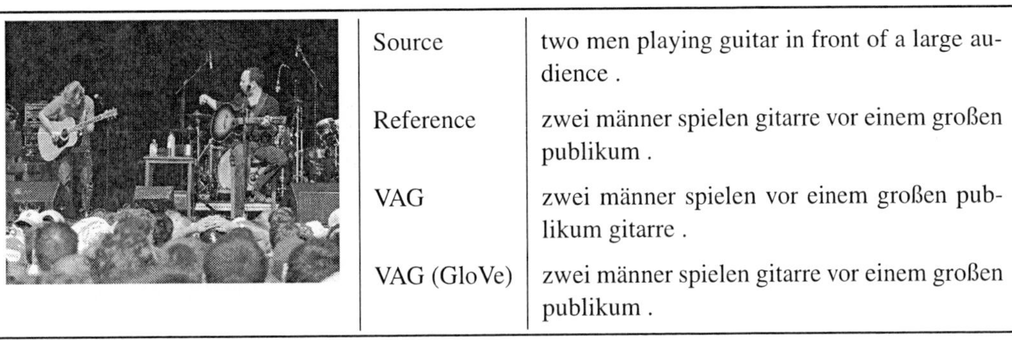

	Source	two men playing guitar in front of a large audience .
	Reference	zwei männer spielen gitarre vor einem großen publikum .
	VAG	zwei männer spielen vor einem großen publikum gitarre .
	VAG (GloVe)	zwei männer spielen gitarre vor einem großen publikum .

Table 5: Examples of English–German translations obtained using test dataset. "(GloVe)" denotes the model with the optimal settings for GloVe.

5.4 Results

Table 3 shows the overall performance of the randomly initialized models and the models initialized with pretrained word embeddings for English–German translation. Though GloVe embeddings show considerable improvement for both in text-only NMT and all types of multimodal NMT, word2vec and FastText embeddings greatly reduce model performance even with some debiasing. With GloVe embeddings, All-but-the-Top debiasing results in further improvement. In particular, IMAGINATION is improved with GloVe embedding initialization (+0.77 BLEU and +0.79 METEOR) and showed further improvement with All-but-the-Top debiasing (+1.62 BLEU and +1.14 METEOR).

Table 4 shows that the combination of GloVe embedding and All-but-the-Top debiasing greatly improves the overall performance of each model for English–French translation. The model with GloVe and All-but-the-Top surpasses the randomly

initialized model by +1.09 BLEU and +0.93 METEOR in the text-only NMT model, by +1.27 BLEU and +0.85 METEOR in the doubly-attentive model, by +0.72 BLEU and +0.69 METEOR in the IMAGINATION model, by +0.16 BLEU and +0.19 METEOR in the VAG-NET model, respectively.

6 Discussion

Word embedding In our study, GloVe performs the best among three word embeddings, while word2vec and FastText do not help multimodal NMT models; the degradation of word2vec is attributed to the cohesiveness of word embeddings and that of FastText the shortage of training data, respectively.

The word embeddings in word2vec are reported to be cohesively clustered and not evenly distributed, while those in GloVe are well distributed (Mimno and Thompson, 2017). This makes it harder to train the model with word2vec rather than the model initialized using random values, as the model with word2vec is required to learn all the

---

[13] https://github.com/toshohirasawa/mmt-emb-init

English $\rightarrow$ German			
BPE	Init	BLEU	METEOR
No	random	35.55	54.87
No	GloVe	**36.36**	**55.17**
Yes	random	35.46	55.30

English $\rightarrow$ French			
BPE	Init	BLEU	METEOR
No	random	57.78	73.21
No	GloVe	**58.45**	**73.59**
Yes	random	56.63	72.38

Table 6: Results of VAG-NET with various settings obtained using Multi30K test2016 dataset for English–German translation (upper) and English–French translation (lower). "BPE" denotes whether a model uses BPE. "Init" denotes the initialization strategy: "random," a model initialized using random values and "GloVe," a model initialized using GloVe embeddings with All-but-the-Top debiasing (English–German) or without debiasing (English–French).

word representations from almost the same value i.e. the mean vector of entire embeddings.

FastText requires more training data than GloVe does, as it learns not only embeddings for words but also those of their subwords. Our pretrained word embeddings are trained using only Wikipedia and do not use Common Crawl; it contains at least 50 times tokens and three times words than Wikipedia does, and is used together with Wikipedia to construct FastText embeddings that improve NMT models (Qi et al., 2018).

Debiasing All-but-the-Top improves most of models for both English–German translation and English–French translation; this may prove the idea suggested in Mu and Viswanath (2018), in which neural network models may not be able to learn the debiasing technique by themselves.

In contrast, models using localized centering only show a comparable performance with models not using debiasing. It is because that the debiased vector has small norm and thus the additional training may break the relation of debiased vectors, as localized centering subtracts the local centroid of a word that is quite similar with the word. This observation is contrary with Hara et al. (2015), in which debiased word embeddings are used without the additional training.

Languages We found that pretrained word embeddings are more useful for English–German translation than for English–French translation. The best models with GloVe embedding surpasses the randomly initialized model by +1.28 BLEU in average for English–German translation, but by only +0.97 BLEU for English–French translation with the optimal settings. This is because the German decoder has more unique words (18,722 for German and 11,219 for French, as listed in Table 2) in the original training dataset, resulting in less in-vocabulary words after restricting the vocabulary and making it difficult for the German decoder learn embeddings from scratch.

BPE BPE is an alternative approach to improve translation quality. Therefore, we compared the VAG-NET model with GloVe embeddings and the VAG-NET model with BPE to validate which approach would contribute more to the overall performance (Table 6). Although BPE does not improve the VAG-NET model for both English–German and English-French translation, GloVe embeddings provide a substantial improvement in both language pairs.

Translation quality To understand the model performance for translating rare words, we computed the F-score of VAG-NET models with various debiasing techniques (Figure 1). Although VAG-NET models with GloVe embeddings outperform the model with random initialization, we do not observe a consistent improvement for rare word translation, as reported in (Qi et al., 2018).

Translation examples Table 5 shows English–German translations generated by VAG-NET models with different initialization strategies. Compared to the model without pretrained word embeddings, the model with GloVe embeddings generates a more fluent sentence.

7 Conclusion

We have explored the use of pretrained word embeddings with various multimodal NMT models. We showed that GloVe embeddings improve the performance of all multimodal translation models, and All-but-the-Top debiasing can result in further improvement.

In the future, we will examine training approaches for word embeddings that are more suitable for multimodal NMT, especially by considering MT evaluation metrics when training word embeddings. For example, fine-tuning word embeddings based on BLEU or other metrics for machine translation could further improve the compatibility of pretrained word embeddings with multimodal NMT models.

Acknowledgment

This work was partially supported by JSPS Grant-in-Aid for Scientific Research (C) Grant Number JP19K12099.

References

Bahdanau, Dzmitry, Kyunghyun Cho, and Yoshua Bengio. 2015. Neural machine translation by jointly learning to align and translate. In *ICLR*.

Bojanowski, Piotr, Edouard Grave, Armand Joulin, and Tomas Mikolov. 2017. Enriching word vectors with subword information. In *TACL*, volume 5, pages 135–146.

Caglayan, Ozan, Mercedes García-Martínez, Adrien Bardet, Walid Aransa, Fethi Bougares, and Loïc Barrault. 2017. NMTPY: A flexible toolkit for advanced neural machine translation systems. *Prague Bull. Math. Linguistics*, pages 15–28.

Caglayan, Ozan, Adrien Bardet, Fethi Bougares, Loïc Barrault, Kai Wang, Marc Masana, Luis Herranz, and Joost van de Weijer. 2018. LIUM-CVC submissions for WMT18 multimodal translation task. In *WMT*, pages 597–602.

Calixto, Iacer, Qun Liu, and Nick Campbell. 2017. Doubly-attentive decoder for multi-modal neural machine translation. In *ACL*, pages 1913–1924.

Cho, Kyunghyun, Bart van Merrienboer, Dzmitry Bahdanau, and Yoshua Bengio. 2014. On the properties of neural machine translation: Encoder–decoder approaches. In *Proceedings of SSST-8, Eighth Workshop on Syntax, Semantics and Structure in Statistical Translation*, pages 103–111.

Denkowski, Michael and Alon Lavie. 2014. Meteor Universal: Language specific translation evaluation for any target language. In *WMT*, pages 376–380.

Dinu, Georgiana, Angeliki Lazaridou, and Marco Baroni. 2015. Improving zero-shot learning by mitigating the hubness problem. In *ICLR, Workshop Track*.

Elliott, Desmond and Àkos Kádár. 2017. Imagination improves multimodal translation. In *IJCNLP*, pages 130–141.

Elliott, Desmond, Stella Frank, Khalil Sima'an, and Lucia Specia. 2016. Multi30k: Multilingual English-German image descriptions. In *Proceedings of the 5th Workshop on Vision and Language*, pages 70–74.

Faruqui, Manaal, Yulia Tsvetkov, Pushpendre Rastogi, and Chris Dyer. 2016. Problems with evaluation of word embeddings using word similarity tasks. In *Proceedings of the 1st Workshop on Evaluating Vector-Space Representations for NLP*, pages 30–35, August.

Grönroos, Stig-Arne, Benoit Huet, Mikko Kurimo, Jorma Laaksonen, Bernard Merialdo, Phu Pham, Mats Sjöberg, Umut Sulubacak, Jörg Tiedemann, Raphael Troncy, and Raúl Vázquez. 2018. The MeMAD submission to the WMT18 multimodal translation task. In *WMT*, pages 603–611.

Hara, Kazuo, Ikumi Suzuki, Masashi Shimbo, Kei Kobayashi, Kenji Fukumizu, and Miloš Radovanović. 2015. Localized Centering: Reducing hubness in large-sample data. In *AAAI*, pages 2645–2651.

He, Kaiming, Xiangyu Zhang, Shaoqing Ren, and Jian Sun. 2016. Deep residual learning for image recognition. In *CVPR*, pages 770–778.

Helcl, Jindřich, Jindřich Libovický, and Dusan Varis. 2018. CUNI system for the WMT18 multimodal translation task. In *WMT*, pages 616–623.

Hirasawa, Tosho, Hayahide Yamagishi, Yukio Matsumura, and Mamoru Komachi. 2019. Multimodal machine translation with embedding prediction. In *NAACL SRW*, pages 86–91.

Mikolov, Tomas, Ilya Sutskever, Kai Chen, Greg S Corrado, and Jeff Dean. 2013. Distributed representations of words and phrases and their compositionality. In *NIPS*, pages 3111–3119.

Mimno, David and Laure Thompson. 2017. The strange geometry of skip-gram with negative sampling. In *EMNLP*, pages 2873–2878.

Mu, Jiaqi and Pramod Viswanath. 2018. All-but-the-Top: Simple and effective postprocessing for word representations. In *ICLR*.

Papineni, Kishore, Salim Roukos, Todd Ward, and Wei-Jing Zhu. 2002. BLEU: a method for automatic evaluation of machine translation. In *ACL*, pages 311–318.

Pennington, Jeffrey, Richard Socher, and Christopher D. Manning. 2014. GloVe: Global vectors for word representation. In *EMNLP*, pages 1532–1543.

Qi, Ye, Devendra Sachan, Matthieu Felix, Sarguna Padmanabhan, and Graham Neubig. 2018. When and why are pre-trained word embeddings useful for neural machine translation? In *NAACL*, pages 529–535.

Radovanović, Miloš, Alexandros Nanopoulos, and Mirjana Ivanović. 2010. Hubs in Space: Popular Nearest Neighbors in High-Dimensional Data. *Journal of Machine Learning Research*, 11:2487–2531.

Rios Gonzales, Annette, Laura Mascarell, and Rico Sennrich. 2017. Improving Word Sense Disambiguation in Neural Machine Translation with Sense Embeddings. In *WMT*, pages 11–19.

Sennrich, Rico, Barry Haddow, and Alexandra Birch. 2016. Neural machine translation of rare words with subword units. In *ACL*, pages 1715–1725.

Zhou, Mingyang, Runxiang Cheng, Yong Jae Lee, and Zhou Yu. 2018. A visual attention grounding neural model for multimodal machine translation. In *EMNLP*, pages 3643–3653.

Translator2Vec: Understanding and Representing Human Post-Editors

António Góis

Unbabel

Lisbon, Portugal

antonio.gois@unbabel.com

André F. T. Martins

Unbabel & Instituto de Telecomunicações

Lisbon, Portugal

andre.martins@unbabel.com

Abstract

The combination of machines and humans for translation is effective, with many studies showing productivity gains when humans post-edit machine-translated output instead of translating from scratch. To take full advantage of this combination, we need a fine-grained understanding of how human translators work, and which post-editing styles are more effective than others. In this paper, we release and analyze a new dataset with document-level post-editing action sequences, including edit operations from keystrokes, mouse actions, and waiting times. Our dataset comprises 66,268 full document sessions post-edited by 332 humans, the largest of the kind released to date. We show that action sequences are informative enough to identify post-editors accurately, compared to baselines that only look at the initial and final text. We build on this to learn and visualize continuous representations of post-editors, and we show that these representations improve the downstream task of predicting post-editing time.

1   Introduction

Computer-aided translation platforms for interactive translation and post-editing are now commonly used in professional translation services (Alabau et al., 2014; Federico et al., 2014; Green et al., 2014; Denkowski, 2015; Hokamp, 2018; Sin-wai, 2014; Kenny, 2011). With the increasing quality of machine translation (Bahdanau et al., 2014; Gehring et al., 2017; Vaswani et al., 2017), the translation industry is going through a transformation, progressively shifting gears from "computer-aided" (where MT is used as an instrument to help professional translators) towards **human-aided translation**, where there is a human in the loop who only intervenes when needed to ensure final quality, and whose productivity is to be optimized. A deep, data-driven understanding of the **human post-editing process** is key to achieve the best trade-offs in translation efficiency and quality. What makes a "good" post-editor? What kind of behaviour shall an interface promote?

There is a string of prior work that relates the difficulty of translating text with the cognitive load of human translators and post-editors, based on indicators such as editing times, pauses, keystroke logs, and eye tracking (O'Brien, 2006; Doherty et al., 2010; Lacruz et al., 2012; Balling and Carl, 2014, see also §6). Most of these studies, however, have been performed in controlled environments on a very small scale, with a limited number of professional translators and only a few sessions. A direct use of human activity data for understanding and representing human post-editors, towards improving their productivity, is still missing, arguably due to the lack of large-scale data. Understanding how human post-editors work could open the door to the design of better interfaces, smarter allocation of human translators to content, and automatic post-editing.

In this paper, we study the behaviour of human post-editors "in the wild" by automatically examining tens of thousands of post-editing sessions at a document level. We show that these detailed editor activities (which we call **action sequences**, §2) encode useful additional information besides just the initial machine-translated text and the final post-edited text. This is aligned to recent findings in other domains: Yang et al. (2017) and Faruqui et al. (2018) have recently shown that Wikipedia page edits can represent interesting linguistic phenomena in language modeling and discourse. While prior work analyzed the cognitive behaviour of post-editors and their productivity by collecting a few statistics, we take a step forward in this paper, using state-of-the-art machine learning techniques to **represent editors in a vector space** (§4). These representations are obtained by training a model to **identify** the editor based on his action sequences (§3). This model achieves high accuracy in predicting the editor's identity, and the learned representations exhibit interesting correlations with the editors' behaviour and their productivity, being effective when plugged as features for **predicting the post-editing time** (§5).

Overall, we use our action sequence dataset to address the following research questions:

1. **Editor identification** (§3): are the post-editors' activities (their action sequences) informative enough to allow discriminating their identities from one another (compared to just using the initial machine-translated text and the final post-edited one)?

2. **Editor representation** (§4): can the post-editors' activities be used to learn meaningful vector representations, such that similar editors are clustered together? Can we interpret these embeddings to understand which activity patterns characterize "good" editors (in terms of translation quality and speed)?

3. **Downstream tasks** (§5): do the learned editor vector representations provide useful information for downstream tasks, such as predicting the time to translate a document, compared to pure text-based approaches that do not use them?

We base our study on editor-labeled action sequences for two language pairs, English-French and English-German, which we make available for future research. In both cases, we obtain positive answers to the three questions above.

2   Post-Editor Action Sequences

A crucial part of our work is in converting raw keystroke sequences and timestamps into **action**

Action	Symbol	Appended Info
Replace	R	new word
Insert	I	new word
Delete	D	old word
Insert Block	BI	new block of words
Delete Block	BD	old block of words
Jump Forward	JF	# words
Jump Back	JB	# words
Jump Sentence Forward	JSF	# sentences
Jump Sentence Back	JSB	# sentences
Mouse Clicks	MC	# mouse clicks
Mouse Selections	MS	# mouse selections
Wait	W	time (seconds)
Stop	S	–

Table 1: Text-editing and non-editing actions.

sequences—sequences of symbols in a finite alphabet that describe word edit operations (insertions, deletions, and replacements), batch operations (cutting and pasting text), mouse clicks or selections, jump movements, and pauses.

Each action sequence corresponds to a single post-editing session, in which a human post-edits a document. The starting point is a set of source documents (customer service email messages), which are sent for translation to Unbabel's online translation service. The documents are split into sentences and translated by a domain-adapted neural machine translation system based on Marian (Junczys-Dowmunt et al., 2018). Finally, each document is assigned to a human post-editor to correct eventual translation mistakes.[1] These post-editing sessions are logged, and all the keystroke and mouse operation events are saved, along with timestamps. A preprocessing script converts these raw keystrokes into word-level action sequences, as we next describe, and a unique identifier is appended that represents the human editor.

The preprocessing for converting the raw character-level keystroke data into word-level actions is as follows. We begin with a sequence of all intermediate states of a document between the machine-translated and the post-edited text, containing changes caused by each keystroke. We track the position of the word currently being edited and store one action summarizing the change in that word. A single keystroke may also

---

[1]The human post-editors are native or proficient speakers of both source and target languages, although not necessarily professional translators. They are evaluated on language skills and subject to periodic evaluations by Unbabel. Editors have access to whole documents when translating, and they are given content-specific guidelines, including style, register, etc.

Source	Hey there, Some agents do speak Spanish, otherwise our system will translate :) Best, <Name>
MT	Bonjour, Certains agents parlent espagnol, sinon notre système *se traduira par* :) Cordialement, <Name>
PE	Bonjour, Certains agents parlent espagnol, sinon notre système **traduit** :) Cordialement, <Name>
Actions	W:23 JSF:1 JF:8 D:se W:2 MC:1 MS:1 JF:1 D:par W:7 MC:1 MS:1 JB:1 R:traduit W:2 MS:1 S:–

Table 2: Example of a document and corresponding action sequence. We mark in *red* the MT words that have been corrected and in **blue** their replacement. The actions used here were W (wait), JSF (jump sentence forward), JF (jump forward), D (delete), MC (mouse clicks), MS (mouse selections), JB (jump back), R (replace) and S (stop).

cause simultaneous changes to several words (e.g. when pasting text or deleting a selected block), and we reserve separate actions for these. Overall, five **text-editing actions** are considered: inserting (I), deleting (D), and replacing (R) a single word, and inserting (BI) and deleting (BD) a block of words. Each action is appended with the corresponding word or block of words, as shown in Table 1.

Other actions, dubbed **non-editing actions**, do not change the text directly. Jump-forward (JF) and jump-backward operations (JB) count the distance in words between two consecutive edits. Another pair of actions informs when a new sentence is edited: a sentence jump (JSF/JSB) indicates that we moved a certain number of sentences forth/back since the previous edit. Mouse clicks (MC) and mouse selections (MS) count their occurrences between two consecutive edits. Wait (W) counts the seconds between the beginning of two consecutive edits. Finally, stop (S) marks the end of the post-editing session.

Since we do not want to rely on lexical information to identify the human post-editors, only the 50 most frequent words were kept (most containing punctuation symbols and stop-words), with the remaining ones converted to a special unknown symbol (UNK). Moreover, the first waiting time is split in two: the time until the first keystroke occurs and, in case the first keystroke is not part of the first action (e.g. a mouse click), a second waiting time until the first action begins.

Table 2 shows an example of a small document, along with the editor's action sequence. The editor began on sentence 2 ("Certains agents...") and the word on position 9, since there was a jump for-

ward of 1 sentence and 8 words. After deleting "se", position 9 became "traduira". Since the editor opted to delete "par" (using a mouse selection) before changing the verb, there is a jump forward of 1 word to position 10. Then we have a jump back of 1 before changing the verb to "traduit".

Datasets. We introduce two datasets for this task, one for English-French (En-Fr) and another for English-German (En-De). For each dataset, we provide the action sequences for full documents, along with an editor identifier. To ensure reproducibility of our results, we release both datasets as part of this paper, available in `https://github.com/Unbabel/ translator2vec/releases/download/ v1.0/keystrokes_dataset.zip`. For anonymization purposes, we convert all editor names and the 50 tokens in the word vocabulary to numeric identifiers. Statistics of the dataset are shown in Table 3: it is the largest ever released dataset with post-editing action sequences, and the only one we are aware of with document-level information.[2] Each document corresponds to a customer service email with an average of 116.6 tokens per document. Each sentence has an average length of 9.4 tokens.

---

[2] The closest comparable dataset was released by Specia et al. (2017) in the scope of the QT21 project, containing 176,476 sentences spanning multiple language pairs (about 4 times less), with raw keystroke sequences being available by request. In contrast to ours, their units are sentences and not full documents, which precludes studying how human post-editors jump between sentences when translating a document.

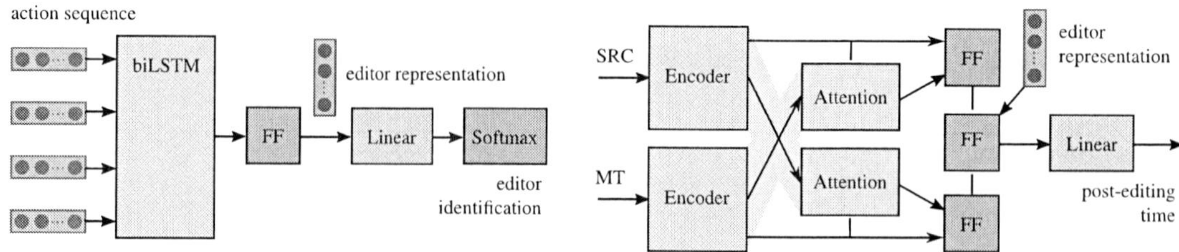

Figure 1: Left: our **Action Seq** model for editor identification. Right: our model for post-editing time prediction.

		# docs	# sents	# words
	train	17,464	154,026	1,895,389
En-Fr	dev	5,514	52,366	659,675
	test	9,441	86,111	1,072,807
	train	17,403	169,478	2,053,407
En-De	dev	6,722	66,521	826,791
	test	9,724	98,920	1,221,319
Total		66,268	627,422	7,729,388

Table 3: Number of documents, sentences, and words in English source text per dataset. There are 149 unique editors across all En-Fr datasets, and 183 in En-De.

3 Editor Identification

We now make use of the dataset just described to answer the three research questions stated at the end of §1, starting with **editor identification**.

3.1 Data Preparation

For this experiment, we took the action sequence dataset described in §2 and selected a small number of human translators for both language pairs who post-edited a number of documents above a threshold: this yielded 6 editors for En-Fr and 7 editors for En-De. To ensure balanced datasets, we filtered them to contain the same number of samples per selected editor. This filtering yielded a total of 998/58/58 training/dev/test documents per editor for En-Fr, and 641/128/72 for En-De.

A random baseline for this dataset would obtain an editor identification accuracy of $1/6 = 16.7\%$ for En-Fr and $1/7 = 14.3\%$ for En-De.

3.2 A Model for Editor Identification

Let $\langle x_1, \ldots, x_L \rangle$ be an action sequence produced by a post-editor y. To identify the editor of a task, we build a model $P(y \mid x_1, \ldots, x_L)$ using a neural network as we next describe (shown in Figure 1). Each action x_i is first associated to a one-hot vector. All numeric actions are grouped

into bins—e.g. waiting times of 200 seconds and higher all correspond to the same one-hot representation. Bins were defined manually, providing higher granularity to small values than to larger ones.[3] Each one-hot is then mapped to a learnable embedding, and the sequence of embeddings is fed to a 2-layer bidirectional LSTM (biLSTM; Hochreiter and Schmidhuber (1997); Graves and Schmidhuber (2005)), resulting in two final states $\overrightarrow{h}, \overleftarrow{h}$. Then we concatenate both, apply dropout (Srivastava et al., 2014) and feed them to a feed-forward layer with a ReLU activation (Glorot et al., 2011) to form a vector h. This vector is taken as the representation of the action sequence. Finally, we define $P(y \mid x_1, \ldots, x_L) = \mathsf{softmax}(Wh + b)$.

We call this model **Action Seq**, since it exploits information from the action sequences.

3.3 Baselines

To assess how much information action sequences provide about human editors beyond the initial (machine translation) and final (post-edited) text, we implemented various baselines which do **not** use fine-grained information from the action sequences. All use pre-trained text embeddings from FastText (Joulin et al., 2017), and they are all tuned for dropout and learning rate:

- One using the machine-translated text only (**MT**). Since this text has not been touched by the human post-editor, we expect this system to perform similarly to the random baseline. The goal of this baseline is to control whether there is a bias in the content each editor receives that could discriminate her identity. It uses word embeddings as input to a biLSTM, followed by feed-forward and softmax layers.

---

[3] We used $\{0, \ldots, 5, 7, 10, 15, 20, 30, 50, 75, 100, 150, 200+\}$ for wait and jump events (in seconds and word positions, respectively); and $\{0, \ldots, 5, 7, 10+\}$ for sentence jumps and mouse events (in sentence positions and clicks).

- Another one using the posted-edited text only (**PE**). This is used to control for the linguistic style of the post-editor. We expect this to be a weak baseline, since although there are positive results on translator stylometry (El-Fiqi et al., 2019), the task of post-editing provides less opportunity to leave a fingerprint than if writing a translation from scratch. The architecture is the same as in the **MT** baseline.

- A baseline combining both MT and PE using a dual encoder architecture (**MT + PE**), inspired by models from dialogue response (Lowe et al., 2015; Lu et al., 2017). This baseline is stronger than the previous two, since it is able to look at the *differences* between the initial and final text produced by the post-editor, although it ignores the process by which these differences have been generated. Two separate biLSTMs encode the two sequences of word embeddings, the final encoded states are concatenated and fed to a feed-forward and a softmax layer to provide the editors' probabilities.

- Finally, a stronger baseline (**MT + PE + Att**) that is able to "align" the MT and PE, by augmenting the dual encoder above with an attention mechanism, inspired by work in natural language inference (Rocktäschel et al., 2016). The model resembles the one in Figure 1 (right), with a softmax output layer and without the editor representation layer. Two separate biLSTMs are used to encode the machine-translated and the post-edited text. The final state of the MT is used to compute attention over the PE, then this attention-weighted PE is concatenated with MT's final state and passed through a feed-forward layer. Symmetrically we obtain a representation from PE's final state and an attention-weighted MT. Finally both vectors are concatenated and turned into editors' probabilities through another feed-forward layer.

Additionally, we prepare another baseline (**Delta**) as a tuple with meta information containing statistics about the difference between the initial and final text (still not depending on the action sequences). This tuple contains the following 5 elements: a count of sentences in the document, minimum edit distance between MT and PE, count of words in the original document, in MT and in PE. Each of these elements is binned and mapped to a learnable embedding. The 5 embeddings are

	En-De (%)	En-Fr (%)
Delta	16.15	26.09
MT	18.21	16.44
PE	27.38	30.00
MT + PE	26.63	31.78
MT + PE + Att	30.12	35.06
Action Seq	**84.37**	**67.07**

Table 4: Results of model and baselines for editor identification. Reported are average test set accuracies of 5 runs, with 7 editors for En-De and 6 editors for En-Fr.

	En-De (%)	En-Fr (%)
Action Seq	**83.31**	**73.16**
w/out editing actions	80.60	69.37
w/out mouse info	75.49	66.38
w/out waiting time	80.42	70.92
w/out 1st waiting time	78.60	71.15
only editing actions	60.20	59.08
only mouse info	56.43	55.06
only waiting time	53.53	44.02
only 1st waiting time	24.22	23.11

Table 5: Ablations studies for editor identification. Reported are average development set accuracies of 5 runs, with 7 editors for En-De and 6 editors for En-Fr.

concatenated into a vector e, followed by a feed-forward layer and a softmax activation.

3.4 Editor Identification Accuracy

Table 4 compares our system with the baselines above. Among the baselines, we observe a gradual improvement as models have access to more information. The fact that the MT baseline performs closely to the random baseline is reassuring, showing that there is no bias in the type of text that each editor receives. As expected, the dual encoder model with attention, being able to attend to each word of the MT and post-edited text, is the one which performs the best, surpassing the random baseline by a large margin. However, none of these baselines have a satisfactory performance on the editor identification task.

By contrast, the accuracies achieved by our proposed model (**Action Seq**) are striking: 84.37% in En-De and 67.07% in En-Fr, way above the closest baselines. This large gap confirms our hypothesis that **the editing process itself contains information which is much richer than the initial and final text only.**

Ablation studies. To understand the importance of each action type in predicting the editor's identity, we conduct a series of ablation studies and report development set accuracies in Table 5. These experiments involve removing mouse information, time information, initial waiting time or editing actions. Also, we try keeping only each of the previous four. We find that all action types contribute to the global accuracy, although to different extents. Also, some action types achieve high performance on their own. Somewhat surprisingly, mouse information alone achieves remarkably high accuracy. Although waiting times also perform well on their own, removing them has little impact on the final score.

4 Editor Representation

The previous section has shown how the action sequences are very effective for identifying editors. As a by-product, the **Action Seq** model used for that task produced an internal vector h that represents the full post-editing session. This suggests a strategy for obtaining **editor representations**: simply *average* all such vectors from each editor. One way of looking at this is regarding editor identification as an auxiliary task that assists us in finding good editor representations. This draws inspiration from previous work, such as Mikolov et al. (2013), as well as its applications to recommendation systems (Grbovic et al., 2015, 2016). In the last two works, an auxiliary task also helps to provide a latent representation of an object of interest.

Visualization of translation sessions. To visualize the vectors h produced during our auxiliary task, we use Parametric t-SNE (Maaten, 2009) for dimensionality reduction. Unlike the original t-SNE (Maaten and Hinton, 2008), the parametric version allows to reapply a learned dimensionality reduction to new data. This way it is possible to infer a 2D structure using the training data, and check how well it fits the test data.

In Figure 2 we show a projection of vectors h for both language pairs, using a t-SNE model learned on the training set vectors; each color corresponds to a different editor. In the training set (used to train both the editor identification model and the Parametric t-SNE) there is one clear cluster for each editor, in both languages. Using test set data, new tasks also form clusters which are closely related to the editors' identity. Some clusters are isolated while others get mixed near their

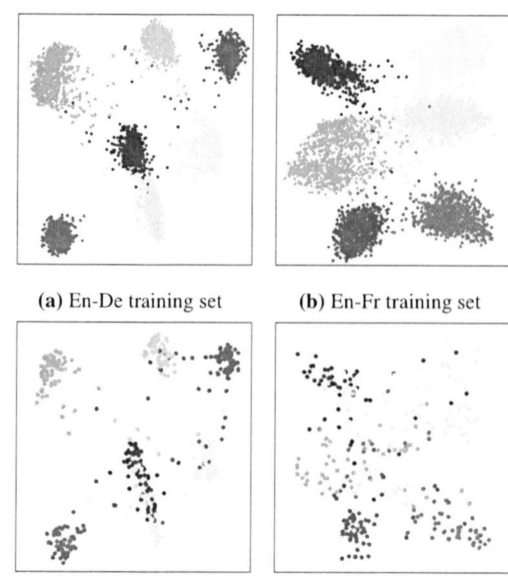

(a) En-De training set **(b)** En-Fr training set

(c) En-De test set **(d)** En-Fr test set

Figure 2: Embeddings of each translation session in the editor identification train and test sets, with editors identified by different colors. For each language, the dimensionality reduction was learned by training parametric t-SNE (Maaten, 2009) on the train data, and then applying it to both train and test data. En-De contains 7 editors, each with 641 train and 72 test samples per editor. En-Fr contains 6 editors, each with 998 train and 58 test samples per editor.

borders, possibly meaning that some editors behave in a more distinctive manner than others.

Visualization of editor representations. To represent an editor with a single vector, we average the h's of all tasks of a given editor to obtain his representation. Figure 3 contains representations for En-Fr editors (similar results have been achieved for En-De editors), using the exact same model as in Figure 2b to produce session embeddings, and the same t-SNE model for visualization. To reduce noise we discard editors with less than 10 samples, keeping 117 out of 149 editors. In Figure 3 we show percentiles for 3 editor features, using one point per editor and setting color to represent a different feature in each panel. In Figure 3a, color represents percentiles of average initial waiting time, and in Figure 3b, percentiles of counts of jump-backs per MT token. We can observe that the model learned to map high waiting times to the left and high counts of jump-backs to the right. In Figure 3c we have mouse activity per user (percentiles of counts of mouse clicks and selections). Here we can see a distribution very similar to that of count of jump-backs.

	Mouse and JB (%)	1st WT and JB (%)
En-Fr	80.75	-39.65
En-De	59.62	-31.11

Table 6: Pearson correlation between two pairs of variables: mouse actions / jump backs and first waiting time / jump backs.

We hypothesize that there are two types of human editors: those who first read the full document and then post-edit it left to right; and those who read as they type, and go back and forth. To check these hypothesis, we measure the Pearson correlation between two pairs of variables in Table 6. Indeed, there is a slight negative correlation between the average initial pause and the count of jump backs per word. This matches intuition, since a person who waited longer before beginning a task will probably have a clearer idea of what needs to be done in the first place. We also present the correlation between the count of mouse events (clicks and selections) and count of jump backs, which we observe to be very high. This may be due to the need to move between distant positions of the document, which is more commonly done with the mouse than with the keyboard.

5 Prediction of Post-Editing Time

Finally, we design a downstream task with the goal of assessing the information contained in each translator's vector h and observing its applicability in a real-world setting. The task consists in predicting the post-editing time of a given job, which has been used as a quality estimation task in previous work (Cohn and Specia, 2013; Specia, 2011). As a baseline, we use the previously described dual encoder with attention (Figure 1, right). The inputs are the word embeddings of the original document and of the machine translation. In the output layer, instead of predicting each editor's logit, we predict the logarithm of the post-editing time per source word, following Cohn and Specia (2013). We use mean squared error as the loss. For our proposed model, we augment this baseline by providing a "dynamic" representation of the human post-editor as described below.

Dynamic editor representations. In order to obtain an editor's embedding in a real-time setting we do the following: For each new translation session, we store its corresponding embedding, keeping a maximum of 10 previous translations per ed-

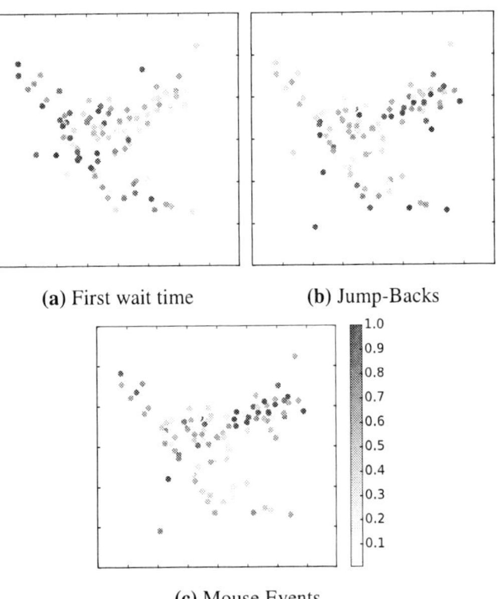

Figure 3: Embeddings of each En-Fr editor, mapped using the same parametric t-SNE as in Figure 2. In 3a we have average pause before beginning for each editor, in percentile. In 3b we have the count of jump-backs per MT token of each editor, also in percentile. In 3c we have percentiles of counts of mouse clicks and selections per editor.

itor. Whenever an editor's embedding is required, we compute the average of his stored translations into a single vector. This allows updating the editors' representations incrementally in a dynamic fashion, coping with the fact that editors change their behaviour over time as they learn to use the translation interface.

To introduce a translator vector h into the previously described baseline, we increase the input size of the feed-forward layer which receives both encoders' outputs, and we introduce h in this step by concatenating it to the encoders' outputs.

Results. Both models are evaluated using Pearson correlation between the predicted and real logtimes. Results in Table 7 confirm our hypothesis that **editor representations can be very effective for predicting human post-editing time**, with consistent gains in Pearson correlation ($+30.11\%$ in En-Fr and $+15.05\%$ in En-De) over the baseline that does not use any editor information. Our approach also allows for initializing and updating editor embeddings dynamically, i.e. without having to retrain the time-prediction model.[4]

---

[4]This experiment also reveals that previous work on translation quality estimation (Specia et al., 2018) using time predictions can have biased results if different types of translators

	Using source text and MT (%)	Adding dynamic editor embedding (%)
En-Fr dev	19.53	**42.98**
test	17.58	**47.69**
En-De dev	27.62	**47.40**
test	23.67	**38.72**

Table 7: Pearson correlation between real and predicted logarithm of time per word in source text.

6 Related Work

There is a long string of work studying the cognitive effort in post-editing machine translation. One of the earliest instances is O'Brien (2006), who investigates the relationship between pauses and cognitive effort in post-editing. This correlation has also been studied by examination of keystroke logs (Lacruz et al., 2012; Lacruz and Shreve, 2014). Our results further confirm this, and also identify other characteristics as a fingerprint of the editors: mouse information and jumps.

More recently, Moorkens and O'Brien (2015) compare novice and professional post-editors in terms of their suitability as research participants when testing new features of post-editing environments. They conclude that professionals are more efficient but less flexible to interface changes, which confirms the existence of several editor profiles, not necessarily ones better than the others.

Other small-scale studies identify editor behaviour during translation. Asadi and Séguinot (2005) distinguish between translators who plan ahead and those who type as they think. Daems and Macken (2019) identify personal preferences between usage of mouse vs. keyboard. De Almeida (2013) studies differences and similarities in editor behaviour for two language pairs, regarding types of edits, keyboard vs. mouse usage and Web searches.

Carl et al. (2011) have shown that human translators are more productive and accurate when post-editing MT output than when translating from scratch. This has recently been confirmed by Toral et al. (2018), who have shown further gains with neural MT compared to phrase-based MT. Koponen et al. (2012) show HTER (Snover et al., 2006) is limited to measure cognitive effort, and suggest post-editing time instead. On the other hand, Herbig et al. (2019) measure cognitive effort subjectively by directly inquiring translators, and then

edit different documents. Our editor representations can be potentially useful for removing this bias.

use a combination of features to predict this cognitive effort – such task could potentially be improved by including translator representations as an additional feature. Blain et al. (2011) take a more qualitative approach to understanding post-editing by introducing a measure based on post-editing actions. Specia (2011) attempts to predict the post-editing time using quality estimation, and Koehn and Germann (2014); Sanchez-Torron and Koehn (2016) study the impact of machine translation quality in post-editor productivity. Tatsumi et al. (2012) study the effect of crowd-sourced post-editing of machine translation output, finding that larger pools of non-experts can frequently produce accurate translations as quickly as experts. Aziz et al. (2012) developed a tool for post-editing and assessing machine translation which records data such as editing time, keystrokes, and translator assessments. A similar tool has been developed by Denkowski and Lavie (2012); Denkowski et al. (2014b), which is able to learn from post-editing with model adaptation (Denkowski et al., 2014a). Our encouraging results on time prediction using editor representations suggests that these representations may also be useful for learning personalized translation models.

Yin et al. (2019) learn representations of single edits, and include a downstream task: applying these edits to unseen sentences. Wikipedia edits have been studied by Yang et al. (2017) and Faruqui et al. (2018). The latter study what can be learned about language by observing the editing process that cannot be readily learned by observing only raw text. Likewise, we study what can be learned about the translation process by observing how humans type, which cannot be readily learned by observing only the initial and final text.

Our work makes a bridge between the earliest studies on the cognitive effort of human post-editors and modern representation learning techniques, towards embedding human translators on a vector space. We draw inspiration on techniques for learning distributed word representations (Mikolov et al., 2013; Pennington et al., 2014), which have also been extended for learning user representations for recommendation systems (Grbovic et al., 2015, 2016). These techniques usually obtain high-quality embeddings by tuning the system for an auxiliary task, such as predicting a word given its context. In our case, we take **editor identification** as the auxiliary task, given a sequence of keytrokes as input. A related problem (but with a completely different goal) is the use of keystroke dynamics for user authentication (Monrose and Rubin, 2000; Banerjee and Woodard, 2012; Kim and Kang, 2018). Unlike this literature, our paper is focused on post-editing of machine-translated text. This is more similar to El-Fiqi et al. (2019), who focus on identifying the translator of a book from his translation style. However, we are not interested in the problem of editor identification per se, but only as a means to obtain good representations.

7 Conclusions

We introduced and analyzed the largest public dataset so far containing post-editing information retrieved from raw keystrokes. We provided strong evidence that these intermediate steps contain precious information unavailable in the initial plus final translated document, by formulating and providing answers to three research questions: (i) that action sequences can be used to perform accurate editor identification; (ii) that they can be used to learn human post-editor vector representations that cluster together similar editors; and (iii) that these representations help downstream tasks, such as predicting post-editing time. In sum, we showed that fine-grained post-editing information is a rich and untapped source of information, and we hope that the dataset we release can foster further research in this area.

Acknowledgments

We would like to thank Carla Parra, Alon Lavie, Ricardo Rei, António Lopes, and the anonymous reviewers for their insightful comments. This work was partially supported by the EU/FEDER programme under PT2020 (contracts 027767 and 038510) and by the European Research Council (ERC StG DeepSPIN 758969).

References

Alabau, Vicent, Christian Buck, Michael Carl, Francisco Casacuberta, Mercedes García-Martínez, Ulrich Germann, Jesús González-Rubio, Robin Hill, Philipp Koehn, Luis Leiva, et al. 2014. Casmacat: A computer-assisted translation workbench. In *Proceedings of the Demonstrations at the 14th Conference of the European Chapter of the Association for Computational Linguistics*, pages 25–28.

Asadi, Paula and Candace Séguinot. 2005. Shortcuts, strategies and general patterns in a process study of nine professionals. *Meta: Journal des traducteurs/Meta: Translators' Journal*, 50(2):522–547.

Aziz, Wilker, Sheila Castilho, and Lucia Specia. 2012. Pet: a tool for post-editing and assessing machine translation. In *LREC*, pages 3982–3987.

Bahdanau, Dzmitry, Kyunghyun Cho, and Yoshua Bengio. 2014. Neural machine translation by jointly learning to align and translate. *arXiv preprint arXiv:1409.0473*.

Balling, Laura Winther and Michael Carl. 2014. *Post-editing of machine translation: Processes and applications*. Cambridge Scholars Publishing.

Banerjee, Salil P and Damon L Woodard. 2012. Biometric authentication and identification using keystroke dynamics: A survey. *Journal of Pattern Recognition Research*, 7(1):116–139.

Blain, Frédéric, Jean Senellart, Holger Schwenk, Mirko Plitt, and Johann Roturier. 2011. Qualitative analysis of post-editing for high quality machine translation. *MT Summit XIII: the Thirteenth Machine Translation Summit [organized by the] Asia-Pacific Association for Machine Translation (AAMT)*, pages 164–171.

Carl, Michael, Barbara Dragsted, Jakob Elming, Daniel Hardt, and Arnt Lykke Jakobsen. 2011. The process of post-editing: a pilot study. *Copenhagen Studies in Language*, 41:131–142.

Cohn, Trevor and Lucia Specia. 2013. Modelling annotator bias with multi-task gaussian processes: An application to machine translation quality estimation. In *Proceedings of the 51st Annual Meeting of the Association for Computational Linguistics (Volume 1: Long Papers)*, volume 1, pages 32–42.

Daems, Joke and Lieve Macken. 2019. Interactive adaptive smt versus interactive adaptive nmt: a user experience evaluation. *Machine Translation*, pages 1–18.

De Almeida, Giselle. 2013. *Translating the posteditor: an investigation of post-editing changes and correlations with professional experience across two Romance languages*. Ph.D. thesis, Dublin City University.

Denkowski, Michael. 2015. *Machine translation for human translators*. Ph.D. thesis, Ph. D. thesis, Carnegie Mellon University.

Denkowski, Michael, Chris Dyer, and Alon Lavie. 2014a. Learning from post-editing: Online model adaptation for statistical machine translation. In *Proceedings of the 14th Conference of the European Chapter of the Association for Computational Linguistics*, pages 395–404.

Denkowski, Michael and Alon Lavie. 2012. Transcenter: Web-based translation research suite. In *AMTA 2012 Workshop on Post-Editing Technology and Practice Demo Session*, page 2012.

Denkowski, Michael, Alon Lavie, Isabel Lacruz, and Chris Dyer. 2014b. Real time adaptive machine translation for post-editing with cdec and transcenter. In *Proceedings of the EACL 2014 Workshop on Humans and Computer-assisted Translation*, pages 72–77.

Doherty, Stephen, Sharon OBrien, and Michael Carl. 2010. Eye tracking as an mt evaluation technique. *Machine translation*, 24(1):1–13.

El-Fiqi, Heba, Eleni Petraki, and Hussein A. Abbass. 2019. Network motifs for translator stylometry identification. *PloS ONE*, 14(2):e0211809.

Faruqui, Manaal, Ellie Pavlick, Ian Tenney, and Dipanjan Das. 2018. Wikiatomicedits: A multilingual corpus of wikipedia edits for modeling language and discourse. In *Proc. of EMNLP*.

Federico, Marcello, Nicola Bertoldi, Mauro Cettolo, Matteo Negri, Marco Turchi, Marco Trombetti, Alessandro Cattelan, Antonio Farina, Domenico Lupinetti, Andrea Martines, et al. 2014. The matecat tool. In *Proceedings of COLING 2014, the 25th International Conference on Computational Linguistics: System Demonstrations*, pages 129–132.

Gehring, Jonas, Michael Auli, David Grangier, and Yann Dauphin. 2017. A convolutional encoder model for neural machine translation. In *Proceedings of the 55th Annual Meeting of the Association for Computational Linguistics (Volume 1: Long Papers)*, volume 1, pages 123–135.

Glorot, Xavier, Antoine Bordes, and Yoshua Bengio. 2011. Deep sparse rectifier neural networks. In *Proceedings of the fourteenth international conference on artificial intelligence and statistics*, pages 315–323.

Graves, Alex and Jürgen Schmidhuber. 2005. Framewise phoneme classification with bidirectional lstm and other neural network architectures. *Neural Networks*, 18(5-6):602–610.

Grbovic, Mihajlo, Nemanja Djuric, Vladan Radosavljevic, Fabrizio Silvestri, Ricardo Baeza-Yates, Andrew Feng, Erik Ordentlich, Lee Yang, and Gavin Owens. 2016. Scalable semantic matching of queries to ads in sponsored search advertising. In *Proceedings of the 39th International ACM SIGIR conference on Research and Development in Information Retrieval*, pages 375–384. ACM.

Grbovic, Mihajlo, Vladan Radosavljevic, Nemanja Djuric, Narayan Bhamidipati, Jaikit Savla, Varun Bhagwan, and Doug Sharp. 2015. E-commerce in your inbox: Product recommendations at scale. In *Proceedings of the 21th ACM SIGKDD International Conference on Knowledge Discovery and Data Mining*, KDD '15, pages 1809–1818, New York, NY, USA. ACM.

Green, Spence, Sida I Wang, Jason Chuang, Jeffrey Heer, Sebastian Schuster, and Christopher D Manning. 2014. Human effort and machine learnability in computer aided translation. In *Proceedings of the 2014 Conference on Empirical Methods in Natural Language Processing (EMNLP)*, pages 1225–1236.

Herbig, Nico, Santanu Pal, Mihaela Vela, Antonio Krüger, and Josef van Genabith. 2019. Multimodal indicators for estimating perceived cognitive load in post-editing of machine translation. *Machine Translation*, pages 1–25.

Hochreiter, Sepp and Jürgen Schmidhuber. 1997. Long short-term memory. *Neural computation*, 9(8):1735–1780.

Hokamp, Christopher M. 2018. *Deep interactive text prediction and quality estimation in translation interfaces*. Ph.D. thesis, Dublin City University.

Joulin, Armand, Edouard Grave, Piotr Bojanowski, and Tomas Mikolov. 2017. Bag of tricks for efficient text classification. In *Proceedings of the 15th Conference of the European Chapter of the Association for Computational Linguistics: Volume 2, Short Papers*, pages 427–431. Association for Computational Linguistics.

Junczys-Dowmunt, Marcin, Roman Grundkiewicz, Tomasz Dwojak, Hieu Hoang,

Kenneth Heafield, Tom Neckermann, Frank Seide, Ulrich Germann, Alham Fikri Aji, Nikolay Bogoychev, André F. T. Martins, and Alexandra Birch. 2018. Marian: Fast neural machine translation in c++. In *Proceedings of ACL 2018, System Demonstrations*, pages 116–121.

Kenny, Dorothy. 2011. Electronic tools and resources for translators. In *The Oxford handbook of translation studies*.

Kim, Junhong and Pilsung Kang. 2018. Recurrent neural network-based user authentication for freely typed keystroke data. *arXiv preprint arXiv:1806.06190*.

Koehn, Philipp and Ulrich Germann. 2014. The impact of machine translation quality on human post-editing. In *Proceedings of the EACL 2014 Workshop on Humans and Computer-assisted Translation*, pages 38–46.

Koponen, Maarit, Wilker Aziz, Luciana Ramos, and Lucia Specia. 2012. Post-editing time as a measure of cognitive effort. *Proceedings of WPTP*, pages 11–20.

Lacruz, Isabel and Gregory M. Shreve. 2014. Pauses and cognitive effort in post-editing. *Post-editing of machine translation: Processes and applications*, page 246.

Lacruz, Isabel, Gregory M Shreve, and Erik Angelone. 2012. Average pause ratio as an indicator of cognitive effort in post-editing: A case study. In *AMTA 2012 Workshop on Post-Editing Technology and Practice (WPTP 2012)*, pages 21–30. AMTA.

Lowe, Ryan, Nissan Pow, Iulian Serban, and Joelle Pineau. 2015. The ubuntu dialogue corpus: A large dataset for research in unstructured multi-turn dialogue systems. *CoRR*, abs/1506.08909.

Lu, Yichao, Phillip Keung, Shaonan Zhang, Jason Sun, and Vikas Bhardwaj. 2017. A practical approach to dialogue response generation in closed domains. *arXiv preprint arXiv:1703.09439*.

Maaten, Laurens. 2009. Learning a parametric embedding by preserving local structure. In *Artificial Intelligence and Statistics*, pages 384–391.

Maaten, Laurens van der and Geoffrey Hinton. 2008. Visualizing data using t-sne. *Journal of machine learning research*, 9(Nov):2579–2605.

Mikolov, Tomas, Ilya Sutskever, Kai Chen, Greg S Corrado, and Jeff Dean. 2013. Distributed repre-sentations of words and phrases and their compositionality. In *Advances in neural information processing systems*, pages 3111–3119.

Monrose, Fabian and Aviel D Rubin. 2000. Keystroke dynamics as a biometric for authentication. *Future Generation computer systems*, 16(4):351–359.

Moorkens, Joss and Sharon O'Brien. 2015. Post-editing evaluations: Trade-offs between novice and professional participants. In *Proceedings of the 18th Annual Conference of the European Association for Machine Translation*.

O'Brien, Sharon. 2006. Pauses as indicators of cognitive effort in post-editing machine translation output. *Across Languages and Cultures*, 7(1):1–21.

Pennington, Jeffrey, Richard Socher, and Christopher Manning. 2014. Glove: Global vectors for word representation. In *Proceedings of the 2014 conference on empirical methods in natural language processing (EMNLP)*, pages 1532–1543.

Rocktäschel, Tim, Edward Grefenstette, Karl Moritz Hermann, Tomáš Kočiský, and Phil Blunsom. 2016. Reasoning about entailment with neural attention. In *Proc. of International Conference on Learning Representations*.

Sanchez-Torron, Marina and Philipp Koehn. 2016. Machine translation quality and post-editor productivity. *AMTA 2016, Vol.*, page 16.

Sin-wai, Chan. 2014. The development of translation technology. *Routledge Encyclopedia of Translation Technology*, page 3.

Snover, Matthew, Bonnie Dorr, Richard Schwartz, Linnea Micciulla, and John Makhoul. 2006. A study of translation edit rate with targeted human annotation. In *Proceedings of association for machine translation in the Americas*, volume 200.

Specia, Lucia. 2011. Exploiting objective annotations for measuring translation post-editing effort. In *Proceedings of the 15th Conference of the European Association for Machine Translation*, pages 73–80.

Specia, Lucia, Kim Harris, Frédéric Blain, Aljoscha Burchardt, Viviven Macketanz, Inguna Skadina, Matteo Negri, , and Marco Turchi. 2017. Translation quality and productivity: A study on rich morphology languages. In *Ma-*

chine Translation Summit XVI, pages 55–71, Nagoya, Japan.

Specia, Lucia, Carolina Scarton, and Gustavo Henrique Paetzold. 2018. Quality estimation for machine translation. *Synthesis Lectures on Human Language Technologies*, 11(1):1–162.

Srivastava, Nitish, Geoffrey Hinton, Alex Krizhevsky, Ilya Sutskever, and Ruslan Salakhutdinov. 2014. Dropout: a simple way to prevent neural networks from overfitting. *The Journal of Machine Learning Research*, 15(1):1929–1958.

Tatsumi, Midori, Takako Aikawa, Kentaro Yamamoto, and Hitoshi Isahara. 2012. How good is crowd post-editing? its potential and limitations. In *AMTA 2012 Workshop on Post-Editing Technology and Practice (WPTP 2012)*, pages 69–77.

Toral, Antonio, Martijn Wieling, and Andy Way. 2018. Post-editing effort of a novel with statistical and neural machine translation. *Frontiers in Digital Humanities*, 5:9.

Vaswani, Ashish, Noam Shazeer, Niki Parmar, Jakob Uszkoreit, Llion Jones, Aidan N Gomez, Łukasz Kaiser, and Illia Polosukhin. 2017. Attention is all you need. In *Advances in Neural Information Processing Systems*, pages 6000–6010.

Yang, Diyi, Aaron Halfaker, Robert Kraut, and Eduard Hovy. 2017. Identifying semantic edit intentions from revisions in wikipedia. In *Proceedings of the 2017 Conference on Empirical Methods in Natural Language Processing*, pages 2000–2010.

Yin, Pengcheng, Graham Neubig, Miltiadis Allamanis, Marc Brockschmidt, and Alexander L. Gaunt. 2019. Learning to represent edits. In *International Conference on Learning Representations (ICLR)*, New Orleans, LA, USA.

Domain Adaptation for MT:
A Study with Unknown and Out-of-Domain Tasks

Hoang Cuong
Agolo, Inc.
cuong.hoang@agolo.com

Abstract

Translation quality could degrade non-gracefully outside the desired domain for MT. Meanwhile, translation requests are often unknown and potentially out-of-domain in practice. This paper shows that having an ecosystem with a range of pre-trained domain-specific MT systems can reduce the effect: a translation task can be out of scope of most pre-trained MT systems, but a few others can be capable of handling the task. But how to obtain the best translation from an ecosystem for such translation requests? We contribute two frameworks to address the problem. Experiments show that our frameworks give the performance in the middle between top rank MT systems with reasonably large-scale ecosystems.

1 Introduction

Translation models have been developed under the assumption that we know the domain at test time in advance, and the domain is strictly relevant to our training data. However, we inevitably will come across test data that is sampled from a different distribution to our training data when using the models in the wild. Another critical thing is that the domain of test data is often unknown in practice (e.g. Google Translate and Microsoft Translators receive translation requests from their users without knowing in advance their interests).

We have not had a solution for this well-known problem yet. Machine Translation (MT) has been advanced by new models, including using Neural Machine Translation (NMT) instead of Statistical Machine Translation (SMT). The hope is that a better translation model would improve the translation in all settings/situations. This, however, is not true. Translation quality could degrade nongracefully outside the desired domain for both NMT and SMT. In fact, it has been known that NMT suffers even harder than SMT when the test data is out-of-domain (Koehn and Knowles, 2017; Chu and Wang, 2018). We also improve MT by using domain adaptation methods (i.e. improving translation system from having a small seed in-domain data such as system interpolation, instance weighting and data selection). In practice, this is not a thorough solution because we do not know the domain of user translation requests in advance.

The contribution of this work is to provide a simple, easy-and-fast-to-deploy, translation model-agnostic[1] solution to the challenging problem. Our approach is to construct an "ecosystem" with a range of pre-trained domain-specific MT systems, each specialized in a certain domain (e.g. Speech, Financial, Food, etc.). Our intuition is that having such an ecosystem could reduce the decrease in translation quality for an outside domain. That is, an out-of-domain translation task can be out of scope of most pre-trained MT systems in the ecosystem. However, with the diversity of domains in a reasonably large ecosystem, we hope there is a chance to have certain pre-trained systems in the ecosystem that can be capable of handling the task well. The larger our ecosystem is, the more likely we have more capable pre-trained MT systems to an out-of-domain task.

The next step is to work on an unsupervised

---

[1]We aim for a solution that works with both NMT, SMT or other translation models.

method that automatically finds the best translations from an ecosystem for every translation request from an unknown and out-of-domain translation task. This is surprisingly difficult. Creating a domain classifier for translation requests provides suboptimal performance, because the target domain is unknown and out-of-domain. System combination could degrade translation quality substantially, as the majority of pre-trained MT systems in the ecosystem are incapable of handling the task. We propose two frameworks to address the problem.

VOTING I involves two separate steps for handling each translation request: First, the request is translated by *all* pre-trained MT systems. Second, the translation output that is most similar to others is returned to the user. An agreement measure is proposed to calculate how similar translation outputs are. The intuition behind VOTING I is that good translations may be similar to the others. That is, because they are good translations, they must be similar to translation references, and therefore it is likely that they are similar to the others as well.

VOTING II selects only a *limited* number of MT systems for decoding. Decoding cost is thus substantially cheaper in VOTING II. The intuition behind VOTING II is that MT systems that are good in a domain tend to agree with each other. However, the expertise parameters of MT systems regarding to an unknown domain are hidden and we thus do not know which MT systems we should select. In VOTING II expertise parameters are initialized randomly and our heuristic learning algorithm consequently updates the parameters during translation. We note that VOTING II works with the assumption that the translation requests would be handled in sequential (not parallel). While this is not true for all cases, it is true when we translate request translations of large documents as one task.

We conduct extensive experiments with *Spanish-English*, *French-English* and *German-English* to support our intuition. Experiments show that VOTING I gives the performance in between the top two systems for medium-scale ecosystem, and in between the top three systems for a large-scale ecosystem. VOTING II performs substantially better than VOTING I and occasionally reaches close to the top Rank 1 MT system for medium-scale ecosystems. Our framework

is scalable and has promising applications to large-scale online translation services.[2]

2 Related Work

This paper discusses a complementary problem to domain adaptation: How to handle unknown and out-of-domain translation tasks. Domain adaptation has been an active topic of research for many years. A survey of domain adaptation for MT can be referred to (Chu and Wang, 2018; Cuong and Sima'an, 2017). Within MT, but the domain of the request is typically known in advance. domain adaptation can be regarded as injecting prior knowledge about the target translation task into learning.

Combination of in-domain data with a general-domain system A common is approach is to combine a system trained on the in-domain data with a general-domain system (Koehn and Schroeder, 2007; Farajian et al., 2017; Kobus et al., 2017; Foster et al., 2010; Shah et al., 2010; Bisazza et al., 2011; Sennrich, 2012b; Razmara et al., 2012; Cuong and Sima'an, 2014a; Cuong and Sima'an, 2015; Sennrich et al., 2013; Haddow, 2013; Hildebrand and Vogel, 2008; Joty et al., 2015; Wang et al., 2018; Khayrallah et al., 2017; Chen et al., 2017; Tars and Fishel, 2018) or to combine the in-domain system with a system trained on a selected subset (Axelrod et al., 2011; Duh et al., 2013; Kirchhoff and Bilmes, 2014; Eetemadi et al., 2015; Chen and Huang, 2016; Wang et al., 2018; van der Wees et al., 2017; Cuong and Sima'an, 2014b).

Meta-information Prior knowledge may also lie in meta-information about training data. This could be document-annotated information (Eidelman et al., 2012; Hu et al., 2014; Hasler et al., 2014; Zhang et al., 2014; Su et al., 2015), and domain-annotated sub-corpora (Chiang et al., 2011; Sennrich, 2012b; Chen et al., 2013; Kothur et al., 2018; Michel and Neubig, 2018; Bapna and Firat, 2019).

Other DA Topics Recent work also performs adaptation by exploiting separate in-domain development sets (Sennrich, 2012a; Carpuat et al., 2013; Mansour and Ney, 2014; Clark et al., 2012; Wang et al., 2012). Rewarding domain invariance is also

---

[2]The code can be downloaded at: github.com/hoangcuong2011/UnsupervisedDomainAdaptation.

another approach to perform unsupervised adaptation (Cuong et al., 2016). Combining several different Machine Translation outputs operating on the same input is also a promising DA approach (Jayaraman and Lavie, 2005; Hildebrand and Vogel, 2008).

Using online methods for adapting MT systems in a scenario where human feedback (e.g. post-edited MT output) is constantly returned has been gaining interest recently (Ortiz-Martínez et al., 2010; Koehn et al., 2014; Denkowski et al., 2014; Bertoldi et al., 2014; Blain et al., 2015; Ortiz-Martínez, 2016; Wuebker et al., 2016; Karimova et al., 2018). Using Bayesian models provides promising results for adapting MT systems (e.g. see (Denkowski et al., 2014; Bertoldi et al., 2014; Blain et al., 2015; Peris and Casacuberta, 2018)). Recently, deploying bandit learning algorithms shows promising results for minimizing the cost of human feedback for improving system performance (e.g. see (Sokolov et al., 2015; Sokolov et al., 2016; Sokolov et al., 2017; Nguyen et al., 2017)).

3 Our Framework

Assume we are given a set of N pre-trained MT systems $\mathbf{m}_1^N = \{m_1, m_2, \ldots, m_N\}$. At test time, our goal is to handle an *unknown* and out-of-domain translation task: $\mathbf{f}_1^K = \{f_1, f_2, \ldots, f_K\}$. Note that the requests may be submitted intermittently by the user, which is common in practice (e.g. as in web-based translation services).

3.1 Voting I

Our first proposed framework is VOTING I. It involves two separate steps. First, each translation request f is translated by *all* pre-trained MT systems. Second, the translation output produced by an MT system that is most similar to others is returned to the user. Note that this approach is quite similar to (Macherey and Och, 2007), only that the approach here is made to be symmetrical.

Technically, the agreement between two translation outputs e_m and $e_{m'}$ produced by two different MT systems m and m' is calculated as the *arithmetic mean* between BLEU+1(e, e') and BLEU+1(e',e):

$$a(e_m, e_{m'}) = \frac{\text{BLEU+1}(e_m, e_{m'}) + \text{BLEU+1}(e_{m'}, e_m).}{2}$$

Here, BLEU+1 (Lin and Och, 2004) is a variant of BLEU for sentence-level assessment (Papineni

et al., 2002). Given that all N MT systems are used to decode each translation request, the average agreement score between one translation output e_m produced by an MT system m and all the others produced by other MT systems m$'$ is calculated as:

$$a(e_m) = \sum_{m' \neq m} \frac{1}{N-1} a(e_m, e_{m'}). \quad (1)$$

VOTING I simply uses the proposed agreement measure to rank translation outputs. As discussed, our assumption is that good translations (e.g. Book, Wikipedia) is likely to be similar to the others. See Table 1 for a positive example we obtain from our experiments with VOTING I .

3.2 Voting II

MT systems can generate similar translations by chance. We show such an example we obtain from our experiments with VOTING I in Table 2 (on the left). There are also cases of "black sheep": a very good translation may be too different from the others. Table 2 (on the right) shows such an example. VOTING I is not able to handle these issues. Applying VOTING I is expensive regarding the decoding cost.

How to address these issues? In our refined framework – VOTING II, we introduce a set of *expertise parameters* of all MT systems: $\Theta_1^N = \{\theta_{m_1}, \theta_{m_2}, \ldots, \theta_{m_N}\}$. Here, expertise parameter θ_m represents how suitable a system m to a certain domain. VOTING II simply selects only the top M MT systems with the highest expertise parameters, instead of using all N MT systems for decoding each translation request. In our experiments, we set $M = 3$.

VOTING II addresses the shortcomings of VOTING I as follows:

- (1) VOTING II explicitly filters bad MT systems for a certain domain;

- (2) VOTING II ranks translation outputs according to a sum of $a(e_m) + \theta_m$ instead of only $a(e_m)$ as in VOTING I;

- and (3) the decoding cost is substantially reduced (with a ratio of $(N - M)/N$). As discussed, VOTING II works with the assumption that the translation requests would be handled in sequential and not parallel (e.g. we translate request translations of large documents as one task).

Medicine	**Input**: aliments et boissons abilify peut se prendre pendant ou en dehors des repas . **Reference**: taking abilify with food and drink abilify can be taken regardless of meals .	
MT System	**Score**	**Translation Output**
Book	**0.70**	**food and drink abilify can take during or outside meals .**
Speech	0.64	food and drink abilify can take yourself for or outside meals .
IT	0.45	aliments and boissons abilify might take in or out of meal .
Bank	0.58	foods and beverages abilify may take during or outside the repas .
News	0.65	foods and drinks abilify can take during or outside the meal .
Wikipedia	0.69	food and drink abilify can be take during or outside the meal .
Legal	0.52	feedingstuffs and beverages abilify may be taken during or outside the meals .
Europarl	0.65	food and drink abilify can take over or outside meals .
Subtitles	0.58	aliments and drinks abilify can take for or out the food .

Table 1: Positive example with VOTING I: Good translations (e.g. Book, Wikipedia) tend to be similar to the others.

Medicine	**Input**: resume des caracteristiques du produit **Reference**: summary of product characteristics		**Input**: étiquetage et notice **Reference**: labelling and package leaflet	
MT System	**Score**	**Translation Output**	**Score**	**Translation Output**
Book	0.62	resume of product characteristics	**0.30**	**labelling and package leaflet**
Speech	**0.78**	**resume of caracteristiques of the product**	0.53	étiquetage and warning
IT	0.77	resume of caracteristiques the product	0.53	tag and notice
Bank	0.46	**summary of characteristics of product**	**0.74**	**étiquetage and notice**
News	**0.78**	**resume of caracteristiques of the product**	**0.74**	**étiquetage and notice**
Wikipedia	0.74	resume the caracteristiques of the product	**0.74**	**étiquetage and notice**
Legal	0.69	resume of the characteristics of the product	0.36	labelling and document
Europarl	0.70	resume the caracteristiques product	**0.74**	**étiquetage and notice**
Subtitles	0.63	resume some caracteristiques the product	**0.74**	**étiquetage and notice**

Table 2: Two negative examples with VOTING I. On the left: bad translations (e.g. IT, Wikipedia, Speech) are also similar to the others by chance. On the right: a case of "black sheep": a very good translation (Book) is too different from the others.

Of course the expertise parameters of MT systems are hidden. The question is how to learn them? The intuition behind VOTING II is that MT systems that are good in a certain domain are likely to agree with each other.

Two models are proposed in this paper to implement the idea. They are in the same spirit: the expertise parameter of each system m is sampled from a posterior distribution $\pi_m(\theta)$: $\theta_m \sim \pi_m(\theta)$. Our heuristic learning algorithm starts in a naive state, and we do not have any a-priori preference for one system over another. The algorithm consequently updates the parameters of the posterior distribution $\pi_m(\theta)$ based on agreement scores for translation outputs produced by system m. The proposed models use different posterior distributions $\pi(\theta)$ for sampling θ. Our goal of proposing different models is to investigate which one that addresses the problem best.

Figure 1 illustrates the framework.

3.2.1 Voting II Real

Our first model (VOTING II - REAL) uses normal distribution to sample expertise parameters. Let us assume a sample of agreement scores from all translation outputs produced by an MT system m as $\mathcal{A}_m = \{a_1, a_2, \ldots, a_{|\mathcal{A}_m|}\}$. Here, $|\mathcal{A}_m|$ denotes the sample size. Let us denote the sample *mean* and sample *variance* as $\bar{\mu}_m$ and δ_m^2.

In VOTING II - REAL, we assume (by way of the Central Limit Theorem) that the expertise parameter of system m is approximately normal with mean $\bar{\mu}_m$ and variance $\delta_m^2/|\mathcal{A}_m|$:

$$\theta_m \sim \mathcal{N}(\bar{\mu}_m, \delta_m^2/|\mathcal{A}_m|). \qquad (2)$$

We propose a heuristic algorithm for learning expertise parameters in VOTING II - REAL:

- Given each translation request f, expertise parameter is first drawn from the posterior distribution for each MT system.

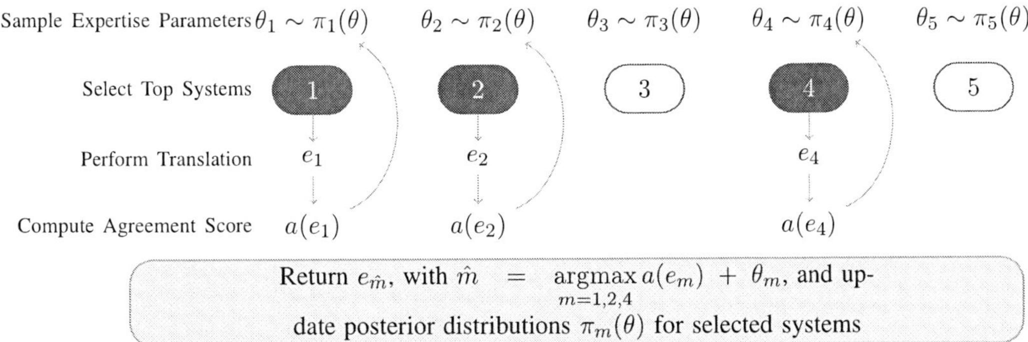

Figure 1: The setup of VOTING II for $N = 5$. Expertise θ is sampled from posterior distribution $\pi(\theta)$ for each system, and three systems are selected. Here we assume the top 3 systems are m_1, m_2 and m_4. Then, agreement scores for their translations are calculated. The translation with the highest agreement is returned. Finally, the posterior distributions are updated for all three selected systems.

- Select top three MT systems m, m' and m'' with the highest expertise parameters and decode translation request f. Let us assume translation outputs are as e_m, $e_{m'}$ and $e_{m''}$ respectively.

- Compute $a(e_m)$, $a(e_{m'})$ and $a(e_{m''})$.

- Add $a(e_m)$ to $\mathcal{A}_m$, $a(e_{m'})$ to $\mathcal{A}_{m'}$ and $a(e_{m''})$ to $\mathcal{A}_{m''}$. Update sample mean $\bar{\mu}_m$ and sample variance δ_m^2 for $\mathcal{A}_m$, $\mathcal{A}_{m'}$ and $\mathcal{A}_{m''}$.

Analysis: MT systems are promoted/demoted explicitly during learning. A high agreement score increases the sample mean for a promoted system, while a low agreement score decreases the sample mean for a demoted system. A promoted system becomes more likely to be selected in later rounds, but it is not the case for a demoted system.

The chance of being selected for MT systems also depends on variance for sampling expertise parameters. The variance effect decreases with sample size $|\mathcal{A}|$. This reflects that the learning becomes gradually more confident about its estimate of expertise parameters.

3.2.2 Voting II Binary

Our second model (VOTING II - BINARY) uses Beta distribution to sample expertise parameters. The parameters of the posterior distribution is updated based on a simplified outcome of agreement scores, which has only two values: $[0, 1]$ (i.e. SUCCESS/FAILURE). This is done by performing a *Bernoulli* trial with success probability exactly as the agreement score.

Let us assume a sample of simplified agreement scores from all translation outputs produced by an MT system m as $\bar{\mathcal{A}}_m = \{\bar{a}_1, \bar{a}_2, \ldots, \bar{a}_{|\bar{\mathcal{A}}_m|}\}$. For this sample, we focus on the numbers of SUCCESSes/FAILUREs instead of the sample *mean* and sample *variance*. Let us denote the numbers as S_m and F_m.

In VOTING II - BINARY, we assume that for a sample of simplified agreement scores $\bar{\mathcal{A}}$, the number of SUCCESSes is the output of a Binomial probability distribution with $|\bar{\mathcal{A}}|$ Bernoulli trials with success probability exactly as expertise parameter θ. We also use the Beta distribution with two hyper-parameters α and β for priors for the expertise parameter θ in VOTING II - BINARY, maintaining uncertainty over their values.

This results in a Beta-Binomial model for VOTING II - BINARY: the expertise parameter θ_m of each MT system m is sample from a Beta distribution with hyper-parameters $S_m + \alpha$ and $F_m + \beta$:

$$\theta_m \sim \mathrm{Beta}(S_m + \alpha, F_m + \beta). \tag{3}$$

In our experiments we set $\alpha = \beta = 1$ for every MT system.

Our heuristic algorithm for learning expertise parameters in VOTING II - BINARY is in the same spirit as in VOTING II - REAL. Given a translation request f, expertise parameters are drawn from the posterior distributions, and top three MT systems m, m' and m'' with the highest expertise parameters are selected to decode f. This results in different translation outputs e_m, $e_{m'}$ and $e_{m''}$ respectively. The update is as follows:

- Compute $a(e_m)$, $a(e_{m'})$ and $a(e_{m''})$.

- Sample $\bar{a}(e_m)$, $\bar{a}(e_{m'})$ and $\bar{a}(e_{m''})$ from

Bernoulli trials with success probability exactly as $a(e_m)$, $a(e_{m'})$ and $a(e_{m''})$ respectively.

- Add $\bar{a}(e_m)$ to $\bar{\mathcal{A}}_m$, $\bar{a}(e_{m'})$ to $\bar{\mathcal{A}}_{m'}$ and $\bar{a}(e_{m''})$ to $\bar{\mathcal{A}}_{m''}$. Update for S_m and F_m for $\bar{\mathcal{A}}_m$, $S_{m'}$ and $F_{m'}$ for $\bar{\mathcal{A}}_{m'}$, $S_{m''}$ and $F_{m''}$ for $\bar{\mathcal{A}}_{m''}$.

Analysis: MT systems are promoted/demoted explicitly during learning: the posterior $\mathrm{Beta}(S+1+\alpha, F+\beta)$ has a higher mean than $\mathrm{Beta}(S+\alpha, F+\beta)$ and the posterior $\mathrm{Beta}(S+\alpha, F+1+\beta)$ has a lower mean than distribution $\mathrm{Beta}(S+\alpha, F+\beta)$.

Both $\mathrm{Beta}(S+1+\alpha, F+\beta)$ and $\mathrm{Beta}(S+\alpha, F+1+\beta)$ have a lower variance than distribution $\mathrm{Beta}(S+\alpha, F+\beta)$. The variance effect thus also decreases with sample size $|\bar{\mathcal{A}}|$.

4 Experiment Design

We conduct experiments with three language pairs: *Spanish-English*, *French-English* and *German-English*. We create different translation ecosystems with a large number (from 6 to 10) of domain-specific MT systems for experiments. Our experiments are extensive with 23 translation tasks in total, which are unknown and out-of-domain. Note that we use NMT for one language pair and SMT for the rest, and the motivation behind this decision is simply that training SMT is somewhat easier than NMT for us.

4.1 Domain-specific MT system

Spanish-English: Our MT system is an attention-based Neural MT system (Bahdanau et al., 2015) for English-Spanish. We use `Nematus` (Sennrich et al., 2016; Sennrich and Haddow, 2016) with 512-dimensional word embeddings and layers. We use a vocab size of $50K$ for both the source and target languages. The vocabulary contains the top word types from all domains combined, and we train on sentences up to length 50. Pervasive dropout (Gal and Ghahramani, 2015) is applied to all vertical and recurrent connections, but not on word types. We optimize MT systems using Adam (Kingma and Ba, 2014) with a learning rate of 0.0001 and use early-stopping to prevent over-fitting. Translations are obtained using beam search with a beam of size 12.

We create a medium scale translation ecosystem with 6 different domain-specific Neural MT systems for Spanish-English. Each MT system is trained on a domain-specific dataset consisting of $250K$ sentence pairs, which is taken from OPUS.

The system is tuned on an in-domain devset with $3K$ sentence pairs. The domains are: *Subtitles* (Domain 1), *Wikipedia* (Domain 2), *Medicine* (Domain 3), *Legal* (Domain 4), *News* (Domain 5), and *Speech* (Domain 6). Each domain has an in-domain test set with $3K$ sentence pairs as translation task.

French-English: The scale of our ecosystem is increased to 10 instead of 6 for experiments with French-English, Our MT systems are with SMT instead of Neural MT systems. Each SMT system is a standard phrase-based approach (Koehn et al., 2003). The language model is a 4-gram model with Kneser-Ney smoothing, estimated by KenLM (Heafield et al., 2013) from in-domain monolingual corpus. We use the k-best batch MIRA to tune MT systems (Cherry and Foster, 2012). Finally, the decoder is MOSES (Koehn et al., 2007).

Each domain-specific SMT system is trained on a domain-specific dataset consisting of $250K$ sentence pairs, and tuned on an in-domain devset with $3K$ sentence pairs taken from OPUS. The domains are: *Book* (Domain 1), *Speech* (Domain 2), *IT* (Domain 3), *Bank* (Domain 4), *News* (Domain 5), *Medicine* (Domain 6), *Wikipedia* (Domain 7), *Legal* (Domain 8), *European Parliament* (Domain 9), *Subtitles* (Domain 10). Similarly, each domain has an in-domain test set with $3K$ sentence pairs as translation task.

German-English: Domain-specific MT systems are constructed differently for German-English. We first train an SMT system on a dataset consisting of $4.1M$ sentence pairs released for WMT 2015 Shared Task. We then optimize the system over 7 different domain-specific devsets with different domains taken from TAUS. The domains are: Consumer Electronics (Domain 1), Hardware (Domain 2), Industrial Electronics (Domain 3), Legal (Domain 4), Professional & Business (Domain 5), Software (Domain 6), Retail Distribution (Domain 7).

The agreement degree between domain-specific MT systems for our German-English translation ecosystem for the pair is expected to be significantly higher than for the other cases.

4.2 Translation Task

Given each translation ecosystem, we are given one task out of the N translation tasks at test time. We evaluate how do we obtain translation quality from an ecosystem with range of remaining $N-1$

Spanish-English

Tasks	Reference						Avg.	Rank 2	Rank 1	Vote I	Vote II	
	MT1	MT2	MT3	MT4	MT5	MT6					Real	Bin.
Task 1	–	14.3	2.2	2.8	22.5	19.4	15.1	19.4	22.5	20.4	22.4	22.1
Task 2	7.0	–	6.2	13.6	31.0	20.3	14.1	20.3	31.0	26.6	29.9	29.5
Task 3	2.3	21.0	–	20.7	17.8	11.3	14.6	20.7	21.0	22.8	23.1	23.0
Task 4	2.7	25.6	8.0	–	22.1	15.1	14.7	22.1	25.6	23.9	24.7	24.4
Task 5	7.6	27.6	4.9	10.9	–	22.6	14.7	22.6	27.6	25.6	26.6	26.6
Task 6	16.1	24.8	4.8	7.2	29.0	–	16.4	24.8	29.0	26.8	26.7	28.2

Table 3: Results for Spanish-English experiments.

French-English

Tasks	Reference										Avg.	Rank 3	Rank 2	Rank 1	Vote I	Vote II	
	MT1	MT2	MT3	MT4	MT5	MT6	MT7	MT8	MT9	MT10						Real	Bin.
Task 1	–	9.6	6.3	9.8	12.2	8.7	11.5	11.7	13.9	5.7	9.9	11.7	12.2	13.9	12.7	13.0	12.5
Task 2	18.3	–	14.8	13.3	27.3	11.4	21.4	10.7	22.3	20.2	17.7	21.4	22.3	27.3	22.5	23.1	23.0
Task 3	16.9	22.9	–	15.6	19.6	14.1	19.9	12.5	17.5	16.1	17.2	19.6	19.9	22.9	19.2	19.2	20.5
Task 4	33.9	21.9	21.5	–	29.0	22.9	26.2	35.0	34.2	11.3	26.2	33.9	34.2	35.0	30.2	29.0	30.3
Task 5	16.0	20.7	11.2	13.2	–	10.7	18.4	12.0	17.9	12.9	14.8	17.9	18.4	20.7	17.5	17.8	16.9
Task 6	26.7	22.5	21.6	24.7	26.9	–	25.0	21.8	22.3	16.8	23.1	25.0	26.7	26.9	25.9	26.2	25.9
Task 7	15.8	18.8	14.1	15.6	20.8	14.9	–	14.8	17.8	14.9	16.4	17.8	18.8	20.8	18.6	19.4	18.1
Task 8	31.4	15.8	11.0	27.3	22.3	15.2	23.6	–	29.4	18.8	20.8	27.3	29.4	31.4	26.6	24.9	27.9
Task 9	21.4	15.1	7.6	15.7	19.5	8.4	16.4	14.8	–	8.6	14.2	16.4	19.5	21.4	19.3	18.9	19.5
Task 10	12.0	23.3	10.7	9.6	22.8	8.3	16.9	8.4	17.3	–	14.4	17.3	22.8	23.3	17.5	17.6	15.5

Table 4: Results for French-English experiments.

5 Results

5.1 Ecosystem Performance

We first investigate how well the ecosystems handle unknown and out-of-domain translation tasks. Tables 3, 4 and 5 present the results (in BLEU). Note that:

- AVG: average of BLEU score of MT systems

- Rank 3, Rank 2, Rank 1: top 3 MT systems

- Vote I: VOTING I method

- Vote II Real: VOTING II method with real reward

- Vote II Bin: VOTING II method with binary reward

As expected, translation quality degrades substantially for most pre-trained MT systems given such a translation task. The *Subtitle*-adapted MT system for Spanish-English (MT 1 - Tables 3) is a notable example to raise the issue: the translation accuracy substantially drops for the other out-of-domain translation tasks (i.e. Task 2 (Wikipedia): 7.0 BLEU score, Task 3 (Medicine): 2.3 BLEU score, Task 4 (Legal): 2.7 BLEU score, Task 5 (News): 7.6 BLEU score, Task 6 (Speech): 16.1 BLEU score).

However, the degradation of each pre-trained MT system is different from the others. For example, the Speech-adapted MT system for Spanish-English (MT 6 - Tables 3) drops their performance significantly for only Task 3 (Medicine) (11.3 BLEU score) and Task 4 (Legal) (15.1 BLEU score). The Speech-adapted MT system is capable of handling other out-of-domain translation tasks (i.e. Task 1 (Subtitles): 19.4 BLEU score, Task 2 (Wikipedia): 20.3 BLEU score, Task 5 (News): 22.6 BLEU score).

For 23 out-of-domain translation tasks in total, our results show that despite the translation quality substantially drops for most pre-trained MT systems, a few pre-trained MT systems are still competitive to handle the tasks. In 21/23 cases, top MT systems with respect to a certain translation task are still able to handle the task well.[3]

This supports our claim: Having a large-scale ecosystem of pre-trained MT systems is very useful for handling out-of-domain tasks in practice. But is it possible to gain competitive performance to top rank MT systems from ecosystem of pre-trained domain-specific systems for unknown and out-of-domain translation tasks? Our experiments show that it is possible with our proposed frameworks.

---

[3]For convenience, we set a BLEU threshold (20) to decide if the MT quality is good or not. In practice, it should not be a good idea to have such a fixed threshold for any domain.

| | German-English | | | | | | | | | | | Vote II | |
| Tasks | Reference | | | | | | | Avg. | Rank 2 | Rank 1 | Vote I | | |
	MT1	MT2	MT3	MT4	MT5	MT6	MT7	All				Real	Bin.
Task 1	–	22.9	23.1	19.8	18.9	23.2	23.0	21.8	23.1	23.2	23.0	23.0	23.0
Task 2	20.2	–	20.5	19.7	19.0	20.8	20.7	20.2	20.7	20.8	20.7	20.7	20.7
Task 3	20.7	20.9	–	18.1	17.4	21.1	20.7	19.8	20.9	21.1	21.0	20.2	20.9
Task 4	28.5	29.0	28.9	–	28.5	29.5	29.4	29.0	29.4	29.5	29.4	29.4	29.3
Task 5	12.6	13.8	13.7	14.8	–	13.4	13.4	13.6	13.8	14.8	13.6	13.6	13.6
Task 6	21.8	23.3	23.2	20.8	20.8	–	22.8	22.1	23.2	23.3	23.0	23.1	23.0
Task 7	32.3	33.5	33.5	28.2	28.2	33.0	–	31.5	33.5	33.5	33.2	33.4	33.3

Table 5: Results for German-English experiments.

| | Spanish-English | | | | | | | Vote II | |
Tasks	MIN	SC	Avg. All	DC	Avg. TRs	Vote I		Real	Bin.
Task 1	2.2	10.9	15.1	18.6	21.0	20.4		22.4	22.1
Task 2	6.2	15.2	14.1	15.7	25.7	26.6		29.9	29.5
Task 3	2.3	18.4	14.6	15.2	20.9	22.8		23.1	23.0
Task 4	2.7	13.9	14.7	13.5	23.9	23.9		24.7	24.4
Task 5	4.9	14.0	14.7	17.3	25,1	25.6		26.6	26.6
Task 6	4.8	17.0	16.4	18.2	26,9	26.8		26.7	28.2

Table 6: A detailed comparison for other baselines (SC: System Combination, DC: Domain Classification, Avg. TR: Average baseline between top rank MT systems (Rank 1 and Rank 2) for Spanish-English.

5.2 Our Framework Performance

Tables 3, 4 and 5 present the results. Note that our models are stochastic, and results for our experiments are averaged among 20 runs. The main findings are:

Voting I substantially outperforms Rank 2 for all cases for Spanish-English. It outperforms Rank 3 for 6/10 tasks for French-English. We would like to emphasize that: (1) this performance is obtained without any knowledge about translation task; and (2) the gap between the best and the worst MT systems for each task in ecosystems is huge (i.e. usually around +20 BLEU score). This validates the idea behind Voting I: Good translations are likely to be similar to the others.

We perform System Combination (SC) by ensembling all NMT systems for the tasks. SC rather gives a poor performance in our setting (Table 6). We should emphasize that the result is rather expected: SC degrades translation quality substantially because most pre-trained MT systems in the ecosystem are incapable of handling the task.[4]

We also create a simple domain classifier (DC) for translation requests: We train different in-domain language models from in-domain mono-lingual corpora, and perform a search to select an MT system from the ecosystem based on their language model probability of each translation request: $\hat{m} = \operatorname*{argmax}_{m=1,...,N} P_m(f)$. DC also rather gives a poor performance in our setting (Table 6). It outperforms the average baseline (Avg. All) in most cases, but its performance is far behind the middle of top rank MT systems (Avg. TRs). The result is unsurprising: it is hard to expect a domain classifier for translation requests provides robust performance for target domain that is not only unknown but also out-of-domain.

Interestingly, Voting I gives the performance at least in the middle between Rank 1 and Rank 2 in 5/6 tasks for Spanish-English, except only Task 1. Meanwhile, the performance is at least in the middle between Rank 1, Rank 2 and Rank 3 in 3/10 tasks for French-English.

Voting II - REAL and Voting II - BINARY perform better than Voting I for 5/6 tasks for Spanish-English. All these frameworks perform substantially better (at least +1.0 BLEU score) than Voting I in 4 cases (Tasks 1, 2, 3 and 5). For French-English, Voting II - REAL and Voting II - BINARY perform at least compatible to Voting I for 6/10 tasks. Each of these frameworks performs better than Voting I for 4/10 tasks.

The results validate the idea behind Voting II: MT systems that are good in a domain tend to agree with each other.

Voting II - REAL usually performs better than Voting II - BINARY. This is reasonable as in Voting II - BINARY, model parameters are updated based on simplified outcome of the agreement scores instead of the agreement scores.

Despite having a different set up for constructing domain-specific MT systems, all our observations are also confirmed for German-English as in Table 5. Voting I gives the performance in the middle between Rank 1 and Rank 2 in 6/7 tasks,

---

[4]We should also note that interpolating all SMT systems gives a rather poor performance as well. This is because of the same reason: most pre-trained MT systems in the ecosystem are incapable of handling the task. We did not report the results here due to space constraints.

except only Task 5. VOTING II provides compatible performance to VOTING I. This is reasonable as when MT systems are close to the others regarding their translation quality, the benefits of reducing the decoding cost is what VOTING II is expected to provide. It is worthy to emphasize that our VOTING frameworks still outperform the average baseline significantly.

5.3 Disadvantage of our method

While the result from our method is impressive, we should be clear about its disadvantage. We found that:

- A generic system trained with all the training data of the different domains normally produces significantly better performance than what our framework provides.

- An indomain MT system trained on in-domain training data normally produces significantly better performance than what our framework provides as well.

Improving our framework to make it work compatible to those stronger baselines is a goal of future research.

6 Conclusion

This work shows that having an ecosystem of pre-trained domain-specific MT systems is not only efficient for in-domain translation tasks, but could be also very useful for out-of-domain translation tasks. More specifically, we show that an out-of-domain translation task can be out-of-scope of most pre-trained adapted MT systems in the ecosystem, but a few others can be still very capable of handling the task. We conduct extensive experiments with different scale (from 6 to 10) ecosystems of pre-trained MT systems to support our claim. We also contribute two frameworks that gain competitive performance to top rank MT systems from ecosystem of pre-trained domain-specific systems for unknown and potentially out-of-domain translation tasks. We hope our study fills an important gap in the domain adaptation literature: making translation ecosystems with domain-adapted MT systems capable of handling unknown and out-of-domain tasks.

Acknowledgement

This work was conducted when the author was at University of Amsterdam, as well as when he was in his visiting research to University of Sheffield. The author would like to thanks many people since then, including: Kashif Shah, Lucia Specia, Joost Bastings, Khalil Simaa'n, Ivan Titov. The author also thanks reviewers for their constructive comments.

References

[Axelrod et al.2011] Axelrod, Amittai, Xiaodong He, and Jianfeng Gao. 2011. Domain adaptation via pseudo in-domain data selection. In *EMNLP*.

[Bahdanau et al.2015] Bahdanau, Dzmitry, Kyunghyun Cho, and Yoshua Bengio. 2015. Neural Machine Translation by Jointly Learning to Align and Translate. In *Proceedings of the International Conference on Learning Representations (ICLR)*.

[Bapna and Firat2019] Bapna, Ankur and Orhan Firat. 2019. Non-parametric adaptation for neural machine translation. *CoRR*, abs/1903.00058.

[Bertoldi et al.2014] Bertoldi, Nicola, Patrick Simianer, Mauro Cettolo, Katharina Wäschle, Marcello Federico, and Stefan Riezler. 2014. Online adaptation to post-edits for phrase-based statistical machine translation. *Machine Translation*.

[Bisazza et al.2011] Bisazza, Arianna, Nick Ruiz, and Marcello Federico. 2011. Fill-up versus interpolation methods for phrase-based smt adaptation. In *IWSLT*.

[Blain et al.2015] Blain, F., F. Bougares, A. Hazem, L. Barrault, and H. Schwenk. 2015. Continuous adaptation to user feedback for statistical machine translation. In *NAACL-HLT (Short Papers)*.

[Carpuat et al.2013] Carpuat, Marine, Hal Daume III, Katharine Henry, Ann Irvine, Jagadeesh Jagarlamudi, and Rachel Rudinger. 2013. Sensespotting: Never let your parallel data tie you to an old domain. In *ACL*.

[Chen and Huang2016] Chen, Boxing and Fei Huang. 2016. Semi-supervised convolutional networks for translation adaptation with tiny amount of in-domain data. In *Conll*.

[Chen et al.2013] Chen, Boxing, Roland Kuhn, and George Foster. 2013. Vector space model for adaptation in statistical machine translation. In *ACL*.

[Chen et al.2017] Chen, Boxing, Colin Cherry, George Foster, and Samuel Larkin. 2017. Cost weighting for neural machine translation domain adaptation. In *Proceedings of the First Workshop on Neural Machine Translation*, pages 40–46. Association for Computational Linguistics.

[Cherry and Foster2012] Cherry, Colin and George Foster. 2012. Batch tuning strategies for statistical machine translation. In *NAACL HLT*.

[Chiang et al.2011] Chiang, David, Steve DeNeefe, and Michael Pust. 2011. Two easy improvements to lexical weighting. In *ACL HLT (Short Papers)*.

[Chu and Wang2018] Chu, Chenhui and Rui Wang. 2018. A survey of domain adaptation for neural machine translation. In *Proceedings of the 27th International Conference on Computational Linguistics*, pages 1304–1319, Santa Fe, New Mexico, USA, August. Association for Computational Linguistics.

[Clark et al.2012] Clark, Jonathan H, Alon Lavie, and Chris Dyer. 2012. One system, many domains: Open-domain statistical machine translation via feature augmentation. *AMTA*.

[Cuong and Sima'an2014a] Cuong, Hoang and Khalil Sima'an. 2014a. Latent domain phrase-based models for adaptation. In *Proceedings of the 2014 Conference on Empirical Methods in Natural Language Processing*. Association for Computational Linguistics.

[Cuong and Sima'an2014b] Cuong, Hoang and Khalil Sima'an. 2014b. Latent domain translation models in mix-of-domains haystack. In *Proceedings of COLING*.

[Cuong and Sima'an2015] Cuong, Hoang and Khalil Sima'an. 2015. Latent domain word alignment for heterogeneous corpora. In *NAACL-HLT*.

[Cuong and Sima'an2017] Cuong, Hoang and Khalil Sima'an. 2017. A survey of domain adaptation for statistical machine translation. *Machine Translation*, 31(4):187–224, December.

[Cuong et al.2016] Cuong, Hoang, Khalil Sima'an, and Ivan Titov. 2016. Adapting to all domains at once: Rewarding domain invariance in smt. In *TACL*.

[Denkowski et al.2014] Denkowski, Michael, Chris Dyer, and Alon Lavie. 2014. Learning from post-editing: Online model adaptation for statistical machine translation. In *EACL*.

[Duh et al.2013] Duh, Kevin, Graham Neubig, Katsuhito Sudoh, and Hajime Tsukada. 2013. Adaptation data selection using neural language models: Experiments in machine translation. In *ACL (Short Papers)*.

[Eetemadi et al.2015] Eetemadi, Sauleh, William Lewis, Kristina Toutanova, and Hayder Radha. 2015. Survey of data-selection methods in statistical machine translation. *Machine Translation*.

[Eidelman et al.2012] Eidelman, Vladimir, Jordan Boyd-Graber, and Philip Resnik. 2012. Topic models for dynamic translation model adaptation. In *ACL (Short Papers)*.

[Farajian et al.2017] Farajian, M. Amin, Marco Turchi, Matteo Negri, and Marcello Federico. 2017. Multi-domain neural machine translation through unsupervised adaptation. In *Proceedings of the Second Conference on Machine Translation*, pages 127–137, Copenhagen, Denmark, September. Association for Computational Linguistics.

[Foster et al.2010] Foster, George, Cyril Goutte, and Roland Kuhn. 2010. Discriminative instance weighting for domain adaptation in statistical machine translation. In *EMNLP*.

[Gal and Ghahramani2015] Gal, Y. and Z. Ghahramani. 2015. A Theoretically Grounded Application of Dropout in Recurrent Neural Networks. *ArXiv e-prints*, December.

[Haddow2013] Haddow, Barry. 2013. Applying pairwise ranked optimisation to improve the interpolation of translation models. In *NAACL HLT (Short Papers)*.

[Hasler et al.2014] Hasler, Eva, Phil Blunsom, Philipp Koehn, and Barry Haddow. 2014. Dynamic topic adaptation for phrase-based mt. In *EACL*.

[Heafield et al.2013] Heafield, Kenneth, Ivan Pouzyrevsky, Jonathan H. Clark, and Philipp Koehn. 2013. Scalable modified kneser-ney language model estimation. In *ACL (Short Papers)*.

[Hildebrand and Vogel2008] Hildebrand, Almut Silja and Stephan Vogel. 2008. Combination of Machine Translation Systems via Hypothesis Selection from Combined N-Best Lists. In *Proceedings of the Eighth Conference of the Association for Machine Translation in the Americas*, pages 254–261.

[Hu et al.2014] Hu, Yuening, Ke Zhai, Vladimir Eidelman, and Jordan Boyd-Graber. 2014. Polylingual tree-based topic models for translation domain adaptation. In *ACL*.

[Jayaraman and Lavie2005] Jayaraman, Shyamsundar and Alon Lavie. 2005. Multi-engine machine translation guided by explicit word matching. In *Proceedings of the ACL 2005 on Interactive Poster and Demonstration Sessions*, ACLdemo '05, pages 101–104, Stroudsburg, PA, USA. Association for Computational Linguistics.

[Joty et al.2015] Joty, Shafiq, Hassan Sajjad, Nadir Durrani, Kamla Al-Mannai, Ahmed Abdelali, and Stephan Vogel. 2015. How to avoid unwanted pregnancies: Domain adaptation using neural network models. In *EMNLP*.

[Karimova et al.2018] Karimova, Sariya, Patrick Simianer, and Stefan Riezler. 2018. A user-study on online adaptation of neural machine translation to human post-edits. *Machine Translation*, 32(4):309–324.

[Khayrallah et al.2017] Khayrallah, Huda, Gaurav Kumar, Kevin Duh, Matt Post, and Philipp Koehn. 2017. Neural lattice search for domain adaptation in machine translation. In *Proceedings of the Eighth International Joint Conference on Natural Language Processing (Volume 2: Short Papers)*, pages 20–25. Asian Federation of Natural Language Processing.

[Kingma and Ba2014] Kingma, Diederik and Jimmy Ba. 2014. Adam: A method for stochastic optimization. *arXiv preprint arXiv:1412.6980*.

[Kirchhoff and Bilmes2014] Kirchhoff, Katrin and Jeff Bilmes. 2014. Submodularity for data selection in machine translation. In *EMNLP*.

[Kobus et al.2017] Kobus, Catherine, Josep Crego, and Jean Senellart. 2017. Domain control for neural machine translation. In *Proceedings of the International Conference Recent Advances in Natural Language Processing, RANLP 2017*, pages 372–378, Varna, Bulgaria, September. INCOMA Ltd.

[Koehn and Knowles2017] Koehn, Philipp and Rebecca Knowles. 2017. Six challenges for neural machine translation. In *Proceedings of the First Workshop on Neural Machine Translation*, pages 28–39. Association for Computational Linguistics.

[Koehn and Schroeder2007] Koehn, Philipp and Josh Schroeder. 2007. Experiments in domain adaptation for statistical machine translation. In *WMT*.

[Koehn et al.2003] Koehn, Philipp, Franz Josef Och, and Daniel Marcu. 2003. Statistical phrase-based translation. In *NAACL HLT*.

[Koehn et al.2007] Koehn, Philipp, Hieu Hoang, Alexandra Birch, Chris Callison-Burch, Marcello Federico, Nicola Bertoldi, Brooke Cowan, Wade Shen, Christine Moran, Richard Zens, Chris Dyer, Ondřej Bojar, Alexandra Constantin, and Evan Herbst. 2007. Moses: Open source toolkit for statistical machine translation. In *ACL*.

[Koehn et al.2014] Koehn, Philipp, Chara Tsoukala, and Herve Saint-Amand. 2014. Refinements to interactive translation prediction based on search graphs. In *ACL (Short Papers)*.

[Kothur et al.2018] Kothur, Sachith Sri Ram, Rebecca Knowles, and Philipp Koehn. 2018. Document-level adaptation for neural machine translation. In *Proceedings of the 2nd Workshop on Neural Machine Translation and Generation*, pages 64–73, Melbourne, Australia, July. Association for Computational Linguistics.

[Lin and Och2004] Lin, Chin-Yew and Franz Josef Och. 2004. Orange: A method for evaluating automatic evaluation metrics for machine translation. In *COLING*.

[Macherey and Och2007] Macherey, Wolfgang and Franz J. Och. 2007. An empirical study on computing consensus translations from multiple machine translation systems. In *Proceedings of the 2007 Joint Conference on Empirical Methods in Natural Language Processing and Computational Natural Language Learning (EMNLP-CoNLL)*, pages 986–995, Prague, Czech Republic, June. Association for Computational Linguistics.

[Mansour and Ney2014] Mansour, Saab and Hermann Ney. 2014. Unsupervised adaptation for statistical machine translation. In *WMT*.

[Michel and Neubig2018] Michel, Paul and Graham Neubig. 2018. Extreme adaptation for personalized neural machine translation. In *Proceedings of the 56th Annual Meeting of the Association for Computational Linguistics (Volume 2: Short Papers)*, pages 312–318, Melbourne, Australia, July. Association for Computational Linguistics.

[Nguyen et al.2017] Nguyen, Khanh, Hal Daumé III, and Jordan Boyd-Graber. 2017. Reinforcement learning for bandit neural machine translation with simulated human feedback. In *Proceedings of the 2017 Conference on Empirical Methods in Natural Language Processing*, pages 1464–1474, Copenhagen, Denmark, September. Association for Computational Linguistics.

[Ortiz-Martínez et al.2010] Ortiz-Martínez, Daniel, Ismael García-Varea, and Francisco Casacuberta. 2010. Online learning for interactive statistical machine translation. In *NAACL-HLT*.

[Ortiz-Martínez2016] Ortiz-Martínez. 2016. Online learning for statistical machine translation. *Comput. Linguist.*

[Papineni et al.2002] Papineni, Kishore, Salim Roukos, Todd Ward, and Wei-Jing Zhu. 2002. Bleu: A method for automatic evaluation of machine translation. In *ACL*.

[Peris and Casacuberta2018] Peris, Álvaro and Francisco Casacuberta. 2018. Active learning for interactive neural machine translation of data streams. In *Proceedings of the 22nd Conference on Computational Natural Language Learning*, pages 151–160, Brussels, Belgium, October. Association for Computational Linguistics.

[Razmara et al.2012] Razmara, Majid, George Foster, Baskaran Sankaran, and Anoop Sarkar. 2012. Mixing multiple translation models in statistical machine translation. In *ACL*.

[Sennrich and Haddow2016] Sennrich, Rico and Barry Haddow. 2016. Linguistic input features improve neural machine translation. In *Proceedings of the First Conference on Machine Translation*, pages 83–91, Berlin, Germany, August. Association for Computational Linguistics.

[Sennrich et al.2013] Sennrich, Rico, Holger Schwenk, and Walid Aransa. 2013. A multi-domain translation model framework for statistical machine translation. In *ACL*.

[Sennrich et al.2016] Sennrich, Rico, Barry Haddow, and Alexandra Birch. 2016. Edinburgh neural machine translation systems for wmt 16. In *Proceedings of the First Conference on Machine Translation*, pages 371–376, Berlin, Germany, August. Association for Computational Linguistics.

[Sennrich2012a] Sennrich, Rico. 2012a. Mixture-modeling with unsupervised clusters for domain adaptation in statistical machine translation. In *EAMT*.

[Sennrich2012b] Sennrich, Rico. 2012b. Perplexity minimization for translation model domain adaptation in statistical machine translation. In *EACL*.

[Shah et al.2010] Shah, Kashif, Loïc Barrault, and Holger Schwenk. 2010. Translation model adaptation by resampling. In *WMT*.

[Sokolov et al.2015] Sokolov, Artem, Stefan Riezler, and Tanguy Urvoy. 2015. Bandit structured prediction for learning from partial feedback in statistical machine translation. In *MTSummit*.

[Sokolov et al.2016] Sokolov, Artem, Julia Kreutzer, Christopher Lo, and Stefan Riezler. 2016. Learning structured predictors from bandit feedback for interactive nlp. In *ACL*.

[Sokolov et al.2017] Sokolov, Artem, Julia Kreutzer, Kellen Sunderland, Pavel Danchenko, Witold Szymaniak, Hagen Fürstenau, and Stefan Riezler. 2017. A shared task on bandit learning for machine translation. In *Proceedings of the Second Conference on Machine Translation*, pages 514–524, Copenhagen, Denmark, September. Association for Computational Linguistics.

[Su et al.2015] Su, Jinsong, Deyi Xiong, Yang Liu, Xianpei Han, Hongyu Lin, Junfeng Yao, and Min Zhang. 2015. A context-aware topic model for statistical machine translation. In *ACL-IJCNLP*.

[Tars and Fishel2018] Tars, Sander and Mark Fishel. 2018. Multi-domain neural machine translation. *CoRR*, abs/1805.02282.

[van der Wees et al.2017] van der Wees, Marlies, Arianna Bisazza, and Christof Monz. 2017. Dynamic data selection for neural machine translation. In *Proceedings of the 2017 Conference on Empirical Methods in Natural Language Processing*, pages 1400–1410. Association for Computational Linguistics.

[Wang et al.2012] Wang, Wei, Klaus Macherey, Wolfgang Macherey, Franz Och, and Peng Xu. 2012. Improved domain adaptation for statistical machine translation. In *AMTA*.

[Wang et al.2018] Wang, R., M. Utiyama, A. Finch, L. Liu, K. Chen, and E. Sumita. 2018. Sentence selection and weighting for neural machine translation domain adaptation. *IEEE/ACM Transactions on Audio, Speech, and Language Processing*, pages 1–1.

[Wuebker et al.2016] Wuebker, Joern, Spence Green, John DeNero, Sasa Hasan, and Minh-Thang Luong. 2016. Models and inference for prefix-constrained machine translation. In *ACL*.

[Zhang et al.2014] Zhang, Min, Xinyan Xiao, Deyi Xiong, and Qun Liu. 2014. Topic-based dissimilarity and sensitivity models for translation rule selection. *JAIR*.

What is the impact of raw MT on Japanese users of Word: preliminary results of a usability study using eye-tracking

Ana Guerberof
ADAPT/SALIS
Dublin City University
ana.guerberof@dcu.ie

Joss Moorkens
ADAPT/SALIS
Dublin City University
joss.moorkens@dcu.ie

Sharon O'Brien
ADAPT/SALIS
Dublin City University
sharon.obrien@dcu.ie

Abstract

This paper presents preliminary results of a study of Japanese native speakers working with the Microsoft Word application in two modalities: the released Japanese version and a machine translated (MT) version (the raw MT strings incorporated into the MS Word interface). To explore the effect of translation modality on task completion, time and satisfaction, an experiment using an eye-tracker was set up with a group of 42 users: 22 native Japanese and 20 native English speakers. The results suggest that Japanese-native speakers have higher completion scores and are more efficient when working with the released versions of the product than with the MT version, but these differences are not significant. Their self-reported satisfaction, however, is significantly higher when working with the released product as opposed to the raw MT version.

1 Introduction

In the commercial arena, the software and localization industries face long-term business challenges. There is an increase in the volume of software to localize, and this software needs to run on several platforms. Moreover, the software is delivered to the user in a rapid cycle, with daily, weekly, and quarterly updates and releases. In parallel, there are continuous advances in machine translation (MT) technology with the full implementation of statistical engines and rapid advances in neural MT solutions.[*] Therefore, it is only logical to marry the use of new technology with localization of software products with the aid of automation where possible, as long as this can be achieved without hindering the user experience and, hence, the commercial viability of that product. Large software corporations have, in fact, implemented MT and post-editing (PE) cycles as part of their localization processes for some time now. However, as MT technology advances, several questions come to mind: is it possible to apply raw (i.e. unedited) MT to certain components of the user interface without hindering the user experience? Where raw MT is employed, how does linguistic quality impact the user experience?

Preliminary results are presented here from a usability experiment involving Japanese and English native speakers using an eye-tracker. The Japanese participants were presented with two Microsoft Word applications: one was the Japanese-released version (referred as HT hereafter), and the other one was a version translated from English into Japanese with MT specifically for this experiment (referred as MT hereafter). English speakers were presented with one Word application (to act as the control group). The different versions (HT, MT and English) are referred as scenarios. Both groups had to perform the same six tasks.

2 Related work

MT and PE have been implemented in some large organizations since the 1980s (the European Commission and the Pan American Health Organization, for example); however, it is only in the last ten years that major software development companies (such as Microsoft, Autodesk, or Google, to name but a few) have included MT in their standard localisation workflows, and subsequently, MTPE has been adopted in many localisation agencies worldwide (Lommel and DePalma, 2016).

Logically, there has been an increase in academic and commercial research to find out more about aspects related to MTPE activity with the translator as the central figure of studies (i.e., De Almeida and O'Brien, 2010; Guerberof, 2012; Moorkens et al., 2015; O'Brien, 2006; Plitt and Masselot, 2010). However, less attention has been paid to end user reception of products processed using MT. In many cases, translators' evaluation of MT output has been considered equivalent to end users' opinions of MT.

Some research has tried to fill this gap by analysing the usability aspect of MT in different products. Experiments have been designed to ascertain whether users understood instructions translated using MT in comparison to those using either the original text or MTPE (Castilho et al., 2014; Doherty and O'Brien, 2012, 2014; O'Brien and Castilho, 2016). The results show that usability is increased when users read either the original text or text that has been post-edited, even with minimal changes (light post-editing), when compared to raw MT output. However, users could complete most tasks by using the latter even if this activity took longer or if the experience was less satisfactory. Results, however, were not equal for all languages tested.

Bowker (2015) studied the difference in user experience when reading text on websites and translatability rules were applied (a set of guidelines applied to the source to improve MT). She found that the user experience of source-language readers decreases when these rules are applied, while that of the target-language readers (Spanish, in this case) increases. As a follow up to this research, Bowker and Buitrago Ciro (2018) replicated this experiment with more participants (Spanish, French Canadian and Italian) with similar findings. When the text was post-edited, however, readers preferred the texts that had been translated without translatability rules applied to the source.

The most extensive research on measuring acceptability of machine translated enterprise content by users was carried out by Castilho as part of her doctoral study (2016). In this work, Castilho shows that the PE quality level has a significant effect on acceptability by German, Chinese and Japanese users of enterprise content. She also highlights, however, that the raw MT versions were usable, and participants were still able to perform the assigned tasks with these instructions. Because of its relevant content (Microsoft Excel) and design, this research draws heavily on Castilho's work.

Castilho and Guerberof (2018) explored reading comprehension for Spanish and Chinese users when using SMT and NMT engines to translate an IELTs (International English Language Testing System) test. The authors found that users from the target languages completed more tasks in less time with a higher level of satisfaction when using translations from the NMT system.

Using a questionnaire, Van Edgom and Pluymaekers (2019) examined how different degrees of PE (minimal, light, moderate, and full) impact the user who read two different types of texts (informative and instructive texts) that had been post-edited. They concluded that different degrees of PE "make a difference" (idem., 168). However, the distinctions between, for example moderate and full PE, was not obvious to the users.

Screen (2019) looked at the English and Welsh language pair. He used an eye-tracker to measure fixations while participants read a post-edited text and a translated text. After this task, the participants rated the texts according to readability and comprehensibility. He found no statistical differences between the two groups.

Although this research feeds from the existing literature, it introduces some novel changes: participants are instructed to complete tasks in a software application in which raw MT is used for the user interface rather than testing the instructions to complete those tasks or the understanding of a "regular" text. Participants are not only queried about their satisfaction and eye-tracked, a retrospective think aloud protocol is put in place after task completion to understand what the participants thought, felt, and did when working with the three scenarios (HT, MT and English).

3 Methodology

To explore the topic of usability and translation modality further, a within-subject experiment was designed to compare MS Word translated from English using raw Japanese MT (MT) and a released version of that same product (HT).

Since the number of participants that were available to participate was limited due to the location and the time available, a within-subject experiment was the best option to have enough participants for a statistical analysis.

3.1 Research questions

This research poses the following questions:

RQ1: Will users perform the same number of successful tasks regardless of the scenario used (English original version, MT, or HT)?

RQ2: Will there be differences in time when participants perform the tasks in the different scenarios (English, MT or HT)?

RQ3: Will the participants be equally satisfied when using the English, MT or HT scenario?

RQ4: Will participants expend different amounts of cognitive effort when performing the tasks in different scenarios?

3.2 Measuring usability

Following specific studies on usability mentioned in this paper (Castilho et al., 2014; Castilho, 2016; Doherty and O'Brien, 2012, 2014), usability was defined as per the ISO/TR 16982 guidelines: "the extent to which a product can be used by specified users to achieve specified goals with effectiveness, efficiency, and satisfaction in a specified content of use" (ISO 2002).[2]

Effectiveness was measured through task completion. Users were presented with tasks to complete through interaction with different components of the user interfaces. The more tasks the user completed following specific instructions, the higher the effectiveness score was (from 0 to 100). The following formula was used to calculate the Effectiveness score:

$$\frac{\#\ tasks\ completed\ successfully}{total\ \#\ tasks} x\ 100 = effectiveness$$

Efficiency was measured considering the tasks that were completed in relation to the time it took to complete those tasks. If less time was invested to complete a task, then the efficiency score was higher, and vice versa. The following formula was used to calculate the efficiency rate:

$$\sum \frac{accuracy}{total\ task\ time\ in\ secs} \times 100$$

$$where\ \frac{task\ successes}{total\ tasks} \times 100 = accuracy$$

Efficiency was also measured in terms of cognitive effort using an eye-tracking device. Fixation duration (total length of fixation in an area of interest or AOI), fixation count (total number of fixations within an AOI) were measured. Eye-tracking has been established as an adequate tool to measure cognitive effort in MT studies (Doherty and O'Brien, 2009; Doherty et al., 2010).

Satisfaction was measured through an IBM After-Scenario Questionnaire (Lewis, 1995) containing a series of statements that users rated. This questionnaire was chosen instead of other frequently used questionnaires such as SUS (Software Usability Scale) or Post-Study System Usability Questionnaire (PSSUQ) because, in this project, two set of tasks (1, 2, 3 and 4, 5, 6) were assessed while the other questionnaires are better suited to rate an entire system. The ASQ has three questions to rate on a 7-point Likert-type scale. This test was modified to address the language factor in two questions to differentiate between the quality in the instructions and in the Word as follows:

1. Overall, I am satisfied with the ease of completing the tasks in this scenario.
2. Overall, I am satisfied with the time it took to complete the tasks in this scenario.
3. Overall, I am satisfied with the instructions given for completing the tasks.
4. Overall, I am satisfied with the language used in the Word menus, dialog boxes and buttons.

The participants could rate between 1 (Strongly agree) to 7 (Strongly disagree). Question 3 was added, even if it does not refer to MS Word specifically, because participants always worked with the Instruction windows visible.

3.3 Content and Design

In collaboration with Microsoft Ireland, the business partner for this research project, the different applications that form part of the Office suite were analyzed. Finally, Word was chosen as the optimal application for the experiment. This was firstly because the study sought to reach as many participants as possible and Word is the most popular application in the suite, and secondly, because it was important to measure the impact of translation modality as opposed to the users' skills or knowledge when using an application, and Word is a relatively easy application to use.

The set of languages analyzed here were English, and Japanese. English was chosen to be used as the control group and Japanese was chosen because it is a language traditionally considered to be difficult for MT.

---

[2] International Organization for Standardization. 2002. ISO/TR 16982: Ergonomics of human-system interaction – Usability methods supporting human centered design. Available on-line http://www.iso.org/iso/iso_catalogue/catalogue_tc/catalogue_detail.htm?csnumber=31176 (last accessed April 2nd 2019)

The software version used was Microsoft Word 2016 MSO (16.0.9126.2315) 32-bit in English and in Japanese. The providers' translation cycle involves MT and full PE. The final quality of the translation delivered by the service provider is equal to publishable quality as defined in the localization instructions and the quality evaluation channels the localization assets go through. It is relevant to note that the localization process might involve translating with no previous reference, but, in general, it includes MT and translation memories, among other reference material, as well as a review cycle.

A specially-devised version of Word was used for the Japanese MT scenario, translated from English using the business partner's highly-customized Microsoft Translator SMT.[3] At the time of implementing this experimental setup, customized Microsoft NMT was not available.

A warm-up task and 6 subsequent tasks were selected. The criteria for selection were that they contained enough text so as to measure the translation modality, that they were coded for telemetry purposes (for a second phase of this experimental project), that they could be performed in all the languages tested (German, Spanish, Japanese and English), and that they were relatively new or non-standard so as to minimize the effect of previous experience.

The warm-up task involved selecting a paragraph and changing the font. The six tasks were: 1) selecting a digital pen and drawing a circle using a defined thickness and color, 2) changing the indentation and spacing for the paragraph (presented to the users), 3) automatically reviewing the document, 4) selecting an option from the Word Options dialog box in the corresponding menu, 5) inserting a section break; and 6) finding the Learning Tools in the corresponding menu and changing the page appearance.

The tasks were evaluated by an English native speaker to test the instructions and the environment. Since it was not possible to analyze the original and translated text with standard readability metrics, a Japanese native speaker evaluated the tasks in the Japanese-released version and in the raw MT environment. This evaluator commented on the high quality of the MT although she signaled the sentences and words that were not idiomatic, wrong, or different from the released version. The errors spotted in the MT scenario in the tasks selected was

comparable to the other languages that were going to be included in the project.

The instructions for the experiment were translated using Microsoft's localization services. They translated the texts following specific instructions to respect the fluency and accuracy of the text and the experimental design.

3.4 Scenarios

Three scenarios (i.e. conditions) were defined for the experiment: MT, HT and English.

The Japanese participants in Group 1 completed three tasks as A) HT, and three tasks as B) MT, while participants in Group 2 were presented the same tasks but in reverse order, that is, B) MT, A) HT. This served to counterbalance the within-subject effect. Between scenarios, there was a brief pause that allowed the researcher to change the Word configuration and recalibrate the eye-tracker.

The English-speaking group were presented with a warm up task and 6 tasks. As with the Japanese group, they had a brief pause between the tasks, replicating the same environment.

3.5 Pre-task questionnaire

The participants were asked to fill in a questionnaire before the experiment. The questionnaire assessed the experience users had in using word-processing applications, Word, their native language and level of English, gender, age, education level, as well as their experience in doing the tasks that were part of the experiment. The questionnaire was provided by email using Google Forms.

3.6 Participants

The criteria for the inclusion of volunteer participants was that they were native speakers, that they were willing to participate in the research and sign a consent form, and that they were frequent users of word processing applications. The participants were recruited through advertisement in social media and email lists within Dublin City University, although the participants were not limited to students or people associated with the university. The participants were given a €20 voucher for their contribution. All participants received a Plain Language Statement and signed an Informed Consent form before the experiment (DCUREC/2017/200).

---

[3] https://hub.microsofttranslator.com/

42 participants took part in the experiment: 20 English-speakers, and 22 Japanese-speakers. 12 Japanese participants were assigned to Group 1 and 10 participants to Group 2.

The reason for the difference in number of Japanese participants is that some eye-tracking data was discarded due to poor recording quality (see Section 3.7). Also, after examination, the data from two EN participants were discarded because of changes in the original set-up (Word version). 75% of participants identified as women and 25% as men. Table 1 shows the age distribution per language.

Age	English	Japanese
18-24	55%	86%
25-34	17%	9%
35-44	28%	5%
Total	18	22

Table 1: Age distribution

The age distribution is important as it might be an indicator of experience with the application. For example, although all of them reported experience using Microsoft Word, the EN group reported a higher level of experience.

Also, when participants were asked about their experience in the 6 experimental tasks, the Japanese group (JP) reported an average experience of 2.1 tasks out of 6 (35.61 %) while the EN group reported an average of 3.8 tasks out of 6 (62.96 %). When they were asked to rate their level of proficiency (i.e. "How would you describe your level of proficiency when working with word-processing applications?"), the average value for the EN was 3.83 in a 5-point Likert scale (1 being Novice and 5 being Very proficient) while the JP selected a 2.14. A Mann-Whitney test for self-reported experience suggests that there is a significant difference in the level of perceived experience between the two groups ($U=24$ and $p<0.05$). JP participants reported significantly lower experience than EN participants.

3.7 Experimental setup

The data recording equipment consisted of a Tobii X60 XL, a wide screen eye-tracker with a 24-inch monitor and 60Hz sampling rate, and a laptop computer (Intel Core 1.7 vPro[tm], 2.00 GHz 2 Core, 4 Logical processors, 8 GB RAM). The laptop was used for stimulus presentation and eye movement recording. The stimuli were presented with a 1600 x 900 resolution. The software used to record and analyze the data was Tobii Studio 3.4.5 1309, Professional Edition. The fixation filter selected was an IV-T Filter provided by the manufacturer. The filter has a velocity threshold of 30 degrees, a maximum time between fixations of 75 ms and a maximum angle of 0.5 degrees. Fixations under 60 ms were discarded.

The participants were calibrated using a nine-point calibration screen (automatic). The participants were recalibrated if the Tobii system reported a poor calibration or if the calibration points were not clearly defined within the calibration grid. The optimal distance to the eye-tracker was set as 67 cm. However, this varied as the participants were not tested using a chin rest to preserve ecological validity during the experiment.

To estimate the cognitive effort using an eye-tracker, two Areas of Interest (AOIs) were defined. One AOI comprised the Instructions windows (25.7%, 369516 px) and the Word application window (74%, 1065165 px). Two participants in the JP group moved the screens slightly, therefore the AOIs for these 2 participants were slightly different for the Instructions (22.81%, 328500px) and the Word application (76.9 %, 1107000px) windows.

To test the quality of the sample, the gaze sample data in the Tobii system and the velocity charts were checked. Moreover, the segments of interest were exported (each segment represented a task timeline therefore six segments were exported per participant) to calculate the eye validity codes within these segments. A minimum 80% gaze sample was required for a recording to be considered valid and to be included in the statistical analysis. This meant that each participant had at least one eye or both eyes on the segments 80 per cent of the time.

3.8 Retrospective Think Aloud

Once the participants had completed the tasks, their gaze data was replayed, and they were asked to comment on what they were doing, thinking or feeling during the experiment. The participants were recorded using Flashback Express 5. The interviews took approximately 15 minutes.

The researcher asked certain questions to elicit responses from the participants, such as How did you find this task? What were you thinking at this point? How was the language in this menu? Had you done this task before? Did you notice any difference in Word when you came back from the pause?

3.9 Statistical methods

To analyze the results graphically and statistically, SAS v9.4 and IBM SPSS Statistics, v24 were used. The statistics decisions were made with a significance value of 0.05.

To determine the effect of the scenario (HT, MT and EN) for each response variable (Effectiveness, Efficiency and Satisfaction), a general linear mixed model (called hereafter a mixed model) was adjusted according to the scenario and task groups (1, 2, 3 vs. 4, 5, 6) and the interaction between the two (Type III Test). The tasks and scenarios are considered fixed factors and the repeated measures of each participant are included in the model (random effects).

4   Results

4.1   Effectiveness

Table 1 shows that HT evinces higher effectiveness scores on average than the MT scenario in both groups of tasks. The EN group has the highest scores. Figure 1 illustrates these figures clearly.

Tasks/Scenarios		N	Mean	Std
1, 2, 3	HT	12	**82.64**	9.70
	MT	10	**74.17**	27.06
	EN	18	**93.98**	12.06
4, 5, 6	HT	10	**46.67**	26.99
	MT	12	**40.28**	29.05
	EN	18	**62.96**	34.09

Table 1: Effectiveness

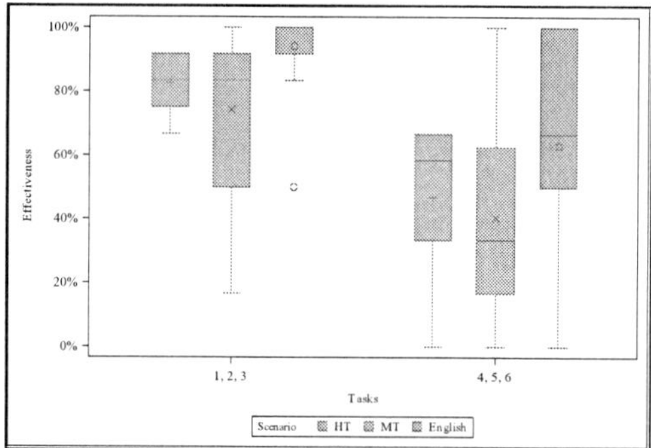

Figure 1: Effectiveness according to scenarios and tasks

A mixed model for effectiveness shows that there are statistically significant differences between scenarios (F(2, 37)=4.26; p=0.0216) and tasks (F(1, 37)=64.73; p<.0001). The estimated mean of effectiveness is 78.47 in EN, 64.65 in HT and 57.22 in MT scenarios.

There are significant differences between scenarios when comparing the EN and MT groups, with 21.25 as the estimated difference. This means that the EN scenario is estimated as 21.25% more effective than the JP MT scenario (in line with findings from Doherty and O'Brien, 2014). The participants in the JP group show higher effectiveness scores in the HT than in the MT scenarios, but this difference is not significant.

Regarding the tasks, the estimated mean is 83.6 in tasks 1, 2, 3 and 49.97 for 4, 5, 6. There are statistically significant differences between tasks. The estimated difference of effectiveness between task 1, 2, 3 and tasks 4, 5, 6 is 33.63%, CI$_{95\%}$=[25.16, 42.09]. The mixed model confirms that tasks 1, 2, 3 were "easier" for participants than tasks 4, 5, 6.

4.2   Efficiency

As with effectiveness, the efficiency was calculated per scenario and task as shown in Table 2 and Figure 2.

Tasks/Scenario		N	Mean	Std
1, 2, 3	HT	12	**31.92**	13.89
	MT	10	**21.13**	8.47
	EN	18	**48.75**	19.27
4, 5, 6	HT	10	**11.88**	9.64
	MT	12	**9.11**	8.08
	EN	18	**21.63**	19.94

Table 2: Efficiency

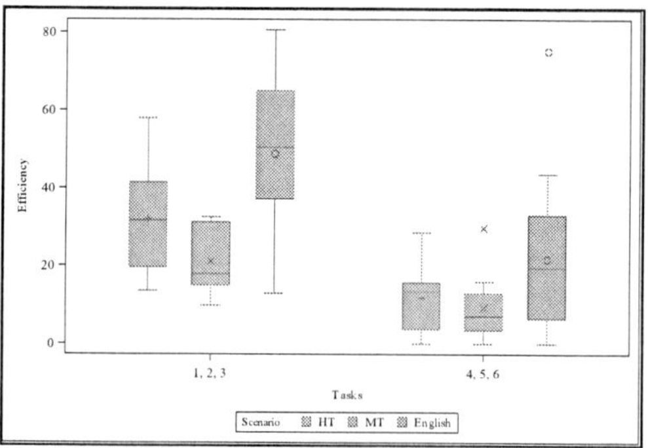

Figure 2: Efficiency according to scenario and tasks

HT shows higher efficiency on average than the MT scenario in both groups of tasks and the EN group shows the highest efficiency scores.

A mixed model shows that there are statistically significant differences between scenarios (F(2,37)=9.9; p=0.0004) and tasks (F=65.25; p<0.0001). (F(1,37)=65.25; p<.0001). The JP group shows more efficiency in the HT than in the MT scenario, however this difference is not significant. The estimated mean of efficiency is 35.19 in EN, 21.90 in HT and 15.12 in MT.

The EN group has a 13.29 estimated difference with the HT scenario, and an estimated 20.07 difference with the MT scenario. There are no significant differences between the HT and MT scenarios in the JP group.

Regarding the tasks, the estimated mean for efficiency is 33.93 for tasks 1, 2, 3 and 14.21 for tasks 4, 5 and 6. There are statistically significant differences between tasks. The estimated difference between 1, 2, 3 and 4, 5, 6 is 19.72, $CI_{95\%}$=[14.78, 24.67].

If efficiency is considered, the participants are statistically more efficient in the EN group than in the JP group (in line with Castilho, 2016 and Doherty and O'Brien, 2014). However, if time is analyzed without considering task completion, there are statistically significant differences only between tasks ($F(1,37)$=20.2; p<.0001) but not between scenarios. The JP group employs less time the HT than in the MT scenario, however this difference is not significant.

The estimated mean of efficiency is 299.61 seconds for tasks 1, 2, 3 and 485.31 seconds for 4, 5, 6. The estimated difference is 185.7 $CI_{95\%}$=[-269.4, -101.99], it took an average of 3 minutes longer to complete tasks 4, 5, 6.

4.3 Satisfaction

The satisfaction was calculated using the four questions from the post-scenario questionnaire that were ranked by the user on a 7-point Likert-type scale where 1 indicated the most satisfaction and 7, the least. Table 3 shows Satisfaction according to scenarios and tasks.

Tasks/Scenarios		N	Mean	Std
1, 2, 3	HT	12	**3.42**	1.42
	MT	10	**3.37**	1.14
	EN	18	**2.13**	1.08
4, 5, 6	HT	10	**3.40**	1.22
	MT	12	**4.56**	1.36
	EN	18	**3.11**	1.22

Table 3: Satisfaction*

Table 3 shows that Japanese participants report being more satisfied in the MT in the first part of the experiment and more satisfied in the HT scenario in the second part of the experiment where the difference is higher. The EN group shows the best satisfaction scores. Figure 3 shows this data clearly.

A mixed model shows that there are statistically significant differences between scenarios ($F(2,37)$=8.08; p=0.0012) and tasks ($F(1,37)$=21.94; p<0.0001. The estimated mean of satisfaction is 2.62 in EN, 3.41 in HT and 3.96 in MT scenarios.

*Lower scores indicate higher satisfaction.

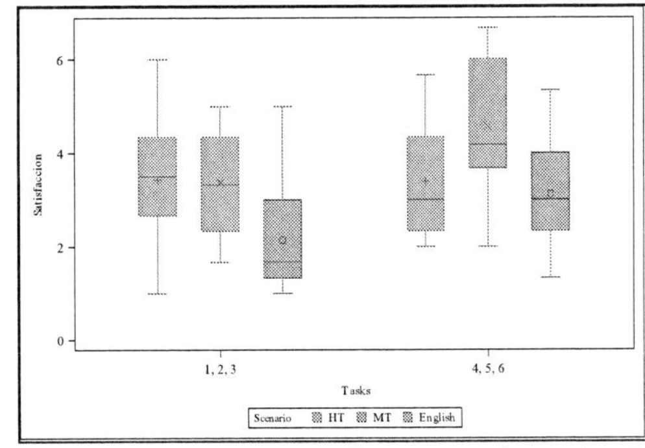

Figure 3: Satisfaction according to scenarios and tasks

There is an estimated difference of -1.34 between EN and MT scenarios, and a -0.55 between HT and MT Scenarios. There are differences between the EN group and the HT scenario (estimated difference=-0.79, stderr=0.38) but this is not significant.

Regarding the tasks, the estimated mean for satisfaction is 2.97 for tasks 1, 2, 3 and 3.69 for tasks 4, 5, 6. There are statistically significant differences between tasks. The estimated difference between 1, 2, 3 and 4, 5, 6 is -0.72, $CI_{95\%}$=[-1.03, -0.41].

The question that specifically addressed the Word application was explored ("Overall, I am satisfied with the language used in the Word menus, dialog boxes and buttons?"). Participants were more satisfied in the HT (M=3.5) than in the MT scenarios (M=4.5). A Wilcoxon signed rank test shows that HT ranks significantly lower than the MT scenario (Z=-2.62, p=0.009). As explained before, a lower score indicates a higher satisfaction. The results show that 3 participants were more satisfied with MT, 12 participants with HT, and in 7 cases MT was ranked alongside HT. If compared to the EN group significant differences are only found with the MT scenario (U= -3.26 and p=0.001).

The results regarding the participants' satisfaction show they are more satisfied in the EN group than in the JP group (in line with Castilho, 2016 and Doherty and O'Brien, 2014). This could be explained by several factors: the language, the experience (EN group was more experienced and the familiarity could explain a higher satisfaction), but also to the way each culture reports satisfaction. The participants in the JP group are significantly more satisfied in the HT than in the MT scenarios and this was particularly true for the most difficult tasks.

4.4 Cognitive Effort

For these groups the fixation duration and count were calculated as indicators of cognitive load. Fixation duration measures the duration of each individual fixation within an AOI in seconds. Table 4 shows the Fixation duration mean for the Word AOI.

Tasks/Scenario		N	Mean in seconds	Std
1, 2, 3	HT	10	**0.22**	0.04
	MT	8	**0.23**	0.03
	EN	18	**0.21**	0.05
4, 5, 6	HT	8	**0.21**	0.03
	MT	10	**0.20**	0.03
	EN	18	**0.18**	0.04

Table 4: Fixation duration mean in Word AOI

The mean value for MT is higher than HT in the first tasks, and lower in the second set of tasks, and EN presents the lowest mean value as illustrated in Figure 4.

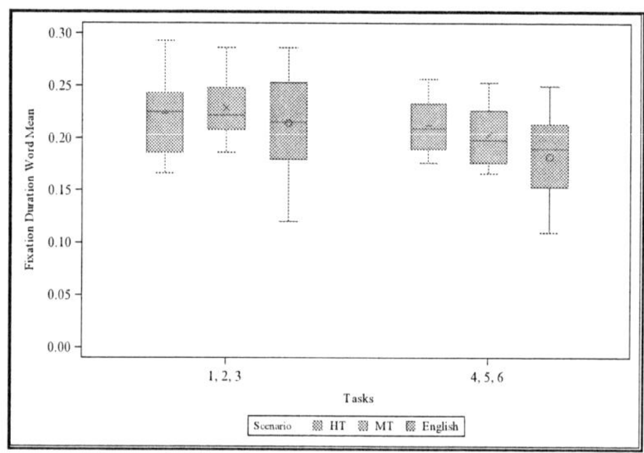

Figure 4: Fixation duration mean in Word AOI

A mixed model shows that there are statistically significant differences ($F_{(2,33)}$=25.01; p<0.0001) between tasks, but not between scenarios or the interaction between scenarios and tasks. The estimated mean fixation duration is 0.22 for tasks 1, 2, 3 and 0.20 for 4, 5, 6 tasks. There is an estimated difference of 0.023 seconds $CI_{95\%}$=[0.014, 0.032].

Fixation count measures the number of times the participant fixates on the Word AOI. Figure 5 shows the average fixation count per participant and tasks. There is a lower number of fixations in HT than in MT for both groups of tasks and the EN group shows a lower number of fixations than the HT scenario in the first 3 tasks but not in the second 3 tasks.

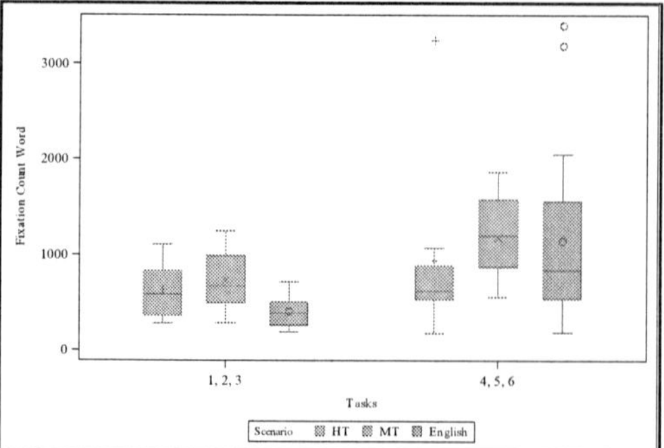

Figure 5: Fixation count in Word AOI

Tasks/Scenario		N	Mean fixations	Std
1, 2, 3	HT	10	**631.40**	300.09
	MT	8	**731.25**	336.08
	EN	18	**404.06**	179.45
4, 5, 6	HT	8	**939.63**	963.72
	MT	10	**1175.60**	439.54
	EN	18	**1142.61**	918.70

Table 4: Fixation duration mean in Word AOI

The estimated fixation count (at logarithmic scale) is 6.29 for tasks 1, 2 and 3 and 6.85 for tasks 4, 5 and 6. There is an estimated of -0.56 fixations (less) in tasks 1, 2, 3 than in 4, 5, 6 $CI_{95\%}$=[-0.78, -.034]. If tasks and scenarios are considered, the estimated mean for the EN 1, 2, 3 tasks in 5.93 and 6.86 for 4, 5 and 6. The estimated differences in the EN group is of -0.93 fixations (less) in the first group of tasks $CI_{95\%}$=[-1.38, -0.49].

Regarding the cognitive load, there are significant differences between the tasks, which indicates that the cognitive load varied depending on the difficulty of the task, but not necessarily due to the scenario (as in Castilho, 2016). This is clear in the EN group where participants had significantly more fixations in the second set of tasks than in the first ones, but the participants were always under the same scenario. The mean fixation duration is lower for tasks 4, 5, 6 and this is surprising since these tasks were more difficult for participants. It could be that participants did not spend more time fixating on an option but fixating on different keywords to try and find the solution. So, although the sum of all fixation durations in seconds was higher for tasks 4, 5 and 6, the mean (when computing N=count of fixations) was lower because there were a lot more fixations in those tasks.

4.5 Mouse clicks

During the experiment, when the participants in the JP group did not understand a word in the MT scenario, they were observed clicking around to try and understand the context of that word.

Therefore, the number of mouse clicks were compared between the HT and MT scenario in the Japanese group. Although HT had a lower number of clicks than the MT scenario (HT=58.86; MT=62.68), there is no statistically significant difference between the two. On 10 occasions, the MT scenario ranks lower than HT, on 11 MT ranks higher than HT, and on 1 occasion they rank equally.

4.6 Retrospective think aloud protocols

At the time of writing this paper, a complete qualitative analysis of these interviews has not been completed, as all interviews are being transcribed for ease of analysis, therefore a summary of the observations during the experiment is provided instead.

The participants from the JP and EN groups reported that they found the first three tasks easier than the second three tasks in general as has been observed in the quantitative analysis. As per the self-reported questionnaire and the results, the JP group reported having more difficulties with certain tasks than the EN group, and less experience with those tasks and Word in general.

Possibly, the most surprising comment after talking to the participants was that when returning from the pause, the JP group did not notice that the Word application was different. The participants were concentrating on the completion of the tasks, and since they were not informed that there was a change in the application, they assumed it was the same one. Having said this, however, participants in the JP group did report that some words were wrong, incorrect or confusing, and that some technical terms posed difficulty in MT. As explained in Section 4.3, the JP group rated the MT scenario lower than the HT scenario, so they were less satisfied when working with MT, especially in tasks 4, 5 and 6.

5 Conclusions and future work

There are differences between the EN and JP group when it comes to effectiveness, efficiency, satisfaction and, to some extent, when it comes to cognitive effort. Translation modality appears to be a factor, especially when the MT scenario is considered for effectiveness and satisfaction.

If the JP group is examined in isolation, there are differences between the MT and HT scenarios, but these are not significant if effectiveness and efficiency are considered. However, when it comes to satisfaction, the difference is significant. This is also in line with what the participants

reported in the RTA protocol; overall, they did not notice a difference between the HT and the MT systems. However, they did notice words that were wrong, strange, confusing in the MT scenario and this is what they remembered when rating their satisfaction in both scenarios. The difference in satisfaction is also larger for more difficult tasks, and this might indicate that the less familiar we are with an application, the more we need the language to be of high quality to understand our way around that application.

Another aspect to consider is that if users cannot complete a high percentage of tasks, their satisfaction score might be lower because they would feel that either they, the instructions, or the language was inadequate. For this reason, it is important to see how participants in different languages and with different experience and successful scores, rate satisfaction.

Nevertheless, even if the number of tasks or the time it took to complete them was not significantly different in both scenarios, Japanese participants felt more satisfied in the HT scenario, and this perceived value is a key factor if customer experience and retention are considered when implementing MT solutions.

Would this have been different if participants were using a system translated with NMT? As we can see from the literature when comparing both paradigms (Bentivogli et al., 2016, Castilho et al. 2017, Castilho and Guerberof, 2018; Toral, Wieling and Way, 2018) improvements in quality have been observed when moving from SMT to NMT systems, but the effect this improvement has on translators/users, if any, is yet to be defined clearly. When reading within software (with a focus on completing a task), as in this experiment, the important factor appears to be key words, i.e. accuracy, not necessarily the fluency of the text, which is where NMT performs better. Therefore, if a raw NMT system is put in place (especially if compared to a highly customized SMT system), users might also notice or be confused by incorrect or unclear terms and report lower satisfaction scores. This remains to be tested.

As mentioned in Section 1, these are preliminary results from a larger project. The next steps are to analyze the data for all the languages and tasks, as well as further exploration of the eye-tracking and qualitative data gathered through the RTA, and the telemetry data collected per scenario.

Acknowledgements

This research was supported by the Edge Research Fellowship programme that has received funding from the EU Horizon 2020 and innovation programme under the MSC grant agreement No. 713567, and by the ADAPT Centre for Digital Content Technology, funded under the SFI Research Centres Programme (Grant 13/RC/2106) and cofounded under the European Regional Development Fund.

This research was also funded by Microsoft Ireland. We would like to thank Glenn Poor and Dag Schmidtke for their support in this pilot experiment.

References

Bentivogli, Luis, Arianna Bisazza, Mauro Cettolo, and Marcello Federico. 2016. Neural versus phrase-based machine translation quality: a case study. arXiv preprint arXiv:1608.04631

Bowker, Lynne. 2015. Translatability and User eXperience: Compatible or in Conflict? Localisation Focus: *The International Journal of Localisation* 14(2): 13-27.

Bowker, Lynne and Jairo Buitrago Ciro. 2018. Localizing websites using machine translation. *The Human Factor in Machine Translation*. Chan Sin-wai, ed. Routledge Studies in Translation. Routledge, Lonad and New York: 8-29.

Castilho, Sheila, and Ana Guerberof Arenas. 2018. Reading comprehension of machine translation output: what makes for a better read? *21st Annual Conference of the European Association for Machine Translation*, Alacant, Spain:79-88.

Castilho, Sheila, Joss Moorkens, Federico Gaspari, Iacer Calixto, John Tinsley, and Andy Way. 2017. Is neural machine translation the new state of the art? *The Prague Bulletin of Mathematical Linguistics*, 108(1): 109–120.

Castilho, Sheila, Sharon O'Brien, Fabio Alves. and Morgan O'Brien. 2014. Does post-editing increase usability? A study with Brazilian Portuguese as Target Language. Proceedings of the *Seventeenth Annual Conference of the European Association for Machine Translation*, Dubrovnik, Croatia, 183–190.

Castilho, Sheila. 2016. Measuring Acceptability of Machine Translated Enterprise Content. PhD Thesis. Dublin City University, Dublin, Ireland.

De Almeida, G. and Sharon O'Brien. 2010. Analysing post-editing performance: correlations with years of translation experience. In *Proceedings of the 14th Annual Conference of the European Association for Machine Translation*, S. Rafael, France.

Doherty, Stephen and Sharon O'Brien. 2009. Can MT output be evaluated through eye tracking? Proceedings of *the Machine Translation Summit XII*, Ottawa, Ontario, Canada, 214-221.

Doherty, Stephen and Sharon O'Brien. 2012. A user-based usability assessment of raw machine translated technical instructions. The Tenth Biennial Conference of the Association for Machine Translation in the Americas. Proceedings, San Diego, 6pp.

Doherty, Stephen and Sharon O'Brien. 2014. Assessing the Usability of Raw Machine Translated Output: A User-Centered Study Using Eye Tracking. *International Journal of Human- Computer Interaction*, 30(1): 40–51.

Doherty, Stephen, Sharon O'Brien and Michael Carl 2010. Eye tracking as an MT evaluation technique. *Machine Translation Magazine*, 24(1): 1-13.

Guerberof, Ana. 2012. Productivity and quality in the post-editing of outputs from translation memories and machine translation. PhD thesis. Universitat Rovira i Virgili, Tarragona. Spain.

Lewis, James R. (1995) IBM Computer Usability Satisfaction Questionnaires: Psychometric Evaluation and Instructions for Use. *International Journal of Human-Computer Interaction*, 7:1, 57-78.

Lommel, Arle R. and Donal A. DePalma. 2016. Post-editing goes Mainstream. Common Sense Advisory. Available on-line http://www.commonsenseadvisory.com/AbstractVi ew/tabid/74/ArticleID/36532/Title/Post-EditingGoesMainstream/Default.aspx (accessed April 4th 2019)

Moorkens, Joss, Sharon O'Brien, Igor A.L. da Silva, Norma de Lima Fonseca, and Fabio Alves. 2015. Correlations of perceived post-editing effort with measurements of actual effort. *Machine Translation*, 29(3): 267–284.

O'Brien, Sharon and Sheila Castilho. 2016. Evaluating the Impact of Light Post-Editing on Usability. Proceedings of the *Tenth International Conference on Language Resources and Evaluation* (LREC 2016), Portorož, Slovenia. 310-316

O'Brien, Sharon. 2006. Eye-tracking and translation memory matches. *Perspectives: Studies in Translatology*, 14(3):185–205.

Plitt, Mirko, and François Masselot. 2010. A productivity test of statistical machine translation post-editing in a typical localization context. *The Prague Bulletin of Mathematical Linguistics*, 23: 7-16

Screen, Benjamin. 2019. What effect does post-editing have on the translation product from an end-user's perspective? *Journal of specialised translation*, (31): 135-157.

Toral, Antonio, Martijn Wieling, and Andy Way. 2018. Post-editing effort of a novel with statistical and neural machine translation. *Frontiers in Digital Humanities*, 5, 9.

van Egdom, Gys Walt and Mark Pluymaekers, M. 2019. Why go the extra mile? How different degrees of post-editing affect perceptions of texts, senders and products among end users. *Journal of specialised translation*, (31), 158-176.

MAGMATic: A Multi-domain Academic Gold Standard with Manual Annotation of Terminology for Machine Translation Evaluation

Randy Scansani
University of Bologna
Forlì, Italy
`randy.scansani@unibo.it`

Luisa Bentivogli
Fondazione Bruno Kessler
Trento, Italy
`bentivo@fbk.eu`

Silvia Bernardini
University of Bologna
Forlì, Italy
`silvia.bernardini@unibo.it`

Adriano Ferraresi
University of Bologna
Forlì, Italy
`adriano.ferraresi@unibo.it`

Abstract

This paper presents MAGMATic (Multi-domain Academic Gold Standard with Manual Annotation of Terminology), a novel Italian–English benchmark which allows MT evaluation focused on terminology translation. The data set comprises 2,056 parallel sentences extracted from institutional academic texts, namely course unit and degree program descriptions. This text type is particularly interesting since it contains terminology from multiple domains, e.g. education and different academic disciplines described in the texts. All terms in the English target side of the data set were manually identified and annotated with a domain label, for a total of 7,517 annotated terms. Due to their peculiar features, institutional academic texts represent an interesting test bed for MT. As a further contribution of this paper, we investigate the feasibility of exploiting MT for the translation of this type of documents. To this aim, we evaluate two state-of-the-art Neural MT systems on MAGMATic, focusing on their ability to translate domain-specific terminology.

1 Introduction

The availability of bilingual versions of course catalogues has started to play a major role for European universities after the Bologna Process and the resulting growth in students' mobility. Course catalogues fall into the category of institutional academic text collections and they usually include degree program and course unit descriptions, where information regarding degree courses and modules are provided to students. Such texts have to be produced and published every year in each country language and in English. Universities would thus undoubtedly benefit from the use of machine translation (MT).

Further proof of the need for an MT engine able to translate course catalogues are two projects funded by the European Commission, namely the Bologna Translation Service[1] (Depraetere et al., 2011), aimed at developing an MT system to translate course catalogues in 9 language combinations, and TraMOOC,[2] aimed at using MT for the translation of massive online open courses from English into eleven European and BRIC languages.

Developing an engine in this field poses several challenges. First, the fact that degree program and course unit descriptions are usually translated by non-native speakers of the target language (Fernandez Costales, 2012) reduces the number of available high-quality and alignable bilingual texts. Moreover, the lack of guidelines and best practices to draft these texts results in substantial unmotivated variation among course catalogues from different universities. Finally, institutional academic texts usually contain terminology from different domains, with disciplinary terms, e.g. *Hydrosilylation*, *Fotoredox catalysis*, for a course on chemistry, appearing together with educational ones - e.g. *ECTS*, *module*.

The potential and challenges mentioned so far make course catalogues an interesting test bed for

---

[1] `https://cordis.europa.eu/project/rcn/191739/factsheet/en`
[2] `http://tramooc.eu/content/scientific-publications`

neural MT (NMT) (Sutskever et al., 2014; Bahdanau et al., 2014). Indeed, in the last few years NMT has delivered considerable improvements in output quality in many respects (Bentivogli et al., 2016), yet not showing clear-cut progresses when it comes to lexis-related issues, e.g. lexical choices, omissions or mistranslations (Castilho et al., 2018). These issues are especially critical for texts rich in domain-specific terminology, or texts containing terms belonging to different domains. Testing an MT engine on course catalogues can provide interesting information on domain-specific terminology handling and on results achievable with a relatively small amount of in-domain resources used to perform domain-adaptation of a neural model.

Whilst assessing systems' ability to correctly translate domain-specific terms is a crucial aspect in MT evaluation, research in the field has to cope with a dearth of publicly available resources specifically tailored to that task. The main contribution of this paper is to provide the MT community with MAGMATic (Multi-domain Academic Gold standard with Manual Annotation of Terminology), a novel Italian–English benchmark which allows MT evaluation focused on terminology translation. The data set comprises 2,056 sentences extracted from course unit and degree program descriptions from four different Italian universities and manually aligned to their English translations. All terms in the English target side of the data set were manually identified and annotated with a domain label, for a total of 7,517 annotated terms, covering 20 different domains related to different disciplines - excluding humanities and with a focus on hard sciences - as well as education and education equipment. These features make the data set a valuable resource to evaluate and analyze systems' performance on terminology translation, thus contributing to shed light on this crucial aspect for MT. MAGMATic is released under a Creative Commons Attribution – Non Commercial – Share Alike 4.0 International license (CC BY-NC–SA 4.0), and is freely downloadable at:

```
https://ict.fbk.eu/magmatic/
```

In the remainder of this paper we describe MAGMATic and illustrate its potential by using it to evaluate two state-of-the-art MT systems (Google Translate and ModernMT), both in terms of overall performance and focusing on their ability to translate domain-specific terminology. After describing related work on term translation evaluation (Section 2), we introduce the main characteristics of MAGMATic (Section 3) and provide results from the evaluation study carried out on the two state-of-the-art MT systems (Section 4).

2 Related work

A number of monolingual annotated data sets for benchmarking terminology extraction and classification techniques have been created along the years for different domains (Kim et al., 2003; Bernier-Colborne and Drouin, 2014; Q. Zadeh and Handschuh, 2014; Astrakhantsev et al., 2015). The situation is much less favourable for terminology translation evaluation. Indeed, the majority of works addressing domain adaptation for MT evaluate systems only in terms of overall performance on a domain-specific test set, while very few studies specifically focus on the engines' ability to translate domain-specific terminology, and thus resort to test sets in which terms are annotated. To the best of our knowledge, only the following manually annotated resources are made available to the community. The BitterCorpus[3] (Arcan et al., 2014a) is a collection of parallel English–Italian documents in the information technology domain in which technical terms in both the source and target sides of the bi-texts are manually marked and aligned. TermTraGS[4] (Farajian et al., 2018) is a sentence-aligned version of the BitterCorpus, which also includes a large training set.

On a different aspect of MT quality evaluation, most of the works comparing NMT with previous paradigms treat correct or wrong lexical choices as one of the main quality indicators (Bentivogli et al., 2016; Bentivogli et al., 2018; Toral and Sánchez-Cartagena, 2017; Castilho et al., 2018; Van Brussel et al., 2018). However, all these works focus on the broader concept of lexical issues without specifically addressing terminology. The MAGMATic data set offers a new opportunity to compare different MT approaches directly on terminology issues.

Finally, regarding the institutional academic scenario, it is worthwhile to point out that neither of the two EU-funded projects mentioned in Sect. 1 – *Bologna Translation Service* and *TraMOOC* – led to the creation of data sets targeted to the evaluation of terminology translation.

---

[3] `https://ict.fbk.eu/bittercorpus/`
[4] `https://gitlab.com/farajian/TermTraGS`

3 Data set description

3.1 Data selection

The text material used in this work was collected from the websites of four Italian universities. All the course unit and degree program descriptions for which the corresponding English version was available were extracted, automatically aligned at sentence level and cleaned with TMop (Jalili Sabet et al., 2016), an open-source software for Translation Memory cleaning.

As an attempt to narrow down the number of domains – and thus the variability of terminology – course catalogues belonging to the humanities and social sciences were excluded, keeping only those catalogues related to scientific disciplines.

Then, a subset of sentence pairs was randomly selected and manually checked to ensure alignment correctness. This procedure resulted in 2,157 Italian–English parallel sentences. Statistics for the data set are summarised in Table 1.

MAGMATic		
	It	**En**
Sent.pairs	2,157	
Tokens	36,162	34,589
Vocabulary	10,207	9,138

Table 1: Size of the MAGMATic data set: number of sentences, number of tokens (i.e. running words) and vocabulary (i.e. number of distinct word types).

3.2 Data annotation

Two expert linguists with a background in translation studies took part in the annotation: one of them annotated the whole data set and the other annotated a portion of it so as to allow inter-annotator agreement assessment (see details in Section 3.4).

Two main annotation tasks were performed on the English target side of the data set, namely *(i)* the identification of the terms and *(ii)* their classification into domain categories. In order to ensure annotation quality and comparability, guidelines were created, tested in a pilot study and then given to the annotators.

Term identification. Both single-word (SW) terms – i.e. terms formed of one word – and multi-word (MW) terms – i.e. terms formed of two or more words – were annotated.

Furthermore, instances of language for general and specific purposes often blur into each other,

making the decision as to what belongs to one or the other prone to subjectivity bias. For this reason, annotators were asked to report on their level of confidence, distinguishing between `sure` terms and `possible` terms, the latter accounting for expressions whose terminological status and specialisation were uncertain. For example, in a description of a course on electronics, *RC-circuit* was identified as a `sure` term and *charge* as a `possible` term. Where contents of a course on chemistry were outlined, *analysis* was categorized as `possible` and *pollutants formation* as `sure`. In sentences describing a course's teaching and evaluation methods, *exam* and *lecture* were labelled as `sure` terms, while *topics* and *notions* were labelled as `possible`. This additional annotation level is particularly useful since it supports more flexible evaluation designs.

Domain annotation. The identified terms were assigned to one of the following categories:

- `Disciplinary`: the term belongs to a disciplinary domain - e.g. *chemical reaction, linear equation, cholinesterase*.

- `Education`: the term belongs to the educational domain - e.g. *module, course, lecturer*.

- `Education equipment`: the term refers to educational equipment that could also be used elsewhere - e.g. *overhead projector, desk*.

While the `education` and `education equipment` categories are univocal, the `disciplinary` category encompasses multiple domains, i.e. multiple scientific disciplines. To assign each term to a specific discipline, we leveraged the names of the degree programs included in the data set: each sentence in the data set was automatically labelled with its corresponding degree program name and all the terms annotated as `disciplinary` in those sentences during the annotation process inherited the sentence domain label by default. Annotators were shown this domain label during the annotation process and asked to signal cases where a discrepancy between the label assigned automatically and the actual domain of one or more terms was observed. In these cases, annotators were asked to manually assign a different label to the term(s), selecting it from the list of degree program names.

	Disciplinary		Education		Equipment		Total
	Sure	Poss.	Sure	Poss.	Sure	Poss.	
SWs	2,298	295	868	323	111	21	3,916
MWs	2,464	359	491	186	85	16	3,601
Total	4,762	654	1,359	509	196	37	
	5,416		1,868		233		7,517
Vocabulary	4,316		686		130		5,132

Table 2: Statistics of the terms annotated in the MAGMATic data sets. Terms in the three domain categories - Disciplinary, Education, Education-equipment (here Equip.) - are further split into the Sure and Possible (Poss.) subcategories. For either of these subcategories, the number of SWs and MWs, and the total number of terms are provided. In the two bottom rows, the total number of terms and the vocabulary (i.e. the number of distinct terms) are given for each category.

The annotation was carried out using the MT-EQuAL annotation tool (Girardi et al., 2014). For each English sentence, the MT-EQuAL interface displays the source sentence and the disciplinary domain retrieved from the name of the university course catalogue. Furthermore, the tool allows the annotators to perform the two annotation steps simultaneously: they mark each term and annotate it (sure/possible distinction and domain category) in a single go. This makes the annotation task efficient and less demanding in terms of effort.

3.3 Annotation statistics

Details regarding the number of terms annotated in the data set are provided in Table 2. In 101 sentences out of 2,157 (see Table 1) no terms were found. We therefore ended up with 2,056 sentence pairs and a total of 7,517 term occurrences, which correspond to 5,132 distinct terms.

The disciplinary category is the largest, while the education equipment category is the smallest. Looking at the proportion between sure and possible terms for each category, it is interesting to note that possible terms are much more frequent in the education category (27.2% of the total terms) than in the disciplinary (12%) or education equipment (15.9%) categories. We can assume that disciplinary or education equipment terms are rarely encountered in everyday language, and are thus easier to identify as terms. On the other hand, education-related terms are also used outside of the domain, making the decision as to their status more difficult.

Looking at SWs and MWs, their number in the data set is approximately the same. However the disciplinary category contains more MWs than SWs, whereas for the two other categories the opposite is the case. This is in line with what was stated above, i.e. disciplinary terms are highly domain-specific, and thus more likely to be MWs than, for example, education ones. The average length of MW terms is 2.44 words.

Comparing the number of term occurrences with the corresponding vocabulary, we see that terms in the education category show a much lower degree of variation than disciplinary terms. Indeed, the type-token ratio amounts to 0.80 for the disciplinary category, 0.37 for education and 0.56 for education equipment. This is due to the fact that the disciplinary category includes multiple domains, and thus a high number of different terms, while education and education equipment terms are stable and repeated across most texts. Also, the 5 most frequent terms in the data set belong to the education category (SWs: *student, course, students, knowledge, lectures*; MWs: *oral exam, end of the course, written test, oral examination, written exam*).

As concerns the specific domains represented in the disciplinary category, we saw in the previous section that the specific domain labels were assigned to the terms by exploiting the names of the degree programs of the universities from which the data set was derived. These names refer to domains with different granularity - e.g. biology, which is more generic, and biotechnology, which is more specific - and thus different size. To obtain a more homogeneous set of domains, we merged the most specific ones with the generic ones where appropriate, e.g. biotechnology was grouped with biology and biomedicine with medicine. This procedure resulted in 20 macro-domain labels with a similar level of granularity.

Examples of the macro-domains are given in Table 3, which shows the 5 most and 5 less populated ones. As we can see in the table, the number of terms included in the most populated domains allow for an extremely thorough terminology evaluation. Also, even if not all of them are displayed here, 9 domains out of 20 include more than 300 annotated terms. Regarding the less populated domains, they appear frequently in translation tasks and only three of them contain less than 100 annotated terms.

Domain	SWs	MWs	Total
Chemistry	345	367	712
Informatics	256	224	480
Physics	184	283	467
Biology	245	212	457
Mechanical engineering	200	210	410
...	...	...	...
Geosciences	62	47	109
Industrial engineering	48	59	107
Astronomy	21	61	82
Law	15	34	49
Institutions	14	11	25

Table 3: The 5 most populated and 5 least populated macro-domains covered in the data set and number of terms in each of them (SW, MW and total).

3.4 Inter-annotator agreement

In order to assess the reliability of the annotations, 220 sentences – corresponding to 10% of the data set – were annotated by a second annotator.

Inter-Annotator Agreement (IAA) was calculated for the two types of manual annotation, namely *(i)* the identification of the terms and *(ii)* their assignment to a domain category.

Agreement was computed on all the identified terms, without taking into account the `sure`/`possible` distinction.

Term identification. Two different types of agreement were calculated, to account for *complete* as well as *partial* agreement. Complete agreement refers to perfect overlap of two terms annotated by different annotators (i.e. exact match), whereas for partial agreement overlap is calculated at the level of the single words composing the term.

The agreement rates – computed using the Dice coefficient[5] (Dice, 1945) – are 0.69 for complete

agreement and 0.79 for partial agreement. Given the high number of MW terms and the strict approach used for complete agreement, results may be considered satisfactory in terms of reliability of the annotations and suitability of the annotation guidelines.

Domain annotation. For the subset of terms for which complete agreement between the two annotators was found (495 terms), we also calculated the agreement on the assigned category label (i.e. `disciplinary, education, education equipment`).

To this end, we computed the standard *kappa coefficient* κ (in Scott's π formulation) (Scott, 1955; Artstein and Poesio, 2008), which measures the agreement between two raters, each of whom classifies N items into C mutually exclusive categories, taking into account the agreement occurring by chance.

The resulting κ value is 0.95, which – according to the standard interpretation of the κ values (Landis and Koch, 1977) – corresponds to "almost perfect" agreement.

4 MT evaluation on MAGMATic

4.1 MT and institutional academic texts

As a first application of our MAGMATic data set, we evaluated translations of course catalogues produced by two state-of-the-art NMT systems, i.e. Google Translate (GT)[6] and ModernMT (MMT)[7].

On the one hand, course catalogues are an ideal test bed for MT, given the multi-domain nature of these texts. On the other hand, being able to apply MT to course catalogues is particularly key for universities, since the increasing students and staff mobility has created the need of translating a large quantity of institutional academic texts into English (see Sect. 1).

Given the lack of in-house (customised) MT systems and of high-quality in-domain parallel data, using such technologies is a big challenge for higher-education institutions. Two ready-to-use state-of-the-art MT systems like MMT and GT thus represent a viable solution for this real-world multi-domain translation scenario. Both of them are based on the state-of-the-art transformer architecture (Vaswani et al., 2017) and trained on a large

---

[5]Note that Dice coefficient has the same value of the F1 measure computed considering either annotator as the reference.

[6]`translate.google.com`
[7]`www.modernmt.eu`

pool of parallel data. Furthermore, MMT implements an adaption mechanism which allows the system to adapt to new data in real time (Bertoldi et al., 2018). This feature represents a particularly interesting option in our scenario, since it would allow universities to leverage new translated data as soon as they are produced. In our evaluation we used the full-fledged commercial version of MMT available through the MateCat tool[8] and and we compared it with the GT online system.[9]

To the best of our knowledge, this contribution represents the first attempt at translating institutional academic texts with NMT.

4.2 Evaluation scenarios

Given the novelty of the application of MT to the translation of course catalogues, we are focusing on two scenarios that we deem realistic for one or more universities willing to use MT:

- First scenario (GT, MMT-I). One or more universities want to use MT for the translation of their course catalogues for the first time, and have no translation memories. At this point, no in-domain bilingual texts are available.

- Second scenario (GT, MMT-II). A university consortium agrees to coordinate their communication strategies. They use CAT tools for translating their course catalogues and produce a reasonable amount of translations, which can be leveraged as shared domain-adaptation data.

In order to address the second scenario, we needed an in-domain data set to be exploited for MT adaptation. To this effect, the parallel data collected from the 4 Italian universities but left out in the creation of MAGMATic (see Sect. 3.1) were used. Statistics for this data set are outlined in Table 4.[10]

Since the online generic version of GT used in this work is not adaptive, it can be tested in the first evaluation scenario only. As a SOTA system, GT provides an external validation of the quality of MMT. Differently, MMT is evaluated in both scenarios to analyse the impact of in-domain data on translation quality.

---

⁸

[8] www.matecat.com
[9] Evaluations were carried out on February 5th, 2019.
[10] The statistics for MAGMATic, which was used as test set, are shown in Table 1.

Domain-adaptation		
	It	**En**
Sent.pairs	40,361	
Tokens	632,223	601,236
Vocabulary	55,458	48,126

Table 4: Size of the domain-adaptation data set: number of sentences, number of tokens (i.e. running words) and vocabulary (i.e. number of distinct word types).

4.3 Evaluation metrics

The MT systems were evaluated both in terms of overall performance and specifically targeting their ability to translate domain terminology.

The bigger picture of the quality achieved with the setup described so far is provided through an automatic evaluation in terms of BLEU score (Papineni et al., 2002).

The evaluation focused on terminology translation is based on the Term Hit Rate (THR) metric (Farajian et al., 2018). THR takes in a list of annotated terms in each reference sentence and looks for their occurrence in the MT output. Then it computes the proportion of terms in the reference that are correctly translated by the MT system. An upper bound of 1 match for each reference term is applied in order not to reward over-generated terms in the MT output.

Similarly to the approach adopted for inter-annotator agreement (see Sect. 3.4), two THR types are computed: *perfect THR* – where a match is scored only if the whole reference term appears in the MT output – and *partial THR*, where the overlap between the reference terms and the MT output is calculated at the level of shared tokens. In this case, function words are removed from the MW terms in the reference, so as to avoid false positives with other function words present in the MT output.

	BLEU ($\uparrow$)
GT	36.90
MMT-I	35.45
MMT-II	43.16

Table 5: BLEU scores for GT and for MMT in both scenarios.

4.4 Evaluation results

A general overview on the quality achieved by GT, MMT-I (first scenario) and MMT-II (second scenario) is provided in Table 5.

Perfect THR								
	GT			MMT-I			MMT-II		
	Overall	SWs	MWs	Overall	SWs	MWs	Overall	SWs	MWs
All	63.72	75.43	50.98	60.97	72.98	47.90	65.33	76.07	53.65
Disc	66.80	79.75	54.91	63.94	77.52	51.47	67.74	80.03	56.50
Edu	55.62	66.33	36.78	53.32	63.48	35.45	59.28	68.01	44.61
Equip	55.78	66.96	36.76	53.31	64.10	34.96	59.11	68.40	43.32
Sure	64.95	76.26	52.76	62.43	73.91	50.06	66.58	77.05	55.30
Poss	57.25	71.20	41.35	53.25	68.23	36.18	58.75	71.05	44.74

Table 6: Perfect THR for GT and the 2 MMT systems. In addition to the overall scores, figures for SWs and MWs are given separately. Results are provided *(i)* for the whole data set (All), *(ii)* split according to the domain category (Disc, Edu, Equip) and *(iii)* distinguishing between `sure` and `possible` terms.

The good results obtained by GT and MMT-I show that NMT can be helpful already in the first scenario, where only generic systems can be used. The huge performance increase of MMT-II (+7.71 wrt MMT-I and +6.26 wrt GT) is even more encouraging in the long-term perspective.

Focusing on the evaluation of terminology translation, perfect and partial THR scores were computed on MAGMATic for GT and the two MMT systems.

Table 6 presents results for Perfect THR. Since MAGMATic contains both SW and MW terms, the table gives the scores for each set separately in addition to the overall score. Also, to allow a more detailed analysis of the systems' behaviour on MAGMATic terms, results are provided by domain category (`disciplinary`, `education`, `equipment`) and in terms of the `sure`/`possible` distinction.

Considering the strict parameters used to calculate perfect THR, the results shown in Table 6 are quite satisfactory. Regarding domain categories, all systems in all scenarios perform far better on `disciplinary` terms. As for term length, SW terms are, as expected, easier to translate than MWs. The most challenging terms for all MT systems are MWs in the `education` and `equipment` categories.

Focusing on the first scenario, we see that GT and MMT have a similar behaviour, since the differences between the two systems (ranging between 2 and 4 THR points) are constant across all the different views of the data. Two exceptions are represented by the `education` and `education equipment` MW terms, for which differences are less marked (respectively 1.33 and 1.8 THR). This seems to indicate that MMT has fewer problems

Partial THR			
	GT	MMT-I	MMT-II
All	76.68	74.91	77.23
Disc	80.40	78.83	80.64
Edu	65.33	63.13	67.49
Equip	65.63	63.30	67.13
Sure	77.74	75.94	78.07
Poss	71.27	69.68	72.96

Table 7: Partial THR for GT and the 2 MMT systems. Only Overall scores are reported, since matches are computed at the token level. Results are provided *(i)* for the whole data set (All), *(ii)* by domain category (Disc, Edu, Equip) and *(iii)* for `sure` and `possible` terms.

translating the most difficult terms in the data set. At the same time, GT outperforms MMT-I by 5.17 THR in the `possible` MW category, showing that MMT-I probably struggles more than GT for words that might not be terms.

Comparing MMT results in the two scenarios sheds light on the specific contributions that in-domain data can bring to terminology translation. First of all, in the second scenario there is an increase of the overall performance on the whole data set (+4.36 THR points). The difference with respect to the first scenario is particularly evident for MW terms (+5.75), suggesting that domain adaptation did not only influence lexical choices, but also helped the system to place terms in the correct position. As a matter of fact, if we look at the partial THR results shown in Table 7, we see that the performance gap between the two systems is narrower. This means that the generic and the adapted MMT systems perform similarly in the generation of the SWs composing a MW, but adapted MMT is better at generating them in the correct order. For example, in one of the segments the annotated MW *classification of living beings* was correctly generated in the second scenario, while in the first one the system produced the MW *living classification*, which is a match only in the partial THR evaluation.

Finally, the biggest improvement can be found for `education` and `equipment` MW terms, which – as we have seen above – are the most challenging for the MT systems.

As a final observation holding for all systems in both THR evaluations, there is a clear drop in performance when progressing from the evaluation of `sure` terms to that of `possible` terms. The remarkably higher performance obtained on the most reliable terms in the data set highlights the importance of having good quality, flexible gold standards to evaluate translation of terminology.

5   Conclusion and further work

In this contribution we have presented MAG-MATic, a gold standard with manually annotated multi-domain terminology. We have described and analised the annotation process and the methods used to check the annotation reliability, and applied the gold standard to the evaluation of NMT in the institutional academic domain.

Given its large size, MAGMATic is able to cover 20 disciplinary domains with a considerable amount of terms each, as well as the education and education equipment domains. Both single-word and multi-word terms are included in this data set, and further distinguished between sure and possible terms. Thanks to these peculiarities, MAG-MATic can fill a gap in the field of MT evaluation, providing a valuable test set for insightful and sound quality assessments based on terminology translation. Besides fitting the purpose of evaluating terminology in an MT output, MAGMATic can also be applied to different use cases, e.g. bilingual terminology extraction from word-aligned bilingual corpora where one of the two languages is English, or domain identification in multi-domain English corpora.

The results obtained with adaptive MT on the translation of course catalogues are encouraging, especially taking into account that this is a first attempt to apply NMT to this scenario, and considering the scarcity of available bilingual data. We believe that further work in this field is therefore warranted. From the point of view of MT evalua-tion, a manual assessment in terms of fluency and adequacy of the outputs produced by MMT and GT could be carried out and its results compared to those described here. This could provide interesting insights into the relationship between correct/incorrect terminology translation and translation quality as perceived by humans. From the point of view of the application scenario, further analyses will be carried out within the second scenario in order to better understand the specific contribution of the in-domain data from each university to the other universities. Finally, in the long-term perspective, we will be able to collect more in-domain data to evaluate the corresponding performance trends of adaptive MT.

References

Arcan, Mihael, Marco Turchi, Sara Tonelli, and Paul Buitelaar. 2014a. Enhancing statistical machine translation with bilingual terminology in a CAT environment. In Al-Onaizan, Yaser and Michel Simard, editors, *Proceedings of AMTA 2014*, Vancouver, BC.

Artstein, Ron and Massimo Poesio. 2008. Inter-coder agreement for computational linguistics. *Computational Linguistics*, 34(4):555–596.

Astrakhantsev, Nikita A., Denis G. Fedorenko, and Denis Yu. Turdakov. 2015. Methods for automatic term recognition in domain-specific text collections: A survey. *Programming and Computer Software*, 41(6):336–349.

Bahdanau, Dzmitry, Kyunghyun Cho, and Yoshua Bengio. 2014. Neural machine translation by jointly learning to align and translate. *arXiv e-prints*, abs/1409.0473, September.

Bentivogli, Luisa, Arianna Bisazza, Mauro Cettolo, and Marcello Federico. 2016. Neural versus phrase-based machine translation quality: a case study. In *Proceedings of the 2016 Conference on Empirical Methods in Natural Language Processing*, pages 257–267. Association for Computational Linguistics.

Bentivogli, Luisa, Arianna Bisazza, Mauro Cettolo, and Marcello Federico. 2018. Neural versus phrase-based MT quality: An in-depth analysis on English-German and English-French. *Computer Speech & Language*, 49:52–70.

Bernier-Colborne, Gabriel and Patrick Drouin. 2014. Creating a test corpus for term extractors through term annotation. *Terminology. International Journal of Theoretical and Applied Issues in Specialized Communication*, 20(1):50–73.

Bertoldi, Nicola, Davide Caroselli, and Marcello Federico. 2018. The ModernMT project. In *Proceedings of the 21st Annual Conference of the European*

Association for Machine Translation (EAMT 2018), Alacant, Spain.

Castilho, Sheila, Joss Moorkens, Federico Gaspari, Rico Sennrich, Andy Way, and Panayota Georgakopoulou. 2018. Evaluating MT for massive open online courses. *Machine Translation*, August.

Depraetere, Heidi, Joachim Van den Bogaert, and Joeri Van de Walle. 2011. Bologna translation service: Online translation of course syllabi and study programmes in English. In Forcada, Mikel L., Heidi Depraetere, and Vincent Vandeghinste, editors, *Proceedings of the 15th Conference of the European Association for Machine Translation*, pages 29–34, Leuven, Belgium.

Dice, Lee Raymond. 1945. Measures of the amount of ecologic association between species. *Ecology*, 26(3):297–302, July.

Farajian, M. Amin, Nicola Bertoldi, Matteo Negri, Marco Turchi, and Marcello Federico. 2018. Evaluation of terminology translation in instance-based neural MT adaptation. In *Proceedings of the 21st Annual Conference of the European Association for Machine Translation*, Alacant, Spain.

Fernandez Costales, Alberto. 2012. The internationalization of institutional websites. In Pym, Anthony and David Orrego-Carmona, editors, *Translation Research Projects*, pages 51–60. Tarragona: Intercultural Studies Group.

Girardi, Christian, Luisa Bentivogli, Mohammad Amin Farajian, and Marcello Federico. 2014. MT-EQuAl: a toolkit for human assessment of machine translation output. In *Proceedings of COLING 2014, the 25th International Conference on Computational Linguistics: System Demonstrations*, pages 120–123, Dublin, Ireland, August. Dublin City University and Association for Computational Linguistics.

Jalili Sabet, Masoud, Matteo Negri, Marco Turchi, José G.C. de Souza, and Marcello Federico. 2016. TMop: a tool for unsupervised translation memory cleaning. In *Proceedings of ACL-2016 System Demonstrations*, pages 49–54.

Kim, J.-D., T. Ohta, Y. Tateisi, and J. Tsujii. 2003. GENIA corpusa semantically annotated corpus for biotextmining. *Bioinformatics*, 19(suppl_1):i180–i182, 07.

Landis, J. Richard and Gary G. Koch. 1977. The measurement of observer agreement for categorical data. *Biometrics*, 33(1).

Papineni, Kishore, Salim Roukos, Todd Ward, and Wei-Jing Zhu. 2002. BLEU: A method for automatic evaluation of machine translation. In *Proceedings of the 40th Annual Meeting on Association for Computational Linguistics*, ACL '02, pages 311–318, Stroudsburg, PA, USA. Association for Computational Linguistics.

Q. Zadeh, Behrang and Siegfried Handschuh. 2014. The ACL RD-TEC: A dataset for benchmarking terminology extraction and classification in computational linguistics. In *Proceedings of the 4th International Workshop on Computational Terminology (Computerm)*, pages 52–63, Dublin, Ireland, August. Association for Computational Linguistics and Dublin City University.

Scott, William A. 1955. Reliability of Content Analysis:The Case of Nominal Scale Coding. *Public Opinion Quarterly*, 19(3):321–325, 01.

Sutskever, Ilya, Oriol Vinyals, and Quoc V. Le. 2014. Sequence to sequence learning with neural networks. In *Proceedings of the 27th International Conference on Neural Information Processing Systems - Volume 2*, NIPS'14, pages 3104–3112, Cambridge, MA, USA. MIT Press.

Toral, Antonio and Víctor M. Sánchez-Cartagena. 2017. A multifaceted evaluation of neural versus phrase-based machine translation for 9 language directions. In *Proceedings of the 15th Conference of the European Chapter of the Association for Computational Linguistics, EACL 2017, Valencia, Spain, April 3-7, 2017, Volume 1: Long Papers*, pages 1063–1073.

Van Brussel, Laura, Arda Tezcan, and Lieve Macken. 2018. A fine-grained error analysis of NMT, PBMT and RBMT output for english-to-dutch. In Calzolari, Nicoletta, Khalid Choukri, Christopher Cieri, Thierry Declerck, Sara Goggi, Koiti Hasida, Hitoshi Isahara, Bente Maegaard, Joseph Mariani, Hélène Mazo, Asuncion Moreno, Jan Odijk, Stelios Piperidis, and Takenobu Tokunaga, editors, *Proceedings of the Eleventh International Conference on Language Resources and Evaluation*, pages 3799–3804. European Language Resources Association (ELRA).

Vaswani, Ashish, Noam Shazeer, Niki Parmar, Jakob Uszkoreit, Llion Jones, Aidan N Gomez, Ł ukasz Kaiser, and Illia Polosukhin. 2017. Attention is all you need. In Guyon, I., U. V. Luxburg, S. Bengio, H. Wallach, R. Fergus, S. Vishwanathan, and R. Garnett, editors, *Advances in Neural Information Processing Systems 30*, pages 5998–6008. Curran Associates, Inc.

Automatic error classification with multiple error labels

Maja Popović
ADAPT Centre
Dublin City University
Ireland
maja.popovic@adaptcentre.ie

David Vilar
Amazon
Germany
dvilar@amazon.com

Abstract

Although automatic classification of machine translation errors still cannot provide the same detailed granularity as manual error classification, it is an important task which enables estimation of translation errors and better understanding of the analyzed MT system, in a short time and on a large scale. State-of-the-art methods use hard decisions to assign single error labels to each word. This work presents first results of a new error classification method, which assigns multiple error labels to each word. We assign fractional counts for each label, which can be interpreted as a confidence for the label. Our method generates sensible multi-error suggestions, and improves the correlation between manual and automatic error distributions.

1 Introduction

Translations produced by machine translation (MT) systems have been evaluated mostly in terms of overall performance scores, either by manual evaluations (ALPAC, 1966; White et al., 1994; Graham et al., 2017; Federmann, 2018) or by automatic metrics (Papineni et al., 2002; Lavie and Denkowski, 2009; Snover et al., 2006; Popović, 2015; Wang et al., 2016). All these overall scores give an indication of the general performance of a given system, but they do not provide any additional information. Translation error analysis, both manual (Vilar et al., 2006; Farrús et al., 2010; Lommel et al.,

2014b) as well as automatic (Popović and Ney, 2011; Zeman et al., 2011), as a way to identify weaknesses of the systems and define priorities for their improvement, has received a fair amount of attention in the MT community. Although automatic error classification still cannot deal with fine-grained error taxonomies, it represents a valuable tool for fast and large scale translation error analysis. With the emergence of neural MT systems, first insights about the differences between the neural approach and the then state-of-the-art statistical phrase-based approach were obtained by using automatic error classification. Bentivogli et al. (2016) analyzed four MT systems for English into German by comparing different TER (Snover et al., 2006) scores and sub-scores, and Toral and Sánchez-Cartagena (2017) applied the WER-based approach proposed by Popović and Ney (2011) for a multilingual and multi-faceted evaluation of eighteen MT systems for nine translation directions including six languages from four different families.

So far, automatic error classification is based on hard decisions about the error class for a given word. Addicter (Zeman et al., 2011) uses a first-order Markov model for aligning reference words with hypothesis words, and Popović and Ney (2011) use WER alignments; both methods assign only one single error label for each word. However, the assumption that each word can be tagged with only one error category can be somewhat restrictive. Human annotators' feedback (Popović and Burchardt, 2011; Lommel et al., 2014a; Klubička et al., 2018) have pointed out that sometimes it is not completely clear what error category should be assigned to a word (e.g. it is difficult to differentiate a lexical error from a missing or extra word, or to decide which word

reference: in some places **rents will even rise**
hypothesis: in some places **even grow rents**

Possible ambiguties:

- which words should be tagged as reordering errors, "rents" or "even"?

- "rise"/"grow" can be reordering errors too, and lexical errors at the same time

- are "will", "rise" and "grow" lexical errors, or "will" and "rise" are missing words and "grow" is an extra word?

Figure 1: Examples of potentially ambiguous error labels both for human annotators as well as for automatic tools: the decision about lexical errors vs missing and extra words, and determining an exact span for reordering errors.

span should be tagged as a reordering issue), or it may be the case that a generated word should be assigned more than one error (e.g. a lexical and a reordering error). Examples of such cases can be seen in Figure 1.

In this work we propose to expand the automatic error classification approach by suggesting multiple error categories for each word. Additionally, with each error category we are able to assign a (fractional) count which intuitively can be interpreted as a confidence for each error category. Since, to the best of our knowledge, this represents the first attempt of multi-label automatic classification, we first explore what kind of multi-error suggestions are generated by our method. We then compare our results with manual error annotations and with the method based on a single WER alignment. As translation corpora with manual error analysis allowing multiple labels are not yet available, we evaluate our method by computing the correlation of the global distribution of errors with human assigned labels. We also try to gain insights about the behaviour of the system and find out that the system makes sensible multi-error suggestions.

2   Error classification method

As starting point for our method we take the approach proposed by Popović and Ney (2011) which is based on a combination of WER and PER statistics on different forms of the words (surface, base forms). WER is defined as (a normalized version of) the edit distance (Levenshtein,

1966), whereas PER is Position-independent word Error Rate which does not take the word order into account. The described method identifies actual words which contribute to WER as well as to two types of PER called "Reference PER" (RPER) and "Hypothesis PER" (HPER) corresponding to recall and precision. The dynamic programming (DP) algorithm for WER enables a simple and straightforward identification of each word which contributes to the edit distance. The WER operations are called "substitutions", "deletions" and "insertions". The PER metric is based on reference and hypothesis word counts without distinguishing which words are deletions, which insertions, and which are substitutions. Therefore two alternative PER-based measures which correspond to the recall and precision are introduced, RPER and HPER. The RPER errors are defined as the words in the reference which do not appear in the hypothesis, and the HPER errors are the words in the hypothesis which do not appear in the reference. Once the WER, RPER and HPER erors have been identified, the base forms for each word are used in order to distinguish the following five error classes:

- inflectional error ("infl"): a word which contributes to WER and PER, but its base form does not

- reordering error ("ord"): a word which contributes to WER but not to PER

- missing word ("miss"): a WER deletion which also contributes to RPER

- extra word ("ext"): a WER insertion which also contributes to HPER

- lexical error ("lex"): a WER substitution which also contributes to RPER/HPER

The edit distance is well defined as a value, and the alignment between the two strings being compared can be obtained as a by-product. However, there are several optimal alignments (or paths in the dynamic programming trellis) that produce the same distance, e.g. often a series of "insertion" and "deletion" operations can be reordered without affecting the resulting distance, or different words can be chosen as "substitution" operations. An example can be seen in Figure 2. How to choose among all the possible alternatives is normally implementation dependent (e.g. the first op-

let	us	see	an	example
_us_	_see_	see	an	example

— — — — — — — — — —

let	us	see		an	example
—	us	see	+see+	an	example

— — — — — — — — — —

let	us		see	an	example
—	us	+see+	see	an	example

Figure 2: Three possible alignments with edit distance 2 between the reference "let us see an example" and the hypothesis "us see see an example". Insertions are marked as +insertion+, deletions as — and substitutions are <u>underlined</u>.

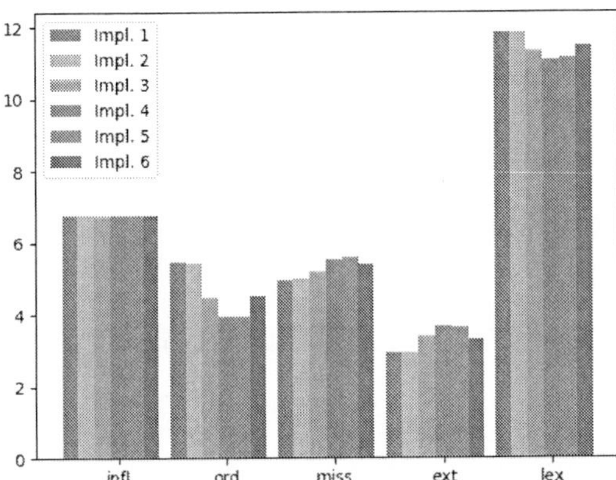

Figure 3: Distribution of error categories using different criteria for selecting the best WER alignments. The height of the bars corresponds to the percentage of each error (words classified as correct are not included), the different colors correspond to different implementations.

eration checked in the code) and does not have any linguistic motivation.

While this discussion may appear academic at first sight, it does have an important effect when these alignments are used for defining error categories. Figure 3 illustrates this effect, where we show 6 different strategies for defining WER alignments (based on different precedence of checking "insertion", "deletion" and "substitution" operations).

On the other hand, the fact that a word can be involved in different WER operations can give additional information to be used for error classification. In this work we take into account all optimal WER alignments and collect statistics of all possible edit operations for each word. We collect the alignment statistics (the counts of each operation for each word) using dynamic programming with memoization (using a Depth-First Search strategy). Further combination with PER counts is applied in the same way as in (Popović and Ney, 2011), but instead of combining it with one single WER operation, it is combined with each possible WER operation on the given word thus providing all possible error classes for this word.

All possible paths for minimal edit distance between the reference and the hypothesis from the example from Figure 2 are presented in Table 1. Minimal edit distance is 2, and it can be reached by three paths. The standard version of the error classification method described in (Popović and Ney, 2011) takes only one path into account, therefore each word in the reference and in the hypothesis is labelled with only one edit operation and thus with one error class. The method proposed in this work collects the edit operations from all paths in the following way:

- deletions are counted only for reference words

- insertions are counted only for hypothesis words

- for each reference word, label counts are collected from each cell in its column in the DP trellis

- for each hypothesis word, label counts are collected for each cell in its row in the DP trellis

In this way, in the example in Table 1 the hypothesis word "see" at the second position has one "substitution" label (from the cell aligned with the reference word "us") as well as one "x"[1] and one "insertion" (from the cell aligned with the reference word "see"). The reference word "see" has two labels "x" (one from the first hypothesis word "see" and one from the second one), however no "insertion" operations.

For each word, each edit operation together with associated PER counts defines an error category as described above. Fractional counts for each error class are obtained by dividing the count of the given error class with the total count of all encountered classes for this word. In our example, the first hypothesis word "see" has three error labels "x" (no edit operations, correct word), "sub" (substitution) and "ins" (insertion) and each of them is seen once. Thus, the total count for this word is 3, and probability for each class is $\frac{1}{3} = 0.33$.

---

[1] We denote with "x" the "match" operation, i.e. when the hypothesis and reference words are the same.

hyp↓	let	us	see	an	example
			ref→		
us	**1 sub** ↘ 2,3 del →	2, 3 x ↘			
see		**1 sub** ↘	2 x ↘ 3 ins ↓		
see			**1,3 x** ↘	2 ins ↓	
an				**1,2,3 x** ↘	
example					**1, 2,3 x** ↘

Table 1: Three possible paths in the dynamic programming trellis for minimal edit distance for the Example from Figure 2: path1 = "sub sub x x x", path2 = "del x x ins x x" and path3 = "del x ins x x x". Standard WER takes only one path (e.g. path1 in bold) into account.

When collecting statistics over a segment or a full corpus, in order to compute the error distributions these fractional counts are summed over all words. Thus, the total amount of errors can be a fractional number as well. Note that we can still normalise it by the total number of words in the segment/document to obtain a normalized error rate, as the fractional counts for each word sum up to 1.

Table 2 presents single and multiple error labels for the potentially ambiguous error categories from Figure 1. It can be seen that the multi-label method assigns multiple error cases to the words which can be ambiguous even for a human annotator.

3 Evaluation setup

We applied the new method as well as the single WER path method described in (Popović and Ney, 2011) to the publicly available test sets from the TERRA corpus (Fishel et al., 2012) and PE2RR corpus (Popović and Arčan, 2016) designed for evaluating automatic error classification. In addition to translation hypotheses and post-edits (PE2RR) or references (TERRA), manual error annotations are also available. The statistics of the test corpora are shown in Table 3.

The main differences between the two data sets are (i) post-edited MT hypotheses are available in PE2RR (and standard reference translations in TERRA), (ii) manual error annotation in PE2RR is based on correcting automatically assigned labels whereas in TERRA it is performed from scratch. All results are reported separately for each of the data sets.

4 Distribution of error labels

Our first experiment aims to explore the nature and frequency of the error label suggestions generated by the new method. The distributions of error labels in the form of relative frequencies are shown in Table 4 for both test sets.

Apart from some small variations, the main tendencies are the same for the two test sets. The majority of multiple labels are double labels, the most frequent ones being "lex+miss", "lex+ext" and "x+reord". They involve the single labels which are, as mentioned in the introduction, reported to be difficult to disambiguate, even for human annotators. Other types of double labels can make sense in certain circumstances but are significantly less frequent. Two types of triple labels are found, too, "x+lex+ext" and "x+lex+miss", but their frequency is also low.

Further analysis of the three most frequent double labels is shown in Table 5. The majority of "lex+miss" labels has the same fractional counts, namely 0.5. For the "lex+ext" label the equal counts are the most frequent in the PE2RR corpus, whereas in the TERRA corpus the majority of instances has higher fractional count for the "lex" category. For both multiple labels and in both corpora, there are much more higher fractional counts for the "lex" category than for "miss" or "ext". As for the "x+reord" label, almost two thirds have a higher count for reordering, one third has equal counts, whereas instances with higher counts for correct word are very rare.

reference	rents	will	even	rise
single labels	reord	lex	reord	lex
multiple labels	reord	lex+miss	x+reord	lex+miss
frac. counts	*1.00*	*0.50+0.50*	*0.25+0.75*	*0.67+0.33*
hypothesis	even	grow	rents	
single labels	reord	lex	reord	
multiple labels	x+reord	lex+ext	reord	
frac. counts	*0.33+0.67*	*0.75+0.25*	*1.00*	

Table 2: Example from Figure 1 with single error labels and with multiple error labels together with their fractional counts.

corpus	hyps	sents	words	langs
PE2RR	11	2896	40138	8
TERRA	7	436	6293	2

Table 3: Statistics of the used error annotated corpora: number of different translation hypotheses, number of sentences in all hypotheses, number of running words in all hypotheses, and number of different language pairs.

5 Comparison with manual error annotations

5.1 Pearson correlations

An automatic error classification method can be used to detect weak and strong points of individual translation systems, as well as to compare different translation systems. In order to estimate and compare the reliability of the error classification methods we compute the Pearson correlation with human annotations in two different ways:

- interClass
  For each translated segment, correlation with the manual annotation is calculated over all error classes.

- interHyp
  For each error class, correlation with manual annotation is calculated over all translation segments.

We compare two methods: single error labels (*single*) and our proposed multi-label method (*frac*). For each of the methods, the extracted error counts are compared with the error counts obtained by manual annotation. For computing error counts on the segment level, we just sum the (fractional) counts.

The correlation coefficients are presented in Table 6. The interClass correlation coefficients are very high for both methods on both corpora, with our proposed *frac* method having better correlation on the TERRA corpus. For the interHyp corre-

lations, there is no difference for inflectional errors between both test sets. Reordering (reord) and lexical (lex) errors as well as correct words (x) have similar correlations on PE2RR and improved correlations on TERRA, whereas the correlation for missing words is improved on both corpora. Correlation for extra words, however, increased on PE2RR data but decreased on TERRA data. Previous work (Popović and Burchardt, 2011) defined this error class as not reliable enough, so further and deeper analysis focused on this class would be a possible direction for future work.

It can be noted that the majority of improvements are achieved on TERRA data, where only standard reference translations are available, and no post-edited MT hypotheses. This scenario represents a more difficult task for automatic classification (as mentioned in Section 3), and it also represents a more realistic scenario – one reference translation can be used for large-scale evaluations involving many different MT systems, whereas producing a post-edited version for each MT system would be very time- and resource-consuming.

5.2 Analysis of differences

The most intuitive method for further analysis of differences between the *single* and *frac* approaches would be to calculate precision and recall for each error label. However standard precision and recall are not convenient metrics for evaluating our method since the manual annotations consist of only one label, so that adding multiple labels would be penalised by this metric (specifically by the precision term).

Thus, in order to better understand the differences between the *single* and *frac* methods, we conducted an ad-hoc analysis. For each word that was assigned more than one error category, we distinguish two cases:

Adding correct information The *single* label

	PE2RR		TERRA	
	label(s)	rel.freq.	label(s)	rel.freq.
single labels	x	71.2	x	43.5
	lex	7.7	lex	17.5
	infl	7.3	reord	7.4
	reord	3.1	infl	5.7
	miss	1.2	miss	1.5
	ext	0.6	ext	0.6
double labels	lex + miss	3.6	lex + miss	11.8
	lex + ext	2.9	lex + ext	6.5
	x + reord	2.1	x + reord	3.9
	x + lex	0.1	x + lex	0.8
	x + infl	0.03	x + miss	0.08
	x + miss	0.02	x + ext	0.08
	x + ext	0.01		
triple labels	x + lex + ext	0.06	x + lex + miss	0.4
	x + lex + miss	0.04	x + lex + ext	0.3

Table 4: Relative frequencies of multiple error labels for PE2RR and TERRA.

	frac counts	PE2RR %	TERRA %
lex + miss	0.50 + 0.50	62.4	52.3
	lex > miss	28.8	40.4
	lex < miss	8.8	7.3
lex + ext	0.50 + 0.50	59.9	42.7
	lex > ext	34.5	53.1
	lex < ext	5.6	4.2
x + reord	0.50 + 0.50	38.1	31.6
	x > reord	0.3	0.8
	x < reord	61.6	67.6

Table 5: Most frequent multiple error labels and the relation between their fractional counts.

was incorrect and the expanded method is able to add the correct label.

Adding noise The *single* label was already correct, therefore the additional labels generated by our method do not improve the system.

Statistics about these two categories are shown in Table 7. Improvements are dependent of the correct error category so no global conclusion can be drawn. The single label method tends to incorrectly label missing and extra words as lexical errors. In this case the additional error labels are helpful, whereas for the true "lex" category they are adding noise. In addition to that, the new method helps identifying correct words which the single method tags as reordering errors.

For both "lex+miss" and "lex+ext", about 15-40% instances are adding information, however even more instances are adding noise (25-60%). The most frequent case is when both manual and single label are "lex" (in which case no additional suggestions are needed), followed by the manual "ext" or "miss" tagged as "lex" (where additional "miss" or "ext" label can be helpful). The third frequent case is when the correct label is "miss" or "ext", and the least frequent case is helping to identify "lex" when it is labelled as "ext" or "miss".

The "x+reord" label mainly helps for correct words labelled as reordering error, especially for TERRA, where a number of superfluous errors are assigned by the automatic system. For PE2RR, this effect is much smaller, whereas introducing multiple label for already correctly labelled reordering errors is dominant.

corpus	method	interClass correlations	infl	reord	ext	lex	miss	x
PE2RR	*single*	.869	.772	.856	.664	.782	.809	.982
	frac	.869	.772	.852	.676	.781	.813	.982
TERRA	*single*	.891	.820	.586	.533	.502	.537	.537
	frac	.936	.820	.602	.520	.521	.610	.544

(header spanning: "interClass correlations" over one column; "interHyp correlations" over infl, reord, ext, lex, miss, x)

Table 6: Pearson correlations comparison between error classes (interClass) and between translation hypotheses (interHyp)

multiple labels	*single*	*man*	*frac* is adding	PE2RR %	TERRA %
lex+miss	miss	lex	inform.	11.4	7.5
	lex	miss	inform.	26.0	12.3
	lex	lex	noise	28.6	21.1
	miss	miss	noise	25.3	9.8
lex+ext	ext	lex	inform.	12.6	4.7
	lex	ext	inform.	19.6	8.1
	lex	lex	noise	39.2	21.1
	ext	ext	noise	18.2	4.7
x+order	reord	x	inform.	24.2	59.4
	x	reord	inform.	1.5	2.3
	x	x	noise	7.9	16.8
	reord	reord	noise	66.1	19.9

Table 7: Percentage of multiple labels which adds information (if *single* label is incorrect but one in the double label is) and those which do not.

6 Summary

In this paper we proposed an automatic error classification method for machine translation based on edit distance which assigns multiple error labels to each word and enables calculating error label probabilities. The main findings of our experiments are:

- The most frequent multiple error labels are "lex+miss" and "lex+ext", followed by "x+reord". These error categories have been reported by human annotators to be difficult to differentiate, thus our method seems to generate sensible multi-error suggestions and to model this effect correctly.

- The use of fractional counts increases the correlation of error distribution with human judgements, especially for the more difficult and more realistic TERRA test set. We explain this as a useful confidence-like measure for the labels, which correlates with the uncertainty on human labels.

The described work offers several possibilities for future work taking better advantage of the fractional counts. One issue we encountered when evaluating our method is that the available data sets for the evaluation of error classification methods have single labels. We tried to evaluate our approach assigning to each word the label with the highest fractional count, but this did not lead to an increase in accuracy (despite the better correlation with error distribution judgements). Given the fact that human annotators' feedback indicates a potential for assigning multiple labels, one interesting direction would be to generate new data sets supporting this labelling scheme and compute standard measures like precision and recall on this data.

Despite of not having ideal evaluation conditions, preliminary manual inspection of the assigned labels gives us confidence that the method will be useful and interesting for further research.

Acknowledgments

This research was supported by the ADAPT Centre for Digital Content Technology at Dublin City University, funded under the Science Foundation Ireland Research Centres Programme (Grant

13/RC/2106) and co-funded under the European Regional Development Fund.

References

ALPAC. 1966. Language and machines. Computers in translation and linguistics.

Bentivogli, Luisa, Arianna Bisazza, Mauro Cettolo, and Marcello Federico. 2016. Neural versus Phrase-Based Machine Translation Quality: a Case Study. In *Proceedings of the 2016 Conference on Empirical Methods in Natural Language Processing (EMNLP 2016)*, pages 257–267, Austin, Texas, November.

Farrús, Mireia, Marta Ruiz Costa-Jussà, José Bernardo Mariño, and José Adrián Rodríguez Fonollosa. 2010. Linguistic-based Evaluation Criteria to Identify Statistical Machine Translation Errors. In *Proceedings of the 14th Annual Conference of the European Association for Machine Translation (EAMT 2010)*, pages 167–173, Saint-Raphael, France, May.

Federmann, Christian. 2018. Appraise evaluation framework for machine translation. In *Proceedings of the 27th International Conference on Computational Linguistics (COLING 2018): System Demonstrations*, pages 86–88, Santa Fe, New Mexico, August.

Fishel, Mark, Ondřej Bojar, and Maja Popović. 2012. Terra: a Collection of Translation Error-Annotated Corpora. In *Proceedings of the Eighth International Conference on Language Resources and Evaluation (LREC 2012)*, pages 7–14, Istanbul, Turkey, May.

Graham, Yvette, Timothy Baldwin, Alistair Moffat, and Justin Zobel. 2017. Can machine translation systems be evaluated by the crowd alone. *Natural Language Engineering*, 23(1):3–30.

Klubička, Filip, Antonio Toral, and Víctor M. Sánchez-Cartagena. 2018. Quantitative fine-grained human evaluation of machine translation systems: a case study on English to Croatian. *Machine Translation*, 32(3):195–215.

Lavie, Alon and Michael J. Denkowski. 2009. The METEOR Metric for Automatic Evaluation of Machine Translation. *Machine Translation*, 23(2-3):105–115, September.

Levenshtein, Vladimir Iosifovich. 1966. Binary Codes Capable of Correcting Deletions, Insertions and Reversals. *Soviet Physics Doklady*, 10:707–710, February.

Lommel, Arle, Maja Popović, and Aljoscha Burchardt. 2014a. Assessing inter-annotator agreement for translation error annotation. In *Proceedings of the LREC Workshop on Automatic and Manual Metrics for Operational Translation Evaluation*, Reykjavik, Iceland, May.

Lommel, Arle Richard, Aljoscha Burchardt, and Hans Uszkoreit. 2014b. Multidimensional quality metrics (mqm): A framework for declaring and describing translation quality metrics. *Tradumàtica: tecnologies de la traducció*, pages 455–463, 12.

Papineni, Kishore, Salim Roukos, Todd Ward, and Wie-Jing Zhu. 2002. BLEU: a Method for Automatic Evaluation of Machine Translation. In *Proceedings of the 40th Annual Meeting of the Association for Computational Linguistics (ACL 2002)*, pages 311–318, Philadelphia, PA, July.

Popović, Maja and Mihael Arčan. 2016. PE2rr Corpus: Manual Error Annotation of Automatically Pre-annotated MT Post-edits. In *Proceedings of the 10th International Conference on Language Resources and Evaluation (LREC 2016)*, Portorož, Slovenia, May.

Popović, Maja and Aljoscha Burchardt. 2011. From human to automatic error classification for machine translation output. In *Proceedings of the 15th International Conference of the European Association for Machine Translation (EAMT 2011)*, Leuven, Belgium, May.

Popović, Maja and Hermann Ney. 2011. Towards automatic error analysis of machine translation output. *Computational Linguistics*, 37(4), December.

Popović, Maja. 2015. chrF: character n-gram F-score for automatic MT evaluation. In *Proceedings of the Tenth Workshop on Statistical Machine Translation (WMT 2015)*, pages 392–395, Lisbon, Portugal, September.

Snover, Matthew, Bonnie J. Dorr, Richard M. Schwartz, and Linnea Micciulla. 2006. A study of translation edit rate with targeted human annotation. In *In Proceedings of the 7th Conference of Association for Machine Translation in the Americas (AMTA 2006)*, pages 223–231, Cambridge, MA, August.

Toral, Antonio and Víctor Manuel Sánchez-Cartagena. 2017. A Multifaceted Evaluation of Neural versus Statistical Machine Translation for 9 Language Directions. In *Proceedings of the 15th Conference of the European Chapter of the Association for Computational Linguistics (EACL 2017)*, Valencia, Spain, April.

Vilar, David, Jia Xu, Luis Fernando D'haro, and Hermann Ney. 2006. Error analysis of statistical machine translation output. In *Proceedings of the 5th International Conference on Language Resources and Evaluation (LREC 2006)*, Genoa, Italy, May.

Wang, Weiyue, Jan-Thorsten Peter, Hendrik Rosendahl, and Hermann Ney. 2016. Character: Translation edit rate on character level. In *Proceedings of the 1st Conference on Machine Translation (WMT 2016)*, pages 505–510, Berlin, Germany, August. Association for Computational Linguistics.

White, John, Theresa OConnell, and Francis OMara. 1994. The ARPA MT evaluation methodologies: evolution, lessons, and future approaches. In *Proceedings of the 1994 Conference of Association for Machine Translation in the Americas (AMTA 1994)*, pages 193–205.

Zeman, Daniel, Mark Fishel, Jan Berka, and Ondrej Bojar. 2011. Addicter: What is wrong with my translations? *The Prague Bulletin of Mathematical Linguistics*, 96:79–88.

Interactive-Predictive Neural Machine Translation through Reinforcement and Imitation

Tsz Kin Lam[*] and **Shigehiko Schamoni**[†,*] and **Stefan Riezler**[†,*]
[*]Computational Linguistics & [†]IWR, Heidelberg University, Germany
{lam,schamoni,riezler}@cl.uni-heidelberg.de

Abstract

We propose an interactive-predictive neural machine translation framework for easier model personalization using reinforcement and imitation learning. During the interactive translation process, the user is asked for feedback on uncertain locations identified by the system. Responses are weak feedback in the form of "keep" and "delete" edits, and expert demonstrations in the form of "substitute" edits. Conditioning on the collected feedback, the system creates alternative translations via constrained beam search. In simulation experiments on two language pairs our systems get close to the performance of supervised training with much less human effort.

1 Introduction

Despite recent success reports on neural machine translation (NMT) reaching human parity (Wu et al., 2016; Hassan et al., 2018), professional use cases of NMT require model personalization where the NMT system is adapted to user feedback provided for suggested NMT outputs (Wuebker et al., 2018; Michel and Neubig, 2018). In this paper, we will focus on the paradigm of interactive-predictive machine translation (Foster et al., 1997; Barrachina et al., 2008) which has been shown to fit easily into the sequence-to-sequence model of NMT (Knowles and Koehn, 2016; Wuebker et al., 2016). The standard interactive-predictive protocol takes a human-corrected prefix as conditioning context in predicting a sentence completion,

which is again corrected or accepted by the human user. Recent work showed in simulation experiments that human effort can be reduced by asking humans for reward signals or validations of partial system outputs instead of for corrections (Lam et al., 2018; Domingo et al., 2017).

Our goal is to combine both feedback modes — corrections and rewards — by treating them as expert demonstrations and reward values in an interactive protocol that combines imitation learning (IL) (Ross et al., 2011) and reinforcement learning (RL) (Sutton and Barto, 2018), respectively, using only limited human edits. A further difference of our framework to standard interactive-predictive NMT is our use of an uncertainty criterion that reduces the amount of feedback requests to the tokens where the entropy of the policy distribution is highest. This idea has been used successfully before in Lam et al. (2018) and Peris and Casacuberta (2018) and connects our work to the area of active learning (Settles and Craven, 2008). Lastly, our framework differs from prior work by allowing model updates based on partial translations.

Our experiments show that weak feedback in form of keep/delete rewards on translation outputs yields consistent improvements of between 2.6 and 4.3 BLEU points over the pre-trained baseline. On one language pair, it even matches the improvements gained by forcing word substitutions from reference translations into the re-decoded output. Furthermore, both feedback scenarios considerably reduce human effort.

2 Related Work

Interactive-predictive translation goes back to early approaches for IBM-type (Foster et al., 1997; Foster et al., 2002) and phrase-based machine translation (Barrachina et al., 2008; Green et al.,

2014). Knowles and Koehn (2016) and Wuebker et al. (2016) presented neural interactive translation prediction — a translation scenario where translators interact with an NMT system by accepting or correcting subsequent target tokens suggested by the NMT system in an auto-complete style. However, in their work the system parameters are not updated based on the prefix. This idea is implemented in Turchi et al. (2017), Michel and Neubig (2018), Wuebker et al. (2018), Karimova et al. (2018), or Peris et al. (2017). In contrast to our work, these approaches use complete post-edited sentences to update their system, while we update our model based on partial translations. Furthermore, our approach employs techniques to reduce the number of interactions.

Our work is also closely related to approaches for interactive pre-post-editing (Marie and Max, 2015; Domingo et al., 2017). The core idea is to ask the translator to mark good segments and use these for a more informed re-decoding, while we integrate constraints derived from diverse human feedback to interactively improve decoding. Additionally, we try to reduce human effort by minimizing the number of feedback requests and by frequent model updates.

Several recent approaches to reinforcement learning from human feedback implement the idea of reinforcing/penalizing a targeted set of actions. Kreutzer et al. (2018) presented an approach were ratings from human users on full translations are used successfully for NMT domain adaptation. Simulations of NMT systems interacting with human feedback have been presented firstly by Kreutzer et al. (2017), Nguyen et al. (2017), or Bahdanau et al. (2017), who apply different policy gradient algorithms, William's REINFORCE (Williams, 1992) or advantage-actor-critic methods (Mnih et al., 2016), respectively. In this paper, we use REINFORCE update strategies for simulated bandit feedback on the sub-sentence level.

González-Rubio et al. (2011; 2012) apply active learning for interactive machine translation, where a user interactively finishes translations of a statistical MT system. Their active learning component decides which sentences to sample for translation and receive supervision for, and the MT system is updated on-line (Ortiz-Martínez et al., 2010). In our algorithm, the active learning component decides which prefixes to receive feedback for based on the entropy of the policy distribution.

3 Learning Interactive-Predictive NMT from Rewards and Demonstrations

As shown in Cheng et al. (2018), IL and RL can be viewed as a single algorithm that only differs in the choice of the oracle, based on objective functions that are defined as the expected value function with respect to the current model's policy π_n in case of RL, and as the expected value function with respect to an expert policy π^* in case of IL. Applied to NMT, both IL and RL are based on a Markov Decision Process where a deterministic sequence of states consisting of the source input and the history of the model's predictions (possibly incorporating expert's demonstrations) serves as conditioning context to predict the respective word, or "action" (Bahdanau et al., 2017).

We instantiate rewards and demonstrations to the feedback types in interactive-predictive translation as follows: In the first case, uncertain words predicted by the system receive a positive or negative reward based on "keep" or "delete" feedback respectively. In the second case, uncertain words can additionally be corrected based on an expert policy in the form of "substitute" feedback associated with a positive reward. This feedback is integrated in context of the model's own predictions by adding rules to constrained beam search decoding (Hokamp and Liu, 2017; Post and Vilar, 2018).[1]

3.1 Learning Objective

We formalize the objective of interactive-predictive NMT as maximizing the value function V of a parametrized policy π_θ, i.e., we seek to maximize the expected (future) reward obtainable from interactions of the NMT system with a human translator who, by editing translations, implicitly assigns rewards $R(\hat{\mathbf{y}})$ to system predictions $\hat{\mathbf{y}}$ given source sentences $\mathbf{x}$:

$$\max_\theta V_{\pi_\theta}(\hat{\mathbf{y}}; \mathbf{x}) = \max_\theta \mathbb{E}_{\hat{\mathbf{y}} \sim \pi_\theta(\cdot|\mathbf{x})}[R(\hat{\mathbf{y}})] \quad (1)$$

---

[1] We observe that the distinction between weak feedback and expert feedback is difficult to make in the "keep" feedback case: on the one hand, this type of feedback refers to an action generated by the system, and on the other hand, it can be seen as a form of expert demonstration. From this perspective, our first system is closer to RL while our second system is closer to IL. For brevity, we will refer to our models as "RL model" and "IL model", respectively.

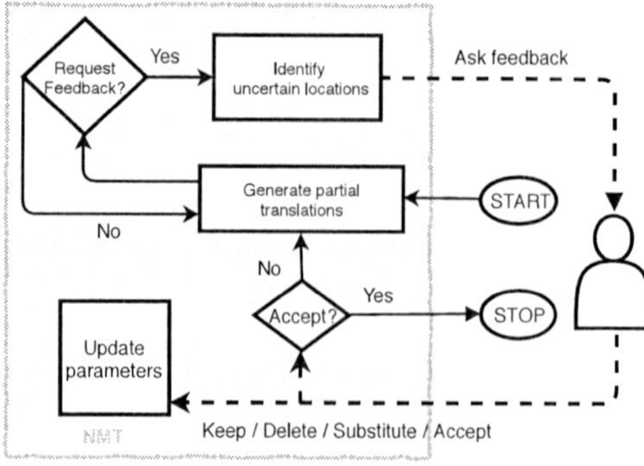

Figure 1: A graphical illustration of the interactive-predictive workflow of our system. Dotted arrows indicate interactions between human and system; solid arrows indicate procedures within the system

Following the policy gradient theorem (Sutton et al., 2000; Bahdanau et al., 2017), its derivative is

$$\nabla_\theta V_{\pi_\theta} = \mathbb{E}_{\hat{\mathbf{y}} \sim \pi_\theta(\cdot|\mathbf{x})} \sum_{t=1}^{T} \sum_{y \in \mathcal{V}} \nabla_\theta \pi_\theta(y|\mathbf{x}, \hat{\mathbf{y}}_{<t}) R(y)$$

(2)

where $\mathcal{V}$ is a vocabulary of target words. In our application, we ask for feedback on a single trajectory at each round of interactions. Similar to Williams (1992), we consider a 1-sample estimate to reduce the inner sum of actions at each time step to the single action $\hat{y}_t$ presented to the user.

Depending on the type of feedback, the instantaneous reward $R(\hat{y}_t)$ for a system translation $\hat{y}_t$ is set to the following values:

$$R(\hat{y}_t) = \begin{cases} 0.5 & \text{if SUBSTITUTE/KEEP,} \\ -0.1 & \text{if DELETE.} \end{cases}$$

(3)

In addition, we found that flooring rewards for tokens that do not receive explicit feedback to a small number[2] stabilizes the training and improves performance on the dev set.

4 Algorithms

In this section, we present the details of our interactive-predictive workflow and describe the system components of our implementation to reduce human effort while maintaining high quality model adaptation. In contrast to existing approaches where full sentences are corrected in each

round, our system stops decoding when the generated segment meets several (un)certainty criteria. Our system then identifies uncertain words within the generated segment and asks the user to edit these words. The idea is to direct the user to possible translation errors in the segment, and to collect feedback on these highly informative locations, effectively implementing an active learning strategy. The collected feedback is used twice: first, it is used to perform an on-line update of the system's parameters, and secondly, it is integrated as rules into constrained beam search. The full translation is reached after several interactive rounds when the translator finally accepts the translation. Figure 1 gives a graphical illustration of the workflow.

4.1 Measuring uncertainty

We define a measure of uncertainty based on the entropy at a time step t given a set of actions $\mathcal{V}$ (i.e., the target vocabulary) where

$$H_t = -\sum_{y \in \mathcal{V}} \pi_\theta(y|\mathbf{x}, \hat{\mathbf{y}}_{<t}) \log \pi_\theta(y|\mathbf{x}, \hat{\mathbf{y}}_{<t}).$$

The idea is that learning from edits on high entropy time steps is more helpful than learning from edits on low entropy time steps, because updating parameters based on uncertain regions better stabilizes the model over time. Furthermore, entropy is computationally simple and far less expensive than external reward estimators such as a quality estimation system, a critic, or a discriminator.

A single token at time step t is considered uncertain if the entropy exceeds a defined threshold ϵ, i.e., $H_t > \epsilon$. We use this criterion to identify informative locations of a partial translation on which the user is asked for feedback.

In case of partial translations, a sequence of length t is considered uncertain if the token at time t is uncertain as defined above, and there is an abrupt change in entropy at t, formally $\frac{H_t - H_{t-1}}{H_{t-1}} > \delta$. Both criteria are applied to determine the length of a partial translation shown to the user.

4.2 Interactive-predictive workflow

Algorithm 1 describes the workflow in our interactive-predictive machine translation scenario. In the first round, the system starts with initial model parameters θ_0, and an empty set of feedback rules ξ, and calls BEAM-SEARCH to first generate an unconstrained partial translation of length t by evaluating the uncertainty criteria in function

---

[2]We apply Gaussian noise with mean 0.1 and standard deviation of 0.05.

Algorithm 1: Interactive-predictive workflow for a single sentence using constrained beam search. *Input:* model parameters θ, source sentence $\mathbf{x}$, beam size k, learning rate α. *Output:* updated θ^*.

```
1  t_prefix ← 1, n ← 1
2  θ_0 ← θ, ξ ← ∅
3  SET-NMT-SOURCE (x)
4  repeat
5    ŷ_1:t ← BEAM-SEARCH (k, t_prefix, T_max, ξ)
6    for i ← 1 to t do
7      if UNCERTAIN-LOCATION (ŷ_1:t, i) then
          Collect feedback rules ξ_i
8      Get rewards for ξ_i ∈ {keep, delete, substitute}
          according to Eq. 3
9      θ_n ← θ_{n-1} + α∇_θ V (Eq. 2)
10     t_prefix ← |ŷ_1:t|, n ← n + 1
11 until ŷ_1:t accepted
```

Algorithm 2: Constrained beam search for uncertain partial translation. *Input:* beam size k, prefix length p, maximum length N, feedback rules ξ. *Output:* partial translation.

```
1  function BEAM-SEARCH (k, p, N, ξ)
2    beam ← DECODER-INIT (k)
3    for t ← 1 to N do
4      scores ← DECODER-STEP (beam)
5      beam ← KBEST (scores, k, ξ)
6      if LENGTH (beam[0]) > p and
         IS-UNCERTAIN (beam[0]) then break
7    return beam[0]
8  function KBEST (scores, k, ξ)
9    scores_c ← APPLY-CONSTRAINTS (scores, ξ)
10   beam ← ARGMAX_k (scores_c)
11   return beam
```

IS-UNCERTAIN. The algorithm then evaluates each token within the partial translation and asks for user feedback if the token is considered uncertain w.r.t. the function UNCERTAIN-LOCATION.

Feedback is captured in form of rules that correspond to edits on specific locations, e.g., KEEP token at position i, DELETE token at position i, or SUBSTITUTE token at position i with another token. After collecting the rewards for feedback rules ξ_i according to Equation 3, the model parameters are updated by taking a gradient step as defined in Equation 2.

The updated system then proceeds to the next round by calling BEAM-SEARCH again, this time with a set of feedback rules ξ to generate a constrained partial translation exceeding the previous length t_{prefix}. The uncertainty criterion of tokens is evaluated again and the user is asked for feedback on these tokens, extending the set of feedback rules ξ, which are used to update the system parameters and generate the next partial translation until the user is satisfied with the translation.

4.3 Constrained beam search

A central component is a modified beam search algorithm that takes positional constraints into account (Algorithm 2). The user constraints force the system to generate alternative translations and can thus be interpreted as an exploration strategy. An efficient alternative exploration strategy is multinomial sampling. In our interactive-predictive scenario, however, it is crucial that translations on locations without explicit user feedback are preserved, and this cannot be modeled easily with multinomial sampling. Beam search on the other hand ensures stable translations due to its deterministic nature, and the idea of constrained beam search provides the tools to improve the translation interactively. As a side effect, higher quality translations can be obtained by increasing the beam size at the cost of computational power.

After initializing k beams, the algorithms generates a partial translation by calling DECODER-STEP to retrieve the next token and score all hypotheses. The constraints (provided in the form of feedback rules) are applied in the function KBEST by filtering out all hypotheses that do not satisfy the constraints before the ARGMAX$_k$ operation selects the k highest scoring remaining hypotheses. The single best partial translation is shown to the user only if two conditions are met: (1) the length exceeds the length of the previous partial translation, and (2) the current partial translation is considered an uncertain sequence. In case one condition is not met, the system iteratively extends the partial translation up to a maximum hypothesis length.

5 Experiments

To demonstrate the effectiveness of our reinforcement and imitation strategies, we simulate the interactive-predictive workflow described in Section 4 in a domain adaptation setup. A human translator is simulated by comparing partial translations with corresponding gold translation to extend the set of feedback rules in every round. In the RL setting, the simulated human translator provides only weak feedback (KEEP and DELETE edits) on tokens generated by the system, while in the IL setting the simulated translator addition-

	Data	Training	train / dev / test	$\varnothing$ en-length
fr-en	EP	pre-training	1.3M / 2k / –	25.5
fr-en	NC	interactive	18.4k / 3k / 5k	22.8
de-en	EP	pre-training	1.7M / 2.7k / –	24.0
de-en	NC	interactive	18.9k / 1k / 2k	22.6

Table 1: Data used in pre- and interactive training for French-English (fr-en) and German-English (de-en).

ally injects expert feedback (SUBSTITUTE edit) by demonstrating how the system should act at a specific time step. In our simulation experiments, we focus on the uncertain tokens of the partial translation. An exact match between the uncertain token and the reference generates a KEEP edit, while differing tokens generate either a DELETE or SUBSTITUTE edit depending on the type of system. Tokens exceeding the sentence length of the reference always receive a DELETE feedback. We refer to the first system as KEEP+DELETE, and the second system as +SUBSTITUTE. While the system parameters are updated online after every such simulated interaction, system evaluation is done by a standard offline translation of an unseen test set.

5.1 Dataset

For pre-training, we use the Europarl (EP) corpus version 5 for the French-English system, and version 7 for German-English. For interactive training, we use the News Commentary (NC) 2006 corpus. Both corpora are publicly available on the WMT13's homepage.[3] All experiments are conducted on two language pairs, i.e., German-English (de-en) and French-English (fr-en). Data sets were tokenized and lowercased using MOSES preprocessing scripts (Koehn et al., 2007). We applied compound splitting on the German source sentences using CDEC's tool (Dyer et al., 2010). Our data sets for interactive training differ from the original News Commentary data splits as follows: (1) we sample a subset of the original training set to reduce the number of parallel sentences to 18,432 for French-English and 18,927 for German-English, and (2) we increase both validation and test set for French-English to 3,001 and 5,014 parallel sentences by moving data from the original training set excluding sentences that were sampled for training. Note that a training set size of less than 19,000 parallel sentences is very small even

in a domain adaptation setup. Table 1 summarizes the statistics of our datasets.

5.2 Model Architecture

We use a single uni-directional LSTM layer with global attention mechanism between encoder and decoder. The dimensionality of the LSTM hidden states and the word embeddings are 500. We build the vocabulary using the most frequent 50,000 words in each language.

The Adam optimizer (Kingma and Ba, 2014) is used in all training scenarios. In supervised training, we use a mini-batch size of 64 and an initial learning rate of 0.001. Starting from the 5th epoch, the rate is reduced by half in each epoch if the validation perplexity increases. In interactive training, we train for a single epoch and apply a constant learning rate of 10^{-5} with a mini-batch size of 1. In all experiments we set entropy parameters to $\epsilon = 1$, $\delta = 0.5$, and use a beam size of 5 during training. For testing, we apply greedy decoding. PyTorch code of our models is publicly available.[4]

5.3 Results and Discussion

On both language pairs, the optimal pre-trained NMT models are obtained in the 6th training epoch, forming the out-of-domain baseline. We also compare our RL/IL strategies with full post-edits simulated by supervised training on the in-domain News Commentary data, forming an in-domain upper bound. We repeated each experiment three times and report mean and standard deviation for both Character-F[5] (ChrF) (Popović, 2015) and corpus BLEU (Papineni et al., 2002).

In the French-English experiments, both our imitation and reinforcement strategies show improvements of more than 3 points in BLEU and 1 point in ChrF over the out-of-domain baseline. Both strategies achieve lower BLEU score than training on full post-edits, in particular, 0.94 points lower in the KEEP+DELETE setting, and 0.58 points lower in +SUBSTITUTE setting. However, both strategies achieve higher ChrF scores, i.e., 0.76 points for KEEP+DELETE and 0.28 points for +SUBSTITUTE. See upper half of Table 2 for a summary.

In the German-English experiments, there is a bigger performance gap between the KEEP+DELETE and the full post-edits system, concretely, 0.64 points in ChrF score and

---

[3] https://www.statmt.org/wmt13/

[4] https://github.com/heidelkin/IPNMT_RL_IL
[5] Using parameters $ngram = 6$ and $\beta = 2$.

Pair	System	ChrF (σ)	ΔChrF	BLEU (σ)	ΔBLEU	$\varnothing$ rounds	$\varnothing$ keep+delete / subst.
fr-en	Pre-trained	61.08	–	24.70	–	–	–
	Full Post Edits	61.96 (0.15)	+0.88	29.10 (0.09)	+4.40	–	–
	KEEP+DELETE	**62.72** (0.11)	+1.64	28.16 (0.14)	+3.46	3.2	13.7 / –
	+SUBSTITUTE	62.24 (0.08)	+1.16	**28.52** (0.10)	+3.82	3.3	1.8 / 5.6
de-en	Pre-trained	59.34	–	22.66	–	–	–
	Full Post Edits	60.24 (0.25)	+0.9	27.40 (0.22)	+4.74	–	–
	KEEP+DELETE	59.57 (0.19)	+0.23	25.28 (0.09)	+2.62	3.3	13.1 / –
	+SUBSTITUTE	**60.73** (0.14)	+1.39	**26.91** (0.1)	+4.25	3.3	1.8 / 5.9

Table 2: Character-F (ChrF), and BLEU test results on the French-English (fr-en) and German-English (de-en) translation tasks. Highest scores on RL and IL systems are printed in bold. The Δ columns indicate the score differences to the pre-trained baseline system. All scores are averaged over three runs with standard deviation σ in parentheses.

2.12 points in BLEU lower than full post-edits. However, the improvement over the pre-trained model amounts to 2.62 BLEU points and 0.25 points in ChrF score. Our +SUBSTITUTE system is comparable in performance to the full post-edits system, yielding a result that is 0.49 lower in BLEU but 0.49 points higher in ChrF. See lower half of Table 2 for the summary.

We also report average numbers of feedback rounds and rules per sentence in Table 2. We optimized the maximum number of allowed feedback rules per round on the dev set and use 9 (fr-en) and 7 (de-en) for the KEEP+DELETE and 3 for the +SUBSTITUTE systems. Even for the simpler model based on only weak feedback, the number of user clicks is between 13.7 and 13.1, which is well below the average target sentence length of 22.8 and 22.6. By allowing expert SUBSTITUTE feedback that actively generates better tokens in the next round the number of rules is reduced to 7.4 and 7.7. Our experiments indicate that focusing on uncertain locations can reduce human translation effort substantially.

Effect of on-line learning. We also examine the effect of on-line learning on average cumulative entropy of the model's policy distribution over time. Figure 2 visualizes the change of entropy during interactive training. At the beginning, the system is in regions of high entropy but quickly learns from human edits and the curves become smooth and monotonic. After this initial phase, the overall better performing French-English task shows consistently lower entropy than the German-English task, indicat-

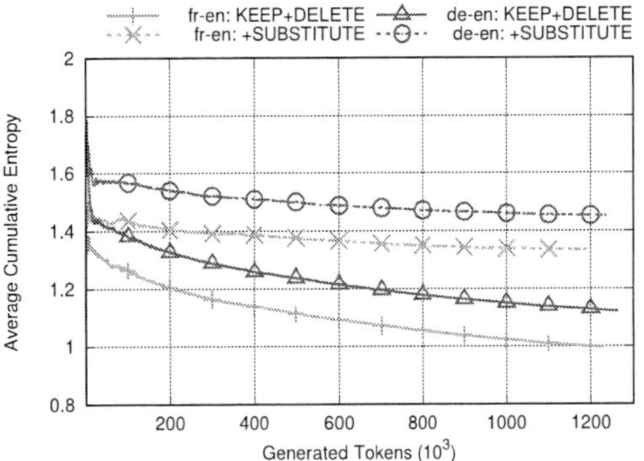

Figure 2: Average cumulative entropy of the model's policy distribution over time during simulated interactive learning. Plots are shown for the French-English (fr-en) and the German-English (de-en) task, and for the KEEP+DELETE and the +SUBSTITUTE system, respectively.

ing a connection between model's entropy and translation quality. However, the comparison between the KEEP+DELETE and the better performing +SUBSTITUTE systems shows the opposite trend and requires a different explanation. We conjecture that the +SUBSTITUTE system's expert demonstrations at uncertain locations help the system to find better translations, but such demonstrations also move the system to higher entropy regions, effectively implementing a useful exploration strategy. In contrast to this, the KEEP+DELETE system always stays in more certain regions by selecting another high probability token if the original token receives a DELETE feedback by the user.

Effect of beam size. The observations on model's entropy over time in the previous paragraph and the implementation details described in Section 4.3 show that our constrained beam search implements exploration in a user-controlled manner. We conjecture that beam size also influences the exploration and should have a different effect on different feedback strategies. We thus conduct additional experiments using beam sizes of 2, 5, 10 and 20 on all language pairs and the two systems. The results are summarized in Figure 3. In both KEEP+DELETE and +SUBSTITUTE systems, a beam size of 2 is sufficient to achieve substantial gains over the baselines in both language pairs. In case of the KEEP+DELETE system, increasing beam sizes only marginally influence the translation performance. In case of the +SUBSTITUTE system, there are considerable gains of almost 1 BLEU point and 1 Character-F point when increasing the beam size from 2 to 5. Here, the larger beam size enables the system to connect the expert demonstrations with better prefixes which helps the system to explore higher scoring trajectories. Increasing the beam size to 10 or 20 further improves performance but the gains are small.

Decoding Speed. The total runtime of each of our simulated interactive experiments is roughly 6 hours when simulated on a Nvidia P40, while training of the KEEP+DELETE system is slightly slower than of the +SUBSTITUTE system due to the higher number of feedback rules. Looking at the sentence level this means the total decoding time of our system for all partial translations of a single sentence is $6 \times 1h/(18{,}432 \times 3.3) = 0.361s$ for the French-English task, and even less for the German-English task. This estimate does not account for the time our system conducts validation tests or constructs simulated feedback, thus the actual average processing time is lower. Knowles and Koehn (2016) argue that beam search is usually too slow to be used for training in interactive live systems, however, recent hardware developments together with our strategy of partial decoding makes constrained beam search applicable even in training. As a side effect, corrections on early time steps reduce the problem of error propagation and thus improve both usability of the system and satisfaction of the translator.

Leveraging BPE or character-level NMT. Our current implementation of interactive-predictive

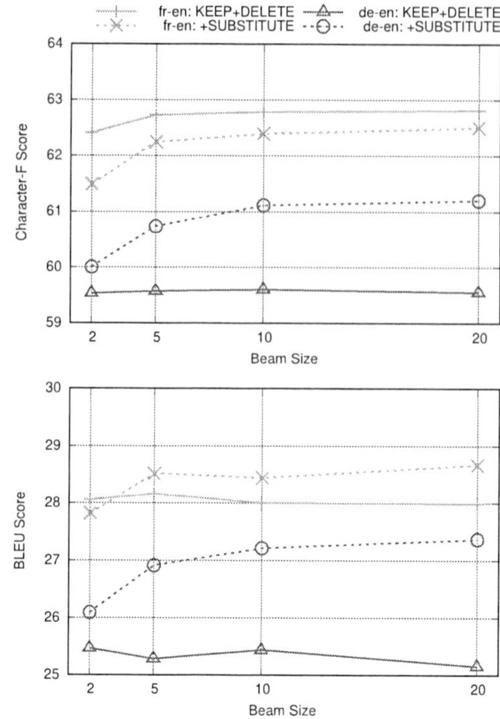

Figure 3: The two figures show the effect of different beam sizes on Character-F score (top) and BLEU score (bottom). We conduct experiments on French-English (fr-en) and German-English (de-en) and both systems (KEEP+DELETE and +SUBSTITUTE). All scores are averaged over two runs.

NMT uses a word-based translation approach and presents word units to users for feedback. An adaptation of our algorithm to sub-word or character level NMT is possible and requires to redistribute the reward associated to the word level to sub-word units or characters, and to maintain their location information in the constrained beam search. We leave this extension to future work.

5.4 Examples

Table 3 illustrates the translation workflow of our interactive-predictive protocol by listing four examples: the upper half shows example translations of the two systems for the German-English task, the lower half shows two examples of the systems for the French-English task.

The first example is taken from the KEEP+DELETE system, where our simulated user provides only KEEP and DELETE feedback on suggested locations. In interactive round 1 on the German-English task, the system stops after

	Source	der kern des problems ist nicht die gesamt‿menge des öls , sondern seine lage .
	Reference	the heart of the problem is not the overall quantity of oil , but its location .
German-English	**Round**	**Partial translation** → FEEDBACK
	1	the core$_2$ → DELETE(2)
	2	the *heart*$_2$ of the problem is not the total$_9$ → KEEP(2), → DELETE(9)
	3	the *heart* of the problem is not the *overall* amount$_{10}$ of oil , but its$_{15}$ → DELETE(10), → KEEP(15)
	4	the *heart* of the problem is not the *overall* volume$_{10}$ of oil , but *its* situation$_{16}$. → DELETE(10, 16)
	5	the *heart* of the problem is not the *overall supply* of oil , but *its position* . → accepted.

	Source	die süd‿koreaner ihrerseits verlassen sich darauf , dass china mit der nuklearen krise in nord‿korea fertig wird .
	Reference	as for the south koreans , they are counting on china to deal with the north korean nuclear crisis .
German-English	**Round**	**Partial translation** → FEEDBACK
	1	the$_1$ south koreans are$_4$ → SUBSTITUTE(1:as, 4:south)
	2	*as* for the$_3$ *south* koreans , china$_7$ → KEEP(3:the), → SUBSTITUTE(7:they)
	3	*as* for *the south* koreans , *they* are relying$_9$ on china to be$_{13}$ → SUBSTITUTE(9:counting, 13:deal)
	4	*as* for *the south* koreans , *they* are *counting* on china to *deal* with the nuclear crisis in north korea . → accepted.

	Source	il est dur d' aimer ou de respecter un peuple et de haïr son état .
	Reference	it is hard to love or respect a people and hate their state .
French-English	**Round**	**Partial translation** → FEEDBACK
	1	it is hard to love$_5$ → KEEP(5)
	2	it is hard to *love* or to$_7$ → DELETE(7)
	3	it is hard to *love* or comply$_7$ with a people and to$_{12}$ hate$_{13}$ their$_{14}$ → DELETE(7, 12, 13, 14)
	4	it is hard to *love* or respect$_7$ a$_8$ people and hatred$_{11}$.$_{12}$ → KEEP(7, 8), → DELETE(11, 12).
	5	it is hard to *love* or *respect a* people and *to hate their state* . → accepted.

	Source	un gouvernement qui n' est pas en mesure d' équilibrer ses propres finances ne peut pas apporter une stabilité macroéconomique .
	Reference	a government that cannot balance its own finances cannot be relied on to provide macroeconomic stability .
French-English	**Round**	**Partial translation** → FEEDBACK
	1	a government that is$_1$ → SUBSTITUTE(4:cannot)
	2	a government that *cannot* balance its own$_7$ → KEEP(7)
	3	a government that *cannot* balance its *own* finances cannot bring$_{10}$ about$_{11}$ macro-economic$_{12}$ stability . → SUBSTITUTE(10:be, 11:relied, 12:on)
	4	a government that *cannot* balance its *own* finances cannot *be relied on* to bring about macro-economic stability . → accepted.

Table 3: Interaction protocol illustrating translation progress of the two learning systems on the German-English task (upper half) and French-English (lower half). For each language pair, the first example illustrates interactions with the KEEP+DELETE system, while the second example shows interactions with the +SUBSTITUTE system. In each round, the user is asked for feedback on uncertain locations of the current partial translation. Tokens printed in blue with their position in subscript indicate uncertain locations. At the end of each round, the system is updated given the user's feedback (KEEP, DELETE, SUBSTITUTE). In the next round, it generates a constrained (partial) translation with respect to this feedback. Tokens generated based on feedback rules are printed in *italics*.

generating the uncertain partial translation "the core" and asks the user for feedback specifically on the term "core". The simulated user returns a DELETE feedback and the system is able to generate the more appropriate translation "heart of the problem" in round 2. In round 3, however, a weakness of the simulated feedback becomes apparent: our user gives a negative DELETE feedback on the token "amount" because the token differs from the given reference word "quantity", even though it is an appropriate translation for the German word "Menge" in this context. The system then generates "volume" in round 4 and "supply" in the final round 5, although both translations are worse than the initially proposed translation "amount". One explanation for this behavior is the way on-line updates are applied to the NMT system: while the constrained beam search implements feedback rules on token level, the on-line updates of the NMT system take place on the word embedding level. An update based on negative feedback actually forces the NMT system to avoid semantically similar words. In the above example, the negative feedback for "amount" downgrades the optimal translation "quantity" because of the semantic similarity of both words, and instead upgrades the more diverse translations "volume" and "supply". In our example, this strategy has an immediate negative impact on translation quality, but it also illustrates the positive exploration effect which is helpful in the long run.

The second example is taken from the +SUBSTI-TUTE system, where the simulated user additionally provides "substitute" feedback. In interactive round 1, the system generates the uncertain partial translation "the south koreans are" and identifies "the" and "are" as uncertain tokens. The user suggests to change "the" to "as", and "are" to "south" by providing SUBSTITUTE feedback. Again, a limitation of our simulation becomes apparent: our simulated substitutions are based on reference translations, but a real translator would not change the given partial translation to "as south korean south". Still, based on the two feedback rules and the on-line update, the NMT system is able to follow a better trajectory in round 2. We observe that SUBSTITUTE feedback is a very strong signal that supports the system to quickly get close to the translation our simulated user has in mind (which is the reference in our simulation).

The French-English task examples illustrate a noteworthy property of our algorithm: In round 3 of the KEEP+DELETE system, the simulated user provides DELETE feedback on the tokens "to hate their" only because they occur at different positions compared to the reference. However, the system is able to recover and re-generate the tokens at the correct position in round 5. A similar behav-

ior can be observed for the +SUBSTITUTE system in round 3, where the phrase "bring about macro-economic" is first substituted and then generated again in the final round 4.

6 Conclusion

In this work, we integrate interactive-predictive NMT with imitation learning and reinforcement learning. Our goal is to merge the human edit process with effort reduction and model learning into a single framework for easier model personalization. Our results indicate that on-line learning from edits on uncertain locations of partial translations can achieve performance comparable to using supervised learning on in-domain data but with substantially less human effort. In the future, we would like to investigate the limitations of entropy-based uncertainty measures, work on the efficiency of the training speed, and conduct field studies with human users.

Acknowledgments.

We would like to thank the anonymous reviewers for their feedback. The research reported in this paper was supported in part by the German research foundation (DFG) under grant RI-2221/4-1.

References

Bahdanau, Dzmitry, Philemon Brakel, Kelvin Xu, Anirudh Goyal, Ryan Lowe, Joelle Pineau, Aaron Courville, and Yoshua Bengio. 2017. An actor-critic algorithm for sequence prediction. In *Proceedings of the 5th International Conference on Learning Representations (ICLR)*, Toulon, France.

Barrachina, Sergio, Oliver Bender, Francisco Casacuberta, Jorge Civera, Elsa Cubel, Shahram Khadivi, Antonio Lagarda, Hermann Ney, Jesús Tomás, Enrique Vidal, and Juan-Miguel Vilar. 2008. Statistical approaches to computer-assisted translation. *Computational Linguistics*, 35(1):3–28.

Cheng, Ching-An, Xinyan Yan, Nolan Wagener, and Byron Boots. 2018. Fast policy learning through imitation and reinforcement. In *Uncertainty in Artificial Intelligence (UAI)*, Monterey, CA, USA.

Domingo, Miguel, Álvaro Peris, and Francisco Casacuberta. 2017. Segment-based interactive-predictive machine translation. *Machine Translation*, 31(4):163–185.

Dyer, Chris, Jonathan Weese, Hendra Setiawan, Adam Lopez, Ferhan Ture, Vladimir Eidelman, Juri Ganitkevitch, Phil Blunsom, and Philip Resnik. 2010. cdec: A decoder, alignment, and learning framework for finite-state and context-free translation models. In *Proceedings of the ACL 2010 System Demonstrations (ACL Demo)*, Uppsala, Sweden.

Foster, George, Pierre Isabelle, and Pierre Plamondon. 1997. Target-text mediated interactive machine translation. *Machine Translation*, 12(1-2):175–194.

Foster, George, Philippe Langlais, and Guy Lapalme. 2002. User-friendly text prediction for translators. In *Proceedings of the Conference on Empirical Methods in Natural Language Processing (EMNLP)*, Philadelphia, PA.

González-Rubio, Jesús, Daniel Ortiz-Martínez, and Francisco Casacuberta. 2011. An active learning scenario for interactive machine translation. In *Proceedings of the 13th International Conference on Multimodal Interfaces (ICMI)*, Barcelona, Spain.

González-Rubio, Jesús, Daniel Ortiz-Martínez, and Francisco Casacuberta. 2012. Active learning for interactive machine translation. In *Proceedings of the 13th Conference of the European Chapter of the Association for Computational Linguistics (EACL)*, Avignon, France.

Green, Spence, Sida I. Wang, Jason Chuang, Jeffrey Heer, Sebastian Schuster, and Christopher D. Manning. 2014. Human effort and machine learnability in computer aided translation. In *Proceedings of the 2014 Conference on Empirical Methods in Natural Language Processing (EMNLP)*, Doha, Qatar.

Hassan, Hany, Anthony Aue, Chang Chen, Vishal Chowdhary, Jonathan Clark, Christian Federmann, Xuedong Huang, Marcin Junczys-Dowmunt, William Lewis, Mu Li, Shujie Liu, Tie-Yan Liu, Renqian Luo, Arul Menezes, Tao Qin, Frank Seide, Xu Tan, Fei Tian, Lijun Wu, Shuangzhi Wu, Yingce Xia, Dongdong Zhang, Zhirui Zhang, and Ming Zhou. 2018. Achieving human parity on automatic chinese to english news translation. *CoRR*, abs/1803.05567.

Hokamp, Chris and Qun Liu. 2017. Lexically constrained decoding for sequence generation using grid beam search. In *ACL*, Vancouver, Canada.

Karimova, Sariya, Patrick Simianer, and Stefan Riezler. 2018. A user-study on online adaptation of neural machine translation to human post-edits. *Machine Translation*, 32(4):309–324.

Kingma, Diederik P and Jimmy Ba. 2014. Adam: A method for stochastic optimization. *CoRR*, abs/1412.6980.

Knowles, Rebecca and Philipp Koehn. 2016. Neural interactive translation prediction. In *North American component of the International Association for Machine Translation (AMTA)*, Austin, TX, USA.

Koehn, Philipp, Hieu Hoang, Alexandra Birch, Chris Callison-Burch, Marcello Federico, Nicola Bertoldi, Brooke Cowan, Wade Shen, Christine Moran,

Richard Zens, et al. 2007. Moses: Open source toolkit for statistical machine translation. In *Proceedings of the 45th Annual Meeting of the Association for Computational Linguistics Companion Volume Proceedings of the Demo and Poster Sessions (ACL Demo)*, Prague, Czech Republic.

Kreutzer, Julia, Artem Sokolov, and Stefan Riezler. 2017. Bandit structured prediction for neural sequence-to-sequence learning. In *Proceedings of the 55th Annual Meeting of the Association for Computational Linguistics (ACL)*, Vancouver, Canada.

Kreutzer, Julia, Joshua Uyheng, and Stefan Riezler. 2018. Reliability and learnability of human bandit feedback for sequence-to-sequence reinforcement learning. In *Proceedings of the 56th Annual Meeting of the Association for Computational Linguistics (ACL)*.

Lam, Tsz Kin, Julia Kreutzer, and Stefan Riezler. 2018. A reinforcement learning approach to interactive-predictive neural machine translation. In *Proceedings of the 21st Annual Conference of the European Association for Machine Translation (EAMT)*, Alicante, Spain.

Marie, Benjamin and Aurélien Max. 2015. Touch-based pre-post-editing of machine translation output. In *Proceedings of the Conference on Empirical Methods in Natural Language Processing (EMNLP)*, Lisbon, Portugal.

Michel, Paul and Graham Neubig. 2018. Extreme adaptation for personalized neural machine translation. In *Proceedings of the 56th Annual Meeting of the Association for Computational Linguistics (ACL)*, Melbourne, Australia.

Mnih, Volodymyr, Adrià Puigdomènech Badia, Mehdi Mirza, Alex Graves, Timothy P. Lillicrap, Tim Harley, David Silver, and Koray Kavukcuoglu. 2016. Asynchronous methods for deep reinforcement learning. In *Proceedings of the 33rd International Conference on Machine Learning (ICML)*, New York, NY.

Nguyen, Khanh, Hal Daumé, and Jordan Boyd-Graber. 2017. Reinforcement learning for bandit neural machine translation with simulated feedback. In *Proceedings of the Conference on Empirical Methods in Natural Language Processing (EMNLP)*, Copenhagen, Denmark.

Ortiz-Martínez, Daniel, Ismael García-Varea, and Francisco Casacuberta. 2010. Online learning for interactive statistical machine translation. In *Human Language Technologies: The 2010 Annual Conference of the North American Chapter of the Association for Computational Linguistics (NAACL-HLT)*, Los Angeles, CA.

Papineni, Kishore, Salim Roukos, Todd Ward, and Wei-Jing Zhu. 2002. Bleu: a method for automatic evaluation of machine translation. In *Proceedings of the*

40th Annual Meeting of the Association for Computational Linguistics (ACL), Philadelphia, PA, USA.

Peris, Álvaro and Francisco Casacuberta. 2018. Active learning for interactive neural machine translation of data streams. In *Proceedings of the 22nd Conference on Computational Natural Language Learning (CoNLL)*, Brussels, Belgium.

Peris, Álvaro, Luis Cebrián, and Francisco Casacuberta. 2017. Online learning for neural machine translation post-editing. *CoRR*, abs/1706.03196.

Popović, Maja. 2015. chrf: character n-gram f-score for automatic mt evaluation. In *Proceedings of the Tenth Workshop on Statistical Machine Translation*, Lisbon, Portugal.

Post, Matt and David Vilar. 2018. Fast lexically constrained decoding with dynamic beam allocation for neural machine translation. In *Proceedings of the 2018 Conference of the North American Chapter of the Association for Computational Linguistics: Human Language Technologies (NAACL-HLT)*, New Orleans, LA, USA.

Ross, Stéphane, Geoffrey J. Gordon, and J. Andrew Bagnell. 2011. A reduction of imitation learning and structured prediction to no-regret online learning. In *Proceedings of the fourteenth international conference on artificial intelligence and statistics (AISTATS)*, Fort Lauderdale, FL, USA.

Settles, Burr and Mark Craven. 2008. An analysis of active learning strategies for sequence labeling tasks. In *Proceedings of the Conference on Empirical Methods in Natural Language Processing (EMNLP)*, Honolulu, Hawaii.

Sutton, Richard S. and Andrew G. Barto. 2018. *Reinforcement Learning. An Introduction*. The MIT Press, second edition.

Sutton, Richard S, David A McAllester, Satinder P Singh, and Yishay Mansour. 2000. Policy gradient methods for reinforcement learning with function approximation. In *Advances in Neural Information Processings Systems (NIPS)*, Denver, CO, USA.

Turchi, Marco, Matteo Negri, M. Amin Farajian, and Marcello Federico. 2017. Continuous learning from human post-edits for neural machine translation. *The Prague Bulletin of Mathematical Linguistics (PBML)*, 108(1):233–244, jun.

Williams, Ronald J. 1992. Simple statistical gradient-following algorithms for connectionist reinforcement learning. *Machine Learning*, 8:229–256.

Wu, Yonghui, Mike Schuster, Zhifeng Chen, Quoc V. Le, Mohammad Norouzi, Wolfgang Macherey, Maxim Krikun, Yuan Cao, Qin Gao, Klaus Macherey, Jeff Klingner, Apurva Shah, Melvin Johnson, Xiaobing Liu, Lukasz Kaiser, Stephan Gouws, Yoshikiyo Kato, Taku Kudo, Hideto Kazawa, Keith Stevens, George Kurian, Nishant Patil, Wei Wang, Cliff Young, Jason Smith, Jason Riesa, Alex Rudnick, Oriol Vinyals, Greg Corrado, Macduff Hughes, and Jeffrey Dean. 2016. Google's neural machine translation system: Bridging the gap between human and machine translation. *CoRR*, abs/1609.08144.

Wuebker, Joern, Spence Green, John DeNero, Sasa Hasan, and Minh-Thang Luong. 2016. Models and inference for prefix-constrained machine translation. In *Proceedings of the 54th Annual Meeting of the Association for Computational Linguistics (ACL)*, Berlin, Germany.

Wuebker, Joern, Patrick Simianer, and John DeNero. 2018. Compact personalized models for neural machine translation. In *Proceedings of the 2018 Conference on Empirical Methods in Natural Language Processing (EMNLP)*, Brussels, Belgium.

An Intrinsic Nearest Neighbor Analysis
of Neural Machine Translation Architectures

Hamidreza Ghader
Informatics Institute,
University of Amsterdam,
The Netherlands
h.ghader@uva.nl

Christof Monz
Informatics Institute,
University of Amsterdam,
The Netherlands
c.monz@uva.nl

Abstract

Earlier approaches indirectly studied the information captured by the hidden states of recurrent and non-recurrent neural machine translation models by feeding them into different classifiers. In this paper, we look at the encoder hidden states of both transformer and recurrent machine translation models from the nearest neighbors perspective. We investigate to what extent the nearest neighbors share information with the underlying word embeddings as well as related WordNet entries. Additionally, we study the underlying syntactic structure of the nearest neighbors to shed light on the role of syntactic similarities in bringing the neighbors together. We compare transformer and recurrent models in a more intrinsic way in terms of capturing lexical semantics and syntactic structures, in contrast to extrinsic approaches used by previous works. In agreement with the extrinsic evaluations in the earlier works, our experimental results show that transformers are superior in capturing lexical semantics, but not necessarily better in capturing the underlying syntax. Additionally, we show that the backward recurrent layer in a recurrent model learns more about the semantics of words, whereas the forward recurrent layer encodes more context.

1 Introduction

Neural machine translation (NMT) has achieved state-of-the-art performance for many language pairs (Bahdanau et al., 2015; Luong et al., 2015b; Jean et al., 2015; Wu et al., 2016; Vaswani et al., 2017). Additionally, it is straightforward to train an NMT system in an end-to-end fashion. This has been made possible with an encoder-decoder architecture that encodes the source sentence into a distributed representation and then decodes this representation into a sentence in the target language. While earlier work has investigated what information is captured by the attention mechanism of an NMT system (Ghader and Monz, 2017), it is not exactly clear what linguistic information from the source sentence is encoded in the hidden distributed representation themselves. Recently, some attempts have been made to shed some light on the information that is being encoded in the intermediate distributed representations (Shi et al., 2016; Belinkov et al., 2017).

Feeding the hidden states of the encoder of different seq2seq systems, including multiple NMT systems, as the input to different classifiers, Shi et al. (2016) aim to show what syntactic information is encoded in the hidden states. They provide evidence that syntactic information such as the voice and tense of a sentence and the part-of-speech (POS) tags of words are being learned with reasonable accuracy. They also provide evidence that more complex syntactic information such as the parse tree of a sentence is also learned, but with lower accuracy.

Belinkov et al. (2017) follow the same approach as Shi et al. (2016) to conduct more analyses about how syntactic and morphological information are encoded in the hidden states of the encoder. They carry out experiments for POS tagging and morphological tagging. They study the effect of different word representations, different layers of the encoder and target languages on the accuracy of their classifiers to reveal the impact of these variables on the amount of the syntactic information captured in the hidden states.

Additionally, there are recent approaches that compare different state-of-the-art encoder-decoder architectures in terms of their capabilities to capture syntactic structures (Tran et al., 2018) and lexical semantics (Tang et al., 2018). These works also use some extrinsic tasks to do the comparison. Tran et al. (2018) use subject-verb agreement and logical inference tasks to compare recurrent models with transformers. On the other hand, Tang et al. (2018) use subject-verb agreement and word sense disambiguation for comparing those architectures in terms of capturing syntax and lexical semantics respectively. In addition to these tasks, Lakew et al. (2018) compare recurrent models with transformers on a multilingual machine translation task.

Despite the approaches discussed above, attempts to study the hidden states more intrinsically are still missing. For example, to the best of our knowledge, there is no work that studies the encoder hidden states from a nearest neighbor perspective to compare these distributed word representations with the underlying word embeddings. It seems intuitive to assume that the hidden state of the encoder corresponding to an input word conveys more contextual information compared to the embedding of the input word itself. But what type of information is captured and how does it differ from the word embeddings? Furthermore, how different is the information captured by different architectures, especially recurrent vs self-attention architectures which use entirely different approaches to capture context?

In this paper, we choose to investigate the hidden states from a nearest neighbors perspective and try to show the similarities and differences between the hidden states and the word embeddings. We collect statistics showing how much information from embeddings of the input words is preserved by the corresponding hidden states. We also try to shed some light on the information encoded in the hidden states that goes beyond what is transferred from the word embeddings. To this end, we analyze how much the nearest neighbors of words based on their hidden state representations are covered by direct relations in WordNet (Fellbaum, 1998; Miller, 1995). For our German side experiments, we use GermaNet (Hamp and Feld-

weg, 1997; Henrich and Hinrichs, 2010). From now on, we use *WordNet* to refer to either Word-Net or GermaNet.

This paper does not directly seek improvements to neural translation models, but to further our understanding of the inside behaviour of these models. It explains what information is learned in addition to what is already captured by embeddings. This paper makes the following contributions:

1. We provide interpretable representations of hidden states in NMT systems highlighting the differences between hidden state representations and word embeddings.

2. We compare transformer and recurrent models in a more intrinsic way in terms of capturing lexical semantics and syntactic structures.

3. We provide analyses of the behaviour of the hidden states for each direction layer and the concatenation of the states from the direction layers.

2 Datasets and Models

We conduct our analysis using recurrent and transformer machine translation models. Our recurrent model is a two-layer bidirectional recurrent model with Long Short-Term Memory (LSTM) units (Hochreiter and Schmidhuber, 1997) and global attention (Luong et al., 2015a). The encoder consists of a two-layer unidirectional forward and a two-layer unidirectional backward pass. The corresponding output representations from each direction are concatenated to form the encoder hidden state representation for each word. A concatenation and down-projection of the last states of the encoder is used to initialize the first state of the decoder. The decoder uses a two-layer unidirectional (forward) LSTM. We use no residual connection in our recurrent model as they have been shown to result in performance drop if used on the encoder side of recurrent model (Britz et al., 2017). Our transformer model is a 6-layer transformer with multi-headed attention of 8 heads (Vaswani et al., 2017). We choose these settings to obtain competitive models with the relevant core components from each architecture.

We train our models for two directions, namely English-German and German-English, both of which use the WMT15 parallel training data. We exclude 100k randomly chosen sentence pairs

English-German				
Model	test2014	test2015	test2016	test2017
Recurrent	24.65	26.75	30.53	25.51
Transformer	26.93	29.01	32.44	27.36

German-English				
Model	test2014	test2015	test2016	test2017
Recurrent	28.40	29.61	34.28	29.64
Transformer	30.15	30.92	35.99	31.80

Table 1: Performance of our experimental systems in BLEU on WMT (Bojar et al., 2017) German-English and English-German standard test sets.

which are used as our held-out data. Our recurrent system has hidden state dimensions of the size of 1,024 (512 for each direction) and is trained using a batch size of 64 sentences. The learning rate is set to 0.001 for the Adam optimizer (Kingma and Ba, 2015) with a maximum gradient norm of 5. A dropout rate of 0.3 has been used to avoid over-fitting. Our transformer model has hidden state dimensions of 512 and a batch size of 4096 tokens and uses layer normalization (Vaswani et al., 2017). A learning rate of 2 changed under warm-up strategy with 8000 warm-up steps is used for Adam optimizer with $\beta_1 = 0.9$, $\beta_2 = 0.998$ and $\epsilon = 10^{-9}$ (Vaswani et al., 2017). The dropout rate is set to 0.1, and no gradient clipping is used. The word embedding size of both models is 512. We apply Byte-Pair Encoding (BPE) (Sennrich et al., 2016) with 32K merge operation.

We train our models until convergence and then use the trained models to translate 100K sentences from a held-out dataset and log the hidden states for later use in our analyses. The 100K held-out data is randomly chosen from the WMT15 parallel training data. The remaining of the WMT15 parallel training data is used as our training data.

Table 1 summarizes the performance of our experimental models in BLEU (Papineni et al., 2002) on different standard test sets. This is to make sure that the models are trustable.

3 Nearest Neighbors Analysis

Following earlier work on word embeddings (Mikolov et al., 2013; Pelevina et al., 2016), we choose to look into the nearest neighbors of the hidden state representations to learn more about the information encoded in them. We treat each hidden state as the representation of the corresponding input token. This way, each occurrence of a word has its own representation. Based on this representation, we compute the list of n nearest neighbors of each word occurrence. We set n

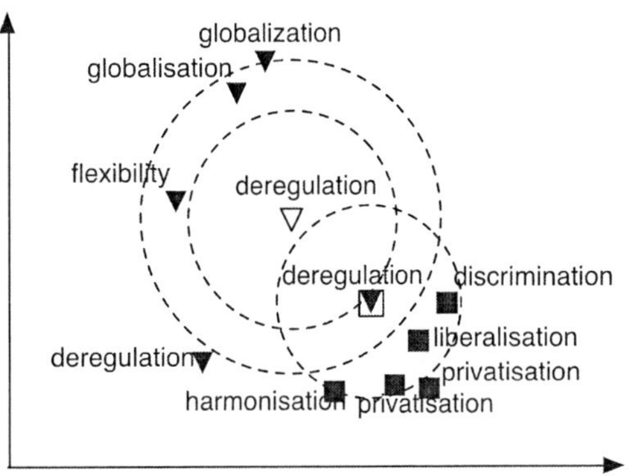

Figure 1: An example of 5 nearest neighbors of two different occurrences of the word "deregulation". Triangles are the nearest neighbors of "deregulation" shown with the empty triangle. Squares are the nearest neighbors of "deregulation" shown with the empty square.

equal to 10 in our experiments. Cosine similarity is used as the distance measure.

In the case of our recurrent neural model, we use the concatenation of the corresponding output representations of our two-layer forward and two-layer backward passes as the hidden states of interest for our main experiments. We also use the output representations of the forward and the backward passes for our direction-wise experiments. In the case of our transformer model, we use the corresponding output of the top layer of the encoder for each word as the hidden state representation of the word.

Figure 1 shows an example of 5 nearest neighbors for two different occurrences of the word "deregulation". Each item in this figure is a specific word occurrence, but we have removed occurrence information for the sake of simplicity.

3.1 Hidden States vs Embeddings

Here, we count how many of the words in the nearest neighbors lists of hidden states are covered by the nearest neighbors list based on the corresponding word embeddings. Just like the hidden states, the word embeddings used for computing the nearest neighbors are also from the same system and the same trained model for each experiment. The nearest neighbors of the word embeddings are also computed using cosine similarity. It should be noted that we generate the nearest neighbors lists for the embeddings and the hidden states separately and never compute cosine similarity between word embeddings and the hidden state representations.

Coverage is formally computed as follows:

$$cp^{H,E}_{w_{i,j}} = \frac{\left|C^{H,E}_{w_{i,j}}\right|}{\left|N^{H}_{w_{i,j}}\right|} \qquad (1)$$

where

$$C^{H,E}_{w_{i,j}} = N^{H}_{w_{i,j}} \cap N^{E}_{w} \qquad (2)$$

and $N^{H}_{w_{i,j}}$ is the set of the n nearest neighbors of word w based on hidden state representations. Since there is a different hidden state for each occurrence of a word, we use i as the index of the sentence of occurrence and j as the index of the word in the sentence. Similarly, N^{E}_{w} is the set of the n nearest neighbors of word w, but based on the embeddings.

Word embeddings tend to capture the dominant sense of a word, even in the presence of significant support for other senses in the training corpus (Pelevina et al., 2016). Additionally, it is reasonable to assume that a hidden state corresponding to a word occurrence captures more of the current sense of the word. Comparing the lists can provide useful insights as to which hidden state-based neighbours are not strongly related to the corresponding word embedding. Furthermore, it shows in what cases the dominant information encoded in the hidden states comes from the corresponding word embedding and to what extent other information has been encoded in the hidden state.

3.2   WordNet Coverage

In addition, we also compute the coverage of the list of the nearest neighbors of hidden states with the directly related words from WordNet. This can shed further light on the capability of hidden states in terms of learning the sense of the word in the current context. Additionally, it could play the role of an intrinsic measure to compare different architectures in their ability to learn lexical semantics. To this end, we check how many words from the nearest neighbors list of a word, based on hidden

states, are in the list of related words of the word in WordNet. More formally, we define R_{w} to be the union of the sets of synonyms, antonyms, hyponyms and hypernyms of word w in WordNet:

$$cp^{H,W}_{w_{i,j}} = \frac{\left|C^{H,W}_{w_{i,j}}\right|}{\left|N^{H}_{w_{i,j}}\right|} \qquad (3)$$

where

$$C^{H,W}_{w_{i,j}} = N^{H}_{w_{i,j}} \cap R_{w} \qquad (4)$$

and $N^{H}_{w_{i,j}}$ is the set of the n nearest neighbors of word w based on hidden state representations.

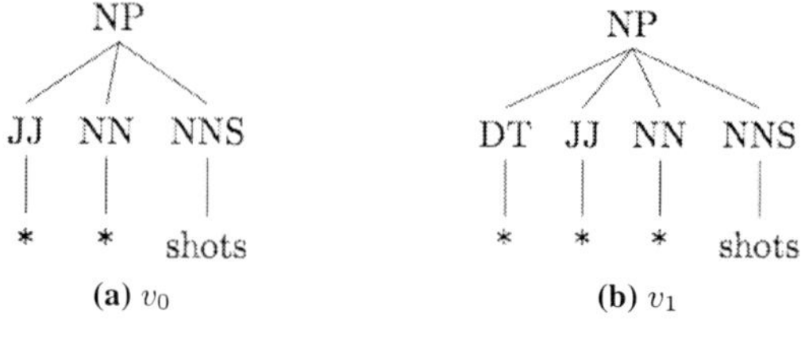

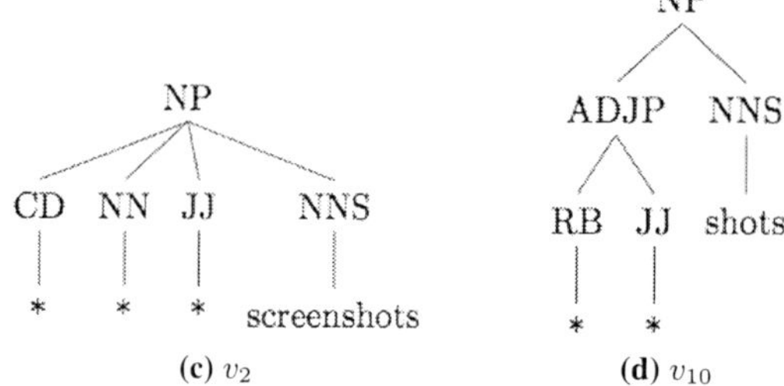

Figure 2: The figure shows the corresponding word and constituent subtree of query hidden state (v_0) and the corresponding word and subtree of the first (v_1) and the second (v_2) and the last (v_{10}) nearest neighbors of it.

3.3   Syntactic Similarity

Recent extrinsic comparisons of recurrent and non-recurrent architectures on learning syntax (Tran et al., 2018; Tang et al., 2018) also motivate a more intrinsic comparison. To this end, we also study the nearest neighbors of hidden states in terms of syntactic similarities. For this purpose, we use the subtree rooting in the smallest phrase constituent above each word, following Shi et al. (2016). This way, we will have a corresponding parse tree for each word occurrence in our corpus. We parse our corpus using the Stanford constituent parser (Zhu et al., 2013). We POS tag and parse our corpus prior to applying BPE segmentation. Then, after applying BPE, we use the same POS tag and the

Model	POS	English-German	σ^2	German-English	σ^2
	All POS	18%	4	24%	7
	VERB	29%	5	31%	5
Recurrent	NOUN	14%	3	19%	8
	ADJ	19%	3	31%	7
	ADV	36%	5	48%	2
	All POS	37%	14	33%	10
	VERB	39%	8	36%	7
Transformer	NOUN	38%	16	31%	14
	ADJ	32%	11	36%	9
	ADV	33%	12	38%	3

Table 2: Percentage of the nearest neighbors of hidden states covered by the list of the nearest neighbors of embeddings.

same subtree of a word for its BPE segments, following Sennrich and Haddow (2016).

To measure the syntactic similarity between a hidden state and its nearest neighbors, we use PARSEVAL standard metric (Sekine and Collins, 1997) as the similarity metric between the corresponding trees. PARSEVAL computes precision and recall by counting the correct constituents in a parse tree with respect to a gold tree and divide the count with the number of constituent in the candidate parse tree and the gold tree, respectively.

Figure 2a shows the corresponding word and subtree of a hidden state of interest, and the rest in Figure 2 shows the corresponding words and subtrees of its three neighbours. The leaves are substituted with dummy "*" labels to show that they do not influence the computed tree similarities. We compute the similarity score between the corresponding tree of each word and the corresponding trees of its nearest nighbors. For example, in Figure 2 we compute the similarity score between the tree in Figure 2a and each of the other trees.

3.4 Concentration of Nearest Neighbors

Each hidden state with its nearest neighbors behaves like a cluster centered around the corresponding word occurrence of the hidden state, whereby the neighboring words give a clearer indication of the captured information in the hidden state. However, this evidence is more clearly observed in some cases rather than others.

The stronger the similarities that bring the neighbors close to a hidden state, the more focused the neighbors around the hidden state are. Bearing this in mind, we choose to study the relation between the concentration of the neighbors and the information encoded in the hidden states.

To make it simple but effective, we estimate the population variance of the neighbors' distance from a hidden state as the measure of the con-centration of its neighbors. More formally, this is computed as follows:

$$v_{w_{i,j}} = \frac{1}{n} \sum_{k=1}^{n} (1 - x_{k,w_{i,j}})^2 \qquad (5)$$

Here n is the number of neighbors and $x_{k,w_{i,j}}$ is the cosine similarity score of the kth neighbor of word w occurring as the jth token of the ith sentence.

4 Empirical Analyses

We train our systems for English-German and German-English and use our trained model to translate a held-out data of 100K sentences. During translation, we log the hidden state representations together with the corresponding source tokens, their sentence and token indices.

We use the logged hidden states to compute the nearest neighbors of the tokens with frequency of 10 to 2000 in our held-out data. We compute cosine similarity to find the nearest neighbors.

In addition to hidden states, we also log the word embeddings from the same systems and the same trained model. Similar to hidden states, we also use embedding representations to compute the nearest neighbors of words. We have to note that in the case of embedding representations we have one nearest neighbor list for each word whereas for hidden states there is one list for each occurrence of a word.

4.1 Embedding Nearest Neighbors Coverage

As a first experiment, we measure how many of the nearest neighbors based on the embedding representation would still remain the nearest neighbor of the corresponding hidden state, as described in Section 3.1, above.

Table 2 shows statistics of the coverage by the nearest neighbors based on embeddings in general and based on selected source POS tags for each

Model	POS	English-German	σ^2	German-English	σ^2
	All POS	24%	6	51%	12
	VERB	49%	9	48%	10
Recurrent	NOUN	19%	3	28%	8
	ADJ	15%	2	60%	12
	ADV	24%	4	23%	1
	All POS	67%	16	74%	10
	VERB	77%	9	70%	9
Transformer	NOUN	65%	18	63%	13
	ADJ	66%	14	81%	9
	ADV	74%	10	35%	5

Table 3: Percentage of the nearest neighbors of hidden states covered by the list of the directly related words to the corresponding word of the hidden states in WordNet.

of our models. To carry out an analysis based on POS tags, we tagged our training data using the Stanford POS tagger (Toutanova et al., 2003). We convert the POS tags to the universal POS tags and report only for POS tags available in WordNet. We use the same POS tag of a word for its BPE segments, as described in the Section 3.3.

The first row of Table 2 shows that only 18% and 24% of the information encoded in the hidden states respectively for English and German is already captured by the word embeddings, in case of our recurrent model. Interestingly, in all cases except ADV, the similarity between the hidden states and the embeddings for the transformer model are much higher, and the increase for nouns is much higher than for the rest. This may be a product of the existence of no recurrence in case of transformer which results in a simpler path from each embedding to the corresponding hidden state. We hypothesize that this means that the recurrent model uses the capacity of its hidden states to encode some other information that is encoded to a lesser extent in the hidden states of the transformer.

4.2 WordNet Coverage

Having observed that a large portion of nearest neighbors of the hidden states are still not covered by the nearest neighbors of the corresponding embeddings, we look for other sources of similarity that causes the neighbors to appear in the list. As the next step, we check to see how many of the neighbors are covered by directly related words of the corresponding word in WordNet.

This does not yield subsets of the nearest neighbors that are fully disjoint with the subset covered by the nearest neighbors from the embedding list. However, it still shows whether this source of similarity is fully covered by the embeddings or whether the hidden states capture information from this source that the embeddings miss.

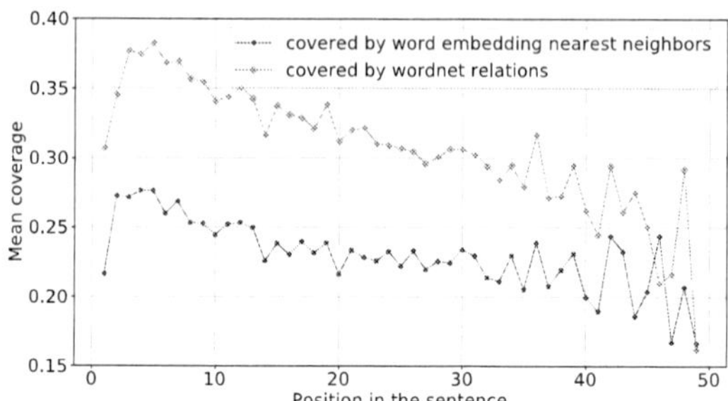

Figure 3: The mean coverage per position of the nearest neighbors of hidden states of the recurrent model; (i) by the nearest neighbors of the embedding of the corresponding word (ii) by WordNet related words of the corresponding word of the hidden state.

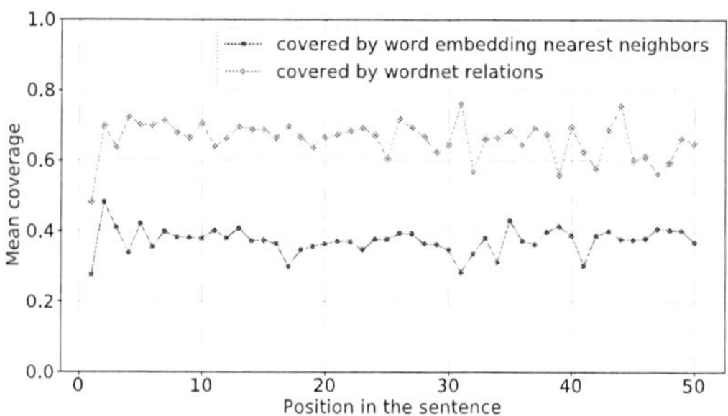

Figure 4: The mean coverage per position of the nearest neighbors of hidden states of the transformer model; (i) by the nearest neighbors of the embedding of the corresponding word (ii) by WordNet related words of the corresponding word of the hidden state.

Table 3 shows the general and the POS-based coverage for our English-German and German-English systems. The transformer model again has the lead by a large margin. The jump for nouns is again the highest, as can be seen in Table 2. This basically means that more words from the WordNet relations of the word of interest are present in the hidden state nearest neighbors of the word. A simple reason for this could be that the hidden states from transformer capture more word semantic than hidden states of the recurrent model. Or

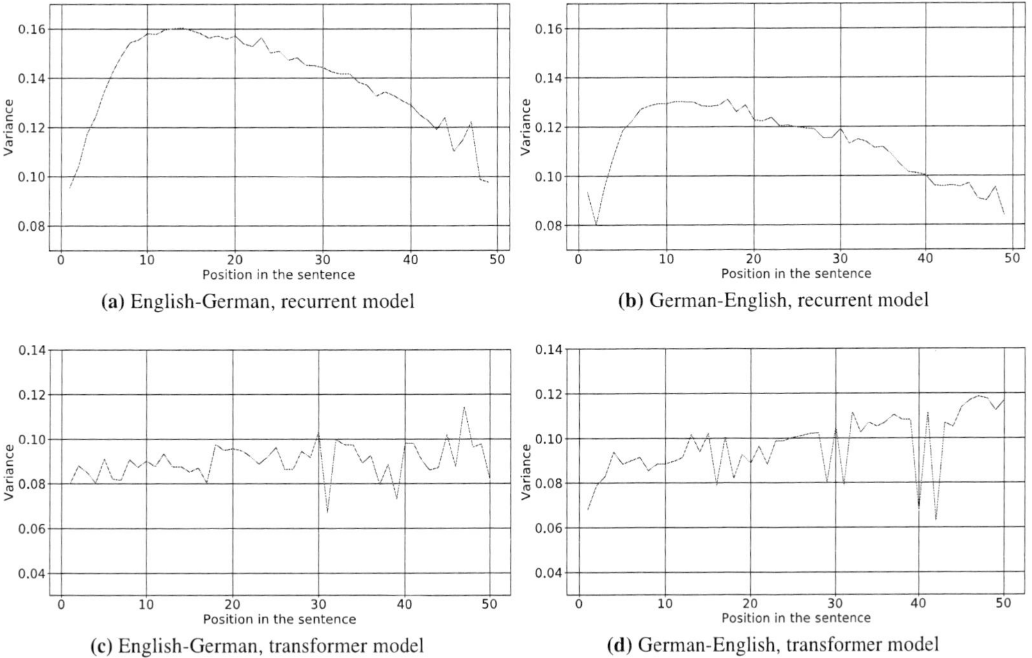

Figure 5: The average variance of cosine distance scores of the nearest neighbors of words per positions.

in other words, the hidden states from the recurrent model capture some additional information that brings different words than WordNet relations of the word of interest to its neighborhood.

To investigate whether recurrency has any direct effect on this, we compute the mean coverage by direct relations in WordNet per position. Similarly, we also compute the mean coverage by embedding neighbors per position. More formally, we write:

$$acp_j^{H,W} = \frac{\sum_{i=1}^m (cp_{w_{i,j}}^{H,W})}{\left|S_{l(s)\geq j}\right|} \tag{6}$$

and

$$acp_j^{H,E} = \frac{\sum_{i=1}^m (cp_{w_{i,j}}^{H,E})}{\left|S_{l(s)\geq j}\right|} \tag{7}$$

respectively for the mean coverage by WordNet direct relations per position and the mean coverage by embedding neighbors per position.

Here $cp_{w_{i,j}}^{H,W}$ and $cp_{w_{i,j}}^{H,E}$ are the values computed in Equation 3 and 1, respectively. The function $l(s)$ returns the length of sentence s and $S_{l(s)\geq j}$ is the set of sentences that are longer than or equal to j.

Figure 3 shows that the mean coverage in both embedding and WordNet cases is first increasing by getting farther from the left border of a sentence, but it starts to decrease from position 5 on-

wards, in case of the recurrent model. This is surprising to see the drop in the coverages, taking into account that the model is a bidirectional recurrent model. However, this may be a reflection of the fact that the longer a sentence, the less the hidden states from the recurrent model are encoding information about the corresponding word.

Figure 4 shows the same mean coverage for the case of hidden states from the transformer model. No decrease in the coverage per position in the case of transformer, confirms our hypothesis that the lower coverage in case of recurrent models is indeed directly in relation with the recurrency.

In order to refine the analysis of the positional behaviour of the hidden states, we compute the average variance per position of the cosine distance scores of the nearest neighbors based on hidden states. To compute this value we use the following definition:

$$Av_j = \frac{\sum_{i=1}^m v_{w_{i,j}}}{\left|S_{l(s)\geq j}\right|} \tag{8}$$

Here $v_{w_{i,j}}$ is the variance estimate as defined in Equation 5, $l(s)$ is the function returning the length of sentence s and $S_{l(s)\geq j}$ is the set of sentences that are longer than or equal to j as mentioned earlier.

Figures 5a and 5b show the average variance per position for the recurrent model. One can see

English-German

Model	Precision	Recall	Matched Brackets	Cross Brackets	Tag Accuracy
Recurrent	0.38	0.38	0.42	0.31	0.46
Transformer	0.31	0.31	0.35	0.28	0.40

German-English

Model	Precision	Recall	Matched Brackets	Cross Brackets	Tag Accuracy
Recurrent	0.12	0.12	0.30	0.80	0.32
Transformer	0.11	0.11	0.28	0.77	0.31

Table 4: Average parse tree similarity (PARSEVAL scores) between word occurrences and their nearest neighbors. Note that the apparent identity of precision and recall values is due to rounding and the very close number of constituents in the corresponding parse tree of words (gold parse trees) and the corresponding parse trees of their nearest neighbors (candidate parse trees).

that the average variance close to the borders is lower than the variance in the middle. This means that the nearest neighbors of the words close to the borders of sentences are more concentrated in terms of similarity score in general. This could mean the information that captures the meaning of those words plays less of a role compared to other information encoded in the corresponding hidden states, especially if we take the information of coverage per position into account. Interestingly, this does not happen in the case of the transformer model (See Figures 5c and 5d).

4.3 Syntactic Similarity

The difference in the patterns observed so far between recurrent and transformer models (with the coverage of embeddings and the WordNet relations), along with the reported superiority of the recurrent model in capturing structure in extrinsic tasks (Tran et al., 2018), lead us to investigate the syntactic similarity between the words of interest and their nearest neighbors. To this end, we use the approach introduced in the Section 3.3 to study syntactic similarity.

Table 4 shows the average similarity between corresponding constituent subtrees of hidden states and corresponding subtrees of their nearest neighbors, computed using PARSEVAL (Sekine and Collins, 1997). Interestingly, the recurrent model takes the lead in the average syntactic similarity. This confirms our hypothesis that the recurrent model dedicates more of the capacity of its hidden states, compared to transformer, to capture syntactic structures. It is also in agreement with the results reported on learning syntactic structures using extrinsic tasks (Tran et al., 2018). We should add that our approach may not fully explain the degree to which syntax in general is captured by each model, but only to the extent to which this is measurable by comparing syntactic structures us-

ing PARSEVAL.

	Embedding		WordNet	
POS	Forward	Backward	Forward	Backward
All	12%	24%	18%	29%
VERB	19%	36%	38%	52%
NOUN	9%	21%	14%	25%
ADJ	13%	22%	12%	17%
ADV	28%	34%	20%	23%

Table 5: Percentage of the nearest neighbors of hidden states, from the forward and backward layers, that are covered by the list of the nearest neighbors of embeddings and the list of the directly related words in WordNet.

4.4 Direction-Wise Analyses

To gain a better understanding of the behaviour of the hidden states in the recurrent model, we repeat our experiments with hidden states from different directions. Note that so far the recurrent hidden states in our experiments were the concatenation of the hidden states from both directions of our encoder.

Table 5 shows the statistics of embedding coverage and WordNet coverage from the forward and the backward layers. As shown, the coverage of the nearest neighbors of the hidden states from the backward recurrent layer is higher than the nearest neighbors based on those from the forward layer.

Furthermore, Figure 6 shows the mean coverage per position of the nearest neighbors of hidden states from the forward and the backward recurrent layers. Figure 6a shows the mean coverage by the nearest neighbors of the corresponding word embedding of hidden states. As shown for the forward layer the coverage degrades as it goes forward to the end of sentences. However, the coverage for the backward layer, except at the very beginning, almost stays constant through sentences. As shown, the coverage for the backward layer is much higher than the coverage for the forward layer showing that it keeps more information from

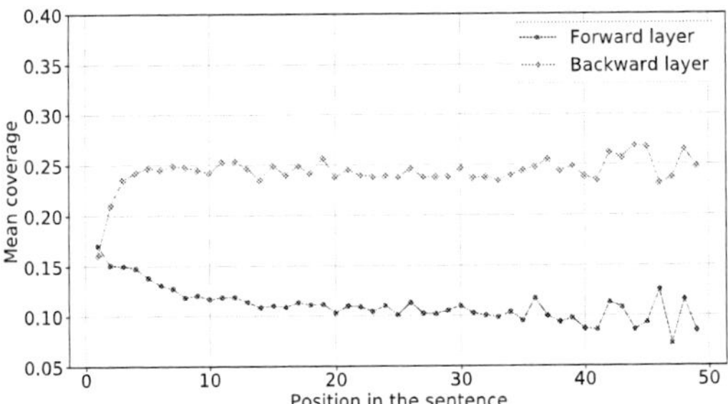

(a) Covered by the nearest neighbors of the embedding of the corresponding word of the hidden state.

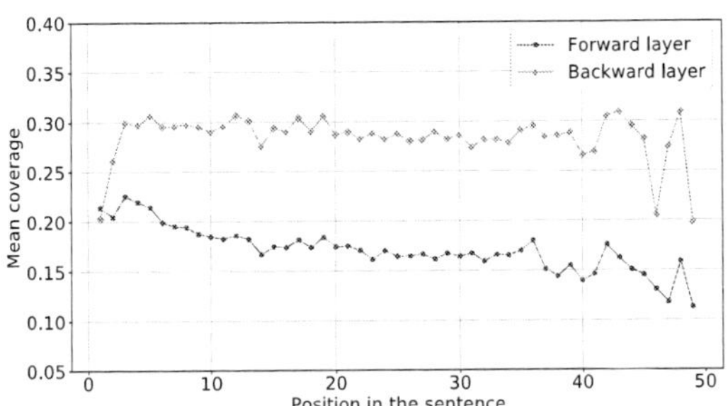

(b) Covered by the directly related words of the corresponding word of the hidden state in WordNet.

Figure 6: The mean coverage per position of the nearest neighbors of hidden states from the forward and backward recurrent layers.

the embeddings compared to the forward layer. The decrease in the forward layer could mean that it captures more context information when moving forward in sentences and forgets more of the corresponding embeddings.

Figure 6b shows the mean coverage by the directly related words, in WordNet, of the corresponding words of hidden states. The difference between the coverage of the nearest neighbors of hidden states from the backward layer comparing to those from the forward layer confirms more strongly that the semantics of words are captured more in the backward layer. This is because here we check the coverage by the directly related words, in the WordNet, of the corresponding words of hidden states.

5 Conclusion

In this work, we introduce an intrinsic way of comparing neural machine translation architectures by looking at the nearest neighbors of the encoder hidden states. Using the method, we compare recurrent and transformer models in terms of capturing syntax and lexical semantics. We show that the transformer model is superior in terms of capturing

lexical semantics, while the recurrent model better captures syntactic similarity.

We show that the hidden state representations capture quite different information than what is captured by the corresponding embeddings. We also show that the hidden states capture more of WordNet relations of the corresponding word than they capture from the nearest neighbors of the embeddings.

Additionally, we provide a detailed analysis of the behaviour of the hidden states, both direction-wise and for the concatenations. We investigate various types of linguistic information captured by the different directions of hidden states in a bidirectional recurrent model. We show that the reverse recurrent layer captures more lexical and semantic information, whereas the forward recurrent layer captures more long-distance, contextual information.

Acknowledgements

This research was funded in part by the Netherlands Organization for Scientific Research (NWO) under project numbers 639.022.213 and 612.001.218.

References

Bahdanau, Dzmitry, Kyunghyun Cho, and Yoshua Bengio. 2015. Neural machine translation by jointly learning to align and translate. In *International Conference on Learning Representations*, San Diego, California, USA, May.

Belinkov, Yonatan, Nadir Durrani, Fahim Dalvi, Hassan Sajjad, and James Glass. 2017. What do neural machine translation models learn about morphology? *arXiv preprint arXiv:1704.03471*.

Bojar, Ondřej, Rajen Chatterjee, Christian Federmann, Yvette Graham, Barry Haddow, Shujian Huang, Matthias Huck, Philipp Koehn, Qun Liu, Varvara Logacheva, et al. 2017. Findings of the 2017 conference on machine translation (wmt17). In *Proceedings of the Second Conference on Machine Translation*, pages 169–214.

Britz, Denny, Anna Goldie, Minh-Thang Luong, and Quoc Le. 2017. Massive exploration of neural machine translation architectures. In *Proceedings of the 2017 Conference on Empirical Methods in Natural Language Processing*, pages 1442–1451. Association for Computational Linguistics.

Fellbaum, Christiane. 1998. *WordNet: An Electronic Lexical Database*. MIT Press, Cambridge, MA.

Ghader, Hamidreza and Christof Monz. 2017. What does attention in neural machine translation pay attention to? In *Proceedings of the Eighth International Joint Conference on Natural Language Processing (IJCNL-2017)*, pages 30–39.

Hamp, Birgit and Helmut Feldweg. 1997. Germanet - a lexical-semantic net for german. In *Proceedings of the ACL workshop Automatic Information Extraction and Building of Lexical Semantic Resources for NLP Applications*.

Henrich, Verena and Erhard Hinrichs. 2010. Gernedit - the germanet editing tool. In Chair), Nicoletta Calzolari (Conference, Khalid Choukri, Bente Maegaard, Joseph Mariani, Jan Odijk, Stelios Piperidis, Mike Rosner, and Daniel Tapias, editors, *Proceedings of the Seventh International Conference on Language Resources and Evaluation (LREC'10)*, Valletta, Malta, may. European Language Resources Association (ELRA).

Hochreiter, Sepp and Jürgen Schmidhuber. 1997. Long short-term memory. *Neural Comput.*, 9(8):1735–1780, November.

Jean, Sébastien, Kyunghyun Cho, Roland Memisevic, and Yoshua Bengio. 2015. On using very large target vocabulary for neural machine translation. In *Proceedings of the 53rd Annual Meeting of the Association for Computational Linguistics and the 7th International Joint Conference on Natural Language Processing (Volume 1: Long Papers)*, pages 1–10, Beijing, China, July. Association for Computational Linguistics.

Kingma, Diederick P and Jimmy Ba. 2015. Adam: A method for stochastic optimization. In *International Conference on Learning Representations (ICLR)*.

Lakew, Surafel Melaku, Mauro Cettolo, and Marcello Federico. 2018. A comparison of transformer and recurrent neural networks on multilingual neural machine translation. In *Proceedings of the 27th International Conference on Computational Linguistics*, pages 641–652. Association for Computational Linguistics.

Luong, Thang, Hieu Pham, and Christopher D. Manning. 2015a. Effective approaches to attention-based neural machine translation. pages 1412–1421, September.

Luong, Thang, Ilya Sutskever, Quoc Le, Oriol Vinyals, and Wojciech Zaremba. 2015b. Addressing the rare word problem in neural machine translation. In *Proceedings of the 53rd Annual Meeting of the Association for Computational Linguistics and the 7th International Joint Conference on Natural Language Processing (Volume 1: Long Papers)*, pages 11–19, Beijing, China, July. Association for Computational Linguistics.

Mikolov, Tomas, Ilya Sutskever, Kai Chen, Greg S Corrado, and Jeff Dean. 2013. Distributed representations of words and phrases and their compositionality. In *Advances in neural information processing systems*, pages 3111–3119.

Miller, George A. 1995. Wordnet: A lexical database for english. *Communications of the ACM*, 38(11):39–41, November.

Papineni, Kishore, Salim Roukos, Todd Ward, and Wei-Jing Zhu. 2002. BLEU: a method for automatic evaluation of machine translation. In *Proceedings of the 40th Annual Meeting of the Association for Computational Linguistics*, pages 311–318.

Pelevina, Maria, Nikolay Arefiev, Chris Biemann, and Alexander Panchenko. 2016. Making sense of word embeddings. In *Proceedings of the 1st Workshop on Representation Learning for NLP*, pages 174–183. Association for Computational Linguistics.

Sekine, Satoshi and Michael J. Collins. 1997. Evalb – Bracket Scoring Program.

Sennrich, Rico and Barry Haddow. 2016. Linguistic input features improve neural machine translation. In *Proceedings of the First Conference on Machine Translation: Volume 1, Research Papers*, pages 83–91. Association for Computational Linguistics.

Sennrich, Rico, Barry Haddow, and Alexandra Birch. 2016. Neural machine translation of rare words with subword units. In *Proceedings of the 54th Annual Meeting of the Association for Computational Linguistics (Volume 1: Long Papers)*, pages 1715–1725. Association for Computational Linguistics.

Shi, Xing, Inkit Padhi, and Kevin Knight. 2016. Does string-based neural mt learn source syntax? In *Proceedings of the 2016 Conference on Empirical Methods in Natural Language Processing*, pages 1526–1534, Austin, Texas, November. Association for Computational Linguistics.

Tang, Gongbo, Mathias Müller, Annette Rios, and Rico Sennrich. 2018. Why self-attention? a targeted evaluation of neural machine translation architectures. In *Proceedings of the 2018 Conference on Empirical Methods in Natural Language Processing*, pages 4263–4272. Association for Computational Linguistics.

Toutanova, Kristina, Dan Klein, Christopher D Manning, and Yoram Singer. 2003. Feature-rich part-of-speech tagging with a cyclic dependency network. In *Proceedings of the 2003 Conference of the North American Chapter of the Association for Computational Linguistics on Human Language Technology-Volume 1*, pages 173–180. Association for Computational Linguistics.

Tran, Ke, Arianna Bisazza, and Christof Monz. 2018. The importance of being recurrent for modeling hierarchical structure. In *Proceedings of the 2018 Conference on Empirical Methods in Natural Language Processing*, pages 4731–4736. Association for Computational Linguistics.

Vaswani, Ashish, Noam Shazeer, Niki Parmar, Jakob Uszkoreit, Llion Jones, Aidan N Gomez, Ł ukasz Kaiser, and Illia Polosukhin. 2017. Attention is all you need. In Guyon, I., U. V. Luxburg, S. Bengio, H. Wallach, R. Fergus, S. Vishwanathan, and R. Garnett, editors, *Advances in Neural Information Processing Systems 30*, pages 5998–6008. Curran Associates, Inc.

Wu, Yonghui, Mike Schuster, Zhifeng Chen, Quoc V Le, Mohammad Norouzi, Wolfgang Macherey, Maxim Krikun, Yuan Cao, Qin Gao, Klaus Macherey, et al. 2016. Google's neural machine translation system: Bridging the gap between human and machine translation. *arXiv preprint arXiv:1609.08144*.

Zhu, Muhua, Yue Zhang, Wenliang Chen, Min Zhang, and Jingbo Zhu. 2013. Fast and accurate shift-reduce constituent parsing. In *Proceedings of the 51st Annual Meeting of the Association for Computational Linguistics (Volume 1: Long Papers)*, pages 434–443. Association for Computational Linguistics.

Improving Neural Machine Translation Using Noisy Parallel Data through Distillation

Praveen Dakwale
Informatics Institute
University of Amsterdam
p.dakwale@uva.nl

Christof Monz
Informatics Institute
University of Amsterdam
c.monz@uva.nl

Abstract

Due to the scarcity of parallel training data for many language pairs, quasi-parallel or comparable training data provides an important alternative resource for training machine translation systems for such language pairs. Since comparable corpora are not of as high quality as manually annotated parallel data, using them for training can have a negative effect on the translation performance of an NMT model. We propose distillation as a remedy to effectively leverage comparable data where the training of a student model on combined clean and comparable data is guided by a teacher model trained on the high-quality, clean data only. Our experiments for Arabic-English, Chinese-English, and German-English translation demonstrate that distillation yields significant improvements compared to off-the-shelf use of comparable data and performs comparable to state-of-the-art methods for noise filtering.

1 Introduction

Traditional machine translation systems are trained on parallel corpora consisting of sentences in the source language aligned to their translations in the target language. However, for many language pairs substantial amounts of high-quality parallel corpora are not available. On the other hand, for many languages, another useful resource known as comparable corpora can be obtained relatively easily in substantially larger amounts. Such comparable corpora can be created by crawling large monolingual data in the source and target languages from multilingual news portals such as Agence France-Presse (AFP), BBC news, Euronews etc. Source and target sentences in these monolingual corpora are then aligned by automatic document and sentence alignment techniques (Munteanu and Marcu, 2005). Such a bitext extracted from comparable data is usually not of the same quality as annotated parallel corpora. Recent research has shown that building models from low-quality data can have a degrading effect on the performance of recurrent NMT models (Khayrallah and Koehn, 2018). Therefore, there is a growing interest in filtering and sampling techniques to extract high-quality sentence pairs from such large noisy parallel texts.

Recently, the "Parallel corpus filtering" (Koehn et al., 2018) shared task was held at WMT-2018. This task aims at extracting high-quality sentence pairs from Paracrawl[1], which is a large noisy parallel corpus. Most of the participants in this task, used rule-based pre-filtering followed by a classifier-based scoring of sentence pairs (Barbu and Barbu Mititelu, 2018; Junczys-Dowmunt, 2018; Hangya and Fraser, 2018). A subset sampled with a fixed number of target tokens is then used to train recurrent NMT systems in order to evaluate the relative quality of the filtered bitexts. Some of the submissions show good translation performance for the German-English translation task by training on the filtered bitext only. In this paper, we propose a strategy to leverage additional low-quality bitexts without any filtering when used in conjunction with a high-quality parallel corpus. Motivated by the "knowledge distillation" frame-

---

[1] https://paracrawl.eu/

Arabic-English (ISI bitext)	
Src:	وقررت وزارة العدل الهولندية ابعاده رغم طلب الاردن تسليمه في اطار قضية تهريب مخدرات.
Trg:	The Dutch justice ministry decided to expel the Iraqi Kurd despite Amman's demand that he be handed over to Jordanian authorities.
Human:	The Dutch Justice Ministry decided to deport him, despite Jordan's request to hand him over as part of a drug smuggling case.
Chinese-English (ISI bitext)	
Src:	美国提出的报复清单是中国政府绝对不能接受的。
Trg:	And the Chinese side would certainly not accept the unreasonable demands put forward by the Americans concerning the protection of intellectual property rights.
Human:	The revenge list proposed by America will definitely not be accepted by Chinese government.
German-English (Paracrawl)	
Src:	Der Elektroden Schalter KARI EL22 dient zur Füllstandserfassung und -regelung von elektrisch leitfähigen Flüssigkeiten .
Tgt:	The KARI EL22 electrode switch is designed for the control of conductive liquids .
Human:	The electrode switch KARI EL22 is used for level detection and control of electrically conductive liquids.

Table 1: Noisy sentence pair example from ISI bitext (Arabic-English and Chinese-English) and Paracrawl (De-En). Fragments in red in either source or target side has no corresponding equivalent fragment on the respective aligned side.

work of Hinton et al. (2014), we propose "distillation" as a strategy to exploit comparable training data for training an NMT system. In our distillation strategy, we first train a teacher model on the clean parallel data, which then guides the training of a final student model trained on the combination of clean and noisy data. Our experimental results demonstrate that for Arabic-English and Chinese-English translation, distillation not only helps to successfully utilize noisy comparable corpora without any performance degradation, but it also outperforms one of the best performing filtering techniques reported in Koehn et al. (2018). In addition, we conduct similar experiments for German-English translation and observe that while simply adding noisy data to the training data pool degrades performance, our distillation approach still yields slight improvements over the baseline.

In Section 2, we discuss the relevant literature in NMT as well as in other deep learning based tasks which aim to utilize low quality training corpus. In Section 3, we provide a brief discussion of the type of noise in the comparable data, the architecture of the NMT model used in our experiments, and the knowledge distillation framework proposed by Hinton et al. (2014). In Section 4, we describe our strategy to use knowledge distillation for training with noisy data. We discuss our experimental settings including datasets and parameters in Section 5 and results in Section 6.

2 Related work

Khayrallah and Koehn (2018) reported that NMT models can suffer substantial degradation from adding noisy bitexts when compared to a baseline model trained on high-quality parallel text only. The "Parallel corpus filtering" (Koehn et al., 2018) task evaluated submissions based on NMT systems trained only on the bitext filtered from Paracrawl. However, given that many language pairs have at least some small amount of high-quality parallel corpora (which is also used by many of the participants to train a classifier for scoring the noisy data), it is important to investigate whether a bitext filtered using these proposed techniques results in any additional improvements in conjunction with the original high-quality data. Filtering techniques involve discarding a sentence pair with low confidence score. However, a sentence pair with a low score may still have fragments in the source and target sentences which can provide useful contexts. Our results show that for a recurrent NMT model, filtering the noisy bitext below a specific threshold using one of the best techniques submitted to the filtering task (known as "Dual conditional cross entropy filtering" (Junczys-Dowmunt, 2018)) yields only small improvements.

In the machine learning literature, various methods have been proposed for efficient learning with label noise. One of the recent methods is the bootstrapping (Reed et al., 2014) approach where improved labels for noisy or unlabeled data can be obtained by predictions of another classifier. For NMT, forward translations of the noisy bitext can be used as a variant of bootstrapping where the target side of the noisy bitext can be replaced by translations of the source sentence obtained by a model trained on the high-quality data. However, a better alternative for NMT would be to use back-translations (Sennrich et al., 2016), i.e., to replace the source side of the noisy bitext by translations of the target side obtained by a model trained in the reverse direction. Our experiments show that although backward translations of noisy data cause lower degradations than the original noisy data, they provide only moderate improvements. Moreover, cleansing the comparable data by back-translation is expensive as it requires the generation of pseudo source sentences using beam search decoding. Fine-tuning (Miceli Barone et al., 2017) is a well-known technique for domain adaptation for NMT but can also be used as a possible solution for training with noisy data where the idea is to first pre-train on noisy data and then continue training on high-quality data.

Our experiments show that when using noisy data for training NMT models, fine-tuning fails to provide any additional improvements. Moreover, bootstrapping based on filtering and back-translation, as explained above, show only small improvements over a model trained on high-quality data only. In order to overcome the dependence on filtering-based data selection or other data cleaning approaches and to leverage all available noisy data, in this paper, we propose knowledge distillation based training on combined clean and noisy sentence pairs.

It is very important to note that, as has been pointed out in Koehn et al. (2018), the aim of *"Parallel corpus filtering"* task proposed at WMT18 was not to select data relevant for a targeted domain, but to focus on the selection of high quality data that is relevant to all domains. Similarly, in this paper, we do not aim to propose a technique for domain adaptation for NMT but to propose a technique to leverage low quality or noisy training data for training high performing NMT models.

Although knowledge distillation has been used as a solution to other problems of NMT such as model compression (Kim and Rush, 2016), domain adaptation (Dakwale and Monz, 2017) or transfer learning for low-resource languages (Chen et al., 2017) and for leveraging noisy data for image recognition (Li et al., 2017), our approach is the first attempt to exploit distillation for training NMT systems with noisy data.

3 Background

3.1 Noise in the training corpora

Khayrallah and Koehn (2018) analyzed the Paracrawl corpus, identifying various types of noise in this corpus. They found that although there are some instances of incorrect language, untranslated sentences, and non-linguistic characters, the majority of noisy samples (around 41%) are misaligned sentences due to faulty document or sentence alignment. This results in alignments of incorrect source to target sentence fragments.

Similarly, a well-known noisy bitext commonly used for training machine translation systems for Arabic-English and Chinese-English is the ISI bitext created by automatically aligning sentences from monolingual corpora extracted from AFP and Xinhua, respectively (Munteanu and Marcu, 2005). This alignment method first searches for articles representing similar stories in two separate monolingual corpora for source and target languages using cross-lingual information retrieval with the help of a dictionary. Then parallel sentences are aligned by calculating word overlaps between each candidate sentence pair followed by a maximum entropy classifier. Since the bitexts are extracted from monolingual corpora for source and target languages, there is rarely any noise due to misspelling, wrong re-ordering or non-linguistic characters. The majority of noise in the resulting aligned bitext is due to limitations of the sentence alignment technique often resulting in sentence pairs which are partial translations of each other with additional fragments on either the source or target side.

Table 1 shows some examples of noisy sentence pairs for German-English (from the Paracrawl corpus) and Arabic-English (from the ISI bitext). The fragments marked red in the source sentence have no correspondence on the target side. We refer the reader to (Khayrallah and Koehn, 2018) and (Munteanu and Marcu, 2005) for a more detailed description of the types of noise in the respective corpora.

3.2 Neural Machine Translation

We employ an NMT system based on Bahdanau et al. (2014). This is a simple encoder-decoder network where both the encoder and decoder are multilayer recurrent neural networks (we use LSTM's). Given an input sentence $[(x_1, x_2, ..., x_n)]$, the encoder converts it into a sequence of hidden state representations $[(h_1, h_2, ..., h_n)]$.

$$h_i = f_{encoder}(x_i, h_{i-1}) \qquad (1)$$

Here, $f_{encoder}$ is an LSTM unit. The decoder is another multi-layer RNN which predicts a target sequence $y = (y_1, y_2, ...y_m)$. The probability of generation of a token y_i at position $'i'$ on the target side is conditioned on the last target token y_{i-1}, the current hidden state of the decoder s_j, and the context vector c_j which is a conditional representation of the source sequence relevant to target position $'i'$. The probability of the sentence is computed as the product of the probabilities of all target tokens.

$$p(\mathbf{y}) = \prod_j^m p(y_j|y_1, ...y_{j-1}, \mathbf{x}) = \prod_j^m g(y_{j-1}, s_j, c_j) \qquad (2)$$

g is a multi-layer feed-forward neural network with a nonlinear transformation. A softmax layer is applied on the output of the feedforward network g, which generates the probability of each word in the target vocabulary. Here, s_j is the hidden state representation corresponding to each token in the target sequence generated by the decoder RNN.

$$s_j = f_{dec}(s_{j-1}, y_{j-1}, c_j) \qquad (3)$$

The context vector c_j is computed using an attention mechanism (Luong et al., 2015) as the weighted sum of the hidden states h_i of the encoder.

$$c_j = \sum_{i=1}^n \alpha_{ji} h_i \qquad (4)$$

where α_{ji} are attention weights corresponding to each encoder hidden state output h_i calculated as follows :

$$\alpha_{ji} = \frac{exp(a(s_{j-1}, h_i))}{\sum_{k=1}^n exp(a(s_{j-1}, h_k))} \qquad (5)$$

Activations $a(s, h)$ are calculated by using a scoring function such as dot product between the current decoder state s_{j-1} and each of the hidden states h_i of the encoder. The end-to-end network is trained by minimizing the negative log-likelihood over the training data. The log-likelihood loss is defined as

$$L_{NLL}(\theta) = -\sum_{j=1}^n \sum_{k=1}^{|V|} (y_j = k) * \log(p(y_j = k|x; \theta)) \qquad (6)$$

Where y_j is the output distribution generated by the network at each time-step and k is the true class label, i.e., the reference target word at each time step selected from a fixed vocabulary V. The outer summation is the total loss computed as the sum over the complete target sequence.

3.3 Knowledge Distillation

Knowledge Distillation is a framework proposed in Hinton et al. (2014) for training compressed "student" networks by using supervision from a large teacher network. Assuming, we have a teacher network with large dimension size trained on a large amount of data, a smaller student network with much smaller dimension size can be trained to perform comparable or even better than the teacher by learning to mimic the output distributions of the teacher network on the same data. This is usually done by minimizing cross-entropy or KL-divergence loss between the two distributions. Formally, if we have a teacher network trained on the same data and with a learned distribution $q(y|x; \theta_T)$, the student network (model parameters represented by θ) can be trained by minimizing the following loss:

$$L_{KD}(\theta, \theta_T) = -\sum_{k=1}^{|V|} \mathrm{KL}\Big(q(y|x; \theta_T) \, p(y|x; \theta)\Big) \qquad (7)$$

where θ_T is the parameter distribution of the teacher network. Commonly, this loss is interpolated with the log-likelihood loss which is calculated with regard to the target labels for the in-domain data:

$$L(\theta, \theta_T) = (1 - \lambda) L_{NLL}(\theta) + \lambda L_{KD}(\theta, \theta_T) \qquad (8)$$

In order to allow the student network to encode the similarities among the output classes, Hinton et al. (2014) suggests to generate a smoother distribution called 'soft-targets' by increasing the temperature of the softmax of both teacher and student network.

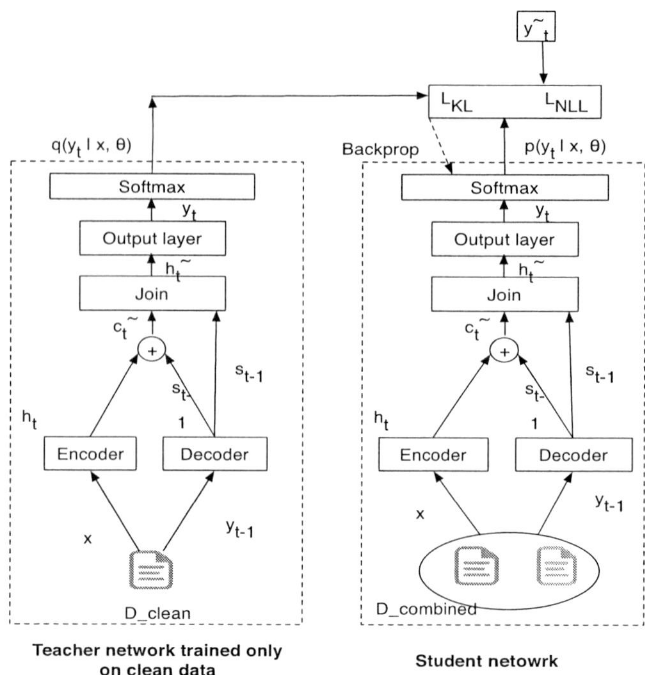

Figure 1: Distillation for noisy data. Both the teacher and student network have same architecture. Teacher network is trained only on the clean data, student network is trained for two losses : L_{NLL} wrt target labels and L_{KL} wrt to output distribution of teacher network

4 Knowledge distillation for noisy data

We discuss the main intuition and idea behind using knowledge distillation for noisy labels. A detailed analysis is given in Li et al. (2017). As shown in Figure 1, the idea is to first train the teacher model f on the clean data D_{clean} and then transfer the knowledge from the teacher to a student network which is trained on the entire dataset D by optimising the following loss:

$$L_D(y_i, f(x_i)) = \lambda l(y_i, f(x_i)) + (1-\lambda)l(s_i, f(x_i)) \tag{9}$$

where $s_i = f_{D_{clean}}(x_i)/\tau$ and τ is the temperature of the softmax. In equation 9, the student model is trained on the combination of two loss functions, the first term is the cross-entropy loss l between the prediction of the student model and the ground truth y_i, while the second term is the cross-entropy or KL-divergence between the output distributions of the student model and the teacher model. λ is a parameter to balance the weight between the two losses. Assuming the second loss to be cross-entropy, Equation 9 can be re-written as:

$$L_D(y_i, f(x_i)) = l(\lambda(y_i) + (1 - \lambda(s_i), f(x_i))) \tag{10}$$

Li et al. (2017) define $y_i^\lambda = \lambda y_i + (1 - \lambda)(s_i, f(x_i))$ as pseudo-label which is a combination of the given noisy label y_i and the prediction s_i from the teacher model. They provide an analysis based on the comparison between the risks involved in training directly on the noisy labels or training on the boot-strapped labels as compared to training on the pseudo label as defined above. They show that training on the pseudo label, for some values of λ defined through distillation, involves lower risks than direct training or bootstrapping. Therefore, a better model can be trained by driving the pseudo labels closer to the ground truth label. In case of comparable corpora training for NMT, instead of learning only from uncertain ground truth labels, the student model also benefits from the predictions of the teacher model while learning to imitate it.

5 Experiments

5.1 Comparisons

We compare our technique to standard scenarios of training on clean and noisy data. Further, we compare to the commonly used strategy of fine-tuning as well as back-translation which is an adapta-

	Clean		Noisy	
	Source	Size	Source	Size
Arabic-English	LDC	300k	ISI bitext	1.1m
Chinese-English	LDC	550k	ISI bitext	550k
German-English	WMT-17	5.1M	Para$_{rn}$	5.1M
German-English	WMT-17	5.1M	Filt$_{toks=100M}$	4.6M

Table 2: Datasets and statistics. Para$_{rn}$ = Randomly sampled subset of Paracrawl. Filt$_{toks=100M}$ = 100 million target token subsample submitted by (Junczys-Dowmunt, 2018)

tion of self-learning or bootstrapping methods. We carry out the following experimental comparisons:

- **Training on parallel data only:** The standard practice in NMT is to train on the high-quality parallel data only. This experiment is also the primary baseline for comparing the proposed method.

- **Training on comparable data only:** We conduct this experiment to demonstrate the substantial difference between the performance of the models trained on only noisy data or only on clean data.

- **Training on combined comparable and parallel data:** This experiment demonstrates the effect of adding comparable data to the baseline training data pool.

- **Fine-tuning:** The standard practice commonly used for domain adaptation. For noisy data, the idea is to first train the model on noisy data and then continue training on clean data.

- **Back-translation:** Back-translation has been proposed as a method to incorporate additional monolingual data for NMT (Sennrich et al., 2016). This is done by training an NMT system in reverse of the desired direction thus obtaining pseudo-source sentences for the additional monolingual target sentences. By applying back-translation, we discard the original source sentence in the comparable data and replace them with the pseudo-source sentences. The back-translated comparable data is then added to the clean parallel data.

- **Dual cross entropy filtering:** As discussed in the introduction, (Junczys-Dowmunt, 2018)) reported the best results for the Parallel Corpus Filtering task for WMT-18. They used the dual cross-entropy method in

which sentence pairs in the noisy corpus are ranked based on forward and backward losses for each sentence pair with respect to NMT models trained on clean data in forward and reverse direction. We consider this filtering method as a competitive baseline for our approach.

Note that back-translation requires beam-search based decoding which is quite expensive for large amount of comparable data.

5.2 Datasets and Parameters

We conduct experiments for Arabic to English, Chinese to English, and German-English NMT. As a commonly used representative of comparable data, we consider all AFP sources from the ISI Arabic-English bitext (LDC2007T08) with a size of 1.1M sentence pairs and Xinhua news sources for the Chinese-English bitext (LDC2007T09) with a size of 550K sentence pairs. Both corpora are created by automatically aligning (Munteanu and Marcu, 2005) sentences from monolingual corpora. For Arabic-English, we compose the parallel data consisting of 325k sentence pairs from various LDC catalogues [2]

For Chinese-English, a parallel text of 550k parallel sentence pairs from LDC catalogues[3] is used. Note that for Arabic-English, the size of the comparable corpus is approximately 4 times that of the parallel data while for Chinese-English, the comparable corpora size is the same as that of the parallel corpus[4]. A byte pair encoding of size 20k is trained on the parallel data for the respective languages. NIST MT05 is used as dev set for both language pairs and MT08, MT09 as test set for Arabic-English and MT-06, MT-08 as test set for Chinese-English. Translation quality is measured in terms of case-sensitive 4-gram BLEU (Papineni et al., 2002). Approximate randomization (Noreen., 1989; Riezler and Maxwell, 2005) is used to detect statistically significant differences.

For German-English, we use high-quality data from the training corpus provided for WMT-17 (Bojar et al., 2017). For the noisy data, we randomly sample a bitext of equal size from the raw

---

[2]LDC2006E25, LDC2004T18, several Gale corpora, LDC2004T17, LDC2005E46 and LDC2004E13.

[3]LDC2003E14, LDC2005T10 and LDC2002E18.

[4]We are aware of the fact that much larger high-quality training data are available for Chinese-English, which result in a higher baseline. However, in order to simulate a scenario where the amount of clean data equals that of the comparable data, we downsample the size for our experiments.

	Arabic-English			Chinese-English		
	MT05	MT08	MT09	MT05	MT06	MT08
Parallel only	57.7	46.1	49.9	28.8	27.5	20.3
Comparable only	48.9 (-8.8)	**32.7** (-13.4)	**36.0**(-13.9)	**11.3**(-12.1)	**10.2**(-17.5)	**5.2** (-15.1)
Combined (Parallel + Comparable)	55.2 (-2.5)	44.2 (-1.9)	**47.9**(-2)	27.7(-1.1)	26.7 (-0.8)	**18.3** (-2)
Parallel +Comparable$_{bck}$	**60.4**(+2.7)	47.5 (+1.4)	**51.0**(+1.1)	**29.1**(+0.3)	27.2(-0.3)	19.8 (-0.5)
Fine-tuning	**56.1**(-1.6)	46.6 (+0.5)	**50.3**(+0.4)	**25.1** (-3.7)	**23.5** (-4)	**17.2** (-3.1)
Dual cross Entropy Filtering						
Parallel +Comparable$_{filt-25\%}$	**59.9** (+2.2)	**47.4** (+1.4)	**51.1** (+1.2)	**19.7**(-9.1)	20.9 (-6.6)	**16.8** (-3.5)
Parallel +Comparable$_{filt-50\%}$	59.2 (+1.5)	46.8 (+0.7)	**50.9**(+1)	20.4 (-8.4)	**21.8**(-5.7)	**17.0** (-3.3)
Parallel+Comparable$_{filt-75\%}$	56.7 (-1)	**44.9** (-1.2)	49.1(-0.8)	**21.5** (-7.3)	**22.3** (-5.2)	**17.5**(-2.8)
Knowledge Distillation						
KD	**62.3** (+4.6)	**48.4** (+2.3)	**52.3**(+2.4)	**29.4** (+0.6)	**28.2** (+0.5)	**21.1** (+0.8)

Table 3: Performance of various training strategies for Arabic/Chinese-English. **Comparable**$_{bck}$ = Back-translated comparable corpora. **KD** =Knowledge distillation. Boldfaced = Significant differences at p < 0.01.

Paracrawl corpus ("very noisy" 1 billion English tokens) similar to Khayrallah and Koehn (2018). To be able to compare with the best filtering method, we also use a bitext of 100M target tokens submitted by Junczys-Dowmunt (2018) (available from the shared task website using a score file) which is filtered using their proposed "Dual cross entropy" score. A BPE of 32k is trained on the WMT-17 training data, newstest15 is used as dev set and newstest16 and newstest17 are used as test set. Table 2 summarizes clean and noisy training data for all language pairs.

We train an LSTM-based encoder-decoder model as described in Luong et al. (2015) using the Open-NMT-python toolkit (Klein et al., 2017), with both embeddings and hidden layers of size 1000. The maximum sentence length is restricted to 80 tokens. Parameters are optimized using Adam with an initial learning rate of 0.001, a decay rate of 0.5 (after every 10k steps), a dropout probability of 0.2 and label smoothing of 0.1. A fixed batch size of 64 is used. Model weights are initialized uniformly within [-0.02, 0.02]. We train for a maximum of 200k steps and select the model with best BLEU score on the development set for the final evaluation and decode with a beam size of 5.

6 Results

First, we compare the primary baseline with direct off-the-shelf use of noisy data without any filtering or noise reduction strategies. As can be seen in Table 3, for both Arabic-English and Chinese-English, the performance of an NMT system trained on comparable data only is substantially worse (up to −13.9 BLEU for Ar-En and −17.5 BLEU for Zh-En) as compared to clean data. Although for Arabic-English, the size of the noisy data is 4 times that of the clean data, while for Chinese-English, it is of equal size. Adding this noisy data to the clean data degrades translation performance (−2 BLEU for both Ar-En and Zh-En). The relative difference between the performance drop between the two language pairs can be attributed to the size of the comparable data.

Replacing the source side of the noisy data with back-translations sightly improves the BLEU score for Arabic-English (up to +1.4) but slightly degrades translation quality for Chinese-English (−0.3 BLEU compared to the baseline). Nevertheless, this is still an improvement over direct off-the-shelf addition of the original noisy bitext. This implies that back-translation replacement does provide some degree of data cleaning.

Fine-tuning for noisy data shows only slight improvements for Ar-En (up to +0.5 BLEU) and none for Zh-En (up to −4 BLEU drop). For both language pairs, we apply the dual cross-entropy filtering method of (Junczys-Dowmunt, 2018) by ranking sentence pairs in the comparable data according to the dual cross entropy and select sub-samples from the top 50% and 75% of the full comparable bitext. Filtering at 50% shows significant (+1 BLEU) improvements for Arabic-English, whereas for Chinese-English this filtering results in performance even worse than adding all data, implying that cross entropy based filtering does not retain high-quality sentences from this

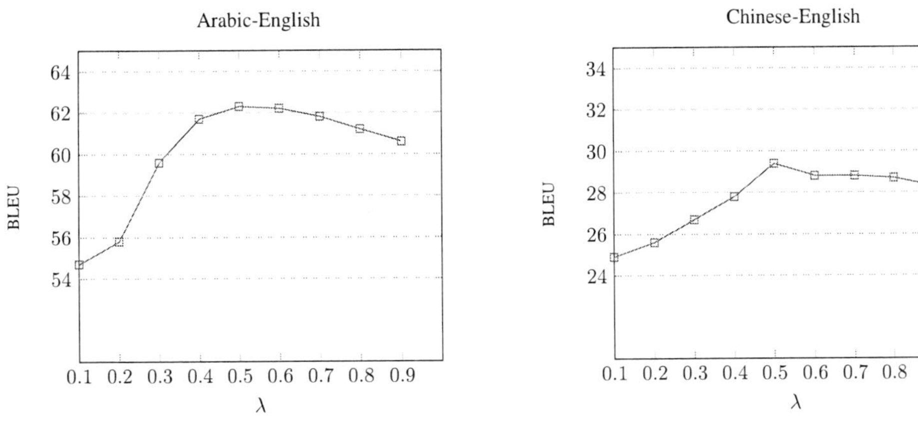

Figure 2: Variation in BLEU score for different values of λ for Arabic-English and Chinese-English

comparable bitext.

On the other hand, the proposed distillation strategy outperforms filtering as well as back-translation replacement for both language pairs. The improvements for Arabic-English are substantially higher ($+4.6$ BLEU for the dev set and $+2.4$ for the test set), while only a small improvement for Chinese-English is observed. Nevertheless, distillation provides significant improvements as compared to direct addition of the noisy data. The improvement with knowledge distillation shown in Table 3 correspond to the best improvements with respect to different values of λ. In Figure 2, we show the effect of varying values for λ (between 0.1 and 0.9) on the translation performance over the development set (MT05). For both the language pairs $\lambda = 0.5$ yields the best performance. As shown in Table 4, for German-English, there is a substantial difference (-16.4 BLEU) between the performance of a model trained on clean data only vs. one trained on randomly sampled Paracrawl data. Khayrallah and Koehn (2018) reported a degradation of up to -9 BLEU when combining clean and noisy data. However, we observe only a 1 BLEU drop for the same setting. Nevertheless, directly adding noisy data seems to provide no additional improvements. Similarly, fine-tuning on the clean data does not show any improvements. On the other hand, applying the proposed distillation over this combined bitext shows slight improvement of 0.3 BLEU over the clean data baseline.

For a comparison with "Dual cross entropy filtering", we use the filtered bitext submitted by Junczys-Dowmunt (2018) and add it to the training data, which also degrades BLEU by -1. Again, applying distillation over this filtered bitext combined with the clean data set shows an improvement of 0.9 BLEU over the clean-data baseline. As shown in Figure 3, we evaluate the performance variation for different values of λ using the 'Randomly sampled (100M target tokens) paracrawl' against the newstest'15 development set. Similar to the other two language pairs, we observe that the best BLEU score is achieved for $\lambda = 0.5$.

7 Conclusion

In this paper, we explored the effectiveness of using comparable training data for neural machine translation. Our experiments show that depending on the size of the noisy data, the performance of an NMT model can suffer significant degradations. Further, we show that noisy cleaning methods such as filtering and back-translation of noisy data show only slight improvements over the baseline. Moreover, fine-tuning fails to show any significant improvements when used for noisy data.

To overcome these problems, we proposed distillation as a remedy to efficiently leverage noisy data for NMT where we train a primary NMT model on the combined training data with knowledge distillation from the teacher network trained on the clean data only. Our experiments show that distillation can help to successfully utilize low-quality comparable data resulting in significant improvements as compared to training directly on the noisy data.

Acknowledgments

This research was funded in part by the Netherlands Organization for Scientific Research (NWO) under project numbers 639.022.213 and

	test15	test16	test17
WMT (Parallel only)	25.2	30.0	26.0
Randomly sampled Paracrawl			
Para_{rn}	**14.6** (-10.6)	**10.2** (-19.8)	9.6 (-16.4)
WMT (Parallel) + Para_{rn}	**24.1**(-1.1)	**29.0** (-1)	25.0 (-1)
Fine-tuning (Para_{rn})	**21.8** (-3.4)	**24.4** (-5.6)	**21.1** (-4.9)
Knowledge distillation (WMT + Para_{rn})	**25.6** (+0.4)	**30.3** (+0.3)	**26.3** (+0.3)
Parcrawl filtered with dual cross entropy			
$\text{Filt}_{toks=100M}$ only	**24.0** (-1.2)	**28.8** (-1.2)	**24.6** (-1.4)
WMT + $\text{Filt}_{toks=100M}$	**24.1** (-1.1)	28.7 (-0.3)	**25.0** (-1)
Fine-tuning ($\text{Filt}_{toks=100M}$)	**23.9** (-1.3)	29.1 (-0.9)	25.1(-0.9)
Knowledge distillation (WMT + $\text{Filt}_{toks=100M}$)	**26.1**(+1.1)	**31.3** (+0.3)	**26.9**(+0.9)

Table 4: German-English results. **WMT** = Only clean Data, **Para_{rn}** = Randomly sampled 5.1 million sentence pairs from Paracrawl. **$\text{Filt}_{toks=100M}$** = 100 million target tokens filtered (Junczys-Dowmunt, 2018)

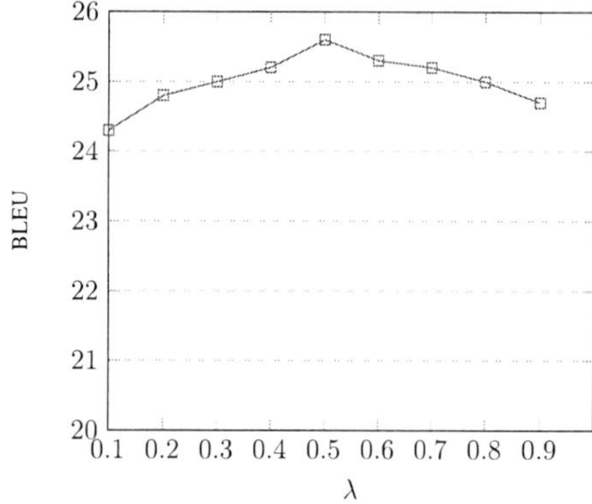

Figure 3: Variation in BLEU score for different values of λ for German-English when trained with randomly sampled paracrawl data

612.001.218.

References

Bahdanau, Dzmitry, Kyunghyun Cho, and Yoshua Bengio. 2014. Neural machine translation by jointly learning to align and translate. *CoRR*, abs/1409.0473.

Barbu, Eduard and Verginica Barbu Mititelu. 2018. A hybrid pipeline of rules and machine learning to filter web-crawled parallel corpora. In *Proceedings of the Third Conference on Machine Translation, Volume 2: Shared Task Papers*, pages 880–884, Belgium, Brussels, October. Association for Computational Linguistics.

Bojar, Ondřej, Rajen Chatterjee, Christian Federmann, Yvette Graham, Barry Haddow, Shujian Huang, Matthias Huck, Philipp Koehn, Qun Liu, Varvara Logacheva, Christof Monz, Matteo Negri, Matt Post, Raphael Rubino, Lucia Specia, and Marco Turchi.

2017. Findings of the 2017 conference on machine translation (wmt17). In *Proceedings of the Second Conference on Machine Translation, Volume 2: Shared Task Papers*, pages 169–214, Copenhagen, Denmark, September. Association for Computational Linguistics.

Chen, Yun, Yang Liu, Yong Cheng, and Victor O.K. Li. 2017. A teacher-student framework for zero-resource neural machine translation. In *Proceedings of the 55th Annual Meeting of the Association for Computational Linguistics (Volume 1: Long Papers)*, pages 1925–1935. Association for Computational Linguistics.

Dakwale, Praveen and Christof Monz. 2017. Fine-tuning for neural machine translation with limited degradation across in-and out-of-domain data. In *Proceedings of the 16th Machine Translation Summit*.

Hangya, Viktor and Alexander Fraser. 2018. An unsupervised system for parallel corpus filtering. In *Proceedings of the Third Conference on Machine Translation, Volume 2: Shared Task Papers*, pages 895–900, Belgium, Brussels, October. Association for Computational Linguistics.

Hinton, Geoffrey, Oriol Vinyals, and Jeff Dean. 2014. Distilling the knowledge in a neural network. In *NIPS 2014 Deep Learning Workshop*.

Junczys-Dowmunt, Marcin. 2018. Dual conditional cross-entropy filtering of noisy parallel corpora. In *WMT*.

Khayrallah, Huda and Philipp Koehn. 2018. On the impact of various types of noise on neural machine translation. In *Proceedings of the 2nd Workshop on Neural Machine Translation and Generation*, Melbourne, Australia. Association for Computational Linguistics.

Kim, Yoon and Alexander M. Rush. 2016. Sequence-level knowledge distillation. In *Proceedings of the*

2016 Conference on Empirical Methods in Natural Language Processing, pages 1317–1327, Austin, Texas, November. Association for Computational Linguistics.

Klein, Guillaume, Yoon Kim, Yuntian Deng, Jean Senellart, and Alexander M. Rush. 2017. Opennmt: Open-source toolkit for neural machine translation. In *Proc. ACL.*

Koehn, Philipp, Huda Khayrallah, Kenneth Heafield, and Mikel L. Forcada. 2018. Findings of the wmt 2018 shared task on parallel corpus filtering. In *Proceedings of the Third Conference on Machine Translation, Volume 2: Shared Task Papers*, pages 739–752, Belgium, Brussels, October. Association for Computational Linguistics.

Li, Yuncheng, Jianchao Yang, Yale Song, Liangliang Cao, Jiebo Luo, and Jia Li. 2017. Learning from noisy labels with distillation. *CoRR*, abs/1703.02391.

Luong, Thang, Hieu Pham, and Christopher D. Manning. 2015. Effective approaches to attention-based neural machine translation. In *Proceedings of the 2015 Conference on Empirical Methods in Natural Language Processing*, Lisbon, Portugal. Association for Computational Linguistics.

Miceli Barone, Antonio Valerio, Barry Haddow, Ulrich Germann, and Rico Sennrich. 2017. Regularization techniques for fine-tuning in neural machine translation. In *Proceedings of the 2017 Conference on Empirical Methods in Natural Language Processing*, pages 1489–1494. Association for Computational Linguistics.

Munteanu, Dragos Stefan and Daniel Marcu. 2005. Improving machine translation performance by exploiting non-parallel corpora. *Comput. Linguist.*, pages 477–504, December.

Noreen., Eric W. 1989. *Computer Intensive Methods for Testing Hypotheses. An Introduction.* Wiley-Interscience.

Papineni, Kishore, Salim Roukos, Todd Ward, and Wei-Jing Zhu. 2002. Bleu: a method for automatic evaluation of machine translation. In *Proceedings of 40th Annual Meeting of the Association for Computational Linguistics*. Association for Computational Linguistics.

Reed, Scott E., Honglak Lee, Dragomir Anguelov, Christian Szegedy, Dumitru Erhan, and Andrew Rabinovich. 2014. Training deep neural networks on noisy labels with bootstrapping. *CoRR*, abs/1412.6596.

Riezler, Stefan and John T. Maxwell. 2005. On some pitfalls in automatic evaluation and significance testing for MT. In *Proceedings of the ACL Workshop on Intrinsic and Extrinsic Evaluation Measures for Machine Translation and/or Summarization.*

Sennrich, Rico, Barry Haddow, and Alexandra Birch. 2016. Improving neural machine translation models with monolingual data. In *Proceedings of the 54th Annual Meeting of the Association for Computational Linguistics (Volume 1: Long Papers)*, pages 86–96. Association for Computational Linguistics.

Exploiting Out-of-Domain Parallel Data through Multilingual Transfer Learning for Low-Resource Neural Machine Translation

Aizhan Imankulova[†]   **Raj Dabre**[‡]   **Atsushi Fujita**[‡]   **Kenji Imamura**[‡]
[†]Tokyo Metropolitan University
6-6 Asahigaoka, Hino, Tokyo 191-0065, Japan
`imankulova-aizhan@ed.tmu.ac.jp`
[‡]National Institute of Information and Communications Technology
3-5 Hikaridai, Seika-cho, Soraku-gun, Kyoto, 619-0289, Japan
`{raj.dabre, atsushi.fujita, kenji.imamura}@nict.go.jp`

Abstract

This paper proposes a novel multilingual multistage fine-tuning approach for low-resource neural machine translation (NMT), taking a challenging Japanese–Russian pair for benchmarking. Although there are many solutions for low-resource scenarios, such as multilingual NMT and back-translation, we have empirically confirmed their limited success when restricted to in-domain data. We therefore propose to exploit out-of-domain data through transfer learning, by using it to first train a multilingual NMT model followed by multistage fine-tuning on in-domain parallel and back-translated pseudo-parallel data. Our approach, which combines domain adaptation, multilingualism, and back-translation, helps improve the translation quality by more than 3.7 BLEU points, over a strong baseline, for this extremely low-resource scenario.

1 Introduction

Neural machine translation (NMT) (Cho et al., 2014; Sutskever et al., 2014; Bahdanau et al., 2015) has enabled end-to-end training of a translation system without needing to deal with word alignments, translation rules, and complicated decoding algorithms, which are the characteristics of phrase-based statistical machine translation (PB-SMT) (Koehn et al., 2007). Although NMT can be significantly better than PBSMT in resource-rich scenarios, PBSMT performs better in low-resource scenarios (Koehn and Knowles, 2017).

Only by exploiting cross-lingual transfer learning techniques (Firat et al., 2016; Zoph et al., 2016; Kocmi and Bojar, 2018), can the NMT performance approach PBSMT performance in low-resource scenarios.

However, such methods usually require an NMT model trained on a resource-rich language pair like French↔English (parent), which is to be fine-tuned for a low-resource language pair like Uzbek↔English (child). On the other hand, multilingual approaches (Johnson et al., 2017) propose to train a single model to translate multiple language pairs. However, these approaches are effective only when the parent target or source language is relatively resource-rich like English (En). Furthermore, the parents and children models should be trained on similar domains; otherwise, one has to take into account an additional problem of domain adaptation (Chu et al., 2017).

In this paper, we work on a linguistically distant and thus challenging language pair Japanese↔Russian (Ja↔Ru) which has only 12k lines of news domain parallel corpus and hence is extremely resource-poor. Furthermore, the amount of indirect in-domain parallel corpora, i.e., Ja↔En and Ru↔En, are also small. As we demonstrate in Section 4, this severely limits the performance of prominent low-resource techniques, such as multilingual modeling, back-translation, and pivot-based PBSMT. To remedy this, we propose a novel multistage fine-tuning method for NMT that combines multilingual modeling (Johnson et al., 2017) and domain adaptation (Chu et al., 2017).

We have addressed two important research questions (RQs) in the context of extremely low-resource machine translation (MT) and our explorations have derived rational contributions (CTs) as follows:

RQ1. What kind of translation quality can we obtain in an extremely low-resource scenario?

CT1. We have made extensive comparisons with multiple architectures and MT paradigms to show how difficult the problem is. We have also explored the utility of back-translation and show that it is ineffective given the poor performance of base MT systems used to generate pseudo-parallel data. Our systematic exploration shows that multilingualism is extremely useful for in-domain translation with very limited corpora (see Section 4). This type of exhaustive exploration has been missing from most existing works.

RQ2. What are the effective ways to exploit out-of-domain data for extremely low-resource in-domain translation?

CT2. Our proposal is to first train a multilingual NMT model on out-of-domain Ja↔En and Ru↔En data, then fine-tune it on in-domain Ja↔En and Ru↔En data, and further fine-tune it on Ja↔Ru data (see Section 5). We show that this stage-wise fine-tuning is crucial for high-quality translation. We then show that the improved NMT models lead to pseudo-parallel data of better quality. This data can then be used to improve the performance even further thereby enabling the generation of better pseudo-parallel data. By iteratively generating pseudo-parallel data and fine-tuning the model on said data, we can achieve the best performance for Japanese↔Russian translation.

To the best of our knowledge, we are the first to perform such an extensive evaluation of extremely low-resource MT problem and propose a novel multilingual multistage fine-tuning approach involving multilingual modeling and domain adaptation to address it.

2   Our Japanese–Russian Setting

In this paper, we deal with Ja↔Ru news translation. This language pair is very challenging because the languages involved have completely different writing system, phonology, morphology, grammar, and syntax. Among various domains, we experimented with translations in the news domain, considering the importance of sharing news between different language speakers. Moreover, news domain is one of the most challenging tasks,

Ru	Ja	En	#sent.	test	Usage development
✓	✓	✓	913	600	313
✓	✓		173	-	173
	✓	✓	276	-	276
✓		✓	0	-	-
✓			4	-	-
	✓		287	-	-
		✓	1	-	-
Total			1,654	-	-

Table 1: Manually aligned News Commentary data.

due to large presence of out-of-vocabulary (OOV) tokens and long sentences.[1] To establish and evaluate existing methods, we also involved English as the third language. As direct parallel corpora are scarce, involving a language such as English for pivoting is quite common (Utiyama and Isahara, 2007).

There has been no clean held-out parallel data for Ja↔Ru and Ja↔En news translation. Therefore, we manually compiled development and test sets using News Commentary data[2] as a source. Since the given Ja↔Ru and Ja↔En data share many lines in the Japanese side, we first compiled tri-text data. Then, from each line, corresponding parts across languages were manually identified, and unaligned parts were split off into a new line. Note that we have never merged two or more lines. As a result, we obtained 1,654 lines of data comprising trilingual, bilingual, and monolingual segments (mainly sentences) as summarized in Table 1. Finally, for the sake of comparability, we randomly chose 600 trilingual sentences to create a test set, and concatenated the rest of them and bilingual sentences to form development sets.

Our manually aligned development and test sets are publicly available.[3]

3   Related Work

Koehn and Knowles (2017) showed that NMT is unable to handle low-resource language pairs as opposed to PBSMT. Transfer learning approaches (Firat et al., 2016; Zoph et al., 2016; Kocmi and Bojar, 2018) work well when a large helping parallel corpus is available. This restricts one of the source or the target languages to be English which, in our case, is not possible. Approaches involving bi-directional NMT modeling is shown to drasti-

---

[1] News domain translation is also the most competitive tasks in WMT indicating its importance.
[2] http://opus.nlpl.eu/News-Commentary-v11.php
[3] https://github.com/aizhanti/JaRuNC

cally improve low-resource translation (Niu et al., 2018). However, like most other, this work focuses on translation from and into English.

Remaining options include (a) unsupervised MT (Artetxe et al., 2018; Lample et al., 2018; Marie and Fujita, 2018), (b) parallel sentence mining from non-parallel or comparable corpora (Utiyama and Isahara, 2003; Tillmann and Xu, 2009), (c) generating pseudo-parallel data (Sennrich et al., 2016), and (d) MT based on pivot languages (Utiyama and Isahara, 2007). The linguistic distance between Japanese and Russian makes it extremely difficult to learn bilingual knowledge, such as bilingual lexicons and bilingual word embeddings. Unsupervised MT is thus not promising yet, due to its heavy reliance on accurate bilingual word embeddings. Neither does parallel sentence mining, due to the difficulty of obtaining accurate bilingual lexicons. Pseudo-parallel data can be used to augment existing parallel corpora for training, and previous work has reported that such data generated by so-called back-translation can substantially improve the quality of NMT. However, this approach requires base MT systems that can generate somewhat accurate translations. It is thus infeasible in our scenario, because we can obtain only a weak system which is the consequence of an extremely low-resource situation. MT based on pivot languages requires large in-domain parallel corpora involving the pivot languages. This technique is thus infeasible, because the in-domain parallel corpora for Ja↔En and Ru↔En pairs are also extremely limited, whereas there are large parallel corpora in other domains. Section 4 empirically confirms the limit of these existing approaches.

Fortunately, there are two useful transfer learning solutions using NMT: (e) multilingual modeling to incorporate multiple language pairs into a single model (Johnson et al., 2017) and (f) domain adaptation to incorporate out-of-domain data (Chu et al., 2017). In this paper, we explore a novel method involving step-wise fine-tuning to combine these two methods. By improving the translation quality in this way, we can also increase the likelihood of pseudo-parallel data being useful to further improve translation quality.

4 Limit of Using only In-domain Data

This section answers our first research question, [RQ1], about the translation quality that we can achieve using existing methods and in-domain par-

Lang.pair	Partition	#sent.	#tokens	#types
Ja↔Ru	train	12,356	341k / 229k	22k / 42k
	development	486	16k / 11k	2.9k / 4.3k
	test	600	22k / 15k	3.5k / 5.6k
Ja↔En	train	47,082	1.27M / 1.01M	48k / 55k
	development	589	21k / 16k	3.5k / 3.8k
	test	600	22k / 17k	3.5k / 3.8k
Ru↔En	train	82,072	1.61M / 1.83M	144k / 74k
	development	313	7.8k / 8.4k	3.2k / 2.3k
	test	600	15k / 17k	5.6k / 3.8k

Table 2: Statistics on our in-domain parallel data.

allel and monolingual data. We then use the strongest model to conduct experiments on generating and utilizing back-translated pseudo-parallel data for augmenting NMT. Our intention is to empirically identify the most effective practices as well as recognize the limitations of relying only on in-domain parallel corpora.

4.1 Data

To train MT systems among the three languages, i.e., Japanese, Russian, and English, we used all the parallel data provided by Global Voices,[4] more specifically those available at OPUS.[5] Table 2 summarizes the size of train/development/test splits used in our experiments. The number of parallel sentences for Ja↔Ru is 12k, for Ja↔En is 47k, and for Ru↔En is 82k. Note that the three corpora are not mutually exclusive: 9k out of 12k sentences in the Ja↔Ru corpus were also included in the other two parallel corpora, associated with identical English translations. This puts a limit on the positive impact that the helping corpora can have on the translation quality.

Even when one focuses on low-resource language pairs, we often have access to larger quantities of in-domain monolingual data of each language. Such monolingual data are useful to improve quality of MT, for example, as the source of pseudo-parallel data for augmenting training data for NMT (Sennrich et al., 2016) and as the training data for large and smoothed language models for PBSMT (Koehn and Knowles, 2017). Table 3 summarizes the statistics on our monolingual corpora for several domains including the news domain. Note that we removed from the Global Voices monolingual corpora those sentences that are already present in the parallel corpus.

---

[4]https://globalvoices.org/
[5]http://opus.nlpl.eu/GlobalVoices-v2015.php

Corpus	Ja	Ru	En
Global Voices[5]	26k	24k	842k
Wikinews[6]	37k	243k	-
News Crawl[7]	-	72M	194M
Yomiuri (2007–2011)[8]	19M	-	-
IWSLT[9]	411k	64k	66k
Tatoeba[10]	5k	58k	208k

Table 3: Number of lines in our monolingual data. Whereas the first four are from the news corpora (in-domain), the last two, i.e., "IWSLT" and "Tatoeba," are from other domains.

We tokenized English and Russian sentences using *tokenizer.perl* of `Moses` (Koehn et al., 2007).[11] To tokenize Japanese sentences, we used `MeCab`[12] with the IPA dictionary. After tokenization, we eliminated duplicated sentence pairs and sentences with more than 100 tokens for all the languages.

4.2 MT Methods Examined

We began with evaluating standard MT paradigms, i.e., PBSMT (Koehn et al., 2007) and NMT (Sutskever et al., 2014). As for PBSMT, we also examined two advanced methods: pivot-based translation relying on a helping language (Utiyama and Isahara, 2007) and induction of phrase tables from monolingual data (Marie and Fujita, 2018).

As for NMT, we compared two types of encoder-decoder architectures: attentional RNN-based model (RNMT) (Bahdanau et al., 2015) and the Transformer model (Vaswani et al., 2017). In addition to standard uni-directional modeling, to cope with the low-resource problem, we examined two multi-directional models: bi-directional model (Niu et al., 2018) and multi-to-multi (M2M) model (Johnson et al., 2017).

After identifying the best model, we also examined the usefulness of a data augmentation method based on back-translation (Sennrich et al., 2016).

PBSMT Systems

First, we built a PBSMT system for each of the six translation directions. We obtained phrase tables from parallel corpus using `SyMGIZA++`[13] with the `grow-diag-final` heuristics for word alignment, and `Moses` for phrase pair extraction. Then, we trained a bi-directional MSD (monotone, swap, and discontinuous) lexicalized reordering model. We also trained three 5-gram language models, using `KenLM`[14] on the following monolingual data: (1) the target side of the parallel data, (2) the concatenation of (1) and the monolingual data from Global Voices, and (3) the concatenation of (1) and all monolingual data in the news domain in Table 3.

Subsequently, using English as the pivot language, we examined the following three types of pivot-based PBSMT systems (Utiyama and Isahara, 2007; Cohn and Lapata, 2007) for each of Ja→Ru and Ru→Ja.

Cascade: 2-step decoding using the source-to-English and English-to-target systems.

Synthesize: Obtain a new phrase table from synthetic parallel data generated by translating English side of the target–English training parallel data to the source language with the English-to-source system.

Triangulate: Compile a new phrase table combining those for the source-to-English and English-to-target systems.

Among these three, triangulation is the most computationally expensive method. Although we had filtered the component phrase tables using the statistical significance pruning method (Johnson et al., 2007), triangulation can generate an enormous number of phrase pairs. To reduce the computational cost during decoding and the negative effects of potentially noisy phrase pairs, we retained for each source phrase s only the k-best translations t according to the forward translation probability $\phi(t|s)$ calculated from the conditional probabilities in the component models as defined in Utiyama and Isahara (2007). For each of the retained phrase pairs, we also calculated the backward translation probability, $\phi(s|t)$, and lexical translation probabilities, $\phi_{lex}(t|s)$ and $\phi_{lex}(s|t)$, in the same manner as $\phi(t|s)$.

We also investigated the utility of recent advances in unsupervised MT. Even though we began with a publicly available implementation of

---

[6]`https://dumps.wikimedia.org/backup-index.html` (20180501)
[7]`http://www.statmt.org/wmt18/translation-task.html`
[8]`https://www.yomiuri.co.jp/database/glossary/`
[9]`http://www.cs.jhu.edu/~kevinduh/a/multitarget-tedtalks/`
[10]`http://opus.nlpl.eu/Tatoeba-v2.php`
[11]`https://github.com/moses-smt/mosesdecoder`
[12]`http://taku910.github.io/mecab`, version 0.996.
[13]`https://github.com/emjotde/symgiza-pp`
[14]`https://github.com/kpu/kenlm`

ID	System	Parallel data			Total size of training data	Vocabulary size
		Ja↔Ru	Ja↔En	Ru↔En		
(a1), (b1)	Ja→Ru or Ru→Ja	12k	-	-	12k	16k
	Ja→En or En→Ja	-	47k	-	47k	16k
	Ru→En or En→Ru	-	-	82k	82k	16k
(a2), (b2)	Ja→Ru and Ru→Ja	12k	-	-	24k	16k
	Ja→En and En→Ja	-	47k	-	94k	16k
	Ru→En and En→Ru	-	-	82k	164k	16k
(a3), (b3)	M2M systems	12k→82k	47k→82k	82k	492k	32k

Table 4: Configuration of uni-, bi-directional, and M2M NMT baseline systems. Arrows in "Parallel data" columns indicate the over-sampling of the parallel data to match the size of the largest parallel data.

unsupervised PBSMT (Lample et al., 2018),[15] it crashed due to unknown reasons. We therefore followed another method described in Marie and Fujita (2018). Instead of short n-grams (Artetxe et al., 2018; Lample et al., 2018), we collected a set of phrases in Japanese and Russian from respective monolingual data using the `word2phrase` algorithm (Mikolov et al., 2013),[16] as in Marie and Fujita (2018). To reduce the complexity, we used randomly selected 10M monolingual sentences, and 300k most frequent phrases made of words among the 300k most frequent words. For each source phrase s, we selected 300-best target phrases t according to the translation probability as in Lample et al. (2018): $p(t|s) = \frac{\exp(\beta \cos(emb(t), emb(s)))}{\sum_{t'} \exp(\beta \cos(emb(t'), emb(s)))}$, where $emb(\cdot)$ stands for a bilingual embedding of a given phrase, obtained through averaging bilingual embeddings of constituent words learned from the two monolingual data using `fastText`[17] and `vecmap`.[18] For each of the retained phrase pair, $p(s|t)$ was computed analogously. We also computed lexical translation probabilities relying on those learned from the given small parallel corpus.

Up to four phrase tables were jointly exploited by the multiple decoding path ability of `Moses`. Weights for the features were tuned using `KB-MIRA` (Cherry and Foster, 2012) on the development set; we took the best weights after 15 iterations. Two hyper-parameters, namely, k for the number of pivot-based phrase pairs per source phrase and d for distortion limit, were determined by a grid search on $k \in \{10, 20, 40, 60, 80, 100\}$ and $d \in \{8, 10, 12, 14, 16, 18, 20\}$. In contrast, we used predetermined hyper-parameters for phrase table induction from monolingual data, following the convention: 200 for the dimension of word and phrase embeddings and $\beta = 30$.

NMT Systems

We used the open-source implementation of the RNMT and the Transformer models in `tensor2tensor`.[19] A uni-directional model for each of the six translation directions was trained on the corresponding parallel corpus. Bi-directional and M2M models were realized by adding an artificial token that specifies the target language to the beginning of each source sentence and shuffling the entire training data (Johnson et al., 2017).

Table 4 contains some specific hyper-parameters[20] for our baseline NMT models. The hyper-parameters not mentioned in this table used the default values in `tensor2tensor`. For M2M systems, we over-sampled Ja→Ru and Ja→En training data so that their sizes match the largest Ru→En data. To reduce the number of unknown words, we used `tensor2tensor`'s internal sub-word segmentation mechanism. Since we work in a low-resource setting, we used shared sub-word vocabularies of size 16k for the uni- and bi-directional models and 32k for the M2M models. The number of training iterations was determined by early-stopping: we evaluated our models on the development set every 1,000 updates, and stopped training if BLEU score for the development set was not improved for 10,000 updates (10 check-points). Note that the development set was created by concatenating those for the individual translation directions without any over-sampling.

Having trained the models, we averaged the last 10 check-points and decoded the test sets with a beam size of 4 and a length penalty which was

---

[15] https://github.com/facebookresearch/ UnsupervisedMT

[16] https://code.google.com/archive/p/ word2vec/

[17] https://fasttext.cc/

[18] https://github.com/artetxem/vecmap

[19] https://github.com/tensorflow/ tensor2tensor, version 1.6.6.

[20] We compared two mini-batch sizes, 1024 and 6144 tokens, and found that 6144 and 1024 worked better for RNMT and Transformer, respectively.

ID	System	Ja→Ru	Ru→Ja	Ja→En	En→Ja	Ru→En	En→Ru
(a1)	Uni-directional RNMT	0.58	1.86	2.41	7.83	18.42	13.64
(a2)	Bi-directional RNMT	0.65	1.61	6.18	8.81	19.60	15.11
(a3)	M2M RNMT	1.51	4.29	5.15	7.55	14.24	10.86
(b1)	Uni-directional Transformer	0.70	1.96	4.36	7.97	20.70	16.24
(b2)	Bi-directional Transformer	0.19	0.87	6.48	10.63	22.25	16.03
(b3)	M2M Transformer	**3.72**	**8.35**	**10.24**	**12.43**	22.10	**16.92**
(c1)	Uni-directional supervised PBSMT	2.02	4.45	8.19	10.27	**22.37**	16.52

Table 5: BLEU scores of baseline systems. **Bold** indicates the best BLEU score for each translation direction.

tuned by a linear search on the BLEU score for the development set.

Similarly to PBSMT, we also evaluated "Cascade" and "Synthesize" methods with uni-directional NMT models.

4.3 Results

We evaluated MT models using case-sensitive and tokenized BLEU (Papineni et al., 2002) on test sets, using `Moses`'s *multi-bleu.perl*. Statistical significance ($p < 0.05$) on the difference of BLEU scores was tested by `Moses`'s *bootstrap-hypothesis-difference-significance.pl*.

Tables 5 and 6 show BLEU scores of all the models, except the NMT systems augmented with back-translations. Whereas some models achieved reasonable BLEU scores for Ja↔En and Ru↔En translation, all the results for Ja↔Ru, which is our main concern, were abysmal.

Among the NMT models, Transformer models (b*) were proven to be better than RNMT models (a*). RNMT models could not even outperform the uni-directional PBSMT models (c1). M2M models (a3) and (b3) outperformed their corresponding uni- and bi-directional models in most cases. It is worth noting that in this extremely low-resource scenario, BLEU scores of the M2M RNMT model for the largest language pair, i.e., Ru↔En, were lower than those of the uni- and bi-directional RNMT models as in Johnson et al. (2017). In contrast, with the M2M Transformer model, Ru↔En also benefited from multilingualism.

Standard PBSMT models (c1) achieved higher BLEU scores than uni-directional NMT models (a1) and (b1), as reported by Koehn and Knowles (2017), whereas they underperform the M2M Transformer NMT model (b3). As shown in Table 6, pivot-based PBSMT systems always achieved higher BLEU scores than (c1). The best model with three phrase tables, labeled "Synthesize / Triangulate / Gold," brought visible BLEU gains with substantial reduction of OOV tokens (3047→1180 for Ja→Ru, 4463→1812 for

System	Ja→Ru	Ru→Ja
PBSMT: Cascade	3.65	7.62
PBSMT: Synthesize	3.37	6.72
PBSMT: Synthesize / Gold	2.94	6.95
PBSMT: Synthesize + Gold	3.07	6.62
PBSMT: Triangulate	**3.75**	7.02
PBSMT: Triangulate / Gold	**3.93**	7.02
PBSMT: Synthesize / Triangulate / Gold	**4.02**	7.07
PBSMT: Induced	0.37	0.65
PBSMT: Induced / Synthesize / Triangulate / Gold	2.85	6.86
RNMT: Cascade	1.19	6.73
RNMT: Synthesize	1.82	3.02
RNMT: Synthesize + Gold	1.62	3.24
Transformer NMT: Cascade	2.41	6.84
Transformer NMT: Synthesize	1.78	5.43
Transformer NMT: Synthesize + Gold	2.13	5.06

Table 6: BLEU scores of pivot-based systems. "Gold" refers to the phrase table trained on the parallel data. **Bold** indicates the BLEU score higher than the best one in Table 5. "/" indicates the use of separately trained multiple phrase tables, whereas so does "+" training on the mixture of parallel data.

Ru→Ja). However, further extension with phrase tables induced from monolingual data did not push the limit, despite their high coverage; only 336 and 677 OOV tokens were left for the two translation directions, respectively. This is due to the poor quality of the bilingual word embeddings used to extract the phrase table, as envisaged in Section 3.

None of pivot-based approaches with uni-directional NMT models could even remotely rival the M2M Transformer NMT model (b3).

4.4 Augmentation with Back-translation

Given that the M2M Transformer NMT model (b3) achieved best results for most of the translation directions and competitive results for the rest, we further explored it through back-translation.

We examined the utility of pseudo-parallel data for all the six translation directions, unlike the work of Lakew et al. (2017) and Lakew et al. (2018), which concentrate only on the zero-shot language pair, and the work of Niu et al. (2018), which compares only uni- or bi-directional models. We investigated whether each translation direction in M2M models will benefit from pseudo-parallel data and if so, what kind of improvement takes place.

| ID | System | Parallel data | | | | Total size of |
		Pseudo	Ja↔Ru	Ja↔En	Ru↔En	training data
#1–#10	Ja*→Ru and/or Ru*→Ja	12k→82k	12k→82k	47k→82k×2	82k×2	984k
	Ja*→En and/or En*→Ja	47k→82k	12k→82k×2	47k→82k	82k×2	984k
	Ru*→En and/or En*→Ru	82k	12k→82k×2	47k→82k×2	82k	984k
	All	All of the above	12k→82k	47k→82k	82k	984k

Table 7: Over-sampling criteria for pseudo-parallel data generated by back-translation.

| ID | Pseudo-parallel data involved | | | | | | BLEU score | | | | | |
	Ja*→Ru	Ru*→Ja	Ja*→En	En*→Ja	Ru*→En	En*→Ru	Ja→Ru	Ru→Ja	Ja→En	En→Ja	Ru→En	En→Ru
(b3)	-	-	-	-	-	-	3.72	8.35	10.24	12.43	22.10	16.92
#1	✓	-	-	-	-	-	•**4.59**	**8.63**	**10.64**	**12.94**	**22.21**	**17.30**
#2	-	✓	-	-	-	-	**3.74**	•**8.85**	10.13	**13.05**	**22.48**	**17.20**
#3	✓	✓	-	-	-	-	•**4.56**	•**9.09**	**10.57**	•**13.23**	**22.48**	•**17.89**
#4	-	-	✓	-	-	-	3.71	8.05	•**11.00**	**12.66**	**22.17**	16.76
#5	-	-	-	✓	-	-	3.62	8.10	9.92	•**14.06**	21.66	16.68
#6	-	-	✓	✓	-	-	3.61	7.94	•**11.51**	•**14.38**	**22.22**	16.80
#7	-	-	-	-	✓	-	**3.80**	**8.37**	**10.67**	**13.00**	**22.51**	•**17.73**
#8	-	-	-	-	-	✓	**3.77**	8.04	**10.52**	12.43	•**22.85**	**17.13**
#9	-	-	-	-	✓	✓	3.37	8.03	10.19	**12.79**	**22.77**	**17.26**
#10	✓	✓	✓	✓	✓	✓	•**4.43**	•**9.38**	•**12.06**	•**14.43**	•**23.09**	**17.30**

Table 8: BLEU scores of M2M Transformer NMT systems trained on the mixture of given parallel corpus and pseudo-parallel data generated by back-translation using (b3). Six "X*→Y" columns show whether the pseudo-parallel data for each translation direction is involved. **Bold** indicates the scores higher than (b3) and "•" indicates statistical significance of the improvement.

First, we selected sentences to be back-translated from in-domain monolingual data (Table 3), relying on the score proposed by Moore and Lewis (2010) via the following procedure.

1. For each language, train two 4-gram language models, using KenLM: an in-domain one on all the Global Voices data, i.e., both parallel and monolingual data, and a general-domain one on the concatenation of Global Voices, IWSLT, and Tatoeba data.

2. For each language, discard sentences containing OOVs according to the in-domain language model.

3. For each translation direction, select the T-best monolingual sentences in the news domain, according to the difference between cross-entropy scores given by the in-domain and general-domain language models.

Whereas Niu et al. (2018) exploited monolingual data much larger than parallel data, we maintained a 1:1 ratio between them (Johnson et al., 2017), setting T to the number of lines of parallel data of given language pair.

Selected monolingual sentences were then translated using the M2M Transformer NMT model (b3) to compose pseudo-parallel data. Then, the pseudo-parallel data were enlarged by over-sampling as summarized in Table 7. Finally, new NMT models were trained on the concatenation of the original parallel and pseudo-parallel data from

scratch in the same manner as the previous NMT models with the same hyper-parameters.

Table 8 shows the BLEU scores achieved by several reasonable combinations of six-way pseudo-parallel data. We observed that the use of all six-way pseudo-parallel data (#10) significantly improved the base model for all the translation directions, except En→Ru. A translation direction often benefited when the pseudo-parallel data for that specific direction was used.

4.5 Summary

We have evaluated an extensive variation of MT models[21] that rely only on in-domain parallel and monolingual data. However, the resulting BLEU scores for Ja→Ru and Ru→Ja tasks do not exceed 10 BLEU points, implying the inherent limitation of the in-domain data as well as the difficulty of these translation directions.

5 Exploiting Large Out-of-Domain Data Involving a Helping Language

The limitation of relying only on in-domain data demonstrated in Section 4 motivates us to explore

---

[21] Other conceivable options include transfer learning using parallel data between English and one of Japanese and Russian as either source or target language, such as pre-training an En→Ru model and fine-tuning it for Ja→Ru. Our M2M models conceptually subsume them, even though they do not explicitly divide the two steps during training. On the other hand, our method proposed in Section 5 explicitly conducts transfer learning for domain adaptation followed by additional transfer learning across different languages.

Domain \ language pair	Direct	One-side shared
in-domain	A, ✓	B, ✓
out-of-domain	C, ×	D, ✓

Table 9: Classification of parallel data.

Lang.pair	Corpus	#sent.	#tokens	#types
Ja↔En	ASPEC	1,500,000	42.3M / 34.6M	234k / 1.02M
Ru↔En	UN	2,647,243	90.5M / 92.8M	757k / 593k
	Yandex	320,325	8.51M / 9.26M	617k / 407k

Table 10: Statistics on our out-of-domain parallel data.

other types of parallel data. As raised in our second research question, [RQ2], we considered the effective ways to exploit out-of-domain data.

According to language pair and domain, parallel data can be classified into four categories in Table 9. Among all the categories, out-of-domain data for the language pair of interest have been exploited in the domain adaptation scenarios (C→A) (Chu et al., 2017). However, for Ja↔Ru, no out-of-domain data is available. To exploit out-of-domain parallel data for Ja↔En and Ru↔En pairs instead, we propose a multistage fine-tuning method, which combines two types of transfer learning, i.e., domain adaptation for Ja↔En and Ru↔En (D→B) and multilingual transfer (B→A), relying on the M2M model examined in Section 4. We also examined the utility of fine-tuning for iteratively generating and using pseudo-parallel data.

5.1 Multistage Fine-tuning

Simply using NMT systems trained on out-of-domain data for in-domain translation is known to perform badly. In order to effectively use large-scale out-of-domain data for our extremely low-resource task, we propose to perform domain adaptation through either (a) conventional fine-tuning, where an NMT system trained on out-of-domain data is fine-tuned only on in-domain data, or (b) mixed fine-tuning (Chu et al., 2017), where pre-trained out-of-domain NMT system is fine-tuned using a mixture of in-domain and out-of-domain data. The same options are available for transferring from Ja↔En and Ru↔En to Ja↔Ru.

We inevitably involve two types of transfer learning, i.e., domain adaptation for Ja↔En and Ru↔En and multilingual transfer for Ja↔Ru pair. Among several conceivable options for managing these two problems, we examined the following multistage fine-tuning.

Stage 0. Out-of-domain pre-training: Pre-train a multilingual model only on the Ja↔En and Ru↔En out-of-domain parallel data (I), where the vocabulary of the model is determined on the basis of the in-domain parallel data in the same manner as the M2M NMT models examined in Section 4.

Stage 1. Fine-tuning for domain adaptation: Fine-tune the pre-trained model (I) on the in-domain Ja↔En and Ru↔En parallel data (fine-tuning, II) or on the mixture of in-domain and out-of-domain Ja↔En and Ru↔En parallel data (mixed fine-tuning, III).

Stage 2. Fine-tuning for Ja↔Ru pair: Further fine-tune the models (each of II and III) for Ja↔Ru on in-domain parallel data for this language pair only (fine-tuning, IV and VI) or on all the in-domain parallel data (mixed fine-tuning, V and VII).

We chose this way due to the following two reasons. First, we need to take a balance between several different parallel corpora sizes. The other reason is division of labor; we assume that solving each sub-problem one by one should enable gradual shift of parameters.

5.2 Data Selection

As an additional large-scale out-of-domain parallel data for Ja↔En, we used the cleanest 1.5M sentences from the Asian Scientific Paper Excerpt Corpus (ASPEC) (Nakazawa et al., 2016).[22] As for Ru↔En, we used the UN and Yandex corpora released for the WMT 2018 News Translation Task.[23] We retained Ru↔En sentence pairs that contain at least one OOV token in both sides, according to the in-domain language model trained in Section 4.4. Table 10 summarizes the statistics on the remaining out-of-domain parallel data.

5.3 Results

Table 11 shows the results of our multistage fine-tuning, where the IDs of each row refer to those described in Section 5.1. First of all, the final models of our multistage fine-tuning, i.e., V and VII, achieved significantly higher BLEU scores than (b3) in Table 5, a weak baseline without using any monolingual data, and #10 in Table 8, a strong baseline established with monolingual data.

---

[22]http://lotus.kuee.kyoto-u.ac.jp/ASPEC/
[23]http://www.statmt.org/wmt18/translation-task.html

ID	Initialized	Out-of-domain data		In-domain data			BLEU score					
		Ja↔En	Ru↔En	Ja↔Ru	Ja↔En	Ru↔En	Ja→Ru	Ru→Ja	Ja→En	En→Ja	Ru→En	En→Ru
(b3)	-	-	-	✓	✓	✓	3.72	8.35	10.24	12.43	22.10	16.92
I	-	✓	✓	-	-	-	0.00	0.15	4.59	4.15	•25.22	•20.37
II	I	-	-	-	✓	✓	0.20	0.70	•14.10	•**17.80**	•28.23	•24.35
III	I	✓	✓	-	✓	✓	0.23	1.07	•13.31	•17.74	•**28.73**	•**25.22**
IV	II	-	-	✓	-	-	•5.44	•10.67	0.12	3.97	0.11	3.66
V	II	-	-	✓	✓	✓	•6.90	•11.99	•14.34	•16.93	•27.50	•23.17
VI	III	-	-	✓	-	-	•5.91	•10.83	0.26	2.18	0.18	1.10
VII	III	-	-	✓	✓	✓	•7.49	•12.10	•**14.63**	•17.51	•28.51	•24.60
I'	-	✓	✓	✓	✓	✓	•5.31	•10.73	•14.41	•16.34	•27.46	•23.21
II'	I	-	-	✓	✓	✓	•6.30	•11.64	•14.29	•16.83	•27.53	•23.00
III'	I	✓	✓	✓	✓	✓	•**7.53**	•**12.33**	•14.19	•16.77	•27.94	•23.97

Table 11: BLEU scores obtained through multistage fine-tuning. "Initialized" column indicates the model used for initializing parameters that are fine-tuned on the data indicated by ✓. **Bold** indicates the best BLEU score for each translation direction. "•" indicates statistical significance of the improvement over (b3).

The performance of the initial model (I) depends on the language pair. For Ja↔Ru pair, it cannot achieve minimum level of quality since the model has never seen parallel data for this pair. The performance on Ja↔En pair was much lower than the two baseline models, reflecting the crucial mismatch between training and testing domains. In contrast, Ru↔En pair benefited the most and achieved surprisingly high BLEU scores. The reason might be due to the proximity of out-of-domain training data and in-domain test data.

The first fine-tuning stage significantly pushed up the translation quality for Ja↔En and Ru↔En pairs, in both cases with fine-tuning (II) and mixed fine-tuning (III). At this stage, both models performed only poorly for Ja↔Ru pair as they have not yet seen Ja↔Ru parallel data. Either model had a consistent advantage to the other.

When these models were further fine-tuned only on the in-domain Ja↔Ru parallel data (IV and VI), we obtained translations of better quality than the two baselines for Ja↔Ru pair. However, as a result of complete ignorance of Ja↔En and Ru↔En pairs, the models only produced translations of poor quality for these language pairs. In contrast, mixed fine-tuning for the second fine-tuning stage (V and VII) resulted in consistently better models than conventional fine-tuning (IV and VI), irrespective of the choice at the first stage, thanks to the gradual shift of parameters realized by in-domain Ja↔En and Ru↔En parallel data. Unfortunately, the translation quality for Ja↔En and Ru↔En pairs sometimes degraded from II and III. Nevertheless, the BLEU scores still retain the large margin against two baselines.

The last three rows in Table 11 present BLEU scores obtained by the methods with fewer fine-tuning steps. The most naive model I', trained on the balanced mixture of whole five types of corpora from scratch, and the model II', obtained through a single-step conventional fine-tuning of I on all the in-domain data, achieved only BLEU scores consistently worse than VII. In contrast, when we merged our two fine-tuning steps into a single mixed fine-tuning on I, we obtained a model III' which is better for the Ja↔Ru pair than VII. Nevertheless, they are still comparable to those of VII and the BLEU scores for the other two language pairs are much lower than VII. As such, we conclude that our multistage fine-tuning leads to a more robust in-domain multilingual model.

5.4 Further Augmentation with Back-translation

Having obtained a better model, we examined again the utility of back-translation. More precisely, we investigated (a) whether the pseudo-parallel data generated by an improved NMT model leads to a further improvement, and (b) whether one more stage of fine-tuning on the mixture of original parallel and pseudo-parallel data will result in a model better than training a new model from scratch as examined in Section 4.4.

Given an NMT model, we first generated six-way pseudo-parallel data by translating monolingual data. For the sake of comparability, we used the identical monolingual sentences sampled in Section 4.4. Then, we further fine-tuned the given model on the mixture of the generated pseudo-parallel data and the original parallel data, following the same over-sampling procedure in Section 4.4. We repeated these steps five times.

Table 12 shows the results. "new #10" in the second row indicates an M2M Transformer model trained from scratch on the mixture of six-way pseudo-parallel data generated by VII and the orig-

No	Initialized	BT	BLEU score					
			Ja→Ru	Ru→Ja	Ja→En	En→Ja	Ru→En	En→Ru
#10	-	(b3)	4.43	9.38	12.06	14.43	23.09	17.30
new #10	-	VII	•6.55	•11.36	•13.77	•15.59	•24.91	•20.55
VIII	VII	VII	•7.83	•12.21	•15.06	•17.19	•28.49	•23.96
IX	VIII	VIII	•8.03	•12.55	•15.07	•17.80	•28.16	•24.27
X	IX	IX	•7.76	•12.59	•15.08	•18.12	•28.18	•24.67
XI	X	X	•7.85	•12.97	•15.26	•17.83	•28.49	•24.36
XII	XI	XI	•8.16	•13.09	•14.96	•17.74	•28.45	•24.35

Table 12: BLEU scores achieved through fine-tuning on the mixture of the original parallel data and six-way pseudo-parallel data. "Initialized" column indicates the model used for initializing parameters and so does "BT" column the model used to generate pseudo-parallel data. "•" indicates statistical significance of the improvement over #10.

Investigation step	Ja→Ru	Ru→Ja
Uni-directional Transformer: (b1) in Table 5	0.70	1.96
M2M Transformer: (b3) in Table 5	3.72	8.35
+ six-way pseudo-parallel data: #10 in Table 8	4.43	9.38
M2M multistage fine-tuning: VII in Table 11	7.49	12.10
+ six-way pseudo-parallel data: XII in Table 12	8.16	13.09

Table 13: Summary of our investigation: BLEU scores of the best NMT systems at each step.

inal parallel data. It achieved higher BLEU scores than #10 in Table 8 thanks to the pseudo-parallel data of better quality, but underperformed the base NMT model VII. In contrast, our fine-tuned model VIII successfully surpassed VII, and one more iteration (IX) further improved BLEU scores for all translation directions, except Ru→En. Although further iterations did not necessarily gain BLEU scores, we came to a much higher plateau compared to the results in Section 4.

6 Conclusion

In this paper, we challenged the difficult task of Ja↔Ru news domain translation in an extremely low-resource setting. We empirically confirmed the limited success of well-established solutions when restricted to in-domain data. Then, to incorporate out-of-domain data, we proposed a multilingual multistage fine-tuning approach and observed that it substantially improves Ja↔Ru translation by over 3.7 BLEU points compared to a strong baseline, as summarized in Table 13. This paper contains an empirical comparison of several existing approaches and hence we hope that our paper can act as a guideline to researchers attempting to tackle extremely low-resource translation.

In the future, we plan to confirm further fine-tuning for each of specific translation directions. We will also explore the way to exploit out-of-domain pseudo-parallel data, better domain-adaptation approaches, and additional challenging language pairs.

Acknowledgments

This work was carried out when Aizhan Imankulova was taking up an internship at NICT, Japan. We would like to thank the reviewers for their insightful comments. A part of this work was conducted under the program "Promotion of Global Communications Plan: Research, Development, and Social Demonstration of Multilingual Speech Translation Technology" of the Ministry of Internal Affairs and Communications (MIC), Japan.

References

Artetxe, Mikel, Gorka Labaka, and Eneko Agirre. 2018. Unsupervised statistical machine translation. In *Proceedings of the 2018 Conference on Empirical Methods in Natural Language Processing*, pages 3632–3642, Brussels, Belgium.

Bahdanau, Dzmitry, Kyunghyun Cho, and Yoshua Bengio. 2015. Neural machine translation by jointly learning to align and translate. In *Proceedings of the 3rd International Conference on Learning Representations*, San Diego, USA.

Cherry, Colin and George Foster. 2012. Batch tuning strategies for statistical machine translation. In *Proceedings of the 2012 Conference of the North American Chapter of the Association for Computational Linguistics: Human Language Technologies*, pages 427–436, Montréal, Canada.

Cho, Kyunghyun, Bart van Merriënboer, Çaglar Gülçehre, Dzmitry Bahdanau, Fethi Bougares, Holger Schwenk, and Yoshua Bengio. 2014. Learning phrase representations using RNN encoder–decoder for statistical machine translation. In *Proceedings of the 2014 Conference on Empirical Methods in Natural Language Processing*, pages 1724–1734, Doha, Qatar.

Chu, Chenhui, Raj Dabre, and Sadao Kurohashi. 2017. An empirical comparison of domain adaptation methods for neural machine translation. In *Proceedings of the 55th Annual Meeting of the Association for Computational Linguistics*, pages 385–391, Vancouver, Canada.

Cohn, Trevor and Mirella Lapata. 2007. Machine translation by triangulation: Making effective use of multi-parallel corpora. In *Proceedings of the 45th Annual Meeting of the Association of Computational Linguistics*, pages 728–735, Prague, Czech Republic.

Firat, Orhan, Kyunghyun Cho, and Yoshua Bengio. 2016. Multi-way, multilingual neural machine translation with a shared attention mechanism. In *NAACL HLT 2016, The 2016 Conference of the North American Chapter of the Association for Computational Linguistics: Human Language Technologies*, pages 866–875, San Diego, USA.

Johnson, Howard, Joel Martin, George Foster, and Roland Kuhn. 2007. Improving translation quality by discarding most of the phrasetable. In *Proceedings of the 2007 Joint Conference on Empirical Methods in Natural Language Processing and Computational Natural Language Learning*, pages 967–975, Prague, Czech Republic.

Johnson, Melvin, Mike Schuster, Quoc Le, Maxim Krikun, Yonghui Wu, Zhifeng Chen, Nikhil Thorat, Fernanda Viégas, Martin Wattenberg, Greg Corrado, Macduff Hughes, and Jeffrey Dean. 2017. Google's multilingual neural machine translation system: Enabling zero-shot translation. *Transactions of the Association for Computational Linguistics*, 5:339–351.

Kocmi, Tom and Ondřej Bojar. 2018. Trivial transfer learning for low-resource neural machine translation. In *Proceedings of the Third Conference on Machine Translation: Research Papers*, pages 244–252, Brussels, Belgium.

Koehn, Philipp and Rebecca Knowles. 2017. Six challenges for neural machine translation. In *Proceedings of the First Workshop on Neural Machine Translation*, pages 28–39, Vancouver, Canada.

Koehn, Philipp, Hieu Hoang, Alexandra Birch, Chris Callison-Burch, Marcello Federico, Nicola Bertoldi, Brooke Cowan, Wade Shen, Christine Moran, Richard Zens, Chris Dyer, Ondrej Bojar, Alexandra Constantin, and Evan Herbst. 2007. Moses: Open source toolkit for statistical machine translation. In *Proceedings of the 45th Annual Meeting of the Association for Computational Linguistics Companion Volume Proceedings of the Demo and Poster Sessions*, pages 177–180, Prague, Czech Republic.

Lakew, Surafel M, Quintino F. Lotito, Matteo Negri, Marco Turchi, and Marcello Federico. 2017. Improving zero-shot translation of low-resource languages. In *Proceedings of the 14th International Workshop on Spoken Language Translation*, pages 113–119, Tokyo, Japan.

Lakew, Surafel M, Mauro Cettolo, and Marcello Federico. 2018. A comparison of transformer and recurrent neural networks on multilingual neural machine translation. In *Proceedings of the 27th International Conference on Computational Linguistics*, pages 641–652, Santa Fe, USA.

Lample, Guillaume, Myle Ott, Alexis Conneau, Ludovic Denoyer, and Marc'Aurelio Ranzato. 2018. Phrase-based & neural unsupervised machine translation. In *Proceedings of the 2018 Conference on Empirical Methods in Natural Language Processing*, pages 5039–5049, Brussels, Belgium.

Marie, Benjamin and Atsushi Fujita. 2018. Unsupervised neural machine translation initialized by unsupervised statistical machine translation. *CoRR*, abs/1810.12703.

Mikolov, Tomas, Ilya Sutskever, Kai Chen, Greg Corrado, and Jeffrey Dean. 2013. Distributed representations of words and phrases and their compositionality. In *Proceedings of the 26th International Conference on Neural Information Processing Systems - Volume 2*, pages 3111–3119, Lake Tahoe, USA. Curran Associates Inc.

Moore, Robert C. and Will Lewis. 2010. Intelligent selection of language model training data. In *Proceedings of the 48th Annual Meeting of the Association for Computational Linguistics (ACL) Short Papers*, pages 220–224, Uppsala, Sweden.

Nakazawa, Toshiaki, Manabu Yaguchi, Kiyotaka Uchimoto, Masao Utiyama, Eiichiro Sumita, Sadao Kurohashi, and Hitoshi Isahara. 2016. ASPEC: Asian scientific paper excerpt corpus. In *Proceedings of the Tenth International Conference on Language Resources and Evaluation*, pages 2204–2208, Portorož, Slovenia.

Niu, Xing, Michael Denkowski, and Marine Carpuat. 2018. Bi-directional neural machine translation with synthetic parallel data. In *Proceedings of the 2nd Workshop on Neural Machine Translation and Generation*, pages 84–91, Melbourne, Australia.

Papineni, Kishore, Salim Roukos, Todd Ward, and Wei-Jing Zhu. 2002. BLEU: A method for automatic evaluation of machine translation. In *Proceedings of the 40th Annual Meeting on Association for Computational Linguistics*, pages 311–318, Philadelphia, USA.

Sennrich, Rico, Barry Haddow, and Alexandra Birch. 2016. Improving neural machine translation models with monolingual data. In *Proceedings of the 54th Annual Meeting of the Association for Computational Linguistics (Volume 1: Long Papers)*, pages 86–96, Berlin, Germany.

Sutskever, Ilya, Oriol Vinyals, and Quoc V. Le. 2014. Sequence to sequence learning with neural networks. In *Proceedings of the 27th International Conference on Neural Information Processing Systems*, pages 3104–3112, Montréal, Canada.

Tillmann, Christoph and Jian-ming Xu. 2009. A simple sentence-level extraction algorithm for comparable data. In *Proceedings of Human Language Technologies: The 2009 Annual Conference of the North American Chapter of the Association for Computational Linguistics*, pages 93–96, Boulder, USA.

Utiyama, Masao and Hitoshi Isahara. 2003. Reliable measures for aligning japanese-english news articles and sentences. In *Proceedings of the 41st Annual Meeting of the Association for Computational Linguistics*, pages 72–79, Sapporo, Japan.

Utiyama, Masao and Hitoshi Isahara. 2007. A comparison of pivot methods for phrase-based statistical machine translation. In *Human Language Technologies 2007: The Conference of the North American Chapter of the Association for Computational Linguistics; Proceedings of the Main Conference*, pages 484–491, Rochester, USA.

Vaswani, Ashish, Noam Shazeer, Niki Parmar, Jakob Uszkoreit, Llion Jones, Aidan N. Gomez, Łukasz Kaiser, and Illia Polosukhin. 2017. Attention is all you need. In *Proceedings of 30th Advances in Neural Information Processing Systems*, pages 5998–6008.

Zoph, Barret, Deniz Yuret, Jonathan May, and Kevin Knight. 2016. Transfer learning for low-resource neural machine translation. In *Proceedings of the 2016 Conference on Empirical Methods in Natural Language Processing*, pages 1568–1575, Austin, USA.

Improving Anaphora Resolution in Neural Machine Translation Using Curriculum Learning

Dario Stojanovski and **Alexander Fraser**
Center for Information and Language Processing
LMU Munich
{stojanovski,fraser}@cis.lmu.de

Abstract

Modeling anaphora resolution is critical for proper pronoun translation in neural machine translation. Recently it has been addressed by context-aware models with varying success. In this work, we propose a carefully designed training curriculum that facilitates better anaphora resolution in context-aware NMT. As a baseline, we train context-aware models as was done in previous work. We leverage oracle information specific to anaphora resolution during training. Following the intuition behind curriculum learning, we are able to train context-aware models which are improved with respect to coreference resolution, even though both the baseline and the improved system have access to exactly the same information at test time. We test our approach using two pronoun-specific evaluation metrics for MT.

1 Introduction

Modeling gender-pronoun agreement and anaphora resolution in machine translation is difficult because most models work on individual sentences. In many cases the antecedent noun is not present in the sentence being translated, but is rather in a preceding sentence. Sentence-external anaphora are a problem in many domains (e.g., consider conversational texts). NMT models can be extended to receive the previous sentences of a document as input. Previous context-aware NMT models include (Jean et al., 2017; Wang

et al., 2017; Tu et al., 2018; Voita et al., 2018; Stojanovski and Fraser, 2018; Zhang et al., 2018a; Miculicich et al., 2018). Previous work on evaluation has shown that context-aware NMT improves over sentence-level baselines, both in terms of BLEU and in terms of metrics tailored for pronoun evaluation (Bawden et al., 2018; Voita et al., 2018; Müller et al., 2018).

In this work, we propose a technique for improving the ability of context-aware models to handle anaphora resolution. The technique is based on curriculum learning (Bengio et al., 2009) which proposes to train neural networks in a similar fashion to how humans learn. Curriculum learning is a method that proposes training neural networks by gradually feeding increasingly more complex data instead of training models by randomly showing data samples.

We borrow on the intuition behind curriculum learning by initially training models with a form of "training wheels", where the anaphora relationships are made explicit. We take the key idea from previous work, which is to use gold-standard reference pronouns as oracles (Stojanovski and Fraser, 2018). We then gradually remove the oracles in consecutive fine-tuning steps, until we have a model working without oracle information. We expect that explicitly showing the reference pronouns in the context will make it easier to model the gender of antecedent nouns and bias the model to do more aggressive anaphora resolution when encountering ambiguous pronouns in the source language (the translation of ambiguous pronouns depends on the antecedent). We experimentally show the importance of the learning rate when training context-aware models with regards to our curriculum learning approach on both pronoun and overall translation performance. For this reason we present experiments training context-aware models with low and high initial learning rates. Note that our approach could be extended to other discourse-level phenomena, provided that useful oracles are easily obtainable. Our main contributions are: 1) We propose a curriculum learning method that supplies oracle information in training (but not testing) to improve anaphora resolution in NMT. 2) We show that our method works when training models with a low learning rate according to different metrics (measuring both MT quality overall and pronoun correctness). 3) We outline best practices for training and fine-tuning context-aware models.

2 Related Work

Several works have proposed methods and models of including contextual information (Wang et al., 2017; Jean et al., 2017; Bawden et al., 2018; Tiedemann and Scherrer, 2017; Maruf and Haffari, 2018; Voita et al., 2018; Stojanovski and Fraser, 2018; Miculicich et al., 2018; Zhang et al., 2018a; Kuang and Xiong, 2018; Kuang et al., 2018). In general, these models make use of extra-sentential attention conditioned on the main sentence being translated and use gates to control the flow of contextual information. The model we use is based on these general concepts as well.

Improvements in BLEU cannot be conclusively attributed to improved anaphora resolution and therefore additional metrics are required. Several works have proposed methods of evaluation and have shown that context-aware NMT achieves improvements. Müller et al. (2018) propose an automatically created challenge set where a model scores German translations of an English source sentence. The source sentences contain an anaphoric third person singular pronoun and the possible translations differ only in the choice of the pronoun in German. Bawden et al. (2018) is an earlier work proposing a manually created challenge set for English and French. Miculicich et al. (2018) evaluate their model's effectiveness on pronoun translation by computing pronoun accuracy based on alignment of hypothesized translations with the reference. Voita et al. (2018) used attention scores which show a tendency of Transformer-based context-aware models to do anaphora resolution. However, Müller et al. (2018) report moderate improvements of the model on their pronoun test set. In order to provide a comprehensive evaluation of our approach, we use BLEU, the pronoun challenge set from Müller et al. (2018), and F_1 score for the ambiguous English pronoun "it" based on alignment.

Previous work on curriculum learning for MT (Kocmi and Bojar, 2017; Zhang et al., 2018b; Wang et al., 2018) proposed methods which feed easier samples to the model first and later show more complex sentences. However, their focus is on improving convergence time while providing limited success on improving translation quality. In contrast with their work, we train models to better handle discourse-level phenomena.

3 Model

We use the Transformer (Vaswani et al., 2017) as a baseline and implement a context-aware model on top of it using Sockeye[1] (Hieber et al., 2018). The main and context sentence encoders are shared up until the penultimate layer, while the last encoder layers are separate. Since the initial layers are shared, the context sentence is marked with a special token so that the encoder knows when a context sentence is being encoded.

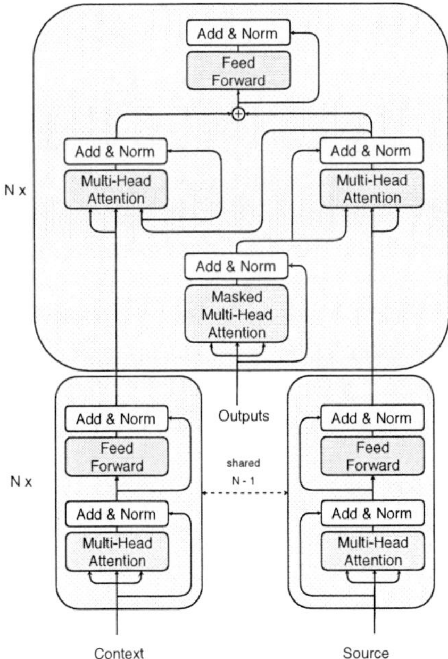

Figure 1: Context-aware model

The decoder layer is based on the standard Transformer decoder. It contains sublayers for

---

[1] https://github.com/awslabs/sockeye

self-attention over the target and multi-head attention (MHA) over the encoded main sentence representation. We further introduce a MHA sublayer over the context representation. The output of the main sentence MHA is used as a query for the MHA over the context which represents the keys and the values. The MHA maps the queries and the keys in order to produce attention weights to score the values. In this way, the context MHA is conditioned on what has been generated until the given time step and on the main sentence. This helps the model to decide where to pay attention to in the context. The outputs of the MHA over the main and context sentences are merged using a gated sum which enables the model to control the flow of information between the main and context sentence. Finally, we apply a feed-forward network. All embeddings in the model including the context embeddings are shared. For further details on the Transformer, we refer to (Vaswani et al., 2017).

4 Curriculum Learning Method

The proposed approach leverages discourse-specific oracles (Stojanovski and Fraser, 2018) in a curriculum learning setting to improve the performance of context-aware models in terms of anaphora resolution on English→German translation. Antecedents to anaphoric pronouns are often in previous sentences. We therefore bias the model to pay more attention to the context when translating pronouns, thus enabling it to do better anaphora resolution. This is facilitated by providing oracle information in the context. Subsequently, oracles are gradually removed with the final result that we finish with a model which is not dependent on oracle information, but which knows that anaphoric pronouns are likely to be resolved by looking at previous sentence context.

4.1 Obtaining oracles

We modify the dataset with oracle information by extracting all pronouns from a reference target sentence and adding them to the corresponding source context sentence. In this work, we only use the previous source sentence. To some extent this is sufficient as in many cases antecedents are relatively close to the corresponding anaphoric pronouns. Distance-based statistics of antecedents in the challenge set (Müller et al., 2018) support this. Previous work (Miculicich et al., 2018; Zhang et al., 2018a) has shown that larger context does

context sentence

The woman told a joke[masculine].

source sentence

It was really funny.

oracle sentence

The woman told a joke.   er[masculine] [SEP] <PRON> It was really funny.

target sentence

Er war wirklich lustig.

Table 1: Oracle example. [SEP] - context separator; <PRON> - pronoun mark token. Glosses for presentation purposes only.

not provide for significant improvements, but these works have not conducted a tailored evaluation of anaphora resolution with regards to machine translation. We leave consideration of further context sentences for future work.

The method of obtaining oracles works as follows. For a given source sentence and reference target sentence we mark all source side pronouns, and extract all target side pronouns and insert them in the context sentence. We mark the pronouns by adding a special token <PRON> before the pronoun. Note that we always mark source side pronouns in the main sentence only (the sentence being translated). In a pure oracle setting, there is no need to mark all source side pronouns. In some sentence pairs, there are no pronouns on the target side and therefore there is no need to mark source pronouns since they don't need to be explicitly translated. However, our goal is through curriculum learning to end up with a non-oracle model and any oracle knowledge is undesirable. The extracted target side pronouns (taken from the main target sentence) are simply inserted at the end of the context sentence.

Consider the example in Table 1. [SEP] is a token marking the end of the context and beginning of the main sentence. The glosses in the examples are not in the actual data samples and are just used for presentation purposes in the paper. In the example in Table 1 we can see that the source sentence contains a pronoun "it" and the target sentence contains a pronoun "er". From the example, it is obvious that "er" is a translation of "it" and "it" is a anaphoric pronoun whose antecedent is present in the previous sentence, namely, "joke".

Given the main sentence alone, it is impossible to determine the appropriate gender of the third person singular pronoun in German. A baseline model will fall back to the data driven prior which tends to be the neuter form "es". However, the translations of "joke" in German, which commonly are "Witz" or "Scherz" are both masculine.

By inserting the correct information to resolve the gender in the context, we bias the model to pay more attention to the context when translating pronouns. This will not be of importance for some English pronouns which are gender independent (e.g., "I"), but it should be helpful for gender-ambiguous pronoun translations such as the English "it" (which must be translated consistently with the antecedent).

4.2 Training curriculum

The training curriculum is designed in order to make use of the oracle information. Previous work has focused on gradually increasing the complexity of the data being fed into a given model. Our approach is conceptually similar in the sense that initially the information for proper anaphora resolution is made explicit. Oracle reference pronouns in the context enable this. It does not necessarily mean that the data examples are less complex, but the model does not need to learn complex pronoun-antecedent relationships at the beginning.

An overview of the general curriculum training steps are:

- train a non-context-aware baseline Transformer model

- use the parameters of the baseline model to initialize the non-context parameters of the context-aware Transformer model

- train the context-aware model with an oracle dataset (gold-standard pronouns in the context)

- fine-tune the model with a dataset where the percentage of oracle samples is gradually lowered

- fine-tune the last model with a non-oracle dataset

We first train a baseline model without giving access to contextual information. The trained parameters are used to initialize the context-aware models (sublayers of the network dealing with

context are randomly initialized). The following step is obtaining oracles for each sample in the dataset and training a model on that data. Resolving the gender of anaphoric pronouns in such a setting is easy. When the model encounters the special token marking a source side pronoun it will learn to look at the context since the gold standard information is there. We specifically put the oracle reference pronouns in the context in order to bias the model to pay attention to the context.

However, applying this model straightforwardly in a realistic setting is not possible because it is biased to rely on the gold standard pronouns. As a result, the next step is fine-tuning this model with context which does not contain the gold standard pronouns, but still has marked source side pronouns. In this way, we still bias the model to look at the context when translating pronouns. However, it is possible it will be difficult for the model to handle the significant change between fine-tuning steps.

As a result, we studied extending the training curriculum with intermediate steps. The initial oracle model is fine-tuned with a dataset where 75% of the samples have oracles. For the remaining samples, we keep the previous sentence and remove the oracle signals. In consecutive steps, we propose to fine-tune the model with a 50% and 25% oracle dataset. We hoped that this would ease the transition and encourage the model to combine the oracle information with the previous sentence. In the final step, we train a model with the previous sentence as context. This step is necessary as the model is still biased to look for the gold standard pronouns. However, we experimentally show that better results are obtained with fewer steps using a low percentage of oracles.

5   Experimental Setup

Following Müller et al. (2018), we conduct experiments on English→German WMT17 data and use newstest2017 and newstest2018 as test sets in addition to the pronoun challenge set. In terms of preprocessing, we tokenize and truecase the data and apply BPE splitting (Sennrich et al., 2016) with 32000 merge operations. We remove all samples where the source, target or context sentence has length over 50. We train small Transformer models as outlined in Vaswani et al. (2017) with 6 encoder and decoder layers. The source code for our models is publicly available [2].

We report mean scores across ten consecutive checkpoints with the lowest average perplexity on the development set (Chen et al., 2018). BLEU scores are computed on detokenized text. Evaluation of pronoun translation is done using two separate metrics. First, we use the challenge set provided by Müller et al. (2018) and report the overall pronoun accuracy. We refer to this metric as challenge set accuracy. The other metric is an F_1 score for "it", which we refer to as reference F_1. We predict translations and then compute micro-average F_1 for "it", using an alignment of the test set input to the reference. We compute alignments using *fastalign* (Dyer et al., 2013). We use all of the training, development and test data for the computation of the alignments. The evaluation was done using the script from Liu et al. (2018).

6 Results

6.1 Baseline

We train a strong Transformer-based baseline which obtains different results than the baseline in Müller et al. (2018). We achieve higher BLEU scores and also observe different challenge set accuracy for the different pronouns, even though the overall score of 47% is similar. All context-aware models are initialized from this strong baseline. We create two setups, i) an initial setup where we train context-aware models with a high learning rate and ii) an improved setup where we train models with a low learning rate.

6.2 Initial setup

As a context-aware baseline (ctx-base), we train a model using the previous source sentence without access to gold standard pronouns. We assumed that a low learning rate could prevent the context-aware models to significantly change the baseline prior pronoun distribution. As a result, we use a high learning rate (10^{-4}) in the fine-tuning step. Training the context-aware baseline for 200K updates provides a small increase in BLEU on newstest, as shown in Table 2. However, large improvements are obtained on the subtitles challenge set. We attribute this to the higher dependency on the context in subtitles which benefits from the increased capability of the context-aware model to diverge from the baseline.

---

[2]https://www.cis.uni-muenchen.de/~dario/projects/curriculum-oracles

	nt17	nt18	challenge
baseline	26.9	40.0	21.7
ctx-base*	27.0†	40.2‡	**22.6†**
ctx-base**	27.2†	**40.4†**	22.0†
pron-25→pron-0*	26.9	39.9	**22.6†**
pron-25→pron-0**	**27.4†**	40.2	22.2†

Table 2: BLEU scores. * - initial learning rate is 10^{-4}, ** - lr=10^{-5}. ctx-base: context-aware baseline, pron-{0,25,50,75}: percentage of samples with oracles. Each pron-{0,25} model fine-tuned for 140K updates. †- improvements statistically significant based on paired bootstrap resampling with p-value < 0.01; ‡- p-value < 0.05

	nt17	challenge
baseline	65.8	36.0
ctx-base*	**67.1**	**45.3**
ctx-base**	65.1	38.1
pron-25→pron-0*	65.2	45.1
pron-25→pron-0**	65.5	40.2

Table 3: Reference F_1 for "it" on newstest2017 and the pronoun challenge set. Notation as in Table 2

However, our curriculum learning approach does not affect performance in this setting. Figure 2 shows that the context-aware baseline achieves 57% challenge set accuracy and the curriculum learning approach only manages to match the score. Figure 2 further depicts that using a high number of oracle pronouns in the dataset decreases performance and that fine-tuning these models with a lower percentage of oracles is not useful. For example, fine-tuning a 25% oracle (pron-25) from the baseline is better than fine-tuning from a 50% oracle considering equal training time. The other oracle settings perform similarly. As a result, the full training curriculum from 100% gradually to 0% oracles is not justified both in terms of computation time or performance. Fine-tuning pron-25→pron-0 for a longer amount of time improved to 58%, but we omit it from the figure since we did not train ctx-base for a comparable amount of time. In terms of reference F_1, shown in Table 3, the context-aware baseline achieves large improvements in comparison to the baseline, both on newstest2017 and the challenge set, but our proposed method fails to increase performance.

6.3 Improved setup

Training context-aware models with a high learning rate improves overall translation quality on subtitles, but not on newstest. The high learning rate allows the model to diverge from the well-

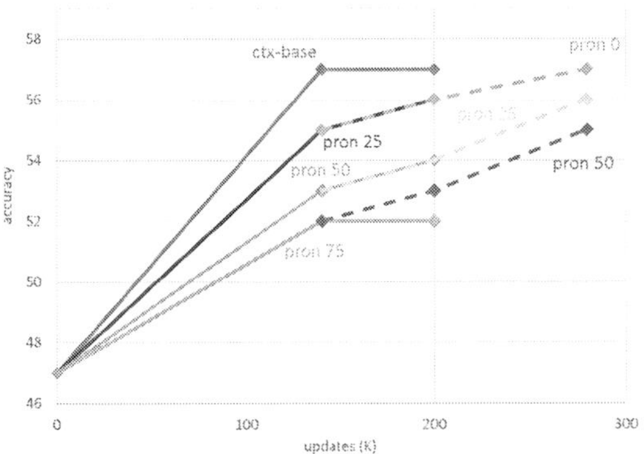

Figure 2: Challenge set accuracy. Full lines show fine-tuning from the baseline and dashed lines from a previous oracle model. Fine-tuning with a lr=10⁻⁴.

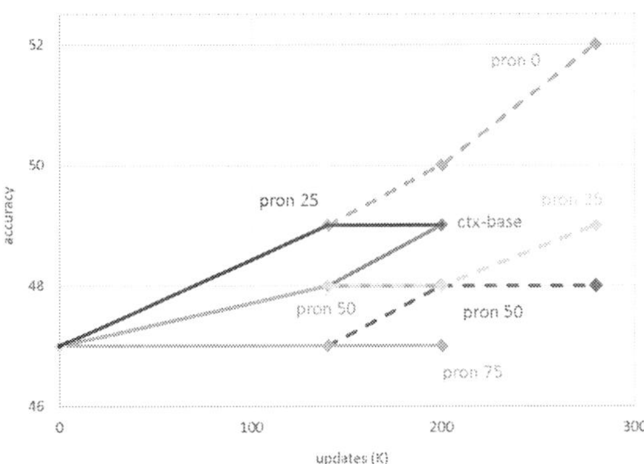

Figure 3: Challenge set accuracy. lr=10⁻⁵.

optimized baseline and this affects performance. We therefore decided to train models with a low learning rate of 10^{-5}. In this setup, the ctx-base improves on newstest and subtitles by 0.3 or 0.4 BLEU. The gains in BLEU are smaller than the ones reported by Müller et al. (2018), but we compare against a stronger baseline.

Unfortunately, performance on pronoun translation is lower. Figure 3 shows that ctx-base improves challenge set accuracy only to 49%. However, in this experimental setup, our curriculum learning approach proved to be effective if we start-off the training curriculum with a lower percentage of oracles. If we train a context-aware baseline (ctx-base) for 200K updates, we get lower performance (49%) than training a 25% oracle (pron-25) for 140K updates and then fine-tuning with a 0% oracle (pron-25→pron-0) for 60K updates (50%). Fine-tuning this model for 140K updates further improves to 52%. Table 3 shows that it is also helpful on reference F_1, providing

a 2.1 improvement over the 38.1 F_1 the ctx-base achieved on the challenge set.

All experiments show that fine-tuning with a high learning rate helps with pronoun translation, but does not benefit from the curriculum learning and lags behind training with a low learning rate in terms of BLEU. Therefore, we conclude that the curriculum learning is useful when improvements on anaphora resolution are desirable at no detrimental cost to overall translation quality.

6.4 Anaphora resolution analysis

We use the challenge set (Müller et al., 2018) to do a more detailed analysis of the models. We previously gave a high-level overview of the models' performance on the challenge set by only reporting the total score. The total score represents the overall accuracy, meaning the percentage of correctly scored examples. However, the challenge set is more comprehensive and offers a more detailed look at different aspects of anaphora resolution. As with the previous results, we report mean scores across ten consecutive checkpoints. We also report the standard deviation since we observed some degree of variance in the results depending on the experimental setup. Each fine-tuning step from the curriculum learning is ran for 140K updates.

6.4.1 Reference pronoun accuracy

Table 4 shows the overall and per-pronoun accuracy. Comparing our Transformer baseline to the one from Müller et al. (2018) showed that our baseline is stronger in terms of translation quality as measured by BLEU. However, in terms of pronoun accuracy as measured by the challenge set, the performance is the same with differences on the per-pronoun accuracy.

Table 4 also shows the detail scores for the context-aware baselines and the curriculum setup where we first train with a 25% oracle and fine-tune with a 0% oracle. Scores are provided for both fine-tuning with a low and high learning rate. The high learning rate context-aware baseline obtains 0.37 on "er", 0.44 on "sie" and a high 0.92 on "es". The curriculum experiment pron-25→pron-0 has similar scores with a lower accuracy on "sie".

The detailed scores also show how the low learning rate models perform. Both, the context-aware baseline and pron-25→pron-0 improve over the baseline. Another aspect that speaks for using fine-tuning with low learning is stability of results. Although the high learning rate models improve

	total	er	sie	es
baseline	0.47 ± 0.003	0.20 ± 0.005	0.32 ± 0.011	0.89 ± 0.005
ctx-base*	0.57 ± 0.007	0.37 ± 0.014	0.44 ± 0.019	0.92 ± 0.005
ctx-base**	0.49 ± 0.003	0.23 ± 0.006	0.35 ± 0.010	0.90 ± 0.004
pron-25→pron-0*	0.57 ± 0.013	0.37 ± 0.027	0.42 ± 0.032	0.92 ± 0.009
pron-25→pron-0**	0.52 ± 0.005	0.26 ± 0.010	0.38 ± 0.010	0.91 ± 0.001

Table 4: Challenge set accuracy for each pronoun. Notation as in Table 2

	intrasegmental	external
baseline	0.73 ± 0.005	0.41 ± 0.004
ctx-base*	0.74 ± 0.011	0.53 ± 0.009
ctx-base**	0.73 ± 0.006	0.43 ± 0.004
pron-25→pron-0*	0.74 ± 0.016	0.53 ± 0.014
pron-25→pron-0**	0.74 ± 0.004	0.46 ± 0.005

Table 5: Challenge set accuracy based on location of antecedent. Notation as in Table 2

fast on anaphora resolution, they are relatively unstable and exhibit fair amount of variance on the challenge set evaluation. This was to some extent observed on BLEU scores as well, but it is less pronounced. A difference in results across different checkpoints is especially observed on "er" and "sie". The experiments with a low learning rate exhibit variance on par with the baseline. This shows that reporting results on the challenge set needs to be carefully executed.

6.4.2 Antecedent location

The challenge set also provides a way of evaluation based on the location of the antecedent. There are two categories, intrasegmental and intersegmental or external. The intrasegmental means that the antecedent is within the main sentence. External refers to examples where the antecedent is in a previous sentence. It is unsurprising to observe that all models, including non-context and context-aware models perform similarly on the intrasegmental score and most of the improvements come from looking at the context, which is what the external score in Table 5 shows.

6.4.3 Antecedent distance

Table 6 shows scores based on the distance of the antecedent. The distance can be 0 (in the main sentence), 1 (in the first previous sentence) or larger. In this work, we only use the first previous sentence, so the results for a distance of 2, 3 or larger are for comparison with previous work. It is again unsurprising that performance does not substantially differ for 2, 3 or >3 since our models do not have direct access to those sentences. Any dif-

ference in results most likely comes from changing the data driven prior of the baseline. All improvements of the context-aware models come from examples where the antecedent is in the first previous sentence. We see that pron-25→pron-0 with a low learning rate obtains high improvements of 0.07 in comparison to the baseline.

6.5 Attention analysis

The model proposed in this work incorporates the contextual representation in each layer in the decoder. This raises the question what layers are responsible for finding the appropriate information for anaphora resolution. Unlike previous RNN-based encoder-decoder architectures which have a single attention mechanism, the Transformer is implemented using multi-head attention. As a result, we first average the attention scores across all attention heads and then visualize the scores.

We do a detailed analysis for separate decoder layers. Figure 4, Figure 5, Figure 6 and Figure 7 show the attention scores from the first, second, third and last layer. The attention scores are from pron-25→pron-0 with a low learning rate.

All context sentences are preceded by the <ctx> token. An interesting phenomena which was also observed in Voita et al. (2018) is that this special token is paid a substantial amount of attention. They interpret this as a way for the model to ignore the context when not needed.

The visualizations show that this is not the case for our model. We observe that the model takes advantage of the fact that the context is used in multiple layers. In the first 3 layers, the models generally pay the highest attention to the appropri-

	0	1	2	3	>3
baseline	0.73 ± 0.005	0.37 ± 0.005	0.47 ± 0.003	0.50 ± 0.004	0.69 ± 0.010
ctx-base*	0.74 ± 0.011	0.54 ± 0.011	0.47 ± 0.005	0.51 ± 0.008	0.72 ± 0.009
ctx-base**	0.73 ± 0.006	0.40 ± 0.005	0.47 ± 0.002	0.50 ± 0.004	0.69 ± 0.008
pron-25→pron-0*	0.74 ± 0.016	0.53 ± 0.017	0.46 ± 0.005	0.50 ± 0.010	0.71 ± 0.008
pron-25→pron-0**	0.74 ± 0.004	0.44 ± 0.007	0.46 ± 0.003	0.50 ± 0.004	0.69 ± 0.004

Table 6: Challenge set accuracy based on distance of antecedent. Notation as in Table 2

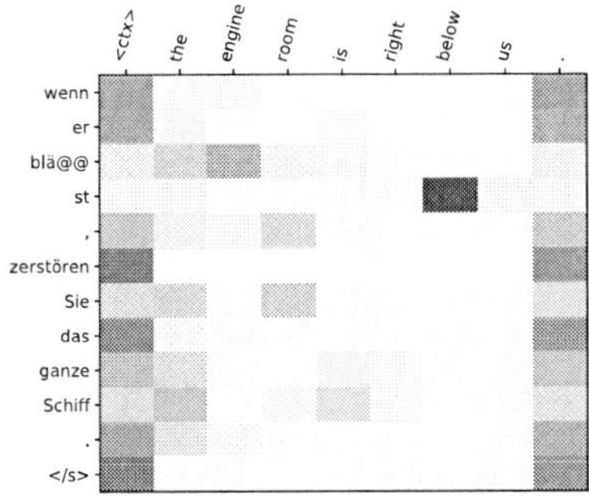

Figure 4: Context attention layer 1

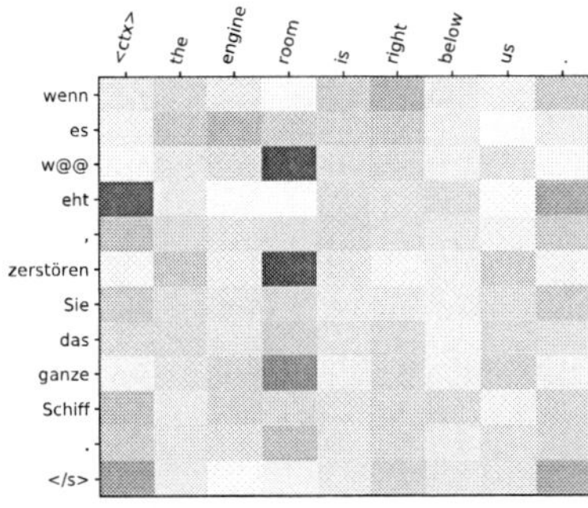

Figure 5: Context attention layer 2

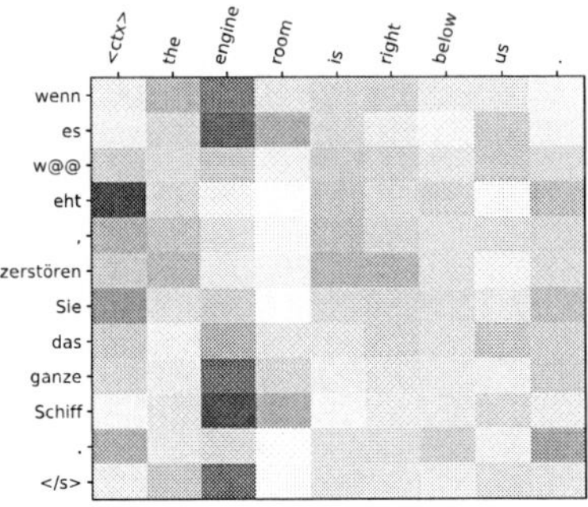

Figure 6: Context attention layer 3

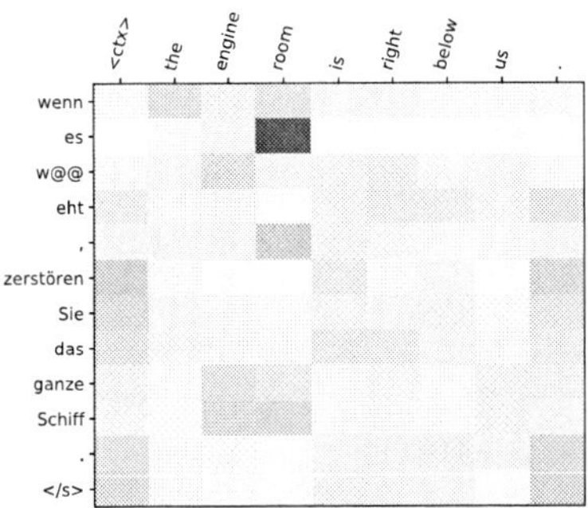

Figure 7: Context attention layer 6

a negative example as the correct German pronoun is "er" while the model generated "es"[3].

In contrast, we didn't observe the same behavior from pron-25→pron-0 with a high learning rate. This model indeed seemed to consistently put attention on the context special token and at the end of the sentence. Attention was paid to the antecedent in the decoder layers by target pronouns, but also by other words in some cases, leading us to assume that the gender information was passed through the decoder. We also assumed that the context special token to some extent represents a summarized representation of the context sentence and contains some gender information. Masking this token when feeding the context encoder representation to the decoder leads to lower results on the challenge set. We leave a more detailed examination of this assumption for future work.

6.5.1 Commonly attended words

We further investigate what words are most commonly attended to by the reference pronouns "er", "sie", "es". We simply compute the total attention score paid to a given context source token by one of the pronouns. We then normalize the scores based on the frequency of the given word.

ate noun, but a lot of attention is paid to irrelevant parts of the previous sentence. However, we see that the attention sharpens in the last layer and the attention over the context mostly focuses on the appropriate tokens. The example we show here is

[3]The translation of engine room in German is a compound word (Maschinenraum or Motorraum) and the gender is inferred from the second part, namely, "Raum". "Raum" is masculine in German, but a more common translation of "room" is "Zimmer" whose gender is neuter.

er	SU@@, Cube, Var@@, Max, ulf, tunnel, text, mur@@, schedule, passport, Jean, painting, bug, President, enemy, Ring, 400@@, temple, spell, state, Frank@@, Key, Cra@@, container, Doctor, Tony, recognized
sie	covers, Body, marble, painting, Machine, church, obviously, Lin@@, gar@@, decision, chamber, party, grie@@, Ara@@, hat@@, humanity, Enterprise, identity, Box, eventually, force, teeth, technology, Anne, tro@@, milk, policy
es	palace, fantastic, Ver@@, Jack@@, Board, article, museum, meeting, seed, So@@, gold, sample, technique, beef, satellite, Dal@@, virus, promise, piano, Jesus, Mac@@, motion, adventure, sounds, Cav@@, match, Ford

Table 7: Frequency based attention analysis

Since we are working on the BPE level, it is sometimes difficult to determine whether the attention score is meaningful, but it gives some indication whether the models are working correctly.

We show the most attended words from the pron-25→pron-0 with a low learning rate. Context words which appeared in a sentence containing a pronoun less than 5 times were removed in order to reduce the probability that some words are attended by chance. We only use the lowercase versions of the pronouns since "Sie" in German can also refer to the polite version of "you" and it cannot easily be disambiguated. We show the source tokens in Table 7. A detailed automatic analysis is problematic because English words can have multiple translations in German and sometimes those translations have different genders. We manually looked at common German translations of the tokens in Table 7. We noticed that in many cases the gender of the translation corresponds to the gender of the pronoun. We also looked at the non-BPE-split tokens and mapped them to German words using the MUSE English-German bilingual dictionary (Lample et al., 2018). We then looked at the gender of the German translations and how often it corresponds to the pronoun gender. The pron-25→pron-0 model performed better compared to the context-aware baseline, meaning a higher percentage of the German translations had gender corresponding to the gender of the pronoun. We leave a more detailed manual evaluation for future work.

7 Conclusion

We devised a curriculum learning approach making use of oracle information to improve anaphora resolution in NMT. Tailoring the data and training curriculum to anaphora resolution is beneficial and can achieve gains against a context-aware baseline. We observed that fine-tuning with low learning rates when applying our curriculum learning method provides a good compromise between overall translation quality and pronoun accuracy. Our method works best with a small number of fine-tuning steps employing smaller percentages of oracles. Our work is a focused contribution showing that curriculum training can be used to improve translation accuracy beyond a starting baseline given oracle information. Our experiments show that using a small learning rate during training is important to obtain improvements.

One aspect of our work that we do not explore is different ways of generating the oracle datasets. We always randomly sampled the sentences that are to be modified with the reference target side pronouns. Future work can investigate more informed ways of creating the oracle datasets. The benefit of this direction is that creating several different random samples of the oracle datasets could provide for more diverse models. This can be very useful for ensembling where larger variety between models is desirable. One could imagine that the variety in the models introduced by this approach is going to be more useful than if we simply train different baselines, context-aware or not.

It is also promising to try our method with other discourse-level phenomena that have easily obtainable oracles. Coherence and cohesion are important aspects of machine translation and improving on those discourse-level phenomena is still challenging for sentence-level models.

Acknowledgments

We would like to thank Dan Bikel and the anonymous reviewers for their valuable input. This project has received funding from the European Research Council (ERC) under the European Union's Horizon 2020 research and innovation programme (grant agreement № 640550).

References

Bawden, Rachel, Rico Sennrich, Alexandra Birch, and Barry Haddow. 2018. Evaluating discourse phenomena in neural machine translation. In *Proceedings of the 2018 Conference of the North American Chapter of the Association for Computational Linguistics: Human Language Technologies, Volume 1 (Long Papers)*, pages 1304–1313. Association for Computational Linguistics.

Bengio, Yoshua, Jérôme Louradour, Ronan Collobert, and Jason Weston. 2009. Curriculum learning. In *Proceedings of the 26th annual international conference on machine learning*, pages 41–48. ACM.

Chen, Mia Xu, Orhan Firat, Ankur Bapna, Melvin Johnson, Wolfgang Macherey, George Foster, Llion Jones, Mike Schuster, Noam Shazeer, Niki Parmar, Ashish Vaswani, Jakob Uszkoreit, Lukasz Kaiser, Zhifeng Chen, Yonghui Wu, and Macduff Hughes. 2018. The best of both worlds: Combining recent advances in neural machine translation. In *Proceedings of the 56th Annual Meeting of the Association for Computational Linguistics (Volume 1: Long Papers)*, pages 76–86. Association for Computational Linguistics.

Dyer, Chris, Victor Chahuneau, and Noah A. Smith. 2013. A simple, fast, and effective reparameterization of ibm model 2. In *Proceedings of the 2013 Conference of the North American Chapter of the Association for Computational Linguistics: Human Language Technologies*, pages 644–648. Association for Computational Linguistics.

Hieber, Felix, Tobias Domhan, Michael Denkowski, David Vilar, Artem Sokolov, Ann Clifton, and Matt Post. 2018. The sockeye neural machine translation toolkit at AMTA 2018. In *Proceedings of the 13th Conference of the Association for Machine Translation in the Americas (Volume 1: Research Papers)*, pages 200–207, Boston, MA, March. Association for Machine Translation in the Americas.

Jean, Sebastien, Stanislas Lauly, Orhan Firat, and Kyunghyun Cho. 2017. Does neural machine translation benefit from larger context? *arXiv preprint arXiv:1704.05135*.

Kocmi, Tom and Ondřej Bojar. 2017. Curriculum learning and minibatch bucketing in neural machine translation. In *Proceedings of the International Conference Recent Advances in Natural Language Processing, RANLP 2017*, pages 379–386. INCOMA Ltd.

Kuang, Shaohui and Deyi Xiong. 2018. Fusing recency into neural machine translation with an inter-sentence gate model. In *Proceedings of the 27th International Conference on Computational Linguistics*, pages 607–617, Santa Fe, New Mexico, USA, August. Association for Computational Linguistics.

Kuang, Shaohui, Deyi Xiong, Weihua Luo, and Guodong Zhou. 2018. Modeling coherence for neural machine translation with dynamic and topic caches. In *Proceedings of the 27th International Conference on Computational Linguistics*, pages 596–606, Santa Fe, New Mexico, USA, August. Association for Computational Linguistics.

Lample, Guillaume, Alexis Conneau, Marc'Aurelio Ranzato, Ludovic Denoyer, and Herv Jgou. 2018. Word translation without parallel data. In *International Conference on Learning Representations*.

Liu, Frederick, Han Lu, and Graham Neubig. 2018. Handling homographs in neural machine translation. In *Proceedings of the 2018 Conference of the North American Chapter of the Association for Computational Linguistics: Human Language Technologies, Volume 1 (Long Papers)*, pages 1336–1345.

Maruf, Sameen and Gholamreza Haffari. 2018. Document context neural machine translation with memory networks. In *Proceedings of the 56th Annual Meeting of the Association for Computational Linguistics (Volume 1: Long Papers)*, pages 1275–1284. Association for Computational Linguistics.

Miculicich, Lesly, Dhananjay Ram, Nikolaos Pappas, and James Henderson. 2018. Document-level neural machine translation with hierarchical attention networks. In *Proceedings of the 2018 Conference on Empirical Methods in Natural Language Processing*, pages 2947–2954. Association for Computational Linguistics.

Müller, Mathias, Annette Rios, Elena Voita, and Rico Sennrich. 2018. A large-scale test set for the evaluation of context-aware pronoun translation in neural machine translation. In *Proceedings of the Third Conference on Machine Translation, Volume 1: Research Papers*, pages 61–72, Brussels, Belgium, October. Association for Computational Linguistics.

Sennrich, Rico, Barry Haddow, and Alexandra Birch. 2016. Neural machine translation of rare words with subword units. In *Proceedings of the 54th Annual Meeting of the Association for Computational Linguistics (Volume 1: Long Papers)*, pages 1715–1725. Association for Computational Linguistics.

Stojanovski, Dario and Alexander Fraser. 2018. Coreference and coherence in neural machine translation: A study using oracle experiments. In *Proceedings of the Third Conference on Machine Translation, Volume 1: Research Papers*, pages 49–60, Brussels, Belgium, October. Association for Computational Linguistics.

Tiedemann, Jörg and Yves Scherrer. 2017. Neural machine translation with extended context. In *Proceedings of the Third Workshop on Discourse in Machine Translation*, pages 82–92.

Tu, Zhaopeng, Yang Liu, Shuming Shi, and Tong Zhang. 2018. Learning to remember translation history with a continuous cache. *Transactions of the Association for Computational Linguistics*, 6:407–420.

Vaswani, Ashish, Noam Shazeer, Niki Parmar, Jakob Uszkoreit, Llion Jones, Aidan N Gomez, Łukasz Kaiser, and Illia Polosukhin. 2017. Attention is all you need. In *Advances in Neural Information Processing Systems*, pages 6000–6010.

Voita, Elena, Pavel Serdyukov, Rico Sennrich, and Ivan Titov. 2018. Context-Aware Neural Machine Translation Learns Anaphora Resolution. In *Proceedings of the 56th Annual Meeting of the Association for Computational Linguistics (Volume 1: Long Papers)*, pages 1264–1274, Melbourne, Australia.

Wang, Longyue, Zhaopeng Tu, Andy Way, and Qun Liu. 2017. Exploiting cross-sentence context for neural machine translation. In *Proceedings of the 2017 Conference on Empirical Methods in Natural Language Processing*, pages 2826–2831.

Wang, Rui, Masao Utiyama, and Eiichiro Sumita. 2018. Dynamic sentence sampling for efficient training of neural machine translation. In *Proceedings of the 56th Annual Meeting of the Association for Computational Linguistics (Volume 2: Short Papers)*, pages 298–304. Association for Computational Linguistics.

Zhang, Jiacheng, Huanbo Luan, Maosong Sun, Feifei Zhai, Jingfang Xu, Min Zhang, and Yang Liu. 2018a. Improving the transformer translation model with document-level context. In *Proceedings of the 2018 Conference on Empirical Methods in Natural Language Processing*, pages 533–542. Association for Computational Linguistics.

Zhang, Xuan, Gaurav Kumar, Huda Khayrallah, Kenton Murray, Jeremy Gwinnup, Marianna J Martindale, Paul McNamee, Kevin Duh, and Marine Carpuat. 2018b. An empirical exploration of curriculum learning for neural machine translation. *arXiv preprint arXiv:1811.00739*.

Improving American Sign Language Recognition with Synthetic Data

Jungi Kim
SYSTRAN Software, Inc.
`jungi.kim@systrangroup.com`

Patricia O'Neill-Brown
U.S. Government
`po17b@icloud.com`

Abstract

There is a need for real-time communication between the deaf and hearing without the aid of an interpreter. Developing a machine translation (MT) system between sign and spoken languages is a multimodal task since sign language is a visual language, which involves the automatic recognition and translation of video images. In this paper, we present the research we have been carrying out to build an automated sign language recognizer (ASLR), which is the core component of a machine translation (MT) system between American Sign Language (ASL) and English. Developing an ASLR is a challenging task due to the lack of sufficient quantities of annotated ASL-English parallel corpora for training, testing and developing an ASLR. This paper describes the research we have been conducting to explore a range of different techniques for automatically generating synthetic data from existing datasets to improve the accuracy of ASLR. This work involved experimentation with several algorithms with varying amounts of synthetic data and evaluations of their effectiveness. It was demonstrated that automatically creating valid synthetic training data through simple image manipulation of ASL video recordings improves the performance of the ASLR task.

1 Introduction

In everyday life, there are situations in which there is the need for deaf and hearing individuals to communicate with one another without the aid of an interpreter. To address this need, we are developing ASL-English MT that enables signers and non-signers to communicate with one another using mobile devices such as smartphones and tablets. The concept is that the signer of ASL signs into the device and the video images are captured, automatically recognized, translated and rendered into both speech and text for the speaker of English. Conversely, using this application, the speaker's speech is automatically recognized and an avatar signing the machine translation in ASL is displayed, which appears along with the English text. This paper outlines our work on the first critical aspect of the problem, which is the development of an automatic sign language recognizer (ASLR). Specifically, we address our research in the area of generating valid synthetic data, a requirement dictated by the lack of sufficient amounts of large-scale annotated data for ASL to English for testing, training and developing ASLR algorithms.

ASL is a visually perceived language based on a naturally evolved system of articulated hand gestures and their placement relative to the body, along with non-manual markers such as facial expressions, head movements, shoulder raises, mouth morphemes, and movements of the body (ASL: A brief description - Lifeprint.com). This language is structured like Japanese: it is a topic-comment language and does not have articles (Nakamura, 2008). See Speers (2002) for an excellent detailed linguistic description of ASL. The challenges involved with the recognition of sign language are akin to those of automatic speech recognition (ASR) (Dreuw et al., 2007). As with speech, for sign language, allophonic variation must be taken into account, since each time a person makes a particular sign, they make tiny variations in how they position their arms and hands. In addition, hand and arm sizes and shapes vary between signers. An effective recognizer must be able to handle these variances as well as the differences in background colors and lighting. To account for these variations, similar to an acoustic range for each type of sound such as each specific vowel, we have developed the concept of a 'bounding box' within which each sign needs to be made for it to be considered that sign as judged by native signers and interpreters. Our plan is to automatically discover the bounding box for each sign through training on images of different signers signing each sign. However, since the datasets available for training algorithms to automatically recognize sign language do not contain a sufficient quantity of signer variation, this research focuses on the automatic creation of valid synthetic data to accurately capture those variations.

In this paper, we discuss our research into the area of automatically generating synthetic data for the ASLR component of an ASL-English MT system. Synthetic data generation has proven to be effective in solving problems such as image classification (Krizhevsky et al., 2012), ASR (Ko et al., 2017), and MT (Sennrich et al., 2016). The approach of using synthetic data to train and test machine learning algorithms is a newly emerging topic of interest and an area of active research in the field of Artificial Intelligence (AI). A popular approach in the attempt to solve this problem is to utilize the generative model in the Generative Adversarial Network (GAN) architecture (Antoniou et al., 2017; Gurumurthy et al., 2017; Bousmalis et al., 2017). However, we experimented with GANs and we found that they generated valid as well as non-valid signs and we were unable to constrain them to automatically generate only valid signs. Therefore, we looked for alternative approaches. This paper discusses our work on developing and testing different techniques for automatically generating valid synthetic data and determining whether synthetic data increases classification accuracy. In particular, we address two key research questions: a) given a very small amount of annotated data for training, how much synthesized data can we utilize for augmenting the training data

without hurting classification performance, and b) would different synthetic data generation methods produce different outcomes for the model performance and if so, what techniques are most suitable and why.

2   Previous Work

A review of the literature reveals different approaches to the development of ASLR. Starner et al. (1998) implemented two Hidden Markov Model based real-time systems for ASLR where one system utilized a desk-mounted camera and the other utilized a hat-mounted camera. Lang et al. (2012) made use of Microsoft's Kinect for recognizing German signs. Chuan et al. (2014) used the palm sized Leap motion sensor for American finger spelling recognition. Dong et al. (2015) designed a color glove-based technique on the Kinect depth sensor for hand segmentation. Tharwat et al. (2015) developed the Arabic Sign Language recognition system where the scale invariant feature transform is used to perform the sign recognition using Neural Network, K-Nearest Neighbors, and Support Vector Machine. Wu et al. (2016) utilized an inertial measurement unit and surface electromyography devices for the recognition of 80 ASL signs. Dai et al. (2017) used gyroscope and accelerometer sensors running on a smartwatch for the recognition of 103 ASL signs. Ma et al. (2018) utilized WiFi packets to estimate hand and finger movements for ASL sign recognition.

There was the approach of developing a sign language recognition system through the training of very large data sets of video clips recorded by multiple signers using a large vocabulary (Koller et al., 2015). Koller's DeepHands model took an unsupervised approach to training a Convolutional Neural Network (CNN) model with 1 million unlabeled hand-shape images and successfully used it to classify Danish, New Zealand, and German signs (Koller et al., 2016). Since it modeled the hands, it could recognize all signs made using the hands and not just those that are finger-spelled, so we leveraged this work to develop a baseline prototype ASLR.

Anantha Rao et al. (2018) implemented Indian Sign Language recognition running in real-time on a mobile phone using hand image segmentation and a feedforward neural net-work. Huang et al. (2018) developed a CNN-based Hierarchical Attention Network with Latent Space in a sequence-to-sequence fashion. In particular, the following studies are similar to our work on the aspect of augmenting training data to improve the performance of CNN models. Molchanov et al. (2015) experimented with the deformation of input data by augmenting reversed ordering and mirroring in the off-line and by augmenting rotating, scaling, shifting, and random dropout in the online for the hand gesture recognition using 3D CNN. Bheda and Radpour (2017) developed CNN-based ASL recognition with data augmentation (rotating and horizontal flipping). These projects applied data augmentation techniques developed for CNN model training; however, they did not evaluate the effectiveness of the techniques nor provide in-depth analyses of their methods. Tao et al. (2018) implemented an ASL alphabet recognition system with a CNN, equipped with a multi-view augmentation and inference scheme. This approach differs from our work in that they exploited a 3D motion capture device and the 3D modeling capability to virtually generate views from different angles, while we opted to utilize a generic input device and 2D techniques. Our approach is to develop the solution so that it is not reliant on special equipment and can run on any tablet, laptop or smartphone.

3 Approach

3.1 Overview of the Baseline System

For this work, we began with a baseline prototype[1] ASLR that we used for developing and testing the hypothesis of data augmentation based on DeepHands using the Kinect Sensor and a graphical user interface to capture the video recordings of people signing in ASL. The Kinect uses multiple cameras in order to capture motions in three dimensions, and utilizes the Kinect 2.0 SDK library, to outputs 25 body joints and their 3D coordinates (Microsoft, 2014). The demo system managed the recording of ASL sign videos of registered users with true labels which were annotated by signers. The demo system was developed by training the system to recognize 50 different signs using these datasets. The recognizer was trained to recognize a single-sign video clip as one of the 50 signs it was trained on. The baseline ASL recognizer consists of the following components: Kinect 2.0 as a

video input device, Kinect SDK for feature extraction, and Kmeans clustering for classification.

For this work, we modified the original baseline system so as to remove the dependency on the Kinect input device to enable the system to train and classify on any 2D video feed or recordings. This enabled us to carry out experiments on a set of ASL video recordings of native ASL signers along with annotations that are made publicly available (Neidle et al., 2012). Being able to do away with specialized recording hardware also opened up the possibility of easily adding or creating more annotated data for training and evaluating the system. As shown in Figure 1, in place of the Kinect device, we utilized OpenPose (Cao et al., 2018) as the input video analysis module of the baseline system. OpenPose[2] is open source software that implements the state-of-the-art multi-person keypoint detection approaches for body, face, hands, and feet. In our preliminary experiments, it was verified that system performance was not degraded when using the features prepared from OpenPose output instead of Kinect output.[3]

3.2 Feature Extraction

OpenPose provides pretrained pose, face, and hand detection models trained on publicly available datasets. We used the pretrained 25-point body pose and 20-point hands detection models. OpenPose models produce the body and hands keypoints for each successfully analyzed frame of an input video clip. Two types of features are extracted for all frames: a) hands 2D coordinate feature and b) DeepHand hand-shape feature. A simple python script was written to automate the feature extraction process from a video clip and its OpenPose output with a tensor flow version of the DeepHand model. This code is available at https://github.com/ Dragonfly-ASL to make our work easily reproducible.

Hands 2Dtracking feature: In the OpenPose analysis output for each video frame, two coordinates (index 4 and 7) out of 25 body keypoints correspond to the right and the left wrists. The two coordinates were normalized with regard to the coordinate of the neck as the origin and the distance between neck and nose as the unit vector. The

---

[1]The baseline prototype and demo systems were developed by the Massachusetts Institute of Technology Lincoln Laboratories (MITLL) under a government contract.

[2]https://github.com/CMU-Perceptual-Computing-Lab/openpose
[3]Top 1 accuracies of the recognizer with Kinect and Open-Pose were 61.8% and 61.5%, respectively.

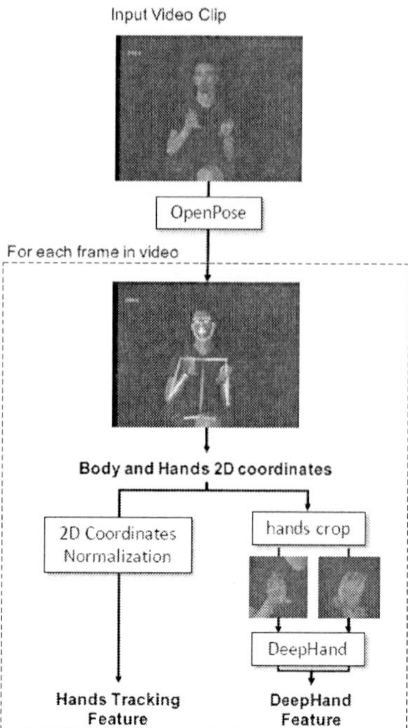

Figure 1: Feature extraction using OpenPose and DeepHand (Example shown from (dataset: ASLLRP-ASLLVD, signer: Brady, sign: CHEM-ISTRY+)[4])

normalized left and right hand coordinates of all frames combined consist of the half of the hands 2D tracking feature. The other half of the hands 2D tracking feature is calculated as the derivative of the normalized 2D coordinates across the time dimension with window size 5. The total dimension of the hands 2D tracking feature is then NumFrames 8, where each hand in a frame is described with a normalized 2D point and its derivative.

DeepHand hand-shape feature: To create handshape features, our baseline system utilizes DeepHand models (Koller et al., 2016), a CNN-based sign language recognizer trained on 1 million hand images. The model was trained to classify input images into 60 fine-grained hand-shape classes. The model performed with 62.8% accuracy on a manually labelled dataset with 3361 images that cover 45 hand-shape classes. The DeepHand takes its architecture after GoogLeNet (Szegedy et al., 2015). The model contains 22 layers, mixed with convolutional, pooling, fully-connected layers. The baseline system utilizes the activation output of one of the internal fully-connected layers, as the compact and abstract representation of the input image.

The activation is of 1,024 dimensions for each hand, resulting in NumFrames $\times$ 2048 in total.

3.3 Classification with K-means Clustering

The baseline ASL classifier was developed using K-means clustering. There were two types of feature representations used for the training data: hands 2D tracking and DeepHand handshape. The K-means clustering algorithm was applied to each of the feature types for all of the video frames in the training data. K-means requires a distance measure between the clustered elements. A simple Euclidean distance was employed: $\text{dist}(p, q) = \sqrt{\sum_{i=1}^{n}(q_i - p_i)^2}$ where p and q are feature representations and n is the feature dimension. Once the clustering was finished, all clusters were calculated for the label probabilities using the distance between all elements in the training data with their annotated labels.

To classify an input video clip, two label probabilities were calculated for each feature type using the K-means clusters. For each feature type, a) the cluster memberships of the input video frames were determined using the same Euclidean distance, b) these distances were multiplied by the cluster's label probabilities, and c) the label probabilities were accumulated and averaged. The final label probabilities for the input video clip were averaged from the label probabilities for each frame. The two label probabilities were then combined as:

$$P_{\text{combined}} = e^{(\ln(P_{\text{HandTracking}}) + \ln(P_{\text{HandShape}}))}$$

P_{combined} is in effect a product of $P_{\text{HandTracking}}$ and $P_{\text{HandShape}}$ but the calculation avoids the risk of underflow. Intuitively speaking, the probabilities for both the 2D hand tracking feature as well as the hand shape feature should be high for the combined probability to be high. Otherwise, if either one of the probabilities is low, then the combined probability stays low.

3.4 Data Augmentation

There is only a very small number of video clips each with a single ASL sign and its sign manually assigned. Therefore, our goal was to augment this data with a large amount of new videos synthesized from the original dataset, so we developed a tool that applies a set of image manipulation operations to all of the frames in a provided video clip. We categorized these 2D image manipulation operations according to their influence in the synthesis process as follows:

- Recording environment anticipation

- Sign and Signer variance anticipation

Depending on the actual usage of the proposed system, we took into account that the recording hardware and environment may vary. For example, ASL signers may use our software on different hardware devices such as their PCs, smartphones, or tablets with different cameras with varying field of view and resolutions, and different recording conditions such as varying levels of lighting and camera zoom and angle settings. These kinds of variances in recording environments may be addressed by training the recognition model with additional data generated with such effects applied to the existing training data. We anticipate that the following image manipulation operations account for such occasions: noise addition or removal, image enhancement, brightness changes, vertical and horizontal skews, etc.

The role of other image manipulation categories is to account for the different ways ASL signs are made by each ASLsigner and the different appearances between the signers in the training data and at the test or use time. There are many image manipulation operations that can potentially address such discrepancy in the training and test conditions. We limited the scope of this work to testing the usefulness of data synthesis within ASL sign recognition and focused on the following two image manipulation operations: Rotate and Zoom.

Each manipulation comes with its own set of parameter ranges and the generation space becomes quite big. For the scope of this experiment, we focused on these two broad sets of synthetic types: a) Random manipulations and parameters selection, and b) Controlled parameter selection (Rotate, Zoom).

Our training and test data were recorded in the identical environment and with identical camera settings. Therefore, we will not be able to verify the effectiveness of the corresponding manipulation operations within the scope of current work. However, we can still demonstrate that training an ASL recognizer with additional synthetically generated data, many times larger in quantity than that of the original data, can still yield a valid model. For this purpose, we have a type of synthetic data whose image manipulation operations and its parameters are chosen and configured with randomness (Figure 2).

Manipulation Operation	Parameter Range
shift-x, shift-y	-10 ~ +10, -3 ~ +3
skew-x, skew-y	-10 ~ +10, -10 ~ +10
rotate	-10 ~ +10
zoom	90% ~ 110%
contrast	0 ~ +3
brightness, saturation, hue	85 ~ 115
DE speckle, enhance	50% probability
normalize, quantize	10% probability
gamma, reduce Noise	0 ~ +2
swirl	-15 ~ +15

Figure 2: Manipulation operations and their parameters were randomly selected for each input video.

For the controlled parameter selections of Rotate and Zoom, three sets of varying ranges and increment steps are selected as below:

- Rotate (degrees angle)

    - Rotate1: $-15° \sim 15°$ (step size 3)
    - Rotate2: $-30° \sim 30°$ (step size 6)
    - Rotate3: $-45° \sim 45°$ (step size 9)

- Zoom (%)

    - Zoom1: $95\% \sim 105\%$ (step size 1)
    - Zoom2: $90\% \sim 110\%$ (step size 2)
    - Zoom3: $85\% \sim 115\%$ (step size 3)

With these varying ranges but with the same amount of generated synthetic data, we did work to gather preliminary evidence to support hypothesis that certain types of image manipulations have greater impact and benefit by helping the synthetic data generation process better address the lack of variability in the limited amount of training data. Through experimentation, we learned that there are certain parameters that are more important than others to ensure that the signs generated are valid.

The complete python script that can produce a synthesized video given an input video clip with a set of various image manipulation options is available at https://github.com/Dragonfly-ASL to make our work easily reproducible

4 Experiments

4.1 Experimental Settings

We trained our ASL recognition models using a publicly available annotated dataset American

Sign Language Lexicon Video Dataset (ASLLVD) (Neidle et al., 2012). ASLLVD consists of almost 10,000 ASL signs signed by 6 native ASL signers. The dataset also comes with human-annotated linguistic information such as gloss labels and handshape labels. Using the entire dataset, we selected videos with glosses that belong to our hand-picked 50 ASL signs, each signed by 6 different signers, making the total dataset size 300. ASLLVD provides videos shot from different angles (front view, side view, close-up), but we only used videos with the front view (Figure 3).

To carry out experiments with varying amount of synthetic data, we trained our ASL recognition model with varying amount (0 or 0%, 1 or 100%, 3 or 300%, 5 or 500%, and 10, 1000%) of synthetic data generated with Random operations and parameter selection method. Another set of experiments was performed to demonstrate the effectiveness of two image manipulation operations (Rotate and Zoom), each with three sets of parameter ranges as described in Section 3.4. For each of the parameter selection strategies (Random, Rotate1 . . . 3, and Zoom1...3), each video clip in the ASLLVD dataset was augmented with up to ten additional synthesized data variants (SYN1...10).

In the preliminary experimentations with the baseline system, it was noted that the hyperparameter K, the number of clusters in the Kmeans algorithm, has a significant impact on the classification performance. For the baseline experiments with 300 ~ 500 annotated data, K was tested with 1,000 ~ 3,000 with increments of 1,000. To account for the increased size in data (300 ~ 3,300), we experimented with K with values 1,000, 2,000, 3,000, and 5,000.

To compare the performance of models, we employ accuracy as our main evaluation measure. Each accuracy is averaged over the scores of 6 signers, each tested with 50 signs evaluated in a cross-validation fashion. For example, we pick one signer at a time whose videos are set as a test input, and evaluate against a model trained with videos of the rest of the signers. Synthetically generated data of the test signer are not included in either the test or the training dataset. To eliminate the impact of random initialization in K-means clustering, each signer's score is averaged over three runs with different K-means initial cluster randomization. This is repeated six times for all signers and the performance is then averaged. Therefore, one accuracy score is an average of 18 independent runs.

4.2 Experimental Results and Analysis

We present the performance evaluation results of all the experiments carried out in this work in Figure 4.

Scores with statistically significant improvements over the Baseline system, measured with the Wilcoxon signed-rank test (N = 50), are marked with † (p < 0.15) and ‡ (p < 0.05). Model configuration with 1,000% synthetic data with the K-means cluster size 3,000 performed the best among all configurations we tried for the current work, and it is shown to have improved most statistically significantly (p = 0.006). To confirm that the performance improvement did not occur by chance from having a good randomly initialized K-means cluster, we carried out additional experiments with the same configuration (K=3,000, SYN10, Rotate1) but with different random seeds two more times. The outcomes of the additional experiments show similar improvements (71.2% and 69.0%).

Figure 5 shows that, with regard to the varying amount of synthetic data in the train (Random-SYN1, 3, 5, 10, equivalent to 0, 100, 300, 500, and 1,000% synthetic data), the performance improvement is not in a linear relationship to the increasing amount of synthetic data in the train set. Rather, the performance first sharply decreases until 300%, then bounces back at 500% and finally outperforms the baseline at 1,000%. Though confirmed for all sizes of K-means cluster, this behavior is rather counter-intuitive. Due to the limited computing resource capacity (256G of RAM) and the way the baseline system was implemented, we could not utilize more than 1,000% synthetic data.

For runs with 1,000% of synthetic data (SYN10), many configurations of Random, Rotate and Zoom present statistically significant improvements over the Baseline. We also observe that certain configurations of Rotate and Zoom also perform better than Random, though none of the Rotate and Zoom configurations outperform Random with statistical significance. Some Rotate runs are worse than Random or even Baseline, indicating that parameter range for the data manipulation operations should be carefully chosen to ensure that the synthesized data still present valid signs. Another observation is that Random configurations performed reasonably well, and it would make a good go-to strategy in general.

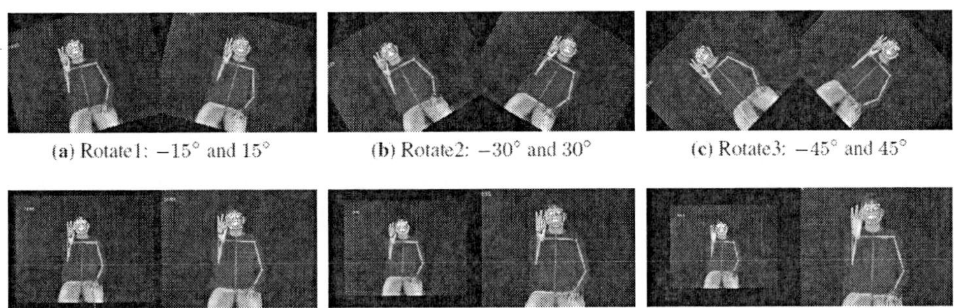

(a) Rotate1: −15° and 15°   (b) Rotate2: −30° and 30°   (c) Rotate3: −45° and 45°

(d) Zoom1: 95% and 105%   (e) Zoom2: 90% and 110%   (f) Zoom3: 85% and 115%

Figure 3: Sample images with minimum and maximum values of Rotate1... 3 and Zoom1... 3 annotated with body and hand keypoints (ASLLVD, Signer: Lana, Sign: FOUR, Frame 67)

| | Baseline | Random | | | SYN10 | | | | | | |
		SYN1	SYN3	SYN5	Random	Rotate1	Rotate2	Rotate3	Zoom1	Zoom2	Zoom3
Dataset size	300	600	1,200	1,800	3,300	3,300	3,300	3,300	3,300	3,300	3,300
Synthetic %	0	100	300	500	1,000	1,000	1,000	1,000	1,000	1,000	1,000
Cluster Size (K) 1,000	62.8	62.0	58.7	61.3	63.0	66.5	65.5	60.7	63.1	65.3	64.5
2,000	67.0	63.2	62.3	63.5	66.9	69.5	65.7	62.3	66.2	68.2†	67.2†
3,000	66.7	64.9	64.1	64.6	67.7†	**71.1‡**	66.6	61.9	66.2†	68.7†	67.7†
5,000	67.1	65.4	64.5	65.1	68.8†	70.5†	68.6†	64.4	67.9†	69.0	68.0†

Figure 4: Top 1 Classification accuracies (%) of the baseline ASL Sign recognizer and recognizers trained with additional synthetic data. Statistically significant improvements over the baseline system with the same cluster size (within the same row) are marked with † (p < 0.15) and ‡ (p < 0.05). We used the Wilcoxon signed-rank test with N = 50. For experiments using the 1,000% of synthetic dataset (SY N10), none of the Rotate and Zoom runs out-performed Random with statistical significance.

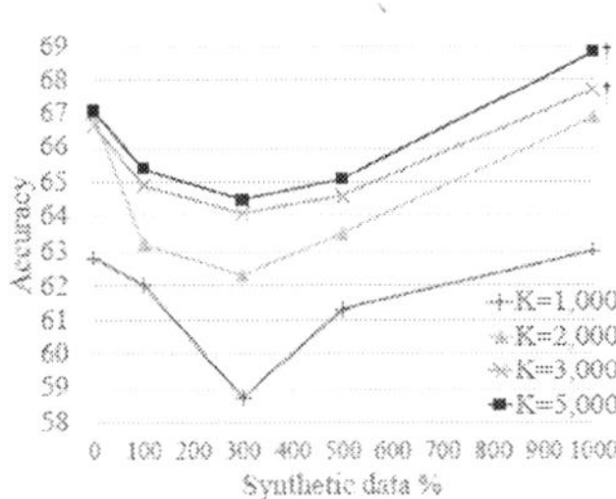

Figure 5: Change in recognition performance with different percentages of synthetic data generated with Random options. † = statistically significant improvement over Baseline (0%).

Though more sensitive to parameter range choices, between Rotate and Zoom, Rotate seems to be more effective in synthetic data generation. We conjecture that this is due to the fact that the 2D coordinates normalization of the hands tracking feature accounts in part for the effect of Zoom. We also speculate that Zoom together with image resizing to make thinner or wider signers should help account for the variances among differently sized and shaped bodies of signers.

We are currently working to further investigate the effectiveness of utilizing greater amounts of synthetic data and combinations of synthetic data generation techniques to identify the most optimal approaches.

In Figure 6, we see the per-sign rank comparison of Baseline and Rotate1 at their best configurations.

Signs with the most positive rank improvement are FOUR, EARTH, and ANY. Signs DEPRESS, CHAT++, and ANSWER were most negatively affected. Figure 7 shows the per-user top 5-ranked signs with their probabilities for input sign FOUR from Baseline (K=5000) and Rotate1 (K=3000). The most-frequently misclassified signs in top 5 rank for input sign 5(a) FOUR from Baseline were 5(b) BEAUTIFUL, 5(c) BLUE, and 5(d) FRIDAY+. Though not shown due to space constraints, the most-frequently misclassified signs in top 5 rank for input sign 6(a) DEPRESS from Baseline (K=5000) and Rotate1 (K=3000) were 6(b) CONFLICT-INTERSECTION, 6(c) DRESS-CLOTHES, and 6(d)EXCITED+. As these figures show, these signs look very similar to each other.

In Figure 8, we observe that the types of motion used by the signers are distinctively different

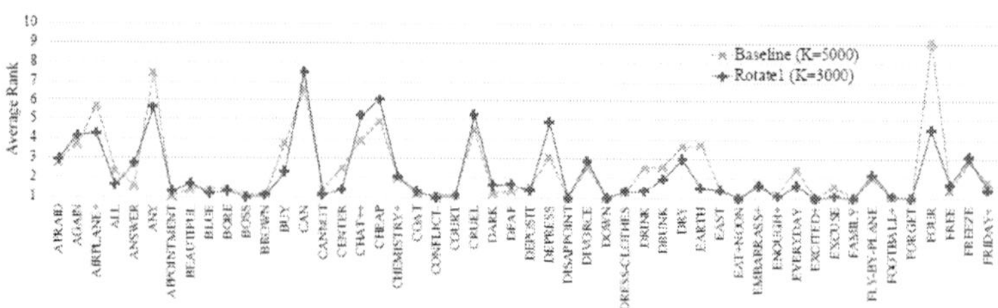

Figure 6: Average ranks of 50 signs for Baseline and Rotate1 (marked with × and marked +, respectively). Lower is better, 24 signs improved in rank (average 0.81), 19 signs degraded (average 0.54), and the ranks for 7 signs did not change.

			Baseline			
Rank	Brady	Dana	Lana	Liz	Naomi	Tyler
1	FOOTBALL+ 0.590	BEAUTIFUL 0.488	**FOUR** 0.982	BEAUTIFUL 0.887	FRIDAY+ 0.922	**FOUR** 0.549
2	BEAUTIFUL 0.0866	BORE 0.159	DOWN 0.0162	DRINK 0.0468	**FOUR** 0.0178	FRIDAY+ 0.395
3	EAT+NOON 0.0865	BLUE 0.152	BLUE 0.00055	FRIDAY+ 0.0357	BLUE 0.0168	BLUE 0.0482
4	BROWN 0.0724	FRIDAY+ 0.0522	ANY 0.000351	BLUE 0.0146	BEAUTIFUL 0.0117	BORE 0.00167
5	EVERYDAY 0.0527	BOSS 0.0405	FRIDAY+ 0.000287	**FOUR** 0.0117	BROWN 0.00873	DRESS-CLOTHES 0.00103
				. . .		
6		**FOUR** 0.0336				
				. . .		
38	**FOUR** 0.000125					

			Rotate1			
Rank	Brady	Dana	Lana	Liz	Naomi	Tyler
1	BEAUTIFUL 0.948	**FOUR** 0.886	**FOUR** 0.864	BEAUTIFUL 0.472	FRIDAY+ 0.838	**FOUR** 0.890
2	FOOTBALL+ 0.0301	FRIDAY+ 0.0286	FRIDAY+ 0.131	FRIDAY+ 0.260	BROWN 0.0876	FRIDAY+ 0.0947
3	BORE 0.00654	DOWN 0.0286	DOWN 0.000766	BROWN 0.0989	BEAUTIFUL 0.0357	DRESS-CLOTHES 0.00584
4	BROWN 0.00267	BLUE 0.0269	DRY 0.000759	DRINK 0.0825	**FOUR** 0.0154	DEAF 0.00236
5	DRINK 0.00265	DRUNK 0.0133	EVERYDAY 0.000722	DISAPPOINT 0.0382	BLUE 0.0105	DISAPPOINT 0.00226
				. . .		
7				**FOUR** 0.00866		
8	**FOUR** 0.00170					

Figure 7: Per-user top 5-ranked signs with their probabilities for test input sign FOUR from Baseline (K=5000) and Rotate1 (K=3000) (Trial 1 result only). For each of the 6 signers, correct rank changed 38→8, 6→1, 1→1, 5→7, 2→4, 1→1.

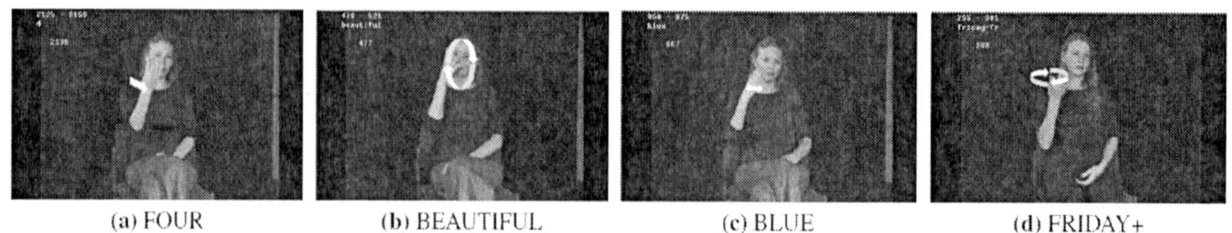

(a) FOUR   (b) BEAUTIFUL   (c) BLUE   (d) FRIDAY+

Figure 8: Most-frequently misclassified signs in top 5 rank for input sign (a) FOUR from Baseline (K=5000) were (b) BEAUTIFUL, (c) BLUE, and (d) FRIDAY+. (ASLLVD, Signer: Liz)

(a) DEPRESS   (b) CONFLICT-INTERSECTION   (c) DRESS-CLOTHES   (d) EXCITED+

Figure 9: Most-frequently misclassified signs in top 5 rank for input sign (a) DEPRESS from Baseline (K=5000) and Rotate1 (K=3000) were (b) CONFLICT-INTERSECTION, (c) DRESS-CLOTHES, and (d) EXCITED+. (ASLLVD, Signers: Brady, Naomi, Tyler, Liz)

from those of FOUR. However, three out of four signs in Figure 9 move two hands in straight lines parallel to the body. We conjecture that this difference in the variations of hand motion affected the usefulness of adding synthetic data created by rotating videos in the plane parallel to the signer. In other words, for the case of FOUR, added synthetic data helped distinguish similarly looking signs because of the different hand motions for these signs, but in the case of DEPRESS, synthetic data created from signs such as CONFLICT-INTERSECTION and DRESS-CLOTHES did not help because the corresponding hand motions, with rotation, did not help and in some cases hurt differentiating those signs from DEPRESS.

5   Conclusions and Ongoing Work

In this work, we explored different strategies for generating synthetic data with the goal of improving ASLR performance, and we experimented with several techniques for the automatic generation of synthetic data in varying amounts. We demonstrated that creating synthetic training data through the simple image manipulation of each frame in ASL video clips helped improve ASLR performance. We anticipate more benefits from utilizing synthetic data for improving the performance of ASL recognizers.

In addition, we are working to extend our automatic generation of synthetic data strategies to the challenge of moving from the lexical level to machine translating videos of ASL sentences and paragraphs into English. In the course of our experimentation and analyses, we discovered a number of issues requiring further investigation. Next, we will experiment with synthetic data of more than 1,000% to the original data to see at what percentage the performance gains begin to diminish. We will also create a better method for generating

valid synthetic data. We plan to do this by defining boundaries of spatial regions that include hand and body motions that constitute a valid sign and developing a synthetic data generation technique from this. Lastly, we will explore adding noise and background variations to the synthetic data generated and verify that these techniques help make ASL systems robust against noisy and poorly lit recording environments.

References

Anantha Rao, G., P. V. V. Kishore, A. S. C. S. Sastry, D. Anil Kumar, and E. Kiran Kumar 2018. Selfie Continuous Sign Language Recognition using Neural Network Classifier. In Proceedings of 2nd International Conference on Micro-Electronics, Electromagnetics and Telecommunications, pages 31–40, Singapore.

Antoniou, Antreas, Amos Storkey, and Harrison Edwards. 2017. Data Augmentation Generative Adversarial Networks. arXiv e-prints, page arXiv: 1711.04340, Nov.

ASL: A brief description - ASL American Sign Language. www.lifeprint.com/asl101/pages-layout/asl1.htm

Bheda, V. and D. Radpour. 2017. Using Deep Convolutional Networks for Gesture Recognition in American Sign Language. arXiv e-prints, October.

Bousmalis, Konstantinos, Nathan Silberman, David Dohan, Dumitru Erhan, and Dilip Krishnan. 2017. Unsupervised Pixel-level Domain Adaptation with Generative Adversarial Networks. In Proceedings of the 2017 Conference on Computer Vision and Pattern Recognition.

Cao, Zhe, Gines Hidalgo, Tomas Simon, Shih-En Wei, and Yaser Sheikh. 2018. OpenPose: Realtime Multi-Person 2D Pose Estimation using Part Affinity Fields. In arXiv preprint arXiv: 1812.08008.

Chuan, C., E. Regina, and C. Guardino. 2014. American Sign Language Recognition Using Leap Motion Sensor. In 2014 13th International Conference on Ma- chine Learning and Applications, pages 541–544, Dec.

Dai, Qian, Jiahui Hou, Panlong Yang, Xiangyang Li, Fei Wang, and Xumiao Zhang. 2017. Demo: The Sound of Silence: End-to-end Sign Language Recognition using Smartwatch. In Proceedings of the 23rd Annual International Conference on Mobile Computing and Network-ing, MobiCom '17, pages 462– 464, New York, NY, USA. ACM.

Dong, C., M. C. Leu, and Z. Yin 2015. American Sign Language alphabet recognition using Microsoft Kinect. In 2015 IEEE Conference on Computer Vision and Pattern Recognition Workshops (CVPRW), pages 44–52, June.

Dreuw, Philippe, David Rybach, Thomas Deselaers, Morteza Zahedi, and Hermann Ney. 2007. Speech Recognition Techniques for a Sign Lan-guage Recognition System. In INTERSPEECH.

Gurumurthy, Swaminathan, Ravi Kiran Sar-vadevabhatla, and R. Venkatesh Babu. 2017. DeLiGan: Generative Adversarial Networks for Diverse and Limited Data. In Proceedings of the 2017 Conference on Com-puter Vision and Pattern Recognition.

Huang, Jie, Wengang Zhou, Qilin Zhang, Houqiang Li, and Weiping Li. 2018. Video-based Sign Language Recognition without Temporal Segmentation. In AAAI.

Ko, T., V. Peddinti, D. Povey, M. L. Seltzer, and S. Khudanpur. 2018. A STUDY ON DATA AUGMENTATION OF REVERBERANT SPEECH FOR ROBUST SPEECH RECOGNITION. In 2017 IEEE International Conference on Acouctics, Speech and Signal Processing (ICASSP), pages 5220–5224, March.

Koller, Oscar, Jens Forster, and Hermann Ney. 2015. Continuous Sign Language Recognition: Towards Large Vocabulary Statistical Recognition Systems Handling Multiple Signers. Computer Vision and Image Understanding, 141:108 – 125

Koller, O., H. Ney, and R. Bowden. 2016. Deep Hand: How to Train a CNN on 1 Million Hand Images When Your Data Is Continuous and Weakly labelled. In 2016 IEEE Conference on Computer Vision and Pattern Recognition (CVPR), pages 3793–3802, June.

Krizhevsky, Alex, Ilya Sutskever, and Geoffrey E. Hinton. 2012. ImageNet Classification with Deep Convolutional Neural Networks. In Proceedings of the 25th International Confer-ence on Neural Information Processing Systems - Volume 1, NIPS'12, pages 1097–1105, USA. Cur-ran Associates Inc.

Lang, Simon, Marco Block-Berlitz, and Raul Rojas. 2012. Sign Language Recognition Using Kinect. pages 394–402, 04.

Ma, Yongsen, Gang Zhou, Shuangquan Wang, Hongyang Zhao, and Woosub Jung. 2018. SignFi: Sign Language Recognition Using WiFi. Proc. ACM Interact. Mob. Wearable Ubiquitous Technol., 2(1):23:1–23:21, March.

ASL: A brief description - ASL American Sign Lan-guage www.lifeprint.com/asl101/pages-layout/asl1.htm

Molchanov, P., S. Gupta, K. Kim, and J. Kautz. 2015. Hand Gesture Recognition with 3D Convolutional Neural Networks. In 2015 IEEE Conference on Computer Vision and Pattern Recognition Workshops (CVPRW), pages 1–7, June.

Nakamura, Karen. 2008. About American Sign Language. In: Deaf Resource Library. http://www.deaflibrary.org/asl.html

Neidle, Carol, Ashwin Thangali, and Stan Sclaroff. 2012. Challenges in Development of the American Sign Language Lexicon Video Dataset (ASLLVD) Cor-pus. In 5th Workshop on the Representation and Pro-cessing of Sign Languages: Interactions between Corpus and Lexicon, LREC 2012.

Sennrich, Rico, Barry Haddow, and Alexandra Birch. 2016. Improving Neural Machine Translation Models with Monolingual Data. In Proceedings of the 54th Annual Meeting of the Association for Computational Linguistics (Volume 1: Long Papers), pages 86–96, Berlin, Ger-many, August. Association for Computational Linguistics.

Speers, D'Armond Lee. 2002. Representation of American Sign Language for Machine Translation. Ph.D. thesis, Georgetown University, Washington, DC, USA. AAI3053310.

Starner, T., J. Weaver, and A. Pentland. 1998. Real-Time American Sign Language Recognition Using Desk and Wearable Computer Based Video. Transactions on Pattern Analysis and Ma-chine Intelligence, 20(12):1371–1375, Dec.

Szegedy, Christian, Wei Liu, Yangqing Jia, Pierre Sermanet, Scott Reed, Dragomir Anguelov, Du-mitru Erhan, Vincent Vanhoucke, and Andrew Rabinovich. 2015. Going deeper with convolutions. In Computer Vision and Pattern Recognition (CVPR).

Tao, Wenjin, Ming C. Leu, and Zhaozheng Yin. 2018. American Sign Language alphabet recognition using Convolutional Neural Networks with mul-tiview augmentation and inference fusion. Engineering Applications of Artificial Intelligence, 76:202 – 213.

Tharwat, Alaa, Tarek Gaber, Aboul Ella Hassanien, M. K. Shahin, and Basma Refaat. 2015. Sift-Based Arabic Sign Language Recognition System. In Abraham, Ajith, Pavel Kromer, and Vaclav Snasel, editors, Afro-European Conference for In-dustrial Advancement, pages 359–370, Cham. Springer International Publishing.

Wu, J., L. Sun, and R. Jafari. 2016. A Wearable System for Recognizing American Sign Language in Real-Time Using IMU and Surface EMG Sensors. IEEE Journal of Biomedical and Health Informatics, 20(5):1281– 1290, Sep

Selecting Informative Context Sentence by Forced Back-Translation

Ryuichiro Kimura[†], **Shohei Iida**[†], **Hongyi Cui**[†], **Po-Hsuan Hung**[†],
Takehito Utsuro[†] **and** **Masaaki Nagata**[‡]
[†]Graduate School of Systems and Information Engineering, University of Tsukuba, Japan
[‡]NTT Communication Science Laboratories, NTT Corporation, Japan

Abstract

As one of the contributions of this paper, this paper first explores the upper bound of context-based neural machine translation and attempt to utilize previously unused context information. We found that, if we could appropriately select the most informative context sentence for a given input source sentence, we could boost translation accuracy as much as approximately 10 BLEU points. This paper next explores a criterion to select the most informative context sentences that give the highest BLEU score. Applying the proposed criterion, context sentences that yield the highest forced back-translation probability when back-translating into the source sentence are selected. Experimental results with Japanese and English parallel sentences from the OpenSubtitles2018 corpus demonstrate that, when the context length of five preceding and five subsequent sentences are examined, the proposed approach achieved significant improvements of 0.74 (Japanese to English) and 1.14 (English to Japanese) BLEU scores compared to the baseline 2-to-2 model, where the oracle translation achieved upper bounds improvements of 5.88 (Japanese to English) and 9.10 (English to Japanese) BLEU scores.

1 Introduction

Recently, neural machine translation (NMT) models (Sutskever et al., 2014; Luong et al., 2015;

Vaswani et al., 2017) have made remarkable progress. Most NMT models are designed to translate a single sentence and do not accept input greater than one sentence, i.e., input sentences that include additional context information. However, recently, several approaches that attempt to translate inputs with more than one sentence have been proposed (Tiedemann and Scherrer, 2017; Libovický and Helcl, 2017; Maruf and Haffari, 2018; Miculicich et al., 2018; Bawden et al., 2018; Voita et al., 2018; Tu et al., 2018). These approaches to context-based NMT models can be roughly categorized according to the width of the context considered in those models. A typical approach is to consider the sentence immediately preceding the source sentence to be translated as the context (Tiedemann and Scherrer, 2017; Libovický and Helcl, 2017; Bawden et al., 2018; Voita et al., 2018). Context-based NMT models can be further categorized according to whether the source and context sentences are encoded using a single (Tiedemann and Scherrer, 2017) or multiple encoders (Libovický and Helcl, 2017; Bawden et al., 2018; Voita et al., 2018). Another approach considers a much wider context than the immediately preceding sentence, e.g., three preceding sentences (Miculicich et al., 2018), preceding sentences within the document (Tu et al., 2018), and all preceding and subsequent sentences within the document (Maruf and Haffari, 2018).

Such approaches to context-based NMT models possibly outperform existing models that only accept a single sentence to be translated. Note that we refer to the model that only accepts a single sentence as a "1-to-1" model. Among these existing models, the 2+2 or 2-to-2 model (Tiedemann and Scherrer, 2017) uses the sentence immediately preceding the source sentence to be translated as

	BLEU		Oracle BLEU	
	Ja-En	En-Ja	Ja-En	En-Ja
1-to-1 (baseline)	15.52	11.48	—	—
2-to-2 (baseline)	16.52	12.36	—	—
selection from 20-best of 2-to-2 (baseline) by 2-to-2 back-translation	16.69 / —	12.61 / —	—	—
1-to-1 + 2-to-2 (immediately preceding sent.)	17.04** / 16.51	13.24** / 12.47	18.15	15.61
1-to-1 + 2-to-2 (1st $\sim$ 5th preceding sents.)	17.25** / 16.67	13.50** / 13.14**	21.09	19.55
1-to-1 + 2-to-2 (1st $\sim$ 5th subsequent sents.)	17.04** / 16.52	13.46** / 13.13**	20.84	19.51
1-to-1 + 2-to-2 (1st $\sim$ 5th preceding + subsequent sents.)	17.26** / 16.68	13.02** / 12.81**	22.40	21.46

Table 1: Evaluation results (maximizing forced back-translation probability / maximizing back-translation sentence-BLEU) ($**$ represents significant difference ($p < 0.01$) against baseline 2-to-2 model)

an extended context. Here the context sentence is concatenated to the source sentence using the $\langle$CONCAT$\rangle$ token. The 2-to-2 model is easy to implement into existing 1-to-1 models: however, it only considers the immediately preceding sentence as context. Thus, it is necessary to consider much wider contexts such as the second through fifth preceding sentences and the first through fifth subsequent sentences. We conducted an empirical study that revealed that, in some cases, among the first through fifth sentences preceding and subsequent to the source sentence, the most informative sentence, i.e, the sentence that returns the highest BLEU score, may not be the sentence immediately preceding the source sentence. We measured oracle BLEU scores by selecting context sentences that give the maximum sentence-BLEU scores among the five preceding and subsequent sentences, as shown in Table 1 and Figure 1. Then, we found that, if we could select the most informative context sentence for a given input source sentence, we can improve translation accuracy by as much as approximately 10 BLEU points, as indicated by the oracle BLEU scores in Table 1 and Figure 1. More specifically, compared to the baseline 2-to-2 model, the oracle translation achieved upper bound improvements of 5.88 (Japanese to English) and 9.10 (English to Japanese) BLEU scores.

Considering this result, within the framework of the 2-to-2 context based NMT model, this study explored how to select the most informative context sentences that give the highest BLEU score among the first five preceding and subse-

quent sentences[1]. Here, we used the Transformer model (Vaswani et al., 2017) as the base 1-to-1 model. To select the translation with the highest BLEU score among the 11 translations (i.e., those translated by the 1-to-1 and 10 2-to-2 models), we propose an approach that selects the translation that yields the highest forced back-translation probability when back-translating into the source sentence. The evaluation results shown in Table 1 demonstrate that the proposed approach achieves significant BLEU score improvements over the baseline 2-to-2 and 1-to-1 models. More specifically, over the baseline 2-to-2 model, the proposed approach achieved significant improvements of 0.74 (Japanese to English) and 1.14 (English to Japanese) BLEU scores.

2 Selective Extended Context Decoding

Tiedemann and Scherrer (2017) proposed the 2-to-2 model, which uses the sentence immediately preceding the source sentence to be translated as the extended context. We extend the 2-to-2 model by considering the first five preceding and first five subsequent sentences. In our extended 2-to-2 context-based NMT model, the immediately preceding sentence, the second through fifth preceding sentences, and the first through fifth subse-

---

[1] An obvious alternative to this approach is to simply employ 3-to-3 (or more) models using an approach similar to the 2-to-2 model that concatenates context sentences using the $\langle$CONCAT$\rangle$ token. However, due to the upper bound restriction of GPU memory, it is impractical to employ such 3-to-3 (or more) models. Furthermore, our preliminary evaluation result also indicates that the 3-to-3 model underperforms compared to the proposed approach.

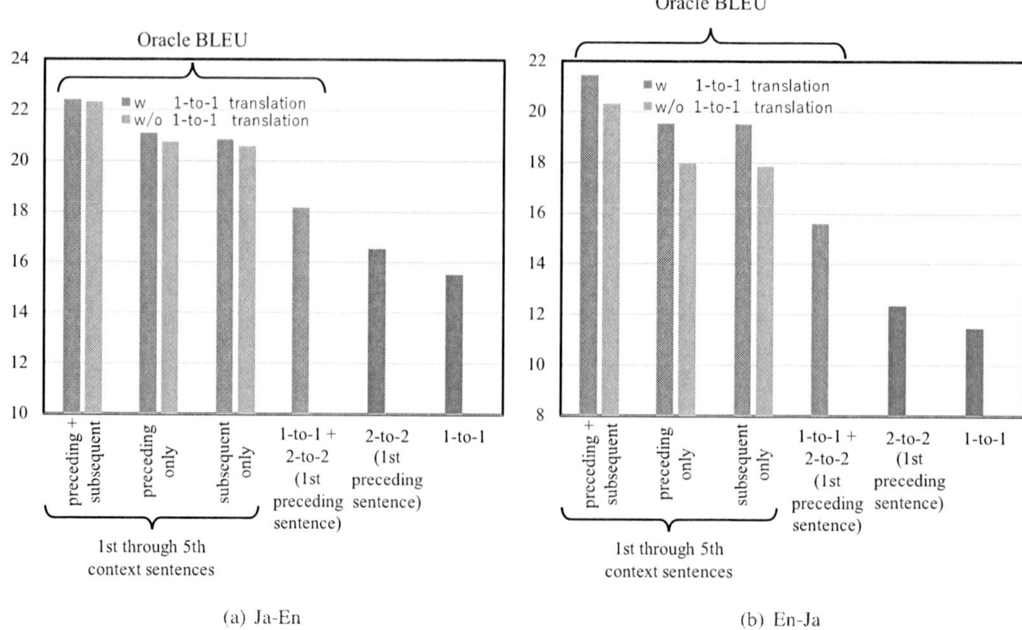

Oracle BLEU

(a) Ja-En   (b) En-Ja

Figure 1: Oracle BLEU and BLEU scores of baseline 2-to-2 ($y_0^{22}(x_{-1}, x_0)$) and 1-to-1 ($y_0^{11}(x_0)$) models

quent sentences are considered candidates for concatenation to the source sentence. Then, among the first through fifth preceding and first through fifth subsequent sentences, we select the most informative context sentences in the 2-to-2 context-based NMT model.

In this framework, this paper employs the notation described below. x_i and y_i ($i = 0, \pm 1, \ldots, \pm 5$) denote the source and target sentences, respectively. x_0 denotes the source sentence to be translated, while y_0 denotes its translation in the target language. x_{-1} denotes the context sentence in the source language immediately preceding x_0, x_i ($i = -2, \ldots, -5$) the second through fifth preceding sentences, and x_i ($i = +1, \ldots, +5$) the first through fifth subsequent sentences. In order to represent the direction of translation as the target language l (x or y in this paper) of the translation, the model m (1-to-1 or 2-to-2) used for the translation, the index i ($i = 0, \pm 1, \ldots, \pm 5$) of the translated sentence, and the source sentence s and the context sentence c in the source language, this paper employs a general notation to represent the translated sentence in the target language as below:

$$l_i^m(c, s).$$

Translation by 1-to-1 Model

For example, the target sentence translated from x_0 by the base 1-to-1 Transformer model is denoted as

$$y_0^{11}(x_0).$$

In this case, the source sentence s is x_0, and is translated without a context sentence. Table 2 shows a typical Japanese subject zero pronoun case improved by the proposed informative context sentence selection approach by forced back-translation, where the bottom line represents the translation by the base 1-to-1 model. In Table 2, $y_0^{11}(x_0)$, i.e., the translation of x_0 by the base 1-to-1 model is:

If we leave now , <u>we</u>'ll never get back .

Here, the base 1-to-1 model fails in the translation of the Japanese zero pronoun subject in x_0, i.e., it is not translated as "you", but translated as "we".

Translation by Baseline 2-to-2 Model

The target sentence translated from x_0 by the baseline 2-to-2 Transformer model which uses the sentence x_{-1} immediately preceding x_0 as the extended context is denoted as

$$y_0^{22}(x_{-1}, x_0).$$

Source sentences		Target sentences		Forced back-translation probability / sentence-BLEU
—		Reference translation:	Walk out now and you may never return .	—
4th preceding sentence x_{-4}:	私に逆らうなら お前 は何もなくなるぞ。 (If you defy me , you will have nothing .)	Translation $y_0^{22}(x_{-4}, x_0)$ by 2-to-2 model:	If you leave , you'll never get back .	$\mathbf{5.8 \times 10^{-8}}$ / **14.99**
Immediately preceding sentence x_{-1}:	それが望みなのか？ (Is that what you want ?)	Translation $y_0^{22}(x_{-1}, x_0)$ by baseline 2-to-2 model:	If we leave now , we'll never get back .	2.8×10^{-10} / 13.55
Source sentence x_0:	出て行けば、戻れなくなるぞ。	Translation $y_0^{11}(x_0)$ by baseline 1-to-1 model:	If we leave now , we'll never get back .	1.3×10^{-8} / 10.57

Table 2: Example improvements over baseline 2-to-2 $y_0^{22}(x_{-1}, x_0)$ (Ja-En)   (a) pronoun translation

In this case, x_0 is concatenated with the immediately preceding sentence x_{-1} as " x_{-1} $\langle$CONCAT$\rangle$ x_0", and the concatenated sentences are translated by the baseline 2-to-2 Transformer model. We denote the translated (concatenated) sentences as follows:

$$y_{-1}^{22}(x_{-1}, x_0) \ \langle\text{CONCAT}\rangle \ y_0^{22}(x_{-1}, x_0)$$

where $y_{-1}^{22}(x_{-1}, x_0)$ and $y_0^{22}(x_{-1}, x_0)$ are the translations of x_{-1} and x_0, respectively. In the case of Table 2, the immediately preceding sentence x_{-1} and the source sentence x_0 are:

x_{-1}: それが望みなのか？
(Is that what you want ?)
x_0: 出て行けば、戻れなくなるぞ。
(Walk out now and you may never return .)

Then, $y_0^{22}(x_{-1}, x_0)$, i.e., the translation of x_0 is:

If we leave now , we'll never get back .

Again, the baseline 2-to-2 model fails in the translation of the Japanese zero pronoun subject in x_0, i.e., it is not translated as "you", but translated as "we".

Translation by 2-to-2 Model with a Context Sentence x_{-4}

Similarly, the first line of Table 2 also shows the target sentence translated from x_0 by the 2-to-2 Transformer model which uses the fourth sentence x_{-4} preceding x_0 as the extended context. In this case, the translated sentence is denoted as

$$y_0^{22}(x_{-4}, x_0).$$

As shown in Table 2, the fourth preceding sentence x_{-4} and the source sentence x_0 are:

x_{-4}: 私に逆らうならお前は何もなくなるぞ。
(If you defy me , you will have nothing .)
x_0: 出て行けば、戻れなくなるぞ。
(Walk out now and you may never return .)

Then, the concatenated sentences "x_{-4} $\langle$CONCAT$\rangle$ x_0" are translated into:

$$y_{-4}^{22}(x_{-4}, x_0) \ \langle\text{CONCAT}\rangle \ y_0^{22}(x_{-4}, x_0).$$

Here, $y_0^{22}(x_{-4}, x_0)$, i.e., the translation of x_0 is:

If you leave , you'll never get back .

This time, the fourth preceding source sentence x_{-4} includes the Japanese pronoun "お前"

(mostly translated as "you" in English in the training corpus): thus, the translation $y_0^{22}(x_{-4}, x_0)$ by the 2-to-2 model successfully includes the translation of the Japanese zero pronoun subject in x_0 as "you". This then contributes to having the highest forced back-translation probability and sentence-BLEU score with the reference translation compared to $y_0^{11}(x_0)$ (translated by the base 1-to-1 model) and $y_0^{22}(x_{-1}, x_0)$ (translated by the baseline 2-to-2 model), in which the Japanese zero pronoun subject is translated as "we" in both cases. This analysis clearly indicates that the baseline 2-to-2 model is insufficient relative to correctly translating Japanese zero pronouns into English.

Translation by 2-to-2 Model with a Context Sentence x_i ($i = \pm1, \ldots, \pm5$)

More generally, in addition to translation $y_0^{11}(x_0)$ obtained by the base 1-to-1 Transformer model, we prepare 10 translated sentences $y_0^{22}(x_{-1}, x_0), \ldots, y_0^{22}(x_{-5}, x_0)$ and $y_0^{22}(x_{+1}, x_0), \ldots, y_0^{22}(x_{+5}, x_0)$ as candidate translations, each of which is generated using the 2-to-2 model based on the standard Transformer model. Each $y_0^{22}(x_i, x_0)$ ($i = \pm1, \ldots, \pm5$) of these 10 translated sentences is generated by the 2-to-2 model, where one of the first through fifth preceding and subsequent sentences x_i ($i = \pm1, \ldots, \pm5$) is used as the context sentence of the 2-to-2 model[2]. In the 2-to-2 model, only one of the five preceding and subsequent sentences x_i ($i = \pm1, \ldots, \pm5$) is concatenated to the source sentence x_0 using the $\langle \text{CONCAT} \rangle$ token as:

$$x_i \ \langle \text{CONCAT} \rangle \ x_0.$$

Then, the concatenated sentences are translated by the 2-to-2 Transformer model. We denote the translated (concatenated) sentences as follows:

$$y_i^{22}(x_i, x_0) \ \langle \text{CONCAT} \rangle \ y_0^{22}(x_i, x_0)$$

where $y_i^{22}(x_i, x_0)$ and $y_0^{22}(x_i, x_0)$ are the translations of x_i and x_0, respectively.

3 Selecting Informative Context Sentences with Maximum Forced Back-translation Probability

In the proposed method of selecting a translation among the 11 candidate translations $y_0^{11}(x_0)$,

$y_0^{22}(x_{\pm1}, x_0), \ldots, y_0^{22}(x_{\pm5}, x_0)$, we select the translation that yields the highest forced back-translation probability when back-translating into the source sentence. In this context, forced back-translation is defined as forced decoding from a translated target sentence to its source sentence.

Here, assume the source sentence x_0 of word length n with a context sentence x_i is given. For the back-translation translation model, we used the 2-to-1 Transformer model with the setup described in Section 5, rather than the 1-to-1 Transformer model. This is simply because, in forced back-translation into x_0, the 2-to-1 model considers both $y_i^{22}(x_i, x_0)$ and $y_0^{22}(x_i, x_0)$, while the 1-to-1 model considers $y_0^{22}(x_i, x_0)$ (translation of the source sentence x_0) only, but not $y_i^{22}(x_i, x_0)$ (translation of the context sentence x_i). We assume that considering both $y_i^{22}(x_i, x_0)$ and $y_0^{22}(x_i, x_0)$ in forced back-translation will yield forced back-translation probabilities that are significantly informative[3].

The forced back-translation probability score of the source sentence word x_j ($1 \leq j \leq n$) of x_0 is expressed as follows.

$$b_j \ = \ -\log p\Big(x_j | x_{<j}, \ y_i^{22}(x_i, x_0),$$
$$y_0^{22}(x_i, x_0) \Big)$$

From $y_i^{22}(x_i, x_0)$ and $y_0^{22}(x_i, x_0)$, the forced back-translation probability score of the entire source sentence x_0 is obtained as the sum of each b_j.

$$B\Big(x_0, \ y_i^{22}(x_i, x_0), \ y_0^{22}(x_i, x_0) \Big) \ = \ \sum_j b_j$$

Similarly, the forced back-translation probability score of the entire source sentence x_0 for the base 1-to-1 model is obtained as below:

$$b_j \ = \ -\log p\Big(x_j | x_{<j}, \ y_0^{11}(x_0) \Big)$$
$$B\Big(x_0, \ y_0^{11}(x_0) \Big) \ = \ \sum_j b_j$$

Finally, among the 11 candidate translations $y_0^{11}(x_0)$, $y_0^{22}(x_{\pm1}, x_0), \ldots, y_0^{22}(x_{\pm5}, x_0)$, we select the translation that yields the highest

---

[2] We examined how many of the 10 translations $y_0^{22}(x_{\pm1}, x_0), \ldots, y_0^{22}(x_{\pm5}, x_0)$ are exactly the same as $y_0^{11}(x_0)$. The rates of cases where none of the 10 translations was exactly the same as $y_0^{11}(x_0)$. were 54% for Japanese to English and 63% for English to Japanese.

[3] In the evaluation discussed in Section 7.1, forced back-translation using the 1-to-1 model achieved merely the same BLEU scores as that of the 2-to-1 model.

forced back-translation probability B when back-translating into the source sentence x_0 as below:

$$\underset{i=0,\pm1,\dots,\pm5}{\operatorname{argmax}} \begin{cases} \mathrm{B}\left(x_0,\ y_0^{11}(x_0)\right) & (i=0) \\ \mathrm{B}\left(x_0,\ y_i^{22}(x_i,x_0),\right. & (i\neq 0) \\ \left. y_0^{22}(x_i,x_0)\right) \end{cases}$$

Employing the forced back-translation probability differs from existing approaches (Rapp, 2009; Li and Jurafsky, 2016; Goto and Tanaka, 2017; Kimura et al., 2017) that incorporate back-translation from the translated target sentence to the source sentence. Rapp (2009) employed the BLEU score between the source sentence and source language sentence back-translated from the target translated sentence in an automatic MT evaluation context. Li and Jurafsky (Li and Jurafsky, 2016) proposed to re-rank decoded translations based on mutual information between source and target sentences x and y i.e., the probabilities $p(y \mid x)$ and $p(x \mid y)$. Goto and Tanaka (2017) and Kimura et al. (2017) also employed the ratio of forced back-translation probabilities in the context of detecting untranslated content in NMT. These approaches differ from the proposed use of the forced back-translation probability[4].

4   Selecting Informative Context Sentences with Maximum Back-translation Sentence-BLEU

Rapp (2009) proposed an approach of using BLEU score between the source sentence and source language sentence back-translated from the target translated sentence in an automatic MT evaluation context. Based on Rapp (2009), we employ another approach to selecting informative context sentences, where back-translation sentence-BLEU is maximized. As in the case of selecting informative context sentences with maximum forced back-translation probability presented in the previous section, candidate translations are the same as those 11 candidates $y_0^{11}(x_0), y_0^{22}(x_{\pm1},x_0),\dots,y_0^{22}(x_{\pm5},x_0)$. For each of those 11 candidate translations, its back-translation back-tran$(i)^5$ into the source language

is given as below:

$$\text{back-tran}(i) =$$
$$\begin{cases} \text{back-tran}^{11}\left(y_0^{11}(x_0)\right)) & (i=0) \\ \text{back-tran}^{21}\left(y_i^{22}(x_i,x_0),\right. & (i\neq 0) \\ \left. y_0^{22}(x_i,x_0)\right) \end{cases}$$

Then, we measure the sentence-BLEU score between the source sentence x_0 and each back-translation. We then select the one that gives the highest sentence-BLEU score.

$$\underset{i=0,\pm1,\dots,\pm5}{\operatorname{argmax}}\ \text{sent-BLEU}\left(x_0,\ \text{back-tran}(i)\right)$$

5   Dataset and Experimental Setup

The dataset used for the oracle translation statistics and the BLEU evaluation comprised 2,083,576 English and Japanese parallel sentence pairs from Opensubtitles 2018 (Lison et al., 2018). Note that we followed Tiedemann and Scherrer (2017) to create the extended context dataset. Here, 90% of the dataset (1,876,624 sentence pairs) was used for training, 5% (104,379 sentence pairs) for development, and 5% (102,573 sentence pairs) for oracle statistics and evaluation. Here, of these 102,573 sentence pairs, only 10,000 pairs were actually used for oracle statistics and evaluation[6] [7]. Throughout the paper, we approximate that all the 2-to-2 models are trained with the immediately preceding sentence as the context.

6   Oracle Translation of Context-based NMT

When measuring the oracle sentence-BLEU score, for each source sentence x_0, we select the sentence

---

translating $y_0^{11}(x_0)$ ($i = 0$), while we used the 2-to-1 Transformer model (denoted as back-tran^{21}) with the setup described in section 5 when back-translating $y_0^{22}(x_i,x_0)$ ($i \neq 0$, i.e., translated from x_0 with a context sentence by the 2-to-2 model).

[6]In training and development, the encoder rejects input sentences (source sentence concatenated with the context sentence for the 2-to-2 models) with greater than 50 tokens. Average token length of the 10,000 pairs for oracle statistics and evaluation is 7.9 (English) and 6.9 (Japanese).

[7]Experimental setup is as follows: Tokenizers are Moses tokenizer (Koehn et al., 2007) for English and MeCab (http://taku910.github.io/mecab/) for Japanese tokenization. OpenNMT-py (Klein et al., 2017) is used for training and testing NMT models. 50,000 vocabulary sizes are employed for both English and Japanese. Embedding sizes are 512. Encoder and decoder are with six layers with batch size as 4,096 and dropout rate as 0.3 and 100,000 steps for training. Adam optimizer (Kingma and Ba, 2015) is used. One NVIDIA Tesla P100 16GB GPU is used. MTEval Toolkit (https://github.com/odashi/mteval) is used to measure BLEU, and Moses decoder's sentence-bleu.cpp is used to measure sentence-BLEU.

---

[4]The proposed approach is included among those that consider a much wider context than the immediately preceding sentence, e.g., the approaches proposed by Miculicich et al. (2018), Tu et al. (2018), and Maruf and Haffari (2018).

[5]For the back-translation translation model, we used the 1-to-1 Transformer model (denoted as back-tran^{11}) when back-

with the maximum sentence-BLEU score among the candidate translations after obtaining 11 candidates ($y_0^{11}(x_0)$ translated by the 1-to-1 model and $y_0^{22}(x_i, x_0)$ ($i=\pm1,\ldots,\pm5$) translated by the 2-to-2 models). Figure 1 shows the oracle BLEU scores for the following seven cases:

(i) among $y_0^{22}(x_i, x_0)$ ($i = \pm1,\ldots,\pm5$) with and without $y_0^{11}(x_0)$

(ii) among $y_0^{22}(x_i, x_0)$ ($i = -1,\ldots,-5$) with and without $y_0^{11}(x_0)$

(iii) among $y_0^{22}(x_i, x_0)$ ($i = +1,\ldots,+5$) with and without $y_0^{11}(x_0)$

(iv) between $y_0^{11}(x_0)$ and $y_0^{22}(x_{-1}, x_0)$

and the BLEU scores of the baseline 1-to-1 ($y_0^{11}(x_0)$) and 2-to-2 models with the immediately preceding sentence as the context ($y_0^{22}(x_{-1}, x_0)$). For all three 2-to-2 model cases with the candidate translation obtained by the 1-to-1 model, the oracle BLEU increased by including $y_0^{11}(x_0)$. Furthermore, the oracle BLEU score increases as more candidates are considered. Table 1 shows that, by considering $y_0^{22}(x_i, x_0)$ ($i = -5,\ldots,-2,+1,\ldots,+5$) in addition to $y_0^{11}(x_0)$ and $y_0^{22}(x_{-1}, x_0)$, the oracle BLEU score improves by approximately four points for Japanese to English and six points for English to Japanese. These results indicate that longer contexts yield obvious benefit for the 2-to-2 context-based NMT model, which is the primary motivation for selecting informative context sentences in that model.

7 Evaluation

7.1 Evaluation Results

For both English to Japanese and Japanese to English directions, Table 1 shows the BLEU scores obtained by selecting the translation candidate that maximizes the forced back-translation and the back-translation sentence-BLEU score. For the proposed method, we compare the following translation candidate cases:[8] (i) between $y_0^{11}(x_0)$ and $y_0^{22}(x_{-1}, x_0)$, (ii) among $y_0^{11}(x_0)$ and $y_0^{22}(x_i, x_0)$ ($i = -1,\ldots,-5$), (iii) among $y_0^{11}(x_0)$ and $y_0^{22}(x_i, x_0)$ ($i = +1,\ldots,+5$), (iv) among $y_0^{11}(x_0)$ and $y_0^{22}(x_i, x_0)$ ($i = \pm1,\ldots,\pm5$). Compared to the BLEU scores of

$y_0^{11}(x_0)$ and $y_0^{22}(x_{-1}, x_0)$, all BLEU scores obtained by the proposed method demonstrate significant improvement ($p < 0.01$), except for the Japanese to English translation obtained by maximizing the back-translation sentence-BLEU score.

By comparing the BLEU scores of $y_0^{11}(x_0)$, $y_0^{22}(x_{-1}, x_0)$, the oracle among them, and the selection between them by maximizing the forced back-translation, the selection between $y_0^{11}(x_0)$ and $y_0^{22}(x_{-1}, x_0)$ by maximizing forced back-translation achieves BLEU scores that are comparable to the oracle BLEU scores. Thus, we conclude that the proposed method contributes to selecting better translation between those candidates. However, the proposed method cannot select informative context sentences among $y_0^{22}(x_i, x_0)$ ($i = -5,\ldots,-2,+1,\ldots,+5$), because the results obtained by adding $y_0^{22}(x_i, x_0)$ ($i = -5,\ldots,-2,+1,\ldots,+5$), to translation candidates $y_0^{11}(x_0)$ and $y_0^{22}(x_{-1}, x_0)$ yields little or no gain in BLEU score. Note that this does not coincide with improving the oracle BLEU score by approximately four points for Japanese to English and six points for English to Japanese with the overall 11 translation candidates. Thus, it can be concluded that further study is required to appropriately select the informative context sentences among the 11 candidates such that the BLEU score becomes much closer to the oracle BLEU score.

Another important comparison with a baseline is also shown as "selection from 20-best of 2-to-2 (baseline) by 2-to-2 back-translation" in Table 1. With this baseline, it is intended to examine whether the five preceding and subsequent sentences introduced in the proposed method are sufficiently informative compared to other well studied translation candidates such as n-best translations. Specifically, the baseline 2-to-2 model with the immediately preceding sentence as the context is employed to generate 20-best translations, and then, out of those generated 20-best translations, the one with the maximum forced back-translation into the source sentence is selected[9]. As shown in Table 1, this baseline performed worse than the proposed approach. From this result, it is obvious that the proposed approach of introducing five preceding and subsequent sentences as the context is

---

[8]Throughout the evaluation results of this paper, when obtaining the forced back-translation probability for y_{11}, we used the 1-to-1 Transformer model as the back-translation translation model.

[9]We compare the 2-to-2 and 2-to-1 models in the step of forced back-translation here, where the 2-to-2 model outperformed the 2-to-1 model. In Table 1, we show the results obtained by the 2-to-2 model.

category of phenomena	Ja-En		En-Ja	
	succeed	fail	succeed	fail
synonymous expression	14	12	17	10
pronoun	**7**	2	2	0
untranslated by baseline	**5**	0	**10**	0
article	0	1	0	0
other	11	2	7	3
manually judged (comparable)	10	18	13	27
(baseline wins)	3	0	1	0
(baseline loses)	0	15	0	10
total	50	50	50	50

Table 3: Distribution of oracle translation phenomena (through manual analysis of 50 examples) (proposed method succeeds / fails in identifying those oracle translations)

category of phenomena	Ja-En		En-Ja	
	2-to-2 wins	1-to-1 wins	2-to-2 wins	1-to-1 wins
synonymous expression	16	20	14	22
pronoun	2	2	1	2
untranslated by 1-to-1	**8**	0	**12**	2
article	1	0	0	0
other	7	8	3	4
manually judged (comparable)	15	15	18	16
(1-to-1 wins)	1	0	2	0
(2-to-2 wins)	0	5	0	4
total	50	50	50	50

Table 4: Distribution of phenomena where baseline 2-to-2 $y_0^{22}(x_{-1}, x_0)$ wins v.s. 1-to-1 $y_0^{11}(x_0)$ wins (through manual analysis of 50 examples)

much more informative than 20-best translations with just the preceding sentence as the context.

7.2 Analysis of Improvements and Errors

To analyze typical cases relative to the improvements and errors of the proposed approach, we randomly select 50 success cases and 50 failure cases when identifying oracle translations using the proposed method. Specifically, we first collect cases where oracle translation is selected from $y_0^{11}(x_0)$ or $y_0^{22}(x_i, x_0)$ $(i = -5, \ldots, -2, +1, \ldots, +5)$, rather than from $y_0^{22}(x_{-1}, x_0)$. Then, from these cases, we randomly select 50 examples for each of the following cases.

(a) Proposed approach (maximizing forced back-translation) successfully identifies collected oracle translations.

(b) Proposed approach (maximizing forced back-translation) fails to identify collected oracle translations.

Then, we manually categorize the 50 examples (for each case) according to the phenomena in Table 3.

For both Japanese to English and English to Japanese, nearly 30~40% are categorized as "synonymous expression", where the proposed approach of maximizing forced back-translation successfully selects the oracle translation that includes the synonymous expression rather than exactly the same expression (as in the reference translation). Due to this synonymous expression, the sentence

has the highest sentence-BLEU score and is selected as the oracle translation. Although this phenomenon is top ranked among others, it is also top ranked among the failure cases. Thus, it is necessary to incorporate other criteria to reduce the failure cases.

For comparison, we also categorize the phenomena of randomly selected 50 cases when the baseline 2-to-2 model outperforms the 1-to-1 model, i.e., translation $y_0^{22}(x_{-1}, x_0)$ by the baseline 2-to-2 model achieves a sentence-BLEU score that is greater than that of translation $y_0^{11}(x_0)$ by the 1-to-1 model. We also categorize the phenomena of randomly selected 50 cases of its opposite, i.e., when the 1-to-1 model outperforms the baseline 2-to-2 model. These results are shown in Table 4. As can be seen, even in the comparison of the baseline 2-to-2 and 1-to-1 models, the "synonymous expression" category is top ranked.

It is interesting to compare the second and third ranked categories, i.e., "pronoun translation" and "untranslated by baseline," among Japanese to English and English to Japanese in Tables 3 and 4. The "pronoun translation" category is ranked high only in the Japanese to English case with the proposed approach (Table 3). Table 2 shows a typical Japanese subject zero pronoun case and its detail is described in section 2. With the "untranslated by baseline / 1-to-1" categories, it is obvious from Table 3 and Table 4 that the proposed approach outperforms the baseline 2-to-2 model for

Source sentences		Target sentences		Forced back-translation probability / sentence-BLEU
—		Reference translation:	Every pain you suffered was punishment for your <u>sins</u> .	—
Immediately preceding sentence x^{-1}:	お前の一挙一動がここにお前を導いた。(Every step you took led you to here .)	Translation $y_0^{22}(x_{-1}, x_0)$ by baseline 2-to-2 model:	Every suffering you suffered was your punishment .	3.4×10^{-19} / 27.64
Source sentence x_0:	お前の受けた全ての苦しみはお前の <u>罪</u> に対する罰だった。	Translation $y_0^{11}(x_0)$ by baseline 1-to-1 model:	All the suffering you've had was your punishment .	5.3×10^{-19} / 16.62
2nd subsequent sentence x^{+2}:	お前の命を奪うために <u>悪魔</u> が送ったものを見よ! (See what the <u>devil</u> has sent to claim you .)	Translation $y_0^{22}(x_{+2}, x_0)$ by 2-to-2 model:	All your suffering was punishment for your <u>sins</u> .	$\underline{5.9 \times 10^{-14}}$ / <u>**57.18**</u>

Table 5: Example improvements over baseline 2-to-2 $y_0^{22}(x_{-1}, x_0)$ (Ja-En)　　(b) untranslated by baseline

both Japanese to English and English to Japanese directions. In addition, the baseline 2-to-2 model outperforms the 1-to-1 model. Thus, it can be concluded that the matter of untranslated content in context-based NMT can be handled consistently by appropriately extending the range of the context considered within a certain framework of context-based NMT models such as the 2-to-2 model. For example, as shown in Table 5, the baseline 2-to-2 model fails to produce the word "sins" in its translation. In contrast, the translation $y_0^{22}(x_{+2}, x_0)$ obtained by the 2-to-2 model with the second subsequent source sentence x_{+2} as the context sentence successfully includes the word "sins," probably because the second subsequent source sentence x_{+2} includes "悪魔" ("devil").

By examining the cases of improvements over the baseline 2-to-2 model, we observe that the essential advantage of the proposed approach is that the measure of forced back-translation probability can distinguish translation errors from relatively acceptable translations, with which the sentence-BLEU score with the reference translation is typically higher than that of the baseline 2-to-2 model. As a result, we conclude that it is unnecessary to consider a context with a much greater number of sentences, such as 3-to-3 (or higher) models.

8 Conclusion

Within the framework of the 2-to-2 context-based NMT model, this paper has explored how to select the most informative context sentences that provide the highest BLEU score among the five preceding and five subsequent sentences. In future, we plan to compare the proposed method to an existing approach (Li and Jurafsky, 2016) that incorporates back-translation into the MT framework. In addition, we plan to incorporate monolingual techniques such as BERT (Devlin et al., 2018) and neural coreference resolution (Lee et al., 2017), to evaluate whether context sentences (i.e., the second through fifth sentences preceding the source sentence and the first through fifth sentences subsequent to the source sentence) are in fact informative. Also, in the context of translation quality estimation techniques (Specia et al., 2015), the proposed approach of estimating the quality of translation by maximizing forced back-translation is novel and has never been studied so far in the task of translation quality estimation.

References

Bawden, R., R. Sennrich, A. Birch, and B. Haddow. 2018. Evaluating discourse phenomena in neural machine translation. In *Proc. NAACL-HLT*, pages 1304–1313.

Devlin, J., M.-W. Chang, K. Lee, and K. Toutanova. 2018. BERT: Pre-training of deep bidirectional transformers for language understanding. In *CoRR*, volume abs/1810.04805.

Goto, I. and H. Tanaka. 2017. Detecting untranslated content for neural machine translation. In *Proc. 1st NMT*, pages 47–55.

Kimura, R., Z. Long, T. Utsuro, T. Mitsuhashi, and M. Yamamoto. 2017. Effect on reducing untranslated content by neural machine translation with a large vocabulary of technical terms. In *Proc. 7th PSLT*, pages 13–24.

Kingma, D. P. and J. Ba. 2015. Adam: A method for stochastic optimization. *Proc. ICLR*.

Klein, G., Y. Kim, Y. Deng, J. Senellart, and A. M. Rush. 2017. OpenNMT: Open-source toolkit for neural machine translation. In *Proc. 55th ACL*, pages 67–72.

Koehn, P., H. Hoang, A. Birch, C. Callison-Burch, M. Federico, N. Bertoldi, B. Cowan, W. Shen, C. Moran, R. Zens, C. Dyer, O. Bojar, A. Constantin, and E. Herbst. 2007. Moses: Open source toolkit for statistical machine translation. In *Proc. 45th ACL*, pages 177–180.

Lee, K., L. He, M. Lewis, and L. Zettlemoyer. 2017. End-to-end neural coreference resolution. In *Proc. EMNLP*, pages 188–197.

Li, J. and D. Jurafsky. 2016. Mutual information and diverse decoding improve neural machine translation. In *CoRR*, volume abs/1601.00372.

Libovický, J. and J. Helcl. 2017. Attention strategies for multi-source sequence-to-sequence learning. In *Proc. 55th ACL*, pages 196–202.

Lison, P., J. Tiedemann, and M. Kouylekov. 2018. Opensubtitles2018: Statistical rescoring of sentence alignments in large, noisy parallel corpora. In *Proc. 11th LREC*, pages 1742–1748, May 7-12, 2018.

Luong, T., H. Pham, and C. D. Manning. 2015. Effective approaches to attention-based neural machine translation. In *Proc. 2015 EMNLP*, pages 1412–1421.

Maruf, S. and G. Haffari. 2018. Document context neural machine translation with memory networks. In *Proc. 56th ACL*, pages 1275–1284.

Miculicich, L., D. Ram, N. Pappas, and J. Henderson. 2018. Document-level neural machine translation with hierarchical attention networks. In *Proc. EMNLP*, pages 2947–2954.

Rapp, R. 2009. The back-translation score: Automatic mt evaluation at the sentence level without reference translations. In *Proc. 47th ACL and 4th IJCNLP*, pages 133–136.

Specia, L., G. Paetzold, and C. Scarton. 2015. Multi-level translation quality prediction with QuEst++. In *Proc. 53rd ACL and 7th IJCNLP System Demonstrations*, pages 115–120.

Sutskever, I., O. Vinyals, and Q. V. Le. 2014. Sequence to sequence learning with neural machine translation. In *Proc. 27th NIPS*, pages 3104–3112.

Tiedemann, J. and Y. Scherrer. 2017. Neural machine translation with extended context. In *Proc. 3rd DiscoMT*, pages 82–92.

Tu, Z., Y. Liu, S. Shi, and T. Zhang. 2018. Learning to remember translation history with a continuous cache. *Transactions of ACL*, 6:407–420.

Vaswani, A., N. Shazeer, N. Parmar, J. Uszkoreit, L. Jones, A. Gomez, L. Kaiser, and I. Polosukhin. 2017. Attention is all you need. In *Proc. 30th NIPS*, pages 5998–6008.

Voita, E., P. Serdyukov, R. Sennrich, and I. Titov. 2018. Context-aware neural machine translation learns anaphora resolution. In *Proc. 56th ACL*, pages 1264–1274.

Memory-Augmented Neural Networks for Machine Translation

Mark Collier
Trinity College Dublin
School of Computer Science and
Statistics, Dublin, Ireland
mcollier@tcd.ie

Joeran Beel
Trinity College Dublin
School of Computer Science and
Statistics, ADAPT Centre, Dublin, Ireland
joeran.beel@tcd.ie

Abstract

Memory-augmented neural networks (MANNs) have been shown to outperform other recurrent neural network architectures on a series of artificial sequence learning tasks, yet they have had limited application to real-world tasks. We evaluate direct application of Neural Turing Machines (NTM) and Differentiable Neural Computers (DNC) to machine translation. We further propose and evaluate two models which extend the attentional encoder-decoder with capabilities inspired by memory augmented neural networks. We evaluate our proposed models on IWSLT Vietnamese→English and ACL Romanian→English datasets. Our proposed models and the memory augmented neural networks perform similarly to the attentional encoder-decoder on the Vietnamese→English translation task while have a 0.3-1.9 lower BLEU score for the Romanian→English task. Interestingly, our analysis shows that despite being equipped with additional flexibility and being randomly initialized memory augmented neural networks learn an algorithm for machine translation almost identical to the attentional encoder-decoder.

1 Introduction

Memory-Augmented Neural Networks (**MANN**) are a new class of recurrent neural network (**RNN**)

that separate computation from memory. The key distinction between MANNs and other RNNs such as Long Short-Term Memory cells (**LSTM**) (Hochreiter and Schmidhuber, 1997) is the existence of an external memory unit. A controller network in the MANN receives input, interacts with the external memory unit via read and write heads and produces output. MANNs have been shown to learn faster and generalize better than LSTMs on a range of artificial sequential learning tasks (Graves et al., 2014; Graves et al., 2016; Sukhbaatar et al., 2015). Despite their success on artificial tasks, LSTM based models remain the preferred choice for many commercially important sequence learning tasks such as handwriting recognition (Graves et al., 2009), machine translation (Wu et al., 2016) and speech recognition (Graves and Jaitly, 2014).

Attentional encoder-decoders (Bahdanau et al., 2014; Luong et al., 2015), where the encoder and decoder are often LSTMs or other gated RNNs such as the Gated Recurrent Unit (Cho et al., 2014b), are a class of neural network models that have achieved state-of-the-art performance on many language pairs for machine translation (Luong and Manning, 2015; Sennrich et al., 2016a). An encoder RNN reads the source sentence one token at a time. The encoder both maintains an internal vector representing the full source sentence and it encodes each token in the source sentence into a vector often assumed to represent the meaning of that token in its surrounding context. The decoder receives the internal vector from the encoder and can read from the encoded source sentence when producing the target sentence.

Attentional encoder-decoders can be seen as a basic form of MANN. The collection of vectors representing the encoded source sentence can be viewed as external memory which is written to by the encoder and read from by the decoder. But attentional encoder-decoders do not have the same range of capabilities as MANNs such as the Neural Turing Machine (**NTM**) (Graves et al., 2014) or Differentiable Neural Computer (**DNC**) (Graves et al., 2016). The encoder RNN in attentional encoder-decoders must write a vector at each timestep and this write must be to a single memory location. The encoder is not able to update previously written vectors and has only one write head. The decoder has read only access to the encoded source sentence and typically just a single read head. Widely used attention mechanisms (Bahdanau et al., 2014; Luong et al., 2015) do not have the ability to iterate through the source sentence from a previously attended location. All of these capabilities are present in NTMs and DNCs.

In this paper we propose two extensions to the attentional encoder-decoder which add several capabilities present in other MANNs. We are also the first that we are aware of to evaluate the performance of MANNs applied directly to machine translation.

2   Background

We briefly review how attention weights are computed for Luong attention (Luong et al., 2015) and how addresses are computed for the NTM. Alternative attention mechanisms have similar computations (Bahdanau et al., 2014) and likewise for alternative MANNs such as DNCs (Graves et al., 2016).

2.1   Luong Attention

At each timestep t during the decoding of an attentional encoder-decoder a weighting $\mathbf{w_t}$ over the encoded source sentence is computed, where $\sum_s w_t(s) = 1$ and $\forall s\ w_t(s) \geq 0$. The predicted token at that timestep during decoding is then a function of the decoder RNN hidden state $\mathbf{h}_t$ and the weighted sum of the encoder hidden states i.e. $\sum_s w_t(s) * \hat{\mathbf{h}}_s$.

The difference between various attention mechanisms is how to compute the weighting $\mathbf{w_t}$. In Luong attention (Luong et al., 2015) the weighting is computed as the softmax over scaled scores for each source sentence token, eq. 2. The scores for each source sentence token are computed as the dot product of decoder RNN hidden state $\mathbf{h}_t$ and encoder RNN hidden state $\hat{\mathbf{h}}_s$ which is first linearly transformed by a matrix $\mathbf{W}_a$.

$$score(\mathbf{h}_t, \hat{\mathbf{h}}_s) \leftarrow \mathbf{h}_t^\top \mathbf{W}_a \hat{\mathbf{h}}_s \qquad (1)$$

$$w_t(s) \leftarrow \frac{\exp(\beta_t * score(\mathbf{h}_t, \hat{\mathbf{h}}_s))}{\sum_{s'} \exp(\beta_t * score(\mathbf{h}_t, \hat{\mathbf{h}}_{s'}))} \qquad (2)$$

2.2   NTM Addressing

Rather than computing weightings over an encoded source sentence, NTMs have a fixed sized external memory unit which is a $N * W$ memory matrix. N represents the number of memory locations and W the dimension of each memory cell. A controller neural network has read and write heads into the memory matrix. Addresses for read and write heads in a NTM are computed somewhat similarly to attention mechanisms. However in addition to being able to address memory using the similarity between a lookup key and memory contents, so called content based addressing, NTMs also have the ability to iterate from current or past addresses. This enables NTMs to learn a broader class of algorithms than attentional encoder-decoders (Graves et al., 2014; Graves et al., 2016).

At each timestep (t), for each read and write head the controller network outputs a set of parameters; a lookup key $\mathbf{k}_t$, a scaling factor $\beta_t \geq 0$, an interpolation gate $g_t \in [0, 1]$, a shift kernel $\mathbf{s}_t$ (s.t. $\sum_k s_t(k) = 1$ and $\forall k\ s_t(k) \geq 0$) and a sharpening parameter $\gamma_t \geq 1$ which are used to compute the weighting $\mathbf{w}_t$ over the N memory locations in the memory matrix $\mathbf{M}_t$ as follows:

$$w_t^c(i) \leftarrow \frac{\exp(\beta_t * K[\mathbf{k}_t, \mathbf{M}_t(i)])}{\sum_{j=0}^{N-1} \exp(\beta_t * K[\mathbf{k}_t, \mathbf{M}_t(j)])} \qquad (3)$$

We can see that $\mathbf{w}_t^c$ is computed similarly to Luong attention and allows for content based addressing. $\mathbf{k}_t$ represents a lookup key into memory and K is some similarity measure such as cosine similarity:

$$K[\mathbf{u}, \mathbf{v}] = \frac{\mathbf{u} \cdot \mathbf{v}}{\|\mathbf{u}\| \cdot \|\mathbf{v}\|} \qquad (4)$$

NTMs enable iteration from current or previously computed memory weights as follows:

$$\mathbf{w}_t^g \leftarrow g_t \mathbf{w}_t^c + (1 - g_t)\mathbf{w}_{t-1} \qquad (5)$$

$$\tilde{w}_t(i) \leftarrow \sum_{j=0}^{N-1} w_t^g(j)s_t(i - j) \qquad (6)$$

$$w_t(i) \leftarrow \frac{\tilde{w}_t(i)^{\gamma_t}}{\sum_{j=0}^{N-1} \tilde{w}_t(j)^{\gamma_t}} \qquad (7)$$

where (5) enables the network to choose whether to use the current content based weights or the previous weight vector, (6) enables iteration through memory by convolving the current weighting by a 1-D convolutional shift kernel and (7) corrects for any blurring occurring as a result of the convolution operation.

The vector $\mathbf{r}_t$ read by a particular read head at timestep t is computed as a weighted sum over memory locations similarly to Luong attention:

$$\mathbf{r}_t \leftarrow \sum_{i=0}^{N-1} w_t(i) * \mathbf{M}_t(i) \qquad (8)$$

An attentional encoder-decoder has no write mechanism. Another way to view this, is that an attentional encoder-decoder has a memory matrix with N equal to the source sentence length and the encoder must always write its hidden state to the memory location corresponding to its position in the source sentence. A NTM does have a write operation, with write addresses determining a weighting over memory locations for the write. Each write head modifies the memory matrix by outputting erase ($\mathbf{e}_t$) and add ($\mathbf{a}_t$) vectors which are then used to softly zero out existing memory contents and write new memory contents through addition:

$$\tilde{\mathbf{M}}_t(i) \leftarrow \mathbf{M}_{t-1}(i)[\mathbf{1} - w_t(i)\mathbf{e}_t] \qquad (9)$$

$$\mathbf{M}_t(i) \leftarrow \tilde{\mathbf{M}}_t(i) + w_t(i)\mathbf{a}_t \qquad (10)$$

3 Proposed Models

We propose two models which bridge the gap between the attentional encoder-decoder and MANNs, extending the attentional encoder-decoder with additional mechanisms inspired by MANNs. We also propose the application of MANNs directly to machine translation.

3.1 Neural Turing Machine Style Attention

The reads from a decoder in an attentional encoder-decoder for machine translation often exhibit monotonic iteration through the encoded source sentence (Bahdanau et al., 2014; Raffel et al., 2017). However widely used attention mechanisms have no way to explicitly encode such a

strategy. NTMs combine content based addressing similar to attention mechanisms with the ability to iterate through memory. We propose a new attention mechanism which combines the content based addressing of Luong attention (Luong et al., 2015) with the ability to iterate through memory from NTMs. For our proposed attention mechanism at each timestep (t) the decoder outputs a set of parameters for each of its read heads: $\mathbf{h}_t$, $\beta_t \geq 0$, $g_t \in [0,1]$, $\mathbf{s}_t$ (s.t. $\sum_k s_t(k) = 1$ and $\forall k\ s_t(k) \geq 0$) and $\gamma_t \geq 1$ which are used to compute the weighting $\mathbf{w}_t$ over encoded source sentence $\hat{\mathbf{h}}_s$ for $s = 1, 2, ...$

$$score(\mathbf{h}_t, \hat{\mathbf{h}}_s) \leftarrow \mathbf{h}_t^\top \mathbf{W}_a \hat{\mathbf{h}}_s \qquad (11)$$

$$w_t^c(s) \leftarrow \frac{\exp(\beta_t * score(\mathbf{h}_t, \hat{\mathbf{h}}_s))}{\sum_{s'} \exp(\beta_t * score(\mathbf{h}_t, \hat{\mathbf{h}}_{s'}))} \qquad (12)$$

$$\mathbf{w}_t^g \leftarrow g_t \mathbf{w}_t^c + (1 - g_t)\mathbf{w}_{t-1} \qquad (13)$$

$$\tilde{w}_t(s) \leftarrow \sum_{j=0}^{N-1} w_t^g(j)s_t(s - j) \qquad (14)$$

$$w_t(s) \leftarrow \frac{\tilde{w}_t(s)^{\gamma_t}}{\sum_{j=0}^{N-1} \tilde{w}_t(j)^{\gamma_t}} \qquad (15)$$

Equations (11) and (12) represent the standard content based addressing of Luong style attention. Equations (13-15) replicate equations (5-7) of the NTM to enable iteration from the currently attended source sentence token $\mathbf{w}_t^c$ or the previously attended token $\mathbf{w}_{t-1}$. As with the NTM equation (14) represents a 1D convolution on the weighting $\mathbf{w}_t^g$ with a convolutional shift kernel which is outputted by the decoder to enable iteration. Equation (15) corrects for any blurring resulting from the 1D convolution. We can see that such an attention mechanism has the content based addressing capability of Luong attention and the same capability to iterate from previously computed addresses as NTMs.

3.2 Memory-Augmented Decoder (M.A.D)

The introduction of attention mechanisms has proved highly successful for neural machine translation. Attention extends the writable memory capacity of the encoder in an encoder-decoder model linearly with the length of the source sentence. This avoids the bottleneck of having to encode the

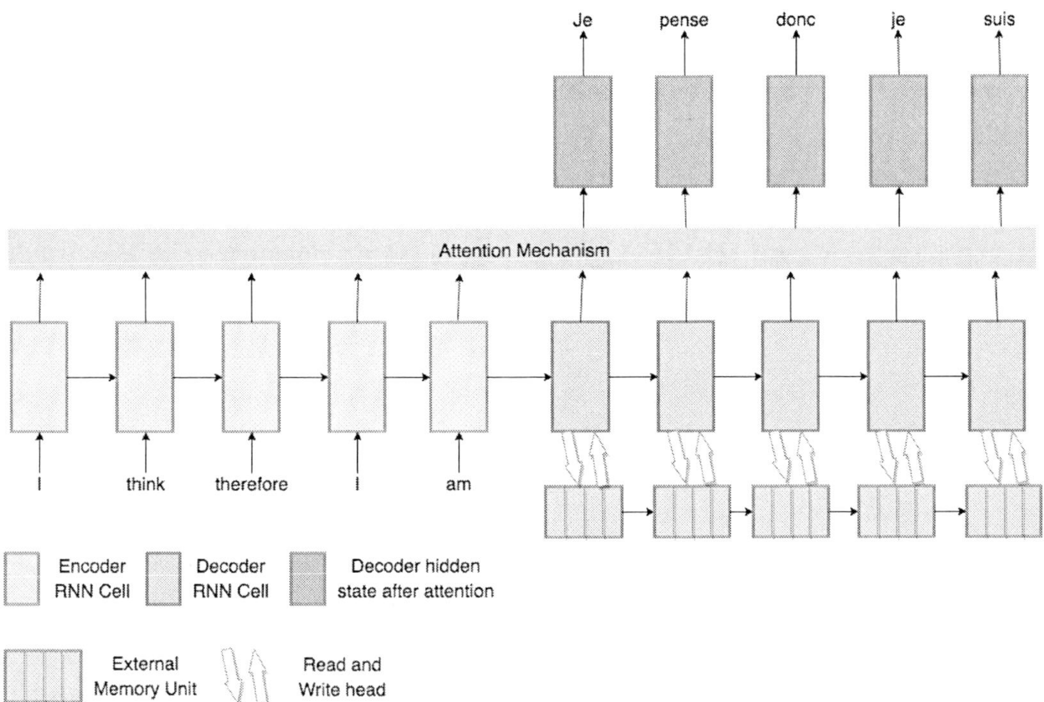

Figure 1: Memory augmented decoder

whole source sentence meaning into the fixed size vector passed from the encoder to decoder (Bahdanau et al., 2014; Cho et al., 2014a). But the decoder in an attentional encoder-decoder must still maintain a history of its past actions in a fixed size vector. We are motivated by the success of attention which extended the memory capacity of the encoder to propose the addition of an external memory unit to the decoder of an attentional encoder-decoder, hence extending the decoder's memory capacity, fig. 1. We still maintain a read-only attention mechanism into the encoded source sentence, however the decoder now has the ability to read and write to an external memory unit. We can set the external memory unit to have a number of memory locations greater than the maximum target sentence length in the corpus, thus scaling the decoder's memory capacity with the target sentence length in a similar vain as to how attention scaled the encoder's memory capacity with source sentence length.

We note that a similar model has been proposed before (Wang et al., 2016), but that in order to train their model the authors propose a pre-training approach based on first training without the external memory unit attached to decoder and then adding

it on. This approach restricts the form of possible memory interactions as it must be possible to add the external memory unit while maintaining the pre-trained weights of the attentional encoder-decoder. We simply make the decoder a NTM with the standard read and write heads into an external memory and an additional read head into the encoded source sentence with the addresses on this read head computed in Luong attention style, but other choices for the addressing mechanism are possible, including DNC style addressing. Following a recent stable NTM implementation (Collier and Beel, 2018) we do not have any problems training our proposed model.

3.3 Pure Memory-Augmented Neural Network

We propose a pure MANN model for machine translation, fig. 2. Under our proposed model a MANN receives the embedded source sentence as input one token at a time and then receives an end of sequence token. The MANN must then output the target sentence. We are motivated by the enhanced performance of MANNs compared to LSTMs on artificial sequence learning tasks (Graves et al., 2014; Graves et al., 2016; Rae et

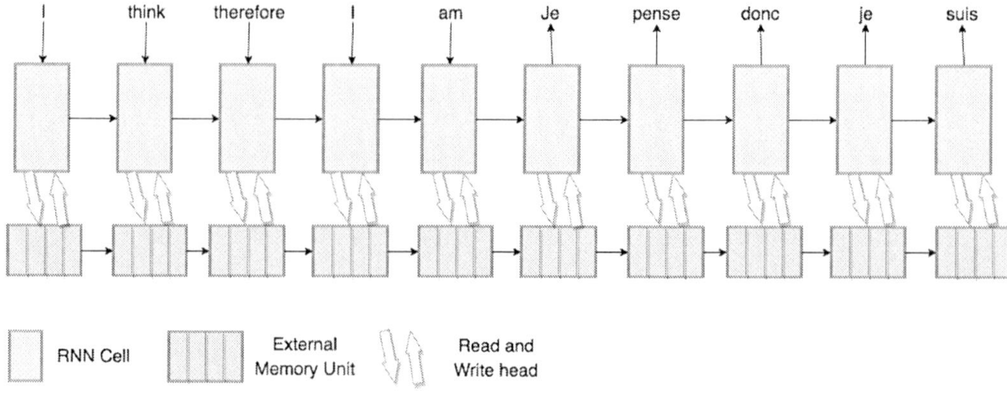

Figure 2: Pure memory augmented neural network for machine translation

al., 2016).

We note that our proposed model has the representational capability to learn a solution similar to an attentional encoder-decoder by simply writing an encoding of each source sentence token to a single memory location and reading the encodings back using content based addressing after the end of sequence token.

We also highlight the differences to the attentional encoder-decoder model. The pure MANN model may have multiple read and write heads each of which uses more powerful addressing mechanisms than popular attention mechanisms. The proposed model may also update previously written locations in light of new information or reuse memory locations if the previous contents have already served their purpose. There is no separation between encoding and decoding and thus only a single RNN is used as the MANN's controller rather than different RNN cells for the encoder and decoder in an encoder-decoder, halving the number of network parameters dedicated to this part of the network.

In this paper for the pure MANN model we use and compare NTMs and DNCs as the choice MANN, however any other MANN with differentiable read and write mechanisms into an external memory unit would be permissible. In both cases we use a LSTM controller. We also compare the use of multiple read and write heads for the NTM model.

4 Methodology

We evaluate our models on two machine translation tasks. As a low resource spoken language task

we use the 2015 International Workshop on Spoken Language's dataset of English to Vietnamese translated TED talks. We follow (Luong and Manning, 2015) in their preprocessing and setup and use their results as a baseline. For training we use TED tst2013, a dataset of 133K sentence pairs. As the validation set we use TED tst2012 and test set results are reported on the TED tst2015 dataset. We use a fixed vocabulary of 17.5K words and 7.7K words for English and Vietnamese respectively. Any words outside the source or target vocabulary are mapped to an unknown token (UNK).

As a medium resource written language task we follow (Sennrich et al., 2016a) in their general setup for the Romanian to English task from the ACL's 2016 First Conference on Machine Translation's, Machine Translation of News Task. We use their results as a baseline. We train our models on the Europarl English Romanian dataset which consists of 600k sentence pairs. We use the newsdev2016 and newstest2016 datasets as the validation and test sets respectively. We Byte Pair Encode (Sennrich et al., 2016b) the source and target languages with 89,500 merge operations. After Byte Pair Encoding, the English vocabulary size is 48,824 sub-words and 65,699 sub-words for the Romanian vocabulary.

For all models we use the Adam optimizer (Kingma and Ba, 2014) with an initial learning rate of 0.001. We train for a fixed number of steps but after each epoch we measure the BLEU score on the validation set and measure the test set performance from the version of the model with the highest validation set BLEU score. For the Vietnamese→English models we train for 14,000

Model	Dev	Test
(Luong and Manning, 2015)	-	23.3
NTM Style Attention	21.5	23.6
M.A.D. (1 R/W head)	21.1	23.1
M.A.D. (2 R/W heads)	21.2	23.8
Pure MANN (NTM - 1 R/W head)	20.9	23.5
Pure MANN (NTM - 2 R/W heads)	21.3	23.5
Pure MANN (DNC - 1 R/W head)	20.6	23.6

Table 1: Vietnamese→English translation results (BLEU) on dev (TED tst2012) and test (TED tst2013) sets. M.A.D ↔ Memory-Augmented Decoder. 1 R/W head means the MANN had 1 read and 1 write head into external memory.

Model	Dev	Test
(Sennrich et al., 2016a)	30.0	29.2
NTM Style Attention	30.0	28.7
M.A.D. (1 R/W head)	29.8	28.9
M.A.D. (2 R/W heads)	29.7	28.3
Pure MANN (NTM - 1 R/W head)	28.9	27.7
Pure MANN (NTM - 2 R/W heads)	28.0	27.3
Pure MANN (DNC - 1 R/W head)	27.8	27.5

Table 2: Romanian→English translation results (BLEU) on dev (newsdev2016) and test (newstest2016) sets. M.A.D ↔ Memory-Augmented Decoder. 1 R/W head means the MANN had 1 read and 1 write head into external memory.

steps and for the Romanian→English models we train for 120,000 steps.

For all models we use beam search with a beam width of 10. We set the dropout rate to 0.3 with no other regularization applied. For both the Vietnamese→English and Romanian→English tasks we follow (Luong and Manning, 2015; Sennrich et al., 2016a) in using a stack of 2 x 512 unit LSTMs as the encoder and decoder for all relevant models and the controller network for the MANNs. For the memory-augmented decoder the number of memory locations is set to 64 and each memory location is a 512 dimensional vector. Whereas for the pure MANN model the number of memory locations is set to 128 with the memory cell size also set to 512.

We implement our model in Tensorflow, extending Google's NMT implementation (Luong et al., 2017), and make it available publicly[1].

5 Results

The test set BLEU scores for the Vietnamese→English translation task are all very similar, with each model's score within the range of 23.1-23.8 BLEU (table 1). Interestingly, despite the pure MANN models seeing the source sentence in a uni-directional fashion (with all other models using bi-directional encoders) the pure MANN models perform on par with the other models.

The attentional encoder-decoder (Sennrich et al., 2016a) has the highest test set BLEU score of all the models for the Romanian→English transla-

tion task (table 2). The proposed extensions to the attentional encoder-decoder result in 0.3-0.9 lower test set BLEU score. For the Romanian→English translation task, the pure MANN model has 1.5-1.9 lower test set BLEU score.

5.1 Analysis

We now examine the attention weights for an attentional encoder-decoder and address computation for the 1 R/W head NTM on a particular Romanian→English translation. The sentence was chosen as it was the first sentence in our test set which had the same translation from both models. We note that the pattern of addresses are typical of the addresses computed on other sentences for both language pairs, but that a single typical example is presented for brevity.

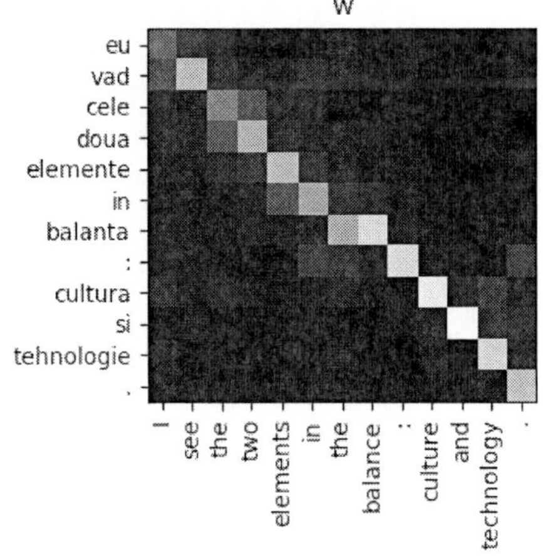

Figure 3: Example attention weights for attentional encoder-decoder

---

[1]https://github.com/MarkPKCollier/
MANNs4NMT

We see that we replicate the monotonic iteration through the source sentence often observed in attention mechanisms (Bahdanau et al., 2014; Raffel et al., 2017) in fig. 3. We note that this pattern of addressing must be computed solely using the content based addressing of the attention mechanism as no iteration capability is available to the attention weight computation.

We now examine how the NTM has computed the addresses for its read and write head in order to arrive at the same resulting translation. Looking first at the write head, fig. 4, we see that as the NTM is shown the source sentence it has learned a very similar strategy to the encoder of an attentional encoder-decoder. In particular we can see that the write head writes an encoded version of the source sentence tokens to successive memory locations, fig. 4a. Interestingly we see that the successive memory locations are computed using the iteration cabability of the NTM as the content based addresses are not significant, fig. 4b and the shift kernel is iterating forward through memory, fig. 4d from the address at the previous timestep as can be seen from the interpolation gate, fig. 4c. If we interpret the encoded source sentence for an attentional encoder-decoder as being written to memory, then this is precisely the form of addresses we would see - except that in the case of a NTM the addressing strategy is learned not hard-coded. This suggests that this particular inductive bias built into the attentional encoder-decoder is a sensible one.

The attentional encoder-decoder leaves the encoded source sentence unchanged during decoding as it has no write mechanism. However we observe that the write head is active during decoding for the NTM, fig. 4a. We see that the NTM uses content based addressing, fig. 4b to write to the memory locations that are previously read from by the read head , fig. 5. This suggests that perhaps the NTM has developed a strategy of marking particular source sentence tokens as completed so as not to retranslate them later during decoding. Interestingly such a mechanism is built directly into the DNC (Graves et al., 2016) and in fact monotonic attention mechanisms have been developed which prevent retranslation of previously translated tokens or preceeding tokens in the source sentence (Raffel et al., 2017). But here of course this strategy is learned from random initialization by the NTM.

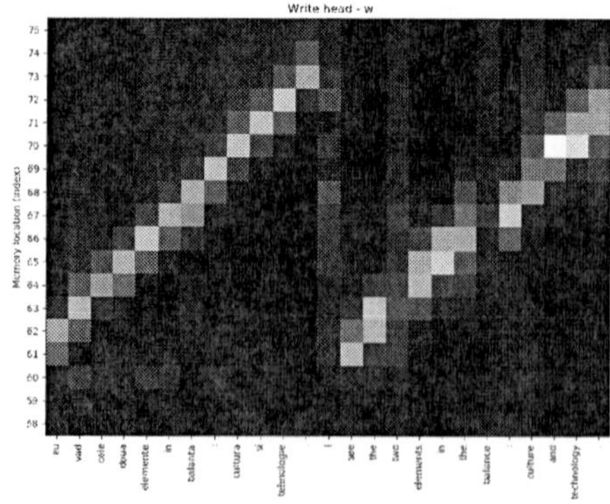

(a) Full address

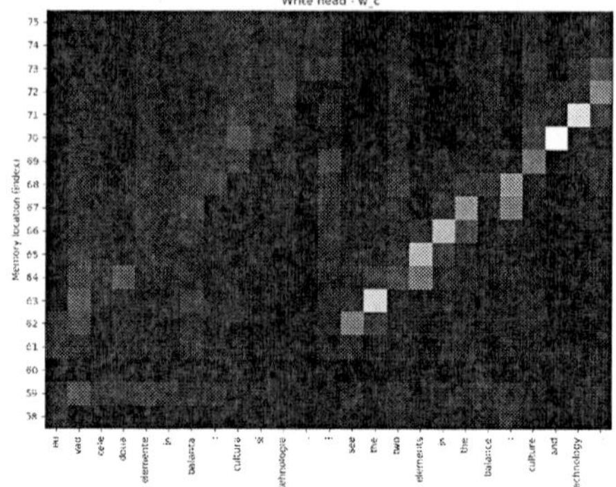

(b) Content based addressing

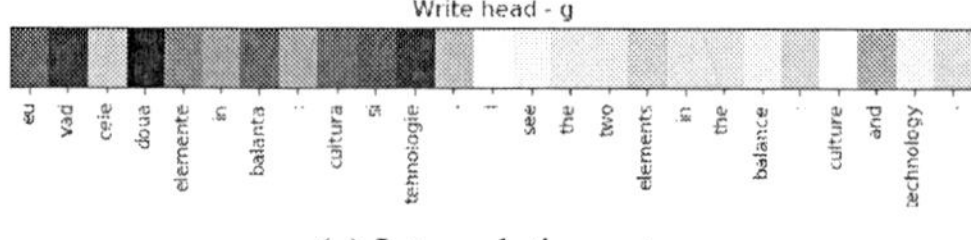

(c) Interpolation gate

(d) Shift kernel

Figure 4: Example write head address computation

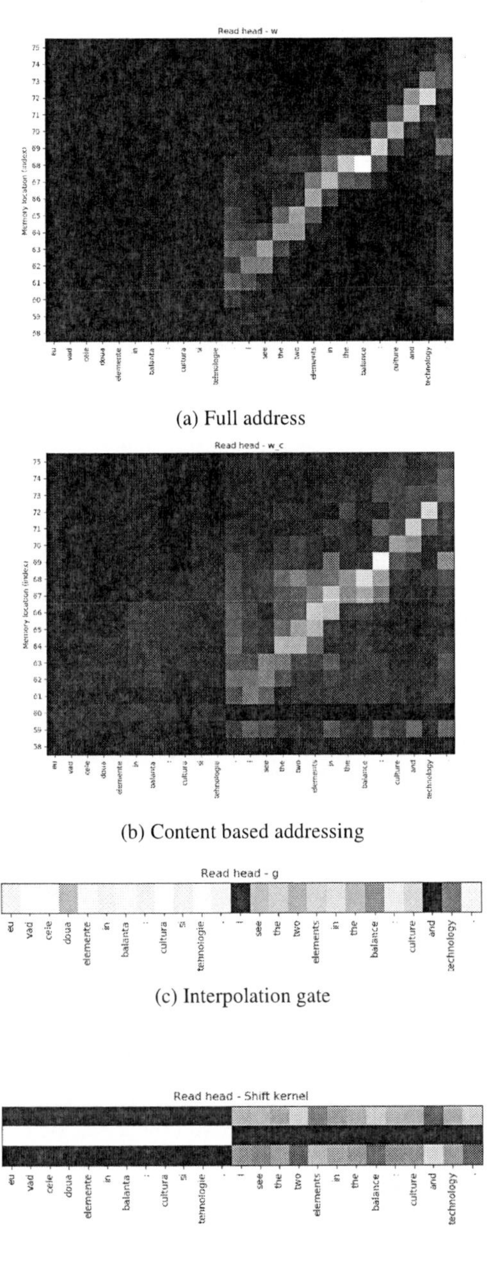

(a) Full address

(b) Content based addressing

(c) Interpolation gate

(d) Shift kernel

Figure 5: Example read head address computation

Having seen that the NTM learns to write the encoded source sentence to successive memory locations we are not surprised that as the predicted sentence is produced the NTM reads the from memory locations similarly to the attentional encoder-decoder. We see that the previously written to memory locations are then read back from, fig. 5a. Interestingly, we see the read head addresses of the NTM as it produces the predicted sentence are heavily determined by its content based addressing, fig. 5b. Thus the NTM does not make significant use of its iteration capability, despite exhibiting the type of monotonic iteration through the source sentence as has been observed with attention mechanisms.

We also note that the read head of the NTM is not particularly focused as the NTM sees the source sentence, fig. 5a. This is somewhat surprising as the results of the read operation are available to the controller at the next timestep and thus could be used to retrieve the encoding of a previous source sentence token or a summary of a section of the source sentence rather than relying on the LSTM controller memory solely for this. We suspect that this behaviour is the result of the read head operation not being available to the write head at the *current* timestep and thus cannot be used to disambiguate the current token as has been the motivation for the successful Transformer NMT model (Vaswani et al., 2017). Thus, we suggest that extending the NTM and other MANNs depth-wise to have successive rather than parallel operations on the memory matrix at each timestep may be a fruitful avenue of future research.

6 Conclusion

We have proposed a series of MANN inspired models for machine translation. Two of these models; NTM Style Attention and the Memory-Augmented Decoder extend the attentional encoder-decoder which has achieved state-of-the-art results on many language pairs. These extensions perform 0.2-0.5 BLEU better than the attentional encoder-decoder alone on the low resource Vietnamese→English translation task and 0.3-0.9 lower BLEU on the Romanian→English translation task. We conclude that a content based addressing mechanism is sufficient to encode a strategy of monotonic iteration through source sentences and that enabling the network to express this strategy directly does not significantly improve translation quality. From the Memory-Augmented Decoder results it appears as though extending the memory capacity of the decoder in an attentional encoder-decoder does not offer an advantage, contrary to previous results (Wang et al., 2016).

Our third proposed model is to just use MANNs directly for machine translation. As far as we are aware we are the first to publish results on MANNs used directly for machine translation.

The pure MANN model performs marginally better, +0.2-0.3 BLEU, than the attentional encoder-decoder for the Vietnamese→English translation task. Performance is 0.3-1.9 BLEU worse for the Romanian→English translation task. We conclude that MANNs in their current form do not improve over the attentional encoder-decoder for machine translation. Our analysis of the algorithm learned by the pure MANN shows that despite being randomly initialized the pure MANN learns a very similar solution to the attentional encoder-decoder.

We note that the performance gap between the pure MANN and attentional encoder-decoder is not very large and that the pure MANN model is very general and does not incorporate any domain specific knowledge. MANNs are a relatively new architecture that have received less attention than encoder-decoder approaches. We expect that with the development of improved MANN architectures, MANNs could achieve state-of-the-art results for machine translation.

Acknowledgements

This publication emanated from research conducted with the financial support of Science Foundation Ireland (SFI) under Grant Number 13/RC/2106.

References

Bahdanau, Dzmitry, Kyunghyun Cho, and Yoshua Bengio. 2014. Neural machine translation by jointly learning to align and translate. *arXiv preprint arXiv:1409.0473*.

Cho, Kyunghyun, Bart van Merrienboer, Dzmitry Bahdanau, and Yoshua Bengio. 2014a. On the properties of neural machine translation: Encoderdecoder approaches. In *Proceedings of SSST-8, Eighth Workshop on Syntax, Semantics and Structure in Statistical Translation*, pages 103–111.

Cho, Kyunghyun, Bart Van Merriënboer, Caglar Gulcehre, Dzmitry Bahdanau, Fethi Bougares, Holger Schwenk, and Yoshua Bengio. 2014b. Learning phrase representations using rnn encoder-decoder for statistical machine translation. *arXiv preprint arXiv:1406.1078*.

Collier, Mark and Joeran Beel. 2018. Implementing neural turing machines. In *International Conference on Artificial Neural Networks*, pages 94–104. Springer.

Graves, Alex and Navdeep Jaitly. 2014. Towards end-to-end speech recognition with recurrent neural networks. In *International Conference on Machine Learning*, pages 1764–1772.

Graves, Alex, Marcus Liwicki, Santiago Fernndez, Roman Bertolami, Horst Bunke, and Jrgen Schmidhuber. 2009. A novel connectionist system for unconstrained handwriting recognition. *IEEE transactions on pattern analysis and machine intelligence*, 31(5):855–868.

Graves, Alex, Greg Wayne, and Ivo Danihelka. 2014. Neural turing machines. *arXiv preprint arXiv:1410.5401*.

Graves, Alex, Greg Wayne, Malcolm Reynolds, Tim Harley, Ivo Danihelka, Agnieszka Grabska-Barwiska, Sergio Gmez Colmenarejo, Edward Grefenstette, Tiago Ramalho, and John Agapiou. 2016. Hybrid computing using a neural network with dynamic external memory. *Nature*, 538(7626):471.

Hochreiter, Sepp and Jrgen Schmidhuber. 1997. Long short-term memory. *Neural computation*, 9(8):1735–1780.

Kingma, Diederik P and Jimmy Ba. 2014. Adam: A method for stochastic optimization. *arXiv preprint arXiv:1412.6980*.

Luong, Minh-Thang and Christopher D Manning. 2015. Stanford neural machine translation systems for spoken language domains. In *Proceedings of the International Workshop on Spoken Language Translation*, pages 76–79.

Luong, Thang, Hieu Pham, and Christopher D Manning. 2015. Effective approaches to attention-based neural machine translation. In *Proceedings of the 2015 Conference on Empirical Methods in Natural Language Processing*, pages 1412–1421.

Luong, Minh-Thang, Eugene Brevdo, and Rui Zhao. 2017. Neural machine translation (seq2seq) tutorial. *https://github.com/tensorflow/nmt*.

Rae, Jack, Jonathan J Hunt, Ivo Danihelka, Timothy Harley, Andrew W Senior, Gregory Wayne, Alex Graves, and Tim Lillicrap. 2016. Scaling memory-augmented neural networks with sparse reads and writes. In *Advances in Neural Information Processing Systems*, pages 3621–3629.

Raffel, Colin, Minh-Thang Luong, Peter J Liu, Ron J Weiss, and Douglas Eck. 2017. Online and linear-time attention by enforcing monotonic alignments. In *International Conference on Machine Learning*, pages 2837–2846.

Sennrich, Rico, Barry Haddow, and Alexandra Birch. 2016a. Edinburgh neural machine translation systems for wmt 16. In *Proceedings of the First Conference on Machine Translation: Volume 2, Shared Task Papers*, volume 2, pages 371–376.

Sennrich, Rico, Barry Haddow, and Alexandra Birch. 2016b. Neural machine translation of rare words with subword units. In *Proceedings of the 54th Annual Meeting of the Association for Computational*

Linguistics (Volume 1: Long Papers), volume 1, pages 1715–1725.

Sukhbaatar, Sainbayar, Jason Weston, and Rob Fergus. 2015. End-to-end memory networks. In *Advances in neural information processing systems*, pages 2440–2448.

Vaswani, Ashish, Noam Shazeer, Niki Parmar, Jakob Uszkoreit, Llion Jones, Aidan N Gomez, Łukasz Kaiser, and Illia Polosukhin. 2017. Attention is all you need. In *Advances in neural information processing systems*, pages 5998–6008.

Wang, Mingxuan, Zhengdong Lu, Hang Li, and Qun Liu. 2016. Memory-enhanced decoder for neural machine translation. In *Proceedings of the 2016 Conference on Empirical Methods in Natural Language Processing*, pages 278–286.

Wu, Yonghui, Mike Schuster, Zhifeng Chen, Quoc V Le, Mohammad Norouzi, Wolfgang Macherey, Maxim Krikun, Yuan Cao, Qin Gao, and Klaus Macherey. 2016. Google's neural machine translation system: Bridging the gap between human and machine translation. *arXiv preprint arXiv:1609.08144*.

An Exploration of Placeholding in Neural Machine Translation

Matt Post[†◊]   **Shuoyang Ding**[†]   **Marianna J. Martindale**[‡]   **Winston Wu**[†]
† Center for Language and Speech Processing, Johns Hopkins University
‡ iSchool, University of Maryland College Park
◊ Human Language Technology Center of Excellence, Johns Hopkins University
`post@cs.jhu.edu, {dings, wswu}@jhu.edu`
`mmartind@umiacs.umd.edu`

Abstract

Phrase-based machine translation provides the system developer with controls that enable fine-grained control over machine translation output. One approach to provide similar control in neural machine translation is *placeholding* (herein called *masking*), which replaces input tokens with masks which are replaced with the original input text in post-processing. But is this a good idea? We undertake an exploration of masking in French–English and Japanese–English using Transformer architectures. We attempt to quantify whether (and where) masking is necessary with analysis of a baseline system, and then explore numerous parameterization of masking, including post-processing techniques for replacing the masks. Our analysis shows this to be a thorny matter; masks solve some problems but are not perfectly translated themselves.

1 Introduction

Neural machine translation generally produces higher quality output than phrase-based machine translation, especially in high-resource training settings and on in-domain data. However, this improvement has come at the expense of a certain loss of control over how words get translated, since there is no longer a direct link between source words, their translation options, and the ordered decoder output. While nearly everyone has considered this trade to be worthwhile, there lingers

src	En 2017 Bernard Arnault a gagné...
mask	En NUM NAME NAME a gagné...
out	In NUM NAME NAME a gagné...
align	In NUM_1 $NAME_1$ $NAME_2$ a gagné...
detok	In 2017 Bernard Arnault won...

Figure 1: A translation pipeline with masking (placeholding). The indexes denote a permutation of each mask type, and may or may not be an explicit part of the tag.

a concern about the stability and dependency of NMT performance. Input words are not all equally important, and there are many settings where one would be willing to sacrifice translation quality for a *translation guarantee* that certain input tokens be translated with perfect recall. Common examples include prices on a product page, names and places in a news article, or contact and location information, and other data types, such as URLs.

One attempt to providing these guarantees is the use of placeholders (or *masks*, the term we will use in this paper), where input tokens in a category are replaced by a masked label token (Figure 1). These are then passed through to the output and replaced with the correct translation in post-processing. This ostensibly guarantees that the input term (or its preferred translation) will correctly appear in the output, while at the same time restoring a capability that was easily handled in the old phrase-based paradigm. At the same time, doing so reflects a lack of confidence in the decoder to get this right. This approach has not received much attention in the research literature.

In this paper, we look at this topic in more detail. We focus our attention on *copy* or *pass-through* tokens, which is to say, input tokens that are not translated, but which are simply copied to the output sentence. This includes many different token types that can be recognized by regular expressions (numbers, URLs, email addresses, and Emojis), as well as types for which we can provide a dictionary.

We ask the following questions:

- Are translation guarantees necessary for these types?

- How effective is masking at producing these guarantees?

We experiment in both high resource (FR→EN) and low-resource (JA→EN) language settings.

2 Related Work

The first application of hard masking in neural machine translation was in Luong et al. (2015) and Long et al. (2016), which address the translation of rare words and technical items, but the approach was largely abandoned when sub-word methods (Sennrich et al., 2016) obviated the need. Most similar to this work in spirit is Crego et al. (2016), who mentioned that masking could be used to translate many "pass-through items" but did not conduct any further analysis towards the problem or the solution.

Another solution for handling pass-through items is to add them as constraints during beam search. A number of approaches introduced modifications to beam search that ensured that desired words would be included in the output (Hokamp and Liu, 2017; Chatterjee et al., 2017; Anderson et al., 2017). One problem with these solutions is that decoding time generally grows very quickly with the number of constraints added. Hasler et al. (2018) showed that even two constraints cause decoding speed to increase by as much as five times. Post and Vilar (2018) introduced a fixed-beam-size variant which is constant in the number of constraints, but the constant overhead is still quite high.

In terms of specific token types, Li et al. (2018), Ugawa et al. (2018) and Grundkiewicz and Heafield (2018) studied NMT models with better handling of named entities, either by adding named entity tags or employing transliteration models. Gotti et al. (2014) analyzed how hashtags are translated in the Canadian government tweet corpus and used insights from the analysis to improve their tweet-oriented machine translation system. Radford et al. (2016) conducted corpus analysis on the alignment between natural language text with Emojis.

match type	examples
template (regex)	numbers, emoji, URLs, email addresses
direct (dict)	names, cities, states, locations

Table 1: Pass-through candidates can be identified at the class level (via regular expressions) or type level (via direct match against a provided dictionary).

3 Masking

Masking is the context-free replacement of a class of input tokens with a single mask token. The idea is to collapse collections of distributionally similar tokens into a single token that the decoder can then be trained to reliably translate.

Because there has been little formal study of these items, there is no consensus on what should be masked (i.e., what the set of pass-through items is). For this work, the set of items to be masked comes from two different sources (Table 1):

- *Template matches.* This refers to sets of items that can be identified by regular expression. We work with numbers, URLs, email addresses, and emoji (a term we use in a general sense to denote extended non-alphabetic character sets).

- *Dictionary matches.* Tokens or sequences of tokens that are always translated the same way. A canonical example is named entities. These are often identified via dictionary lookup.

Dictionary matches typically contain items that are in fact translated, but we focus on the subset of word tokens that are instead passed through.

3.1 Demasking

At inference time, the masked tokens in the decoder output must be replaced with the corresponding source tokens. This *demasking* requires aligning the masks in the decoder output to the masks in the decoder input. Once this is done, recovering the original token identities for replacement is trivial. However, computing the mask alignment is not necessarily easy. We therefore explore two solutions to it: *indexing* and *bipartite matching*. Each of these solutions has its own benefits and problems.

Indexing The indexing approach (Crego et al., 2016) incorporates an index in each mask token:

EMAIL becomes EMAIL1, EMAIL2, and so on. Ideally, the decoder learns to output indexed mask tokens as a bijective permutation of the input mask tokens. The source tokens for each output mask are easily recovered in this scenario, but the downside is that there are now an unbounded number of masks which are all different to the decoder.

Bipartite matching Without indexes, we must produce our own alignment. We propose a general solution based on weighted bipartite matching. This approach takes as input a matrix of weights that assigns a score to each (source token, target token) pair. These weights can be obtained in different ways; for example, from the decoder attention weights, or from an external alignment model.

The task is to convert these weights into a set of hard alignments between the input and decoder output masks. We do this by formulating the problem as a bipartite graph problem (Algorithm 1. For each subset of masks with the same label, we use alignment scores as the edge weights, and execute the bipartite graph matching algorithm to find the best hard alignment scheme. These alignments can then be used to demask the output tokens.

Our approach guarantees an alignment for each target mask. If there are fewer target than source masks, an input token will be erroneously used multiple times.

Obtaining weights Obtaining weights to use with bipartite matching is not straightforward. We experiment with two approaches:

- *Averaged attention scores.* We average source attention scores across all decoder heads and layers in our model.

- *External aligner.* We run a version of fast-align (Dyer et al., 2013).

Both have problems. We use Transformers (Vaswani et al., 2017) in our experiments, but multi-head Transformer attention is not the same thing as alignment (Jain and Wallace, 2019). Fast-align is fast and easy to use at inference time, but it is a variant of IBM Model 2 (Brown et al., 1993) and the HMM model (Vogel et al., 1996). Therefore, its translation model cannot distinguish among mask permutations, and its impoverished distortion model is not well-suited to the task of recovering permutations of identical masks. However, we consider both approaches worth testing on this coarser alignment task, where we are only concerned with

---

Algorithm 1: Bipartite Matching Demasking

Input: source sentence $\mathcal{S} = \{s_0, \ldots, s_{I-1}\}$,
  target sentence $\mathcal{T} = \{t_0, \ldots, t_{J-1}\}$,
  soft alignment matrix $\mathcal{A}$ of size $I \times J$

Output: demasked target sentence $\mathcal{T}'$

$\mathcal{T}' = \mathcal{T}$;

for *each unique mask label m in $\mathcal{T}$* **do**

  $\mathcal{C} = \emptyset$; // competing masks

  for *(s_i, t_j) in $\mathcal{S} \times \mathcal{T}$* **do**

    if *s_i, t_j are both masks and both belong to category m* **then**

      $\mathcal{C} = \mathcal{C} \cup \{(s_i, t_j)\}$;

    end

  end

  extract bipartite graph $\mathcal{G}$ corresponding to $\mathcal{C}$ using the weights from $\mathcal{A}$;

  conduct bipartite matching $\mathcal{M}$ on $\mathcal{G}$;

  for *match (s_i, t_j) in $\mathcal{M}$* **do**

    substitute t_j in $\mathcal{T}'$ with the unmasked source token corresponding to s_i;

  end

end

return $\mathcal{T}'$;

---

alignment of a handful of well-attested types, and not all the words in the sentence pair.

4 Experiment Setup

4.1 Data

Our evaluation follows the WMT 2019 Robustness Task,[1] except that we use MTNT data (Michel and Neubig, 2018) *for evaluation only*. This includes MTNT/train, which we excluded from training in part because many of the masked items we would like to evaluate occur most frequently in this dataset. Table 2 contains information about all data sets.

For French–English training data, we use Europarl (Koehn, 2005, v7) and News Commentary (v10), and a portion of the UN Corpus. Due to its large size, we do not add all of the UN data, but add only lines that have a mask other than NUMBER, which includes about 1.1 million lines. This is crucial for the experiments since there is not enough masked data without this addition. We also include the WMT 2015 newstest test set for evaluation.

We also conduct limited experiments on Japanese–English. We follow Michel & Neubig in combining KFTT (Neubig, 2011), JESC (Pryzant

---

[1] www.statmt.org/wmt19/robustness.html

Dataset	French–English		Japanese–English	
	sents	words	sents	words
Europarl v.7	2.0m	50.2m	-	-
News commentary v.10	200k	4.4m	-	-
UN (complete)	12.8m	316.2m	-	-
→ UN (dict masks)	1.1m	33.8m	-	-
KFTT	-	-	440k	9.7m
JESC	-	-	3.2m	21m
TED Talks	-	-	241k	4.0m
newstest2014	3,003	69k	-	-
MTNT1.1/valid	886	34k	965	19k
newstest2015	1,500	25k	-	-
MTNT1.1/train	19k	660k	6,506	128k
MTNT1.1/test	1,022	16k	1,001	11k

Table 2: Pre-tokenization data sizes in sentence and English words for FR–EN and JA–EN training (top), validation (middle), and testing (bottom).

et al., 2017), and TED Talks (Cettolo et al., 2012) data.

4.2 Masks

We obtain our set of mask types from two sources: a set of regular expressions, and a dictionary extracted from the training data.

Regular expressions We built a set of regular expressions to identify the following mask types: NUMBER, EMOJI, EMAIL, and URL.

A difficulty with developing these regular expressions is their interaction with other steps in the pipeline. One first has to choose whether to apply masking before or after tokenization. A natural place is afterwards, but this requires that the tokenizer not split up the items we wish to mask, which in turn requires one to apply a set of regular expressions to exempt portions of the input segment.[2] As a result, we apply all masks to the raw data and modify tokenization and subword splitting code to not split up masks.

Dictionary We also want to test how well the system translates named entities. We identify these items by running the Stanford NER tagger on the English side of all the training data (including the complete UN corpus). We then construct a dictionary from all entries satisfying the following constraints, which simplify the masking and demasking

process. Each entity:

- should be labeled as one of the following category: PERSON, LOCATION, ORGANIZATION, CITY, COUNTRY;

- must be found verbatim in the non-English side of the parallel sentence;[3] and

- must contain at least one word not among the most frequent 10k words in the training data.

Table 3 shows the statistics of pass-through items in MTNT dataset captured by our regular expression and named entity dictionary.

4.3 Synthetic Data

A problem apparent from Table 3 is that there simply aren't many instances for many of the mask types, which impedes investigation. MTNT/train has the most examples for many types, but for EMAIL, URL, COUNTRY, and even CITY, there are fewer than 1k, and often barely any at all.

To address this problem, we synthesize larger tests that allow us to see how often various types are translated correctly in the baseline system. For each mask, m, we identify all sentence pairs (s, t) in the training data for which one of the words was masked as m, ensuring the mask is in both the source and reference. Call this set D_m. Next, we build a set V_m of all tokens that get masked as m:

$$V_m = \{p \mid \text{mask(p)} = m\}$$

---

[2]The Moses tokenizer, which is applied with default settings in many scenarios, segments URLs into many pieces, due to a weak and buggy "protected patterns" file.

[3]This requirement limits our ability to identify Japanese entities, but it prevents errors from transliteration and/or alignment

Mask	French–English				Japanese–English		
	train	WMT15	MTNT$_{\text{test}}$	MTNT$_{\text{train}}$	train	MTNT$_{\text{test}}$	MTNT$_{\text{train}}$
NUMBER	1,926,726	210	238	16,562	64,635	121	1,014
EMOJI	5,434	1	5	131	2,057	11	352
EMAIL	20,751	0	0	0	1	0	0
URL	38,655	0	0	26	175	0	5
CITY	186,902	39	16	824	13	0	0
COUNTRY	34,205	1	0	7	12	0	0
LOCATION	409,109	41	24	1,598	155	0	2
ORG.	369,297	73	46	1,896	507	0	40
PERSON	845,116	131	60	3,395	179	0	3

Table 3: Entity counts across all data. For training data, the counts are "true" counts, that is, they are only counted for tokens that appeared on both the source and target sides of the data. For test sets, the counts are produced by matching only against the source. For most entity types, data is quite sparse.

We then produce a new test set by repeating the following procedure 5,000 times:

1. Sample a sentence pair $d \in D_m$;

2. Twenty separate times, do

   (a) Sample one of the positions with mask m in d (there may be only one);

   (b) Sample a term $s \in V_m$;

   (c) Create a new sentence pair by inserting s into d.

This yields synthetic datasets of 100k sentences. Table 7 contains examples.

4.4 Models

Our baseline NMT system is a 4-layer transformer trained with Sockeye (Hieber et al., 2017). We use the following settings for training both French–English and Japanese–English models: eight attention heads, model size of 512, feed-forward layer size 2048, three-way tied embeddings, layer normalization applied before attention, dropout and a residual connection added afterwards, a batch size of 4096 words, and the learning rate initialized to 0.0002. We compute checkpoints every 5000 updates, and train until validation likelihood does not increase for ten consecutive checkpoints.

For preprocessing, we first apply the Moses scripts that normalize punctuation, remove non-printing characters, and tokenize.[4] We learn a subword model using byte-pair encoding (Sennrich et al., 2016) with 32k merge operations. No recasing is applied to either source- or target-language text.

For alignment-based demasking, we trained two fast-align models, one in each language direction, using default parameters. We then combine them with the `grow-diag-final-and` heuristic.

Source Factors We also experiment with source factors (Sennrich and Haddow, 2016) applied to the baseline (unmasked) system. Source factors are separate embeddings that are learned from annotations applied to the input tokens. For each of the types NUMBER, EMAIL, and URL, instead of masking, we added a distinct binary source factor. We also experimented with two ways of combining factors: *concatenation* and *summing*. Concatenation was described in Sennrich et al.; we learn an embedding of size 4 for each factor, and concatenate with the subword embeddings. For summing, we instead embed each factor to size 512, and sum together all factors for each input token.

5 Results

We compute BLEU on detokenized, cased outputs using the standardized BLEU scoring script, sacre-BLEU (Post, 2018).[5] The results on all test sets can be found in Table 4. We provide the same-data baseline score from Michel and Neubig (2018) as an anchor point for evaluating the models.

In no masking situation is there any improvement in BLEU score over the baseline system. In fact, adding masks seems to uniformly cost the models in

---

[4] With the options `-no-escape` and using a version of the Moses `basic-protected-patterns` file modified to protect masks.

[5] Shared portion of signature: `BLEU +case.mixed +numrefs.1 +smooth.exp +tok.13a +version.1.2.20`.

System	French–English			JA–EN	
	WMT15	MTNT$_{test}$	MTNT$_{train}$	MTNT$_{test}$	MTNT$_{train}$
Michel & Neubig (Base)	-	23.2	-	6.6	-
baseline	32.0	28.1	28.7	8.2	6.5
indexed masking	31.8	27.4	27.0	8.0	6.6
masking (fast-align)	31.9	27.9	*	8.1	*
masking (attention)	31.9	28.0	27.5	8.1	5.4
source factors (concat)	32.0	28.1	28.3	8.2	6.0
source factors (summed)	32.4	28.4	29.1	8.2	6.7

Table 4: BLEU scores on test sets. The score take from Michel & Neubig is the system *not* trained on MTNT/train, since we did not train on that in this paper, instead reserving it for analysis.

type	WMT	MTNT /test	MTNT /train	synth
NUMBER	91.1	95.2	94.8	-
EMOJI	*0*	*0*	5.2	-
EMAIL	-	-	-	96.9
URL	-	-	*91.7*	91.3
CITY	*100*	*92.3*	95.1	98.4
COUNTRY	*100*	-	*50.0*	90.2
LOCATION	*100*	*100*	87.9	-
ORG.	98.4	*100*	93.6	-
PERSON	99.2	100	94.9	-

Table 5: FR–EN baseline recall scores (against the reference) for each data type when decoding with the baseline system. Hyphens (-) indicate no data being available, and *italics* indicate counts for which there were fewer than 50 instances (Table 3). The synthetic dataset is discussed in Section 6.3.

terms of BLEU score, from small drops of a tenth of a point or so (for WMT15 and Japanese), to large drops of about half a BLEU point on FR-EN MTNT. We do, however, see BLEU score increases of about a third of a point when using summed source factors.[6]

BLEU is important, but is too coarse of a metric to draw conclusions from in this situation that deals with relatively rare phenomena. We turn now to a more fine-grained analysis.

6 Baseline Analysis

We begin with an analysis of the performance of the baseline system on all the mask types in our study. Table 5 reports, for each type, the percentage

of time that the baseline system correctly translated tokens that were in both the source and reference.

6.1 NUMBER

Numbers are by far the most frequent category type, and additionally for many scenarios numbers are considered to be one of the data types that are important to correctly translate. How well are numbers translated?

On WMT15, there are 210 instances of numbers that are matched by our regular expression and exist in both the French input and the English reference. On these numbers, the baseline system achieves an accuracy of 91.2%, leaving only 18 instances of missed masks. Of these, the vast majority are fine: 12 are found in written form in the system output (e.g., *twelve* instead of 12), and four are localization effects of time (e.g., *14:30 → 2:30 PM*). Accounting for these, the accuracy is 99.0%.

Turning to MTNT/test, we find an accuracy of 92.2% on 219 masked instances, with 17 of them translated incorrectly. Of these, 11 are fine (written substitutions), and many are the result of the decoder entering a "language modeling mode", where it generates output that has little to do with the input (Koehn and Knowles, 2017). A few are actually wrongly translated: *15 jours* gets translated as *fortnight*, and *1h de sommeil* ("one hour of sleep") is mistranslated.

Finally, we look at MTNT/train, where there are many more masks, especially numbers. MTNT/train is an unusual dataset. There are many input segments with hundreds or over a thousand words, often containing multiple sentences, due to the way the data was collected (Michel and Neubig, 2018, penultimate paragraph of §3.4) There is also a lot of repetition: some input sentences

---

[6]Recall that these are applied only to numbers, email addresses, and URLs, and that these terms are not masked, but instead have the standard tokenization and subword-splitting regime applied to them.

type	# of digits				
	1	**2**	**3**	**4**	*****
correct	203	9	0	1	2
missing	6	8	1	6	0
wrong	1	5	0	0	2
total	210	23	1	87	4

Table 6: Counts of error types made by the baseline system on FR–EN MTNT/train on 1-, 2-, 3-, and 4-digit integers, and other numbers (*), looking only at system outputs with 50 or fewer words. *missing* and *wrong* denote errors where the number is either dropped or mistranslated by the baseline system. *correct* sentences were fine but not identical (e.g., "1,000" and "1000" or "1" and "one").

are repeated three or four times, leading to skewed statistics. It is also quite informal, and since we had no such data in our training data, we often observed the NMT model again entering "language model mode". The accuracy is 95.7% on 10,040 instances with system outputs with 50 or fewer words.

We analyze the 325 instances where our method reports an error (Table 6).[7] The error counts are produced by counting all instances where a number matching our pattern is found in both the French source and English reference, but not in our system output. We break down the analysis by number type: integers with one to four digits, and all others.

It is clear that the analysis from above holds: the majority of items marked incorrect by automatic matching are actually fine (65%). The six missing 4-digit numbers seem to be a quirk of the data: six of the source sentences have X *Edition* at the start of the input and reference (for some year X), with no punctuation, and it gets dropped. The handful of other errors are similar to those described above. If we remove the bad lines, and count as correct the sentences we identify, the new recall for numbers on MTNT/train is 98.8%.

The baseline JA-EN system does not perform nearly as well as the FR-EN system. The accuracy for numbers is only 49.3% on MTNT/test and 61.2% on MTNT/train. However, we see the same pattern of mismatches that are not errors (e.g., numbers spelled out or formatted slightly differently). Accounting for these, the recall on MTNT/test jumps to 67.1%. This is still much lower than we see for French, but not unexpected given the drastic difference in BLEU score.

---

[7]This is after throwing out 103 instances where the input was multiline or the NMT output was garbage, perhaps due to out-of-domain effects.

The bottom line on these test sets is that numbers appear to be correctly passed-through or translated the majority of the time in the high resource setting. They are also often correctly translated in context-sensitive ways. However, they are not perfect.

6.2 EMOJI

We use the term *emoji* broadly to indicate special characters that are outside the phonetic alphabet. Emoji are a unique type of data, because they are typically single Unicode codepoints. If these codepoints were not in the training data, they will be untranslatable. This is precisely what happens in WMT15, where the single instance

> *L'introduction   mi-septembre   par Apple^{TM} d'écrans plus grand pour...*

is mistranslated. Emoji are therefore a unique candidate for masking.

6.3 EMAIL, URL, CITY, and COUNTRY

These four categories have almost no data in the test sets, so we instead analyze the synthetic data (§4.1). The synthetic data provides us with 5,000 sentence contexts with 20 different instances, totalling nearly 100k samples (Table 7). We translate each of these sentences with the baseline system, and check whether the entity type is in the system output. The results can be found above in the last column of Table 5.

We focus here on EMAIL and URL. Note that these are types which should almost always be passed through, and not translated. Yet the baseline system mistranslates 3.1% of email addresses and 8.7% of URLs. The reason likely has to do with the MT preprocessing pipeline: both tokenization and subword processing mangle these types into long sequences of tokens. On average, URLs are transformed into 14.1 subword tokens (the longest is 125 tokens), versus 3.9 subword tokens for the average vocabulary item.

Looking at the outputs, we see that URLs are usually translated nearly perfectly, except for a small mistranslated or dropped piece (Table 8). But for these types, a single character mis-translation renders the entire item useless.

6.4 LOCATION, ORG., and PERSON

These three categories are a bit unusual, since we are restricting our attention to instances that have the same surface form in both French and English (instead of using a translation dictionary). All of

Présidence de l'Union européenne : `http://europa-eu-un.org`
Présidence de l'Union européenne : `http://www.fao.org/figis/servlet/static?`
`xml=CCRF_prog.xml&dom=org&xp_nav=2,3`
Présidence de l'Union européenne : `www.all4syria.org`
Présidence de l'Union européenne : `http://www.njcl.fi/1_2006/commentary1.pdf`

Prière de prendre contact avec le Groupe du Journal, à l'adresse `journal@un.org`.
Prière de prendre contact avec le Groupe du Journal, à l'adresse `frank.X@univie.ac.at`.
Prière de prendre contact avec le Groupe du Journal, à l'adresse `jferex@eclac.cl`.
Prière de prendre contact avec le Groupe du Journal, à l'adresse `chungrx@un.org`.

Table 7: Substitutions for URL (top) and EMAIL (bottom). The original is in bold. Personal email addresses have been slightly modified.

sys:	`http://www.cbs.nl/NR/rdonlyres/D1716A60-0D13-4281-BED6-3607514888AD/`
ref:	`http://www.cbs.nl/NR/rdonlyres/D1716A60-0D13-4281-BED6-360751488AD/`
sys:	`www.fao.org/forestry/fo/fra/index.jsp`
ref:	`www.fao.org/forestry/fo/fra/index.jp`
sys:	`qualityws.ht`
ref:	`qualitativeyws.ht`
sys:	`http://www.tebtebba.org/tebtebba_files/ipr/racism.htm`
ref:	`http://www.tebba.org/tebtebba_files/ipr/racism.htm`

Table 8: Mistranslated URLs.

them display similar patterns: extremely high accuracies in all three test sets (WMT15, MTNT/test, and MTNT/train). We took the most prevalent category, PERSON, and manually examined the error cases. Of the 131 tokens tagged as PERSON in MTNT/test, seven did not appear in the reference, leaving 123 instances, on which the baseline system achieved 99.2% accuracy, missing only one. The single missed instance translated *Jean-Pierre Bernajuzan* as *Mr Bernajuzan*.

No mistakes were made on MTNT/test. MTNT/train is more difficult to analyze, but many of the missing instances were caused by multiline inputs where the NMT system stopped translating after the first sentence of the input.

In summary, for these categories, the baseline system does very well. But again, it's not perfect.

6.5 Source Factors

We applied source factors to types NUMBER, EMAIL, and URL in the baseline system. From Table 4, this seems to have had no effect on BLEU scores when using the embedding concatenation described in (Sennrich and Haddow, 2016), except for a minor drop on MTNT/train. When summing the factors, however, we see a small improvement in BLEU score on all three test sets. However, there

type	indexed		unindexed		
	1	2+	1	2+	3+
NUMBER	98.5	95.9	98.5	97.7	97.7
EMOJI	91.4	74.0	98.8	92.0	100
EMAIL	-	-	-	-	-
URL	100	-	100	-	-
CITY	98.9	97.6	97.6	97.1	96.4
COUNTRY	100	100	100	100.0	-
LOCATION	98.6	92.0	99.0	93.6	90.7
ORG.	98.9	90.7	98.2	93.8	91.7
PERSON	98.3	82.1	98.5	97.3	96.7

Table 9: FR–EN recall scores (against the reference) for masking on MTNT/train, broken down between indexing and (attention-based) not-indexing, and between sentences that have only a single (1) or multiple (2+) instances of a mask.

was no improvement in entity-based recall scores over the baseline analysis in Table 5.

7 Masking

Masking has the potential to achieve 100% accuracy on masked entities. However, its success depends on a number of pieces: (1) the masks need to be translated correctly (i.e., one-for-one with the input masks), and (2) for unindexed masking, they need to be correctly aligned.

Table 9 looks into (1). It displays masks recall scores on the MTNT/train test set, broken down between indexed and unindexed masking, and between sentences with exactly one instance of each mask, or more than one (2+). For unindexed masking, we also display recall for masks appearing 3+ times in a single sentence. We see that masks are not perfectly translated, but that unindexed masking does a slightly better job of it. And the numbers are somewhat better than those of the baseline system in Table 5, though for some labels they are not that different. Performance degrades with more masks of the same type, in all instances except EMOJI (where there are only 18 3+ instances).

		reference		reference	
		mono	not	mono	not
system	mono	61	18	67	20
	not	7	2	1	0

Table 10: Demasked permutations for the attention-based (left) and alignment-based (right) approaches. Mono/not denotes whether the text of the decoder output (rows) and reference (columns) was monotonic with respect to the input.

Demasking Section 3.1 described two approaches to aligning masks: decoder attention and post-alignment via fast-align. This use case proves similarly difficult to analyze for a number of reasons. On WMT15 (where we expect the neat text to present the simplest case), there are 88 instances where a single mask type appears more than once in a sentence. We break down the analysis into whether or not the permutations of the text in the (a) system output and (b) reference were monotonic (with respect to the input text). (Note that in the case of non-monotonic permutations, we are not guaranteed that the system and reference line up.) The results are in Table 10, and are largely inconclusive. There is not a lot of data to determine whether permutations are correctly restored, and there does not appear to be much difference between the two approaches.

8 Conclusions

We began this paper wondering whether "translation guarantees" for certain word types were necessary, and whether masking was an appropriate tool for guaranteeing them. The answer is not as clear-cut as we would have liked. Masking (or placeholding) is sometimes viewed as a way of ensuring or increasing the chances that a particular entity type is correctly translated. Our experiments on different test sets with a modern Transformer architecture on French–English and (to a lesser extent) Japanese–English show that this is often not the case. Masked systems do not reliably translate masks, which is likely why Crego et al. mention the use of constraints to ensure masks are output. And in any case, the baseline system does a decent job of translating many of these types already. The recall numbers between the baseline and masked systems (Tables 5 and 9) all range in the mid-90s across multiple test sets.

Another issue is that the set of items that should be masked cannot be perfectly predicted. As we saw with types like NUMBER, many numbers should not in fact be passed through, but require translation, in ways that are often mediated by context. Using masks for such types is akin to a vote of "no confidence" in the decoder, which seems not to be justified. This also seems to be the case for other entity-based types, which are handled well by the baseline system.

However, we have seen that unindexed masking can do a good job of passing items through, compared to Crego et al. (2016)'s indexed system. In situations where it is better to drop the identified term than to mistranslate it, unindexed masking may be preferable. This includes terms like emojis and extended character sets, and email addresses and URLs. The former are important to mask because otherwise the characters will be outside the decoder character set; one could alternately augment the training data with all emoji types, but this could be difficult and error-prone, especially as new characters are introduced all the time. Email addresses and URLs cause complications with tokenization, can get broken up into many subword pieces, and can also be hard to reliably detokenize. It makes sense to translate these items as a single entity, making masking the clear option for this.

There are many avenues we have not explored in this paper. For example, adding a source factor to masked tokens might help increase the reliability of mask translation. An even better approach may be to use special loss functions to further encourage the decoder to get marked tokens right. One could also use constrained decoding (Hokamp and Liu, 2017; Post and Vilar, 2018) to ensure that desired items (or masks) are placed in the output.

References

Anderson, Peter, Basura Fernando, Mark Johnson, and Stephen Gould. 2017. Guided open vocabulary image captioning with constrained beam search. In *Proceedings of the 2017 Conference on Empirical Methods in Natural Language Processing*, pages 936–945, Copenhagen, Denmark, September. Association for Computational Linguistics.

Brown, Peter F., Stephen A. Della Pietra, Vincent J. Della Pietra, and Robert L. Mercer. 1993. The mathematics of statistical machine translation: Parameter estimation. *Computational Linguistics*, 19(2):263–311.

Cettolo, Mauro, Christian Girardi, and Marcello Federico. 2012. Wit3: Web inventory of transcribed and translated talks. In *Conference of European Association for Machine Translation*, pages 261–268.

Chatterjee, Rajen, Matteo Negri, Marco Turchi, Marcello Federico, Lucia Specia, and Frédéric Blain. 2017. Guiding neural machine translation decoding with external knowledge. In *Proceedings of the Second Conference on Machine Translation*, pages 157–168, Copenhagen, Denmark, September. Association for Computational Linguistics.

Crego, Josep Maria, Jungi Kim, Guillaume Klein, Anabel Rebollo, Kathy Yang, Jean Senellart, Egor Akhanov, Patrice Brunelle, Aurelien Coquard, Yongchao Deng, Satoshi Enoue, Chiyo Geiss, Joshua Johanson, Ardas Khalsa, Raoum Khiari, Byeongil Ko, Catherine Kobus, Jean Lorieux, Leidiana Martins, Dang-Chuan Nguyen, Alexandra Priori, Thomas Riccardi, Natalia Segal, Christophe Servan, Cyril Tiquet, Bo Wang, Jin Yang, Dakun Zhang, Jing Zhou, and Peter Zoldan. 2016. Systran's pure neural machine translation systems. *CoRR*, abs/1610.05540.

Dyer, Chris, Victor Chahuneau, and Noah A. Smith. 2013. A simple, fast, and effective reparameterization of IBM model 2. In *Proceedings of the 2013 Conference of the North American Chapter of the Association for Computational Linguistics: Human Language Technologies*, pages 644–648, Atlanta, Georgia, June. Association for Computational Linguistics.

Gotti, Fabrizio, Philippe Langlais, and Atefeh Farzindar. 2014. Hashtag occurrences, layout and translation: A corpus-driven analysis of tweets published by the canadian government. In *Proceedings of the Ninth International Conference on Language Resources and Evaluation, LREC 2014, Reykjavik, Iceland, May 26-31, 2014.*, pages 2254–2261.

Grundkiewicz, Roman and Kenneth Heafield. 2018. Neural machine translation techniques for named entity transliteration. In *Proceedings of the Seventh Named Entities Workshop, NEWS@ACL 2018, Melbourne, Australia, July 20, 2018*, pages 89–94.

Hasler, Eva, Adrià de Gispert, Gonzalo Iglesias, and Bill Byrne. 2018. Neural machine translation decoding with terminology constraints. In *Proceedings of the 2018 Conference of the North American Chapter of the Association for Computational Linguistics: Human Language Technologies, Volume 2 (Short Papers)*, pages 506–512, New Orleans, Louisiana, June. Association for Computational Linguistics.

Hieber, Felix, Tobias Domhan, Michael Denkowski, David Vilar, Artem Sokolov, Ann Clifton, and Matt Post. 2017. Sockeye: A toolkit for neural machine translation. *CoRR*, abs/1712.05690.

Hokamp, Chris and Qun Liu. 2017. Lexically constrained decoding for sequence generation using grid beam search. In *Proceedings of the 55th Annual Meeting of the Association for Computational Linguistics (Volume 1: Long Papers)*, pages 1535–1546, Vancouver, Canada, July. Association for Computational Linguistics.

Jain, Sarthak and Byron C. Wallace. 2019. Attention is not Explanation. In *Proceedings of the 2019 Conference of the North American Chapter of the Association for Computational Linguistics: Human Language Technologies, Volume 1 (Long and Short Papers)*, pages 3543–3556, Minneapolis, Minnesota, June. Association for Computational Linguistics.

Koehn, Philipp and Rebecca Knowles. 2017. Six challenges for neural machine translation. In *Proceedings of the First Workshop on Neural Machine Translation*, pages 28–39, Vancouver, August. Association for Computational Linguistics.

Koehn, Philipp. 2005. Europarl: A parallel corpus for statistical machine translation. In *MT summit*, volume 5, pages 79–86.

Li, Zhongwei, Xuancong Wang, AiTi Aw, Eng Siong Chng, and Haizhou Li. 2018. Named-entity tagging and domain adaptation for better customized translation. In *Proceedings of the Seventh Named Entities Workshop, NEWS@ACL 2018, Melbourne, Australia, July 20, 2018*, pages 41–46.

Long, Zi, Takehito Utsuro, Tomoharu Mitsuhashi, and Mikio Yamamoto. 2016. Translation of patent sentences with a large vocabulary of technical terms using neural machine translation. In *Proceedings of the 3rd Workshop on Asian Translation, WAT@COLING 2016, Osaka, Japan, December 2016*, pages 47–57.

Luong, Thang, Ilya Sutskever, Quoc Le, Oriol Vinyals, and Wojciech Zaremba. 2015. Addressing the rare word problem in neural machine translation. In *Proceedings of the 53rd Annual Meeting of the Association for Computational Linguistics and the 7th International Joint Conference on Natural Language Processing (Volume 1: Long Papers)*, pages 11–19, Beijing, China, July. Association for Computational Linguistics.

Michel, Paul and Graham Neubig. 2018. MTNT: A testbed for machine translation of noisy text. In *Proceedings of the 2018 Conference on Empirical Methods in Natural Language Processing*, pages 543–553. Association for Computational Linguistics.

Neubig, Graham. 2011. The Kyoto free translation task. http://www.phontron.com/kftt.

Post, Matt and David Vilar. 2018. Fast lexically constrained decoding with dynamic beam allocation for neural machine translation. In *Proceedings of the 2018 Conference of the North American Chapter of the Association for Computational Linguistics: Human Language Technologies, Volume 1 (Long Papers)*, pages 1314–1324, New Orleans, Louisiana, June. Association for Computational Linguistics.

Post, Matt. 2018. A call for clarity in reporting bleu scores. In *Proceedings of the Third Conference on Machine Translation: Research Papers*, pages 186–191, Belgium, Brussels, October. Association for Computational Linguistics.

Pryzant, Reid, Yongjoo Chung, Dan Jurafsky, and Denny Britz. 2017. JESC: japanese-english subtitle corpus. *CoRR*, abs/1710.10639.

Radford, Will, Ben Hachey, Bo Han, and Andy Chisholm. 2016. : telephone: : person: : sailboat: : whale: : okhand: ; or "call me ishmael" - how do you translate emoji? In *Proceedings of the Australasian Language Technology Association Workshop 2016, Melbourne, Australia, December 5 - 7, 2016*, pages 150–154.

Sennrich, Rico and Barry Haddow. 2016. Linguistic input features improve neural machine translation. In *Proceedings of the First Conference on Machine Translation: Volume 1, Research Papers*, pages 83–91, Berlin, Germany, August. Association for Computational Linguistics.

Sennrich, Rico, Barry Haddow, and Alexandra Birch. 2016. Neural machine translation of rare words with subword units. In *Proceedings of the 54th Annual Meeting of the Association for Computational Linguistics (Volume 1: Long Papers)*, pages 1715–1725, Berlin, Germany, August. Association for Computational Linguistics.

Ugawa, Arata, Akihiro Tamura, Takashi Ninomiya, Hiroya Takamura, and Manabu Okumura. 2018. Neural machine translation incorporating named entity. In *Proceedings of the 27th International Conference on Computational Linguistics, COLING 2018, Santa Fe, New Mexico, USA, August 20-26, 2018*, pages 3240–3250.

Vaswani, Ashish, Noam Shazeer, Niki Parmar, Jakob Uszkoreit, Llion Jones, Aidan N Gomez, Ł ukasz Kaiser, and Illia Polosukhin. 2017. Attention is all you need. In Guyon, I., U. V. Luxburg, S. Bengio, H. Wallach, R. Fergus, S. Vishwanathan, and R. Garnett, editors, *Advances in Neural Information Processing Systems 30*, pages 5998–6008. Curran Associates, Inc.

Vogel, Stephan, Hermann Ney, and Christoph Tillmann. 1996. HMM-based word alignment in statistical translation. In *COLING 1996 Volume 2: The 16th International Conference on Computational Linguistics*.

Controlling the Reading Level of Machine Translation Output

Kelly Marchisio[*] and **Jialiang Guo**[*] and **Cheng-I Lai** and **Philipp Koehn**
Center for Language and Speech Processing
Johns Hopkins University
{kellym,guo,clai24,phi}@jhu.edu

Abstract

Today's machine translation systems output the same translation for a given input, despite important differences between users. In practice, translations should be customized for each reader, for instance when translating for children versus in a business setting. In this paper, we introduce the task of reading level control to machine translation, and provide the first results. Our methods can be used to raise or lower the reading level of output translations. In our first approach, source-side sentences in the training corpus are tagged based on the reading level (readability) of the matching target sentences. Our second approach alters the traditional encoder-decoder architecture by specifying a joint encoder and separate decoders for simple and complex decoding modes, with training data partitioned by reading level. We demonstrate control over output readability score on three test sets in the Spanish–English language direction.

1 Introduction

Though the goal of machine translation is to generate semantically accurate translations from one language to another, there are other factors which affect whether a translation is "good". One often-neglected factor is the reading level of the translation—different contexts require different reading levels. When translating for less-skilled readers, one may desire a translation with common vocabulary and simple sentence structures. In a professional setting, however, one often requires concise language with advanced vocabulary and syntactic structure.

For instance, when translating a Spanish web page about machine translation to an English-speaking 7-year-old, one might output, "machine translation is a way to take a sentence from one language and turn it into a sentence in another language". When advertising new machine translation software to a potential investor, one might explain, "machine translation is the automated process by which a sentence in a source language can be converted into a sentence in another language". Both sentences carry the same meaning and do not require specialist technical knowledge, but decreasing the complexity in the first makes it easier for a child to understand, and increasing the complexity in the second makes it sound more professional and sophisticated. Furthermore, for native speakers of low-resource languages where machine translation quality may currently be poor but who can read basic phrases in a second language where translation quality is high, they may prefer to read a lower complexity but semantically accurate translation in their second language over an inaccurate, garbled message in their native tongue.

In this paper, we introduce the task of reading level control (readability control) to machine translation. We develop two methodologies that control the reading level of a translation in the Spanish–English language direction, focusing on lexical complexity as a first step. For professional settings, we aim to produce advanced vocabulary. For less-skilled readers, the translation should use simple words while maintaining the meaning of the source sentence. Accordingly, we build a system where a user can specify the reading level ("sim-

---

[*] Equal contribution

ple" or "complex") of the translation they wish to be output. Future work should examine controlling other factors that affect the readability of a sentence, such as syntactic structure.

2 Background: Readability Tests

To quantitatively evaluate the reading level of English sentences, we use three commonly-used automated readability[1] tests.

2.1 Dale-Chall Readability

The Dale-Chall (DC) readability score utilizes a list of 3000 common English words, which captures lexical information of text (Chall and Dale, 1995). Words not in the list are considered "difficult". The metric is computed using the percentage of difficult words and the average number of words per sentence, as below:

$$0.1579\left(\frac{\#\text{difficult words}}{\#\text{words}}\times100\right)+0.0496\left(\frac{\#\text{words}}{\#\text{sentences}}\right)$$

2.2 Flesch-Kincaid Grade Level

One of the most widely-used readability metrics, Flesch-Kincaid Grade Level (FKG) approximately corresponds to grade level in the US schooling system (Kincaid et al., 1975). The score considers only two basic features of the text—the average number of words per sentence and the average number of syllables per word. It is computed as below:

$$0.39\left(\frac{\#\text{words}}{\#\text{sentences}}\right) + 11.8\left(\frac{\#\text{syllables}}{\#\text{words}}\right) - 15.59$$

2.3 Flesch Reading Ease

We also evaluate translations with Flesch Reading Ease (FRE) (Flesch, 1948), where higher scores indicate "easier" text. FRE was the basis for FKG, and is computed as:

$$206.835 - 1.015\left(\frac{\#\text{words}}{\#\text{sentences}}\right) - 84.6\left(\frac{\#\text{syllables}}{\#\text{words}}\right)$$

2.4 Readability Tests for Other Languages

Apart from the three tests above for English, there are many readability tests available for other languages, such as Amstad readability index for German (Amstad, 1978), GulpEase index for Italian (Lucisano and Piemontese, 1988), and LIX for a wide range of languages (Björnsson, 1968). There

are also various approaches to reading level scoring based on machine learning and natural language processing techniques (François and Miltsakaki, 2012).

In this work, we focus on the three traditional English readability tests mentioned above as a first step for the Spanish–English language direction. Though the readability tests aren't perfect, they achieve good results in our work and are easy to implement. We anticipate that our general frameworks will work with various target languages and readability scorers, provided the corresponding readability tests effectively estimate reading level.

3 Factors Affecting the Reading Level of the Output Translation

At test time, it is reasonable to anticipate that advanced vocabulary and phrases in a source sentence will be translated into advanced vocabulary and phrases in a target sentence, and simple lexical features of a source to simple lexical features in a target. This leads to a problem in the typical setting where there is a single source document at test time. Since the source has fixed complexity, users do not have control over the reading level of the output. As a result, we must find other ways of controlling output reading level besides altering the source.

In this section, we demonstrate that the reading level of output translations is also affected by the overall reading level of target-side sentences during training. We train four OpenNMT (Klein et al., 2017) default RNN models on four separate training corpora in the Spanish–English language direction. The corpora have different overall target-side readability (Table 1). We then test the readability of each model's translation of WMT newstest2013[2] (Table 2). Please see Section 5 for implementation details and description of datasets.

Corpus	DC	FKG	FRE
OpenSubtitles	3.43	2.28	89.39
OpenSubtitles+Europarl	6.08	7.27	69.43
ParaCrawl	7.92	11.17	56.43
Europarl	8.80	12.41	48.94

Table 1: Overall readability scores of the target-side sentences in different training corpora. Lower DC score, lower FKG score, and higher FRE score indicate simpler sentences.

---

[1] Throughout this paper, we use the terms "readability", "reading level", and "text complexity" interchangeably.

[2] http://www.statmt.org/wmt13/translation-task.html

	DC	FKG	FRE
gold	8.11	9.49	59.83
OpenSubtitles	7.09	8.25	67.52
OpenSubtitles+Europarl	7.61	9.15	63.40
Europarl	7.75	9.48	61.84
ParaCrawl	7.92	9.36	61.11

Table 2: Effect of the training corpus on translation readability for newstest2013. Lower DC score, lower FKG score, and higher FRE score indicate simpler sentences.

Examining Tables 1 and 2, we observe that the readability of the translation tends to mimic the readability of the target sentences in the training corpus. This effect inspired us to partition the training data into "simple" and "complex" subsets so the model can learn how sentences of lower and higher reading level should look.

4   Proposed Approaches

In this paper, we develop two training methods which allow some control over the reading level of machine translation output.

4.1   Data Tagging

Inspired by Sennrich et al. (2016)'s work controlling politeness, our first approach utilizes a short text token added to the end of each source-side training sentence, which corresponds to the matching target-side sentence's readability. The intuition behind this method is that the attention mechanism will learn to pay attention to the complexity token when decoding in the simple or complex setting.

A token indicating whether each training sentence pair is of low or high reading level is used if the target sentence meets a preset readability threshold. A third token indicating intermediate reading level is added to sentences that do not meet the chosen thresholds, so that the model can learn other knowledge—such as a better language model and alignment—from these examples.

The data tagging approach requires no customization of model architecture or training procedure. At test time, we append a "simple" or "complex" token to the test source sentences to specify the desired reading level of the output. We choose tokens that are unlikely to appear in the target language to avoid overloading the symbols with multiple meanings.

4.2   Double-Decoder

The second approach is an encoder-decoder model with a shared encoder and two decoders—one for "complex" decoding, and the other for "simple" decoding as shown in Figure 1. When training a complex sentence, the joint encoder is paired with the "complex" decoder and loss is calculated based on that encoder-decoder pair. For a simple sentence, the encoder is paired with the "simple" decoder. In this way, the encoder learns a shared representation for all source sentences, while separate decoders tune themselves to sentences that have the desired reading level. At inference time, we pass a flag indicating whether we want the output to be "simple" or "complex". The corresponding decoder then translates the test set.

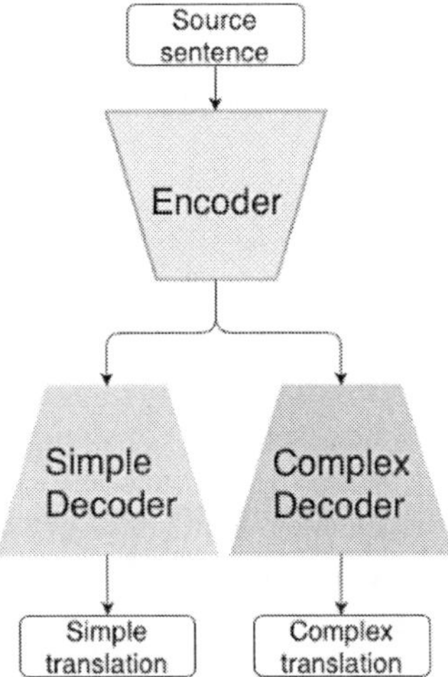

Figure 1: Encoder-decoder model with separate decoders for simple vs. complex output settings.

4.3   Data Selection

4.3.1   Partitioning by Readability Level

We use a method of data selection to partition our data into "simple" and "complex" training sets. We first score the readability of each target-side sentence in the corpus. Next, we select which sentences to include in the training sets based on their percentile rank for readability. For instance, in the 30-30 setting for the double-decoder architecture, we include the bottom 30% of available training sentences as the simple set, the top 30% as the complex set, and discard the remaining sentences. In the data tagging approach, we equivalently tag the bottom and top 30% as simple/complex, and the remaining as neutral. We experiment with multiple thresholds.

4.3.2 Oversampling

Though more extreme data partitioning endows more effective control over output readability, it also brings potential problems; the data tagging approach has limited "simple" and "complex" examples from which to gain knowledge about reading level, and the double-decoder approach discards so much data that it could suffer translation quality degradation. We therefore use oversampling to reinforce the effect of data with extreme readability. For the data tagging approach, we use an extreme data partition (e.g., 15-15) and oversample all examples tagged as "simple" or "complex"; for the double-decoder approach, we use the 50-50 data partition but oversample the extreme parts (top 15% and bottom 15%).

5 Technical Implementation

5.1 Datasets

We use three Spanish–English training sets: the European Parliament Proceedings (Europarl) (Koehn, 2005), OpenSubtitles2018 (OS) corpus (Lison and Tiedemann, 2016), and ParaCrawl[3]. Europarl contains transcripts of European Parliamentary proceedings, OpenSubtitles2018 is a corpus of movie subtitles, and ParaCrawl consists of data scraped from the web.

For training each model and for the preliminary experiments in Table 2, we use either: $\sim$2 million randomly-selected lines from OpenSubtitles2018, the $\sim$2 million line Europarl training set, a concatentaion of the aforementioned two corpora (OS+Europarl), or 14.7 million randomly-selected lines from ParaCrawl.

Development sets are: 10,000 held-out lines from OpenSubtitles2018 for the OpenSubtitles baseline, newstest2012 for the Europarl baseline, the concatenation of newstest2012 and the OpenSubtitles development set for the OS+Europarl baseline, and 3,000 held-out lines from ParaCrawl for the ParaCrawl baseline. Double-decoder models are validated by assessing the performance of each decoder separately on the development set.

The test sets are newstest2013 (3,000 lines), a combined test set of newstest2013 plus 10,000 held-out lines from OpenSubtitles2018, and 3,000 held-out lines from ParaCrawl.

5.2 Data Preprocessing

All data were punctuation-normalized, tokenized, truecased, and cleaned to a maximum sentence length of 100 words using the standard Moses scripts (Koehn et al., 2007). We applied BPE (Sennrich et al., 2015) to all data using 32,000 merge operations. Training and development data were again cleaned with `clean-corpus-n.perl` using default parameters and a maximum length of 100 BPE tokens.

To select "simple" and "complex" data for the two approaches, we apply the data selection method of Section 4.3 using the Dale-Chall readability score. All readability scores in this work were calculated after removing BPE, detruecasing, and detokenizing the data.

5.3 Models & Training

The basic model architecture is the default RNN-based encoder-decoder model with attention (Luong et al., 2015) from OpenNMT. The encoder and decoder are two-layer LSTMs (Hochreiter and Schmidhuber, 1997) with a 500-dimension hidden size and 500-dimension word embeddings. The models were trained with batch size 64 using stochastic gradient descent with the default initial learning rate of 1.0. We decay the learning rate by a factor of 0.5 starting at 50,000 steps, and further decay every subsequent 10,000 steps.

Each model was trained until performance on the validation set ceased to improve. For testing, we chose the model with lowest validation perplexity. For double-decoder models, lowest perplexity did not typically occur at the same timestep for simple and complex decoders. In that case, we chose a model that had good performance on both validation sets.

Readability was scored using the textstat[4] implementations of the Dale-Chall, Flesch-Kincaid (Grade Level), and Flesch Reading Ease formulas. BLEU was scored using `multi-bleu-detok.perl` from the Moses toolkit (Koehn et al., 2007). Statistical significance was assessed using SciPy (Jones et al., 2001).

6 Results

6.1 Quantitative Results

Tables 3 and 4 show the readability performance of data tagging and double-decoder approaches on

---

[3]https://ParaCrawl.eu/releases.html, version 1

[4]https://github.com/shivam5992/textstat

newstest2013 at different levels of data partitioning. (For example, a 30-30 partition corresponds to the case where the bottom/top 30% of data are labeled as simple/complex.) "Baseline" hereafter refers to the single encoder-decoder model trained on the original, unpartitioned dataset. These tables demonstrate effective control over average output readability for both approaches. We also conducted two-tailed paired samples t-tests[5] which demonstrated that DC, FKG, and FRE results in both decoding modes are significantly different from the baseline (p<0.001).

Partition	Mode	DC	FKG	FRE	BLEU
-	gold	8.11	9.49	59.83	-
-	baseline	7.92	9.36	61.11	27.38
50-50	simple	7.72	9.15	62.87	27.32
	complex	8.21	9.53	59.72	27.27
30-30	simple	7.45	8.98	64.41	27.14
	complex	8.58	9.79	57.57	27.09
15-15	simple	7.26	8.80	65.60	26.74
	complex	8.72	9.83	56.57	26.62
15-15*	simple	6.96	8.45	67.78	25.91
	complex	8.96	9.93	55.42	25.47
13-13	simple	7.23	8.82	65.69	26.71
	complex	8.69	9.82	56.68	26.74

Table 3: Performance on newstest2013 of data tagging approach trained on ParaCrawl. DC, FKG, and FRE are readability measures (lower indicates simpler for DC/FKG, and higher for FRE). e.g., 7.72 is the average DC score of the output in simple mode using a 50-50 partition. 15-15* means oversampling the top/bottom 15% of data (3x). All DC/FKG/FRE results are significant (p<0.001).

For all models, translations in complex mode are slightly shorter than in simple mode, and have slightly more bytes per word. In the data-tagging 15-15 mode, complex mode translations averaged 18.4 words per line, versus 19.3 in simple mode. The bytes-per-word were 6.0 and 5.7 for complex and simple mode, respectively. As data splits became less aggressive, the difference decreased. This suggests that in complex mode, the models attempt to be more concise while using longer words.

Figure 2 demonstrates that as the constraints for categorizing a sentence as "simple" or "complex" become more strict, the gap widens between the mean readability score in simple mode and com-

[5]https://docs.scipy.org/doc/scipy-1.1.0/
reference/generated/scipy.stats.ttest_
rel.html

Partition	Mode	DC	FKG	FRE	BLEU
-	gold	8.11	9.49	59.83	-
-	baseline	7.92	9.36	61.11	27.38
50-50	simple	7.57	9.00	63.71	26.41
	complex	8.30	9.59	59.16	26.71
50-50*	simple	7.41	8.87	64.59	25.71
	complex	8.43	9.66	58.46	26.01
30-30	simple	7.22	8.60	66.18	25.56
	complex	8.72	9.84	56.79	25.89
20-20	simple	6.69	7.97	69.75	23.51
	complex	9.05	9.99	54.99	24.08
15-15	simple	5.93	7.30	74.24	20.85
	complex	9.36	10.16	53.19	22.04

Table 4: Performance on newstest2013 of double-decoder models trained on ParaCrawl data. In the 50-50* setting, 50% of data is designated "simple", 50% "complex", and the most extreme 15% of simple/complex data are oversampled (3x). All DC/FKG/FRE results are significant (p<0.001).

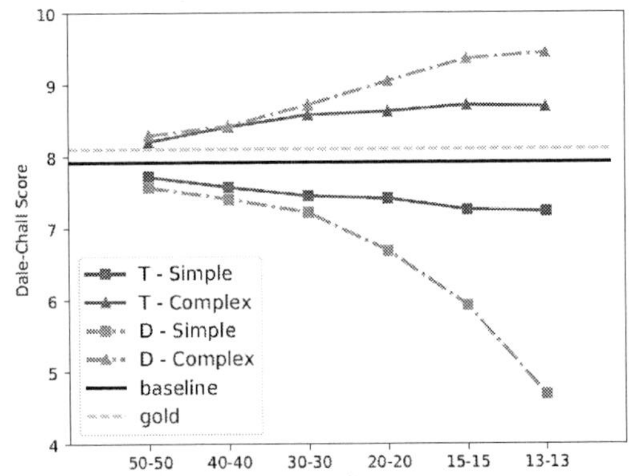

Figure 2: Readability results of newstest2013 translation in simple and complex mode for data tagging (T) and double-decoder (D) models trained on ParaCrawl.

plex mode. This holds for all three readability metrics, on all three test sets and the two training corpora that with which we experimented.

In Table 3, we see little negative effect on BLEU (Papineni et al., 2002) for the data tagging approach. In Table 4, however, we see that BLEU suffers as the double-decoder model receives less data. In the 13-13 partition, BLEU drops to 18.52 in simple mode, when the simple decoder receives only ∼1.9 million sentences, many of which are very short.

Table 5 compares the two approaches with different training and test sets, reporting the difference between the baseline Dale-Chall score and the readability of translated test sets in simple and complex modes. We observe that both methods

Training Corpus	Approach	Test Set		
		ParaCrawl	**OpenSubtitles+Europarl**	**Newstest2013**
ParaCrawl	T-15/15	-0.84 / +0.73	-0.74 / +2.79	-0.67 / +0.79
	D-15/15	**-2.41 / +1.53**	**-1.74 / +4.36**	**-1.99 / +1.44**
OpenSubtitles+Europarl	T-40/40	-0.90 / +0.61	-0.64 / **+2.67**	-0.80 / **+0.70**
	D-40/40	**-1.99 / +0.66**	**-1.11** /+2.53	**-1.69** / +0.67

Table 5: Performance of high-performing models with double-decoder (D) and data tagging (T) approaches on three test sets. The left/right number is the difference in Dale-Chall score between the baseline and the simple/complex translation. Model with the larger difference is bolded.

System	BLEU	Human Eval
Baseline	27.38	6.54
Weaker Baseline	24.34	5.64
Complex	24.08	5.75
Simple	23.51	5.84

Table 6: Average model score in human evaluation for models trained on Paracrawl. Complex and Simple represent complex and simple modes for the double-decoder approach with a 20-20 data partition.

work well for all six train-test pairs, and that the double-decoder method generally makes the simple translations simpler and the complex translations more complex, than the data tagging approach.

6.2 Qualitative Results

The qualitative examples in Tables 7 were produced when translating newstest2013 using the data tagging and double-decoder approaches.

We observe from the examples that both approaches successfully control the complexity of output sentences. Furthermore, the baseline appears an appropriate intermediary between the two complexity levels; For the baseline translation "This attitude is a deplorable vision of future.", the data tagging approach changes *"deplorable vision"* to *"terrible view"* in simple mode to decrease complexity. In complex mode, however, the model changes *"is"* to *"implies"* to make the sentence even more complex, keeping *"deplorable vision"*. We also see change in sentence structure. For example, in simple mode the data tagging approach produces, *"there is..."*, while in complex mode it produces, *"...occurred"* or *"...existed"*.

In the double-decoder approach we observe some loss in meaning for certain sentences as the threshold for training sentences to be qualified as simple or complex becomes more restrictive.

6.3 Human Evaluation

We performed human evaluation to determine whether the lower BLEU score observed in more extreme data-partitioning conditions in the double-decoder approach was the result of true loss in translation quality, or desirable swapping of simple/complex words. We randomly sampled 50 translations from newstest2013 and obtained the translations from the double-decoder 20-20 partition setting, along with the baseline model and a weaker baseline trained to achieve comparable BLEU to that of the double-decoder approach. Nine English-speaking adults each scored approximately one-third of the sampled translations on a 10-point scale so that each translation received three scores. Reviewers were instructed to score how well each translation matched the meaning of the reference, along with the fluency of the translation. Examples were presented in blocks with the reference translation followed by the four system translations in a random order for each block. Participants each scored 15 or 20 blocks.

In Table 6, we show the average score that translations from each system received. We observe that while the drop in BLEU in Table 4 reflects some lowered translation quality as judged by human reviewers, the loss in quality is smaller than the BLEU depreciation makes it seem. When compared to a baseline model with comparable BLEU to that of the "simple" and "complex" modes (the "weaker" baseline), the double-decoder approaches fair better in human evaluation despite having lower BLEU scores. This indicates that BLEU over-penalizes models trained to control readability level, and that readability-controlled translations are better than they appear based on BLEU alone.

Note that in this section we only performed human evaluation on outputs from the double-

Src	*Por este motivo, no creo que se haya producido una ruptura tan drástica como en el caso de Libia.*
Ref	*Therefore I do not think that this was as dramatic a fracture as was the case in the matters regarding Libia.*
Baseline	For this reason, I don't believe that there was such a drastic rupture as in the case of Libya.
Simple	For this reason, I don't believe that **there is** a drastic **break** as in Libya.
Complex	For this reason, I don't believe that a drastic **rupture occurred** as in Libya's case.
Src	*Esta actitud supone una deplorable visión de futuro.*
Ref	*This is woefully short-sighted.*
Baseline	This attitude is a deplorable vision of future.
Simple	This attitude **is** a **terrible view** of the future.
Complex	This attitude **implies** a **deplorable vision** of future.
Src	*Pero mis provocaciones están dirigidas a que se inicie una conversación.*
Ref	*But my provocations are aimed at starting conversation.*
Baseline	But my provocations are directed to start a conversation.
Simple	But my provocations are **meant** to **start** a conversation.
Complex	But my provocations are **directed** to **initiate** a conversation.
Src	*No todos se sienten contentos con el hecho de que...*
Ref	*Not everyone is happy that...*
Baseline	Not everyone feels happy with the fact that...
Simple	**Not everyone feels happy** with the fact that...
Complex	**Not all are satisfied** with the fact that...

Table 7: Example translations of newstest2013 in simple/complex mode from models trained on ParaCrawl (15-15). The first two examples come from the data tagging approach (15-15), and the second two come from the double-decoder approach (15-15).

decoder 20-20 model (which had a ∼3–4 BLEU drop compared to the baseline) whereby we do observe some loss in translation quality from the baseline. However, for the models which achieve very similar BLEU scores to the baseline, such as the data-tagging 50-50 and 30-30 model, there may be no loss in translation quality. Human evaluation could verify this notion.

6.4 Attention Visualization

In Figure 3, we see a heatmap of attention when the data tagging approach translated the same sentence in simple and complex modes. When choosing the word "*adversely*" in complex mode versus "*negatively*" in simple mode, we see attention placed on the complexity indicator tags "*czxc*" and "*szxc*". This suggests that the model attended to the complexity tag when deciding which word to use.

In many cases, however, the difference in word choice is not reflected by attention to the complexity tag. This could be because the difference in attention values is too small for humans to detect the color difference in the heatmap. A more plausible explanation is that information about the reading level has been passed to the hidden states at all positions by the bi-LSTM, so that the decoder doesn't need to pay attention to the complexity token (the last hidden state) to make different word choices.

6.5 Adaption to Multiple Reading Level Setting

Our approaches can be adapted to the multiple reading level setting. We experimented using the data tagging approach with the data equally-partitioned into five reading levels (Reading Level A-E), with A being the lowest and E the highest. The results are given in Table 8. We observe effective control over reading level at this finer level of granularity. Similar BLEU scores to that of the baseline indicate that different modes maintain translation quality.

6.6 Analysis and Discussion

We have demonstrated success both raising and lowering the reading level of test sets using two different methods. The results on multiple test sets and training corpora suggest that our methods are general and applicable beyond the scope

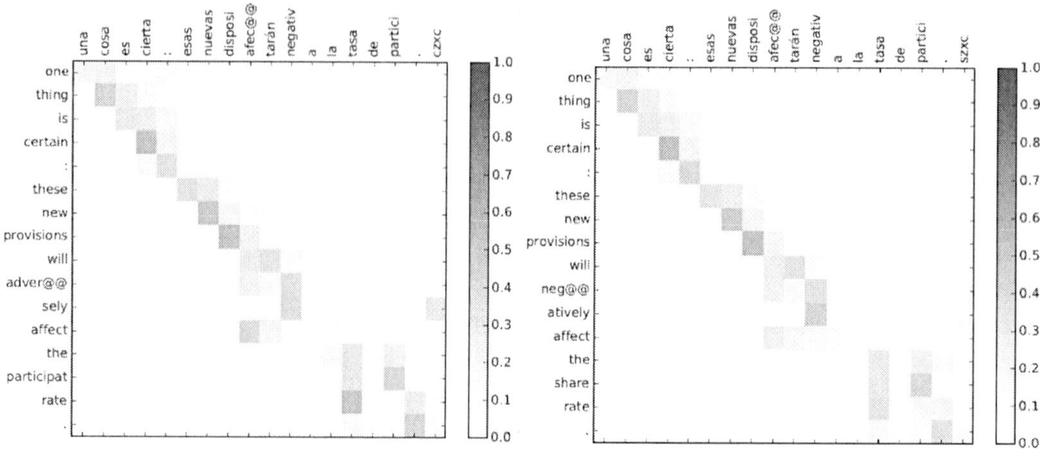

Figure 3: Attention visualization in simple vs. complex mode of data tagging approach (40-40 partition, trained on ParaCrawl).

Specified Readability	FKG	DC	BLEU
Baseline	9.36	7.92	27.38
Reading Level A	8.66	7.22	26.81
Reading Level B	9.01	7.67	27.14
Reading Level C	9.34	8.10	27.29
Reading Level D	9.61	8.49	27.12
Reading Level E	10.03	9.06	26.17

Table 8: Readability performance of the data tagging method at five levels of readability, trained on ParaCrawl and tested on newstest2013.

of the datasets we chose. Our qualitative examples demonstrate that though BLEU score depreciates, some of the decrease reflects correct changes towards our goal of adjusting reading level.

Translations in "simple" mode sometimes end early or are too short (in the double-decoder ParaCrawl 15-15 model, specifically). Simple training sentences tend to be shorter than complex training sentences, which may teach the simple decoder to produce short sentences.

We observe that the double-decoder is generally able to pull the mean readability of sentences translated in simple vs. complex mode farther apart than the data tagging approach. The separated decoders become more specialized towards creating sentences of particular relative readability levels, which may explain this observation.

We also observed the data tagging approach retaining higher BLEU than the double-decoder. We suspect this is because in the data tagging approach, we retain sentences of an intermediate complexity level during training, and this extra data helps maintain high BLEU. On the other hand, the double-decoder model with a 15-15 data partition receives ~2.2 million simple sentences and ~2.2 million complex sentences. This means that the encoder is trained on less than 30% of the data as the baseline, and each decoder is trained on approximately 15% of the data. This lower-data condition likely contributes to the lower BLEU score for double-decoder models, and explains why the data tagging approach does not suffer the same loss in BLEU. This also suggests that the data tagging approach may be preferable in low-resource settings. That said, human evaluators rated translations from the double-decoder approach higher than a baseline with similar BLEU performance.

7   Related Work

Our work is similar to style transfer and work controlling style during natural language generation (e.g., (Carlson et al., 2017; Fu et al., 2017; John et al., 2018; Ficler and Goldberg, 2017)), and to the text simplification literature (e.g., (Napoles and Dredze, 2010; Nisioi et al., 2017)). In style transfer, NMT methods using double-decoder architectures have been used, for instance, to output formal vs. informal or positive vs. negative versions of a source sentence (e.g., (Fu et al., 2017; Prabhumoye et al., 2018)). Sennrich et al. (2016) use tokens similar to our complexity tags in NMT to specify politeness in their English-German output. Vanmassenhove et al. (2018) and Kobus et al. (2016) retain gender information and domain information, respectively, in NMT through a tag to improve the translation quality.

As far as we are aware, we are the first authors to use NMT to both reduce and increase the complexity of translations. Unlike most of the text simplification literature, we simplify output cross-linguistically and also increase text complexity. In statistical machine translation, Stymne et al. (2013) translate and simplify output, while Niu et al. (2017) control formality in French–English translation. Štajner and Popović (2016) investigate how simplifying source-side sentences affects adequacy and fluency in English–Serbian translation. Interestingly, we notice qualitative similarities between our "complex" translations and the formal output of Niu et al. (2017), though the authors did not frame these qualitative differences as increases in complexity.

Prior work in machine translation and NLP has focused on readability assessment and text simplification. For readability assessment, a data-driven method is proposed in Le et al. (2018) for assessing the readability of document text, whereas Ciobanu et al. (2015) investigated the readability of the MT system output with standard metrics. Jones et al. (2005) also investigated the readability of MT and ASR system output but with human evaluation. As for text simplification, Hardmeier et al. (2013) proposes a document-level decoder for SMT and mentioned a case study that utilizes document-wide features to improve the readability of text. Contrary to Stymne et al. (2013), Xu et al. (2016) designed a new training objective for SMT text simplification. Similar to Le et al. (2018), Ciobanu et al. (2015), and Jones et al. (2005), we adopted evaluation metrics for assessing the MT output. However, the readability constraint is taken into account during training in our proposed approaches. Stymne et al. (2013) introduces document-level features such as type/token ratios and lexical consistency as input to the MT system. On the other hand, our approaches at most require an additional simplicity/complexity tag. Different from Xu et al. (2016) in which new training objective is proposed for text simplification, our NMT training objective remains the same.

8 Conclusion

In this work, we are the first authors to address the important task of controlling the reading level of machine translation output, and provide the first results. This work is important for practitioners who wish to control the simplicity or complexity of text that their machine translation system produces.

We develop two methods for controlling the reading level of output translations in NMT. Both of our proposed models successfully increase or decrease the reading level of multiple test sets when trained on different corpora, and have good qualitative results. Furthermore, our human evaluation indicates that the readability-level controlled translations are better than a baseline which had higher BLEU.

Notably, our data tagging approach can be deployed immediately on existing NMT systems with no architectural changes. We demonstrate a trade-off between more effective control of reading level and BLEU score, particularly with the double-decoder approach. As the data partition becomes more aggressive, the difference in reading level between the two modes increases, but BLEU score drops. We show that this effect can be mitigated by oversampling.

In the future, we plan to experiment with different language pairs and readability scorers. We also plan to discard sentences with very low readability scores and filter training corpora to exclude low-quality examples, which Junczys-Dowmunt (2018) demonstrated can severely degrade model performance. We expect these methods will help us retain better BLEU. Furthermore, we will use the state-of-the-art transformer model which we expect to provide improved BLEU and greater control over reading level in the data tagging method, because the complexity tag will contribute to each word's representation via self-attention (Vaswani et al., 2017).

Finally, we observed exciting effects related to formality which are outside the scope of this paper. Particularly when training on Europarl and Open-Subtitles2018 data, we observed that sentences trained in "complex" mode appeared more formal than those trained in "simple" mode; most contractions were removed, and words appeared more formal. We plan to repeat these experiments, and have observed promising first results.

Acknowledgements

The authors would like to thank Jason Eisner, Huda Khayrallah, Shuoyang Ding, Arya McCarthy, and Rebecca Knowles for their insightful comments and advice. We also thank our anonymous reviewers for their helpful comments.

References

Amstad, Toni. 1978. *Wie verständlich sind unsere Zeitungen?* Studenten-Schreib-Service.

Björnsson, Carl-Hugo. 1968. *Läsbarhet: hur skall man som författare nå fram till läsarna?* Bokförlaget Liber.

Carlson, Keith, Allen Riddell, and Daniel Rockmore. 2017. Zero-shot style transfer in text using recurrent neural networks. *arXiv preprint arXiv:1711.04731*.

Chall, Jeanne Sternlicht and Edgar Dale. 1995. *Readability revisited: The new Dale-Chall readability formula*. Brookline Books.

Ciobanu, Alina Maria, Liviu P Dinu, and Flaviu Pepelea. 2015. Readability assessment of translated texts. In *Proceedings of the International Conference Recent Advances in Natural Language Processing*, pages 97–103.

Ficler, Jessica and Yoav Goldberg. 2017. Controlling linguistic style aspects in neural language generation. *arXiv preprint arXiv:1707.02633*.

Flesch, Rudolph. 1948. A new readability yardstick. *Journal of applied psychology*, 32(3):221.

François, Thomas and Eleni Miltsakaki. 2012. Do nlp and machine learning improve traditional readability formulas? In *Proceedings of the First Workshop on Predicting and Improving Text Readability for target reader populations*, pages 49–57. Association for Computational Linguistics.

Fu, Zhenxin, Xiaoye Tan, Nanyun Peng, Dongyan Zhao, and Rui Yan. 2017. Style transfer in text: Exploration and evaluation. *arXiv preprint arXiv:1711.06861*.

Hardmeier, Christian, Sara Stymne, Jörg Tiedemann, and Joakim Nivre. 2013. Docent: A document-level decoder for phrase-based statistical machine translation. In *ACL 2013 (51st Annual Meeting of the Association for Computational Linguistics); 4-9 August 2013; Sofia, Bulgaria*, pages 193–198. Association for Computational Linguistics.

Hochreiter, Sepp and Jürgen Schmidhuber. 1997. Long short-term memory. *Neural computation*, 9(8):1735–1780.

John, Vineet, Lili Mou, Hareesh Bahuleyan, and Olga Vechtomova. 2018. Disentangled representation learning for non-parallel text style transfer. *arXiv preprint arXiv:1808.04339*.

Jones, Eric, Travis Oliphant, Pearu Peterson, et al. 2001–. SciPy: Open source scientific tools for Python.

Jones, Douglas, Edward Gibson, Wade Shen, Neil Granoien, Martha Herzog, Douglas Reynolds, and Clifford Weinstein. 2005. Measuring human readability of machine generated text: three case studies in speech recognition and machine translation. In *Acoustics, Speech, and Signal Processing, 2005. Proceedings.(ICASSP'05). IEEE International Conference on*, volume 5, pages v–1009. IEEE.

Junczys-Dowmunt, Marcin. 2018. Microsoft's submission to the WMT2018 news translation task: How I learned to stop worrying and love the data. *CoRR*, abs/1809.00196.

Kincaid, J Peter, Robert P Fishburne Jr, Richard L Rogers, and Brad S Chissom. 1975. Derivation of new readability formulas (automated readability index, fog count and flesch reading ease formula) for navy enlisted personnel.

Klein, Guillaume, Yoon Kim, Yuntian Deng, Jean Senellart, and Alexander M. Rush. 2017. OpenNMT: Open-source toolkit for neural machine translation. In *Proc. ACL*.

Kobus, Catherine, Josep Crego, and Jean Senellart. 2016. Domain control for neural machine translation. *arXiv preprint arXiv:1612.06140*.

Koehn, Philipp, Hieu Hoang, Alexandra Birch, Chris Callison-Burch, Marcello Federico, Nicola Bertoldi, Brooke Cowan, Wade Shen, Christine Moran, Richard Zens, et al. 2007. Moses: Open source toolkit for statistical machine translation. In *Proceedings of the 45th annual meeting of the ACL on interactive poster and demonstration sessions*, pages 177–180. Association for Computational Linguistics.

Koehn, Philipp. 2005. Europarl: A parallel corpus for statistical machine translation. In *MT summit*, volume 5, pages 79–86.

Le, Dieu-Thu, Cam-Tu Nguyen, and Xiaoliang Wang. 2018. Joint learning of frequency and word embeddings for multilingual readability assessment. In *Proceedings of the 5th Workshop on Natural Language Processing Techniques for Educational Applications*, pages 103–107.

Lison, Pierre and Jörg Tiedemann. 2016. Opensubtitles2016: Extracting large parallel corpora from movie and tv subtitles.

Lucisano, Pietro and Maria Emanuela Piemontese. 1988. Gulpease: una formula per la predizione della difficoltà dei testi in lingua italiana. *Scuola e città*, 3(31):110–124.

Luong, Minh-Thang, Hieu Pham, and Christopher D Manning. 2015. Effective approaches to attention-based neural machine translation. *arXiv preprint arXiv:1508.04025*.

Napoles, Courtney and Mark Dredze. 2010. Learning simple wikipedia: A cogitation in ascertaining abecedarian language. In *Proceedings of the NAACL HLT 2010 Workshop on Computational Linguistics and Writing: Writing Processes and Authoring Aids*, pages 42–50. Association for Computational Linguistics.

Nisioi, Sergiu, Sanja Štajner, Simone Paolo Ponzetto, and Liviu P Dinu. 2017. Exploring neural text simplification models. In *Proceedings of the 55th Annual Meeting of the Association for Computational Linguistics (Volume 2: Short Papers)*, volume 2, pages 85–91.

Niu, Xing, Marianna Martindale, and Marine Carpuat. 2017. A study of style in machine translation: Controlling the formality of machine translation output. In *Proceedings of the 2017 Conference on Empirical Methods in Natural Language Processing*, pages 2814–2819.

Papineni, Kishore, Salim Roukos, Todd Ward, and Wei-Jing Zhu. 2002. Bleu: a method for automatic evaluation of machine translation. In *Proceedings of the 40th annual meeting on association for computational linguistics*, pages 311–318. Association for Computational Linguistics.

Prabhumoye, Shrimai, Yulia Tsvetkov, Ruslan Salakhutdinov, and Alan W Black. 2018. Style transfer through back-translation. *arXiv preprint arXiv:1804.09000*.

Sennrich, Rico, Barry Haddow, and Alexandra Birch. 2015. Neural machine translation of rare words with subword units. *arXiv preprint arXiv:1508.07909*.

Sennrich, Rico, Barry Haddow, and Alexandra Birch. 2016. Controlling politeness in neural machine translation via side constraints. In *Proceedings of the 2016 Conference of the North American Chapter of the Association for Computational Linguistics: Human Language Technologies*, pages 35–40.

Štajner, Sanja and Maja Popović. 2016. Can text simplification help machine translation? In *Proceedings of the 19th Annual Conference of the European Association for Machine Translation*, pages 230–242.

Stymne, Sara, Jörg Tiedemann, Christian Hardmeier, and Joakim Nivre. 2013. Statistical machine translation with readability constraints. In *Proceedings of the 19th Nordic Conference of Computational Linguistics (NODALIDA 2013); May 22-24; 2013; Oslo University; Norway. NEALT Proceedings Series 16*, number 085, pages 375–386. Linköping University Electronic Press.

Vanmassenhove, Eva, Christian Hardmeier, and Andy Way. 2018. Getting gender right in neural machine translation. In *Proceedings of the 2018 Conference on Empirical Methods in Natural Language Processing*, pages 3003–3008, Brussels, Belgium, October-November. Association for Computational Linguistics.

Vaswani, Ashish, Noam Shazeer, Niki Parmar, Jakob Uszkoreit, Llion Jones, Aidan N Gomez, Łukasz Kaiser, and Illia Polosukhin. 2017. Attention is all you need. In *Advances in Neural Information Processing Systems*, pages 5998–6008.

Xu, Wei, Courtney Napoles, Ellie Pavlick, Quanze Chen, and Chris Callison-Burch. 2016. Optimizing statistical machine translation for text simplification. *Transactions of the Association for Computational Linguistics*, 4:401–415.

A Call for Prudent Choice of Subword Merge Operations in Neural Machine Translation

Shuoyang Ding† **Adithya Renduchintala**† **Kevin Duh**†‡
† Center for Language and Speech Processing
‡ Human Language Technology Center of Excellence
Johns Hopkins University
{dings, adi.r}@jhu.edu kevinduh@cs.jhu.edu

Abstract

Most neural machine translation systems are built upon subword units extracted by methods such as Byte-Pair Encoding (BPE) or wordpiece. However, the choice of *number of merge operations* is generally made by following existing recipes. In this paper, we conduct a systematic exploration on different numbers of BPE merge operations to understand how it interacts with the model architecture, the strategy to build vocabularies and the language pair. Our exploration could provide guidance for selecting proper BPE configurations in the future. Most prominently: we show that for LSTM-based architectures, it is necessary to experiment with a wide range of different BPE operations as there is no typical optimal BPE configuration, whereas for Transformer architectures, smaller BPE size tends to be a typically optimal choice. We urge the community to make prudent choices with subword merge operations, as our experiments indicate that a sub-optimal BPE configuration alone could easily reduce the system performance by 3–4 BLEU points.

1 Introduction

While achieving state-of-the-art results, it is a common constraint that Neural Machine Translation (NMT) (Sutskever et al., 2014; Bahdanau et al., 2015; Luong et al., 2015; Vaswani et al., 2017) systems are only capable of generating a closed set of symbols. Systems with large vocabulary sizes are too hard to fit onto GPU for training, as the word embedding is generally the most parameter-dense component in the NMT architecture. For that reason, subword methods, such as Byte-Pair Encoding (BPE) (Sennrich et al., 2016), are very widely used for building NMT systems. The general idea of these methods is to exploit the pre-defined vocabulary space optimally by performing a minimum amount of word segmentations in the training set.

However, very few existing literature carefully examines what is the best practice regarding application of subword methods. As hyper-parameter search is expensive, there is a tendency to simply use existing recipes. This is especially true for the *number of merge operations* when people are using BPE, although this configuration is closely correlated with the granularity of the segmentation on the training corpus, thus having direct influence on the final system performance. Prior to this work, Denkowski and Neubig (2017) recommended 32k BPE merge operation in their work on trustable baselines for NMT, while Cherry et al. (2018) contradicted their study by showing that character-based models outperform 32k BPE. Both of these studies are based on the LSTM-based architectures (Sutskever et al., 2014; Bahdanau et al., 2015; Luong et al., 2015). To the best of our knowledge, there is no work that looks into the same problem for the Transformer architecture extensively.[1]

In this paper, we aim to provide guidance for this hyper-parameter choice by examining the interaction between MT system performance with the choice of BPE merge operations under the *low-*

---

[1] For reference, the original Transformer paper by Vaswani et al. (2017) used BPE merge operations that resulted in 37k joint vocabulary size.

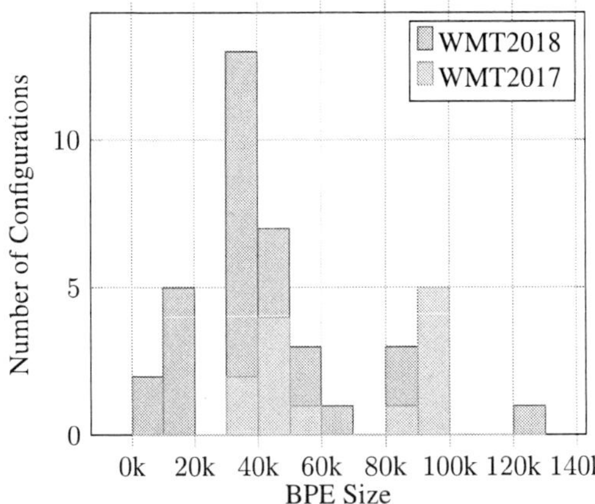

Figure 1: Histogram of BPE merge operations used for in WMT papers from 2017-2018.

resource setting. We conjecture that lower resource systems will be more prone to the performance variance introduced by this choice, and the effect might vary with the choice of model architectures and languages. To verify this, we conduct experiments with 5 different architecture setup on 4 language pairs of IWSLT 2016 dataset. In general, we discover that there is no typical optimal choice of merge operations for LSTM-based architectures, but for Transformer architectures, the optimal choice lays between 0–4k, and systems using the traditional 32k merge operations could lose as much as 4 points in BLEU score compared to the optimal choice.

2   Related Work

Currently, the most common subword methods are BPE (Sennrich et al., 2016), wordpiece (Wu et al., 2016) and subword regularization (Kudo, 2018). Subword regularization introduces Bayesian sampling method to incorporate more segmentation variety into the training corpus, thus improving the systems' ability to handle segmentation ambiguity. Yet, the effect of such method is not very thoroughly tested. In this work we will focus on the BPE/wordpiece method. Because the two methods are very similar, throughout the rest of the paper, we will refer to the BPE/wordpiece method as *BPE method* unless otherwise specified.

To the best of our knowledge, no prior work systematically reports findings for a wide range of systems that cover different architectures and both directions of translation for multiple language pairs. While some work has conducted experiments with different BPE settings, they are generally very lim-

ited in the range of configurations explored. For example, Sennrich et al. (2016), the original paper that proposed the BPE method, compared the system performance when using 60k separate BPE and 90k joint BPE. They found 90k to work better and used that for their subsequent winning WMT 2017 new translation shared task submission (Sennrich et al., 2017). Wu et al. (2016), on the other hand, found 8k–32k merge operations achieving optimal BLEU score performance for the wordpiece method. Denkowski and Neubig (2017) explored several hyperparameter settings, including number of BPE merge operations, to establish strong baseline for NMT on LSTM-based architectures. While Denkowski and Neubig (2017) showed that BPE models are clearly better than word-level models, their experiments on 16k and 32k BPE configuration did not show much difference. They therefore recommended "32K as a generally effective vocabulary size and 16K as a contrastive condition when building systems on less than 1 million parallel sentences". However, while studying deep character-based LSTM-based translation models, Cherry et al. (2018) also ran experiments for BPE configurations between 0–32k, and found that the system performance deteriorates with the increasing number of BPE merge operations. Recently, Renduchintala et al. (2018) also showed that it is important to tune the number of BPE merge operations and found no typical optimal BPE configuration for their LSTM-based architecture while sweeping over several language pairs in the low-resource setting. It should be noticed that the results from the above studies actually contradict with each other, and there is still no clear consensus as to what is the best practice for BPE application. Moreover, all the work surveyed above was done with LSTM-based architectures. To this day, we are not aware of any work that explored the interaction of BPE with the Transformer architecture.

To give the readers a better landscape of the current practice, we gather all 44 papers that have been accepted by the research track of Conference of Machine Translation (WMT) through 2017 and 2018. We count different configurations used in a single paper as separate data points. Hence, after removing 8 papers for which BPE is irrelevant, we still manage to obtain 42 data points, shown in Figure 1. It first comes to our attention that 30k–40k is the most popular range for the number of BPE merge operations. This is mostly driven by the popularity of two configurations: 30k and 32k. 80k–100k is also pretty popular, which is largely due to configurations 89.5k and 90k. Upon closer examination, we realized that most papers that used 90k were following the configuration in Sennrich et al. (2017), the winning NMT system in the WMT 2017 news translation shared task, but this setup somehow became less popular in 2018. On the other hand, although we are unable to confirm a clear trend-setter, 30k–50k always seems to be a common choice. Moreover, although smaller BPE size got more popular among configurations in 2018, none of the work published in WMT has ever explored BPE size lower than 6k. All of the above observations support our initial claim that we as a community have not yet systematically investigated the entire range of BPE merge operations used in our experiments.

3 Analysis Setup

Our goal is to compare the impact of different numbers of BPE merge operations on multiple language pairs and multiple NMT architectures. We experiment with the following BPE merge operation setup: 0 (character-level), 0.5k, 1k, 2k, 4k, 8k, 16k, and 32k, on both translation directions of 4 language pairs and 5 architectures. Additionally, we include 6 more language pairs (with 2 architectures) to study the interaction between linguistic attributes and BPE merge operations.

3.1 Dataset

Our experiments are conducted with the all the data from IWSLT 2016 shared task, covering translation of English (en) from and into Arabic (ar), Czech (cs), French (fr) and German (de). As this dataset contains multiple dev and test sets, we concatenate all the dev sets into a single dev set and do the same for the test set as well. To increase language coverage, we also conduct extra experiments with 6 more language pairs from the TED corpus (Qi et al., 2018). We use Brazilian Portuguese (pt), Hebrew (he), Russian (ru), Turkish (tr), Polish (pl) and Hungarian (hu) as our extra languages, paired with English. All the data are tokenized and true-cased using the accompanying script from Moses decoder (Koehn et al., 2007) before training and applying BPE models.[2]

We use subword-nmt[3] to train and apply BPE

to our data. Unless otherwise specified, all of our BPE models are trained on the concatenation of the source and target training corpus, i.e. the *joint BPE* scheme in Sennrich et al. (2016). We use SacreBLEU (Post, 2018) to compute BLEU score.[4]

3.2 Architecture

We build our NMT system with fairseq (Ott et al., 2019). We use two pre-configured architectures in fairseq for our study, namely `lstm-wiseman-iwslt-de-en` (referred to as `tiny-lstm`) and `transformer-iwslt-de-en` (referred to as `deep-transformer`), which are the model architecture tuned for their benchmark system trained on IWSLT 2014 German-English data. However, we find (as can be seen from Table 1) that the number of parameters in `lstm-tiny` is a magnitude lower than `deep-transformer` mainly due to the fact that the former has a single-layer uni-directional encoder and a single-layer decoder, while the later has 6 encoder and decoder layers. For a fairer comparison we include a `deep-lstm` architecture with 6 encoder and decoder layers which roughly matches the number of parameters in `deep-transformer`. To study the effect of BPE on relatively smaller architectures, we also include `shallow-transformer` and `shallow-lstm` architectures, both with 2 encoder and decoder layers. The `shallow-lstm` also use bidirectional LSTM layers in the encoder. These two architectures also roughly match each other in terms of number of parameters. With these 5 architectures, we believe we have covered a wide range of common choices in NMT architectures, especially in low-resource settings. We use Adam optimizer (Kingma and Ba, 2014) for all the experiments we run. For Transformer experiments, we use the learning rate scheduling settings in Vaswani et al. (2017), including the inverse square root learning rate scheduler, 4000 warmup updates and initial warmup learning rate of 1×10^{-7}. For most LSTM experiments, we just use learning rate 0.001 from the start and reduce the learning rate by half every time the loss function fails to improve on the development set. However, we find that for `deep-lstm` architecture, such learning rate schedule tends to be unstable, which is very similar to training Transformer without the warmup

---

[2]Data processing scripts available at `https://github.com/shuoyangd/prudent-bpe`.

[3]`https://pypi.org/project/subword-nmt/0.3.5/`

[4]SacreBLEU signature:BLEU+case.mixed+numrefs.1+ smooth.exp+tok.13a+version.1.2.12.

	bi-dir	d_{enc}	d_{dec}	d_{emb}	l	N_h	N_p
shallow-transformer	N/A	512	512	512	2	4	18.8M
deep-transformer	N/A	512	512	512	6	4	39.8M
tiny-lstm	no	256	256	256	1	1	5.6M
shallow-lstm	yes	384	384	384	2	1	16.4M
deep-lstm	yes	384	384	384	6	1	35.3M

Table 1: Information of the 5 architectures used for analysis. **bi-dir** is a boolean representing whether the encoder is bidirectional. d_{enc}, d_{dec} and d_{emb} are dimension of encoder, decoder and source/target word embedding, respectively. l is the number of encoder/decoder layers. N_h is the number of attention heads, while N_p is the number of parameters of the model at 8k BPE merge operations.

learning rate schedule. Applying the same warmup schedule as Transformer experiments works for most `deep-lstm` architecture except for de-en experiments as BPE size 16k and 32k, for which we have to apply 8000 warmup updates. Per the experiment setting in Vaswani et al. (2017), we also apply label smoothing with $\varepsilon_{ls} = 0.1$ for all of our Transformer experiments.

4 Analysis

4.1 Analysis 1: Architectures

Table 2 shows the BLEU score for Transformer systems with BPE merge operations ranging from 0 to 32k. The Transformer experiments show a clear trend; large BPE settings of 16k-32k are *not* optimal for low-resource settings. We see that regardless of the direction of translation, the best BLEU score for Transformer-based architectures are somewhere in the 0-1k range. Although there is not much drop for 2k-4k, there is generally a drastic performance drop as the number of BPE merge operation is increased beyond 8k. It should also be noted that the difference between the best and the worst performance is around 3 BLEU points (refer to the δ column in Table 2), larger than the improvements claimed in many machine translation papers.

Table 3 shows the BLEU score for LSTM-based architectures trained with BPE merge operations ranging from 0 to 32k. Among the three tables, the `shallow-lstm` architecture has the minimal variation with regard to different merge operation choices. For `tiny-lstm`, we observe a drastic performance drop between BPE merge operations 0/500 or 500/1k. But aside from these two settings, the variation is of similar scale to `shallow-lstm`. For `deep-lstm`, the variation is even larger than the Transformer architectures, and compared to `tiny-lstm` and `shallow-lstm`, the optimal BPE configuration

shifts to BPE sizes on the smaller end. However, we have also noticed that the overall absolute BLEU score of `deep-lstm` is lower than `shallow-lstm` despite more parameter is being used. We conjecture that the larger variation and lower BLEU score from the `deep-lstm` experiments is largely due to the overfitting effect on the small training data. Despite this effect, moving from tiny to deep model, we observe a trend that deeper models tends to make use of smaller BPE size better. In general, we conclude that unlike Transformer architecture, there is no typical optimal BPE configuration setting for the LSTM architecture. Because of this noisiness, we urge that future work using LSTM-based baselines tune their BPE configuration in a wider range on a development set to the extent possible, in order to ensure reasonable comparison.

4.2 Analysis 2: Joint vs Separate BPE

Another question that is not extensively explored in the existing literature is whether *joint BPE* is the definitive better approach to apply BPE. The alternative way, referred to here as separate BPE, is to build separate models for source and target side of the parallel corpus. Sennrich et al. (2016) conducted experiments with both joint and separate BPE, but these experiments were conducted with different BPE size, and not much analysis was conducted on the separate BPE model. Huck et al. (2017) is the only other work we are aware of that used with separate BPE models for their study. It was mentioned that their joint BPE vocabulary of 59500 yielded a German vocabulary twice as large as English, which is an undesirable characteristic for their study.

Before comparing the system performance, we would like to systematically understand how the resulting vocabulary is different when jointly and separately applying BPE. Table 4 shows the two

		0	0.5k	1k	2k	4k	8k	16k	32k	δ
deep-transformer	ar-en	30.3	30.8	30.6	30.5	30.4	29.8	28	27.5	3.3
	cs-en	24.6	23.3	23.0	22.7	21.2	22.6	20.6	21.0	4.0
	de-en	28.1	28.6	28.0	28.4	27.7	27.5	26.7	25.2	3.4
	fr-en	28.8	29.8	29.6	29.3	28.7	28.5	27.5	26.6	3.2
	en-ar	12.6	13.0	12.1	12.3	11.8	11.3	10.7	10.6	2.4
	en-cs	17.3	17.1	16.7	16.4	16.1	15.6	14.7	13.8	3.5
	en-de	26.1	27.4	27.4	26.1	26.3	26.1	25.8	23.9	3.5
	en-fr	25.2	25.6	25.3	25.5	25.3	24.7	24.1	22.8	2.8
shallow-transformer	ar-en	26.4	27.9	28.7	28.5	28.6	27.7	26.2	25.5	3.2
	cs-en	22.4	22.6	22.3	21.8	21.7	21.1	21.1	20.1	2.5
	de-en	25.5	27.4	27.1	27.3	27.1	25.9	24.6	23.7	3.7
	fr-en	26.3	28.0	28.9	28.0	28.0	27.4	26.1	26.1	2.7
	en-ar	11.7	11.2	11.5	11.0	11.3	10.5	9.5	9.0	2.7
	en-cs	16.4	16.7	16.0	16.2	14.4	14.2	13.9	13.9	2.8
	en-de	23.8	25.7	25.4	25.3	25.2	24.3	24.1	22.1	3.6
	en-fr	23.5	24.7	25.1	24.6	24.5	23.8	22.7	22.1	3.0

Table 2: BLEU score for Transformer architectures with multiple BPE configurations. Each score is color-coded by its rank among scores from different BPE configurations in the same row. δ is the difference between the best and worst BLEU score of each row.

		0	0.5k	1k	2k	4k	8k	16k	32k	δ
tiny-lstm	ar-en	20.6	22.1	22.4	23.0	24.1	24.2	24.2	24.0	3.6
	cs-en	17.8	19.1	18.8	19.0	19.2	19.5	20.7	19.1	2.9
	de-en	21.1	22.5	23.2	23.1	23.1	23.1	23.6	23.0	2.5
	fr-en	21.8	25.3	25.3	25.4	25.1	25.3	25.1	24.7	3.6
	en-ar	8.5	8.7	9.3	8.8	8.8	8.6	8.8	8.8	0.8
	en-cs	11.5	12.3	13.7	13.2	13.0	14.1	14.4	13.2	2.9
	en-de	18.2	20.8	21.4	21.1	21.9	21.6	21.0	21.6	3.7
	en-fr	19.9	20.4	20.7	21.8	21.3	21.0	21.3	21.3	1.7
shallow-lstm	ar-en	27.5	27.2	27.1	27.6	27.4	26.7	27.5	26.3	1.3
	cs-en	22.2	22.2	22.2	22.9	22.7	23.0	22.8	21.6	1.4
	de-en	25.7	25.9	26.0	25.9	26.4	26.3	26.1	26.5	0.8
	fr-en	27.6	26.7	27.7	28.4	27.9	27.7	28.5	27.5	1.8
	en-ar	11.0	11.0	10.7	10.4	10.6	10.6	10.4	10.1	0.9
	en-cs	16.1	15.7	15.8	15.3	15.8	15.5	15.8	15.6	0.8
	en-de	24.9	25.1	23.9	24.2	25.4	25.2	25.5	25.0	1.6
	en-fr	24.3	23.8	23.7	24.2	23.5	24.1	23.9	23.0	1.3
deep-lstm	ar-en	21.2	25.7	27.2	27.1	25.6	24.8	25.1	22.9	4.3
	cs-en	19.8	22.0	18.5	21.1	20.9	21.2	20.3	15.8	6.2
	de-en	25.7	25.2	24.9	24.1	24.5	23.5	23.5	23.1	2.6
	fr-en	25.6	26.8	27.1	26.0	26.9	25.6	17.9	22.8	9.2
	en-ar	10.9	10.2	10.3	7.5	9.5	9.4	7.2	8.0	3.7
	en-cs	13.7	14.6	15.3	14.6	12.2	12.6	11.9	12.6	3.4
	en-de	22.4	24.9	23.6	23.9	22.4	24.0	24.3	23.4	2.5
	en-fr	23.1	22.9	23.5	23.1	22.2	22.0	18.0	20.0	5.5

Table 3: BLEU score for LSTM architectures with multiple BPE configurations. Each score is color-coded by its rank among scores from different BPE configurations in the same row. δ is the difference between the best and worst BLEU score of each row.

		Char	Separate BPE			Joint BPE		
			2k	8k	32k	2k	8k	32k
ar-en	src	0.49k	2.48k	8.47k	32.36k	2.46k	7.98k	26.11k
	tgt	0.24k	2.23k	8.17k	30.45k	1.27k	4.06k	13.45k
fr-en	src	0.30k	2.30k	8.26k	31.23k	2.18k	7.14k	24.48k
	tgt	0.23k	2.22k	8.16k	30.40k	1.94k	6.10k	20.45k

Table 4: Vocabulary size after applying separate and joint BPE for ar-en and fr-en language pair.

		Best Sep.	Best Joint	Worst Sep.	Worst Joint
tiny-lstm	ar-en	24.3	24.2	20.6	20.6
	cs-en	20.2	20.7	17.8	17.8
	de-en	23.3	23.6	21.1	21.1
	fr-en	25.0	25.4	21.8	21.8
	en-ar	9.1	9.3	8.3	8.5
	en-cs	15.2	14.4	11.5	11.5
	en-de	21.8	21.9	18.2	18.2
	en-fr	21.1	21.8	19.9	19.9
deep-transformer	ar-en	31.0	30.8	26.8	27.5
	cs-en	24.6	24.6	19.0	20.6
	de-en	28.1	28.6	24.8	25.2
	fr-en	28.8	29.8	27.3	26.6
	en-ar	12.0	13.0	9.6	10.6
	en-cs	17.3	17.3	13.0	13.8
	en-de	27.3	27.4	23.8	23.9
	en-fr	24.0	25.6	22.5	22.8

Table 5: Best and worst BLEU score with `tiny-lstm` and `deep-transformer` for joint and separate BPE models.

most typical cases for this comparison, namely the Arabic-English language pair and the French-English language pair. The reason these two language pairs are typical is that for Arabic-English, the scripts of the two languages are completely different, while the French and English scripts only have minor difference. It could be seen that for Arabic-English language pair, the Arabic vocabulary size is always roughly twice the size of the English vocabulary. Upon closer examination, we see that roughly half of the Arabic vocabulary is consisted of English words and subwords, scattering over around 2% of the lines in the Arabic side of the training corpus.[5] Hence, for most sentence pairs in the training data, the *effective* Arabic and English vocabulary under joint BPE model is still roughly the same size. On the other hand, because of extensive subword vocabulary sharing, at lower

BPE size, the vocabulary size for French and English is always roughly the same as the number of BPE merge operations regardless of separate or joint BPE. However, this equality starts to diverge as more BPE merge operations are conducted, because the vocabulary difference between French and English starts to play out in this scenario. Unlike Arabic-English, it is hard to predict what is the resulting BPE size from the number of merge operations used, because it is hard to know how many resulting subwords will be shared between the two languages.

Table 5 shows our experimental results with separate/joint BPE and our base architectures.[6] With the configurations we explore, the difference between the best separate/joint BPE performance seems minimal. On the other hand, while the worst BPE configuration remains the same for separate BPE models, we see even worse performance for Transformer at 32k separate BPE most of the time. We think this is a continuation of the trend observed in our main results, as the vocabulary size tends to be even larger than joint BPE when applying separate BPE models.

Given the negligible difference in model performance, we think it is not necessary to sweep BPE merge operations for both joint and separate settings. It is sufficient to focus on the setting that makes the most sense for the task at hand, and focus on hyper parameter search within that setting.

4.3 Analysis 3: Languages

We are interested in what properties of the language have the most impact on the variance of BLEU score with regard to different BPE configurations. For our main experiments, we can already see a pretty consistent trend that for `deep-transformer` architecture, 0.5k and 32k merge operations always roughly correspond to the best and worst BPE configurations, respectively.

---

[5]These English tokens are generally English names, URLs or other untranslated concepts or acronyms.

[6]We only run experiments on 2k, 8k and 32k to save computation time.

	0.5k	32k	δ		0.5k	32k	δ
pt-en	36.3	34.7	1.6	**en-pt**	38.5	35.6	2.9
he-en	31.1	28.6	2.5	**en-he**	26.2	22.9	3.3
tr-en	20.9	17.8	3.1	**en-tr**	13.0	9.8	3.2
ru-en	19.9	18.0	1.9	**en-ru**	19.1	16.6	2.5
pl-en	19.3	16.7	2.6	**en-pl**	16.7	13.4	3.3
hu-en	20.8	16.8	4.0	**en-hu**	16.0	12.6	3.4

Table 6: BLEU score for the 6 extra language pairs in multilingual-TED dataset with `deep-transformer` architecture.

	coef.	std. error	p-value
f_1	0.575	1.345	0.677
f_2	-0.460	1.345	0.738
f_3	-1.998	1.983	0.333
f_4	0.304	0.360	0.415
f_5	1.060	0.639	0.123
f_6	1.169	0.516	0.043
f_7	0.913	0.314	0.013
f_8	0.340	0.367	0.373
f_9	1.280	0.755	0.116

Table 7: Coefficient from regression analysis and their corresponding standard error and p-values. f_1 and f_2 are source and target type/token ratio, respectively. f_3 is alignment ratio. f_4–f_6 are binary features for source-side morphological type (fusional, introflexive and agglutinative) and f_7–f_9 are the same for target.

To add more data points, we assume 0.5k and 32k are always the best and the worst configurations and build systems with these two configurations with both translation directions of 6 more languages pairs, namely, translating of English into and out of Brazilian Portuguese (pt), Hebrew (he), Russian (ru), Turkish (tr), Polish (pl) and Hungarian (hu). Table 6 shows the result with these 6 language pairs. We note that our observation for the 4 language pairs generalize well for the extra 6 language pairs, and we observe a similar magnitude of performance drop as the other language pairs moving from 0.5k to 32k.

To acquire insights for the aforementioned problem, we conduct a linear regression analysis using the linguistic features of the the 10 language pairs as independent variables and BLEU score difference between 0.5k and 32k merge operation settings as the dependent variable.[7] The linguistic features of our interest are described as follows:

- **Type/Token Ratio**: Taken from Bentz et al.

(2016) this is the ratio between number of token types and the number of tokens in the training corpus, ranging $[0, 1]$. These are computed separately for source and target language and denoted as f_1 and f_2 respectively.

- **Alignment Ratio**: Also taken from Bentz et al. (2016), this is the relative difference between the number of many-to-one alignments and one-to-many alignments in the training corpus, ranging $[-1, 1]$. We follow the same alignment setting as in Renduchintala et al. (2018). This is computed together for each parallel training corpus and denoted as f_3.

- **Morphological Type**: We then use a set of binary features to indicate if a language exhibits a certain morphological patterns. We take morphological features from Gerz et al. (2018), where for each language a morphological type from the following categories was assigned: *Isolating*, *Fusional*, *Introflexive* and *Agglutinative*. None of the languages we use exhibit *Isolating* morphology which leaves us with 6 binary features. The features f_4, f_5 and f_6 indicates the presence (or absence) of *fusional*, *introflexive* and *agglutinative* morphological patterns respectively for the source language and f_7, f_8, f_9 indicate the same for the target side.

The 9 features are re-normalized to the $[0, 1]$ region with the min-max normalization. Our linear regression analysis is conducted with Ordinary Least Squares (OLS) model in the Python statsmodels[8] package.

Table 7 shows the regression result. Surprisingly, we don't see any strong correlation between the type/token ratio, alignment ratio and the variance in BPE. On the other hand, the regression points out that having agglutinative language on the source side and fusional language on the target side increases such variance. While we have seen significant BPE variances for all the experiments with Transformer, we think future work should be especially cautious with systems that translate out of agglutinative language and into fusional language (note that English is classified as fusional language in this regime).

4.4 Analysis 4: Variance with Random Seeds

Since our experiments are under low-resource settings, it is important to examine whether the trends

---

[7]Note that for language pairs in our main results, these may not necessarily the best or the worst system. But the readers shall see that the difference is pretty minimal.

[8]`https://pypi.org/project/statsmodels/0.9.0/`

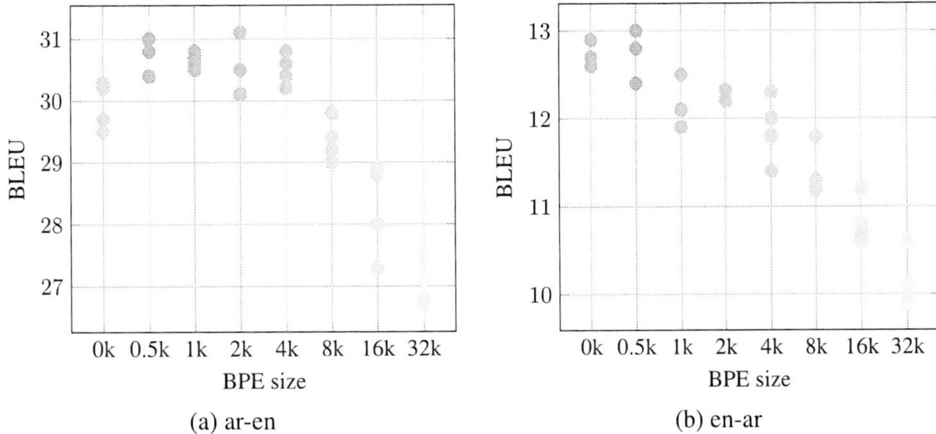

(a) ar-en   (b) en-ar

Figure 2: Scatter plots for the variance analysis of `deep-transformer` system. Each dot in the plot represents the BLEU score for one random restart, while the color code follows the result ranking of its corresponding system configuration in Table 2.

we observe above are due to different system configurations or mostly variance of random seeds. As it is expensive to re-run all the systems multiple times, we only conduct such analysis on the `deep-transformer` architecture and ar-en and en-ar language pairs. We choose to focus on Transformer architecture because we observe more consistent trend for Transformer than LSTM. Hence, it is more interesting to see how well it holds against the randomness in training. To conduct such analysis, we run each system configuration for three more times with different random seeds resulting in four points for each system configuration.

Figure 2 shows the scatter plots of BLEU scores for each random restart under each system configuration. Ideally, the BLEU scores from multiple random restarts of the system configurations should preserve the same ranking as the results in Table 2. It can be seen that, the results from the top-3 BPE configurations are often clustered together (indicating low variance) and the rankings of the other configurations are preserved pretty well. Specifically, even best instances among multiple random restarts with 16k and 32k BPE merge operations fall pretty far from those with top configurations, further verifying our previous observations on the Transformer architecture.

4.5 Analysis 5: High-Resource Setting

While this paper focuses on low-resource settings, we conduct one set of experiments with a high-resource language pair to see if our results generalize to high-resource settings. This experiment is conducted with all WMT 2017 Russian-English

(ru-en) data except the UN dataset, which includes 2.61M sentence pairs in total. We use the test sets from news translation shared task of WMT 2012-2016 as the development data and test on WMT 2017 test set. Due to computation constraints, we only experiment with `deep-transformer` architecture. All the other configurations are exactly the same as the low-resource experiments.

Table 8 summarizes the results. First, notice that the overall variance of results under different BPE configurations is relatively smaller than the low-resource experiments, verifying our intuition that it is especially important to tune BPE size under low-resource settings. Besides, the trend in this setting is also very different from what is shown in Table 2. Specifically, the best results are often obtained with larger BPE sizes, which explains why these configurations were preferred by previous analysis. It could hence be concluded that the analysis results in this paper should *not* be generalized to high-source settings. We leave comprehensive analysis with high-resource language pairs for future work.

5 Conclusion

We conduct a systematic exploration over various numbers of BPE merge operations to understand its interaction with system performance. We conduct this investigation over 5 different NMT architectures including encoder-decoder and Transformer, and 4 language pairs in both translation directions. We leave systematic study on the effect of BPE on high-resource settings and more language pairs, especially morphologically isolating languages, for

	0	0.5k	1k	2k	4k	8k	16k	32k	δ
ru-en	29.3	30.4	30.0	30.3	30.6	30.9	31.0	30.9	1.7
en-ru	28.0	29.1	29.1	29.5	29.5	29.8	30.0	30.0	2.0

Table 8: BLEU score for `deep-transformer` architecture under high-resource setting, with multiple BPE configurations. Each score is color-coded by its rank among scores from different BPE configurations in the same row. δ is the difference between the best and worst BLEU score of each row.

future work. Subword regularization could also be studied in this manner.

Based on the findings, we make the following recommendations for selecting BPE merge operations in the future:

- For Transformer-based architectures, we recommend the sweep be concentrated in the $0 - 4k$ range.

- For Shallow LSTM architectures, we find no typically optimal BPE merge operation and therefore urge future work to sweep over $0 - 32k$ to the extent possible.

- We find no significant performance differences between joint BPE and seperate BPE and therefore recommend BPE sweep be conducted with either of these settings.

Furthermore, we strongly urge that the aforementioned checks be conducted when translating into fusional languages (such as English or French) or when translating from agglutinative languages (such as Turkish).

Our hope is that future work could take the experiments presented here to guide their choices regarding BPE and wordpiece configurations, and that readers of low-resource NMT papers call for appropriate skepticism when the BPE configuration for the experiments appears to be sub-optimal.

Acknowledgments

This work is supported in part by the Office of the Director of National Intelligence, Intelligence Advanced Research Projects Activity (IARPA), via contract #FA8650-17-C-9115. The views and conclusions contained herein are those of the authors and should not be interpreted as necessarily representing the official policies, either expressed or implied, of the sponsors.

References

Bahdanau, Dzmitry, Kyunghyun Cho, and Yoshua Bengio. 2015. Neural machine translation by jointly learning to align and translate. In *3rd International Conference on Learning Representations, ICLR 2015, San Diego, CA, USA, May 7-9, 2015, Conference Track Proceedings*.

Bentz, Christian, Tatyana Ruzsics, Alexander Koplenig, and Tanja Samardzic. 2016. A comparison between morphological complexity measures: typological data vs. language corpora. In *Proceedings of the Workshop on Computational Linguistics for Linguistic Complexity (CL4LC)*, pages 142–153.

Cherry, Colin, George Foster, Ankur Bapna, Orhan Firat, and Wolfgang Macherey. 2018. Revisiting character-based neural machine translation with capacity and compression. In *Proceedings of the 2018 Conference on Empirical Methods in Natural Language Processing, Brussels, Belgium, October 31 - November 4, 2018*, pages 4295–4305.

Denkowski, Michael J. and Graham Neubig. 2017. Stronger baselines for trustable results in neural machine translation. In *Proceedings of the First Workshop on Neural Machine Translation, NMT@ACL 2017, Vancouver, Canada, August 4, 2017*, pages 18–27.

Gerz, Daniela, Ivan Vulić, Edoardo Maria Ponti, Roi Reichart, and Anna Korhonen. 2018. On the relation between linguistic typology and (limitations of) multilingual language modeling. In *Proceedings of the 2018 Conference on Empirical Methods in Natural Language Processing*, pages 316–327, Brussels, Belgium, October-November. Association for Computational Linguistics.

Huck, Matthias, Simon Riess, and Alexander M. Fraser. 2017. Target-side word segmentation strategies for neural machine translation. In *Proceedings of the Second Conference on Machine Translation, WMT 2017, Copenhagen, Denmark, September 7-8, 2017*, pages 56–67.

Kingma, Diederik P and Jimmy Ba. 2014. Adam: A method for stochastic optimization. *arXiv preprint arXiv:1412.6980*.

Koehn, Philipp, Hieu Hoang, Alexandra Birch, Chris Callison-Burch, Marcello Federico, Nicola Bertoldi, Brooke Cowan, Wade Shen, Christine Moran, Richard Zens, Chris Dyer, Ondrej Bojar, Alexandra Constantin, and Evan Herbst. 2007. Moses: Open source toolkit for statistical machine translation. In *ACL 2007, Proceedings of the 45th Annual Meeting of the Association for Computational Linguistics, June 23-30, 2007, Prague, Czech Republic*.

Kudo, Taku. 2018. Subword regularization: Improving neural network translation models with multiple subword candidates. In *Proceedings of the 56th Annual Meeting of the Association for Computational Linguistics, ACL 2018, Melbourne, Australia, July 15-20, 2018, Volume 1: Long Papers*, pages 66–75.

Luong, Thang, Hieu Pham, and Christopher D. Manning. 2015. Effective approaches to attention-based neural machine translation. In *Proceedings of the 2015 Conference on Empirical Methods in Natural Language Processing, EMNLP 2015, Lisbon, Portugal, September 17-21, 2015*, pages 1412–1421.

Ott, Myle, Sergey Edunov, Alexei Baevski, Angela Fan, Sam Gross, Nathan Ng, David Grangier, and Michael Auli. 2019. fairseq: A fast, extensible toolkit for sequence modeling. *arXiv preprint arXiv:1904.01038*.

Post, Matt. 2018. A call for clarity in reporting bleu scores. In *Proceedings of the Third Conference on Machine Translation: Research Papers*, pages 186–191, Belgium, Brussels, October. Association for Computational Linguistics.

Qi, Ye, Devendra Singh Sachan, Matthieu Felix, Sarguna Padmanabhan, and Graham Neubig. 2018. When and why are pre-trained word embeddings useful for neural machine translation? In *Proceedings of the 2018 Conference of the North American Chapter of the Association for Computational Linguistics: Human Language Technologies, NAACL-HLT, New Orleans, Louisiana, USA, June 1-6, 2018, Volume 2 (Short Papers)*, pages 529–535.

Renduchintala, Adithya, Pamela Shapiro, Kevin Duh, and Philipp Koehn. 2018. Character-aware decoder for neural machine translation. *CoRR*, abs/1809.02223.

Sennrich, Rico, Barry Haddow, and Alexandra Birch. 2016. Neural machine translation of rare words with subword units. In *Proceedings of the 54th Annual Meeting of the Association for Computational Linguistics, ACL 2016, August 7-12, 2016, Berlin, Germany, Volume 1: Long Papers*.

Sennrich, Rico, Alexandra Birch, Anna Currey, Ulrich Germann, Barry Haddow, Kenneth Heafield, Antonio Valerio Miceli Barone, and Philip Williams. 2017. The university of edinburgh's neural MT systems for WMT17. In *Proceedings of the Second Conference on Machine Translation, WMT 2017, Copenhagen, Denmark, September 7-8, 2017*, pages 389–399.

Sutskever, Ilya, Oriol Vinyals, and Quoc V. Le. 2014. Sequence to sequence learning with neural networks. In *Advances in Neural Information Processing Systems 27: Annual Conference on Neural Information Processing Systems 2014, December 8-13 2014, Montreal, Quebec, Canada*, pages 3104–3112.

Vaswani, Ashish, Noam Shazeer, Niki Parmar, Jakob Uszkoreit, Llion Jones, Aidan N. Gomez, Lukasz Kaiser, and Illia Polosukhin. 2017. Attention is all you need. In *Advances in Neural Information Processing Systems 30: Annual Conference on Neural Information Processing Systems 2017, 4-9 December 2017, Long Beach, CA, USA*, pages 6000–6010.

Wu, Yonghui, Mike Schuster, Zhifeng Chen, Quoc V. Le, Mohammad Norouzi, Wolfgang Macherey, Maxim Krikun, Yuan Cao, Qin Gao, Klaus Macherey, Jeff Klingner, Apurva Shah, Melvin Johnson, Xiaobing Liu, Lukasz Kaiser, Stephan Gouws, Yoshikiyo Kato, Taku Kudo, Hideto Kazawa, Keith Stevens, George Kurian, Nishant Patil, Wei Wang, Cliff Young, Jason Smith, Jason Riesa, Alex Rudnick, Oriol Vinyals, Greg Corrado, Macduff Hughes, and Jeffrey Dean. 2016. Google's neural machine translation system: Bridging the gap between human and machine translation. *CoRR*, abs/1609.08144.

The Impact of Preprocessing on Arabic-English Statistical and Neural Machine Translation

Mai Oudah, Amjad Almahairi[†] and Nizar Habash
Computational Approaches to Modeling Language Lab
New York University Abu Dhabi, UAE
[†]Element AI, Canada
{mai.oudah,nizar.habash}@nyu.edu
amjad.almahairi@elementai.com

Abstract

Neural networks have become the state-of-the-art approach for machine translation (MT) in many languages. While linguistically-motivated tokenization techniques were shown to have significant effects on the performance of statistical MT, it remains unclear if those techniques are well suited for neural MT. In this paper, we systematically compare neural and statistical MT models for Arabic-English translation on data preprecossed by various prominent tokenization schemes. Furthermore, we consider a range of data and vocabulary sizes and compare their effect on both approaches. Our empirical results show that the best choice of tokenization scheme is largely based on the type of model and the size of data. We also show that we can gain significant improvements using a system selection that combines the output from neural and statistical MT.

1 Introduction

Neural machine translation (NMT) has been rapidly attracting the attention of the research community for its promising results (Cho et al., 2014b; Bahdanau et al., 2014; Wu et al., 2016; Vaswani et al., 2017). NMT is composed of two neural networks, an encoder and a decoder, where the encoder is fed a sentence from the source language and the decoder generates its translation, word by word, in the target language. Recently, NMT

has been shown to outperform other MT systems in many language pairs, e.g. German-English, French-English and Basque-English (Escolano et al., 2017; Dahlmann et al., 2017; Unanue et al., 2018). While Arabic MT has been mostly developed under statistical MT (SMT), NMT has also been applied and studied recently (Habash and Sadat, 2006; Almahairi et al., 2016; Durrani et al., 2017).

Linguistically-motivated tokenization has shown to have a significant effect on SMT, particularly in the case of morphologically rich languages like Arabic (Habash and Sadat, 2006). However, it remains unclear if such techniques are well suited for NMT, where language-agnostic tokenizations, e.g. byte-pair encoding (BPE) (Sennrich et al., 2016), are widely used. Almahairi et al. (2016) has looked into Arabic SMT and NMT, achieving the highest accuracy using the Penn Arabic Treebank (ATB) tokenization, with 51.2 and 49.7 BLEU points for SMT and NMT, respectively.

In this paper, we study the impact of different preprocessing techniques in Arabic-English MT on both SMT and NMT, by examining various prominent tokenization schemes. We conduct learning curve experiments to study the interaction between data size and the choice of tokenization scheme. We study the performance under morphology-based and frequency-based tokenization schemes, provided by MADAMIRA (Pasha et al., 2014) and BPE, respectively, on in-domain data. In addition, we evaluate the best performing models on out-of-domain data. Our results show that the utilization of BPE for SMT can be effective and allows achieving a good performance even with a small vocabulary size of 20K. Moreover, the results show that the performance of NMT is especially sensitive to the size of data. We notice that NMT suffers with long sentences, and thus, we utilize system selection, which yields significant improvements over both approaches. Our best system significantly outperforms previous results reported on the same in-domain test data by +4 BLEU points (Almahairi et al., 2016).

The rest of the paper is organized as follows. The related work is presented in Section 2. Section 3 describes our proposed approach. Section 4 illustrates the experimental settings. The results are reported in Section 5. In Section 6, we discuss our findings. Finally, we conclude the paper and mention the future work in Section 7.

2 Related Work

Many studies have compared the performance of different MT models on translation tasks (Unanue et al., 2018; Almahairi et al., 2016; Durrani et al., 2017). However, the data preprocessing was not unified across those models. For example, BPE is only applied to the training data utilized by the NMT system, but not SMT (Almahairi et al., 2016; Durrani et al., 2017).

Habash and Sadat (2006) investigated and compared across some preprocessing schemes for Arabic, describing and evaluating different methods for combining them. The main preprocessing schemes were Simple Tokenization, Decliticization (degrees 1 to 3), and Arabic Treebank Tokenization. Decliticization of degree 2 outperformed the rest when applied individually. They reported improvement in MT performance when combining different schemes together.

Almahairi et al. (2016) compared NMT and SMT on Arabic translation, and showed that NMT performs comparably to SMT. The best performance is achieved when Penn Arabic Treebank (ATB) tokenization is used with 51.19 and 49.70 BLEU points for SMT and NMT, respectively.

The idea of system selection for MT exists in the literature, but mostly for model selection under the same approach (SMT or NMT) (Devlin and Matsoukas, 2012; Salloum et al., 2014).

3 Approach

In our study, we systematically compare SMT and NMT on the following dimensions.

3.1 Source Language Tokenization

Much research has shown the importance of tokenization and orthographic normalization for SMT and NMT, as they deal with data sparsity (El Kholy and Habash, 2012; Habash and Sadat, 2006; Zalmout and Habash, 2017). Tokenization schemes can either be morphology-based or statistical/frequency-based (Pasha et al., 2014; Sennrich et al., 2016). We investigate both in the context of Arabic MT, both separately and in combination, to observe their interaction. We normalize Alif 'ا' and Ya 'ي' in all schemes, where Hamza is removed from the variants of Hamzated Alif (e.g. 'أ','إ') to become 'ا', the Alif Maqsura 'ى' is replaced with Ya 'ي' and the diacritics are removed.

Morphology-based This tokenization scheme relies on the linguistic rules of the source language. We explore three schemes under this category (Habash and Sadat, 2006; Zalmout and Habash, 2017): 1) Simple Tokenization (Raw) that splits off punctuation and numbers; 2) Penn Arabic Treebank (ATB) Tokenization, which splits all clitics except definite articles; 3) Decliticization (D3), which splits all clitics.

Frequency-based We use byte-pair encoding (BPE) (Sennrich et al., 2016), which is an iterative compression approach that replaces the most frequent pair of characters in a sentence with a unique sequence of characters. It allows for a fixed-size vocabulary representation. Figure 1 shows an example across Raw and Tok schemes with/without BPE on top.

3.2 Training Data Size

We conduct a learning curve experiment to explore how much both Arabic-English SMT and NMT can benefit from adding more training data with each tokenization scheme. Habash and Sadat (2006) have conducted a similar learning curve study for SMT. Each tokenization scheme may result in a different number of tokens per sentence; hence, a sentence-length filter will discard more sentences from more verbose schemes. This would lead to some schemes having access to more words than others. Therefore, we adopt El Kholy and Habash (2012)'s approach of filtering training parallel data based on the D3 scheme as a reference scheme for selecting sentences of length up to 100

Setting	Sentence
Original	قال أحمد أبو حميدة أنّنا نرتاح اليوم ونوزع المهام على الأفراد.
Raw	قال احمد ابو حميدة اننا نرتاح اليوم و نوزع المهام علي الافراد .
ATB	قال احمد ابو حميدة ان +نا نرتاح اليوم و+ نوزع المهام علي الافراد .
D3	قال احمد ابو حميدة ان +نا نرتاح ال+ يوم و+ نوزع ال+ مهام علي ال+ افراد .
Raw+BPE	قال ا حمد ابو حمي@@ دة اننا نر@@ تاح اليوم ونو@@ زع المهام علي الافراد .
ATB+BPE	قال احمد ابو حمي@@ دة ان +نا ن@@ ر@@ تاح اليوم و+ نو@@ زع المهام علي الافراد .
D3+BPE	قال احمد ابو حميدة ان +نا ن@@ رت@@ اح ال+ يوم و+ نو@@ زع ال+ مهام علي ال+ افراد .
Translation	Today we are resting and distributing the new posts, said Ahmad Abou Hamida.

Figure 1: Tokenization schemes applied to an example.

tokens. Thus, the same sentences will be selected across different tokenization schemes.

3.3 Target Language Resources

We design the training so that both systems will have access to the same additional target language resources besides the target side of the training parallel corpus. In SMT, target language resources are used to build language models for fluency improvement. Whereas, many works have proven pretrained word embeddings to be useful in neural network models (Qi et al., 2018), and therefor, the same additional TLR are used to learn pretrained word embeddings that support the decoder in NMT. Here, the $tgt++$ designation next to the system name indicates the use of additional TLR.

3.4 Input Length and System Selection

Many have reported NMT performing worse with long sentences (Cho et al., 2014a; Koehn and Knowles, 2017), which was caught in our error analysis and thus we explored combining the two MT systems via a system selection approach, where the selection of either translation is based on which is closer to the input length as a criterion. Whereas the sentence BLEU score is the criterion in the Oracle system selection.

4 Experimental Settings

4.1 Datasets

The training dataset contains 1.2M sentence pairs in newswire (NW) domain from three Linguistic Data Consortium (LDC) resources: LDC2004T18, LDC2004T14, and LDC2007T08. For tuning, we use LDC2010T12 (MT04), which consists of 1,075 sentence pairs in NW and government documents. As for the in-domain testing, we use LDC2010T14 (MT05), which consists of 1,056 sentence pairs in NW, and has four English reference translations. We look into the performance of the systems in out-of-domain data using LDC2014T02 (MT12), which consists of 1,535 sentence pairs mostly web collection, and has four English reference translations.

4.2 Preprocessing

MADAMIRA (Pasha et al., 2014) is utilized for morphology-based tokenization of the source side. Sennrich et al. (2016)'s BPE implementation is used for learning and applying BPE models. We set vocabulary size to 20K in BPE learning after exploring multiple vocabulary sizes, including 10K, 20K and 30K, where the 20K setting achieved comparable results to the 30K and outperformed the 10K. Each BPE model is trained on source side of training data of the respective experiment. While Moses' (Koehn et al., 2007) tokenizer and lowercaser are used for preparing the target side.

4.3 SMT settings

We use Moses 3.0 (Koehn et al., 2007) to train SMT models with maximum phrase length of 8 tokens. Two versions of the language model are examined: 1) trained solely on the target side of the training dataset, and 2) trained on the target side and the English Gigaword 5th edition.

4.4 NMT settings

We use the encoder-decoder with the *general* global attention architecture as introduced by Lu-

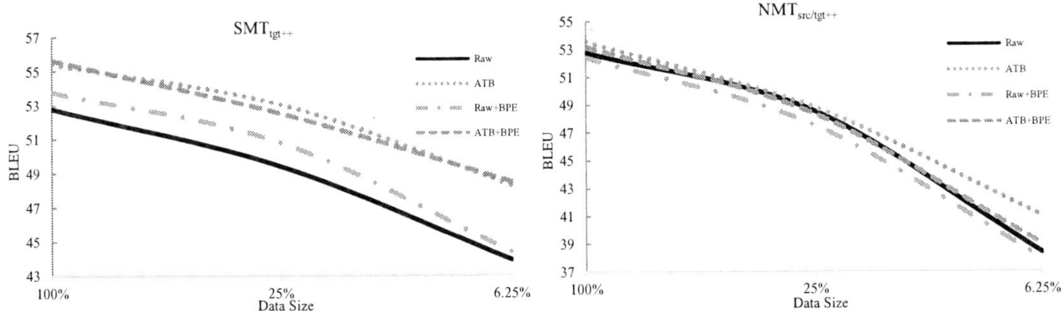

Figure 2: The performance on in-domain test (MT05) under different settings with different training data sizes.

	#Vocab	SMT_{tgt++}	CI	$\text{NMT}_{scr/tgt++}$	CI	P-value
Raw	331K	52.78	$\pm$ 0.98	52.76	$\pm$ 1.24	0.412
ATB	208K	55.42	$\pm$ 1.07	**53.54**	$\pm$ 1.20	0.002
D3	190K	54.66	$\pm$ 1.02	53.51	$\pm$ 1.20	0.027
Raw+BPE	20K	53.78	$\pm$ 1.10	52.41	$\pm$ 1.17	0.003
ATB+BPE	20K	**55.64**	$\pm$ 1.11	53.18	$\pm$ 1.15	0.001
D3+BPE	20K	54.59	$\pm$ 1.07	53.38	$\pm$ 1.16	0.018

Table 1: Comparing Raw, ATB and D3 Tokenized cases without/with BPE on in-domain test (MT05), in terms of BLEU scores, where the Confidence Interval (CI) and P-value are reported. Bold font highlights best results by SMT and NMT.

ong et al. (2015). All the NMT models have been trained using OpenNMT toolkit (Klein et al., 2017) with no restriction on input's vocabulary. We use long short-term memory units (LSTM) (Hochreiter and Schmidhuber, 1997), with hidden units of size 500 and two layers in both the encoder and decoder. The word embedding vector size for source/target is 300.

English pretrained word embeddings were trained as skip-gram model (Mikolov et al., 2013) via gensim tool (Rehurek and Sojka, 2010) with settings: (size=300, window=8, min count=5) on English Gigaword 5th edition (Graff and Cieri, 2003) dataset. Arabic embeddings were trained on the Arabic Gigaword 5th edition (Parker et al., 2011) via FastText (Bojanowski et al., 2017), which showed better performance with morphologically rich languages (Erdmann et al., 2018). We give the designation of $_{src/tgt++}$ to the system that uses both embeddings.

4.5 Evaluation Metrics

The evaluation results are reported in case insensitive BLEU scores (Papineni et al., 2002) with their confidence intervals (CI) and p-values. Bootstrap resampling is used to compute statistical significance intervals (Koehn, 2004).

5 Results

5.1 Preprocessing and Learning Curve

We examine Raw, ATB and D3 with and without BPE applied on top, across a learning curve where smaller sets of our training data (1.2M) are considered at 25% (300K) and 6.25% (75K) tokens. Figure 2 illustrates the learning curve results for Raw (baseline) and ATB (overall best), with and without BPE. Figure 2 shows the importance of training data availability, especially for NMT, and also that BPE impact can be seen in both systems, which we find interesting. Moreover, SMT is shown to be far more sensitive to preprocessing than NMT.

Table 1 shows the best systems' results when 100% of the training data is tokenized by Raw, ATB and D3, with and without BPE on top of it, for SMT and NMT. It shows ATB+BPE and ATB to achieve the best results for SMT and NMT, respectively, which we find interesting as BPE is usually associated with NMT. The p-value indicates whether the difference between SMT and NMT results under the same tokenization scheme is statistically significant or not. The statistical significance is illustrated with p-value < 0.05. SMT_{tgt++} and $\text{NMT}_{scr/tgt++}$ have comparable results at the baseline. As expected, using more data for LM

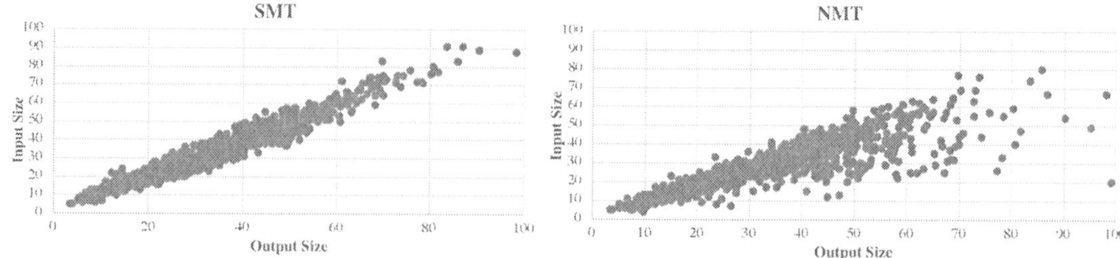

Figure 3: The input size vs. output size in SMT and NMT, respectively, on MT05 with ATB tokenization. We notice that in NMT parts of the input sentences are dropped and not translated at all, which motivates the length-based selection.

$\mathbf{SMT}_{tgt++}$		$\mathbf{NMT}_{scr/tgt++}$		**System Selection**	**Oracle**
Setting	BLEU	Scheme	BLEU	BLEU	BLEU
ATB+BPE	55.64	ATB	53.54	**56.18**	61.26

Table 2: BLEU score of the length-based system selection (using best models of SMT and NMT) when applied on in-domain test (MT05).

$\mathbf{SMT}_{tgt++}$		$\mathbf{NMT}_{scr/tgt++}$		**System Selection**	**Oracle**
Scheme	BLEU	Scheme	BLEU	BLEU	BLEU
ATB+BPE	35.11	ATB	36.56	**37.96**	39.11

Table 3: BLEU score of the length-based system selection (using best models of SMT and NMT) when applied on out-of-domain test (MT12).

produces better results as well as the increase in training data size. Using pretrained word embeddings for both languages improve the NMT results significantly compared to only target ones by two BLEU points. As shown in Table 3, the best $\mathrm{NMT}_{scr/tgt++}$ model (using ATB) outperforms SMT_{tgt++} model (using ATB+BPE) by 1.5 BLEU against MT12 in the out-of-domain testing.

5.2 Error analysis

Error analysis has shown that NMT output is more fluent than SMT's, especially with short sentences (< 50 tokens), in contrast to long sentences where coverage and accuracy drop, which support related work. Figure 3 shows dropping in NMT output size as the input size increases, especially < 40 tokens, while SMT keeps more consistent output to the input size. So we explore system selection based on the closeness to the input length as well as Oracle results, where the selection is based on the highest output BLEU score. Tables 2 and 3 show the results of length-based system selection on best models in SMT and NMT when applied to in-domain test (MT05) and out-of-domain testing (MT12), respectively, which illustrate im-

provements over the original BLEU scores.

Figure 4 illustrates five examples, where either SMT or NMT output is selected based on the output length compared to the source input size. In Example 1, the SMT output is selected over the NMT one as the NMT system drops the phrase after the comma and only translates the part before, however, fluently. Example 2, which represents much longer sentence, SMT output is selected over NMT, which translates the saying and drops the rest of the sentence. On the other hand, in Examples 3 and 4, NMT output is selected over SMT's for being the closest to the source input in terms of length. Furthermore, Example 5 represents a case where the system selection approach fails to select the better prediction (in terms of BLEU score) for the final output based on the source-output length comparison.

6 Discussion

We notice that morphology-based tokenization schemes improve the performance of MT systems regardless of the MT approach, but in different levels. The difference in scheme choice is less im-

<table>
<tr><td colspan="2" align="center">Example 1</td></tr>
<tr><td>Input</td><td dir="rtl">و+ كرر القول ان البرنامج النووي الايراني سلمي و+ ان ايران لا تسعي الي التزود ب+ قنبلة ذرية , كما تؤكد الولايات المتحدة .</td></tr>
<tr><td>SMT*</td><td>and repeated that iran ' s nuclear program is peaceful and that iran is not seeking to acquire an atomic bomb , as the united states alleges .</td></tr>
<tr><td>NMT</td><td>he repeated that iran ' s nuclear program was peaceful and iran was not seeking to acquire atomic bomb .</td></tr>
<tr><td>Human</td><td>he repeated that iran ' s nuclear program is peaceful and that iran is not trying to acquire an atomic bomb as the united states claims .</td></tr>
<tr><td colspan="2" align="center">Example 2</td></tr>
<tr><td>Input</td><td dir="rtl">1 - 3 (اف ب) ـ قال الناطق الرسمي ب+ اسم وزارة الخارجية الاردنية رجب السقيري ان جميع دول الجوار العراقي س+ تشارك في الاجتماع الذي س+ يعقد في عمان الخميس المقبل علي مستوي وزراء الخارجية ب+ استثناء ايران التي س+ تشارك ب+ وفد يراس +ه مساعد وزير الخارجية للشوون الدولية و+ القانونية .</td></tr>
<tr><td>SMT*</td><td>oman 3 - 1 (afp) - the jordanian foreign ministry spokesman recep UNK that all iraqi neighboring countries will participate in the meeting , which will be held in amman next thursday at the level of foreign ministers , with the exception of iran , which would participate with a delegation led by assistant foreign minister UNK international and legal .</td></tr>
<tr><td>NMT</td><td>jordan will take part in a meeting of foreign ministers in amman on thursday , except for iran , a foreign ministry spokesman said .</td></tr>
<tr><td>Human</td><td>amman 1 - 3 (afp) - jordanian foreign ministry spokesperson rajab sukayri has said that all of iraq ' s neighboring countries will be taking part in thursday ' s meeting in amman at foreign minister level , with the exception of iran which will be represented by a delegation headed by the foreign minister ' s assistant for legal and international affairs .</td></tr>
<tr><td colspan="2" align="center">Example 3</td></tr>
<tr><td>Input</td><td dir="rtl">و+ لم يتسن التحقق من صحة البيان .</td></tr>
<tr><td>SMT</td><td>he could not verify the authenticity of the statement .</td></tr>
<tr><td>NMT*</td><td>the authenticity of the statement could not be verified .</td></tr>
<tr><td>Human</td><td>the authenticity of the statement could not be verified .</td></tr>
<tr><td colspan="2" align="center">Example 4</td></tr>
<tr><td>Input</td><td dir="rtl">و+ تهدف المحادثات النووية السداسية التي توقفت منذ سبتمبر الماضي الي حل القضية النووية سلميا علي شبه الجزيرة الكورية .</td></tr>
<tr><td>SMT</td><td>and designed six-party nuclear talks which have been stalled since last september to peacefully solve the nuclear issue on the korean peninsula .</td></tr>
<tr><td>NMT*</td><td>the six-party nuclear talks , which have been stalled since last september , are aimed at resolving the nuclear issue peacefully on the korean peninsula .</td></tr>
<tr><td>Human</td><td>the six-party nuclear talks , which stopped last september , are aimed at a peaceful settlement of the nuclear issue on the korean peninsula .</td></tr>
<tr><td colspan="2" align="center">Example 5</td></tr>
<tr><td>Input</td><td dir="rtl">و+ حضر الرئيسان السوداني عمر البشير و+ الجنوب افريقي ثابو مبيكي مراسم التوقيع</td></tr>
<tr><td>SMT*</td><td>the two presidents attended the omar al-beshir and south african president thabo mbeki the signing ceremony</td></tr>
<tr><td>NMT</td><td>sudanese president omar al-beshir and south african president thabo mbeki attended the signing ceremony</td></tr>
<tr><td>Human</td><td>the sudanese president umar bashir and the south african president thabo mbeki attended the signing ceremonies</td></tr>
</table>

Figure 4: Examples from MT05, with SMT and NMT outputs when ATB is used as a scheme. The * designation next to the system name indicates the decision of the system selection.

pactful on NMT; compared with SMT. The improvement range for NMT is 1.13 BLEU, while for SMT the range is 2.86 BLEU. While Raw results are almost the same for SMT and NMT; ATB improves both NMT and SMT; but the improvement is higher for SMT. Adding BPE helps SMT, while lowering vocabulary size. The effect of BPE on NMT is insignificant, which is a surprising result since BPE is often associated with NMT. Also, we significantly improve on Almahairi et al. (2016)'s results by more than three BLEU points.

Length-based system selection improves over both NMT and SMT results in in-domain and out-of-domain cases, significantly in the later, which indicates a hybrid MT system may be promising. Moreover, the huge jump in performance with Oracle selection shows that there is still room for potential improvement in system designs, for better accuracy and fluency. More TLR allow for better results in MT systems. When both Arabic and English pretrained word embeddings are used, the performance improves by more than two BLEU points compared to English only.

7 Conclusion and Future Work

In this paper, we study the impact of various preprocessing techniques to Arabic-English MT under SMT and NMT, where various prominent tokenization schemes are examined. We conduct a learning curve analysis of the different preprocessing settings with incremental training data size, where ATB scheme performs consistently well along the learning curve. Moreover, we implemented a length-based system selection to deal with NMT's struggle with short sentences, and significant improvements. The empirical results show that the choice of tokenization scheme can be optimized based on the type of model to train and the data available. We also gain significant improvements using length-based system selection that combines the output from neural and statistical MT. Our results significantly outperform the ones reported in the prior work when applied to in-domain test (MT05). As future work, we plan to examine training data of general domain with linguistically-motivated tokenization schemes to study further their impact on NMT under different neural models. Also, exploring sophisticated system selection schemes for potential improvement.

Acknowledgments

The support and resources from the High Performance Computing Center at New York University Abu Dhabi are gratefully acknowledged.

References

Almahairi, Amjad, Kyunghyun Cho, Nizar Habash, and Aaron Courville. 2016. First result on Arabic neural machine translation. *arXiv preprint arXiv:1606.02680*.

Bahdanau, Dzmitry, Kyunghyun Cho, and Yoshua Bengio. 2014. Neural machine translation by jointly learning to align and translate. *arXiv e-prints*, abs/1409.0473.

Bojanowski, Piotr, Edouard Grave, Armand Joulin, and Tomas Mikolov. 2017. Enriching word vectors with subword information. *Transactions of the Association for Computational Linguistics*, 5:135–146.

Cho, Kyunghyun, Bart Van, Dzmitry Bahdanau, and Yoshua Bengio. 2014a. On the properties of neural machine translation: Encoder-decoder approaches. In *Proceedings of SSST-8 Eighth Workshop on Syntax Semantics and Structure in Statistical Translation*, pages 103–111. Association for Computational Linguistics.

Cho, Kyunghyun, Bart van Merrienboer, Caglar Gulcehre, Dzmitry Bahdanau, Fethi Bougares, Holger Schwenk, and Yoshua Bengio. 2014b. Learning phrase representations using rnn encoder–decoder for statistical machine translation. In *Proceedings of the 2014 Conference on Empirical Methods in Natural Language Processing (EMNLP)*, pages 1724–1734. Association for Computational Linguistics.

Dahlmann, Leonard, Evgeny Matusov, Pavel Petrushkov, and Shahram Khadivi. 2017. Neural machine translation leveraging phrase-based models in a hybrid search. *CoRR*.

Devlin, Jacob and Spyros Matsoukas. 2012. Trait-based hypothesis selection for machine translation. In *Proceedings of the 2012 Conference of the North American Chapter of the Association for Computational Linguistics: Human Language Technologies*, NAACL HLT 12, pages 528–532. Association for Computational Linguistics.

Durrani, Nadir, Fahim Dalvi, Hassan Sajjad, and Stephan Vogel. 2017. Qcri machine translation systems for iwslt 16. *CoRR*.

El Kholy, Ahmed and Nizar Habash. 2012. Orthographic and morphological processing for English–Arabic statistical machine translation. *Machine Translation*, 26(1-2):25–45.

Erdmann, Alexander, Nasser Zalmout, and Nizar Habash. 2018. Addressing noise in multidialectal word embeddings. In *Proceedings of Conference of the Association for Computational Linguistics*, Melbourne, Australia.

Escolano, Carlos, Marta Costa-jussa, and Jose Fonollosa. 2017. The talp-upc neural machine translation system for german/finnish-english using the inverse direction model in rescoring. In *Proceedings of the Second Conference on Machine Translation*, pages 283–287. Association for Computational Linguistics.

Graff, David and Christopher Cieri. 2003. English gigaword, ldc catalog no ldc2003t05. Linguistic Data Consortium, University of Pennsylvania.

Habash, Nizar and Fatiha Sadat. 2006. Arabic preprocessing schemes for statistical machine translation. In *HLT-NAACL*.

Hochreiter, Sepp and Jürgen Schmidhuber. 1997. Long short-term memory. *Neural Comput.*, 9(8):1735–1780, November.

Klein, Guillaume, Yoon Kim, Yuntian Deng, Jean Senellart, and Alexander Rush. 2017. Opennmt: Open-source toolkit for neural machine translation. In *Proceedings of ACL 2017 System Demonstrations*, pages 67–72. Association for Computational Linguistics.

Koehn, Philipp and Rebecca Knowles. 2017. Six challenges for neural machine translation. In *Proceedings of the First Workshop on Neural Machine Translation*, pages 28–39. Association for Computational Linguistics.

Koehn, Philipp, Hieu Hoang, Alexandra Birch, Christopher Callison-Burch, Marcello Federico, Nicola Bertoldi, Brooke Cowan, Wade Shen, Christine Moran, Richard Zens, Christopher Dyer, Ondrej Bojar, Alexandra Constantin, and Evan Herbst. 2007. Moses: open source toolkit for statistical machine translation. In *Proceedings of the 45th Annual Meeting of the Association for Computational Linguistics Companion Volume Proceedings of the Demo and Poster Sessions*, pages 177–180, Prague, Czech Republic.

Koehn, Philipp. 2004. Statistical significance tests for machine translation evaluation. In *Proceedings of EMNLP*, Barcelona, Spain.

Luong, Thang, Hieu Pham, and Christopher Manning. 2015. Effective approaches to attention-based neural machine translation. In *Proceedings of the 2015 Conference on Empirical Methods in Natural Language Processing*, pages 1412–1421. Association for Computational Linguistics".

Mikolov, Tomas, Kai Chen, Greg Corrado, and Jeffrey Dean. 2013. Efficient estimation of word representations in vector space. *CoRR*, abs/1301.3781.

Papineni, Kishore, Salim Roukos, Todd Ward, and Wei-Jing Zhu. 2002. BLEU: a Method for Automatic Evaluation of Machine Translation. In *Proceedings of the 40th Annual Meeting of the Association for Computational Linguistics*, pages 311–318, Philadelphia, PA.

Parker, Robert, David Graff, Ke Chen, Junbo Kong, and Kazuaki Maeda. 2011. Arabic Gigaword Fifth Edition. LDC catalog number No. LDC2011T11, ISBN 1-58563-595-2.

Pasha, Arfath, Mohamed Al-Badrashiny, Ahmed El Kholy, Ramy Eskander, Mona Diab, Nizar Habash, Manoj Pooleery, Owen Rambow, and Ryan Roth. 2014. Madamira: A fast, comprehensive tool for morphological analysis and disambiguation of arabic. In *In Proceedings of LREC*.

Qi, Ye, Devendra Singh, Matthieu Felix, Sarguna Janani, and Graham Neubig. 2018. When and why are pre-trained word embeddings useful for neural machine translation? *CoRR*.

Rehurek, Radim and Petr Sojka. 2010. Software framework for topic modelling with large corpora. In *Proceedings of the LREC 2010 Workshop on New Challenges for NLP Frameworks*, pages 45–50, Valletta, Malta. ELRA.

Salloum, Wael, Heba Elfardy, Linda Alamir-Salloum, Nizar Habash, and Mona Diab. 2014. Sentence level dialect identification for machine translation system selection. In *Proceedings of the 52nd Annual Meeting of the Association for Computational Linguistics*, pages 772–778.

Sennrich, Rico, Barry Haddow, and Alexandra Birch. 2016. Neural machine translation of rare words with subword units. In *Proceedings of the 54th Annual Meeting of the Association for Computational Linguistics (Volume 1: Long Papers)*, pages 1715–1725. Association for Computational Linguistics.

Unanue, Inigo, Lierni Arratibel, Ehsan Borzeshi, and Massimo Piccardi. 2018. English-basque statistical and neural machine translation. In *Proceedings of the Eleventh International Conference on Language Resources and Evaluation (LREC 2018)*, Paris, France. European Language Resources Association (ELRA).

Vaswani, Ashish, Noam Shazeer, Niki Parmar, Jakob Uszkoreit, Llion Jones, Aidan N. Gomez, Lukasz Kaiser, and Illia Polosukhin. 2017. Attention is all you need. *CoRR*, abs/1706.03762.

Wu, Yonghui, Mike Schuster, Zhifeng Chen, Quoc V. Le, Mohammad Norouzi, and Wolfgang Macherey. 2016. Googles neural machine translation system: Bridging the gap between human and machine translation. *CoRR*, abs/1609.08144.

Zalmout, Nasser and Nizar Habash. 2017. Optimizing Tokenization Choice for Machine Translation across Multiple Target Languages. *The Prague Bulletin of Mathematical Linguistics*, 108:257–270, June.

Lost in Translation:
Loss and Decay of Linguistic Richness in Machine Translation

Eva Vanmassenhove   **Dimitar Shterionov**   **Andy Way**

ADAPT, School of Computing, Dublin City University, Dublin, Ireland
`firstname.lastname@adaptcentre.ie`

Abstract

This work presents an empirical approach to quantifying the loss of lexical richness in Machine Translation (MT) systems compared to Human Translation (HT). Our experiments show how current MT systems indeed fail to render the lexical diversity of human generated or translated text. The inability of MT systems to generate diverse outputs and its tendency to exacerbate already frequent patterns while ignoring less frequent ones, might be the underlying cause for, among others, the currently heavily debated issues related to gender biased output. Can we indeed, aside from biased data, talk about an algorithm that exacerbates seen biases?

1 Introduction

Berman (2000) observed that the translation process consists of deformation processes, one of which he refers to as 'quantitative impoverishment', a loss of lexical richness and diversity. Although mitigated by a human translator, this loss is to some extent inevitable as it is hard to respect the multitude of signifiers and constructions when translating one language into another. While Berman (2000) studied the decrease of lexical richness of human translations (HTs) from a theoretical point of view, Kruger (2012) demonstrated using empirical methods that there is indeed a lexical loss when comparing translations to original texts. In the field of Machine Translation (MT), Klebanov and Flor (2013) showed that Statistical MT (SMT) suffers considerably more from lexical loss than HTs in a study focused on lexical tightness and text cohesion. We are not aware of any other research in this direction.

As generating accurate translations has been the main objective of current MT systems, maintaining lexical richness and creating diverse outputs has understandably not been a priority. Nevertheless, the issue of lexical loss in MT might at the same time be a symptom and a cause of a more serious issue underlying the current systems. The difference between a one-to-many relationship such as the one illustrated in Figure 1, is very different from the one illustrated in Figure 2 or Figure 3 from a (human) translator point of view. However, from a statistical point of view, they are not always clearly distinguishable. When presented with an ambiguous sentence, like 'I am intelligent' or 'See?' where there is little context to decide on a particular target variant of the same source word, it essentially boils down to the same thing: picking the translation that maximizes the probability over the entire sentence. As such, the loss of richness and diversity and the exacerbation of already frequent patterns might not simply be limited to the loss of (near) synonyms or rare words, but could also be the underlying cause of, for example, the inability of statistical MT systems to handle morphologically richer language correctly (Vanmassenhove et al., 2016; Passban et al., 2018), the already observed issues with gender bias (Vanmassenhove et al., 2018) in MT output or the difficulties of dealing with agglutinative languages (Unanue et al., 2018).

The inability of neural models to generate diverse output has already been observed for tasks involving language generation, where creating intrinsically diverse outputs is more of a necessity.

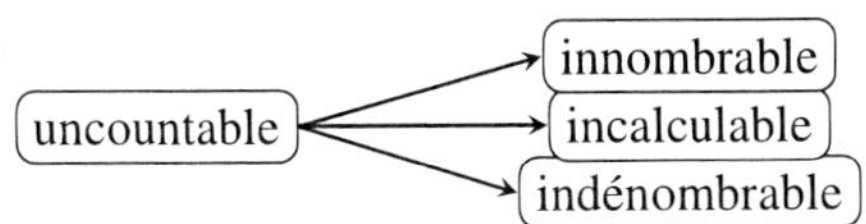

Figure 1: One-to-many relation between an English source word and some of its possible French translations

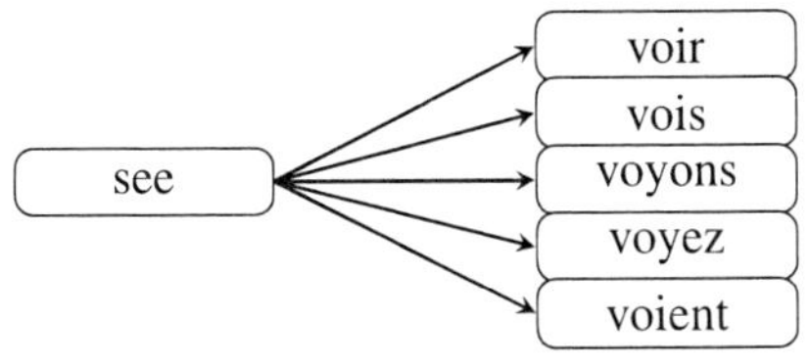

Figure 2: *One-to-many* relation between English verb 'see' and its conjugations in French

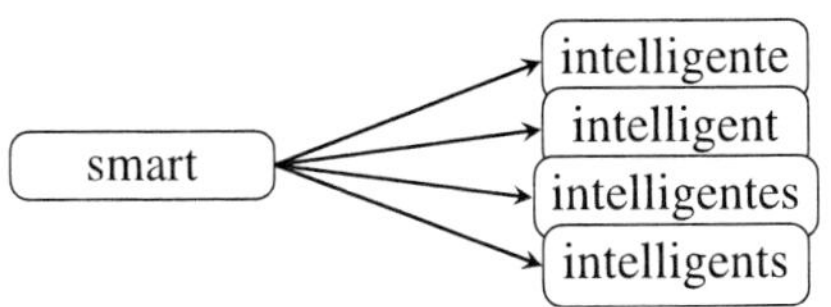

Figure 3: *One-to-many* relation between English adjective 'smart' and its male and female counterparts in French

However, from a translation point of view, the ability of MT systems to be (1) consistent and (2) learn and generalize well are –compared to previous MT systems– the biggest asset of NMT. We however, hypothesize that this type of generalization might as well have serious drawbacks and that diversity, although not deemed a priority, is of importance for the field of MT as well. Overgeneralization over a seen input and the exacerbation of dominant forms might not only lead to a loss of lexical choice, but could also be the underlying cause of gender bias exacerbation. Although, in the context of gender, some researchers have already alluded to the existence of so-called 'algorithmic bias' (Zhao et al., 2017; Prates et al., 2019), no empirical evidence has been provided so far.

With our empirical approach, comparing the lexical diversity of different MT systems and further analyzing the frequencies of words, we aim to shed some light on the relation between the loss of diversity and the exacerbation or loss of certain words. Thus, the first objective of our work is to verify how NMT compares to SMT and HT in terms of lexical richness or the loss thereof. The second objective is to quantify to what extent the different MT architectures favour translations that are more frequently observed in the training data.

The structure of the paper is the following: related work is described in Section 2; Our hypothe- ses are defined in details in Section 3; information on the data and the MT systems used in our experiments is provided in Section 4; Section 5 discusses the results of our experiments and finally, we conclude and provide some ideas for future work in Section 6.

2 Related Work

In the field of linguistics, Berman (2000) researched the so-called deforming tendencies that are inherent to the act of translation. Although these tendencies can be mitigated by the (human) translator, they are to a large extent inevitable. Quantitative impoverishment (or lexical loss), is one of the tendencies mentioned. Kruger (2012) compared human-translated to comparable non-translated English texts and found the translations to be more simplified in terms of language use than the original writings.

In the field of MT, the concept of lexical loss/diversity and its importance is indirectly related to the research of Wong and Kit (2012) on cohesion. They illustrated the relevance of the under-use of linguistic devices (super-ordinates, meronyms, synonyms and near-synonyms) for SMT in terms of cohesion. More closely related to our work is the work of Klebanov and Flor (2013) who presented findings regarding the loss of associative texture by comparing original and back-translated texts, references and system translations and a set of different MT systems. Although the destruction of the underlying networks of signification might be, to some extent, unavoidable in any translation process, the work of Klebanov and Flor (2013) shows that SMT specifically suffers from lexical loss, more than HT.

Lexical diversity or the loss thereof has also been used as a feature to estimate the quality of MT systems. Bentivogli et al. (2016) used lexical diversity, measured by using the type-token ratio (TTR), as an indicator of the size of vocabulary as well as the variety of subject matter in a text. Their experiments compared SMT to NMT and the results suggested that NMT is better able to cope with lexical diversity than SMT.

3 Hypothesis

Data-driven statistical MT paradigms[1] are concerned with (i) identifying the most probable target words, phrases, or sub-word units given a source-language input sentence and the preceding decoded information, via the translation model, and (ii) chaining those words, phrases or sub-word units in a way that maximizes the likelihood of the generated sentence with respect to the grammatical and stylistic properties of the target language, via the language model. In NMT, where translation and language modeling are co-occurring in the decoder, it boils down to finding the most likely word at each time step.

Our hypothesis is that the inherent nature of data-driven MT systems to generalise over the training data has a quantitatively distinguishable negative impact on the word choice, expressed by favouring more frequent words and disregarding less frequent ones. We hypothesize that the most visible effect of such bias is to be found in the word frequencies and the disappearance (or 'non-appearance') of scarce words. Apart from a general effect on lexical diversity, such behaviour might also lead to the disappearance or amplified use of certain morphological variants of the same word, accounting, for example, for the already observed over-use of male forms in ambiguous sentences, the preference for certain verb forms over other less frequent ones (3rd person $> 1^{st}$ person), or the difficulties of MT systems to appropriately handle morphologically richer target languages in general.

Because NMT handles translation and language modelling (or alignment) jointly (Bahdanau et al., 2015; Vaswani et al., 2017), which makes it harder to optimize compared to SMT, we further hypothesise that NMT is more susceptible to problems related to overgeneralisation.

We present our experiments and analyses in Section 4 and Section 5.

4 Empirical evaluation

To test our hypothesis we built three types of MT systems and analysed their output for two language pairs on Europarl (Koehn, 2005) data. The language pairs are English $\rightarrow$ French (EN-FR) and English $\rightarrow$ Spanish (EN-ES). We

Language pair	Train	Test	Dev
EN–FR	1,467,489	499,487	7,723
EN–ES	1,472,203	459,633	5,734

Table 1: Number of parallel sentences in the train, test and development splits for the language pairs we used.

trained attentional RNN (Bahdanau et al., 2015), Transformer (Vaswani et al., 2017) and Moses MT (Koehn et al., 2007) systems. To draw more general conclusions on the effects of bias propagation and loss of lexical richness, we assessed output from seen (during training) and unseen data.

Data We used +/- 2M sentence pairs from the Europarl corpora for each of the language pairs. We randomised the order of the sentence pairs and split the data into train, test and development sets, filtering out empty lines. Details on the different datasets can be found in Table 1. We chose to include large quantities of data in our test sets – the unseen data – in order to maximise the language variability and explore general tendencies.

MT systems For each of the three MT architectures we first trained a standard MT system (the forward or FF system) on the original data. For the RNN and Transformer systems we used OpenNMT-py. The systems were trained for 150K steps, saving an intermediate model every 5000 steps. We scored the perplexity of each model on the development set and chose the one with the lowest perplexity as our best model, used later for translation. The options we used for the neural systems are as follows:

- RNN: size: 512, RNN type: bidirectional LSTM, number of layers of the encoder and of the decoder: 4, attention type: mlp, dropout: 0.2, batch size: 128, learning optimizer: adam (Kingma and Ba, 2014) and learning rate: 0.0001.

- Transformer: number of layers: 6, size: 512, transformer_ff: 2048, number of heads: 8, dropout: 0.1, batch size: 4096, batch type: tokens, learning optimizer adam with $\text{beta}_2 = 0.998$, learning rate: 2.

All neural systems have the learning rate decay enabled and their training is distributed over 4 nVidia 1080Ti GPUs. The selected settings for the RNN systems are optimal according to (Britz et al., 2017); for the Transformer we use the set-

---

[1] Despite the fact that often phrase-based SMT is labeled as 'statistical' and contrasted to 'neural' MT or NMT, we ought to stress that both approaches are in fact *statistical*.

Language pair	SRC	TRG
EN–FR	113,132	131,104
EN–ES	113,692	168,195

Table 2: Training vocabularies for the English, French and Spanish data used for our models.

Lang. pair	EN*			FR*/ES*		
	RNN	SMT	Trans.	RNN	SMT	Trans.
EN–FR	28,742	106,441	40,321	36,991	123,770	42,309
EN–ES	27,349	118,362	40,629	39,805	138,193	44,545

Table 3: Vocabularies of the English translation from the REV systems, used as source for the BACK systems and the French/Spanish output from the BACK systems.

tings suggested by the OpenNMT community[2] as the optimal ones that lead to quality on par with the original Transformer work (Vaswani et al., 2017).

For the SMT systems we use Moses (Koehn et al., 2007) with default settings and a 5-gram language model with pruning of bigrams. Each system is further tuned with MERT (Och and Ney, 2003) until convergence or for a maximum of 25 iterations.

For the neural systems, we opted not to use subword units as is typically done for NMT. This is because we focus on the word frequencies in the translations and do not want any algorithm for splitting into sub-word units to add extra variability in our data. To construct the dictionaries we use all words in our training data. Table 2 (first two columns) shows the training vocabularies for the source and target sides.

To assess how MT amplifies bias and loss of lexical richness, along with the original-data systems, we trained MT with backtranslated (BT) data, which is typically used to complement original data for MT training when the quantity of the original data is not sufficient for reaching high translation quality (Sennrich et al., 2016; Poncelas et al., 2018).

We first trained MT systems for the reverse language directions, i.e. for FR–EN and ES–EN. We used the same data sets, but reversed the associations of the source and the target with FR/ES → EN instead of EN → FR/ES. We then used these *reversed* (*REV* or *rev*) systems to translate the training set: the same set used for training the FF systems and the REV systems. That is, we use a system trained on (say) FR–EN data to translate the same FR set into English (EN*). The aim is to see what is the impact of the underlying algorithms on the data in the most-favourable scenario; when the data has already been seen. With the translated English target data, we trained new systems for the EN*→FR and EN*→ES directions, where the source data was the backtranslated set. We refer to these systems with *BACK* and use the suffix *back* to denote them. We end up with what can

be seen as a combination of back-translation and round-trip-translation. See Figure 4 for a visualization of the pipeline of systems.

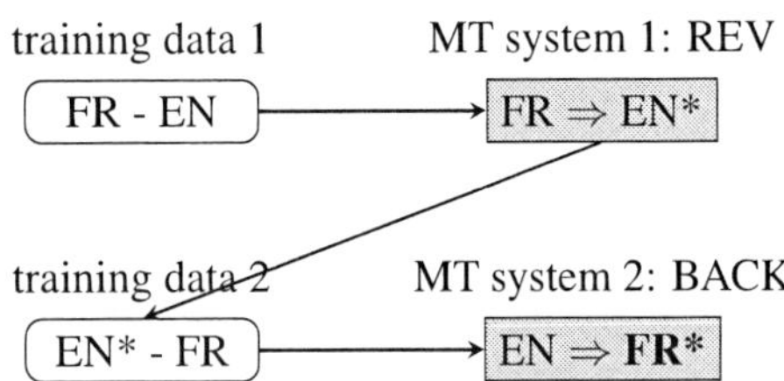

Figure 4: Back-translated data pipeline.

For the REV and BACK systems we used the same settings as for the FF ones. However, at this stage, the source side of the training data is different and thus impacts the learnable vocabulary. Table 3 presents the source-side vocabulary sizes for the RNN, SMT and Transformer systems. These are in practice the number of distinct words of the translations produced by the REV systems. Compared to Table 2, this table clearly shows how source and target vocabularies are comparable in the original datasets, but translating the same original English dataset with the neural REV systems (RNN and Transformer) results in a huge drop in vocabulary size; with the SMT REV systems the decrease is still significant, but not as profound as in the former cases.

In Table 4 we present automatic evaluation scores – BLEU (Papineni et al., 2002) and TER (Snover et al., 2006) – for the 12 analysed systems. For completeness we present BLEU and TER for the REV systems in Table 5, although we do not consider them in our analysis. For the test set we performed a statistical significance test using the *multeval* tool (Clark et al., 2011). For $p < 0.05$ all results in Table 4 are statistically significant.

In what follows we use the following denotations to indicate the system we refer to: `{src}-{trg}-{system}-{dir}`, where `{src}` indicates the source language 'en', that is English, `{trg}` indicates the target languag – 'fr'

---

[2] `http://opennmt.net/OpenNMT-py/FAQ.html`

System	Dev set		Test set	
reference	BLEU↑	TER↓	BLEU↑	TER↓
en-fr-rnn-ff	33.7	50.7	33.8	51.0
en-fr-smt-ff	35.9	50.4	35.7	50.7
en-fr-trans-ff	35.9	**49.5**	36.0	**49.4**
en-fr-rnn-back	32.8	52.1	33.0	52.1
en-fr-smt-back	35.2	51.0	35.0	51.3
en-fr-trans-back	**36.3**	49.8	**36.3**	49.9
en-es-rnn-ff	37.4	45.3	37.9	45.3
en-es-smt-ff	38.5	45.8	38.6	45.9
en-es-trans-ff	**39.4**	**44.5**	**39.5**	**44.5**
en-es-rnn-back	36.0	47.0	36.3	47.0
en-es-smt-back	38.0	46.5	38.0	46.5
en-es-trans-back	**39.4**	45.2	39.3	45.5

Table 4: Automatic evaluation scores (BLEU, TER) for all MT systems.

for French and 'es' for Spanish – and the system is one of 'HT' for human translation, 'smt' for SMT, 'rnn' for the RNN models and 'trans' for the Transformer models; {dir} is one of 'ff' to indicate that the system is the forward, trained on the original data, 'back' to indicate that the system is trained with back-translated data or 'rev' to denote that it is the reverse system, trained after swapping source and target (the human translation has no dir index).

System reference	BLEU↑	TER↓
en-fr-rnn-rev	33.3	50.2
en-fr-smt-rev	36.5	47.1
en-fr-trans-rev	**36.8**	**46.8**
en-es-rnn-rev	37.8	45.0
en-es-smt-rev	39.2	44.0
en-es-trans-rev	**40.4**	**42.7**

Table 5: Automatic evaluation scores (BLEU and TER) for the REV systems.

Evaluated output In total we trained 18 MT systems. To assess the validity of our hypothesis and to provide a quantitative analysis of the investigated phenomena, we use the outputs from the FF and the BACK systems; the REV systems are used just to generate the backtranslated data.

5 Analysis

In the analysis we compare word frequencies of the original target data to the translation output of the forward (FF) and backward (BACK) MT systems. We investigate two scenarios: (i) *seen* and (ii) *unseen* data. For (i) we translate the original source side of the training set (i.e. the English sentences) with the FF and with the BACK systems. The reason behind performing this kind of test is that since the MT system has seen this data during training, any loss of lexical richness and/or bias exacerbation are due to the inherent workings of the systems. That is, the observed differences between lexical diversity on seen data can only be attributed to the algorithm itself. For (ii) we are evaluating the lexical diversity on the (unseen) test set. This evaluation scenario is the one that gives us an indication of the overall lexical diversity of the translations produced by MT systems as compared to the data they were trained on.

Language diversity score Lexical diversity (LD) refers to the amount or range of different words that are used in a text. The greater that range, the higher the diversity. Although LD has many applications (neuropathology, data mining, language acquisition), coming up with a robust index to quantify it has proven to be a difficult task. A comparison between different measures of LD (McCarthy and Jarvis, 2010) concluded by saying that, although there is no consensus yet, LD can be assessed in different ways, with each measurement having its own assets and drawbacks. Therefore, we evaluated LD by using four different widely used metrics: type/token ratio (TTR) (Templin, 1975), Yule's K (in practice, we use the reverse Yule's I) (Yule, 1944), and the measure of textual lexical diversity (MTLD) (McCarthy, 2005).

The easiest lexical richness metric is TTR. TTR is the ratio of the types, i.e. total number of *different* words in a text to its tokens, i.e. the total number of words. A high/low TTR indicates a high/low degree of lexical diversity. While TTR is one of the most widely used metrics, it has some drawbacks linked to the assumption of a linear relation between the types and the tokens. Because of that, TTR is only valid when comparing texts of a similar size, as it decreases when texts become longer due to repetitions of words (Brezina, 2018).

Yule's characteristic constant, or Yule's K, is a probability model of the changes that take place in the lexical frequency spectrum of a text as the text becomes longer. Yule's K and its reverse Yule's I are considered to be more immune to fluctuations related to text length than TTR (Oakes and Ji, 2013).

Another metric used to study lexical richness and diversity is MTLD. The difference with the two previous methods is that MTLD is evaluated sequentially as the mean length of sequential word strings in a text that maintain a given TTR value

(McCarthy, 2005). A more recent study by McCarthy and Jarvis (2010) shows that MTLD is the most robust with respect to text length.

Our metrics are presented in Table 6 and Table 7. Higher/lower scores indicate higher/lower lexical richness. Table 6 shows the metrics for the human and the machine translations of the training set, i.e. the seen data, and Table 7 shows the scores for the human (HT) and the machine translations of the test sets, i.e. the unseen data. Due to the large number of output words, e.g. the rnn-ff translation of the EN–FR test set contains 14 561 653 words, and the low vocabulary size relative to the total number of words, our TTR scores are quite low. For readability and for ease of comparison we present these scores multiplied by a factor of 1000. We tested pairwise statistical significance through bootstrap sampling following (Koehn, 2004). The scores for all MT variants are significantly different from the HT variant.

Translation	Yules I	TTR * 1000	MTLD
en-fr-HT	*9.2793*	*2.9277*	*127.1766*
en-fr-rnn-ff	0.7107	0.8656	109.4506
en-fr-smt-ff	6.7492	2.6442	118.1239
en-fr-trans-ff	1.1768	1.0925	120.5179
en-fr-rnn-back	0.7587	0.8776	116.8942
en-fr-smt-back	**7.8738**	**2.7496**	120.9909
en-fr-trans-back	1.0325	1.0172	**121.5801**
en-es-HT	*12.3065*	*3.7037*	*99.0850*
en-es-rnn-ff	0.6298	0.9394	89.3562
en-es-smt-ff	7.3249	3.1170	95.1146
en-es-trans-ff	1.0022	1.1581	**96.2113**
en-es-rnn-back	0.7355	0.9829	95.7198
en-es-smt-back	**8.1325**	**3.2166**	95.1479
en-es-trans-back	0.9162	1.1014	95.0886

Table 6: Lexical richness metrics (Train set).

Translation	Yules I	TTR * 1000	MTLD
en-fr-HT	33.6709	5.7022	124.1889
en-fr-rnn-ff	4.4766	2.1969	106.1370
en-fr-smt-ff	21.1230	4.8034	113.9262
en-fr-trans-ff	6.5352	2.5957	118.9642
en-fr-rnn-back	5.1490	2.3092	112.9991
en-fr-smt-back	**25.7705**	**5.1254**	117.6979
en-fr-trans-back	6.7921	2.6287	**119.1729**
en-es-HT	48.2366	7.6151	97.0591
en-es-rnn-ff	4.7988	2.6250	85.4589
en-es-smt-ff	24.6771	5.9171	92.6397
en-es-trans-ff	6.7967	3.0432	**94.4709**
en-es-rnn-back	6.0098	2.8357	92.4704
en-es-smt-back	**28.0153**	**6.1887**	92.3310
en-es-trans-back	7.3824	3.1483	92.8928

Table 7: Lexical richness metrics (Test set).

Word frequencies and bias In order to prove/disprove our hypothesis, along with investigating lexical richness, we aim to investigate to what extent MT systems propagate bias in the output. This we assess by whether more/less frequent words in the human translation have higher/lower frequency in the MT output (see Section 3). As soon as we started training the BACK systems, the first thing we observed was the reduced vocabularies from the FF systems. The loss of certain words (in the case of unknown words, the RNN and Transformer systems would generate the `<unk>` token) already suggests biased MT. Comparing Table 2 and Table 3, we see that a lot of words are not accounted for in all systems, but that the RNN and Transformer models suffer the most. We believe this is due to the fact that NMT systems' advantage over more traditional systems, namely its ability to generalize and learn over the entire sentence, has a negative affect on lexical diversity, particularly for the least frequent words.

Due to the differences in vocabularies and sentence lengths of the generated translations, in order to conduct a realistic comparison of the frequencies we applied 3 post-processing steps on the collected data: (i) we accounted for sentence variability by normalizing the frequency of each word (in the HT or the MT output) by the length of sentences in which it appears, (ii) we normalized the frequency of each word (in the HT or the MT output) by the accumulated frequency, reducing each frequency to a probability, and (iii) to account for the missing words in the MT output we counted words with zero frequencies separately. In addition, we need to make a distinction between frequent and non-frequent words. While this is a hard task in itself, here we commit to the average normalized word frequency of the human translation.

Once we applied the aforementioned post-processing we compactly represent our data in six classes:

- *Frequency increase of frequent words*: for a frequent word in the HT, its frequency in the MT is higher. We denote this class using '+ +' symbol combination. This class also indicates positive bias exacerbation.

- *Frequency decrease of frequent words*: for a frequent word in the HT, its frequency in the MT is lower (but not zero). We denote this class using '+ −' symbol combination.

- *Frequency increase of non-frequent words*: for a non-frequent word in the HT, its frequency in the MT is higher. We denote this class using '− +' symbol combination.

- *Frequency decrease of non-frequent words*: for a non-frequent word in the HT, its frequency in the MT is lower (but not zero). We denote this class using '− −' symbol combination. This class indicates negative bias exacerbation.

- *Zero frequency of frequent words*: a frequent word in the HT, does not appear in the MT. We denote this class using '+ 0' symbol combination.

- *Zero frequency of non-frequent words*: a non-frequent word in the HT, does not appear in the MT. We denote this class using '− 0' symbol combination. This class indicates negative bias exacerbation.

For each of these classes we count the (normalized) number of words, and we accumulate the absolute value of the differences for each of these cases. We present our results for the training data in Table 8, Table 10 and for the test data – in Table 9, Table 11. The numbers in Table 8 and Table 9 can be interpreted as the amount of translated words with higher, lower or zero frequency compared to the human translation.[3] The numbers in Table 10 and Table 11 quantify the differences between frequencies; they indicate the amount of increase or decrease in the frequencies presented by an MT system as compared to the HT. To derive information from these numbers, one should compare the '+ +' to '+ −' and '− +' to '− −' and '+ 0' to '− 0'.

System	+ +	+ -	- +	- -	+ 0	- 0
en-fr-rnn-ff	3710	3023	10157	18683	10	95519
en-fr-smt-ff	3362	3381	32577	46714	0	45068
en-fr-trans-ff	3839	2901	12398	24403	3	87558
en-fr-rnn-back	3356	3372	13009	17253	15	94097
en-fr-smt-back	3246	3496	34111	43472	1	46776
en-fr-trans-back	3482	3254	14610	20962	7	88787
en-es-rnn-ff	4667	3532	9929	19149	41	130875
en-es-smt-ff	4276	3963	39817	56169	1	63967
en-es-trans-ff	4626	3601	11379	25698	13	122876
en-es-rnn-back	4265	3951	13716	17872	24	128365
en-es-smt-back	4006	4233	39636	51831	1	68486
en-es-trans-back	4288	3929	14295	22032	23	123626

Table 8: Frequency exacerbation and decay count (Train set)

System	+ +	+ -	- +	- -	+ 0	- 0
en-fr-rnn-ff	2917	2335	10653	15400	11	57623
en-fr-smt-ff	2652	2610	20587	26949	1	36140
en-fr-trans-ff	2997	2264	12537	17430	2	53709
en-fr-rnn-back	2642	2610	13513	14963	11	55200
en-fr-smt-back	2577	2684	22604	26608	2	34464
en-fr-trans-back	2701	2554	14932	17101	8	51643
en-es-rnn-ff	3541	2669	10636	16425	27	75113
en-es-smt-ff	3252	2982	23389	29057	3	49728
en-es-trans-ff	3508	2716	12069	19046	13	71059
en-es-rnn-back	3241	2971	14394	15847	25	71933
en-es-smt-back	3163	3072	24547	28389	2	49238
en-es-trans-back	3256	2967	15160	18606	14	68408

Table 9: Frequency exacerbation and decay count (Test set)

System	+ +	+ -	- +	- -	+ 0	- 0
en-fr-rnn-ff	840.76	687.16	46.36	115.27	1.47	83.22
en-fr-smt-ff	664.86	555.60	31.17	119.64	0.00	20.79
en-fr-trans-ff	663.00	552.74	49.98	108.63	0.40	51.20
en-fr-rnn-back	770.72	680.73	83.68	96.68	2.19	74.81
en-fr-smt-back	620.67	525.26	40.36	112.35	0.13	23.29
en-fr-trans-back	639.69	568.68	75.88	90.25	1.05	55.58
en-es-rnn-ff	733.44	535.15	42.54	117.47	4.93	118.43
en-es-smt-ff	547.86	423.87	33.22	129.73	0.12	27.35
en-es-trans-ff	587.22	436.02	47.61	119.98	1.37	77.46
en-es-rnn-back	677.23	564.31	94.47	101.57	2.92	102.90
en-es-smt-back	561.03	438.09	44.31	133.35	0.12	33.78
en-es-trans-back	548.37	438.33	72.27	98.11	2.33	81.87

Table 10: Accumulated frequency differences (Train set)

Remarks on automatic evaluation The summary of our results allows us to draw the following conclusions:

1. *Lexical richness* All metrics and results presented in Table 6 and Table 7 and for both language pairs indicate that neither of the MT systems reaches the lexical richness of the HT. While SMT systems (for both language pairs) retain more language richness according to two out of the three metrics (Yule's I and TTR) than the neural methods, the MTLD scores indicate that the Transformer systems lead to translations of higher lexical richness. This we may account for the different numbers of distinct words produced by SMT and neural systems, which may be favoured by Yule's I and TTR. However, consistently, the worst systems are the RNN ones.

2. *Automatic quality evaluation vs. lexical richness*: The results in Table 4 show that the Transformer systems perform best. The only lexical richness metric that corroborates the BLEU and TER scores is MTLD. This observation can act as a future research direction for integrating or improving quality evaluation metrics of MT to

---

[3]Note that these numbers are normalized for fair comparison.

System	+ +	+ -	- +	- -	+ 0	- 0
en-fr-rnn-ff	827.07	655.81	68.84	133.21	2.48	104.41
en-fr-smt-ff	790.41	640.60	60.98	156.94	0.13	53.71
en-fr-trans-ff	662.76	533.83	73.15	123.07	0.31	78.70
en-fr-rnn-back	751.49	655.35	112.32	114.16	2.28	92.01
en-fr-smt-back	679.17	551.88	64.50	142.50	0.34	48.96
en-fr-trans-back	625.59	548.18	104.26	107.39	1.41	72.88
en-es-rnn-ff	726.16	509.28	67.76	134.45	4.16	146.04
en-es-smt-ff	679.08	503.57	70.86	169.33	0.38	76.67
en-es-trans-ff	592.32	414.37	73.00	134.59	1.84	114.52
en-es-rnn-back	653.89	533.03	128.86	119.04	4.22	126.46
en-es-smt-back	630.86	462.82	74.19	165.11	0.31	76.81
en-es-trans-back	538.03	415.49	103.32	118.89	2.40	104.57

Table 11: Accumulated frequency differences (Test set)

accommodate for lexical richness by possibly adopting features from MTLD.

3. *Bias* To understand how the inherent probabilistic nature of PB-SMT and NMT systems exacerbates (or not) the bias, we rely on the result in Table 8, Table 9, Table 10 and Table 11. More precisely, we focus on the comparison between '[+ +]' and '[+ −]', and the '[− +]' and '[− −]' classes as well as the values in the '[+ 0]' and '[− 0]' classes. One could simplify the analysis by joining the latter two classes together with '[+ −]' and '[− −]'. However, their independent analysis carries more important information. Precisely, we see that all of the systems lose less frequent words, indicated by the low numbers for the '[+ 0]' class for both the training and the test set translations. Second, not all MT systems produce more words with higher frequencies (for the Train set: en-fr-PB-SMT-ff with 3362 vs 3381, en-fr-PB-SMT-back with 3246 vs 3496 and en-es-PB-SMT-back with 4006 vs 4233; for the test set: en-fr-PB-SMT-back with 2577 vs 2684), but the accumulative normalized frequency for such words is higher than that of the HT. The accumulated frequency differences indicate that MT systems are indeed biased towards these more frequent words. This observation, together with the fact that all MT systems suffer from loss of less frequent words, further supports our hypothesis that MT systems target learning the more frequent words and disregard the less frequent ones.

4. *Seen and unseen data* We divided our experiments over seen and unseen data. From the perspective of lexical richness we see the same trends in both cases, although a slight decrease

can be observed for the unseen test set (measured by the MTLD metric). With regards to the word frequencies comparing '+ +' and '+ −' classes in Table 10 and Table 11 we see similar trends. Furthermore, more words are lost altogether when translating the unseen test set.

It should be stressed that in this work we looked at the frequency of words, and as such the RNN and Transformer models we trained are not optimized according to state-of-the-art settings. In particular, no BPE is used to account for out-of-vocabulary problems, and the vocabularies have not been restricted prior to training (typically the vocabulary of an NMT system consists of the K, e.g. 50k most frequent words/tokens).

Another observation that we ought to note is that the BACK systems score quite high not only based on word frequencies and lexical richness metrics, but also based on the evaluation metrics presented in Table 4. We assume this is due to the fact that the simplified source (translated by the REV systems) changes the complexity of the learned association. We plan to further investigate these systems.

Semi-manual evaluation To obtain a more concrete image of the observed bias exacerbation by MT, we looked into the translations of 15 random English words: 'picture', 'create', 'states', 'happen', 'genuine', 'successful', 'also', 'reasons', 'membership', 'encourage', 'selling', 'site', 'vibrant', 'still' and 'event'. This evaluation does not have the intention to be exhaustive, as the general tendencies of the systems have already been discussed in the previous sections. However, looking into some actual translations produced by the systems does further clarify the exacerbation effect of the learning algorithm.

Let us first look at the Spanish translations of the English word 'picture', presented in Figure 5. The original data shows quite a lot of diversity as 'picture' can be translated into among others 'imagen', 'imágenes', 'visión', 'foto', 'fotografías' and 'fotos'. However, when we look at the output of the EN–ES MT systems, we see that all of them use the most frequent translation –'imagen'– even more frequently than in the original data. This comes at the expense of the other translation variants. Although the second most frequent translation ('imágenes') is still frequent, all others show a decrease and the least frequent ones disappear entirely.

Similar, though slightly different patterns are observed for the translations of the other words we examine. Also presented in Figure 5 are the translations of the English verb 'happen' into the Spanish verbs 'ocurrir', 'suceder', 'pasar', 'acontecer' and 'pasarse' and the English conector 'also' into 'también', 'además' and 'igualmente'. Again, the graphs show how the most frequent translation(s) gain in relative frequency at the cost of less frequent options.

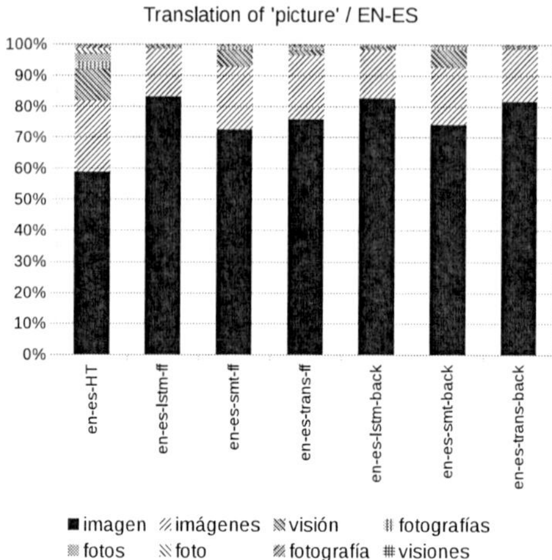

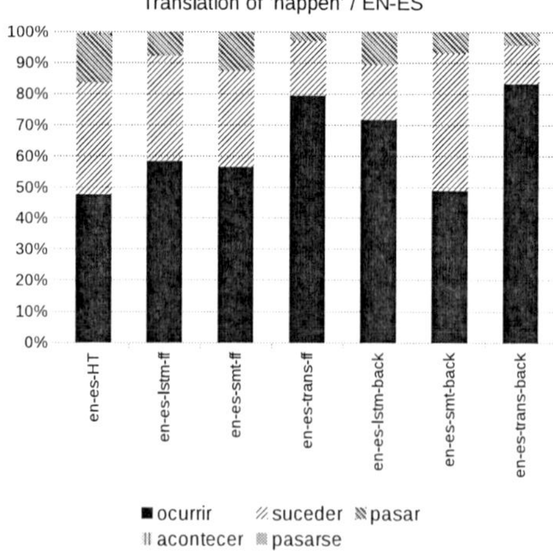

Figure 5: Relative frequencies of the Spanish translations of the English words 'picture' and 'happen'.

6   Conclusions and Future Work

This work investigates bias exacerbation and loss of lexical richness through the process of MT. We analyse the problem of loss of lexical richness using a number of LD metrics on the output of 12 different MT systems: SMT, RNN and Transformer models for EN–FR and EN–ES with original and back-translated data.

Via our experiments and their subsequent analysis, we observe that the process of MT causes a general loss in terms of lexical diversity and richness when compared to human-generated text. This confirms our first hypothesis. Furthermore, we investigate how this loss comes about and whether it is indeed the case that the more frequent words observed in the input occur even more in the output, negatively affecting the frequency of less seen events or words by causing them to become even rarer events or causing them to disappear altogether. Our analysis shows that MT paradigms indeed increase/decrease the frequencies of more/less frequent words to such extend that a very large amount of words are completely 'lost in translation'. We believe, this demonstrates indeed that current systems overgeneralize and thus, we deem it appropriate to speak of a form of algorithmic bias.

Overall, the RNNs systems are among the worst performing in terms of LD, although we do need to take into account that, for the sake of comparison, we did not use BPE, which might gave the neural models a disadvantage compared to the SMT systems. While Transformer models are the best ones according to the evaluation metrics, SMT seems to retain the most lexical richness according to the LD metrics we used (TTR, Yule's I and MTLD).

As research on language generation has already accounted for the lack of diverse outputs, in the future, we aim to lock into potential solutions to overgeneralization of current trnaslation models. However, allowing for a certain degree of randomness while maintaining a strong learning (and thus generalizing) ability is a very complex and potentially contradictory task.

Acknowledgements

This work has been supported by the Dublin City University Faculty of Engineering & Computing under the Daniel O'Hare Research Scholarship scheme and by the ADAPT Centre for Digital Content Technology, which is funded under the SFI Research Centres Programme (Grant 13/RC/2106).

References

Bahdanau, Dzmitry, Kyunghyun Cho, and Yoshua Bengio. 2015. Neural Machine Translation by Jointly Learning to Align and Translate. In *Proceedings of International Conference on Learning Representations (ICLR2015)*, San Diego, USA, May.

Bentivogli, Luisa, Arianna Bisazza, Mauro Cettolo, and Marcello Federico. 2016. Neural versus Phrase-Based Machine Translation Quality: a Case Study. In *Proceedings of the 2016 Conference on Empirical Methods in Natural Language Processing, EMNLP*, pages 257–267, Austin, Texas, USA, November.

Berman, Antoine. 2000. Translation and the Trials of the Foreign. In *The Translation Studies Reader*. Routledge London.

Brezina, Vaclav. 2018. *Statistics in Corpus Linguistics: A Practical Guide*. Cambridge University Press.

Britz, Denny, Anna Goldie, Minh-Thang Luong, and Quoc Le. 2017. Massive Exploration of Neural Machine Translation Architectures. In *Proceedings of the Association for Computational Linguistics (ACL)*, pages 1442–1451, Vancouver, Canada, July–August.

Clark, Jonathan H, Chris Dyer, Alon Lavie, and Noah A Smith. 2011. Better Hypothesis Testing for Statistical Machine Translation: Controlling for Optimizer Instability. In *Proceedings of the 49th Annual Meeting of the Association for Computational Linguistics (ACL): Human Language Technologies: short papers, Volume 2*, pages 176–181, Portland, Oregon, USA, June.

Kingma, Diederik P. and Jimmy Ba. 2014. Adam: A Method for Stochastic Optimization. In *Proceedings of the 3rd International Conference on Learning Representations: Poster Session*, Banff, Canada, April.

Klebanov, Beata Beigman and Michael Flor. 2013. Associative Texture is Lost in Translation. In *Proceedings of the Workshop on Discourse in Machine Translation*, pages 27–32, Sofia, Bulgaria, August.

Koehn, Philipp, Hieu Hoang, Alexandra Birch, Chris Callison-Burch, Marcello Federico, Nicola Bertoldi, Brooke Cowan, Wade Shen, Christine Moran, Richard Zens, Chris Dyer, Ondrej Bojar, Alexandra Constantin, and Evan Herbst. 2007. Moses: Open-Source Toolkit for Statistical Machine Translation. In *Proceedings of the 45th Annual Meeting of the Association of Computational Linguistics (ACL)*, pages 177–180, Prague, Czech Republic, June.

Koehn, Philipp. 2004. Statistical significance tests for machine translation evaluation. In *Proceedings of the 2004 Conference on Empirical Methods in Natural Language Processing, (EMNLP 2004), A meeting of SIGDAT, a Special Interest Group of the ACL, held in conjunction with ACL 2004*, pages 388–395, Barcelona, Spain, July.

Koehn, Philipp. 2005. Europarl: A Parallel Corpus for Statistical Machine Translation. In *Proceedings of The Tenth Machine Translation Summit*, pages 79–86, Phuket, Thailand, September.

Kruger, Haidee. 2012. A Corpus-Based Study of the Mediation Effect in Translated and Edited Language. In *Target. International Journal of Translation Studies, Volume 24:2*, pages 355–388. John Benjamins Publishing Company, Amsterdam, The Netherlands.

McCarthy, Philip M and Scott Jarvis. 2010. MTLD, vocd-D, and HD-D: A Validation Study of Sophisticated Approaches to Lexical Diversity Assessment. In *Behavior Research Methods, Volume 2:2*, pages 381–392. Springer, Berlin, Germany.

McCarthy, Philip M. 2005. An Assessment of the Range and Usefulness of Lexical Diversity Measures and the Potential of the Measure of Textual, Lexical Diversity (MTLD). In *PhD Thesis, Dissertation Abstracts International, Volume 66:12*. University of Memphis, Memphis, Tennessee, USA.

Oakes, Michael P and Meng (eds) Ji. 2013. Quantitative Methods in Corpus-Based Translation Studies: A Practical Guide to Descriptive Translation Research. In *Studies in Corpus Linguistics, Volume 51*, page 361. John Benjamins Publishing Company, Amsterdam, The Netherlands.

Och, Franz Josef and Hermann Ney. 2003. A Systematic Comparison of Various Statistical Alignment Models. In *Computational Linguistics, Volume 29:1*, pages 19–51. MIT Press, Cambridge, Massachusetts, USA.

Papineni, Kishore, Salim Roukos, Todd Ward, and Wei-Jing Zhu. 2002. BLEU: a Method for Automatic Evaluation of Machine Translation. In *Proceedings of the 40th Annual Meeting on Association for Computational Linguistics (ACL)*, pages 311–318, Philadephia, PA, USA, July.

Passban, Peyman, Andy Way, and Qun Liu. 2018. Tailoring Neural Architectures for Translating from Morphologically Rich Languages. In *Proceedings of the 27th International Conference on Computational Linguistics (COLING)*, pages 3134–3145, Santa Fe, New-Mexico, USA, August.

Poncelas, Alberto, Dimitar Shterionov, Andy Way, Gideon Maillette de Buy Wenniger, and Peyman Passban. 2018. Investigating Backtranslation in Neural Machine Translation. In *Proceedings of the 21st Annual Conference of the European Association for Machine Translation (EAMT)*, pages 249–258, Alacant, Spain, May.

Prates, Marcelo OR, Pedro HC Avelar, and Luis Lamb. 2019. Assessing Gender Bias in Machine Translation–A Case Study with Google Translate. In *Neural Computing and Applications*. Springer, Berlin, Germany, March.

Sennrich, Rico, Barry Haddow, and Alexandra Birch. 2016. Improving Neural Machine Translation Models with Monolingual Data. In *Proceedings of the 54th Annual Meeting of the Association for Computational Linguistics (ACL): Long Papers*, pages 86–96, Berlin, Germany, August.

Snover, Matthew, Bonnie Dorr, Richard Schwartz, Linnea Micciulla, and John Makhoul. 2006. A Study of Translation Edit Rate with Targeted Human Annotation. In *Proceedings of Association for Machine Translation in the Americas (AMTA) 200:6*, pages 223–231, Austin, Texas, USA, October.

Templin, Mildred C. 1975. *Certain Language Skills in Children: Their Development and Interrelationships*. Greenwood Press, Westport, Connecticut, USA.

Unanue, Inigo Jauregi, Lierni Garmendia Arratibel, Ehsan Zare Borzeshi, and Massimo Piccardi. 2018. English-Basque statistical and neural machine translation. In *Proceedings of the Eleventh International Conference on Language Resources and Evaluation (LREC-2018)*, pages 880–885, Miyazaki, Japan, May.

Vanmassenhove, Eva, Jinhua Du, and Andy Way. 2016. Improving Subject-Verb Agreement in SMT. In *Proceedings of the Fifth Workshop on Hybrid Approaches to Translation: HyTra (EAMT)*, Riga, Latvia, June.

Vanmassenhove, Eva, Christian Hardmeier, and Andy Way. 2018. Getting Gender Right in Neural Machine Translation. In *Proceedings of the 2018 Conference on Empirical Methods in Natural Language Processing (EMNLP)*, pages 3003–3008, Brussels, Belgium, Novemebr–October.

Vaswani, Ashish, Noam Shazeer, Niki Parmar, Jakob Uszkoreit, Llion Jones, Aidan N Gomez, Ł ukasz Kaiser, and Illia Polosukhin. 2017. Attention is All you Need. In *Proceedings of The Thirty-first Annual Conference on Neural Information Processing Systems 30 (NIPS)*, pages 5998–6008, Long Beach, CA, USA, December.

Wong, Billy and Chunyu Kit. 2012. Extending Machine Translation Evaluation Metrics with Lexical Cohesion to Document Level. In *Proceedings of the 2012 Joint Conference on Empirical Methods in Natural Language Processing and Computational Natural Language Learning (EMNL)*, pages 1060–1068, Jeju Island, Korea, July.

Yule, G. Udny. 1944. *The Statistical Study of Literary Vocabulary*. Cambridge University Press, Cambridge, USA.

Zhao, Jieyu, Tianlu Wang, Mark Yatskar, Vicente Ordonez, and Kai-Wei Chang. 2017. Men also Like Shopping: Reducing Gender Bias Amplification Using Corpus-Level Constraints. In *Proceedings of the 2017 Conference on Empirical Methods in Natural Language Processing (EMNL)*, pages 2979–2989, Copenhagen, Denmark, September.

Identifying Fluently Inadequate Output
in Neural and Statistical Machine Translation

Marianna J. Martindale† Marine Carpuat‡ Kevin Duh° Paul McNamee°
†iSchool, ‡Dept. of Computer Science, University of Maryland, College Park, USA
°HLTCOE, Johns Hopkins University, Baltimore, USA
`mmartind@umiacs.umd.edu, marine@cs.umd.edu`
`kevinduh@cs.jhu.edu, mcnamee@jhu.edu`

Abstract

With the impressive fluency of modern machine translation output, systems may produce output that is fluent but not adequate (*fluently inadequate*). We seek to identify these errors and quantify their frequency in MT output of varying quality. To that end, we introduce a method for automatically predicting whether translated segments are fluently inadequate by predicting fluency using grammaticality scores and predicting adequacy by augmenting sentence BLEU with a novel Bag-of-Vectors Sentence Similarity (BVSS). We then apply this technique to analyze the outputs of statistical and neural systems for six language pairs with different levels of translation quality. We find that neural models are consistently more prone to this type of error than traditional statistical models. However, improving the overall quality of the MT system such as through domain adaptation reduces these errors.

1 Introduction

Recent work has shown that well-trained, in-domain neural machine translation (NMT) systems can produce translations that, at the sentence level, are rated on par with human reference translations (Hassan Awadalla et al., 2018). Part of this success comes from the impressive improvements in fluency of NMT output compared to previous MT paradigms (Bentivogli et al., 2016; Toral and Sánchez-Cartagena, 2017; Koehn and Knowles,

2017). However, NMT has also been shown to sometimes produce output that is low adequacy and even unrelated to the input–particularly when not trained on sufficient in-domain data (Koehn and Knowles, 2017). Because of NMT's uncanny ability to produce fluent output, these translations may not just be inadequate but *fluently inadequate*. The fluency of *fluently inadequate* translations may mislead users into trusting the content based on fluency alone–particularly in the context of other fluent and adequate translations (Martindale and Carpuat, 2018).

Mitigating the effects of fluently inadequate translations first requires understanding the scale of the problem and what situations are likely to generate these errors. The general success and high system level quality of NMT suggests that fluently inadequate translations are rare, but we cannot say how rare without a means of automatically identifying *potentially* fluently inadequate translations in large collections of MT output.

In this work, we propose a method to automatically detect fluently inadequate translations based on the underlying characteristics of fluency and adequacy. We view fluently inadequate translations as translations that are fluent, well-formed sentences that could have been written by a human, and that do not preserve the meaning of the reference. In practice, given a reference translation r and MT hypothesis h, we consider h to be fluently inadequate if $fluency(h) > \tau_f$ and $adequacy(h, r) < \tau_a$, where τ_a and τ_f are minimum fluency and adequacy thresholds respectively. We define novel fluency and adequacy metrics for this purpose, building on prior work on grammaticality detection and comparisons of multisets applied to word embeddings (Section 2).

We conduct two sets of experiments. First, we

evaluate the fluency and adequacy metrics, establishing that they can be used for the task of detecting fluently inadequate translations, and set thresholds τ_a and τ_f empirically in Sections 3.1 and 3.2. We then conduct an automatic analysis to assess how frequent these errors are in neural and statistical machine translation (SMT) systems for a variety of languages and varying levels of model quality and train/test domain match. We find that fluently inadequate translations are more common in NMT overall, especially when there is less training data and when there is a mismatch between training and test data.

2 Approach

2.1 Predicting Fluency

We propose to score fluency using metrics introduced for the related task of detecting grammaticality, which scores the well-formedness of a sentence. Lau et al (2016) take an unsupervised, language modeling approach to predicting grammaticality. Based on the intuition that well-formedness errors will be caused by one or more incorrect or out of place words, they introduce scores based not only on sentence probability, but also on scores that focus on lowest word probabilities in a segment. Specifically, given a 5-gram language model, the following scores are computed:

$$Mean\ LP = \frac{\sum_{n=1:N} \log p_5(w_n|w_{n-1}, ...)}{N} \quad (1)$$

$$Norm\ LP = \frac{\sum_{n=1:N} \log p_5(w_n|w_{n-1}, ...)}{\sum_{n=1:N} \log p_1(w_n)} \quad (2)$$

$$Word\ LPmin_n = min_n \left\{ -\frac{\log p_5(w)}{\log p_1(w)} \right\} \quad (3)$$

$$Word\ LP_{n\%} = \frac{\sum_{w \in LP_{n\%}} -\frac{\log p_5(w)}{\log p_1(w)}}{|LP_{n\%}|} \quad (4)$$

$$Word\ LP_{mean} = \frac{\sum_{n=1:N} -\frac{\log p_5(w_n)}{\log p_1(w_n)}}{N} \quad (5)$$

where $logp_5$ is the 5-gram log probability, w_n is the nth word and N is the number of words in the sentence. $Mean\ LP$ is the sentence n-gram log probability, normalized by length. $Norm\ LP$ is the sentence n-gram log probability, normalized by sentence unigram log probability. The other metrics are focused on probability of individual words given the preceding words. Each word's 5-gram log probability is normalized by its unigram probability ($logp_1$), $Word\ LPmin_n$ is the nth lowest normalized word probability, $LP_{n\%}$ is the lowest $n\%$ normalized word probabilities. Because there may be outliers that score artificially low, we introduce an additional variant, $Word\ LP_{mid}$, which uses LP_{mid}, the middle 50% of the normalized word probabilities:

$$Word\ LP_{mid} = \frac{\sum_{w \in LP_{mid}} -\frac{\log p_5(w)}{\log p_1(w)}}{|LP_{mid}|} \quad (6)$$

We expect that fluently inadequate output is being influenced by the training data more than the input text, so we build our language model based on the target side of the system training data rather than a large generic language model.

2.2 Predicting Adequacy

BLEU (Papineni et al., 2002) is a widely accepted baseline measure of MT quality at the system level and, as such, is an obvious choice for a baseline adequacy metric. However, it may not be well suited for this task. Segments with high BLEU scores more closely match the reference, indicating high adequacy, but translations that receive a lower BLEU score may be inadequate or they may be adequate with different word choice. For the purpose of detecting fluently inadequate translations, we can be confident that a segment with a high BLEU score is adequate, but low BLEU scores do not necessarily imply low adequacy.

To account for cases where a translation may be adequate but receive a low BLEU score, we need an adequacy metric that will be less affected by word choice. This suggests the need for comparing semantic representations rather than matching strings. For our baseline vector-based metric, we use the common, simple approach of comparing sentence embeddings generated by averaging the word embeddings for each word in the sentence. However, this approach does not directly compare any of the word vectors, only their sum, and there are many unrelated sentences that could produce the same sentence vector. We introduce an alternative word embedding based measure of sentence similarity that overcomes this flaw to produce more a reliable adequacy metric, bag-of-vectors sentence similarity (BVSS).

BVSS Metric   BVSS is an application of Saga (Similarity AGregation Application) introduced by Knox (2015). The Saga approach frames a task as an information similarity problem. Given a measure of information I for a multiset, the similarity between two multisets, X and Y, is the proportion of information from the union of X and Y that is found in both X and Y:

$$S(X,Y) = \frac{I(X) + I(Y) - I(X \cup Y)}{I(X \cup Y)} \quad (7)$$

The information measure in Saga uses single-linkage agglomerative clustering (Florek et al., 1951). If the items in a multiset are clustered according to similarity, more clusters indicate more disparate items and, therefore, more information. When we compare two multisets of items, X and Y, we first cluster each multiset separately to get $I(X)$ and $I(Y)$. We then pool all of the items and cluster again to get $I(X \cup Y)$. If the items in X are similar to the items in Y, those items will cluster together yielding fewer clusters than if they were different.

A nice feature of this approach is that in addition to the undirected similarity, we can modify Equation 7 to a directed form. The directed similarity to X of Y would be given by the proportion of information in Y that also appears in X:

$$S_X(Y) = \frac{I(X) + I(Y) - I(X \cup Y)}{I(Y)} \quad (8)$$

To compare sentences with this approach, we treat a sentence as a multiset of words and determine the similarity of words using the cosine similarity of their embeddings. Replacing X and Y in equation 7 with S for MT system output and R for reference gives us the *BVSS* metric:

$$BVSS(S,R) = \frac{I(S) + I(R) - I(S \cup R)}{I(S \cup R)} \quad (9)$$

The directed form provides a way to measure when information is lost (i.e., the reference has more information than the MT output) or hallucinated (the MT output has more information than the reference). We will use *BVSS-reference* and *BVSS-system* to refer to these directed similarities.

BVSS-reference is the proportion of the information in the reference that is also in the MT output and *BVSS-system* is the proportion of the information in the MT output that is also in the reference:

$$BVSS_{reference} = \frac{I(S) + I(R) - I(S \cup R)}{I(R)} \quad (10)$$

$$BVSS_{system} = \frac{I(R) + I(S) - I(R \cup S)}{I(S)} \quad (11)$$

3   Detection Method Evaluation

Since there is no existing dataset with manual annotation of fluently inadequate translations, we first evaluate our fluency and adequacy prediction approaches comparing against direct assessment scores from WMT16 (Bojar et al., 2016) as 2016 was the only year in which human fluency judgments were collected. We then use our automated fluency scores on reference translations and automated adequacy scores on synthetic low adequacy "translations" to determine thresholds for high fluency and dubious adequacy.

3.1   Fluency Experiments

Task   For WMT16, fluency judgments were collected for Czech-English (CS-EN), German-English (DE-EN), Finnish-English (FI-EN), Romanian-English (RO-EN), Russian-English (RU-EN), and Turkish-English (TR-EN) in the news shared task. Annotations were collected with the goal of system-level reliability, so many segments only have one judgment. To improve reliability, we use only segments where there are two or more judgments.

Model setup   Fluency scores are based on a 5-gram language model. We built a 5-gram KenLM (Heafield, 2011; Heafield et al., 2013) language model using the monolingual news training data from WMT16.

Results   For each of the metrics described in section 2.1, we calculated the Pearson correlation with the direct assessment scores for each of the language pair data sets and for all the data combined. Results are shown in Table 1. Although these correlations are lower than we would like, we find that for all language pairs and for the combined data, $WordLP_{mid}$ yields the highest correlation, so we will use this formula for our fluency prediction metric.

Fluency Metric	CS-EN	DE-EN	FI-EN	RO-EN	RU-EN	TR-EN	All
$Mean LP$	0.32619	0.21290	0.27686	0.25831	0.22792	0.32402	0.26974
$Norm LP$	0.41271	0.26721	0.25297	0.22797	0.27404	0.2496	0.28037
$Word LP min_1$	0.04490	0.01192	0.05817	0.02359	0.05289	0.04036	0.03745
$Word LP min_2$	0.28831	0.23004	0.21382	0.21216	0.24384	0.20712	0.23121
$Word LP_{25\%}$	0.40021	0.25993	0.23916	0.20506	0.28920	0.21564	0.26748
$Word LP_{50\%}$	0.32168	0.26854	0.22640	0.19729	0.25738	0.20799	0.24382
$Word LP_{mean}$	0.38227	0.29371	0.26660	0.22748	0.30028	0.25658	0.28609
$Word LP_{mid}$	**0.42543**	**0.34306**	**0.34907**	**0.31295**	**0.34471**	**0.38615**	**0.35872**

Table 1: Pearson correlation between each of the fluency prediction metrics and the human fluency direct assessment scores for each language and across all languages.

	CS-EN	DE-EN	FI-EN	RO-EN	RU-EN	TR-EN	All
Percent fluent	59.22%	59.70%	56.79%	58.04%	60.80%	48.81%	57.21%
Precision	65.35	63.36	59.62	62.06	66.22	52.37	61.42
Recall	90.97	87.29	91.56	92.20	87.67	87.77	89.38
F1	76.06	73.42	72.21	74.18	75.45	65.60	72.81

Table 2: Precision, recall, and F1 on fluent translations for $Word LP_{mid}$ on system outputs for each language pair and on all system outputs. The percentage of outputs that were labeled fluent based on the human fluency judgments is also provided for reference.

Setting the fluency threshold Because our goal is to correctly label sentences as fluently inadequate rather than to provide an exact score, we must select a fluency threshold τ_f to label a translation as "fluent". To determine this threshold, we computed the $Word LP_{mid}$ scores for the reference translation sentences in the WMT16 news training data. To cover most examples while allowing for variance in human judgments, the threshold is set at the point where 90% of reference segments would be labeled as fluent. Precision, recall, and F1 scores for $Word LP_{mid}$, are shown in Table 2. Across all data sets we see high recall but the precision is not as high. Although this suggests that this metric might overestimate the fluency of translations, we are more concerned with comparing between systems than with the raw scores.

3.2 Adequacy Experiments

Task and Data We assess adequacy metrics using the direct assessment adequacy scores and system outputs for all language pairs from WMT16 (Bojar et al., 2016). Adequacy judgments were collected for all submitted systems in all language pairs in the news shared task. These annotations were used to determine the system rankings in the news task and as gold standard quality judgments for the metrics shared task. For the metrics task, enough annotations were collected for each system-produced segment to establish segment-level reliability, while only enough judgments for system-level reliability were collected for the remainder of the segments for the news task. Because we need segment-level reliability, we use only the metrics subset of the data as gold standard human judgments, and we use the reference translations from the news subset in generating synthetic inadequate examples.

We use the standardized human direct assessment adequacy scores from WMT16 (Bojar et al., 2016) as gold standard in determining how well each adequacy metric correlates with human judgments. However, for binary questionable/acceptable adequacy judgments, we must be sure that the inadequate examples are clearly inadequate regardless of fluency and other MT quirks. The high correlation between human judgments of fluency and adequacy in Callison-Burch et al (2007) and Graham et al (2017) may indicate that human adequacy judgments are influenced by fluency, lowering the adequacy scores of disfluent translations. To ensure that our inadequate examples are truly inadequate, we rely on synthetic examples. We generate synthetic low adequacy translations by randomly selecting pairs of reference translations from the WMT16 news task

Adequacy Metric	CS-EN	DE-EN	FI-EN	RO-EN	RU-EN	TR-EN	All
BLEU	0.54275	0.41975	0.41460	0.48410	0.45093	0.50346	0.46242
Averaged Embeddings	0.43905	0.18998	0.31218	0.36303	0.23545	0.30257	0.29584
BVSS	0.61286	0.47068	**0.51856**	**0.56164**	**0.55478**	**0.58858**	**0.54306**
BVSS-Reference	**0.62178**	**0.47877**	0.49006	0.55619	0.51949	0.56264	0.53643
BVSS-System	0.53773	0.38887	0.45177	0.47698	0.50288	0.53687	0.46925

Table 3: Pearson correlation between each of the adequacy prediction metrics and the human adequacy direct assessment scores for each language and across all languages.

	Prec.	Recall	F1
BLEU	94.33	99.08	96.65
Averaged Embeddings	84.56	**99.15**	91.28
BVSS	**99.39**	99.04	**99.22**
BVSS-Reference	99.00	99.03	99.01
BVSS-System	99.17	99.03	99.10
BLEU+BVSS	**99.61**	**99.81**	**99.71**

Table 4: Precision, recall, and F1 on BLEU, BVSS, BVSS-Reference, BVSS-System, and BLEU with BVSS and BVSS-System on the questionable adequacy test set with thresholds calculated based on predicted adequacy scores for the synthetic low adequacy dev data.

and treating one as synthetic MT output and the other as reference. We split these synthetic examples into dev and test sets. The dev synthetic examples are used in choosing the binary acceptable/questionable adequacy threshold τ_a as described below. The test synthetic examples are used as the questionable adequacy items in our adequacy precision/recall test set, with acceptable adequacy items chosen from actual WMT16 submissions. Because we are looking for extreme inadequacy and the systems in WMT16 were of competitively high quality, we use segments with direct assessment scores in the top 90% as acceptable adequacy in the test set.

Model setup Our vector-based metrics are based on word embeddings. We use the pre-trained aligned Wikipedia fastText word vectors (Joulin et al., 2018; Bojanowski et al., 2017).

Results For each metric defined in Section 2.2, we calculated the Pearson correlation with the direct assessment scores for each of the WMT16 language pair data sets and for all the data sets combined (Table 3). The averaged sentence embeddings had the lowest correlation across all lan-

guage pairs. BVSS-System performed similarly well compared to BLEU, but BVSS and BVSS-Reference both outperformed BLEU.

Setting the adequacy threshold As with fluency, our goal for the adequacy metric is to correctly label a sentence as questionable adequacy rather than to provide an exact score. We used each candidate adequacy metric described in section 2.2 to score the segments in the synthetic low adequacy dev set, and set adequacy threshold τ_a for each metric such that 99% of dev set examples would be labeled inadequate. The precision, recall, and F1 on the synthetic test set using this threshold for each metric is shown in Table 4. We see that as with correlation scores, the Averaged Embeddings have much lower precision than BLEU or any of the BVSS metrics, and the BVSS metric have higher precision than BLEU.

Because of the potentially complementary differences in BLEU and BVSS, we also tested combinations of BLEU and the highest-performing vector-based metric, BVSS. We combine the metrics by marking a translation as questionable adequacy only if both metrics would label it as questionable. We see a slight improvement in F1 with the combination, and we adopt this metric for labeling segments as questionable adequacy.

3.3 Selected Scoring Method

Based on the fluency and adequacy evaluations in Sections 3.1 and 3.2, we select $WordLP_{mid}$ and the BLEU+BVSS combination to label segment translations as fluently inadequate.

The results on segment level fluency and adequacy prediction tests show that neither metric is perfect at the segment level. However, the impact of segment-level errors is lessened when segment level scores are aggregated to compare across systems.

Data source	Arabic	Chinese	Farsi	German	Korean	Russian
Subtitles	30M	11M	6.2M	22M	1.4M	26M
UN v1	18M	-	-	-	-	-
WMT17	-	25M	-	5.8M	-	25M
LDC	1.3M	-	-	-	-	-
All General	49M	36M	6.2M	28M	1.4M	51M
TED	174K	169K	114K	152K	164K	180K
TED Test	1982	1982	1982	1982	1982	1982

Table 5: Number of segments in General Domain and TED training and test data for all languages

4 System-Level Analysis of Fluently Inadequate Translations

Koehn and Knowles (2017) showed that in out-of-domain and low-resource settings NMT produces lower quality output than SMT and they include examples where the NMT produced translations that were fluent but unrelated to the input. We seek to quantify this observation by estimating how often such fluently inadequate translations occur in SMT and NMT systems in different domain mismatch and training data settings. We score the output of 36 MT systems according to the percentage of fluently inadequate translations using the method described above.

4.1 MT Systems

We use a set of neural and phrase-based statistical MT models built from the same general domain data and adapted to translate a more specific domain, namely, transcripts of TED talks. We selected six languages to cover a range of resource availability scenarios and language families: Arabic, Chinese, Farsi, German, Korean and Russian.

4.1.1 Data

The number of segments of training and test data for each language is summarized in Table 5. The same tokenization was performed for all systems for a given language, and the tokenized data was split into subwords for NMT training using byte pair encoding (BPE) (Sennrich et al., 2016). The BPE models were trained separately on the source and target language with 30K BPE symbols.

All languages used data from the OpenSubtitles[1] corpus (Tiedemann, 2009) in the General domain training and dev data sets. The Chinese, German, and Russian models used additional parallel corpora from WMT17[2] (Bojar et al., 2017). For the Arabic models, we added data from the Linguistic Data Consortium (LDC)[3] and the UN v1 corpus[4] (Ziemski et al., 2016).

The domain for the In-Domain and Domain-Adapted models was TED talks. Training, dev, and test sets for the domain were from the Multi-target TED Talks Task (MTTT) corpus (Duh, 2018). All systems, regardless of training setting, were tested on the TED domain test set.

Fluency scores for each system were generated based on a language model built on the English side of its primary training data. As noted in Section 2.1, it is important that the language model match the training data, and we expect this to be particularly true when the test set is out-of-domain. We therefore use only the General domain data for both the General models and the adapted models, while the In-Domain models use the in-domain training data. Thresholds were calculated in a similar manner to the thresholds on the WMT16 data: thresholds for $WordLP_{mid}$ were calculated based on the General domain training data and thresholds for sentence BLEU and BVSS based on synthetic data built from the TED training data.

4.1.2 Statistical MT Systems

The statistical systems were built using the Apache Joshua toolkit[5] (Post et al., 2015). We tested three SMT models for each language: Joshua General, Joshua In-Domain, and Joshua Domain-Adapted, which were trained respectively on the General domain data, on the TED training data and on both. Language models for all systems were built from the English side of the training data. The Domain-Adapted model was tuned

---

[1] http://www.opensubtitles.org/
[2] http://www.statmt.org/wmt17/translation-task.html
[3] LDC2004T18, LDC2007T08, and LDC2012T09
[4] UN v1 is included in the Russian and Chinese WMT17 data
[5] http://cwiki.apache.org/confluence/display/JOSHUA/

	Arabic	**German**	**Farsi**	**Korean**	**Russian**	**Chinese**
Joshua General	23.50	30.65	13.41	6.34	24.49	14.79
Joshua TED Only	24.49	28.72	16.56	9.81	21.85	13.32
Joshua Adapted	27.11	31.35	17.71	10.24	25.23	15.70
Sockeye General	29.6	34.59	22.22	11.56	**28.6**	15.92
Sockeye TED Only	27.42	32.25	21.31	14.4	22.9	16.18
Sockeye Adapted	**35.37**	**39.9**	**27.92**	**17.22**	**28.6**	**20.37**

Table 6: BLEU scores for all systems

on TED dev data.

4.1.3 Neural MT Systems

The neural systems were built using Sockeye[6] (Hieber et al., 2017). The systems used two LSTM layers in both encoder and decoder with hidden size 512 and word embeddings dimension 512. We used a batch size of 4096 and created a checkpoint every 4000 mini-batches. Our systems employed the Adam optimizer (Kingma and Ba, 2014) with an initial learning rate of 0.0003. As with the SMT, we built three models for each language: Sockeye General, Sockeye In-Domain, and Sockeye Domain-Adapted. The Sockeye General and In-Domain models were trained with the same data as the corresponding SMT models. The Sockeye Domain-Adapted models were trained using continued training on TED data starting from the Sockeye General model as in Luong at al (2015) and Freitag and Al-Onaizan (2016).

4.2 System Analyses

We compute the percentage of fluently inadequate translations in the system output of all MT and SMT systems to determine the effect of MT paradigm and training data on the occurrence of fluently inadequate translations.

Although the language pair and system varies, we can directly compare the output of the systems because the test data for all systems is from the *Multi-target* TED corpus. Note that in the corpus, the source is English and the other languages are translations while our task is translating into English. This means that if there are human translation errors or non-literal translations, the source will be inconsistent across languages but the reference will be the same. Table 7 shows English references for two different segments in Farsi and Chinese that yielded fluently inadequate MT output, along with their corresponding source and system

outputs. For some segments the human translation (our source) may have slightly different meaning from the original (our reference), but the fluently inadequate examples we seek to identify are much further in meaning from both the source and reference. For instance, in the Chinese-English example the Chinese adds information that must be inferred from context in the original English. The Chinese literally translates to "Crow parents also teach their children these kinds of skills." The Sockeye TED and Joshua outputs reflect this additional information, but the Sockeye General output is fluent but completely unrelated to the reference.

Figure 1 shows the percent of segments labeled as fluently inadequate for each system. Even the highest percentage (Chinese-English Sockeye General) is less than 2%. Based on the high recall and low precision scores for the fluency metric in Section 3.1, we expect that we are overpredicting fluently inadequate translations so the actual percentage may be even lower. This confirms that these errors are indeed rare.

We also see from Figure 1 that the NMT models for Korean and Chinese, the languages most typologically different from English, have the highest levels of fluently inadequate translations on out-of-domain models. Although they have similarly high percentages of fluently misleading and similar amounts of in-domain training data, the Chinese domain-adapted model improves much more than the Korean domain-adapted model.

We compare the percent fluently inadequate segments to system BLEU scores in Figure 2. Based on the definition of our metric for fluently inadequate translations, translations with high sentence BLEU cannot be labeled fluently inadequate, so we expect a strong negative correlation between system BLEU and the percent fluently inadequate. We do see this negative correlation, but we can also see a clear difference in the percent fluently inadequate for the SMT vs NMT systems.

---

[6]http://github.com/awslabs/sockeye

System	FA-EN Example	ZH-EN Example
Source	انگیزه های زیرکانه تری داشته باشید	乌鸦 父母 还 教会 自己 的 孩子 这样 的 技巧 呢 。
Reference	get smarter incentives .	parents seem to be teaching their young .
Joshua General	terry زیرکانه have motives .	parents also teach their children the skills like this ?
Joshua TED	you have the انگیزه زیرکانه needed	parents crow can also teach our kids that the skills that .
Joshua Adapted	terry motives inspired .	the parents teach their children such skills .
Sockeye General	have a more subtle motivator .	**i 'm afraid i 'm not going to have to go to bed .**
Sockeye TED	**there 's a lot of gamers .**	and the crow parents taught their kids like this .
Sockeye Adapted	have smarter motivations .	and their parents also taught their children how to do it .

Table 7: Reference translation and example translations from the Farsi-English and Chinese-English systems. Fluently inadequate examples in bold.

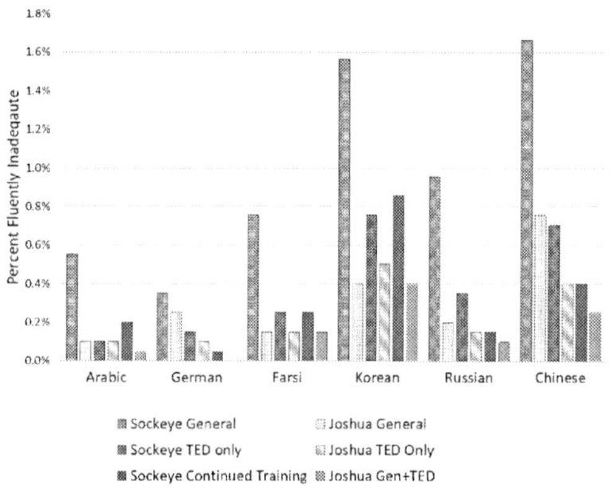

Figure 1: Segments labeled as fluently inadequate for General, TED, and Domain-Adapted Sockeye and Joshua models for all languages.

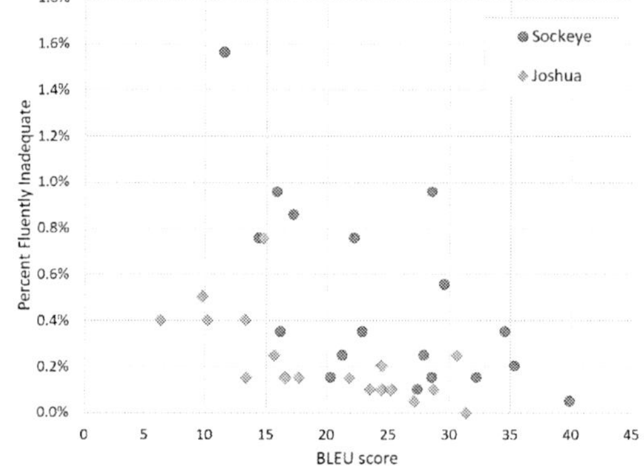

Figure 2: Segments labeled as fluently inadequate vs BLEU score for all Sockeye and Joshua models for all languages.

The NMT systems with low BLEU scores have much higher percentage of fluently inadequate translations than the similarly low-scoring SMT systems. This follows the suggestion in Koehn and Knowles (2017) that NMT is more prone to producing output that is disconnected from the source text when trained with insufficient or out-of-domain data. Indeed, we can see in Figure 1 that the NMT consistently has a higher percentage of fluently inadequate translations than the SMT.

Because our fluency metric relies on language models very similar to the language models used in the SMT systems, we might suspect that the fluency metric is biased towards the SMT models, potentially making SMT output more likely to be labeled as fluently inadequate. However, Figure 3 shows that the NMT systems still consistently have more segments labeled as fluent compared to SMT systems with similar BLEU score. This agrees with prior work showing that NMT output is more fluent than SMT and suggests that while the fluency metric likely leads to overprediction of fluently inadequate translations, it does not do so in a way that favors one paradigm over the other.

We also measured the percentage of fluently inadequate translations on the development set during training. Figure 4 shows that the percent fluently inadequate levels off very quickly, flattening after a few checkpoints on the in-domain model.

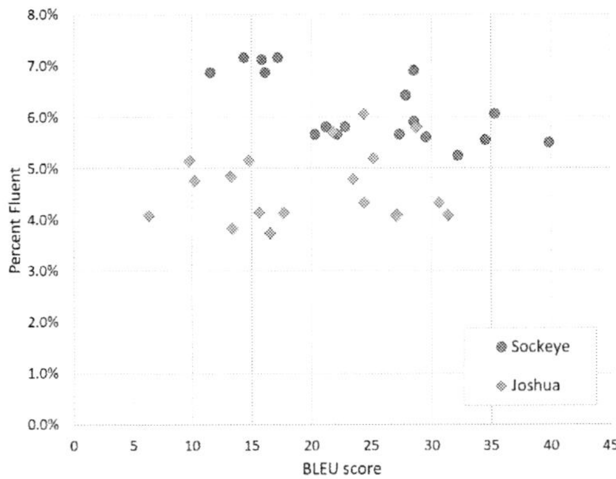

Figure 3: Segments labeled as fluent vs BLEU score for all Sockeye and Joshua models for all languages.

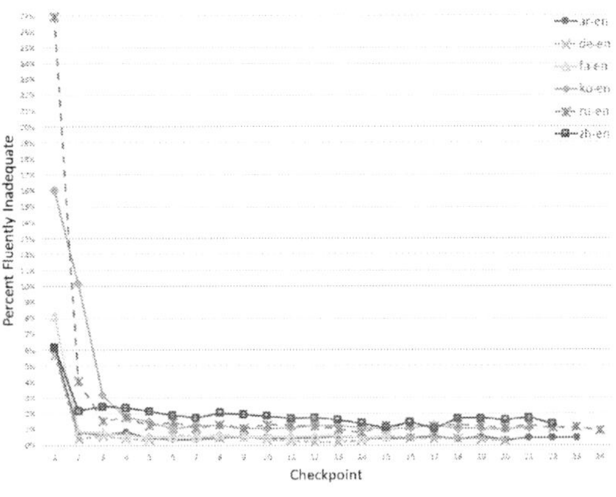

Figure 4: Percent fluently inadequate at each checkpoint during in-domain training

5 Related Work

MT quality metrics are judged based on their correlation with human judgments, and recently that has meant human adequacy judgments (Bojar et al., 2017). This indicates that any of the common MT metrics such as BLEU (Papineni et al., 2002) or METEOR (Banerjee and Lavie, 2005) may also serve as baseline adequacy scores. However, they incorporate elements of fluency while we wish to separate fluency and adequacy.

Adequacy is, essentially, semantic equivalence and the goal of SemEval's Semantic Textual Similarity (STS) task is to measure the degree of semantic equivalence between two sentences (Cer et al., 2017). The cross-lingual version of the task is similar enough to quality estimation that one of the data sets for 2017 actually came from the WMT quality estimation task. However, the STS systems performed much worse on the MT data than when tested on the Stanford Natural Language Inference (SNLI) Corpus data for the same language pair, with the top system achieving a correlation of only 34 compared to 83. These models are also complex and for use in combination with fluency, we prefer a simpler approach for this study.

Although grammaticality focuses on well-formedness while fluency includes all aspects of "sounding natural," the metrics used to predict grammaticality may still prove to be good measures of fluency. Lau et al (2016) take an unsupervised, language modeling approach to the task of predicting grammaticality as described in Section 2.1. They used two types of test data. One was generated by round-tripping sentences through Google Translate and the other was generated by extracting example sentences from a syntax textbook. The MT-generated English data is most similar to our problem, and the most effective models for that data were the word-based scores from the language model.

6 Conclusion

We have introduced an approach to automatically detect fluently inadequate translations in machine translation output based on automatic fluency and adequacy metrics. Applying this technique to a diverse set of statistical and neural MT systems, we found that although fluently inadequate translations are rare, NMT does appear to be consistently more prone to this type of error compared to SMT. Improving the match between training and test with continued training on in-domain data reduces these errors. These findings raise several questions for future work: How often are fluently inadequate translations actually misleading to human users? How can we detect fluently inadequate translations without reference translations?

Acknowledgments

This work is supported in part by an Amazon Web Services Machine Learning Research Award. The views contained herein are those of the authors and should not be interpreted as necessarily representing the official policies, either expressed or implied, of the sponsors. Part of this work was done at the JHU SCALE 2018 workshop and we would like to thank all our team members for helpful discussions, particularly John Farina and David Yuen.

References

Banerjee, Satanjeev and Alon Lavie. 2005. METEOR: An automatic metric for MT evaluation with improved correlation with human judgments. In *Proceedings of the ACL workshop on intrinsic and extrinsic evaluation measures for machine translation and/or summarization*, volume 29, pages 65–72.

Bentivogli, Luisa, Arianna Bisazza, Mauro Cettolo, and Marcello Federico. 2016. Neural versus phrase-based machine translation quality: a case study. In *Proceedings of the 2016 Conference on Empirical Methods in Natural Language Processing*, pages 257–267, Austin, Texas. Association for Computational Linguistics.

Bojanowski, Piotr, Edouard Grave, Armand Joulin, and Tomas Mikolov. 2017. Enriching word vectors with subword information. *Transactions of the Association for Computational Linguistics*, 5:135–146.

Bojar, Ondřej, Rajen Chatterjee, Christian Federmann, Yvette Graham, Barry Haddow, Matthias Huck, Antonio Jimeno Yepes, Philipp Koehn, Varvara Logacheva, Christof Monz, Matteo Negri, Aurelie Neveol, Mariana Neves, Martin Popel, Matt Post, Raphael Rubino, Carolina Scarton, Lucia Specia, Marco Turchi, Karin Verspoor, and Marcos Zampieri. 2016. Findings of the 2016 Conference on Machine Translation. In *Proceedings of the First Conference on Machine Translation*, pages 131–198, Berlin, Germany, Aug. Association for Computational Linguistics.

Bojar, Ondřej, Rajen Chatterjee, Christian Federmann, Yvette Graham, Barry Haddow, Shujian Huang, Matthias Huck, Philipp Koehn, Qun Liu, Varvara Logacheva, Christof Monz, Matteo Negri, Matt Post, Raphael Rubino, Lucia Specia, and Marco Turchi. 2017. Findings of the 2017 Conference on Machine Translation (WMT17). In *Proceedings of the Second Conference on Machine Translation, Volume 2: Shared Task Papers*, pages 169–214, Copenhagen, Denmark. Association for Computational Linguistics.

Callison-Burch, Chris, Cameron Fordyce, Philipp Koehn, Christof Monz, and Josh Schroeder. 2007. (Meta-) Evaluation of Machine Translation. In *Proceedings of the Second Workshop on Statistical Machine Translation*, pages 136–158, Prague, Czech Republic, Jun. Association for Computational Linguistics.

Cer, Daniel, Mona Diab, Eneko Agirre, Inigo Lopez-Gazpio, and Lucia Specia. 2017. Semeval-2017 task 1: Semantic textual similarity-multilingual and cross-lingual focused evaluation. In *Proceedings of SemEval 2017*.

Duh, Kevin. 2018. The multitarget ted talks task. http://www.cs.jhu.edu/~kevinduh/a/multitarget-tedtalks/.

Florek, Kazimierz, Jan Łukaszewicz, Julian Perkal, Hugo Steinhaus, and Stefan Zubrzycki. 1951. Sur la liaison et la division des points d'un ensemble fini. In *Colloquium Mathematicae*, volume 2, pages 282–285.

Freitag, Markus and Yaser Al-Onaizan. 2016. Fast domain adaptation for neural machine translation. *arXiv preprint arXiv:1612.06897*.

Graham, Yvette, Timothy Baldwin, Alistair Moffat, and Justin Zobel. 2017. Can machine translation systems be evaluated by the crowd alone. *Natural Language Engineering*, 23(1):3–30.

Hassan Awadalla, Hany, Anthony Aue, Chang Chen, Vishal Chowdhary, Jonathan Clark, Christian Federmann, Xuedong Huang, Marcin Junczys-Dowmunt, Will Lewis, Mu Li, Shujie Liu, Tie-Yan Liu, Renqian Luo, Arul Menezes, Tao Qin, Frank Seide, Xu Tan, Fei Tian, Lijun Wu, Shuangzhi Wu, Yingce Xia, Dongdong Zhang, Zhirui Zhang, and Ming Zhou. 2018. Achieving Human Parity on Automatic Chinese to English News Translation, Mar.

Heafield, Kenneth, Ivan Pouzyrevsky, Jonathan H Clark, and Philipp Koehn. 2013. Scalable modified kneser-ney language model estimation. In *Proceedings of the 51st Annual Meeting of the Association for Computational Linguistics (Volume 2: Short Papers)*, volume 2, pages 690–696.

Heafield, Kenneth. 2011. Kenlm: Faster and smaller language model queries. In *Proceedings of the Sixth Workshop on Statistical Machine Translation*, pages 187–197. Association for Computational Linguistics.

Hieber, Felix, Tobias Domhan, Michael Denkowski, David Vilar, Artem Sokolov, Ann Clifton, and Matt Post. 2017. Sockeye: A toolkit for neural machine translation. *arXiv preprint arXiv:1712.05690*.

Joulin, Armand, Piotr Bojanowski, Tomas Mikolov, Hervé Jégou, and Edouard Grave. 2018. Loss in translation: Learning bilingual word mapping with a retrieval criterion. In *Proceedings of the 2018 Conference on Empirical Methods in Natural Language Processing*.

Kingma, Diederik P. and Jimmy Ba. 2014. Adam: A method for stochastic optimization. *CoRR*, abs/1412.6980.

Knox, Steven W. 2015. Extending pairwise element similarity to set similarity efficiently. Presentation at MAA MathFest, Washington, DC, 8.

Koehn, Philipp and Rebecca Knowles. 2017. Six Challenges for Neural Machine Translation. In *Workshop on Neural Machine Translation*, Vancouver, BC. arXiv: 1706.03872.

Lau, Jey Han, Alexander Clark, and Shalom Lappin. 2016. Grammaticality, acceptability, and probability: A probabilistic view of linguistic knowledge. *Cognitive Science*, 41(5):1202–1241.

Luong, Minh-Thang, Hieu Pham, and Christopher D
Manning. 2015. Effective approaches to attention-
based neural machine translation. *arXiv preprint
arXiv:1508.04025*.

Martindale, Marianna J. and Marine Carpuat. 2018.
Fluency Over Adequacy: A Pilot Study in Measur-
ing User Trust in Imperfect MT. In *Proceedings of
the 13th Conference of The Association for Machine
Translation in the Americas*, pages 13–25, Boston,
MA, USA, March.

Papineni, Kishore, Salim Roukos, Todd Ward, and Wei-
Jing Zhu. 2002. BLEU: a method for automatic
evaluation of machine translation. In *Proceedings of
the 40th annual meeting on association for computational linguistics*, pages 311–318. Association for
Computational Linguistics.

Post, Matt, Yuan Cao, and Gaurav Kumar. 2015.
Joshua 6: A phrase-based and hierarchical statistical machine translation system. *The Prague Bulletin
of Mathematical Linguistics*.

Sennrich, Rico, Barry Haddow, and Alexandra Birch.
2016. Neural machine translation of rare words with
subword units. In *Proceedings of the 54th Annual
Meeting of the Association for Computational Linguistics (Volume 1: Long Papers)*, pages 1715–1725.
Association for Computational Linguistics.

Tiedemann, Jörg. 2009. News from opus-a collection
of multilingual parallel corpora with tools and interfaces. In *Recent advances in natural language processing*, volume 5, pages 237–248.

Toral, Antonio and Víctor M. Sánchez-Cartagena.
2017. A Multifaceted Evaluation of Neural versus
Phrase-Based Machine Translation for 9 Language
Directions. In *Proceedings of the 15th Conference
of the European Chapter of the Association for Computational Linguistics*, volume 1, pages 1063–1073,
Valencia, Spain. Association for Computational Linguistics.

Ziemski, Michal, Marcin Junczys-Dowmunt, and
Bruno Pouliquen. 2016. The united nations parallel corpus v1. 0. In *LREC*.

Character-Aware Decoder for Translation
into Morphologically Rich Languages

Adithya Renduchintala[*] and **Pamela Shapiro**[*] and **Kevin Duh** and **Philipp Koehn**
Department of Computer Science
Johns Hopkins University
{adi.r,pshapiro,phi}@jhu.edu kevinduh@cs.jhu.edu

Abstract

Neural machine translation (NMT) systems operate primarily on words (or subwords), ignoring lower-level patterns of morphology. We present a *character-aware* decoder designed to capture such patterns when translating into morphologically rich languages. We achieve character-awareness by augmenting both the softmax and embedding layers of an attention-based encoder-decoder model with convolutional neural networks that operate on the spelling of a word. To investigate performance on a wide variety of morphological phenomena, we translate English into 14 typologically diverse target languages using the TED multi-target dataset. In this low-resource setting, the character-aware decoder provides consistent improvements with BLEU score gains of up to +3.05. In addition, we analyze the relationship between the gains obtained and properties of the target language and find evidence that our model does indeed exploit morphological patterns.

1 Introduction

Traditional attention-based encoder-decoder neural machine translation (NMT) models learn *word-level* embeddings, with a continuous representation for each unique word type (Bahdanau et al., 2015). However, this results in a long tail of rare words for which we do not learn good representations. More recently, it has become standard prac-

tice to mitigate the vocabulary size problem with Byte-Pair Encoding (BPE) (Gage, 1994; Sennrich et al., 2016). BPE iteratively merges consecutive characters into larger chunks based on their frequency, which results in the breaking up of less common words into "subword units."

While BPE addresses the vocabulary size problem, the spellings of the subword units are still ignored. On the other hand, purely *character-level* NMT translates one character at a time and can implicitly learn about morphological patterns within words as well as generalize to unseen vocabulary. Recently, Cherry et al. (2018) show that very deep character-level models can outperform BPE, however, the smallest data size evaluated was 2 million sentences, so it is unclear if the results hold for low-resource settings and when translating into a range of different morphologically rich languages. Furthermore, tuning deep character-level models is expensive, even for low-resource settings.[1]

A middle-ground alternative is character-*aware* word-level modeling. Here, the NMT system operates over words but uses word embeddings that are sensitive to spellings and thereby has the ability to learn morphological patterns in the language. Such character-aware approaches have been applied successfully in NMT to the *source-side* word embedding layer (Costa-jussà and Fonollosa, 2016), but surprisingly, similar gains have not been achieved on the target side (Belinkov et al., 2017).

While source-side character-aware models only need to make the *source embedding layer* character-aware, on the target-side we require both the *target embedding layer* and the *softmax layer* [2]

---

[1]The dropout rate was found to be critical in Cherry et al. (2018), and each tuning run takes much longer due to longer sequence lengths.

[2]Also referred to as generator, final output layer or final linear

to be character-aware, which presents additional challenges. We find that the trivial application of methods from Costa-jussà and Fonollosa (2016) to these target-side embeddings results in significant drop in performance. Instead, we propose mixing compositional and standard word embeddings via a gating function. While simple, we find it is critical to successful target-side character awareness.

It is worth noting that unlike some purely character-level methods our aim is not to generate novel words, though this method can function on top of subword methods which do so (Shapiro and Duh, 2018). Rather, the character-aware representations decrease the sparsity of embeddings for rare words or subwords, which are a problem in low-resource morphologically rich settings. We summarize our contribution as follows:

1. We propose a method for utilizing character-aware embeddings in an NMT decoder that can be used over word or subword sequences.

2. We explore how our method interacts with BPE over a range of merge operations (including word-level and purely character-level) and highlight that there is no "typical BPE" setting for low-resource NMT.

3. We evaluate our model on 14 target languages and observe consistent improvements over baselines. Furthermore, we analyze to what extent the success of our method corresponds to improved handling of target language morphology.

2 Related Work

NMT has benefited from character-aware word representations on the source side (Costa-jussà and Fonollosa, 2016), which follows language modeling work by Kim et al. (2016) and generate source-side input embeddings using a CNN over the character sequence of each word. Further analysis revealed that hidden states of such character-aware models have increased knowledge of morphology (Belinkov et al., 2017). They additionally try using character-aware representations in the target side embedding layer, leaving the softmax matrix with standard word representations, and found no improvements.

Our work is also aligned with the character-aware models proposed in (Kim et al., 2016), but

we additionally employ a gating mechanism between character-aware representations and standard word representations similar to language modeling work by (Miyamoto and Cho, 2016). However, our gating is a learned type-specific vector rather than a fixed hyperparameter.

There is additionally a line of work on purely character-level NMT, which generates words one character at a time (Ling et al., 2015; Chung et al., 2016; Passban et al., 2018). While initial results here were not strong, Cherry et al. (2018) revisit this with deeper architectures and sweeping dropout parameters and find that they outperform BPE across settings of the merge hyperparameter. They examine different data sizes and observe improvements in the smaller data size settings—however, the smallest size is about 2 million sentence pairs. In contrast, we look at a smaller order of magnitude data size and present an alternate approach which doesn't require substantial tuning of parameters across different languages.

Finally, Byte-Pair Encoding (BPE) (Sennrich et al., 2016) has become a standard preprocessing step in NMT pipelines and provides an easy way to generate sequences with a mixture of full words and word fragments. Note that BPE splits are agnostic to any morphological pattern present in the language, for example the token `politely` in our dataset is split into `pol+itely`, instead of the linguistically plausible split `polite+ly`.[3] Our approach can be applied to word-level sequences and sequences at any BPE merge hyperparameter greater than 0. Increasing the hyperparameter results in more words and longer subwords that can exhibit morphological patterns. Our goal is to exploit these morphological patterns and enrich the word (or subword) representations with character-awareness.

3 Encoder-Decoder NMT

An attention-based encoder-decoder network (Bahdanau et al., 2015; Luong et al., 2015) models the probability of a target sentence $\mathbf{y}$ of length J given a source sentence $\mathbf{x}$ as:

$$p(\mathbf{y} \mid \mathbf{x}) = \prod_{j=1}^{J} p(y_j \mid \mathbf{y}_{0:j-1}, \mathbf{x}; \boldsymbol{\theta}) \qquad (1)$$

where $\boldsymbol{\theta}$ represents all the parameters of the network. At each time-step the j'th output token is

---

projection.

[3] We observe this split when merge parameter was 15k.

generated by:

$$p(y_j \mid \mathbf{y}_{0:j-1}, \mathbf{x}) = \text{softmax}(\mathbf{W_o s}_j) \qquad (2)$$

where $\mathbf{s}_j \in \mathbb{R}^{D \times 1}$ is the decoder hidden state at time j and $\mathbf{W_o} \in \mathbb{R}^{|\mathcal{V}| \times D}$ is the weight matrix of the softmax layer, which provides a continuous representation for target words. $\mathbf{s}_j$ is computed using the following recurrence:

$$\mathbf{s}_j = \tanh(\mathbf{W_c}\,[\mathbf{c}_j; \tilde{\mathbf{s}}_j]) \qquad (3)$$
$$\tilde{\mathbf{s}}_j = f([\mathbf{s}_{j-1}; \mathbf{w_s}^{y_{j-1}}; \tilde{\mathbf{s}}_{j-1}]) \qquad (4)$$

where f is an LSTM cell.[4] $\mathbf{W_s} \in \mathbb{R}^{|\mathcal{V}| \times E}$ is the target-side embedding matrix, which provides continuous representations for the previous target word when used as input to the RNN. Here, $\mathbf{w_s}^{y_{j-1}} \in \mathbb{R}^{1 \times E}$ is a row vector from the embedding matrix $\mathbf{W_s}$ corresponding to the value of y_{j-1}. $\mathcal{V}$ is the target vocabulary set, D is the is the RNN size and E is embedding size. Often these matrices $\mathbf{W_o}$ and $\mathbf{W_s}$ are tied.

The context vector $\mathbf{c}_j$ is obtained by taking a weighted average over the concatenation of a bidirectional RNN encoder's hidden states.

$$\mathbf{c}_j = \sum_{i=1}^{I} \alpha_i, \mathbf{h}_i \qquad (5)$$

$$\alpha_i = \frac{\exp\left(\tilde{\mathbf{s}}_j^{\top} \mathbf{W_a h}_i\right)}{\sum_l \exp\left(\tilde{\mathbf{s}}_j^{\top} \mathbf{W_a h}_l\right)} \qquad (6)$$

The attention matrix $\mathbf{W_a} \in \mathbb{R}^{D \times H}$ is learned jointly with the model, multiplying with the previous decoder state and bidirectional encoder state $\mathbf{h}_i \in \mathbb{R}^{H \times 1}$, normalized over encoder hidden states via the softmax operation.

4 Character-Aware Extension

In this section we detail the incorporation of character-awareness into the two decoder embedding matrices $\mathbf{W_o}$ and $\mathbf{W_s}$. To begin, we consider an example target side word (or subword in the case of preprocessing with BPE), cat. In both $\mathbf{W_o}$ and $\mathbf{W_s}$, there exist row vectors, $\mathbf{w_o}^{cat}$ and $\mathbf{w_s}^{cat}$ that contain the continuous vector representation for the word cat. In a traditional NMT system, these vectors are learned as the entire network tries to maximize the objective in Equation 1. The objective does not require the vectors $\mathbf{w_o}^{cat}$

---

[4]Note that our notation diverges from Luong et al. (2015) so that $\mathbf{s}_j$ refers to the state used to make the final predictions.

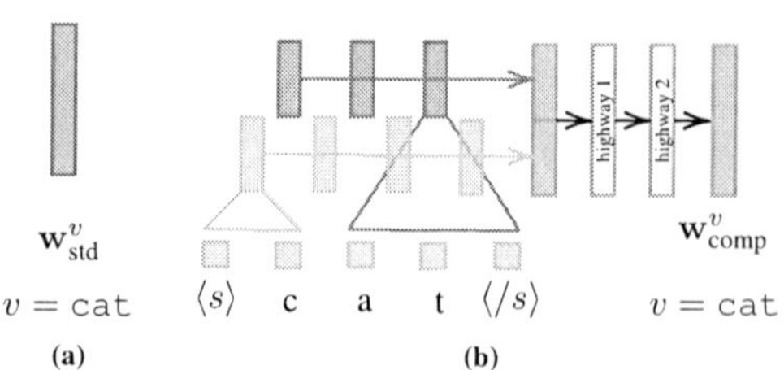

Figure 1: Different approaches to generating embeddings. (a) standard word embedding that treats words as a single symbol. (b) CNN-based composition function. We use multiple CNNs with different kernel sizes over the character embeddings. The resulting hidden states are combined into a single word embedding via max pooling. Note that (b) shows only 2 convolution filters for clarity, in practice we use 4.

and $\mathbf{w_s}^{cat}$ to model any aspect of the spelling of the word. Figure 1a illustrates a simple non-compositional word embedding.

At a high level, we can view our notion of character-awareness as a composition function $\text{comp}(.; \omega)$, parameterized by ω, that takes the character sequence that makes up a word (i.e. its spelling) as input and then produces a continuous vector representation:

$$\mathbf{w}_{\text{comp}}^{\text{cat}} = \text{comp}(\langle s \rangle, \text{c}, \text{a}, \text{t}, \langle /s \rangle; \omega) \qquad (7)$$

ω is learned jointly with the overall objective. Special characters $\langle s \rangle$ and $\langle /s \rangle$ denote the beginning and end of sequence respectively.

Figure 1b illustrates our compositional approach to generating embeddings (Kim et al., 2016). First, a character-embedding layer converts the spelling of a word into a sequence of character embeddings. Next, we apply 4 convolution operations, with kernel sizes $3, 4, 5$ and 6, over the character sequence and the resulting output matrix is max-pooled. We set the output channel size of each convolution to $\frac{1}{4}$ of the final desired embedding size. The max-pooled vector from each convolution is concatenated to create the composed word representation. Finally, we add highway layers to obtain the final embeddings.

4.1 Composed & Standard Gating

The composition is applied to every type in the vocabulary and thus generates a complete embedding matrix (and softmax matrix). In doing so, we assume that *every* word in the vocabulary has a vector representation that can be composed from its spelling sequence. This is a strong assumption as many words, in particular high frequency words, are not normally compositional, e.g. the substring

ing in `thing` is not compositional in the way that it is in `running`. Thus, we mix the compositional and standard embedding vectors. We expect standard embeddings to better represent the meaning of certain words, such has function words and other high-frequency words. For each word v in the vocabulary we also learn a gating vector $\mathbf{g}^v \in [0,1]^{1 \times D}$.

$$\mathbf{g}^v = \sigma(\mathbf{w}^v_{\text{gate}}) \quad (8)$$

Where, σ is a sigmoid operation and type-specific parameters $\mathbf{w}^v_{\text{gate}}$ are jointly learned along with all the other parameters of the composition function. These parameters are regularized to remain close to 0 using dropout. [5] Our final mixed word representation for each word $v \in \mathcal{V}$ is given by:

$$\mathbf{w}^v_{\text{mix}} = \mathbf{g}^v \odot \mathbf{w}^v_{\text{std}} + (\mathbf{1.} - \mathbf{g}^v) \odot \mathbf{w}^v_{\text{comp}} \quad (9)$$

Where $\mathbf{w}^v_{\text{mix}}$ is the final word embedding, $\mathbf{w}^v_{\text{std}}$ is the standard word embedding, $\mathbf{w}^v_{\text{comp}}$ is the embedding by the composition function and $\mathbf{g}^v$ is the type-specific gating vector for the v'th word. The weight matrix is obtained by stacking the word vectors for each word $v \in \mathcal{V}$. The same representation is used for the target embedding layer and the softmax layer i.e. we set $\mathbf{w_o}^{\text{cat}} = \mathbf{w_s}^{\text{cat}} = \mathbf{w}^{\text{cat}}_{\text{mix}}$, when $v = \text{cat}$. Thus, tying the composition function parameters for the softmax weight matrix and the target-side embedding matrix.

Experiments comparing the standard embedding model and the compositional embedding model with and without gating are summarized in Table 1. Row "C" shows the performance of naively using the composition function (which works in the source-side) on the target-side. We observe a catastrophic drop in BLEU (-14.62) compared to a standard NMT encoder-decoder. The Character-aware gated model(CG), however, outperforms the baseline by 0.91 BLEU points suggesting that the CNN composition function and standard embeddings work in a complementary fashion.

4.2 Large Vocabulary Approximation

In Equation 2 of the general NMT framework, the softmax operation generates a distribution over the output vocabulary. Our character-aware model requires a much larger computation graph as we apply convolutions (and highway layers) over the

---

[5] However, in practice we found that this regularization did not affect performance noticeably in this setting.

Composition Method	BLEU
Std. (no composition)	26.84
C (without gating)	12.22
CG (target embedding only)	26.61
CG (softmax embedding only)	27.16
CG (both)	**27.75**

Table 1: Experiments to determine the effectiveness of composition based embeddings and gated embeddings. We used en-de language pair from the TED multi-target dataset. Std. is our baseline with standard word embeddings, model C is the composition only model and CG combines the character-aware (composed) embedding and standard embedding via a gating function.

spellings (character embeddings) of entire target vocabulary, placing a limitation on the target vocabulary size for our model. Which is problematic for word-level modeling (without BPE).

To make our character-aware model accommodate large target vocabulary sizes, we incorporate an approximation mechanism based on (Jean et al., 2015). Instead of computing the softmax over the entire vocabulary, we uniformly sample 20k vocabulary types and the vocabulary types that are present in the training batch.

During decoding, we compute the forward pass $\mathbf{W_o s}_j$ in Equation 2 in several splits of the target vocabulary. As no backward pass is required we clear the memory (i.e. delete the computation graph) after each split is computed.

5 Experiments

We evaluate our character aware model on 14 different languages in a low-resource setting. Additionally, we sweep over several BPE merge hyperparameter settings from character-level to fully word-level for both our model and the baseline and find consistent gains in the character-aware model over the baseline. These gains are stable across all BPE merge hyperparameters all the way up to word-level where they are the highest.

5.1 Datasets

We use a collection of TED talk transcripts (Duh, 2018; Cettolo et al., 2012). This dataset has languages with a variety of morphological typologies, which allows us to observe how the success of our character-aware decoder relates to morphological complexity. We keep the source language fixed as English and translate into 14 different languages, since our focus is on the decoder. The training sets for each vary from 74k sentences pairs for

Language	BPE Sweep			@ 30k BPE			@ Word-level		
	Std(Best BPE)	CG(Best BPE)	Δ	Std	CG	Δ	Std	CG	Δ
cs	20.57 (7.5k)	21.41 (7.5k)	+0.84	18.73	21.28	+2.55	18.44	21.49	+3.05
uk	15.79 (7.5k)	16.60 (30k)	+0.81	14.27	16.60	+2.33	12.94	15.30	+2.36
pl	16.76 (15k)	18.00 (30k)	+1.24	15.98	18.00	+2.02	15.49	17.20	+1.71
tr	15.11 (7.5k)	15.83 (30k)	+0.72	13.82	15.83	+2.01	12.58	14.75	+2.17
hu	16.61 (3.2k)	17.23 (15k)	+0.62	15.45	17.21	+1.76	14.18	16.52	+2.34
he	23.36 (3.2k)	23.86 (30k)	+0.50	22.47	23.86	+1.39	21.26	23.01	+1.75
pt	37.85 (15k)	38.35 (30k)	+0.50	37.05	38.35	+1.30	37.13	38.36	+1.23
ar	16.22 (7.5k)	16.28 (30k)	+0.06	15.05	16.28	+1.23	14.45	16.05	+1.60
de	27.37 (7.5k)	28.12 (30k)	+0.75	26.94	28.12	+1.21	26.84	27.75	+0.91
ro	24.02 (3.2k)	24.20 (15k)	+0.18	22.88	24.00	+1.12	22.39	23.27	+0.88
bg	31.63 (7.5k)	32.20 (15k)	+0.57	30.92	31.90	+0.98	30.18	31.43	+1.25
fr	35.97 (1.6k)	36.17 (7.5k)	+0.20	35.31	35.92	+0.61	35.28	36.01	+0.73
fa	12.94 (30k)	13.52 (30k)	+0.58	12.94	13.52	+0.58	12.85	12.79	-0.06
ru	19.28 (30k)	19.61 (30k)	+0.33	19.28	19.61	+0.33	17.60	19.04	+1.44

Table 2: Best BLEU scores swept over 6 different BPE merge setting (1.6k, 3.2k, 7.5k, 15k, 30k, 60k), and at a standard setting of 30k. We notice a consistent improvement across languages and settings of the merge operation parameter.

Ukrainian to around 174k sentences pairs for Russian (provided in Appendix A), but the validation and test sets are "multi-way parallel", meaning the English sentences (the source side in our experiments) are the same across all 14 languages, and are about 2k sentences each. We filter out training pairs where the source sentence was longer that 50 tokens (before applying BPE). For word-level results, we used a vocabulary size of 100k (keeping the most frequent types) and replaced rare words by an <UNK> token.

5.2 NMT Setup

We work with OpenNMT-py (Klein et al., 2017), and modify the target-side embedding layer and softmax layer to use our proposed character-aware composition function. A 2 layer encoder and decoder, with 1000 recurrent units were used in all experiments The embeddings sizes were made to match the RNN recurrent size. We set the character embedding size to 50 and use four CNNs with kernel widths $3, 4, 5$ and 6. The four CNN outputs are concatenated into a compositional embeddings and gated with a standard word embedding. The same composition function (with shared parameters) was used for the target embedding layer and the softmax layer.

We optimize the NMT objective (Equation 1) using SGD.[6] An initial learning rate of 1.0 was used for the first 8 epochs and then decayed with a decay rate of 0.5 until the learning rate reached a minimum threshold of 0.001. We use a batch size

Lang	Char-Shallow	Char-Deep	CG (30k BPE)	Δ
uk	4.77	13.34	16.60	+3.26
cs	11.16	18.45	21.28	+2.83
de	23.89	25.93	28.12	+2.19
bg	26.40	29.81	31.90	+2.09
tr	5.29	13.94	15.83	+1.89
pl	10.65	16.31	18.00	+1.69
ru	14.63	18.01	19.61	+1.60
ro	21.58	22.45	24.00	+1.55
pt	35.00	37.06	38.35	+1.29
hu	2.51	16.02	17.21	+1.19
fr	32.71	34.76	35.92	+1.16
fa	7.44	12.73	13.52	+0.79
ar	3.58	15.89	16.28	+0.39
he	22.28	23.87	23.86	-0.01

Table 3: BLEU scores (lowercased) comparing character-level models against CG when used on 30k BPE sequences. We show that without sweeping BPE, CG generally outperforms purely character-level methods, even when the purely character-level networks are deepened as was shown to help in Cherry et al. (2018).

of 80 for our main experiments. At the end of each epoch we checkpoint and evaluate our model on a validation datset and used validation accuracy as our model selection criteria for test time. During decoding, a beam size of 5 was chosen for all the experiments.

5.3 Results

We provide case insensitive BLEU scores for our main experiments, comparing our character-aware model (CG) against a baseline model that uses only standard word (and subword) embeddings. We divide the results of our model's performance into three parts: (i) over a sweep of BPE merge operations, including a commonly used setting of 30k merge operations (ii) with word-level source and

---

[6]SGD outperformed both Adam and Adadelta. Others have found similar trends, see Bahar et al. (2017) and Maruf and Haffari (2018).

target sequences and finally, (iii) against a purely character-level model.

5.3.1 BPE Results

Part 1 of Table 2 compares the best BLEU score obtained by the baseline model, after performing a BPE sweep from 1.6k to 60k, to the best BLEU obtained by CG after sweeping over the same BPE range. While our study focuses on the target side, BPE (with the same number of merge operations) was applied to both source and target for our experiments. We find that after this sweep, CG outperforms the baseline in all 14 languages. The exhaustive table of results for these experiments is presented in Appendix A.

No Typical BPE Setting

Additionally, we see that the BPE setting that achieves best BLEU in the baseline model varies considerably from 1.6k to 30k depending on the target language, indicating that *there is no "typical" BPE for low-resource settings*. In the CG model, however, performance was usually best at 30k. Part 2 of Table 2 compares the baseline and CG at BPE of 30k where CG performs optimally.

We find that our CG model consistently outperforms the baseline for almost all BPE merge hyperparameters across all 14 languages. Figure 2 shows the gains observed by the CG model as we sweep over BPE merge operations. While the baseline model does slightly better than CG at small BPE settings for a few languages (all points below the 0 value), a majority of the points show positive gains.

5.3.2 Word-Level Results

In Part 3 of Table 2 we show results with our approximation for word level. While our best results are generally with BPE, we note that we get the biggest relative gains using our method at the word level, which we expect is due to always having the whole word to learn character patterns over. For the CG model, in 60k BPE and word-level settings we used the large vocabulary approximation discussed in Section 4.2.

5.3.3 Character-Level Results

Finally, in Table 3, we compare two character-level models against our CG model at 30k BPE. The shallow character-level model used 2 encoder and decoder layers with 1000 recurrent units, while the deep model used 6 encoder and decoder

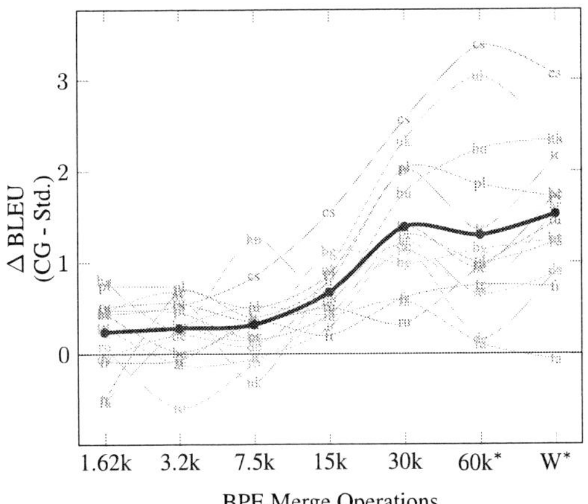

Figure 2: Plot of the difference between the BLEU scores from CG model and baseline model at various BPE settings for each of the 14 languages (shown in color, with language identifier). The bold black line shows the average difference across the languages for each BPE setting.

Features	Corpus-dependent			Corpus-independent	
	TT	**A**	**H**	**UT**	**UTC**
Correlation	0.04	0.59	0.67	0.80	0.49

Table 4: The Pearsons correlation between the features and the relative gain in BLEU obtained by the CG model. See Section 6 for details regarding features.

layers with 512 recurrent units .[7] Furthermore, the improved results from the deep model were only attainable using the Fairseq toolkit with Noam optimization and 100 warmup steps (Gehring et al., 2017). As Table 3 shows, our CG model with 30k BPE compares favorably to even deep character-level models for this low-resource setting.

6 Analysis

We are interested in understanding whether our character-aware model is exploiting morphological patterns in the target language. We investigate this by inspecting the relationship between a set of hand-picked features and improvements obtained by our model over the baseline at word-level inputs. These features fall into two categories, *corpus-dependent* and *corpus-independent*. We following Bentz et al. (2016), and extract features known to correlate with human judgments of morphological complexity. The following corpus-dependent features were used:

---

[7]Increasing the recurrent size for deep models resulted in significant drop in BLEU scores. We set the dropout rate to 0.1.

(i) Type-Token Ratio (TT): the ratio of the number of word types to the total number of word tokens in the target side. We note that a large corpus tends to have a smaller type-token ratio compared to small corpus.

(ii) Word-Alignment Score (A): computed as $A = \frac{|\text{many-to-one}| - |\text{one-to-many}|}{|\text{all-alignments}|}$. One-to-one, one-to-many and many-to-one alignment types are illustrated in Figure 3.[8] We intuit that a morphologically poor source language (like English) paired with a richer target language should exhibit more many-to-one alignments—a single word in the target will contain more information (via morphological phenomena) that can only be translated using multiple words in the source.

(iii) Word-Level Entropy (H): computed as $H = \sum_{v \in \mathcal{V}} p(v) \log p(v)$ where v is a word type. This metric reflects the average information content of the words in a corpus. Languages with more dependence on having a large number of word types rather than word order or phrase structure will score higher.

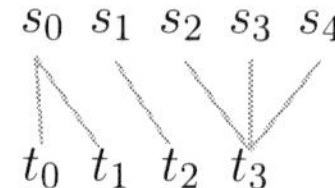

Figure 3: Example of one-to-many (s_0 to t_0, t_1), one-to-one (s_1 to t_2) and many-to-one (s_2, s_3, s_4 to t_3) alignments. For this example $A = (3 - 2)/6$.

For the corpus-independent features we used a morphological annotation corpus called UniMorph (Sylak-Glassman et al., 2015). The UniMorph corpus contains a large list of inflected words (in several languages) along with the word's lemma and a set of morphological tags. For example, the French UniMorph corpus contains the word `marchai` (walked), which is associated with its lemma, `marcher` and a set of morphological tags {**V**, **IND**, **PST**, **1**, **SG**, **PFV**}. There are 19 such tags in the French UniMorph corpus. A morphologically richer language like Hungarian, for example, has 36 distinct tags. We used the number of distinct tags (UT) and the number of different tag combinations (UTC) that appear in the UniMorph corpus for each language. Note that

we do not filter out words (and its associated tags) from the UniMorph corpus that are absent in our parallel data. This ensures that the UT and UTC features are completely corpus independent.

The Pearson's correlation between these hand-picked features and relative gain observed by our model is shown in Table 4. For this analysis we used the relative gain obtained from the word-level experiments. Concretely, the relative gain for Czech was computed as $\frac{21.49 - 18.44}{18.44}$ We see a strong correlation between the corpus-independent feature (UT) and our model's gain. Alignment score and Word Entropy are also moderately correlated. Surprisingly, we see no correlation to type-token ratio.

As the correlation analysis only examines the relation between BLEU gains and an *individual* feature, we further analyzed how the features *jointly* relate to BLEU gains. We fitted a linear regression model, setting the relative gains as the predicted variable y and the feature values as the input variables $\mathbf{x}$, with the goal of studying the linear regression weights ϕ.[9] We used feature-augmented domain adaptation where we consider each language as a domain (Daumé III, 2007), allowing the model to find a set of "general" weights as well language-specific weights that best fit the data (Equation 11). The general feature weights can be interpreted as being indicative of the overall trends in the dataset across all the languages, while the language-specific weights indicate language deviation from the overall trend.

$$\mathcal{L}(\phi) = \sum_{i \in \mathcal{I}} |y_i - \tilde{y}_i|^2 - \lambda |\phi|^2 \tag{10}$$

$$\tilde{y}_i = \phi_{\text{ALL}}^T \mathbf{x}_i + \phi_i^T \mathbf{x}_i \tag{11}$$

Where, y is the true relative gain in BLEU, $\tilde{y}$ is the predicted gain, $\mathbf{x}$ is a vector of input feature values, ϕ_{ALL} and ϕ_i are the general and language-specific weights, and i indexes into the set of languages in our analysis. We set λ to 0.05.

The matrix of learned weights ϕ is visualized in Figure 4. The first row of weights correspond to the "general" weights that are used for all the languages, followed by language-specific weights sorted by relative gain.

While the general weights align with the correlation results (Table 4), this analysis also shows that the UTC weight for Czech and Turkish are

---

[8]We use FastAlign (Dyer et al., 2013) for word alignments with the grow-diag-final-and heuristic from (Och and Ney, 2003) for symmetrization.

[9]The input features were min-max normalized for the regression analysis.

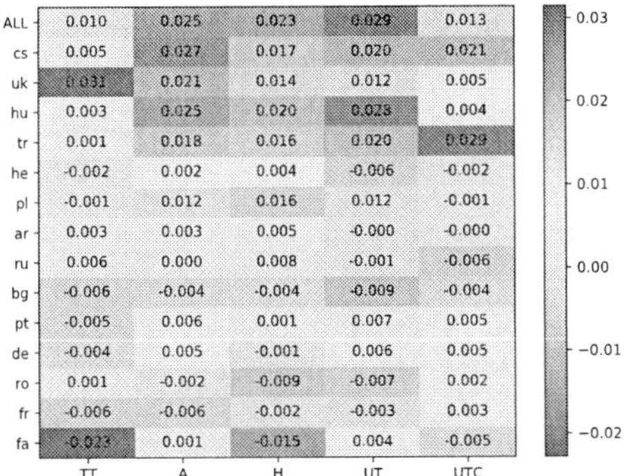

Figure 4: Feature weights of the feature-augmented language adapted linear regression model. The first row represents the "general" set of weights used for all of the languages. Each row below are the language-adapted weights that only "fire" for that specific language.

	here he is : leonardo **da vinci** .
Src	here he is : leonardo **da vinci** .
Ref	h*A hw – lywnArdw **dA fyn$y** .
Std	hnA hw : lywnArdw **dA dA** .
CG	hnA hw : lywnArdw **dA fy+n$y** .
Src	i 'm the **mexican** in the family .
Ref	AnA **Almksyky** fy AlEA}lp .
Std	AnA **mksy+Any** fy AlEA}lp .
CG	AnA **Almksy+ky** fy AlEA}lp .
Src	there was going to be a national **referendum** .
Ref	wtm AlAEdAd lAHrA' **AstftA'** $Eby .
Std	sykwn hnAk **f+tA'** wTny .
CG	sykwn hnAk **Ast+f+tA'** wTny .
Src	there are ordinary **heroes** .
Ref	fhnAk **AbTAl** TbyEywn .
Std	hnAk **ASdqA'** EAdy .
CG	hnAk **AbTAl** EAdyyn .

Table 5: Examples from En-Ar, transliterated with the Buckwalter schema. We show the version of our model and the English using '+' to denote where BPE splits words up, while BPE has not been applied to the target reference.

much larger than any of the other languages' and indeed we can verify that these languages have 194 and 300 different tag combinations while the average tag combinations is $\approx$ 110.

From the corpus-dependent features, word alignment score strongly predicts the gain in BLEU scores. For Czech, Ukrainian, Turkish, Hungarian, and Polish we see additional weight placed on this feature. A similar trend can be seen for the word-entropy feature. While type-token ratio does not exhibit a strong overall trend, we see that Ukrainian and Farsi are outliers.

Our correlation and regression analysis strongly suggest that CG character-aware modeling helps the most when the target language has inherent morphological complexity and that it does indeed have the ability to handle morphological patterns present in the target languages.

6.1 Qualitative Examples

We additionally look at specific examples of where our model is outperforming the baseline in the case of 30k BPE in En-Ar. We see a few trends, which we show examples of in Table 5. The first trend, corresponding to the first example, is that it gets names better. This might be because Arabic is not written in the Latin alphabet, and the spelling-aware model may be able to transliterate better.

Another trend is that CG gets the endings of rare words correct, in particular when the BPE segmentation is *not* according to morpheme boundaries. The second example illustrates this, where the word for "Mexican" appears in the training data broken up by BPE with various morphological endings, all of which are spelled beginning

with "ky" in the second subword. The morpheme boundaries here would be "Al+mksyk+y." Note that CG also gets the definite article "Al" correct while the baseline does not.

Finally, we see a pattern where our model does better for words which are rare and appear both with and without the definite article "Al." Our third example in Table 5 illustrates this with an infrequent word, the word for "referendum", which gets broken up into subwords. In particular, the first subword sometimes has an "Al" attached in the training data. Our model is able to translate this subword, while the baseline skips the subword altogether, outputting two subwords that alone are not a valid word. Again, the word is not broken up along morpheme boundaries by BPE. Here there would be no way to break this word up into morphological segments—it consists of non-concatenative derivational morphology. This occurs again in the fourth example in the word for "heroes," where the baseline predicts the word for "friends." In this case the word was not split up by BPE, but similarly it is rare but occurs with the definite article attached in the training data as well.

7 Conclusion

We extend character-aware word-level modeling to the decoder for translation into morphologically rich languages. Our improvements were attained by augmenting the softmax and the target embedding layers with character-awareness. We also find it critical to add a gating function to balance compositional embeddings with standard embeddings. We evaluate our method on a low-resource dataset translating from English into 14 languages, and on top of a spectrum of BPE merge operations. Furthermore, for word-level and higher merge hyperparameter settings, we introduced an approximation to the softmax layer. We achieve consistent performance gains across languages and subword granularities, and perform an analysis indicating that the gains for each language correspond to morphological complexity.

For future work, we would like to explore how our methods might be of use in higher-resource settings. Furthermore, it would be interesting to see how these methods might interact with multilingual systems and if they might be able to improve what information is shared between related languages.

Acknowledgements

This project originated at the Machine Translation Marathon 2018. We thank the organizers and attendees for their support, feedback and helpful discussions during the event. This work is supported in part by the Office of the Director of National Intelligence, IARPA. The views contained herein are those of the authors and do not necessarily reflect the position of the sponsors.

References

Bahar, Parnia, Tamer Alkhouli, Jan-Thorsten Peter, Christopher Jan-Steffen Brix, and Hermann Ney. 2017. Empirical investigation of optimization algorithms in neural machine translation. *The Prague Bulletin of Mathematical Linguistics*, 108(1):13–25.

Bahdanau, Dzmitry, Kyunghyun Cho, and Yoshua Bengio. 2015. Neural machine translation by jointly learning to align and translate. *International Conference on Learning Representations*.

Belinkov, Yonatan, Nadir Durrani, Fahim Dalvi, Hassan Sajjad, and James Glass. 2017. What do neural machine translation models learn about morphology? In *Proceedings of the 55th Annual Meeting of the Association for Computational Linguistics (Volume 1: Long Papers)*, pages 861–872. Association for Computational Linguistics.

Bentz, Christian, Tatyana Ruzsics, Alexander Koplenig, and Tanja Samardzic. 2016. A comparison between morphological complexity measures: typological data vs. language corpora. In *Proceedings of the Workshop on Computational Linguistics for Linguistic Complexity (CL4LC)*, pages 142–153.

Cettolo, Mauro, Christian Girardi, and Marcello Federico. 2012. Wit3: Web inventory of transcribed and translated talks. In *Conference of European Association for Machine Translation*, pages 261–268.

Cherry, Colin, George Foster, Ankur Bapna, Orhan Firat, and Wolfgang Macherey. 2018. Revisiting character-based neural machine translation with capacity and compression. In *Proceedings of the 2018 Conference on Empirical Methods in Natural Language Processing*, pages 4295–4305.

Chung, Junyoung, Kyunghyun Cho, and Yoshua Bengio. 2016. A character-level decoder without explicit segmentation for neural machine translation. In *Proceedings of the 54th Annual Meeting of the Association for Computational Linguistics (Volume 1: Long Papers)*, pages 1693–1703.

Costa-jussà, Marta R and José AR Fonollosa. 2016. Character-based neural machine translation. In *Proceedings of the 54th Annual Meeting of the Association for Computational Linguistics (Volume 2: Short Papers)*, pages 357–361.

Daumé III, Hal. 2007. Frustratingly easy domain adaptation. In *Proceedings of the 45th Annual Meeting of the Association of Computational Linguistics*, pages 256–263, June.

Duh, Kevin. 2018. The multitarget ted talks task. http://www.cs.jhu.edu/~kevinduh/a/multitarget-tedtalks/.

Dyer, Chris, Victor Chahuneau, and Noah A Smith. 2013. A simple, fast, and effective reparameterization of ibm model 2. In *Proceedings of the 2013 Conference of the North American Chapter of the Association for Computational Linguistics: Human Language Technologies*, pages 644–648.

Gage, Philip. 1994. A new algorithm for data compression. *C Users J.*, 12(2):23–38, February.

Gehring, Jonas, Michael Auli, David Grangier, Denis Yarats, and Yann N Dauphin. 2017. Convolutional Sequence to Sequence Learning. *ArXiv e-prints*, May.

Jean, Sébastien, Kyunghyun Cho, Roland Memisevic, and Yoshua Bengio. 2015. On using very large target vocabulary for neural machine translation. In *Proceedings of the 53rd Annual Meeting of the Association for Computational Linguistics and the 7th International Joint Conference on Natural Language Processing (Volume 1: Long Papers)*, pages 1–10.

Kim, Yoon, Yacine Jernite, David Sontag, and Alexander M Rush. 2016. Character-aware neural language models. In *30th AAAI Conference on Artificial Intelligence, AAAI 2016*.

Klein, Guillaume, Yoon Kim, Yuntian Deng, Jean Senellart, and Alexander M. Rush. 2017. Opennmt: Open-source toolkit for neural machine translation. In *Proceedings of the 55th Annual Meeting of the Association for Computational Linguistics, ACL 2017, Vancouver, Canada, July 30 - August 4, System Demonstrations*, pages 67–72.

Ling, Wang, Isabel Trancoso, Chris Dyer, and Alan W
Black. 2015. Character-based neural machine translation. *arXiv preprint arXiv:1511.04586*.

Luong, Thang, Hieu Pham, and Christopher D. Manning. 2015. Effective approaches to attention-based
neural machine translation. In *Proceedings of the
2015 Conference on Empirical Methods in Natural
Language Processing, EMNLP 2015, Lisbon, Portugal, September 17-21, 2015*, pages 1412–1421.

Maruf, Sameen and Gholamreza Haffari. 2018. Document context neural machine translation with memory networks. In *Proceedings of the 56th Annual
Meeting of the Association for Computational Linguistics (Volume 1: Long Papers)*, volume 1, pages
1275–1284.

Miyamoto, Yasumasa and Kyunghyun Cho. 2016.
Gated word-character recurrent language model. In
*Proceedings of the 2016 Conference on Empirical
Methods in Natural Language Processing*, pages
1992–1997.

Och, Franz Josef and Hermann Ney. 2003. A systematic comparison of various statistical alignment models. *Computational linguistics*, 29(1):19–51.

Passban, Peyman, Qun Liu, and Andy Way. 2018. Improving character-based decoding using target-side
morphological information for neural machine translation. In *Proceedings of the 2018 Conference of
the North American Chapter of the Association for
Computational Linguistics: Human Language Technologies, Volume 1 (Long Papers)*, volume 1, pages
58–68.

Sennrich, Rico, Barry Haddow, and Alexandra Birch.
2016. Neural machine translation of rare words with
subword units. In *Proceedings of the 54th Annual
Meeting of the Association for Computational Linguistics, ACL 2016, August 7-12, 2016, Berlin, Germany, Volume 1: Long Papers*.

Shapiro, Pamela and Kevin Duh. 2018. Bpe and
charcnns for translation of morphology: A cross-
lingual comparison and analysis. *arXiv preprint
arXiv:1809.01301*.

Sylak-Glassman, John, Christo Kirov, Matt Post, Roger
Que, and David Yarowsky. 2015. A universal
feature schema for rich morphological annotation
and fine-grained cross-lingual part-of-speech tagging. In *International Workshop on Systems and
Frameworks for Computational Morphology*, pages
72–93. Springer.

A   More Detailed Results

In Table 6, we provide the number of training sentences for each language.

In Table 7, we provide the full experiments of our sweep of BPE for both standard and our CG embeddings. In our baseline, we see a divergence in trends across languages while sweeping over BPE merge hyperparameters—Czech (cs), Turkish (tr), and Ukrainian (uk) for example, are highly sensitive to the BPE merge hyperparameter. On the other hand, for languages like French (fr) and Farsi (fa), the performance is mostly consistent across different BPE merge hyperparameters.

Language	Number of sentences
Czech (cs)	81k
Ukrainian (uk)	74k
Hungarian (hu)	108k
Polish (pl)	149k
Hebrew (he)	181k
Turkish (tr)	137k
Arabic (ar)	168k
Portuguese (pt)	147k
Romanian (ro)	155k
Bulgarian (bg)	159k
Russian (ru)	174k
German (de)	146k
Farsi (fa)	106k
French (fr)	149k

Table 6: Number of sentences in training data for each language

L	M	Char-Shallow	Char-Deep	BPE (Subwords) 1.6k	3.2k	7.5k	15k	30k	60k	Word-Level
cs	Std.	11.16	18.45	20.28	20.51	20.57	19.60	18.73	17.60	18.44
	CG	-	-	20.71	21.04	21.41	21.14	21.28	20.97	**21.49**
uk	Std.	4.77	-	13.35	15.51	15.79	15.36	14.27	12.50	12.94
	CG	-	-	13.80	16.16	15.48	16.28	**16.60**	15.54	15.30
hu	Std.	2.51	16.02	15.77	16.33	15.62	16.61	15.45	14.81	14.18
	CG	-	-	16.58	16.61	16.88	**17.23**	17.21	17.05	16.52
pl	Std.	10.65	16.31	16.14	16.40	16.34	16.76	15.98	15.47	15.49
	CG	-	-	16.88	17.12	16.84	17.63	**18.00**	17.32	17.20
he	Std.	22.28	23.87	23.07	23.36	23.32	22.76	22.47	21.84	21.26
	CG	-	-	23.52	23.38	23.65	23.33	**23.86**	22.78	23.01
tr	Std.	5.29	13.94	14.92	14.58	15.11	14.75	13.82	13.69	12.58
	CG	-	-	14.42	15.25	15.51	15.54	**15.83**	15.05	14.75
ar	Std.	3.58	15.89	15.66	15.67	16.22	15.70	15.05	14.86	14.45
	CG	-	-	15.96	15.55	16.17	15.99	**16.28**	15.53	16.05
pt	Std.	35.00	37.06	37.47	37.53	37.61	37.85	37.05	37.11	37.13
	CG	-	-	37.94	37.98	37.77	38.28	**38.35**	38.11	38.36
ro	Std.	21.58	22.45	23.48	24.02	23.72	23.78	22.88	22.73	22.39
	CG	-	-	23.55	23.42	23.61	**24.20**	24.00	23.38	23.27
bg	Std.	26.40	29.81	31.17	31.41	31.63	31.09	30.92	30.44	30.18
	CG	-	-	31.43	31.71	31.81	**32.20**	31.90	31.58	31.43
ru	Std.	14.63	-	18.17	18.71	19.05	18.80	19.28	18.28	17.60
	CG	-	-	18.68	19.26	19.40	19.30	**19.61**	19.23	19.04
de	Std.	23.89	25.93	26.98	27.34	27.37	27.23	26.94	27.21	26.84
	CG	-	-	26.94	27.55	27.46	27.89	**28.12**	27.37	27.75
fa	Std.	7.44	12.73	12.87	12.71	12.86	12.94	12.94	13.20	12.85
	CG	-	-	12.35	12.98	13.38	13.36	**13.52**	13.31	12.79
fr	Std.	32.71	34.76	35.97	35.75	35.82	35.90	35.31	35.33	35.28
	CG	-	-	35.89	35.68	**36.17**	36.10	35.92	36.08	36.01

Table 7: BLEU scores (case insensitive) for a standard embedding encoder-decoder baseline (Std), and character-aware model, composed embedding combined with standard embedding (CG) for 14 languages and various BPE merge hyperparameters. For purely character-level we only train the standard model as CG would not have a sequence of characters to compose. For BPE of 60k and word-level we use the softmax approximation described. We see that CG obtains the best result in all languages.

Improving Translations by Combining Fuzzy-Match Repair with Automatic Post-Editing

John E. Ortega
Universitat d'Alacant
E-03071, Alacant, Spain
jeo10@alu.ua.es

Felipe Sánchez-Martínez
Universitat d'Alacant
E-03071, Alacant, Spain
fsanchez@dlsi.ua.es

Marco Turchi
Fondazione Bruno Kessler
Trento, Italy
turchi@fbk.eu

Matteo Negri
Fondazione Bruno Kessler
Trento, Italy
negri@fbk.eu

Abstract

Two of the more predominant technologies that professional translators have at their disposal for improving productivity are machine translation (MT) and computer-aided translation (CAT) tools based on translation memories (TM). When translators use MT, they can use automatic post-editing (APE) systems to automate part of the post-editing work and get further productivity gains. When they use TM-based CAT tools, productivity may improve if they rely on fuzzy-match repair (FMR) methods. In this paper we combine FMR and APE: first a FMR proposal is produced from the translation unit proposed by the TM, then this proposal is further improved by an APE system specially tuned for this purpose. Experiments conducted on the translation of English texts into German show that, with the two combined technologies, the quality of the translations improves up to 23% compared to a pure MT system. The improvement over a pure FMR system is of 16%, showing the effectiveness of our joint solution.

1 Introduction

In recent times, research has shown that translators can be more productive when applying state-of-the-art post-editing techniques (Isabel, 2017). In many cases, the state-of-the-art techniques are applied to improve translation proposals from a translation memory (TM) or directly produced by a ma-

chine translation (MT) system. Post-editing techniques can be automated and seamlessly integrated into the typical translation pipeline for productivity gains. Two such techniques: fuzzy-match repair (FMR) (Ortega et al., 2016) and automatic post-editing (APE) (Chatterjee et al., 2017) have shown to be effective without the initial intervention of the translator by offering a *repaired* translation proposal from a TM in the case of FMR, and an improved MT output in the case of APE.

FMR is an automatic post-editing technique typically used with TM-based computer-aided translation (CAT) tools. In TM-based CAT, the translator is offered a translation proposal that comes from a translation unit (a pair of parallel segments) whose source segment is similar to the segment to be translated. When the source segment in the translation unit and the segment to be translated are not identical, which happens very often, the translation proposal needs to be post-edited in order to create the final translation. FMR aims to provide *repaired* translation hypotheses to reduce the post-editing effort of the original translation proposals by using another source of bilingual information such as an MT system. Some approaches to FMR, like the one by Koehn and Senellart (2010), heavily depend on the specific MT system type being used for repairing. Others, such as the one by Ortega et al. (2016) use an agnostic, black-box, MT system in such a way that the user would only choose from several repaired hypothesis proposals.

APE aims to correct the errors present in a machine-translated text before showing it to the translator or post-editor. As motivated by Parton et al. (2012), an APE system can help to improve MT output by exploiting information that is not available during translation, or by performing a deeper text analysis, and by adapting the output of a general-purpose MT system to the lexicon/style requested in a specific application domain. In doing so, APE aims to provide professional translators with improved MT output quality to reduce (human) post-editing effort.

In this paper, we show that APE could be used to improve sentence-level proposals from FMR when FMR is used as a device to create new translations from a TM. As shown in Figure 1, FMR is first used to produce a repaired translation proposal and then APE is used as a tool to improve the quality of the proposal. We demonstrate that the combination of these two techniques can significantly boost translation quality. It outperforms both a competitive neural MT system and FMR alone, and its performance reaches nearly that of methods relying on the reference (i.e. oracle) translations.

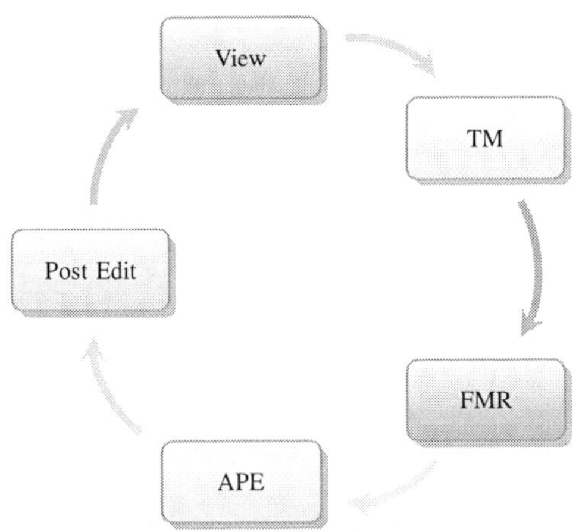

Figure 1: Seamless addition of fuzzy-match repair (FMR) and automatic post-editing (APE) in a traditional computer-aided translation (CAT) pipeline. The post editor is presented with several hypotheses created from a translation memory (TM) proposal through fuzzy-match repair (FMR) and automatic post-editing (APE).

Our work provides an in-depth analysis of which technique would work best under "typical" translation scenarios by testing several combinations of the two post-editing techniques. Our analysis includes various checkpoints of evaluation including industry standards and human-level reviews. In order to better describe our process, we organize the paper as follows. First, in Section 2 we review the relevant work where both technologies (FMR and APE) have been used. Second, in Section 3, we dig deeper into the motivation and methodology of our work and show how the two technologies could be "glued" together to form a new system that is added in a modular way to a traditional CAT pipeline. Third, in Section 4 we describe our ex-

perimental settings in detail. Fourth, we present our results in Section 5. We use BLEU and TER as metrics to evaluate the quality of our translations. We also perform error analysis and human reviews. Then, we measure the systems quantitatively using a word-measurement like word-error rate to show performance. Finally, in Section 6 we give some conclusions and plan on doing in the future.

2 Related work

In this section we describe approaches related to both FMR and APE. It is worth noting that, to the best of our knowledge, FMR and APE have not previously been combined together.

2.1 Fuzzy-match repair

FMR aims to reduce the post-editing effort of translation proposals retrieved from a TM. To do so FMR techniques rely on a source of bilingual information, usually MT, to automatically *repair* a translation proposal by modifying those parts of the proposal that otherwise should be post-edited by the translator. The idea of FMR points back to papers by Kranias and Samiotou (2004) and Hewavitharana et al. (2005) whose approaches were based on the location of anchor points via alignment of words and relied heavily on the inner workings of the MT system they used. Improvements over time led way to advances that used phrase-based MT (Simard and Isabelle, 2009; Koehn and Senellart, 2010). Work has gradually advanced and various FMR methods have been proposed that share one common theme: locating and repairing sub-segments in the translation proposal. Later works (Dandapat et al., 2011; Ortega et al., 2016), on the other hand, can use *any* MT system as a black-box.

Knowles et al. (2018) recently performed a comparison of the nature of MT systems for their use in FMR. In particular, they contrast the quality of FMR output using neural MT and phrase-based MT. Most importantly, they show that neural MT may not be appropriate if it is not trained on in-domain data. Other novel works, like the work by Bulté et al. (2018), include FMR as a primary part of a system integrating MT and TM. Lastly, Ortega et al. (2018) have found a statistical way to select the best MT system to use in black-box FMR.

2.2 Automatic post-editing

Automatic post-editing is the task of correcting recurring errors from an MT system by learning from human corrections. Starting from the seminal work by (Simard et al., 2007), the problem has been tackled as a "monolingual translation" task in which the MT output must be translated into an improved text in the target language. Under this definition, the "parallel data" used for training an APE system consist of triplets of the form (source, target, post-edited target) rather than the (source, target) pairs normally used in MT. Following the translation-based approach, initial solutions relied on the phrase-based paradigm (Simard et al., 2007; Dugast et al., 2007; Terumasa, 2007; Pilevar, 2011; Béchara et al., 2011; Chatterjee et al., 2015; Chatterjee et al., 2016). However, in the past couple of years, top results have been achieved by neural architectures (Pal et al., 2016; Junczys-Dowmunt and Grundkiewicz, 2016; Chatterjee et al., 2017; Junczys-Dowmunt and Grundkiewicz, 2017; Tebbifakhr et al., 2018).

Recent advancements made by participants in the APE shared task organized within the Conference on Machine Translation (WMT) have shown the capability of APE systems to significantly improve the performance of a black-box MT system gaining up to seven BLEU points (Bojar et al., 2017; Chatterjee et al., 2018a).

The neural approaches proposed share common traits such as using multi encoders (one for the source and one for the MT segments) and leveraging artificial data (round-trip translations) to maximize results. The APE system used in this paper proposes a novel approach extending the original technology implemented by the best performing system at the WMT 2016 APE shared task (Chatterjee et al., 2017).

2.3 Combination of approaches

We briefly describe a few combinations of approaches and systems that are usually used in different scenarios, such as FMR and APE, and that could be considered novel and related to our work. The first, and probably the most relevant work, is based on MT quality estimation (QE) and APE. Chatterjee et al. (2018b) combine MT QE and APE in three different ways: one in which sentence-level MT QE is used to activate an APE system, a second one in which word-level MT QE is used to guide the APE system, and a third one that uses

MT QE to choose between the original MT output and its post-edited version. Additionally, Tan et al. (2017) attempts to correct a common problem in APE known as "overcorrection" (i.e. systems' tendency to completely re-translate the MT output, also rephrasing parts that are already correct). They do this by specifying two models (called neural post-editing models). Then, they use MT and QE to help select one of the models for the translation. This by no means is related to fuzzy-match repair; however, the idea of combining several systems around APE is similar to what we are doing.

Hokamp (2017) includes word-level MT QE features as additional inputs to an APE system and trains several neural models using different input representations, but sharing the same output space. These models are finally ensembled together and tuned for APE and MT QE.

3 TM repairing through FMR and APE

Our system is a two-step process that can be added to any TM-based CAT tool that has access to a source of bilingual information (SBI), such as a black-box MT system. The first step of our process is to use the translation unit whose source segment is most similar to the segment to be translated as input to FMR that, in turn, uses the SBI for repairing and proposing new translation hypotheses not present in the TM. These proposals could then be treated as input to a second APE step that is used to output the best final possible hypotheses. In this section, we first describe more formally how FMR and APE are used. Then, we provide an example (Table 1) in the last sub-section that illustrates how APE can be used to improve an FMR translation proposal.

3.1 Fuzzy-match repair

The FMR method devised by Ortega et al. (2016) can generate a set of fuzzy-match repair hypotheses from a translation unit (s, t) and the segment to be translated s' by using any available SBI. For our experiments, we use MT[1] as a black-box SBI.

Their method first identifies mismatched words between s and s', that is, the words they do not have in common. This is done by using the alignment between the words in s and s' obtained as a by-product of the computation of the word-based edit distance (Levenshtein, 1966) between s and

---

[1]Other SBIs that could be used are sub-segment translation memories, bilingual dictionaries or phrase tables.

s': mismatched words are left unaligned. SBIs are then used to translate into the target language sub-segment pairs of s and s' containing mismatched words. The sub-segments pairs to be translated are obtained by using the phrase-pair extraction algorithm used in phrase-based statistical MT to obtain bilingual phrase pairs (Koehn, 2010, section 5.2.3). The translations obtained for the sub-segments of s are used to identify the sub-segment in t that needs to be modified, and the translation of the sub-segments of s' to identify the way they should be modified. In this way, a set of *patching operators* is built. Each patching operator consists of a sub-segment σ of s, a sub-segment σ' of s' aligned with σ, a sub-segment τ of t to be repaired, and a sub-segment τ', the translation of σ', to be used for repairing. By combining these patching operators, a set of fuzzy-match repaired hypothesis is generated. For a detailed description of their method, we refer the reader to the work by Ortega et al. (2016).

3.2 Automatic post-editing

The APE system used in this paper is a re-implementation of the multi-source attention-based encoder-decoder system (Chatterjee et al., 2017) that achieved the best performance in the automatic evaluation at the APE shared task at WMT 2016.[2] This system uses two different encoders to independently process the source and the MT segments. Each encoder consists of a bi-directional GRU and has its own attention layer that is used to compute the weighted context. To obtain a single context, the two context vectors are combined via a feed-forward network. The obtained context is used to compute the classical attention model (Bahdanau et al., 2015). To regularize the multi-source network and to avoid over-fitting, a shared dropout is applied to the hidden state of both encoders and to the merged context. This architecture has shown to be particularly effective in the APE task, and its multi-source structure makes it particularly suitable for the FMR post-editing task.

3.3 FMR with APE

The integration of FMR and APE does not require that the two ideas share any code behind the scenes; so, both can be seen as black box mechanisms for improving translation proposals from the TM. For this paper, FMR first creates several

Source:	article 18 , paragraph 1 , of the co2 act
TM:	article **45** , paragraph 1 , of the co2 **ordinance**
FMR:	artikel 18 absatz 1 der co2-verordnung
APE:	artikel 18 absatz 1 des co2-gesetzes
Ref:	artikel 18 , absatz 1 des co2-gesetzes

Table 1: An example of how fuzzy-match repair (FMR) and automatic post-editing (APE) could work together to improve a translation memory (TM) proposal.

new proposals based on the original TM proposals. Then, APE uses those proposals as the base to produce even better proposals.

Table 1 shows an example of how a source sentence from our TM is modified first by FMR and then by APE. First, FMR repairs the TM proposal by replacing two words (*45* and *ordinance*); notice that FMR incorrectly translates *co2 act* as *co2-verordnung*. APE then takes the FMR proposal and produces an improved translation, *co2-gesetzes*, which is closer to the reference translation. The final result is a more adequate translation that needs fewer post-edits by the final user.

4 Experimental Settings

We experiment with various combinations of FMR and APE using a phrase-based MT system as a SBI for FMR. In addition, we use APE on the output of two MT systems, a phrase-based MT system and a neural MT system, as a point of comparison. This section goes over the details of the data and systems we used. One of our goals in this paper is to show that by using freely-available data found on the Internet, which is the case for small businesses that do not have in-house data and cannot afford more expensive data sets, our system achieves good results despite results from previous work (Knowles et al., 2018; Chatterjee et al., 2018b) that have shown that training MT systems on in-domain data, especially in the case of a neural MT system, can be advantageous.

4.1 Data

Our entire dataset is based on 4,000 randomly selected sentences from the DGT translation memory (DGT-TM-release 2018).[3] The TM is available in several languages containing many translation units.[4] In our evaluation, we use the English–German (EN–DE) TM extracted with the formal

---

[2] `http://www.statmt.org/wmt16/`

[3] `ec.europa.eu/jrc/en/`
`language-technologies/`
`dgt-translation-memory`

[4] For some statistics about this TM, please visit `wt-public.emm4u.eu/Resources/DGT-TM_`

DGT extraction methodology mentioned on their website.

FMR is used to generate repaired translation hypotheses for these 4,000 sentences by using the whole EN–DE DGT TM to look for translation units to repair; it is worth noting that the whole DGT TM is not used in any way by the APE system. FMR hypotheses are generated for each of the 4,000 segments by looking in the whole DGT TM for the translation unit (s, t) whose source segment s is the most similar to the segment to be translated s'. The similarity between s' and s is computed as the *fuzzy match score*, which in turn is based on the word-based edit distance (Levenshtein, 1966) between s and s'. If a translation unit with a fuzzy match score above 60%[5] is found, it is used for FMR; otherwise, the Moses (Koehn et al., 2007) MT system is used to translate s'.

Of the 4,000 sentences selected at random from the DGT TM, 2,500 are randomly selected and used to fine-tune the APE system (see Section 4.3), 500 are used for development, and 1,000 for testing. Altogether, about 350 sentences are not successfully repaired by FMR; in those cases, we used the output of Moses.

4.2 Machine translation systems

We use the phrase-based statistical MT system Moses (Koehn et al., 2007) as a SBI for FMR; it has shown to perform well in previous experiments and in the black-box setting (Knowles et al., 2018). As a term of comparison we use Moses and the neural MT system Nematus (Sennrich et al., 2016) as baselines; we leave for future work the inclusion of a neural MT system as a SBI for FMR. It is worth noting that the phrase-based MT system performed better on the APE module than the neural MT system (see Table 2).

With Moses we use pre-trained models downloaded from `www.statmt.org/moses/ RELEASE-3.0/models/`. By using pre-trained models, we try to replicate what most users in a corporate setting would choose, at least as a first iteration, in absence of advanced knowledge to build the MT models by their own.

Nematus is trained on a collection of datasets belonging to different domains. This is done to resemble a typical industrial scenario where a translation system is trained on a large collection of data

that may or may not match the test domain. In particular, we use domain-specific parallel corpora from the European Central Bank, Gnome, JRC-Acquis, KDE4, OpenOffice, PHP and Ubuntu,[6] and generic training sets obtained from the CommonCrawl dataset[7] and Europarl.[8] The Europarl corpus can be considered an in-domain dataset because it belongs to the same domain of the DGT TM collection.

To train Nematus, the training corpus is first processed using byte pair encoding (BPE) (Sennrich et al., 2016), so that the less frequent words are segmented into their sub-word units, resulting in vocabularies of maximum size of 90k entries, or 90k BPE operations. The size of word embeddings and hidden layers is set, respectively, to 500 and 1024. Source and target dropout are both set to 10%, whereas, encoder and decoder hidden states and embedding dropout is set to 20%. The learning rate is set to 0.001. The cost is computed on mini-batches of 100 sentence pairs with maximum length of 50 tokens, extracted from the randomly shuffled data after each epoch. The models are optimized using Adagrad (Duchi et al., 2011) and every 10,000 mini-batches they are evaluated with BLEU on the 500-sentence-pairs development set.

4.3 APE settings

The APE system is trained on the eSCAPE corpus (Negri et al., 2018), a collection of ~7M triplets (source, MT output and reference), where the MT outputs have been created by a phrase-based MT system. It consists of datasets belonging to different domains and it is filtered by removing duplicates and too short (3 words) or too long (60 words) segments.

To adapt the generic APE system to the FMR task, the model is fine-tuned (Luong and Manning, 2015) on 2,500 triplets (see Section 4.1), where the source input is paired with the repaired translation proposal produced by FMR.

Similar to the neural MT system, the APE system is trained on sub-word units by using BPE. The APE vocabulary is created by selecting 50k most frequent sub-words. Word embedding and GRU hidden state size is set to 1024. Network parameters are optimized with Adagrad with a learning rate of 0.01. Source and target dropout is set to

---

`Statistics.pdf`

[5]We use 60% fuzzy-match as a starting point threshold; in future work, we plan on trying with higher thresholds.

[6]All available at `opus.lingfil.uu.se`.

[7]`www.statmt.org/wmt13/ training-parallel-commoncrawl.tgz`

[8]`www.statmt.org/europarl/`

10%, whereas, encoder and decoder hidden states, weighted source context, and embedding dropout is set to 20%. After each epoch, the training data is shuffled and the batches are created after sorting 2,000 samples in order to speed-up the training. The batch size is set to 100 samples, with a maximum sentence length of 60 sub-words. The fine-tuning step is performed using the same parameters of the generic training.

4.4 Combined FMR and APE settings

Our FMR approach is identical to the FMR approach presented by Ortega et al. (2016). The only things that change are the MT system used as SBI, the language pair and the TM used. The output produced for experimentation by FMR is a list of translated segments that serve as input to the APE system. In particular, we experiment with two main FMR outputs for APE integration:

- an **oracle** experiment that chooses the best possible repaired translation hypothesis for each segment s' by computing the word-based edit distance between the repaired translation and the reference translation;

- a **randomized** experiment that, for each segment s', choses at random a repaired translation from the whole set of repaired translation hypotheses. On average, there are nearly 5 hypotheses per source segment s'. We use a random selection method because of its simplicity and because the chance of choosing the best hypothesis is around 20%.

4.5 Evaluation setting

For evaluating the combination of FMR and APE, we use two major metrics: BLEU (Papineni et al., 2002) and translation edit rate (TER) (Snover et al., 2006). We report on BLEU because it is a centerpiece of the development of MT systems, and on TER because it is the primary evaluation metric at the WMT APE shared task.

In addition to automatic evaluation metrics, we introduce a human evaluator: a native German speaker. This evaluator is not a translator; yet, does have a background in natural language processing and evaluation.[9] We report the evaluator's overall evaluation on the best performing systems in our results and offer it as an extra evaluation metric of

performance. The hope is to better understand the target language and how well the various systems perform under a native eye.

We provided a random set of 1,000 samples to the evaluator, where each sample is made of a sentence pair and its translations provided by each system presented in Table 3. Each sentence pair is rated by assigning quality scores on a 5-point scale (1 being the worst and 5 the best). The evaluator was told to rate the quality of translations and, thus, was given the final translation from the four systems but not the original human reference translation. Additionally, the evaluator was asked to provide an explanation of why each system's translation did not seem correct. Correctness was determined as a system's translation being exactly what was expected for the source sentence (a 5-star rating) or not at all (a 1-star rating).

5 Results

In this section we present results broken down into two different sub-sections to highlight the performance of the final combination system from the 1) system level and 2) human perspective. In Section 5.1 we report two major MT metrics: BLEU and TER. Then, in Section 5.2, the evaluator's feedback is taken into account while analyzing specific text anomalies that were found in the evaluation.

5.1 Metric-based analysis

Table 2 shows results that compare the use of MT, FMR, and APE for translation. They contain two main FMR configurations: **FMR Rand** – selecting a translation hypothesis at random, and **FMR Oracle** – using the hypothesis from FMR that is the nearest to the reference translation in terms of word-error rate. We also provide three variants obtained by combining FMR with APE (**FMR-APE**; see Section 4.4). The first three rows of Table 2 represent baseline experiments without the use of FMR or APE. We consider them as our baseline experiments because they are: the output of the phases-based MT system Moses (**PBMT**), the neural MT system Nematus (**NMT**), and the translation proposal as found in the translation memory (**TM**). APE is then measured alone using the two MT systems (PBMT and NMT) in the two rows **Phrase-based MT-APE** and **NMT-APE**. FMR alone is evaluated after that in the **FMR RAND** and **FMR Oracle**

---

[9]For economic and timing reasons, we only present evaluation from a single evaluator.

System	BLEU	TER
PBMT	39.62	49.74
NMT	51.54	36.75
TM	64.95	25.42
Phrase-based MT-APE	60.02	31.60
NMT-APE	56.58	33.77
FMR Rand	58.38	32.17
FMR Oracle	68.36	23.03
FMR-APE Rand	66.56	26.20
FMR-APE Oracle	80.54	15.60
FMR-APE Oracle-Rand	**74.44**	**20.26**

Table 2: Performance of three baseline approaches (use of a phrase-based MT system, use of a neural MT system, and use of the TM proposal without repairing), of the use of APE to better the MT outputs, the use of FMR alone when the translation hypothesis is selected at random or using an oracle, and of different combinations of FMR and APE.

rows. Then, the combination of FMR and APE with a random FMR hypothesis choice and an oracle (**FMR-APE Rand** and **FMR-APE Oracle**) is presented. Lastly, we present **FMR-APE Oracle-Rand**, which is our best approximation of FMR with APE that uses the randomly chosen hypothesis from FMR for each source segment as additional training data to the APE system.

The TM baseline approach performs the best when compared to the two MT systems (+~25 BLEU points over the phrase-based MT and +~13 over the neural MT). We attribute the performance of the TM approach to the fact that the DGT-TM is highly repetitive: it is quite likely that a match with a high fuzzy match score is found. The TM matches account for more than 70% of the 1,000 test segments; that is, for 70% of the segments there is a translation unit for which the fuzzy match score is above 60%. The TM baseline does quite well when matched; and, when it is not matched, Moses is used to translate the entire sentence.

FMR Rand is significantly below the TM approach, showing that there is a need for a better strategy to choose the best FMR repaired hypothesis in absence of a reference translation to propose to a post-editor. Selecting from hypotheses at random in FMR can generate low-quality segments that could reduce a post-editor's trust in the method. With the oracle selection (FMR Oracle), we notice a significant boost in performance (+4 BLEU points over the TM and +10 over the FMR Rand method). However, the oracle solution should only be considered as an upper bound for

optimum FMR hypothesis selection purposes. We leave a better selection method for FMR based on quality estimation for future work.

When combining FMR with APE, in both cases (FMR-APE Rand and Oracle) and by a large margin (+8 BLEU points for Rand and +12 for Oracle), APE improves translation quality with respect to FMR alone. The APE gain allows the FMR Rand method to also outperform the TM approach. At a closer look, APE seems to have a larger effect on the FMR Oracle than on FMR Rand. We believe that the random selection of hypotheses produces segments with few common characteristics that make it harder for APE to learn a strict correction pattern. For validation, we use the FMR-APE Oracle model as a training mechanism for APE because it contains hypotheses chosen by looking at the reference (FMR-APE Oracle-Rand in Table 2).[10] Results when using the FMR-APE Oracle as training for the APE model are the best and outperform both TM and FMR-APE Rand (+10 and +8 BLEU points). We consider this to be the best adaptation of FMR.

APE gains can be classified into two main categories: (1) addition of missing parts and (2) lexical substitution. In the former, since APE accepts the source and the MT sentences, APE inserts parts that are not present in the FMR output. In one example, the source sentence *"30 October 2015"* is translated by the FMR as *"30 2015"*, discarding the word *"October"* that is re-inserted by the APE system, thus matching the reference sentence *"30 Oktober 2015"*. The latter category (lexical substitution) is mainly related to the identification of the correct word and it is very important when dealing with one or more TMs, where two suggestions can only differ by one word. In another example, the source sentence *"Regulation 2015 / 7"* is translated by the FMR as *"Verordnung 2015 / 8"*, introducing a wrong number for the month. Leveraging the source, the APE is able to set the correct value matching the reference *"Verordnung 2015 / 7"*.

We report also on word-error rate (WER) in Figure 2 to get a better idea of how many words were actually modified by each system. Interestingly, the WER by most of the systems does not beat the TM score. We believe that this is due to the fact that the TM score is actually a mix of the TM and the phrase-based MT system; recall that Moses is

---

[10]Note that this strategy can be used in production because the training data relies on parallel data where the reference/oracle translation is available.

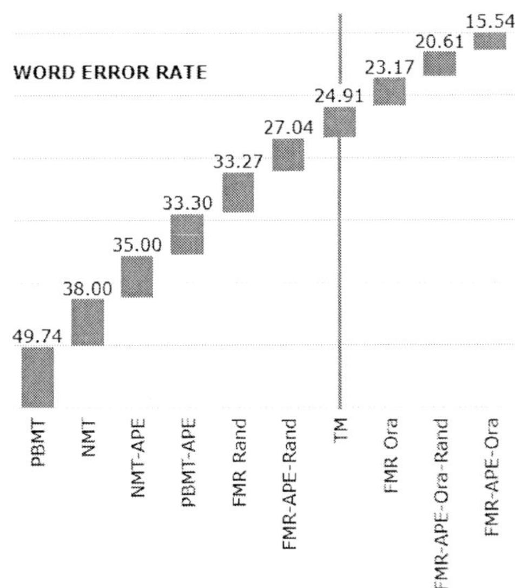

Figure 2: Word error rate (WER) for all of the systems. The best scoring system according to Table 2 (the FMR-APE Oracle-Rand system) also performs best according to the WER score of 20.61 on the top right.

Best System	Human Rating
TM	2.84
Phrase-based MT-APE	2.82
FMR Oracle	2.90
FMR-APE Oracle-Rand	3.67

Table 3: Average human evaluation for the best system combining FMR and APE. Translations were rated using a 5-point scale, 1 being the worst and 5 the best.

used when a good-enough translation unit is not found. Nonetheless, the best scoring systems are the FMR-APE combination systems.

5.2 Human-based analysis

The three measurements (BLEU, TER, and WER) show how well our best system performs and would probably be enough to show that it is worthwhile to combine FMR with APE. However, we passed the translations from our best performing systems to a native German evaluator (non-professional) well-versed in machine translation and natural language processing. Table 3 shows a quick overview of how the best systems perform: the human evaluation score is in line with the automatic metrics reported above.

We also asked the human evaluator to provide general comments on each of the best-performing systems. We did this to get a better idea of the types of errors each system made. Below is an overview of what the evaluator found.

TM. The most common error, accounting for nearly 30% of the incorrect cases from the TM, was "missing" or "wrong" data which describes typical information in the parliamentary texts like an article changing from 33 to 45. This is one of the reasons that a translator would like to use a TM because the translator would typically only have to change the numbers in those situations. There are also a few comments such as "wrong" part-of-speech, e.g. an adjective or noun being wrong.

Phrase-based MT-APE. Unlike the TM, we see some common phrase-based MT mistakes such as "noun cases wrong" that account for more than 15% of the total incorrect words. Also, since Moses marks untranslatable words as "UNK", we find that the evaluator noticed those anomalies made up 20% of the word-based issues. In addition to the normal mistakes, the evaluator noticed that on the order of 35% of the translations just "did not make sense", even more than the TM. That could be coupled with another finding, "repetition", to form what seems to be somewhat common in phrase-based MT-backed APE systems.

FMR Oracle. The best FMR was not immune to issues either. This could be due to the MT systems used. Many of the errors were similar to the Phrase-based MT-APE system; however, other errors were reported such as "punctuation is weird" and "important" words are missing. However, in more cases than others, it seems that the "FMR Oracle" system gets the underlying meaning correct.

FMR-APE Oracle-Rand. This system performed the best in all cases. We consider this to be the most important finding of this paper. While there were comments concerning UNK symbols (typical of the phrase-based MT translations), we saw some issues of morphology such as problems with inflection. For the most part, the evaluator made few comments because the translations were easier to understand than all other systems.

6 Conclusion

In this paper, we proposed a two-step process able to generate improved translations. The approach relies on the combination of two techniques: fuzzy match repair (FMR) and automatic post-editing (APE). Given a translation unit and the segment to be translated, the FMR module creates a set of fuzzy-match repair hypotheses. The selected hypothesis is then fed as input to the APE system that fixes its errors. When compared against neural MT, a TM-based approach and FMR alone, the combined solution outperforms all these methods indicating the effectiveness of the proposed technique. We measure performance using common, industry-wide MT performance metrics: BLEU and TER. We also show how WERs for our experiments nearly correlate with the BLEU and TER scores. In addition to BLEU, TER, and WER, we provide a human rating from a native German speaker as insight into how the best-performing systems fair to the average reader (not necessarily a translator). By combining FMR and APE, we provide easy, seamless access to FMR and APE for translators and post-editors.

We believe that the combination of two orthogonal technologies like FMR and APE could improve most stand-alone post-editing systems. We have been able to get decent gains by seamlessly juxtaposing two post-editing techniques in a straightforward way. Clearly, other system combinations (including using APE before FMR or even with the TM) should be tried along with the introduction of other language pairs as is done in the original FMR work (Ortega et al., 2016).

Along this direction, in future we plan on going the next step by combining yet another system with FMR and APE: quality estimation. One can easily imagine how quality estimation could be used both as a precursor and a post-validator for FMR and APE. Lastly, we will also use both MT systems as SBIs for FMR to increase the coverage and the chances to build successful patching operators, and a quality-estimation inspired approach to select the best hypothesis among the set of hypotheses produced by the FMR method used.

Acknowledgements

We thank Katharina Kann for providing native German translation ratings for several MT systems during evaluation. John E. Ortega's work was partially supported by the Universitat d'Alacant. Felipe Sánchez-Martínez's work was founded by the Spanish Government through the EFFORTUNE project (project number TIN2015-69632-R).

References

Bahdanau, Dzmitry, Kyunghyun Cho, and Yoshua Bengio. 2015. Neural machine translation by jointly learning to align and translate. In *ICLR*.

Béchara, Hanna, Yanjun Ma, and Josef van Genabith. 2011. Statistical post-editing for a statistical mt system. In *MT Summit*, volume 13, pages 308–315.

Bojar, O., R. Chatterjee, C. Federmann, Y. Graham, B. Haddow, S. Huang, M. Huck, P. Koehn, Q. Liu, V. Logacheva, C. Monz, M. Negri, M. Post, R. Rubino, L. Specia, and M. Turchi. 2017. Findings of the 2017 conference on machine translation (wmt17). In *WMT17*, pages 169–214.

Bulté, Bram, Tom Vanallemeersch, and Vincent Vandeghinste. 2018. M3tra: integrating tm and mt for professional translators.

Chatterjee, Rajen, Marion Weller, Matteo Negri, and Marco Turchi. 2015. Exploring the planet of the apes: a comparative study of state-of-the-art methods for mt automatic post-editing. In *Proceedings of the 53rd Annual Meeting of the Association for Computational Linguistics and the 7th International Joint Conference on Natural Language Processing (Volume 2: Short Papers)*, volume 2, pages 156–161.

Chatterjee, Rajen, José G. C. de Souza, Matteo Negri, and Marco Turchi. 2016. The FBK Participation in the WMT 2016 Automatic Post-editing Shared Task. In *Proceedings of the First Conference on Machine Translation*, pages 745–750, Berlin, Germany, August. Association for Computational Linguistics.

Chatterjee, Rajen, M. Amin Farajian, Matteo Negri, Marco Turchi, Ankit Srivastava, and Santanu Pal. 2017. Multi-source Neural Automatic Post-Editing: FBK's participation in the WMT 2017 APE shared task. In *Proceedings of the Second Conference on Machine Translation, Volume 2: Shared Task Papers*, pages 630–638, Copenhagen, Denmark, September. Association for Computational Linguistics.

Chatterjee, Rajen, Matteo Negri, Raphael Rubino, and Marco Turchi. 2018a. Findings of the WMT 2018 Shared Task on Automatic Post-Editing. In *Proceedings of the Third Conference on Machine Translation, Volume 2: Shared Task Papers*, pages 723–738, Belgium, Brussels, October. Association for Computational Linguistics.

Chatterjee, Rajen, Matteo Negri, Marco Turchi, Frédéric Blain, and Lucia Specia. 2018b. Combining quality estimation and automatic post-editing to enhance machine translation output. In *Proceedings of the 13th Conference of the Association for Machine Translation in the Americas (Volume 1: Research Papers)*, volume 1, pages 26–38.

Dandapat, Sandipan, Sara Morrissey, Andy Way, and Mikel L. Forcada. 2011. Using example-based MT to support statistical MT when translating homogeneous data in a resource-poor setting. In *Proceedings of the 15th conference of the European Association for Machine Translation*, pages 201–208. Leuven, Belgium.

Duchi, John, Elad Hazan, and Yoram Singer. 2011. Adaptive Subgradient Methods for Online Learning and Stochastic Optimization. *Journal of Machine Learning Research*.

Dugast, L., J. Senellart, and P. Koehn. 2007. Statistical post-editing on systran's rule-based translation system. In *Proceedings of the Second Workshop on Statistical Machine Translation*, pages 220–223.

Hewavitharana, Sanjika, Stephan Vogel, and Alex Waibel. 2005. Augmenting a statistical translation system with a translation memory. In *Proceedings of the 10th conference of the EAMT on 'Practical applications of machine translation'*, pages 126–132, Carnegie Mellon University, Pittsburgh, USA.

Hokamp, C. 2017. Ensembling factored neural machine translation models for automatic post-editing and quality estimation. In *WMT17*, pages 647–654.

Isabel, Lacruz, 2017. *Cognitive Effort in Translation, Editing, and Post-editing*, chapter 21, pages 386–401. Wiley-Blackwell.

Junczys-Dowmunt, M. and R. Grundkiewicz. 2016. Log-linear combinations of monolingual and bilingual neural machine translation models for automatic post-editing. In *WMT16*, pages 751–758.

Junczys-Dowmunt, Marcin and Roman Grundkiewicz. 2017. An exploration of neural sequence-to-sequence architectures for automatic post-editing. *arXiv preprint arXiv:1706.04138*.

Knowles, R., J. E Ortega, and P. Koehn. 2018. A comparison of machine translation paradigms for use in black-box fuzzy-match repair. In *AMTA 2018*, volume 1, pages 249–255.

Koehn, P. and J. Senellart. 2010. Convergence of translation memory and statistical machine translation. In *AMTA Workshop on MT Research and the Translation Industry*, pages 21–31.

Koehn, P., H. Hoang, A. Birch, C. Callison-Burch, M. Federico, N. Bertoldi, B. Cowan, W. Shen, C. Moran, R. Zens, C. Dyer, O. Bojar, A. Constantin, and E. Herbst. 2007. Moses: Open source toolkit for statistical machine translation. In *Proceedings of the 45th Annual Meeting of the ACL on Interactive Poster and Demonstration Sessions*, pages 177–180.

Koehn, Philipp. 2010. *Statistical Machine Translation*. Cambridge University Press, New York, NY, USA, 1st edition.

Kranias, L. and A. Samiotou. 2004. Automatic translation memory fuzzy match post-editing: a step beyond traditional TM/MT integration. In *Proceedings of the Fourth International Conference on Language Resources and Evaluation*, pages 331–334, Lisbon, Portugal.

Levenshtein, V.I. 1966. Binary codes capable of correcting deletions, insertions and reversals. *Soviet Physics Doklady.*, 10(8):707–710.

Luong, M. and C. D Manning. 2015. Stanford neural machine translation systems for spoken language domains. In *Proceedings of the International Workshop on Spoken Language Translation*.

Negri, Matteo, Marco Turchi, Rajen Chatterjee, and Nicola Bertoldi. 2018. eSCAPE: a Large-scale Synthetic Corpus for Automatic Post-Editing. In *Proceedings of the Eleventh International Conference on Language Resources and Evaluation (LREC 2018)*, may.

Ortega, J. E., F. Sánchez-Martínez, and M. L. Forcada. 2016. Fuzzy-match repair using black-box machine translation systems: what can be expected? In *AMTA 2016, vol. 1*, pages 27–39.

Ortega, John E, Weiyi Lu, Adam Meyers, and Kyunghyun Cho. 2018. Letting a neural network decide which machine translation system to use for black-box fuzzy-match repair.

Pal, Santanu, Sudip Kumar Naskar, Mihaela Vela, and Josef van Genabith. 2016. A neural network based approach to automatic post-editing. In *Proceedings of the 54th Annual Meeting of the Association for Computational Linguistics (Volume 2: Short Papers)*, volume 2, pages 281–286.

Papineni, K., S. Roukos, T. Ward, and W. Zhu. 2002. Bleu: a method for automatic evaluation of machine translation. In *ACL 2002*, pages 311–318.

Parton, Kristen, Nizar Habash, Kathleen McKeown, Gonzalo Iglesias, and Adrià de Gispert. 2012. Can Automatic Post-Editing Make MT More Meaningful? In *Proceedings of the 16th Annual Conference of the European Association for Machine Translation*, pages 111–118.

Pilevar, Abdol Hamid. 2011. Using Statistical Post-editing to Improve the Output of Rule-based Machine Translation System. *International Journal of Computer Science and Communication*.

Sennrich, Rico, Barry Haddow, and Alexandra Birch. 2016. Neural machine translation of rare words with subword units. In *Proceedings of the 54th Annual Meeting of the Association for Computational Linguistics (Volume 1: Long Papers)*, pages 1715–1725.

Simard, M. and P. Isabelle. 2009. Phrase-based machine translation in a computer-assisted translation environment. *Proceeding of the Twelfth Machine Translation Summit (MT Summit XII)*, pages 120–127.

Simard, Michel, Cyril Goutte, and Pierre Isabelle. 2007. Statistical Phrase-Based Post-Editing. In *Proceedings of the Annual Conference of the North American Chapter of the Association for Computational Linguistics*, pages 508–515.

Snover, M., B. Dorr, R. Schwartz, L. Micciulla, and J. Makhoul. 2006. A study of translation edit rate with targeted human annotation. In *AMTA*, volume 200.

Tan, Yiming, Zhiming Chen, Liu Huang, Lilin Zhang, Maoxi Li, and Mingwen Wang. 2017. Neural post-editing based on quality estimation. In *Proceedings of the Second Conference on Machine Translation*, pages 655–660.

Tebbifakhr, Amirhossein, Ruchit Agrawal, Rajen Chatterjee, Matteo Negri, and Marco Turchi. 2018. Multi-source transformer with combined losses for automatic post editing. In *Proceedings of the Third Conference on Machine Translation, Volume 2: Shared Task Papers*, pages 859–865, Belgium, Brussels, October. Association for Computational Linguistics.

Terumasa, Ehara. 2007. Rule Based Machine Translation Combined with Statistical Post Editor for Japanese to English Patent Translation. In *Proceedings of the XI Machine Translation Summit*, pages 13–18.

Post-editing Productivity with Neural Machine Translation: An Empirical Assessment of Speed and Quality in the Banking and Finance Domain

Samuel Läubli [1,3]   Chantal Amrhein [1,3]   Patrick Düggelin [1]

Beatriz Gonzalez [2]   Alena Zwahlen [1]   Martin Volk [1,3]

[1] TextShuttle AG   [2] Migros Bank AG

[3] Institute of Computational Linguistics, University of Zurich

Abstract

Neural machine translation (NMT) has set new quality standards in automatic translation, yet its effect on post-editing productivity is still pending thorough investigation. We empirically test how the inclusion of NMT, in addition to domain-specific translation memories and termbases, impacts speed and quality in professional translation of financial texts. We find that even with language pairs that have received little attention in research settings and small amounts of in-domain data for system adaptation, NMT post-editing allows for substantial time savings and leads to equal or slightly better quality.

1 Introduction

The use of neural networks for sequence transduction (Kalchbrenner and Blunsom, 2013; Sutskever et al., 2014; Bahdanau et al., 2015) has led to astounding progress in the field of machine translation (MT), establishing a new level of quality in applications such as automatic news translation (Sennrich et al., 2016b; Hassan et al., 2018). Nevertheless, the creation of publication-grade translations still requires human involvement (Läubli et al., 2018; Toral et al., 2018a), and previous work has explored human–machine collaboration in the form of post-editing, where human experts revise machine translated text where necessary.

Empirical investigations of post-editing productivity with NMT are still scarce, especially for language combinations that do not include English as

either the source or target language. In this paper, we describe and discuss the results of a productivity test of domain-adapted NMT with the in-house translation team of Migros Bank, a mid-sized financial institution based in Zurich, Switzerland. We evaluate the use of NMT under typical working conditions, focussing on two rarely explored language pairs—German (DE) to French (FR) and Italian (IT)—and texts from a specialised domain: banking and finance. We show that using NMT in combination with translation memories (TMs) and terminology databases (TBs) enables professional translators to work faster with no loss (or slight gains) in quality, even with limited in-domain data for system adaptation.

2 Background

Early assessments of post-editing productivity were focussed on technical texts. While a study by Krings (1994) with user manuals for technical appliances and rule-based MT found mixed results, interest in post-editing grew with the advent of statistical MT (SMT), which enabled time savings of up to 40 % in film subtitling (Volk, 2008; de Sousa et al., 2011) and software localisation (Plitt and Masselot, 2010). Subsequent work concluded that significant time savings can also be achieved in more complex domains such as legal (Federico et al., 2012) or marketing texts (Läubli et al., 2013).

Many productivity tests explored either translation from or into English (e. g., Plitt and Masselot, 2010), or translation between closely related languages such as Swedish and Danish (e. g., Volk, 2008). Green et al. (2013) conducted a large-scale experiment from English into three target languages with different canonical word order: Arabic (VSO), French (SVO), and German

Text	Topic	Source Words	Coverage FR				Coverage IT			
			100 %	90 %	80 %	R	100 %	90 %	80 %	R
A	Funding	1108	8.94	0.54	6.59	14.69	9.57	1.17	6.59	15.89
B	Funding	1006	2.58	3.68	4.17	9.23	1.29	1.69	1.39	3.93
C	Investing	1059	6.80	2.08	1.89	10.18	4.25	3.31	3.02	9.64
D	Investing	1077	14.48	10.58	0.84	24.68	7.24	15.51	3.06	23.65

Table 1: Source texts (DE) and their TM coverage in the target languages (FR, IT). Fuzzy bands include 90.00–99.99 % (referred to as 90 %) and 80.00–89.99 % (referred to as 80 %) matches. Coverage coefficients R indicate the percentage of translated words available in the TM for each text, considering 80–100 % matches.

(SOV). While post-editing was significantly faster than translation from scratch for all combinations, it is unclear whether their findings would equally apply to language pairs that do not include English, particularly if less MT training material is available. We investigate two language pairs that have received little attention in post-editing research: DE–FR and DE–IT.

The effect of using NMT rather than SMT on translation productivity has not yet been conclusively assessed. One of the first studies contrasting NMT and SMT quality found that NMT produces less morphological, lexical, and word order errors, thus reducing post-editing effort by 26 % in English to German subtitle translation (Bentivogli et al., 2016). However, post-editing effort was measured with HTER (Snover et al., 2006), a distance-based metric. Castilho et al. (2017) found that although more fluent, post-editing NMT rather than SMT output did not save time in an educational domain due to a higher number of omissions, additions, and mistranslations. Conversely, time savings doubled with NMT (+36 %) compared to SMT (+18 %) in literary translation (Toral et al., 2018b). The number of studies on NMT post-editing productivity is still limited, and further studies are needed, not least because findings obtained with different domains and language combinations are difficult to compare. The present study contributes data on NMT post-editing speed and quality in the financial domain.

Previous productivity tests used different experimental designs. In early work, Krings (1994) found that post-editing of rule-based MT resulted in a decrease in translation time by 7 % when translators used pen and paper, but an increase by 20 % when they used a computer instead. Plitt and Masselot (2010) and Green et al. (2013) compared post-editing to translation from scratch, using purpose-built web interfaces that showed one source sentence at a time, paired with a target text box that was either populated with MT or empty. Proponents of field tests have argued that while improving control of extraneous variables, such designs reduce experimental validity in that they isolate translators from tools long indispensable in professional workflows, namely software workbenches that show multiple sentences at a time and suggestions from TMs and TBs (Federico et al., 2012; Läubli et al., 2013). We chose an in-situ design where translators had access to the tools and resources known from their daily work.

3 Assessment of Translation Productivity

We conducted a productivity test of domain-adapted NMT on the premises of Migros Bank. Subjects translated texts under two experimental conditions. In TM-ONLY, they used the translation workbench known from their their daily work, including a domain-specific TM, a domain-specific TB, and any online services (except machine translation) of choice. The same setup was used in POST-EDIT, except that sentences with no fuzzy match of at least 80 % in the TM were populated with MT within the translation workbench. We did not show MT where high fuzzy matches were available because editing high fuzzy matches is more efficient (Sánchez-Gijón et al., 2019).

Materials We used four German source texts from Migros Bank. The texts had not been translated by any of the translators involved in the experiment before, and had been excluded from the MT training material (see below). The TMs contained several exact and high fuzzy matches for each text (Table 1).

To pretranslate sentences in POST-EDIT, we trained WMT17-style bi-RNN systems (Sennrich et al., 2017) using the `marian` toolkit (Junczys-Dowmunt et al., 2016). The training material consisted of 6 million out-of-domain segments from publicly available OPUS corpora (Tiede-

Subject	Text	Seq.	MT	Words/h	Quality
FR-1	A	1	No	520.37	4.00
FR-1	B	2	No	630.82	5.50
FR-1	C	3	Yes	909.88	5.00
FR-1	D	4	Yes	602.56	5.00
FR-2	A	1	Yes	987.00	4.50
FR-2	B	2	Yes	1237.13	3.50
FR-2	C	3	No	682.64	4.00
FR-2	D	4	No	505.40	4.50
Average TM-ONLY			No	584.81	4.50
Average POST-EDIT			Yes	934.14	4.50
Difference (%)				59.74	0.00

(a) DE–FR

Subject	Text	Seq.	MT	Words/h	Quality
IT-1	A	1	No	389.41	4.00
IT-1	B	2	No	398.71	4.00
IT-1	C	3	Yes	647.87	4.50
IT-1	D	4	Yes	393.14	4.00
IT-2	A	1	Yes	401.19	5.50
IT-2	B	2	Yes	536.09	5.50
IT-2	C	3	No	553.00	5.50
IT-2	D	4	No	469.56	5.50
Average TM-ONLY			No	452.67	4.75
Average POST-EDIT			Yes	494.57	4.88
Difference (%)				9.26	0.13

(b) DE–IT

Table 2: Experimental conditions and results: the number of target words produced per hour (Words/h) and averaged overall impression scores (Quality) as assigned by two expert raters per translation.

mann, 2009), as well as 385'320 and 186'647 in-domain segments for FR and IT, respectively. We filtered both in- and out-of-domain segments through a set of mostly length-based heuristics (Zwahlen et al., 2016), and oversampled the former as a simple means of domain adaptation. While this has proven effective in other contexts (e. g., Sennrich et al., 2016a), we note that translation quality could likely be improved by means of more advanced techniques such as fine-tuning (Luong and Manning, 2015) or multi-domain modelling (Chu et al., 2017).

Subjects A total of four professional translators took part in the productivity test, two each for the target languages FR (FR-1, FR-2) and IT (IT-1, IT-2). All were members of Migros Bank's internal translation team. They were therefore familiar both with the software used and with the language and terminology of the documents to be translated. FR-1, who joined the organisation shortly before the experiment, was less experienced than the other participants. All subjects had been post-editing outputs of the MT systems used in the experiment (see above) for three months, and had received four hours of post-editing training.

Procedure Each subject translated the four German source texts in the same order. Conditions were counterbalanced (Table 2). Subjects were first briefed about the purpose and data collected during the experiment. They were then given 60 minutes to work on each text, which we announced would likely not be enough to translate all sentences. There were 10-minute breaks between working blocks, and a 30-minute break in the mid-

dle of the experiment. A post-experimental survey concluded the experiment.

We encountered no problems with data collection, with the exception of a temporary failure of IT-1's screen in the last working block. The device went into standby mode, which was not reported immediately and resulted in a total interruption of 4 minutes, which we deducted from the respective session before calculating translation speed as shown in Table 2.

3.1 Speed

We report translation speed as the number of target words produced per hour. To account for TM matches, we derive a TM coverage coefficient R for each text:

$$R = 1a + 0.9b + 0.8c, \tag{1}$$

where a is the percentage of 100 %, b the percentage of 90 %, and c the percentage of 80 % TM matches. We then adjust the number of words W translated in each experimental block as

$$W^* = (1 - R)\,W. \tag{2}$$

This approximation assumes uniform distribution of TM matches within texts.

Results are shown in Table 2. FR subjects produced 584.81 and 934.14 words per hour in TM-ONLY and POST-EDIT, respectively, an increase of 59.74 %. The difference was less marked in IT, with 452.67 and 494.57 words per hour produced in TM-ONLY and POST-EDIT, respectively (9.26 %).

Criterion	DE–FR		DE–IT	
	TM-ONLY	POST-EDIT	TM-ONLY	POST-EDIT
Coherence	4.75	5.25	5.00	5.00
Cohesion	4.75	4.50	5.25	5.00
Grammar	4.75	4.75	4.75	4.88
Style	4.50	5.00	5.00	5.00
Cultural adequacy	4.50	4.75	4.50	4.75
Overall Impression	4.50	4.50	4.75	4.88

Table 3: Detailed quality assessment results. Each cell is an average over eight scores: four translations scored by two expert raters. Overall impression was graded separately; it is not an average over the other criteria.

While focussing on descriptive statistics due to small sample size, we also fit linear-mixed effects models for inferential analysis. Carter and Wojton (2018) show that very small sample sizes can attain sufficient power when a single fixed effect factor is of interest, albeit at a greater risk of type I errors. We use experimental condition (TM-ONLY vs. POST-EDIT) as the fixed effect factor, and random intercepts for subjects and texts. The models show no deviation from homoscedasticity or normality in visual inspection of residual plots and Shapiro-Wilk tests. Likelihood ratio tests show a significant main effect of experimental condition in FR ($\chi^2(1) = 9.74, p < .01$), but not IT ($\chi^2(1) = 0.93, p = .33$).

3.2 Quality

The translations produced in the experiment were reviewed by university lecturers in professional translation, who were remunerated at standard hourly rates. Experts did not know which translations were produced using MT. The quality of each translation was independently assessed by two experts, who assigned scores on a 6-point scale (1 = worst, 6 = best) for coherence, cohesion, grammar, style, cultural adequacy, and overall impression.

Results are shown in Table 3. Each cell is an average over 8 scores: 4 texts evaluated by two experts. Note that experts assigned separate scores for overall impression, which may therefore deviate from the average over scores for the other criteria. Average per-text scores for overall impression are included in Table 2.

Considering overall impression, experts did not find a difference in quality between texts produced with and without MT in FR. In IT, texts translated with MT received slightly higher scores (+0.13). MT improved coherence (+0.50), style (+0.50), and cultural adequacy (+0.25) in FR, as well as grammar (+0.13) and cultural adequacy (+0.25) in IT. Cohesion, on the other hand, was found to be better in texts produced without MT in both FR (−0.25) and IT (−0.25).

4 Discussion

While the minimum speed hardly differed between TM-ONLY and POST-EDIT , the latter allowed for higher average and maximum speed. In FR, the highest speed measured in POST-EDIT was 1237.13 words per hour (FR-2, text B), as opposed to 682.64 words per hour in TM-ONLY (FR-2, text C). In IT, the maximum speed in POST-EDIT was 647.87 words (IT-1, text C), and 553.00 words per hour in TM-ONLY (IT-2, text C).

Three out of four translators were faster in POST-EDIT on average. IT-2 did not benefit from MT: With an average speed of 511.28 words per hour in TM-ONLY and 468.64 words per hour in POST-EDIT, the subject was 8.34 % slower. Previous research has shown that not all translators benefit equally from MT (e. g., Plitt and Masselot, 2010; Koehn and Germann, 2014), which calls for large sample sizes in productivity tests (Green et al., 2013). Although improving robustness, involving a large number of translators is not always possible in practice – in our case, the in-house translation team had no more than four members, and involving external translators would have introduced other confounds (such as domain knowledge) that are hard to control for. We also note that IT-2 produced translations of above-average quality (Tables 2, 3), suggesting that MT may be less beneficial when aiming for maximum quality.

Another observation that warrants discussion is the difference in productivity between the two target languages. Again, one possible explanation is the small number of participants and measurements. A larger number of measurements would allow more accurate conclusions to be drawn as to whether the maximum speed achieved in FR (FR-2, text B) is to be treated as an outlier, or if translators will repeatedly achieve a throughput of more than 1,000 words per hour with MT. Moreover, the DE–IT engine was trained with less in-domain material than the DE–FR engine. This resulted in lower raw MT quality for IT, which in turn may have resulted in lower productivity.[1] Screen recordings also showed that IT translators made more stylistic changes to MT outputs, but apart from slightly higher quality scores overall (Table 3), we cannot quantify this finding and leave a more detailed analysis to future work.

With respect to quality, our results confirm previous findings that post-editing leads to similar or better translations (e. g., Green et al., 2013). An interesting nuance is that we find a slight, but consistent decrease in textual coherence within post-edited translations in both language pairs. As the research community is increasingly focussing on document-level MT, translation workbench providers will need to ensure integrability for future experimentation in real-life settings.

5 Conclusion

We have assessed the impact of NMT on translation speed and quality in the banking and finance domain. Despite working with language pairs that have received limited attention in research contexts and employing a simple means of domain adaptation, the use of NMT enabled professional translators to work faster: 59.74 % in DE–FR and 9.26 % in DE–IT. Unlike a number of previous studies, these improvements are not relative to translation from scratch, but to translation with domain-specific TMs and TBs within a customary translation workbench, which sets a higher baseline in terms of translation speed.

NMT did not have a negative impact on quality. To the contrary, scores assigned by expert raters were slightly higher for post-edited DE–IT translations. Screen recordings showed that IT translators devoted more time to stylistic changes of NMT output, underpinning the importance of translator training in cases where NMT is to be used to optimise throughput rather than quality.

Another factor that likely contributed to the dif-

ference between time savings in DE–FR and DE–IT is that roughly half as much in-domain training data was available for the latter. While further investigation will be needed to determine the impact of in-domain data volume and more advanced domain adaptation techniques, our results suggest that NMT has the potential of increasing translation productivity even with complex text types, little-researched language pairs, and limited amounts of in-domain training data. The present study contributes empirical evidence for DE–FR and DE–IT translation of financial texts, and we hope to encourage similar investigations with other languages and domains.

References

Bahdanau, Dzmitry, Kyunghyun Cho, and Yoshua Bengio. 2015. Neural machine translation by jointly learning to align and translate. In *Proceedings of ICLR*.

Bentivogli, Luisa, Arianna Bisazza, Mauro Cettolo, and Marcello Federico. 2016. Neural versus phrase-based machine translation quality: a case study. In *Proceedings of EMNLP*. Austin TX, USA, pages 257–267.

Carter, Kristina A. and Heather M. Wojton. 2018. The effect of extremes in small sample size on simple mixed models: A comparison of level-1 and level-2 size. Technical Report NS D-8965, IDA, Alexandria VA, USA.

Castilho, Sheila, Joss Moorkens, Federico Gaspari, Iacer Calixto, John Tinsley, and Andy Way. 2017. Is Neural Machine Translation the New State of the Art? *The Prague Bulletin of Mathematical Linguistics* 108:109–120.

Chu, Chenhui, Raj Dabre, and Sadao Kurohashi. 2017. An empirical comparison of domain adaptation methods for neural machine translation. In *Proceedings of ACL*. Vancouver, Canada, pages 385–391.

de Sousa, Sheila C. M., Wilker Aziz, and Lucia Specia. 2011. Assessing the post-editing effort for automatic and semi-automatic translations of dvd subtitles. In *Proceedings of RANLP*. Hissar, Bulgaria, pages 97–103.

Federico, Marcello, Alessandro Cattelan, and Marco Trombetti. 2012. Measuring user productivity in machine translation enhanced computer assisted translation. In *Proceedings of AMTA*. San Diego CA, USA.

Green, Spence, Jeffrey Heer, and Christopher D. Manning. 2013. The efficacy of human post-editing for language translation. In *Proceedings of CHI*. Paris, France.

Hassan, Hany, Anthony Aue, Chang Chen, Vishal Chowdhary, Jonathan Clark, Christian Federmann, Xuedong Huang, Marcin Junczys-Dowmunt, William Lewis, Mu Li, Shujie Liu, Tie-Yan Liu, Renqian Luo, Arul Menezes, Tao Qin, Frank Seide, Xu Tan, Fei Tian, Lijun Wu, Shuangzhi Wu, Yingce Xia, Dongdong Zhang, Zhirui Zhang, and Ming

---

[1] However, Koehn and Germann (2014) find that between-subjects variance is higher than between-systems variance in post-editing.

Zhou. 2018. Achieving human parity on automatic chinese to english news translation. *arXiv preprint* 1803.05567.

Junczys-Dowmunt, Marcin, Tomasz Dwojak, and Hieu Hoang. 2016. Is neural machine translation ready for deployment? A case study on 30 translation directions. In *Proceedings of IWSLT*. Tokyo, Japan.

Kalchbrenner, Nal and Phil Blunsom. 2013. Recurrent continuous translation models. In *Proceedings of EMNLP*. Seattle, Washington, USA, pages 1700–1709.

Koehn, Philipp and Ulrich Germann. 2014. The impact of machine translation quality on human post-editing. In *Proceedings of the EACL 2014 Workshop on Humans and Computer-assisted Translation*. Gothenburg, Sweden, pages 38–46.

Krings, Hans P. 1994. *Texte reparieren: Empirische Untersuchungen zum Prozeß der Nachredaktion von Maschinenübersetzungen*. Habilitation thesis, Universität Hildesheim, Hildesheim, Germany.

Luong, Minh-Thang and Christopher D. Manning. 2015. Stanford neural machine translation systems for spoken language domain. In *Proceedings of IWSLT*. Da Nang, Vietnam.

Läubli, Samuel, Mark Fishel, Gary Massey, Maureen Ehrensberger-Dow, and Martin Volk. 2013. Assessing post-editing efficiency in a realistic translation environment. In *Proceedings of the 2nd Workshop on Post-Editing Technology and Practice (WPTP)*. Nice, France, pages 83–91.

Läubli, Samuel, Rico Sennrich, and Martin Volk. 2018. Has machine translation achieved human parity? A case for document-level evaluation. In *Proceedings of EMNLP*. Association for Computational Linguistics, Brussels, Belgium, pages 4791–4796.

Plitt, Mirko and François Masselot. 2010. A productivity test of statistical machine translation post-editing in a typical localisation context. *Prague Bulletin of Mathematical Linguistics* 93:7–16.

Sennrich, Rico, Alexandra Birch, Anna Currey, Ulrich Germann, Barry Haddow, Kenneth Heafield, Antonio Valerio Miceli Barone, and Philip Williams. 2017. The University of Edinburgh's neural MT systems for WMT17. In *Proceedings of WMT*. Copenhagen, Denmark.

Sennrich, Rico, Barry Haddow, and Alexandra Birch. 2016a. Edinburgh neural machine translation systems for WMT 16. In *Proceedings of WMT*. Berlin, Germany, pages 371–376.

Sennrich, Rico, Barry Haddow, and Alexandra Birch. 2016b. Neural Machine Translation of Rare Words with Subword Units. In *Proceedings of ACL*. Berlin, Germany, pages 1715–1725.

Snover, Matthew, Bonnie Dorr, Rich Schwartz, Linnea Micciulla, and John Makhoul. 2006. A study of translation edit rate with targeted human annotation. In *Proceedings of AMTA*. Boston MA, USA.

Sutskever, Ilya, Oriol Vinyals, and Quoc V. Le. 2014. Sequence to sequence learning with neural networks. In *Proceedings of NIPS*. Montreal, Canada, pages 3104–3112.

Sánchez-Gijón, Pilar, Joss Moorkens, and Andy Way. 2019. Post-editing neural machine translation versus translation memory segments. *Machine Translation* (4 April 2019).

Tiedemann, Jörg. 2009. News from OPUS – A collection of multilingual parallel corpora with tools and interfaces. In *Proceedings of RANLP*. Borovets, Bulgaria, pages 237–248.

Toral, Antonio, Sheila Castilho, Ke Hu, and Andy Way. 2018a. Attaining the unattainable? Reassessing claims of human parity in neural machine translation. In *Proceedings of WMT*. Association for Computational Linguistics, Belgium, Brussels, pages 113–123.

Toral, Antonio, Martijn Wieling, and Andy Way. 2018b. Post-editing effort of a novel with statistical and neural machine translation. *Frontiers in Digital Humanities* 5(9).

Volk, Martin. 2008. The automatic translation of film subtitles: a machine translation success story? In J Nivre, M Dahllöf, and B Megyesi, editors, *Resourceful Language Technology: Festschrift in Honor of Anna Sågvall Hein*, Uppsala University, Uppsala, Sweden, Studia Linguistica Upsaliensia, pages 202–214.

Zwahlen, Alena, Olivier Carnal, and Samuel Läubli. 2016. Automatic TM cleaning through MT and POS tagging: Autodesk's submission to the NLP4TM 2016 shared task. *arXiv preprint* 1605.05906.

Post-editese: an Exacerbated Translationese

Antonio Toral

Center for Language and Cognition
University of Groningen
The Netherlands
`a.toral.ruiz@rug.nl`

Abstract

Post-editing (PE) machine translation (MT) is widely used for dissemination because it leads to higher productivity than human translation from scratch (HT). In addition, PE translations are found to be of equal or better quality than HTs. However, most such studies measure quality solely as the number of errors. We conduct a set of computational analyses in which we compare PE against HT on three different datasets that cover five translation directions with measures that address different translation universals and laws of translation: simplification, normalisation and interference. We find out that PEs are simpler and more normalised and have a higher degree of interference from the source language than HTs.

1 Introduction

Machine translation (MT) is nowadays widely used in industry for dissemination purposes by means of post-editing (PE, also referred to as PEMT in the literature), a machine-assisted approach to translation that results in notable increases in translation productivity compared to unaided human translation (HT), as shown in numerous research studies, e.g. Plitt and Masselot (2010).

In theory, one would claim that HTs[1] and PE translations are clearly different, since, in the translation workflow of the latter, the translator is primed by the output of an MT system (Green et al., 2013), resulting in a translation that should then contain, to some extent, the footprint of that MT system. Because of this, one would conclude that HT should be preferred over PE, as the former should be more natural and adhere more closely to the norms of the target language. However, many research studies have shown that the quality of PE is comparable to that of HT or even better, e.g. Koponen (2016), and, according to one study (Bowker and Buitrago Ciro, 2015), native speakers do not have a clear preference for HT over PE.

In this paper we conduct a set of computational analyses on several datasets that contain HTs and PEs, involving different language directions and domains as well as PE performed according to different guidelines (e.g. full versus light). Our aim is to find out whether HT and PE differ significantly in terms of different phenomena. Since previous research has proven the existence of translationese, i.e. the fact that HT and original text exhibit different characteristics, our current research can be framed as a quest to find out whether there is evidence of *post-editese*, i.e. the fact that HT (or translationese) and PE would be different.

The characteristics of translationese can be grouped along the so-called universal features of translation or translation universals (Baker, 1993), namely simplification, normalisation (also referred to as homogeneisation) and explicitation. In addition to these three, interference is recognised as a fundamental law of translation (Toury, 2012): "phenomena pertaining to the make-up of the source text tend to be transferred to the target text". In a nutshell, compared to original texts, translations tend to be simpler, more standardised, and

[1]By HT we refer to translations produced by a human from scratch, i.e. without the assistance of an MT system or any other computer-assisted technology, e.g. translation memories.

more explicit and they retain some characteristics that pertain to the source language.

In this study then we study the existence of post-editese by conducting a set of computational analyses that fall into three[2] out of these four categories. With these analyses we aim to answer a number of research questions:

- **RQ1**. Does post-editese exist? I.e. is there evidence that PE exhibits different characteristics than HT?

- **RQ2**. If the answer to RQ1 is yes, then which are the main characteristics of PE? I.e. how does it differ from HT?

- **RQ3**. If the answer to RQ1 is yes, then, are there different post-editeses? I.e. are there any characteristics that distinguish the post-editese produced by MT systems that follow different paradigms (rule-based, statistical phrase-based and neural)?

The rest of this paper is organised as follows. Section 2 provides an overview of the related work. Section 3 covers the experimental setup and the experiments conducted. Finally, Section 4 presents our conclusions and suggests lines of future work.

2 Related Work

Many research studies carried out during the last decade have compared the quality of HT and PE. These have shown that the quality of PE is comparable to that of HT, e.g. García (2010), or even better, e.g. Guerberof (2009) and Plitt and Masselot (2010). In these studies quality is typically measured in terms of the number of mistakes in each translation condition. However, they do not take into account other relevant aspects that may flag important differences between HTs and PEs, such as the perspective of the end-user or the presence of different phenomena in both types of translations. A recent strand of work targets precisely these, (i) by collecting the preference of end users between HT and PE and (ii) by analysing the characteristics of both types of translations. In the following subsections we report on recent work conducted in both of these two research lines.

2.1 Preference between HT and PE

Fiederer and O'Brien (2009) compared HT and PE for the English-to-German translation of text from a software user manual. Participants ranked both conditions equally for clarity, PE higher than HT for accuracy and HT higher than PE for style. When asked to choose their favourite translation, HT obtained a higher percentage of preferences than PE: 63% to 37%.

Bowker (2009) presented French- and English-speaking minorities in Canada four translations (HT, full PE, light PE and raw MT) of three short governmental texts (approximately 325 words) written in a relatively clear, neutral style with reasonably short sentences. Preference took into account not only the quality of the translations but also the time and cost required to produce them. The results were rather different for each group. In the French-speaking minority group 71% preferred HT versus 29% PE (21% full and 8% light). However, half of the participants were language professionals, which skewed the results. In fact, when they were removed the results changed drastically: 56% preferred HT versus 44% PE (29% full, 15% light). As for the English minority, 8% preferred HT versus 87% PE (38% full, 49% light) and 4% raw MT.

Bowker and Buitrago Ciro (2015) presented Spanish-speaking immigrants in Canada with four translations (HT, full PE, light PE and raw MT) of three short texts (301 to 380 words) containing library-related information and asked them which they prefered. PE and HT attained a similar number of preferences; 49% of respondents preferred PE (24% full and 25% light, respectively) compared to 42% who preferred HT. Raw MT lagged considerably behind with the remaining 9% of the preferences.

Green et al. (2013) assessed the quality of HT versus PE for Wikipedia articles translated from English into Arabic, French and German. Quality was measured by means of preference, done by ranking on isolated sentences via crowdsourcing. PE was found significantly better for all translation directions.

2.2 Characteristics of HT and PE

Daems et al (2017) used HT and PE news translated from English into Dutch. They presented them to translation students and colleagues, whose task was to identify which translations were PE. They also tried an automated approach, for which they built a classifier with 55 features using surface forms and linguistic information at lexical, syntac-

---

[2]Explicitation is not addressed in our experiments.

Dataset	Direction	PE type	MT systems	# Sent. pairs	Domain
Taraxü	en→de	Light[3]		272	
	de→en		2 SMT, 2 RBMT	240	News
	es→de[4]			101	
IWSLT	en→de	Light	4 NMT, 4 SMT	600	Subtitles
	en→fr		2 NMT, 3 SMT		
MS	zh→en	Full	1 NMT[5]	1,000[6]	News

Table 1: Information about the datasets used in the experiments

tic and semantic levels. No proof of the existence of post-editese was found, either perceived (students) or measurable (classifier).

Čulo and Nitzke (2016) compared MT, PE and HT in terms of terminology and found that the way terminology is used in PE is closer to MT than to HT and has less variation than in HT.

Farrell (2018) identified MT markers (i.e. "translation solutions which occurred with a statistically significantly higher frequency in PEMT than in HT") in short texts from Wikipedia translated from English into Italian and found that MT tends to choose a subset of all the possible translation solutions (the most frequent ones) and that this is the case also, to some extent, in PEs. HTs and PEs were also compared in terms of number of errors, which were found to be comparable, corroborating the findings of the literature covered at the beginning of this section.

Our contribution falls into this research line, to which we contribute a computational study whose analyses are chosen to align to translation universals and laws of translation and that covers multiple languages and domains.

3 Experiments

In this section we first describe the datasets used (Section 3.1), and then report on each of the experiments that we carried out in the subsequent subsections: lexical variety (Section 3.2), lexical density (Section 3.3), length ratio (Section 3.4) and

part-of-speech sequences (Section 3.5).

3.1 Datasets

We make use of three datasets in all our experiments: Taraxü (Avramidis et al., 2014), IWSLT (Cettolo et al., 2015; Mauro et al., 2016) and Microsoft "Human Parity" (Hassan et al., 2018), henceforth referred to as MS. These datasets cover five different translation directions that involve five languages:[7] English↔German, English→French, Spanish→German and Chinese→English. In addition, this choice of datasets allows us to include a longitudinal aspect into the analyses since there are state-of-the-art MT systems from almost one decade ago (in Taraxü), from three and four years ago (IWSLT) and from just one year ago (MS). Table 1 shows detailed information about each dataset, namely its translation direction(s), type of PE done, paradigm of the MT system(s) used, number of sentence pairs and domain of its text.

We note the following two limitations in some of the datasets:

- Mismatch of translator competence. Both PE and HT are carried out by professional translators in two of the datasets (Taraxü and MS). However, in the remaining one, IWSLT, professional translators do PE, while the translators doing HT are not necessarily professionals[8]. Thus, if we find differences between PEs and HTs, for this dataset this may not be (entirely) due to the two translations procedures leading to different translations but (also) to the different translations being produced by translators with different levels of proficiency.

---

[3] "Translators were asked to perform only the minimal post-editing necessary to achieve an acceptable translation quality." (Avramidis et al., 2014)

[4] This dataset contains an additional translation direction (de→es) which is not used here due to its small size; 40 sentence pairs.

[5] The MT systems used in the MT and in the PE condition are not the same. The one in the MT condition is the best system in Hassan et al. (2018) while the one in the PE condition is Google Translate, again as provided in Hassan et al. (2018).

[6] The original dataset contains 2,001 sentences. We only use the subset in which the source text is original instead of translationese (Toral et al., 2018).

[7] In the tables and experiments we will refer to languages with their ISO-2 codes.

[8] "We accept all fluently bilingual volunteers as translators", https://translations.ted.com/TED_Translator_Resources:_Main_guide#Translation

Translation type	Dataset and translation direction					
	Taraxü			IWSLT		MS
	de→en	en→de	es→de	en→de	en→fr	zh→en
HT	0.26	0.27	0.31	0.20	0.16	0.14
PE	**-2.05%**	**-1.81%**	**†-1.27%**	**-3.86%**	**-1.17%**	**-4.76%**
MT	-2.94%	-3.62%	-5.91%	-10.93%	-6.04%	-6.96%
PE-NMT				-4.21%	-1.88%	-4.76%
PE-SMT	**-1.59%**	**-1.31%**	**†-1.03%**	**-3.50%**	**-0.70%**	
PE-RBMT	-2.79%	-2.04%	-3.05%			
NMT				-12.22%	-8.18%	-7.33%
SMT	**-2.36%**	**-2.36%**	**-6.42%**	**-9.63%**	**-4.61%**	
RBMT	-3.08%	-4.26%	-7.78%			

Table 2: TTR scores for HT and relative differences for PE and MT. For directions with more than one MT system, the result shown in rows PE and MT uses the average score of all the PEs or MT outputs, respectively. The best result (highest TTR) in each group of rows is shown in bold. If a † is not shown then the TTR for HT is significantly higher than the TTRs for all the translations in that cell (the 95% confidence interval of the TTR of HT, obtained with bootstrap resampling, is higher and there is no overlap).

- Source language being translationese. In two of the datasets (MS and IWSLT), the source language and the language in which those texts were originally written is the same. This is not the case however for Taraxü, for which the original language of the source texts is Czech. We can still compare MT to PE although we need to take into account that these texts are easier for MT than original texts (Toral et al., 2018). However the comparison between PE (or MT) and HT is problematic since the HT was not translated from the source language but from another language (Czech).

3.2 Lexical Variety

We assess the lexical variety of a translation (MT, PE or HT) by calculating its type-token ratio (TTR), as shown in equation 1.

$$TTR = \frac{number\ of\ types}{number\ of\ tokens} \tag{1}$$

Farrell (2018) observed that MT tends to produce a subset of all the possible translations in the target language (the ones used most frequently in the training data). Therefore, we hypothesise the TTR of MT, and by extension that of PE too, to be lower than that of HT. If this is the case, then PE would be, in terms of lexical variety, simpler than HT.

Table 2 shows the results for each dataset and language direction. In all cases the lexical variety in PE is lower than in HT, and again in all cases, that of MT is lower than that of PE. This could

be interpreted as follows: (i) lexical variety is low in MT because these systems prefer the translation solutions most frequently used in the training data; (ii) a post-editor will add lexical variety to some degree, but because MT primes him/her, the resulting translation will not achieve the level of lexical diversity that is attained in HT.

We now look at the results of PE and MT for different MT paradigms. In the Taraxü dataset we can compare rule-based and statistical MT systems. Rule-based MT has a lower TTR in all three translation directions of this dataset and this is then reflected in a lower TTR again when a system of this paradigm is used for post-editing. In the IWSLT dataset we can confront statistical and neural MT systems. In all cases the lexical variety of neural MT is lower than that of statistical MT. Again, the same trend shows when we look at their PEs. This is perhaps a surprising result, since NMT systems outperformed SMT in the IWSLT dataset, in terms of HTER (Cettolo et al., 2015).

3.3 Lexical Density

Lexical density measures the amount of information present in a text by calculating the ratio between the number of content words (adverbs, adjectives, nouns and verbs) and its total number of words, as shown in equation 2.

$$lex\_density = \frac{number\ of\ content\ words}{number\ of\ total\ words} \tag{2}$$

Translationese has been found to have a lower percentage of content words than original texts,

Translation Type	Dataset and translation direction					
	Taraxü			IWSLT		MS
	de→en	en→de	es→de	en→de	en→fr	zh→en
HT	0.55	0.53	0.53	0.48	0.46	0.59
PE	-1.00%	-2.48%	**-4.31%**	**-3.46%**	-1.24%	**-0.46%**
MT	**-0.81%**	**-0.69%**	-4.53%	-5.14%	**-0.94%**	-2.37%
PE-NMT				-3.88%	-1.47%	-0.46%
PE-SMT	**-0.54%**	-2.87%	-4.78%	**-3.04%**	**-1.09%**	
PE-RBMT	-1.46%	**-2.09%**	**-3.84%**			
NMT				-6.31%	-3.14%	-2.37%
SMT	**-0.80%**	**0.14%**	-3.45%	**-3.98%**	**0.53%**	
RBMT	-0.83%	-1.51%	-5.61%			

Table 3: Lexical density scores for HT and relative differences for PE and MT. For directions with more than one MT system, the result shown in rows PE and MT uses the average score of all the PEs or MT outputs, respectively. The best result (highest density) in each group of rows is shown in bold.

thus being, from this point of view, lexically simpler (Scarpa, 2006). To identify and count content words we tag the target sides of the datasets with their parts-of-speech (PoS) using UDPipe (Straka et al., 2016), a PoS tagger that uses the Universal PoS tagset.[9] Then we assess the lexical density of each translation (HT, PE and MT) using this PoS-tagged version[10] of the datasets.

Table 3 shows the results. In both PE and MT the lexical density is lower than in HT. However between PE and MT, there is no systematic distinction. When inspecting PEs using different MT paradigms, we do not find any clear trend between SMT and RBMT, but one such trend shows up when we inspect SMT and NMT: in the two comparisons we can establish in our dataset (the two translation directions in the IWSLT dataset), PE-NMT leads to a lower lexical density than PE-SMT. Finally, looking at MT outputs produced by different types of MT systems, we observe that both RBMT and NMT lead to lower lexical densities than SMT.

3.4 Length Ratio

Given a source text ST and a target text TT, i.e. TT is a translation of the ST (HT, PE or MT), we compute the absolute difference in length (measured in characters) between the two, normalised by the length of the ST, as shown in equation 3.

$$length\ ratio = \frac{|length_{ST} - length_{TT}|}{length_{ST}} \quad (3)$$

Because (i) MT results in a translation of similar length to that of the ST,[11] and PE is primed by the MT output while (ii) a translator working from scratch (HT) may translate more freely in terms of length, we hypothesise that the difference in absolute length is smaller for MT and PE than it is for HT. If this is true, it would be a case of interference in PE, as the typical length of sentences translated with this method would be similar to the length used in the source text.

We compute this ratio at sentence level and average over all the sentences of the dataset. Table 4 shows the results for each dataset and language direction. The results in datasets Taraxü and MS match our hypothesis; in both datasets the length ratio is lower for PE and MT than it is for HT. This is also the case for MT in dataset IWSLT. However, in the results for PE in dataset IWSLT, the ratio of PE is actually higher than that of HT for en→fr, which seems to contradict our hypothesis. This may be attributed to the difference in translation proficiency between the translators that did HT and those that did PE that we commented upon in Section 3.1. The latter are professional, while the first could be non-professional. It is known

---

[9] https://universaldependencies.org/u/pos/
[10] UDPipe's PoS tagging F1-score is over 90% for all the three target languages considered: de, en and fr (Straka and Straková, 2017, Table 2)

[11] This is necessary the case for RBMT and SMT as the number of TL tokens they can produce per each SL token is limited; e.g. the longest a translation with SMT can be is the number of tokens in the ST multiplied by the longest phrase in the phrase table, which is typically 7. NMT does not have this limitation, so we do not argue in this direction for that MT paradigm.

Dataset	Direct.	Length ratio		
		HT	PE	MT
Taraxü	de→en	0.16	‡-38.5%	†-36.9%
	en→de	0.22	‡-33.4%	‡-38.5%
	es→de	0.17	*-25.2%	-21.0%
IWSLT	en→de	0.17	-3.4%	†-18.8%
	en→fr	0.18	6.7%	-10.9%
MS	zh→en	1.41	‡-9.9%	‡-9.1%

Table 4: Length ratio scores for HT and relative differences for PE and MT. For directions with more than one MT system, the result shown in columns PE and MT uses the average length ratio of all the PEs or MT outputs, respectively. * indicates that the score for HT is significantly higher with $\alpha = 0.05$ († with $\alpha = 0.01$ and ‡ with $\alpha = 0.001$) than the scores of all the PEs/MTs represented in the cell, based on one-tailed paired t-tests.

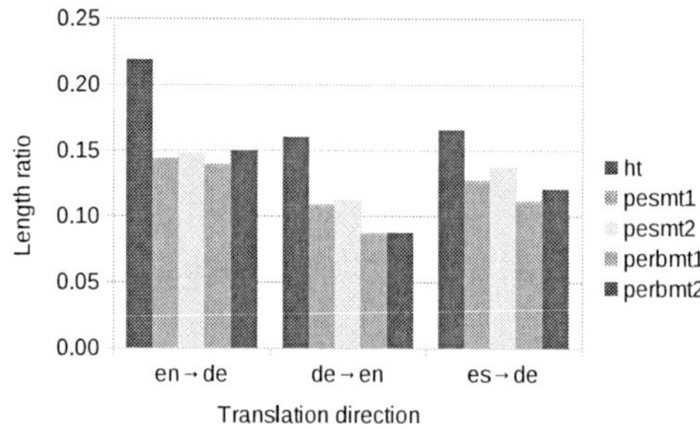

Figure 1: Length ratio for HT and PEs in the Taraxü dataset.

that non-professional translators tend to produce more literal translations, whose length should then be similar to that of the source text.

We now look at the length ratio of PEs that use different MT systems. Figure 1 shows the length ratios of HTs and PEs that use different MT paradigms (SMT and RBMT) in the Taraxü dataset. While for one of the translation direction (en→de) the ratio of PE-SMT and PE-RBMT are similar, the two PE-RBMT systems have lower length ratios than the two PE-SMT systems in the other two translation directions.

3.5 Part-of-Speech Sequences

We assess the interference of the source language on a translation (HT, PE and MT) by measuring how close the sequence of PoS tags in the translation is to the typical PoS sequences of the source language and to the typical PoS sequences of the target language. If the sequences of PoS tags used in a translation A are more similar to the typical sequences of the source language than the sequences of another translation B, that could be an indica-

tion that A has more interference from the source language than B.

Given a PoS-tagged translation T, a language model of a PoS-tagged corpus in the source language LM_{SL} and a language model of a PoS-tagged corpus in the target language LM_{TL}, we calculate the difference of the perplexities of T with respect to both language models, as shown in equation 4.

$$PP\_diff = PP(T, LM_{SL}) - PP(T, LM_{TL}) \tag{4}$$

A high result for a translation T would indicate that T is dissimilar to the source language (high perplexity with respect to the source language) and similar to the target language (low perplexity with respect to the target language). Conversely, a low result would indicate that T is similar to the source language (low perplexity with respect to the source language) and dissimilar to the target language (high perplexity with respect to the target language).

Because MT systems are known to perform less reordering than human translators (Toral and Sánchez-Cartagena, 2017), our hypothesis is that MT outputs, and by extension PEs, are more similar in terms of PoS sequences to the source language than HTs are. This would mean that PEs and MT outputs have more interference in terms of PoS sequences than HTs.

For each language in our datasets (de, en, es, fr and zh), we PoS tag a monolingual corpus[12] with UDPipe, the PoS tagger already introduced in Section 3.3.[13]

We then build language models on these PoS tagged data with SRILM (Stolcke, 2002), considering n-grams up to $n = 6$, using interpolation and Witten-Bell smoothing.[14] Because we use the Uni-

---

[12] The corpora used for the different languages belong to the same domain, news. We use corpora of roughly the same size (around 100MB of text). This leads to corpora of between 1,617,527 sentences (es) and 2,187,421 (de).

[13] While in Section 3.3 we PoS-tagged the target side of the datasets, in this experiment we PoS-tag both the source and target sides. UDPipe's PoS tagging F1-score is over 90% for four of the five languages involved (de, en, es and fr) and 83% for the remaining one: zh (Straka and Straková, 2017, Table 2). Given the lower performance of PoS tagging for zh, the results involving this language should be taken with caution.

[14] The more advanced smoothing method Kneser-Ney did not work because the count-of-count statistics in our datasets are not suitable for this smoothing method, which may be due to the very small size of our vocabulary: the Universal Dependencies PoS tagset.

Translation Type	Dataset and translation direction					
	Taraxü			IWSLT		MS
	de→en	en→de	es→de	en→de	en→fr	zh→en
HT	5.12	5.09	9.41	5.01	2.47	17.23
PE	**-13.84%**	**-11.29%**	**-8.58%**	**-6.26%**	**-2.03%**	-3.26%
MT	-33.65%	-32.25%	-20.71%	-18.66%	-11.07%	**-3.1%**
PE-NMT				**-3.41%**	**-1.40%**	-3.26%
PE-SMT	**-11.72%**	-13.37%	-10.48%	-9.10%	-2.46%	
PE-RBMT	-15.95%	**-9.20%**	**-6.68%**			
NMT				**-5.89%**	**-2.58%**	-3.10%
SMT	**-30.07%**	-41.71%	-26.30%	-31.43%	-7.95%	
RBMT	-37.24%	**-22.80%**	**-15.13%**			

Table 5: Perplexity difference scores for HT and relative differences for PE and MT. For directions with more than one MT system, the result shown in rows PE and MT uses the average score of all the PEs or MT outputs, respectively. The best result (highest perplexity) in each group of rows is shown in bold.

versal PoS tagset, the set of PoS tags is the same for all the languages, which means that all our language models share the same vocabulary.

Table 5 shows the results. In terms of HT versus PE and MT, we observe similar trends to those observed earlier for lexical variety (Table 2), namely MT obtains the lowest perplexity difference score and HT the highest, with PE lying somewhere between the two. The only exception to this is seen in the MS dataset, where the value for MT is slightly higher than that for PE (-3.1% versus -3.26%). It should be taken into account, as already explained in Section 3.1, that the MT systems in the MT and PE conditions are different in this dataset, with the one in the MT condition being substantially better (Hassan et al., 2018). Overall, we interpret these results as MT being the translation type that contains the most interference in terms of PoS sequences, followed by PE.

We now look at the PE and MT results under different MT paradigms. Comparing SMT and NMT, the results indicate that the latter has less interference, both in PE and MT conditions. This corroborates earlier research that compared SMT and NMT in terms of reordering (Bentivogli et al., 2016). We do not find clear trends when comparing SMT and RBMT though.

4 Conclusions and Future Work

We have carried out a set of computational analyses on three datasets that contain five translation directions with the aim of finding out whether post-edited translations (PEs) exhibit different phenomena than human translations from scratch (HTs). In other words, whether there is evidence of the existence of *post-editese*. The analyses conducted measure aspects related to translation universals and laws of translation, namely simplification, normalisation and interference. With these analysis, we find evidence of post-editese (RQ1), whose main characteristics (RQ2) we summarise as follows:

- PEs have lower lexical variety and lower lexical density than HTs. We link these to the simplification principle of translationese. Thus, these results indicate that *post-editese* is lexically simpler than translationese.

- Sentence length in PEs is more similar to the sentence length of the source texts, than sentence length in HTs. We link this finding to interference and normalisation: (i) PEs have interference from the source text in terms of length, which leads to translations that follow the typical sentence length of the source language; (ii) this results in a target text whose length tends to become normalised.

- Part-of-speech (PoS) sequences in PEs are more similar to the typical PoS sequences of the source language, than PoS sequences in HTs. We link this to the interference principle: the sequences of grammatical units in PEs preserve to some extent the sequences that are typical of the source language.

In the paper we have not considered only HTs and PEs but also MT outputs, from the MT systems that were the starting point to produce the PEs. This to corroborate a claim in the literature (Green et al., 2013), namely that in PE the translator is primed by the MT output. We expected then to find similar trends to those found in PEs also in MT outputs and this was indeed the case in all four experiments. In two of the experiments, lexical variety and PoS sequences, the results of PE were somewhere in the middle between those of HT and MT. Our interpretation is that a post-editor improves the initial MT output in terms of variety and PoS sequences, but due to being primed by the MT output, the result cannot attain the level of HT, and the footprint of the MT system remains in the resulting PE.

We have also looked at different MT paradigms (rule-based, statistical and neural), to find out whether these lead to different characteristics in the resulting PEs (RQ3). Neural MT diminishes to some extent the interference in terms of PoS sequences, probably because it is better at reordering (Bentivogli et al., 2016). Statistical MT has obtained better results than the other two MT paradigms in terms of lexical variety, and also better than neural MT, but on par with rule-based MT, in lexical density.

In a nutshell, we have found that PEs tend to be simpler and more normalised and to have a higher degree of interference from the source text than HTs. This seems to be caused because these characteristics are already present in the MT outputs that are the starting point of the PEs. We find thus evidence of *post-editese*, which can be thought of as an exacerbated translationese.

While PE is very useful in terms of productivity, which arguably is the main reason behind its wide adoption in industry, the findings of this paper flag a potential issue. Because PEs are simpler and have a higher interference from the source language than HTs, the extensive use of PE rather than HT may have serious implications for the target language in the long term, for example that it becomes impoverished (simplification) and overly influenced by the source language (interference). At the same time, we have shown that these issues cannot be attributed to PE *per se* but that they originate in the MT systems used as the starting point for PE. Identifying these issues might be then the first step for further research on addressing these problems in current state-of-the-art MT systems.

Throughout the paper, we have assumed that lexical diversity and density correlate directly with translation quality; i.e. the more diverse and dense a translation the better. In this regard, we acknowledge that in translation there is a tension between diversity and consistency, especially in technical translation. At the same time, none of our datasets falls under the domain of technical texts.

We also acknowledge that our study is based on rather superficial linguistic features, either at surface or morphological level (PoS tags). For future work, therefore, we plan to explore the use of additional features, especially relying on deeper linguistic analyses. In addition, we plan to study the overlap between multiple HTs and PEs for the same text, to assess whether it is higher between PEs, which would indicate a higher degree of homogeneisation.

Another line we would like to pursue is that of automatic discrimination between PE and HT. While this has been shown to be possible with a high degree of accuracy between original texts and HTs, this is not the case for PE versus HT in the attempts conducted to date (Daems et al., 2017).

Finally, we would like to point out that all our code and data are publicly released,[15] so we encourage interested parties to use these resources to conduct further analyses.

Acknowledgments

I would like to thank Luisa Bentivogli, Joke Daems, Michael Farrell, Lieve Macken and Maja Popović for pointing me to relevant datasets and related papers and for insightful discussions on the topic of this paper. I would also like to thank the reviewers; their comments have definitely led to improve this paper.

References

Avramidis, Eleftherios, Aljoscha Burchardt, Sabine Hunsicker, Maja Popovic, Cindy Tscherwinka, David Vilar, and Hans Uszkoreit. 2014. The taraxü corpus of human-annotated machine translations. In *LREC*, pages 2679–2682.

Baker, Mona. 1993. Corpus linguistics and translation studies: Implications and applications. *Text and technology: In honour of John Sinclair*, 233:250.

Bentivogli, Luisa, Arianna Bisazza, Mauro Cettolo, and Marcello Federico. 2016. Neural versus phrase-based machine translation quality: a case study. In Su, Jian, Xavier Carreras, and Kevin Duh, editors, *Proceedings of the 2016 Conference on Empirical*

---

[15] https://github.com/antot/posteditese_mtsummit19

Methods in Natural Language Processing, EMNLP 2016, Austin, Texas, USA, November 1-4, 2016, pages 257–267. The Association for Computational Linguistics.

Bowker, Lynne and Jairo Buitrago Ciro. 2015. Investigating the usefulness of machine translation for newcomers at the public library. *Translation and Interpreting Studies*, 10(2):165–186.

Bowker, Lynne. 2009. Can machine translation meet the needs of official language minority communities in canada? a recipient evaluation. *Linguistica Antverpiensia, New Series–Themes in Translation Studies*, (8).

Cettolo, Mauro, Jan Niehues, Sebastian Stüker, Luisa Bentivogli, Roldano Cattoni, and Marcello Federico. 2015. The iwslt 2015 evaluation campaign. In *IWSLT 2015, International Workshop on Spoken Language Translation*.

Daems, Joke, Orphée De Clercq, and Lieve Macken. 2017. Translationese and post-editese : how comparable is comparable quality? *LINGUISTICA ANTVERPIENSIA NEW SERIES-THEMES IN TRANSLATION STUDIES*, 16:89–103.

Farrell, Michael. 2018. Machine Translation Markers in Post-Edited Machine Translation Output. In *Proceedings of the 40th Conference Translating and the Computer*, pages 50–59.

Fiederer, Rebecca and Sharon O'Brien. 2009. Quality and machine translation: A realistic objective. *The Journal of Specialised Translation*, 11:52–74.

Garcia, Ignacio. 2010. Is machine translation ready yet? *Target. International Journal of Translation Studies*, 22(1):7–21.

Green, Spence, Jeffrey Heer, and Christopher D Manning. 2013. The efficacy of human post-editing for language translation. *Chi 2013*, pages 439–448.

Guerberof, Ana. 2009. Productivity and quality in mt post-editing. In *MT Summit XII-Workshop: Beyond Translation Memories: New Tools for Translators MT*. Citeseer.

Hassan, Hany, Anthony Aue, Chang Chen, Vishal Chowdhary, Jonathan Clark, Christian Federmann, Xuedong Huang, Marcin Junczys-Dowmunt, Will Lewis, Mu Li, Shujie Liu, Tie-Yan Liu, Renqian Luo, Arul Menezes, Tao Qin, Frank Seide, Xu Tan, Fei Tian, Lijun Wu, Shuangzhi Wu, Yingce Xia, Dongdong Zhang, Zhirui Zhang, and Ming Zhou. 2018. Achieving Human Parity on Automatic Chinese to English News Translation. https://arxiv.org/abs/1803.05567.

Koponen, Maarit. 2016. Is machine translation post-editing worth the effort? A survey of research into post-editing and effort. *Journal of Specialised Translation*, 25(25):131–148.

Mauro, Cettolo, Niehues Jan, Stüker Sebastian, Bentivogli Luisa, Cattoni Roldano, and Federico Marcello. 2016. The iwslt 2016 evaluation campaign. In *International Workshop on Spoken Language Translation*.

Plitt, Mirko and François Masselot. 2010. A productivity test of statistical machine translation post-editing in a typical localisation context. *The Prague bulletin of mathematical linguistics*, 93:7–16.

Scarpa, Federica. 2006. Corpus-based quality-assessment of specialist translation: A study using parallel and comparable corpora in english and italian. *Insights into specialized translation–linguistics insights. Bern: Peter Lang*, pages 155–172.

Stolcke, Andreas. 2002. Srilm-an extensible language modeling toolkit. In *Seventh international conference on spoken language processing*.

Straka, Milan and Jana Straková. 2017. Tokenizing, pos tagging, lemmatizing and parsing ud 2.0 with udpipe. In *Proceedings of the CoNLL 2017 Shared Task: Multilingual Parsing from Raw Text to Universal Dependencies*, pages 88–99, Vancouver, Canada, August. Association for Computational Linguistics.

Straka, Milan, Jan Hajic, and Jana Straková. 2016. Udpipe: Trainable pipeline for processing conll-u files performing tokenization, morphological analysis, pos tagging and parsing. In *LREC*.

Toral, Antonio and Víctor M. Sánchez-Cartagena. 2017. A multifaceted evaluation of neural versus phrase-based machine translation for 9 language directions. In *Proceedings of the 15th Conference of the European Chapter of the Association for Computational Linguistics: Volume 1, Long Papers*, pages 1063–1073, Valencia, Spain, April. Association for Computational Linguistics.

Toral, Antonio, Sheila Castilho, Ke Hu, and Andy Way. 2018. Attaining the unattainable? reassessing claims of human parity in neural machine translation. In *Proceedings of the Third Conference on Machine Translation, Volume 1: Research Papers*, pages 113–123, Belgium, Brussels, October. Association for Computational Linguistics.

Toury, Gideon. 2012. *Descriptive translation studies and beyond: Revised edition*, volume 100. John Benjamins Publishing.

Čulo, Oliver and Jean Nitzke. 2016. Patterns of terminological variation in post-editing and of cognate use in machine translation in contrast to human translation. In *Proceedings of the 19th Annual Conference of the European Association for Machine Translation, EAMT 2017, Riga, Latvia, May 30 - June 1, 2016*, pages 106–114. European Association for Machine Translation.

Author Index